D1351545

# REVIVAL IN ROSE STREET

BY

**IAN L. S. BALFOUR**

# REVIVAL IN ROSE STREET:

# CHARLOTTE BAPTIST CHAPEL, EDINBURGH,

# 1808–2008

BY

**IAN L. S. BALFOUR**

© IAN L. S. BALFOUR

ISBN 978-1-904429-11-1

Published in 2007
by
Rutherford House
Edinburgh

Designed and Typeset
by
Freight Design
Glasgow

Printed in China
by
Phoenix Publishing

# Contents

# Preface

## Lay participation

Histories of churches tend to be the story of successive ministries. While the pastors of Charlotte Chapel have a prominent place in this book, and rightly so, it is hoped that the wealth and diversity of lay involvement will come through equally strongly. This was the plea of the editor of *The Baptist Quarterly* in October 2002:

*As a denomination, Baptists rightly prioritize Luther's concept of 'the priesthood of all believers'. Nevertheless a latent clericalism, coupled with an over-focus on religion in its Sunday suit, are still widely pervasive. Pick up the history of a local church and you will see what I mean, with the predominant emphasis on ministers and Sunday ministries. This is understandable because this is where the records are most complete, but it does not help to answer the vital question: what difference does it make to the people in the pews in their Monday to Saturday lives that they have worshipped in a Baptist Church on Sunday? This is an essential aspect of our history about which we need to know more.*

*The Baptist Quarterly*, 39 (2002), p. 365.

Lay participation was an outstanding feature of the Chapel during the whole of the twentieth century, and still is. The Chapel has come a long way since all work stopped for five months in 1870, with the laconic comment in the church register: 'the pastor was ill'. When preaching through the life of Abraham in 1996, Peter Grainger came to the death of Abraham's wife, Sarah, in Genesis 23. He commented:

*We're told very little about the patriarchal family in the 37 years between the birth of Isaac and the death of Sarah. There is only one story we know anything about and that is the testing of Abraham. Other than that we know nothing of those 37 years. What did they do? Well, they lived their normal lives; they tended sheep and goats and herds; they traded with people; they went through the necessities of life.... And we know nothing at all of Sarah in this whole period. Yet, while she is in the background of the story, she must have been in the foreground of the daily routine of life in the family of God in the Promised Land.*

25 August 1996, evening service.

How truly the same could be said about Charlotte Chapel. There have been many 'Sarahs', whose contribution has gone unrecorded. Most have preferred it that way, wishing their Christian service to be anonymous, but without them the life and the witness of the Chapel would long since have withered away.

*The activity behind Harvest Thanksgiving is typical of the contribution that dozens of self-effacing lay people make to the life of the Chapel – encouraging contributions, preparing the platform, bringing fruit and flowers and taking gifts to the homes of housebound members.*

During every Sunday service, week in and week out, an open Bible is illuminated at the front of the church as a visible reminder of the centrality of Scripture in the life of the congregation. This is not overlooked, even among the harvest gifts.

## Charlotte Baptist Chapel?

Is it Charlotte Chapel or Charlotte Baptist Chapel? When the Scottish Episcopalians built the original Chapel in 1796, they named it Charlotte Chapel because of its proximity to Charlotte Square. Christopher Anderson kept the name when he bought the building from them in 1818. Chapels in Scotland were generally places of worship for Roman Catholics – the English pairing of church and chapel has no parallel here. Lest people assumed that the Chapel was a Roman Catholic church, publicity material over the years has often used Charlotte Baptist Chapel, but, overall, the two phrases have appeared more or less equally.

Since the autumn of 2005, when a new logo was adopted, symbolizing the words 'Charlotte Chapel, Conspicuous for Christ', the shorter phrase has predominated. People from England, accustomed to referring to churches by the first part

*The phrase 'Charlotte Baptist Chapel' has often been used in publicity material, as on this signpost in Castle Street (removed when the street was pedestrianized in 2005). However, the east wall of the present Chapel, built in 1912, has the shorter name.*

of their name, tend to say 'Charlotte', but the church is also popularly known as 'CC'.

Whoever designed the plaque on Christopher Anderson's portrait, which hangs in the vestry, kept his options open by engraving Charlotte (Baptist) Chapel, while the 1908 centenary brochure had Charlotte Chapel (Baptist). An Edinburgh newspaper's obituary for Christopher Anderson, the founder and first pastor, summed up his sentiments in words with which many would concur: 'He would have gone joyfully across the seas to carry the message of salvation to dying men; but, as he often said, he would not cross the street to make a Baptist.'

### Acknowledgement

The writer is indebted to the Rev. David Searle, formerly warden of Rutherford House, Edinburgh, for taking the manuscript of this book through to publication. Many others, too numerous to name here, have provided information and documents. Their contribution is acknowledged by repeating the chestnut story of the preacher who plagiarized the sermons of others, without identifying his sources. One of his congregation, who was not only well read but blessed with an excellent memory, used to mutter audibly: 'That was C.H. Spurgeon', or: 'He got that from Martyn Lloyd-Jones'. One day, in exasperation, the preacher rounded publicly on his critic: 'Will you shut up?', which elicited the response: 'Now, that sounds more like himself.' The writer hopes that many will recognize their contribution in the book; if the narrative becomes tedious, they are entitled to say: 'Now, that sounds like himself.'

The title *Revival in Rose Street* is used with the permission of the family of the Rev. William Whyte, who wrote a history of the Chapel to 1953 under that name. His book (now out of print) was launched at a reception given by Alex Cameron in his home in the summer of 1976. The text of it is reproduced on the CD under William Whyte.

*The first* Revival in Rose Street *was launched at a reception in 1976, at which this picture was taken; from left to right, Fergus Brown, Rev. William Whyte, the writer, David Murray and Alex Cameron, all elders of the Chapel at the time.*

### To see more of their names

Limitations on space mean that very few lay people can be named in the narrative. Those who have made the Chapel their life-work might reasonably expect to find mention of it, but that would expand the book beyond reasonable size – there are so many of them. The writer was under the same restriction when he contributed a chapter to *The Baptists in Scotland* in 1988. One reviewer said of it: 'Probably some who were deeply involved would prefer … to see more of their own names.' That is fair comment about this book as well. Office-bearers, superintendents, organists, missionaries and others in full-time Christian work, together with the leaders of the Young Peoples Meeting, are listed on the CD provided with the book.

### References

Sources are given for indented quotations only; other citations, and extended footnotes, are on the CD; a list at the end of every chapter gives the topics available on it for that chapter.

### Two centuries on

What might Christopher Anderson, who constituted the church in 1808, and who purchased the original Charlotte Chapel building in 1818, feel about its bicentenary? From his writings, three things may reasonably be deduced:

He would be delighted at the emphasis on evangelism, both at home and abroad. Christopher Anderson was first and foremost an evangelist, seeking souls for Christ.

He would commend the teaching ministry, the regular public exposition of Scripture. Christopher Anderson was a learned man, who sought to build a stable congregation. There is, and always has been, a strain of scholarship running through this Chapel, an important ingredient in the life of the church.

He would appreciate the breadth of the Chapel's interests. Christopher Anderson was a Baptist, but he co-operated with all good men and women of evangelical belief.

To set the scene for the founding of the church that became Charlotte Chapel, Chapter 1 gives a brief survey of Baptist life and Baptist churches in Edinburgh before Christopher Anderson.

*Charlotte Baptist Chapel in 1998, with Edinburgh Castle in the background; photograph taken when the building opposite the Chapel was demolished during renovation of the Roxburghe Hotel.*

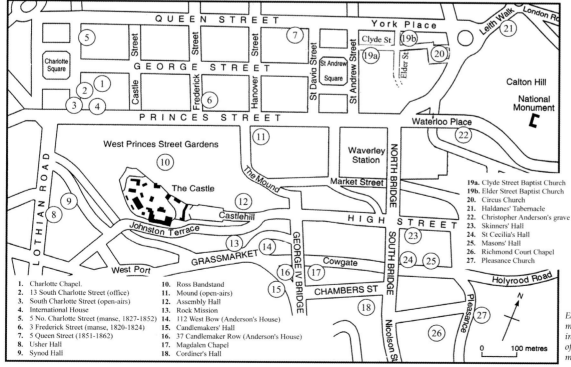

1.  Charlotte Chapel.
2.  13 South Charlotte Street (office)
3.  South Charlotte Street (open-airs)
4.  International House
5.  5 No. Charlotte Street (manse, 1827-1852)
6.  3 Frederick Street (manse, 1820-1824)
7.  5 Queen Street (1851-1862)
8.  Usher Hall
9.  Synod Hall
10. Ross Bandstand
11. Mound (open-airs)
12. Assembly Hall
13. Rock Mission
14. 112 West Bow (Anderson's House)
15. Candlemakers' Hall
16. 37 Candlemaker Row (Anderson's House)
17. Magdalen Chapel
18. Cordiner's Hall

19a. Clyde Street Baptist Church
19b. Elder Street Baptist Church
20. Circus Church
21. Haldanes' Tabernacle
22. Christopher Anderson's grave
23. Skinners' Hall
24. St Cecilia's Hall
25. Masons' Hall
26. Richmond Court Chapel
27. Pleasance Church

*Edinburgh – a modern map, with places of interest for the history of Charlotte Chapel marked.*

# Chapter 1
# Baptist pioneers in Edinburgh (1643–1799)

## The first Baptists in Edinburgh

### Individual Baptists

The first Baptist known to visit Edinburgh was inhospitably received – he was thrown into jail for his beliefs. As Gilbert Gardin from Banchory in Aberdeenshire walked along the High Street in Edinburgh in 1643, he was seized and hustled into the Tolbooth prison. There he remained, one honest man among thieves and rogues, for 18 months. His father was a sheriff but no influence could release him, because he was openly a Baptist. The Reformation in Scotland had been entirely Presbyterian in character, with no toleration for Baptists or other Independents. The stern John Knox denounced believers' baptism and religious liberty as 'maist horribill and absurd'.

*The Tolbooth prison, adjoining St Giles Cathedral, where Gilbert Gardin was incarcerated in 1643 for being a Baptist. Sir Walter Scott's novel* Heart of Midlothian *made it world-famous. It was Edinburgh's main prison until 1817.*

Although Gardin is the first known by name, there were 'watterdippers' in Edinburgh in 1624 and 'sectaries, quakers, and anabaptists' about the same time. Suppressed by both church and state, they held tenaciously to their beliefs. The General Assembly of the Church of Scotland was so alarmed that in 1647 it published a book against believers' baptism, trying to stop any more of 'this pest' from crossing the Tweed from England. Nevertheless,

Baptists and Baptist sympathisers were active in Edinburgh in 1651, despite Presbyterian disapproval, although there is no record of them meeting together as a church.

## The first Baptist church in Edinburgh

The first Baptist church in Edinburgh was constituted in 1652, not by indigenous Scots but by chaplains and soldiers in Oliver Cromwell's army of occupation. Among the troops stationed in Edinburgh and in Leith were a number of Baptists. The Commonwealth Parliament encouraged religious toleration, so the military not only worshipped in their camps, but they also arranged evangelistic services in the community. This led to the formation of a Baptist church in 1652, which met in Leith and in Edinburgh on alternate Sundays – one congregation, but meeting in two locations for the convenience of the believers in the two communities.

 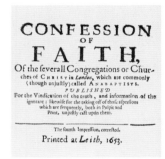

*Cromwell's New Model Army was based in the Citadel in Leith, of which only the main port (gate) has survived. It is directly opposite the pedestrian entrance to the Scottish Government in Commercial Street, Leith; there is an explanatory plaque on the wall.*

*A Confession of Faith by churches 'which are commonly (though unjustly) called Anabaptists' was printed at Leith in March 1653, 'for the edification of the churches, the dispersal of public prejudice and the dissemination of truths the Baptists so ardently espouse.'*

While soldiers formed the majority of the membership, some local people were converted and baptized by immersion and joined the church in February 1653. Baptisms took place in the Water of Leith and among those 'dippit at Bonnington Mill, betwixt Leith and Edinburgh, were both men and women of good rank. Some days there would be sundry hundred persons attending that action and fifteen persons baptized in one day by the Anabaptists.' Among them was Lady Craigie Wallace, who maintained her testimony until her death in 1663. When her brother (who was not sympathetic) visited her shortly before she died, he found her 'very sharp but exceedingly perverse in her opinion of anabaptisme' and she 'expressed unto me her assurance of mercy and salvation through Jesus Christ'.

The Protectorate Army left Edinburgh in November 1659, taking away the chaplains who had acted as pastors, and leaving few to carry on a Baptist witness. Those who did were marked out and persecuted. Charles II ordered proclamations against Anabaptists and Quakers to be read at the market crosses of the royal burghs on 2 January 1661, with instructions 'to apprehend any such persons as shall frequent such meetings'. In 1672, he gave royal assent to a law that subjected the parents of any child unbaptised after 30 days to heavy fines. As an encouragement to sheriffs, they were allowed to pocket the fines, so many native Baptists either fled to England or renounced their beliefs. Extant references to Baptists in Edinburgh are both sparse and derogatory over the next hundred years, as the Presbyterians resumed control of religion. The Covenanters fought to the death against the Establishment, but they did so for purer Presbyterianism and had no sympathy for Baptists or other Independents.

*The two hundred and fiftieth anniversary of the founding of the Keiss Baptist Church was commemorated in the year 2000 by a group visiting Keiss. They viewed the ruins of the castle, in which the first church met in 1750, sang some of Sir William Sinclair's hymns, and inspected the 1854 church buildingx (not in this photograph), which the Keiss church still owns.*

While there is no record of organized Baptist witness in Edinburgh between 1659 and 1765, home groups may have met for fellowship; some individuals publicly refused to conform, such as Thomas Lendon. He had been an officer in

Cromwell's army but he liked Edinburgh and when the army withdrew, he resigned his commission and set up as a merchant here. His Baptist views were well known and during the occasional disciplining of those who refused to attend the National Church, he was imprisoned from time to time. However, he was still taking an active part in public life 29 years later, still well known for his Baptist beliefs.

## The second Baptist church in Edinburgh

On New Year's Day 1750, 30 people in the village of Keiss in Caithness were baptized as believers and formed a Baptist church – the first in Scotland since Cromwell's day. It is relevant to this book because its founder, Sir William Sinclair, was compelled by financial troubles to sell his estate in Caithness and he lived in Edinburgh from 1763 until his death here five years later – his grave is in the Canongate churchyard. A Baptist church was formed in 1765 in the Magdalen Chapel in the Cowgate, next paragraph.

The second Baptist church in Edinburgh originated when Robert Carmichael, the minister of an Old Scots Independent congregation in Candlemakers' Hall (where Christopher Anderson's father and grandparents were active members) became convinced from the Scriptures that baptism was for believers only and that it should be by immersion. Soon after that, when he was asked

*The Magdalen Chapel, 41 Cowgate, housed the first enduring Baptist church in Edinburgh, founded in 1765; Baptists worshipped there until 1774. It is open to the public and is worth a visit.*

## Chapter 1
Baptist pioneers in Edinburgh (1643-1799)

to baptize an infant, Carmichael and seven others withdrew from the Independent church in May 1765 and formed a new fellowship in the nearby Magdalen Chapel.

As they did not know at that stage about either Sir William Sinclair or the church in Keiss, Carmichael arranged to be baptized in London in October 1765. On his return to Edinburgh, he baptized four men and three women in the Water of Leith at Canonmills on 25 November 1765; a reporter for *The Scots Magazine* saw two of the seven baptisms [original wording retained]:

*On Monday November 25 an Antipaedobaptist administered the ordinance of Baptism to two adults in the water of Lieth hard by Canonmills near Edinburgh in the following manner the two persons being first stripped were cloathed with long black gowns and then went into the water along with their Minister who after repeating some words in their ordinary form took them by the nape of the neck plunged them down over head and ears and keept them for a little time wholly under the water.*

1 *The Scots Magazine*, **November 1765.**

These are the first known baptisms in Edinburgh since Cromwell's troops left in November 1659. Thus began the church – the first enduring Baptist church in Edinburgh – that after various moves is today the Bristo Baptist Church at the top of Orchard Brae on the Queensferry Road. In 1796-8, it had a significant influence on the life of Christopher Anderson, the founder of the church that became Charlotte Chapel. He attended for these two years, as a teenager; his concern at some of its policies led him to start another type of Baptist church in Edinburgh, as described in the next chapter.

*In the summers of 1984 and 1985, Charlotte Chapel sponsored Sunday afternoon Baptist Heritage Trails. In this picture, a retired Baptist minister (George Hossack) describes the grave of Archibald McLean and explains McLean's influence on Christopher Anderson, who attended McLean's church for two years as a teenager.*

It is now time to look at the early life of Christopher Anderson, who, at the age of 26, founded the church whose bicentenary in 2008 is celebrated by this book.

## Christopher Anderson

### Christopher Anderson's family
Christopher Anderson, the youngest of five sons, was born on 19 February 1782 in his parents' home at 112 West Bow, Edinburgh, at its junction with the Grassmarket. His father, William Anderson, had an ironmonger's business at 110 West Bow, and they lived over the shop. The shop door and windows are arched, and the house enters from the vennel on the right of the photograph. The Bowfoot Well, erected by the Town Council in 1674 and refurbished in 1861, still stands in front of the premises.

*A contemporary sketch and a recent photograph of the Anderson's home at number 112 West Bow, above the ironmonger's shop at 110, which is now a café.*

Because of delicate health (probably a tubercular condition), Christopher's early years were, on medical advice, spent in the country, boarding with a cottager at Polton, near Lasswade, about six miles south of Edinburgh. He returned to the city at the age of 14, and was apprenticed to an ironmonger at the Royal Exchange in the High Street. However, after four years of his five-year indenture, he was allowed to leave in order to take up a four-year contract as a clerk in the Edinburgh Friendly Insurance Company. His maternal uncle was the manager and a large shareholder; the intention was that Christopher would, in due course, succeed him as manager. He was therefore assured of a comfortable position, with an income of £300-£400 a year, secured for life. Anyone with that much to spend was considered rather important in Edinburgh in 1800.

*The Grassmarket and the West Bow formed the main western thoroughfare into the Old Town in Christopher Anderson's day; his house was behind the lamppost at the right of the 1904 photograph. The coloured picture was taken in 2001 from the window of 112 West Bow, where Christopher Anderson lived until he was 21.*

### Edinburgh in Christopher Anderson's youth

Edinburgh in 1800 was an exciting place – architecturally, culturally and religiously. Architecturally, the New Town was under construction. For the previous two hundred years, Edinburgh had been confined for security reasons within city walls, so that expansion had to be upward rather than outward. One could walk from east to west of old Edinburgh in ten minutes and from north to south in less. Tenements of sixteen storeys were common; in the Royal Mile alone, forty-eight thousand people lived cheek by jowl in bustling, dirty, overcrowded skyscrapers – aristocrats, judges, merchants, apothecaries, fleshers, bakers, publicans, servants and labourers. There was no running water and no sanitation – water had to be drawn from street wells and waste was collected in buckets. The Edinburgh custom of throwing the day's slops out of upstairs windows as the St Giles' belfry sounded 10 p.m., with the perfunctory warning cry 'gardyloo' (*gardez l'eau*: 'look out – water'), had recently been stopped, but the closes still had open gutters.

### The New Town

After the collapse of the Jacobite Rebellion of 1745-6, new building became possible outside the traditional defensive walls; men of vision, led by the Lord Provost, expanded northward into the New Town and southward into George Square. By 1800, the New Town had reached Heriot Row and the southern suburbs had spread beyond the Meadows. As

part of this expansion, a Scottish Episcopalian congregation, meeting in cramped conditions in a hall in West Register Street, planned to build a new church, 'next to South Charlotte Street, to be called Charlotte Chapel', named after the queen of the day. They wanted to be at the heart of the New Town.

Charlotte Chapel was ready for occupation in 1796; the congregation steadily increased in number and influence. In 1818, they moved across Princes Street and built St John's, the magnificent church that still graces the West End. As described in Chapter 3, Christopher Anderson seized the opportunity of purchasing the vacant premises and kept the name Charlotte Chapel. The New Town continued to expand – living in a self-contained house with airy apartments instead of sharing a common entrance, and with the servants consigned to basement or attic, was much more attractive than the cramped, ill-ventilated flats in the Old Town, where family and servants constantly rubbed shoulders. It also had something to do with keeping up with the Joneses. The population of Edinburgh increased by 78 per cent in the first 30 years of the new century.

*Edinburgh in the mid-eighteenth century was a compact burgh, protected on three sides by city walls and, on the fourth side, by the Nor' Loch. The High Street ran down the spine of the hill to the Netherbow Port (gate) at the eastern end.*

The original Charlotte Chapel was a neat, symmetrical, but unpretentious building, with a pretty octagon in the centre of the roof. Princes Street and George Street were entirely residential in 1796 and all buildings had to be three storeys high, with a sunken area in front. Rose Street, the service road between Princes Street and George Street, was permitted to have only two storeys. In the photograph, the church officer (caretaker) is standing at the front door and his wife at the side door, which was the entrance to their house below the building. This Chapel was demolished in 1911 and replaced by the present one on the same site.

*Charlotte Chapel almost as it was in 1796 – the only differences are the notice board and the electric light globes over the gallery windows, which were twentieth-century additions.*

## Edinburgh's Golden Age

Edinburgh in 1800 was also an exciting place culturally – a flowering of literary, artistic and scientific energy known as Edinburgh's Golden Age – now called the Scottish Enlightenment. The novelist Sir Walter Scott, the portrait painters Sir Henry Raeburn and Allan Ramsay, the philosopher David Hume and the economist Adam Smith were all living and working in the city. The poet Robert Burns had twice stayed for six months and had visited five other times; the printer of Burns' Edinburgh edition, William Smellie, produced the first *Encyclopaedia Britannica*. Nothing like it had been seen in Edinburgh before; William Cullen, a world-renowned physicist, Adam Ferguson, the founder of modern sociology, Joseph Black, the pioneering chemist, James Hutton, the father of modern geology and William Robertson, the founder of modern historiography, together with jurists, literary critics, anthropologists and agricultural improvers, made Edinburgh famous in Europe and America. Robert and James Adam established themselves as internationally renowned architects, while James Craig designed the New Town.

Alongside this prosperity, however, went massive seasonal unemployment and desperate poverty. The lowest classes of Edinburgh society laboured in conditions approaching serfdom. With them in mind Christopher Anderson wrote to his brother, Robert, on 6 June 1806: 'I propose ... to collect an audience out of those who are poor, or who are unaccustomed to attend any place of worship, and bring them to repentance.'

For evangelical Christians, Edinburgh's Golden Age had and still has a downside. At the time, it led the National Church into a genteel but insipid form of Christianity, which became known as Moderatism, against which evangelicals battled for generations to come. Culture and moral rectitude was exalted as the objective of the church rather than personal salvation through evangelism, which was denounced as fanaticism. The continuing downside was illustrated by the millennium celebrations for the year 2000. The *Sunday Times* asked Scottish opinion-formers to nominate the Scot of the millennium. When the sceptic philosopher David Hume, 'acknowledged as the father of the Scottish Enlightenment', topped the poll above William Wallace, Robert the Bruce, Robert Burns, Sir Walter Scott, Alexander Graham Bell or Sir Alexander Fleming, the leader of Scotland's Roman Catholics, Cardinal Winning, wrote to the editor in protest. Hume, he pointed out, by exalting human reason over religious faith and by questioning the existence of God, contributed to 'the moral meltdown which is modern European culture'. The *Sunday Times* retaliated with a personal attack on the Cardinal, employing the tactic: if you can't get the ball, get the man.

*Christopher Anderson was converted (next chapter) during evangelistic services held in the Circus, a former variety theatre. It was later destroyed by fire and replaced by the Theatre Royal, seen in this 1931 picture to the left of St Mary's Roman Catholic Cathedral (opened in 1813). The Cathedral acquired the theatre site in 1956 and built its present extension and car park on it.*

## The Circus

Edinburgh in 1800 was also an exciting place religiously. James Haldane and his brother Robert, well-to-do Church of Scotland laymen, had been converted in 1794. When they discovered that their church was not interested in mission, they took over a variety theatre called the Circus at the head of Leith Walk, and began preaching the gospel in July 1798 – a user-friendly outreach. The Haldanes' chief aim was 'the conversion of the undecided'.

*The Haldanes' Tabernacle in Greenside Place, at the top of Leith Walk, was used for Christian services between 1801 and 1864; in 1914, it was a furniture warehouse (upper photo). In 1929, it was replaced by the Playhouse Cinema (lower photo), now the Playhouse Theatre.*

The Circus services were so well supported that in January 1799, the Haldanes formed the New Congregational Church and inducted James Haldane as pastor. The service lasted for five hours and 'the crowded audience gave close attention to the end'; one wonders how many today would still be giving close attention after five hours. The New Congregational Church prospered so greatly that in 1801, Robert Haldane built a large Tabernacle on the other side of Leith Walk, the

site of the present Playhouse Theatre. Christopher Anderson attended both the Circus and the Tabernacle and learned much from the preaching there.

Additional information on the following topics, mentioned in this chapter, is available on the CD.

Baptist distinctive principles
Baptist Heritage Trail
Charlotte Chapel as an Episcopal church
Christopher Anderson's early years
Christopher Anderson's home
Circus
Cromwell's army of occupation
Gilbert Gardin
Haldane brothers
Haldanes' Tabernacle
Old Scots Independent congregation
Rose Street
Sir William Sinclair

# Chapter 2
# Christopher Anderson to 1806 (1799–1806)

## Christopher Anderson's conversion and 'call'

### The Andersons' family church

Christopher Anderson's parents were members of the Old Scots Independent congregation that Carmichael and seven others had left in 1765, to form the Baptist church mentioned in Chapter 1. The Independent church met in Candlemakers' Hall, at the junction of Candlemaker Row and what is now George IV Bridge. They believed in lay leadership (only), which Christopher later described as 'worthy but uneducated'. However, the family habit of going to church, taking notes of the sermons and discussing them later at home, gave Christopher a good grounding in the Christian faith, although his absorbing passion was music and dancing until he reached the age of 17.

*Candlemakers' Hall, which Christopher Anderson attended with his father at 36 Candlemaker Row, was built in 1722 and is still occupied (restored 1929), with the date over the blue door. The statue in the foreground is the world's best-known Skye terrier – Greyfriars Bobby.*

During Christopher's apprenticeship as an ironmonger, all five Anderson brothers found greater spiritual vitality in the Baptist church, formed in the Magdalen Chapel and now meeting in Richmond Court. Three of the brothers stayed there, but in 1798 the youthful and still unconverted Christopher and his older brother James, a medical practitioner, began to attend the services in the Circus. It was here that Christopher, listening at the age of 17 to the exposition of Scripture under James Haldane, was first convicted of sin and then 'called by grace'.

His conversion was sudden and complete. He recorded in his diary: 'it seemed as if the preacher was speaking to me personally'. He began 'to realise the vanity of the world and all its pleasures' and wrote: 'Thursday 3rd or Friday 4th July [1799, aged 17], I first began to know, in some small measure, my interest in the Redeemer and the joys of religion.' On 2 August 1799, he came into full assurance of salvation and 'from that hour was rarely troubled with doubts'. His nephew and biographer, Hugh Anderson, having quoted these extracts from his uncle's diary, added in his own words: 'Repeatedly has he stated to Christian friends that in his case the sensible transition from darkness to God's marvellous light, from the spirit of bondage to the spirit of adoption, was nearly instantaneous. In less than one hour he was conscious of the change, and was seldom afterwards troubled with doubts respecting its reality.'

### Christopher Anderson's baptism

Christopher and his brother James joined the New Congregational Church (as the Circus was now known), and during the formative months of his Christian character, Christopher sat under the Haldanes' ministry. In the winter of 1799-1800, he got to know two Baptist students from England, who were finishing their training for the ministry at Edinburgh University. From them he learned the scriptural basis for believers' baptism by immersion, and became convinced that this was the right course for him to follow. He would have been baptized in the Baptist church, where three of his brothers were members, but baptism there involved membership and he was not happy at several aspects of their church policy, as described below. In March 1801, one of the students baptized Christopher Anderson (aged 19) and several women members of the New Congregational Church.

The unexpected consequence was their expulsion from membership of that church, because it practised infant baptism and there was strong prejudice at that time against Baptists, not only among Presbyterians but also among Independents. Across the West Bow from the Andersons' shop was a good friend of the family, John Campbell, another ironmonger and an associate of James Haldane. He came across to Christopher's father, 'to condole with him on the apostasy of his children', as he put it, four out of the five having become Baptists. 'No, Johnnie', said the good man, 'rejoice with me rather that all my sons are now the sons of God.'

*James Alexander Haldane, under whose preaching Christopher Anderson was converted. He was the first pastor of the Circus and then of the Tabernacle, which Christopher attended during his formative years.*

### Scotch Baptists and English Baptists

During the spring of 1801, the group that had been excluded from membership of the Haldanes' church met on Wednesday evening with the two English students, for prayer and Christian fellowship in Cordiners' Hall, near the university. From these students, Christopher Anderson learned about English Baptist churches, where leadership was by an ordained minister, in contrast to the Scotch Baptists, who had a plurality of lay elders, functioning as a team of co-pastors.

'English' and 'Scotch' had no racial or nationalist meaning in this context, but indicated a difference in church management in two respects. (1) English Baptists believed that a church should have a minister, supported by them, who would not engage in business except for study and prayer and the ministry of the Word, and who would devote his energies entirely to his congregation. Scotch Baptists insisted on lay pastors (always two or more in each church, working as a team), who carried on their trades and professions during the week and received no financial aid from the church. Furthermore, the lay pastors encouraged any men present to pray or to speak, calling it 'mutual exhortation'. Both groups had a plurality of lay deacons; it was the role of the pastor or elder that differentiated them. (2) English Baptists saw no warrant in the New Testament for ordinances other than baptism and the Lord's Supper, while the Scotch Baptists had a weekly love-feast.

Christopher Anderson became increasingly convinced that both Scripture and common sense encouraged a local church to have a full-time pastor. He recognized that small congregations might not afford this, but that was different from insisting, on principle, on lay pastors. Anderson did not accept that 'a man can attend to the Church of God, his family, and a worldly calling, and do justice to all'. Furthermore, he was disappointed at the Edinburgh Scotch Baptists' lack of outreach and evangelism. He recognized that they were good people in themselves, but 'I long to see more zeal for the glory of God and more diligence in devising and using means for gathering in the ordained unto eternal life'. (That was the Edinburgh situation, not necessarily true elsewhere.)

### Leader of the group

When the two students left Edinburgh in May 1801 for the university summer vacation, Christopher Anderson, although only 19 years of age, took over leadership of the group. He displayed considerable force of character, and a contemporary described him as 'ever the leader, never the led'. He was the only one of the group who felt free to pray publicly. During the summer of 1801, the terminal illness of his older brother, William, deepened his own consecration. William's serene death, at the age of 27, left a lasting impression on Christopher who, together with William's young wife, watched as he died.

As the winter of 1801 approached, the small group invited a student from the Bristol Academy (later Bristol Baptist College) to come to Edinburgh for six months, with a view to starting an English Baptist church in Edinburgh. The student, William Gray, was pastor-elect of a Baptist church in Wiltshire; Christopher and his friends supported him during his six months here from November 1801 to May 1802. They hired the Masons' Hall at the junction of Blackfriars Wynd with the Cowgate and held services on Sunday, both morning and evening, and on one night during the week. It was not a wise choice of location. The Scotch Baptists were now meeting in St Cecilia's Hall, not a hundred yards from the Masons' Hall; they looked on this new venture with suspicion, as did the Presbyterian and Independent churches around. In consequence, the congregations were small, especially in the morning, and seldom exceeded one hundred, while often there were not more than 20.

Here, on Thursday 10 December 1801, young Christopher Anderson preached his first sermon. His text was: 'All things whatsoever ye shall ask in prayer, believing, ye shall receive.' He was conscious of the poor figure he made, as he described it, but at the same time he wrote in his diary: 'Spoke with greater freedom than I could have expected. Oh, heavenly Father, may I grow in humility.' After that, he took the Thursday evening exhortation, as it was called, alternately with one of the two English students who had been so influential during the academic year 1800-1 and who had come back to the university for 1801-2.

After William Gray returned south, the Cowgate venture was given up, but Christopher continued the mid-week meeting in a private house. Although unable to take communion in the Tabernacle, which was for members only, he resumed attendance at the public Sunday services. It was the deliberate policy of the Haldanes, both in the Circus and then in the Tabernacle, to invite influential English evangelical preachers, from a variety of denominations, to supply the pulpit. Christopher Anderson greatly appreciated hearing so many different voices on a regular basis, and he learned a great deal from them – not least about the breadth and width of Evangelicalism.

### Baptist church membership

Word reached Edinburgh that an English Baptist church had been started in Glasgow in November 1801, with 30 members under James Lister as pastor. This was the second such church in Scotland; an earlier one had been formed in Paisley, but Glasgow was nearer to Edinburgh than Paisley and Christopher Anderson joined the Glasgow church in October 1802. He was invited to preach on the following Sunday, which he did from Philippians 2:5, on Humility.

English Baptist churches were dependent on their full-time pastors, and when James Lister accepted a 'call' to Liverpool in 1803, the church in Glasgow did not survive beyond 1806. As Charlotte Chapel has discovered many times over the years, effective congregational participation goes hand in hand with strong leadership, which guides enthusiastic but possibly divisive members of the congregation for the good of the whole. It was 1819 before another English Baptist church was formed in Glasgow; when it was, they asked Christopher Anderson to conduct the ordination.

### 'Call' to full-time Christian service

Andrew Fuller, secretary of the Baptist Missionary Society, preached in the Circus one October Sunday morning in 1799, two months after Christopher Anderson's conversion. Christopher's heart was stirred for overseas missionary service, particularly in India.

*Andrew Fuller had a great influence on Christopher Anderson. He encouraged him to preach the gospel freely to the unconverted, and to form an English Baptist church in Edinburgh.*

Over the next two years, Christopher Anderson thought more and more about joining William Carey in Serampore, Bengal; in 1802 the challenge became irresistible. For the previous nine years, Carey's work had been preparatory, but now the first converts had been baptized, a church of 33 believers had been formed, a printing press had been set up and the first translation of the New Testament into Bengali had been issued. Converts were being trained to evangelise their fellow-countrymen, itinerant preaching was taking place in the vernacular, and schools were being established.

On 15 July 1802, Christopher wrote in his diary:

*Most of my relations being now acquainted with my desire
to go as a missionary, except my father, I was afraid he might
hear of it from some other quarter. I felt uneasy at telling
him of it, but as I had noted it at the beginning of this journal,
I asked him to read it. When he had done so, all he said was
that he did not know what to say.*

---

1 Hugh Anderson, *The Life and Letters of Christopher Anderson*
(William P. Kennedy, Edinburgh, 1854), pp. 20-21.

Christopher Anderson's sense of 'call' was taken a stage
further at the beginning of September 1802. Andrew Fuller
came to Edinburgh for the second time, again on behalf of
the Baptist Missionary Society. Christopher had a half-hour
discussion with him, and was greatly encouraged; however,
Dr James Anderson doubted whether his brother's physical
constitution could bear the strain of a tropical climate.
Christopher wrote in his diary on 1 January 1803: 'The height
of my ambition is to serve God in the Gospel of His Son, but
when, where or how I do not fully see. Perhaps the Lord will
make my way clear in the course of this year.'

In March 1803, he decided it was India. Andrew Fuller
advised him to complete his four years' engagement with the
Edinburgh Friendly Insurance Company, while applying to
the Baptist Missionary Society in time for their spring
meeting in 1804. On receiving this letter, Christopher
Anderson gave the office a year's notice that he would leave
in June 1804, at the end of his contract. His maternal uncle,
whose hopes for the future of the office had centred on his
nephew, was not pleased. Christopher had anticipated this
and had induced his older brother, James, to break the news
of his intention. His uncle, who was a member of the
National Church, had no sympathy with Christopher's
project, could not understand his motives and was greatly
troubled by this frustration of his plan for his nephew's
settlement in life.

Although they still had concerns whether Christopher was
physically fit for work in India, the Society accepted him as a
student on probation. As soon as he was free from his duties
in his uncle's office in July 1804, he commenced a course of
study at his own expense. He engaged a tutor in Greek for
three months, and then from October 1804 to April 1805, he

studied logic, moral philosophy and chemistry at the University
of Edinburgh, as well as keeping up his tuition in Greek.

*Christopher Anderson's mother was the daughter of a wealthy Edinburgh merchant,
Alexander Moubray. The family home, Moubray House, at Trunk's Close, 53 High
Street, is probably Edinburgh's oldest extant dwelling. The adjoining building in this
1900 photograph is known as John Knox's house.*

## Christopher Anderson's independence

Christopher Anderson's father died in December 1804.
While grieving for his loss, Christopher, aged 22, felt released
from an obligation that had worried him – as the only
unmarried son, he had stayed with, and been company for,
his father; 'the prospect of going to a distant land was a severe
trial to an affectionate son'. Two months later, his mother,
who had been in an Institution in Musselburgh since shortly
after Christopher's birth, died. Her merchant father had
provided generously for his invalid daughter, and when the
capital passed on her death to her only surviving child,
Christopher was financially secure for life. (His four half-
brothers were from William Anderson's first marriage.) His
income was less than it would have been as manager of the
insurance company, but it was sufficient for all his needs. He
kept on the family home, which was now at 37 Candlemaker
Row, to provide for his widowed sister-in-law, Mrs Margaret
Anderson, and her young daughter. She acted as his
housekeeper, both before he went to England in May 1805
and again on his return to Edinburgh in August 1806.

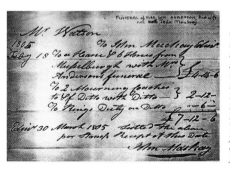

*Christopher Anderson
hardly knew his mother.
She was unwell from
shortly after his birth
in 1782, and was
looked after in an
Institution in
Musselburgh until
her death in 1805.
This receipt for her
funeral cortege is one
of the few surviving
family papers.*

### Cordiners' Hall

At the end of the university year in April 1805, Christopher spent a short time evangelising in the Highlands. On his return, he and four fellow Baptists formed themselves, on the first Sunday in May, into a church that they believed followed the New Testament pattern, namely that practised by English Baptists. They hired Cordiners' Hall, where the newly baptized Christopher, and the others baptized with him, had met with the two English students on Wednesday evening in April and May 1801. Christopher Anderson preached and administered the Lord's Supper on 5 May 1805 and again on the following Sunday.

*Cordiners' Hall, here painted by Skene, was in West College Street; the site is now part of the Royal Scottish Museum. Five believers, led by Christopher Anderson, constituted an English Baptist church there in May 1805.*

It was then time for Christopher to leave for Olney, a village in Buckinghamshire, where he and several other young men were to prepare for service with the Baptist Missionary Society. He still hoped to join William Carey at Serampore. The easiest way to reach Olney from Edinburgh in 1805 was to sail from Leith to London, and then take a horse-drawn coach. To travel all the way by coach took four days and was expensive at nearly £5 per person. Sailing from Leith continued to be the most popular route from Edinburgh to London until the railway line was opened via Newcastle in 1846.

## Christopher Anderson's fifteen months in England

### A change of direction

Shortly after Christopher Anderson reached Olney in June 1805 (having stayed for a few weeks with friends in London, and then in Bristol, on the way), his mentor, Andrew Fuller, was in Edinburgh on missionary society business. After an interview with Christopher's brother, James, and others, Fuller strongly recommended that on health grounds he should think of ministry in this country rather than in tropical Serampore. In September 1805, Christopher reluctantly accepted this advice; he decided to return to Edinburgh and pastor the little church that he had constituted in Cordiners' Hall, which was growing in number.

His friends supported this decision, but advised that before settling down to his life's work in Edinburgh, he should spend the winter in Bristol and attend the Baptist Academy, as it was then called, the only Baptist training college in Great Britain at that time. As he had rejected the Scotch Baptist model, which was the norm in Scotland, he needed time to formulate clearly in his own mind the structure of the church that he anticipated pastoring on his return to Edinburgh. Accordingly, his study arrangements in Bristol were left flexible enough for him to experience as many styles of worship and structures of churches as possible during his stay, and to meet some of the major figures among English Evangelicals.

### Pan-evangelical influences

Three of Christopher Anderson's early experiences – in family, in the Tabernacle and finally in Bristol – gave him a breadth of vision that was lacking in many of his contemporaries in Edinburgh. Before tracing his return to his native city, and the establishment of the church that became Charlotte Chapel, it is worth noting these three influences on him.

First, he was fortunate in the role model of his father. Not only did he give permission for Christopher and his brothers to transfer their allegiance from the Old Scots Independent congregation, where they had been brought up, to the Scotch Baptist Church and then, in James' and Christopher's cases, to the Circus, but he responded positively to Christopher's baptism, as mentioned above. This tolerance toward the views of others, and Christopher's ability to work with Christians who shared only some of his views, can be traced in embryo to the wise nurture of his father. Secondly, in the Circus and in the Tabernacle, Christopher was (as mentioned earlier) exposed to evangelical preachers from a variety of ecclesiastical backgrounds – including the Anglican Charles Simeon of Cambridge. This developed Christopher's pan-evangelical sympathies and his ability to work with Christians from a variety of traditions in other parts of the United Kingdom.

*Leith Docks, from where Christopher Anderson sailed to London in 1805 to prepare for missionary service.*

Thirdly, he took many preaching engagements while in Bristol, and visited many places, illustrated by his choice of worship on Christmas Day, 1805:

*Went to the Catholic Chapel with Mr Pearson. Saw high mass performed. ... went to Temple Church in the evening. The service was interspersed with music vocal and instrumental; ... performed by a full band ... trumpet, drum &c!*

2 Anderson, *Life and Letters*, p. 46.

He was deeply impressed by the strength of the Western Association of Particular Baptist churches, when he attended their annual meeting in Devon in June 1805 – nearly 50 churches from the south and west of England were represented, and he noted their vigour, fervour and animation. His positive experience of churches co-operating for mission and mutual support stood him in good stead when similar developments were, later, proposed for Scotland as well (Chapter 5).

The only formal learning that Christopher Anderson received, after leaving school, was during his 15 months in England, observing the ministry and church government of the English Baptists, together with his earlier year at the University of Edinburgh and two more terms after his return (Chapter 3); the remainder of his massive knowledge was self-acquired. He never did see India, but four men and one woman from the church that he founded in Edinburgh worthily represented him there; Helen Mack, who was at Serampore for some years from 1828, may have been the first woman from Scotland to serve on the mission field.

### Religion in Edinburgh in 1806
Christopher Anderson wrote to his brother, Charles, on 23 May 1806, as he was completing his ministerial training in Bristol: 'We think of purchasing Richmond Court meeting-house, and inviting the poor as well as others to hear the Gospel', and to another brother, Robert, on 6 June 1806: 'We begin in opposition to no party. One of my principal desires and designs being to convert sinners from the error of their ways, and bring them to repentance.' To understand Christopher Anderson's mission statement (as it would now be called), a snapshot of the religious scene in Edinburgh in 1806 will be helpful.

Religious life in Edinburgh, as Christopher Anderson contemplated starting his ministry here, showed two contrasting pictures – on the one hand, a deep concern by some for spiritual life, evidenced by generous support for evangelistic and philanthropic efforts at home and abroad, and, on the other hand, much apathy and formalism. Nearly every 'respectable' person was a member of some church and took communion at least once a year. Many considered that annual payment of seat rent, together with dropping a coin onto the plate on Sunday, fully discharged their religious obligations. Such people made no effort to bring in outsiders; external decorum was important to them, and they regarded innovations like tract distribution and Sunday Schools and lay preaching as intrusions into the sphere of the regular ministry. Nevertheless, there was much genuine piety in many homes – family worship was common, and children were expected to commit to memory large portions of catechism, psalms and prose passages from the Bible.

There were 39 Protestant churches in Edinburgh, providing sitting accommodation for about half of the population. Seventeen of these, with 26 ministers, belonged to the National Church. Most of the landed proprietors and their dependants supported the Episcopal church, which had, as well as Charlotte Chapel, a large church in the Cowgate and five smaller ones elsewhere. The Roman Catholics had two small chapels in Blackfriars Wynd.

Christopher Anderson was familiar with three of the other 15 Protestant churches in Edinburgh. As mentioned, he was brought up in the Old Scots Independent congregation in Candlemakers' Hall, and as a teenager he went with his brothers to the Scotch Baptists for a while. Then, in 1798, he began to attend the Haldanes' church in the Circus and, later, their Tabernacle at the top of Leith Walk. The Haldanes established about eight small congregations in the city over the next few years, three of which continued and five of which were short-lived. There were two English Baptist churches – Cordiners' Hall (above) and Skinners' Hall (Chapter 3); the Cameronians, Bereans, Methodists and Glasites all had one congregation each. These churches differed little in doctrine from each other and from the Presbyterians by whom they were surrounded, except that only the Baptist churches practised believers' baptism by immersion.

## Non-religion in Edinburgh in 1806

There were, however, many unchurched people in Edinburgh in 1806. A Parliamentary Commission noted that out of 162,292 people surveyed, 76,630 belonged to the National Church, 71,271 belonged to dissenting churches (that is, other Presbyterians, Episcopalians, the Haldane churches, Methodists, Baptists, etc.) and 14,391 had no church connection. However, only 74,795 (less than half) attended church regularly. About 45,000 of those who 'rarely attended' were deemed by the Commission to be 'capable of attending but habitually absented themselves from public worship'. Those who never attended or who were not even on a church roll were 'almost entirely confined to the poorer classes and chiefly to the very lowest'. It was for them that Christopher

Anderson started the church while later became Charlotte Chapel. The Commission recorded four reasons why the poor did not attend church:

They had no decent clothing, and stayed away because of 'the importance attached by the poorer classes in Scotland to being well dressed on suitable occasions'. They were embarrassed, and 'rather than encounter that feeling they will stay at home'.

Those who worked hard for six days a week looked forward to Sunday as a day on their own.

The best seats in church attracted high seat-rents, so the lower-rated seats, and those made available without charge for the poor, 'made those who occupy them marked and distinguished from the rest of the congregation'. Of the four reasons given by the poor for not attending church, this was the one about which they felt most passionately.

The principal reason, which even the poorest admitted frankly was the real one, was total indifference to what the churches stood for. They lived in grinding poverty and were 'so absorbed in their own sufferings that they have no thoughts to bestow on other subjects'.

*These sketches of what the well-dressed in Edinburgh wore in the early 1800s makes the poor's sense of inadequacy understandable.*

The first and third reasons given by the poor for not attending church in 1806 – that they were embarrassed at not having suitable clothing and that they resented sitting in designated pews – were echoed in Charlotte Chapel's annual report a hundred years later; the church secretary remarked in 1909:

*Our churches are too stiff and respectable. The poorly attired men and women are in many places frowned upon by the fashionable worshippers whose pews they invade. Pew rents are also a stumbling block ... our building has been made as attractive as a building of this kind can be. The church is open to whoever likes to come. A glad welcome awaits all.*

3 *Charlotte Chapel Record* (Edinburgh, 1907-), 1910, p. 35.

Christopher Anderson would have been delighted.

Additional information on the following topics, mentioned in this chapter, is available on the CD.

Christopher Anderson's brothers
Christopher Anderson's 'call' to full-time Christian service
Christopher Anderson's conversion
Christopher Anderson's evangelising in the Highlands
Christopher Anderson's fifteen months in England
Christopher Anderson's parents
Christopher Anderson's view of James Haldane
Cordiners' Hall – Baptist use
Cordiners' Hall – location
Edinburgh churches in 1806
Haldane brothers
Helen Mack
Margaret Anderson
Old Scots Independent congregation
Richmond Court
Serampore
Skinners' Hall
William Gray in Edinburgh

# Chapter 3
## Richmond Court Chapel (1806–1818)

### Edinburgh Baptist churches in 1806

**Room for another one**

As Christopher Anderson prepared to return to Edinburgh at the age of 24, he was aware that the character of the Old Town was changing. The well-to-do were moving into the New Town, leaving the unsanitary tenement buildings for tradesmen, shopkeepers, labourers and others who could not afford to be upwardly mobile. It was they whom Anderson wished to reach, as he thought about purchasing Richmond Court Chapel. It lay within easy reach of all parts of the Old Town, and he wanted 'to invite the poor as well as others to hear the Gospel'.

There were already three Baptist churches in Edinburgh, but Christopher Anderson did not wish to link up with the largest of them, the Scotch Baptists. He had attended there in his teens and two of his brothers were members. However, he deliberately founded a new church, the one now known as Charlotte Chapel, in order to correct two shortcomings (as he saw it) of the Scotch Baptists – their insistence on lay pastors and their weekly love-feast. He had an additional concern about the Edinburgh congregation – not Scotch Baptists generally – their lack of evangelistic zeal. He was determined that the church which he pastored should have a professional ministry, should observe only the two New Testament ordinances of baptism and communion, and should have an active concern for those outside the faith – in other words, an English Baptist church.

There were two such churches in Edinburgh. A former Presbyterian minister had started an English Baptist church in Skinners' Hall in 1796. He was, however, 'most exclusive in his Church fellowship'; as Christopher Anderson surveyed the Edinburgh scene in 1806, he commented: 'they are still, I suppose, going on in the same monastic style'. The founding minister was about to emigrate to America, but Anderson had never associated with them previously and they held no attraction for him now.

The third Baptist church in Edinburgh was the small group in Cordiners' Hall, which Christopher Anderson and four fellow-Baptists had constituted as a church just before he left Edinburgh for Olney in May 1805. In July of that year, they told Andrew Fuller, who was visiting Edinburgh and who worshipped with them, that they would like to 'call' Christopher Anderson to be their pastor. They welcomed him warmly on his return to Edinburgh in August 1806 and he, for his part, hoped they would be the nucleus of a new outreach through the purchase of Richmond Court. He was disappointed to find that although the group had grown in number to a dozen members during his absence, they were at sixes-and-sevens on small points of doctrine, with consequent 'loss of their zeal for the preaching of the gospel to sinners'. They had also adopted mutual exhortation – any men present could pray or speak – so they had become, in effect, a Scotch Baptist church without the love-feast.

**Skinners' Hall**

Christopher Anderson attended Cordiners' Hall on Sunday morning and afternoon for some weeks, but only as a member, not as their pastor. He now saw no future for himself in Cordiners' Hall and so, wishing to preach the gospel more effectively while he negotiated the purchase of Richmond Court, he hired Skinners' Hall in Skinners' Close in early September 1806. He began to preach there on Sunday evening – the small English Baptist congregation mentioned above did not have an evening service. Skinners' Hall, since demolished, was just to the south of the present Crowne Plaza hotel, at the junction of the High Street with Blackfriars Street (then Blackfriars Wynd), which runs steeply down from the High Street to the Cowgate. Rapidly increasing attendances on Sunday evening encouraged him to press ahead with his plan for the larger premises of Richmond Court.

*I have invited the poor – the respectable part have come of course; and, all circumstances considered, there is great cause for gratitude. I hope that when I get into Richmond Court, which will be in a few weeks, that the cause will prosper.*

1 Anderson, *Life and Letters*, p. 46.

On 7 October, he and two women withdrew completely from the church in Cordiners' Hall and concentrated their efforts on Skinners' Hall. They were further encouraged when two young men from the Bristol Academy arrived for the new academic year at the university. The group met regularly on Monday evening for Bible study, and Christopher greatly enjoyed their company.

### Richmond Court Chapel

When Richmond Court Chapel was opened in 1787, it was the first place of worship in Scotland to have been purpose-built by Baptists – the Scotch Baptists. They moved into it from the Magdalen Chapel and occupied it until 1802, when it became too small. They then made a series of moves, which led them, in due course, to become the present Bristo Baptist Church on Queensferry Road. The vacant premises were ideal for Christopher Anderson to begin his life's work – there was a house on the ground floor, and a hall on the upper floor with accommodation for 400. It lay in a respectable suburb on the southeast of the city, called the Pleasance, not far from the High Street. At that time there was no other place of worship in the vicinity, which was important because Anderson did not wish to build on another man's foundation. If a church was to be formed, in which 'the two positive divine ordinances, Baptism and the Lord's Supper' were observed, his wish was 'that the great majority [of the members] should ever be his own children in the faith of Jesus Christ'.

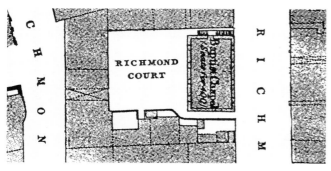

*Richmond Court Chapel. These 1911 photographs show the front and the back of the Chapel, not easily distinguishable from the neighbouring tenements, although, as the ordnance survey map shows, a narrow lane separated them. The wording on the map is 'Baptist Chapel (seats for 400)'.*

The open area gave Richmond Court its name; from it, a pend onto Richmond Place led to Hill Place (still there) and so to Nicolson Street. By 1911, the buildings had deteriorated and look rather dingy in the photographs. The area was re-developed after the Second World War, and the site of the Chapel is now a drying-green for the new houses.

## November 1806–January 1808

### O Lord! Send now prosperity

Christopher Anderson paid £365 out of his own pocket for Richmond Court Chapel, and took possession of it in November 1806. After carrying out some repairs, he opened it for public worship and preaching on Sunday 23 November. His diary for the opening Sunday reads: 'Preached in Richmond Court Chapel for the first time this morning from Psalm 37:4; in the evening from Psalm 102:16. Place pretty well filled. O Lord! send now prosperity.' After his second Sunday, he wrote to a friend: 'Our audience in the morning is not so good as in the evening of course. I was afraid that when I came to Richmond Court, I should find the place much too large, but now I fondly hope not, at least for the evening.'

The address on Sunday evening was directly evangelistic, and enquirers were invited from the pulpit to call on the preacher at his home on Monday evening. After the excitement of the opening of the building, progress was slow. Attendance in February 1807 was 50-70 on Sunday morning and 200-300 on Sunday evening, but Christopher Anderson was not aware of any conversions. His biographer explained why comparatively few of the hundreds who attended the services were baptized and joined the church – these being synonymous events for converts; while Christopher Anderson's preaching was attractive, his direct appeal to the conscience, and his urgent exhortation to immediate repentance toward God and faith in the Lord Jesus Christ, presented a challenge that not many were prepared to accept personally. In addition to services on Sunday morning and evening, Christopher Anderson conducted a prayer meeting with a devotional talk on Thursday evening.

He took a fortnight's break in April 1807, although it was far from a holiday. He went to Kilwinning, to deputize while his friend George Barclay collected funds in England for a new chapel. Christopher Anderson preached nearly every day, in and around Kilwinning, and was assiduous in visiting the sick. He was at home in any company, having that lofty bearing and even a sense of superiority that stemmed from the Norman heritage on his mother's side. He had lost much of his Scottish accent during his time in England – not purposely, he said, because he noted that English congregations enjoyed his accent as long as his speech was grammatical. Christopher Anderson's preaching was easy and sometimes animated, but generally slow, solemn, and impressive, and he held the attention of his hearers.

Richmond Court's strategic location for Edinburgh's Old Town and its expanding southern suburbs was recognized by the Scotch Baptists, not only when they built it but, having sold it to Christopher Anderson in 1806 because they had outgrown it, they purpose-built the Pleasance Chapel, in nearby Arthur Street, in 1811.

*Richmond Place, like Arthur Street in this photograph, lay in the shadow of Arthur's Seat, in an area known (still) as the Pleasance. The buildings were pulled down after the Second World War, and replaced by modern homes.*

## Slow progress

On Christopher Anderson's return to Edinburgh at the end of April 1807, three of those who had been attending Richmond Court were converted – the first fruits of his ministry there. A month later, he reported that 'attendance has not increased of late, yet the adherents seem to be steady, and a good deal interested.' However, by mid-August, he was depressed that numbers were not increasing, either with new attenders or with converts; he began to wonder whether the cause was viable. Several English churches, learning that he had not yet settled into a pastorate, pressed him to consider moving south; he 'remembered the happiness of having from 300 to 700 hearers'.

As there was no one whom he could consult in Edinburgh, he wrote at length to his friend Andrew Fuller, for advice on two connected matters. First, he was aware that the few who were committed to the cause were becoming unsettled by his own uncertainty about his future. They wanted him to form a church and to become their pastor, which would secure his stay in Edinburgh. Secondly, because of the impoverished nature of the congregation, he had to support himself financially and maintain the building from his own resources. If he formed a church with people who 'however willing, were inadequate' to underwrite it, how long could the church continue?

*When I gave up my worldly employment, and was afterwards led to cease from thinking of going to a warm climate, my next immediate desire was to be useful at home.... I resolved to look about and not be too hasty in fixing on a situation which might be for life. Edinburgh presented itself, and seemed to claim my attention; you know under what circumstances. I have therefore tried, and, on the whole, had no occasion to repent, but to bless God for His kindness. My idea was, to spend a part of what I had in supporting myself until it might please the Lord to raise up friends to whom this would be reckoned no burden.... I am still able to proceed in the same way, but shall not be always. And my difficulty is, what explanations would it be prudent to make?*

2 Anderson, *Life and Letters*, p. 75.

Andrew Fuller replied encouragingly. He narrated his own early struggles and suggested that Christopher should form a church with the resources that he had, even if he had to resign if money ran out. 'The consciousness of having done your utmost, will be a satisfaction.'

Andrew Fuller's advice coincided with some further conversions in Richmond Court. As one after another – the total between 1806 and 1808 was eventually 12 – gave satisfactory proof of new birth, they were baptized by Christopher Anderson, in the open air in the Water of Leith near Stockbridge and usually during the afternoon of a weekday, but on one occasion at 7 a.m. The owner of one of the many mills on the Water of Leith was a Scotch Baptist, and he provided facilities in a quiet part of the river beside his mill. At the first baptism of which he has left a note, Christopher Anderson addressed between 50 and 70 spectators in the open air at Stockbridge. It may seem odd for the Scotch Baptists to have built a Baptist church (Richmond Court) without a baptistry, but the position was the same in northern England – there were only two baptistries at this time in the whole of Lancashire and Yorkshire, although Baptist churches were numerous in both counties. The first in Scotland was when the Scotch Baptists built their Pleasance Chapel in Edinburgh in 1811 (page 17).

*There is no photograph of Christopher Anderson baptizing in the Water of Leith, although cameras were available in Edinburgh from 1843; this 1890 scene is representative of an outdoor baptism. Fords for mills in the Water of Leith (lower picture) provided the necessary depth of water.*

## Early days in Richmond Court

Shortly before his death, Christopher Anderson described the 14 months between the purchase of Richmond Court in

November 1806 and the constitution of the church in January 1808.

*The one idea in my own mind was the conversion of sinners. I intimated from the pulpit that I should be at home on Monday evenings, and would be happy to see any one who chose to call; but that there were two subjects on which I could hold no conversation in the first instance – Baptism and Church Government.* [Anderson's reason for saying that is explained on page 27.]

*Others I informed, that I should never be known as a man that enticed Christians away from other Churches, whether Baptist or Independent; that I should never be known as a stealer of sheep. My object was very different. My desire was to gather those to the Redeemer who were not already gathered.*

*In the course of the following year the word was remarkably acknowledged of God, so that after meeting at Richmond Court from November 1806, about twelve souls seemed to be brought home to God. There were four others, including myself, sixteen in all. To them I explained again and again my views of a Christian Church – that I thought we had simply two positive divine ordinances to observe, Baptism and the Lord's Supper; but that I believed it to be at once the duty and high privilege of a Church to support its own pastor, in order that he may give himself wholly to the work.*

---

3 Anderson, *Life and Letters*, p. 81.

## 'Call' to Christopher Anderson

Meantime, Christopher Anderson broadened his education by accompanying one of the Bristol students, who had come back for the university session of 1807-8, to lectures on civil history and anatomy. In December 1807, the 13 baptized believers who were attending Richmond Court issued a formal 'call' to him to constitute a church and to become their pastor. As he had been expecting this – he would not on principle have taken the initiative – he was able to give an affirmative answer almost immediately. Two of them had been with him from the commencement of his attempt to start an English Baptist cause in Edinburgh, and the other 11 had been brought to the Saviour through his teaching and had been baptized by him.

Of the 13 who signed the 'call', 8 were women and 5 were men. From the start of Christopher Anderson's evangelistic work until the conclusion of his ministry, women put the men to shame by their support and their faithfulness. As noted earlier, it was two women who assisted him in Skinners' Hall in October 1806. When he retired from the pulpit in 1851, there were 132 members of Charlotte Chapel – 103 women and 29 men. Eleven of the men had wives in membership, so there were 92 women, who either did not have husbands or whose husbands were not committed to the work. There were only 18 men in the corresponding position. None of the women acted as trustees or as deacons and they took no part in the pulpit ministry. We know nothing about them except their names and addresses, but clearly they were the backbone of the church. They were the 'Sarahs' referred to in the Preface.

## Constitution of the church

Christopher Anderson's ordination took place on Thursday 21 January 1808, when he was aged 25. On the following Sunday, 24 January, 16 baptized believers met around the Lord's Table in Richmond Court, and constituted the church that is now Charlotte Chapel. In addition to Christopher Anderson and the 13 who had signed the 'call', a friend was present and also a young man who had been baptized that morning. 'I preached to them from "Now we live, if ye stand fast in the Lord", explaining the serious connection between us – showing that the church had a serious part to perform. ... We sat down at the Lord's Table together, sixteen in number, and some of them were for supposing there never had been anything like it before, as out of the sixteen there were twelve who had never partaken of the Lord's Supper before.'

One might wonder why the 12 who had been converted over the previous nine months in Richmond Court had never yet had communion. Christopher Anderson explained this in his letter to Andrew Fuller in August 1807, setting out his dilemma about the way ahead. 'Are not, then, the only two methods which I can adopt, to go on preaching as hitherto, without forming a closer connexion, until we have a more permanent prospect? or, to proceed in observing the Lord's Supper, in the faith of God appearing on our behalf? Which of these does my dear brother think most eligible?' In other words, communion was, in Anderson's view, an ordinance to be observed only by those who had formally constituted a church.

## Growth

Three more joined the church over the next three months, all by conversion, while another five or eight were enquirers. Christopher Anderson described the congregation as 'affectionate, simple-hearted and godly people ... mostly young'. By March 1809, the membership had risen to 31, nearly all converted through his ministry. In December 1809, 40 were meeting weekly for communion – that is 40 in membership – of which Anderson thought he 'might have been useful to about 26'.

Christopher Anderson later described a typical service in Richmond Court: 'when I first began, I had to do so in the pulpit all alone. It was easy for me then to sing, so that each service I had the whole to do. Sing, read, pray, sing, preach, sing, and pray.' He followed the practice of most churches at the time, in having a plate at the door, for worshippers to deposit their offering as they arrived – 'their first act of public worship on entering the sanctuary'. An eccentric character called Robert Flockhart narrated how 'the man on the plate would not let me in' after he had created a disturbance in Richmond Court on the previous Sunday.

This practice continued when the congregation moved from Richmond Court to Charlotte Chapel in 1818. Christopher Anderson told a Parliamentary Commission in 1836: 'The ordinary collections at the doors are applied to the regular purposes of the church, lighting and repairs. There are no hired servants attached to the church. The cleaning is done by a member, who lives rent-free below the church.' There was also a box in the front lobby of Charlotte Chapel, lettered Visitors Offertory, for occasions when the plate was not set out. Church-door collections lasted until May 1904, when the deacons decided to pass bags along the pews as part of the worship, morning and evening.

In July 1809, Christopher Anderson asked a lay friend to take the evening service in Richmond Court, so that he himself could preach the gospel in the open air in Leith Links, a popular park. He must have been encouraged by the experiment, because after that he frequently preached either there or in Bruntsfield Links on summer evenings, both on Sunday and on weekday evenings. Whether in the pulpit at Richmond Court or in the open air or in the mail-coach on his many tours of Scotland, England and Ireland,

Christopher Anderson was before and above all else an evangelist, and a markedly successful one.

He did not, however, ignore wider interests. In March 1809, he again accompanied one of the English students to the University of Edinburgh, this time to classes on moral philosophy, logic, chemistry and universal history; he enjoyed them, but commented that Bible study was still 'my favourite pursuit'.

### Christopher Anderson's advice to enquirers

Christopher Anderson did not believe in visiting people regularly in their homes, but after the Lord's Supper, which was dispensed at a special service every Sunday afternoon for baptized believers only, he went from pew to pew and offered counsel, comfort and advice. In addition, he was 'at home' to callers on Monday evening. He recorded, meticulously but by initials or first name only, the advice he gave to enquirers, and his notes show the variety of people who called at the manse. Returning to Edinburgh in March 1812, after spending two months in Liverpool, he wrote: 'Whenever I come back, and Monday evening arrives, then inquirers appear again. I think the Church is in a good state.'

One of the enquirers was a Highlander, who had heard Anderson preach to a large audience on the North Inch at Perth, during his evangelising in the Highlands in August 1810. Although he was a good-living man, he was convicted of sin as he reflected on the challenge that the preacher had presented. None of the Perth clergy was able to give him assurance of salvation or peace of heart, so he decided to move himself and his family to Edinburgh, in the hope of finding the evangelist whose message had awakened his conscience. Knowing neither the name nor the denomination of the visitor to Perth, and being unable to read or write – he was a labourer – he spent Sunday after Sunday patiently going round all the chapels and churches in Edinburgh, including Roman Catholic and Quaker. After many months, he came to Richmond Court. Fortunately Christopher Anderson, who was often out of town or preaching in the open air, was in the pulpit that day, and the Highlander instantly recognized the voice that he had heard so powerfully on the Inch at Perth. Following Monday evening discussions, he was soundly converted, baptized, joined the church and set up in Edinburgh as a cobbler. At the mid-week meetings in Richmond Court, he became one of the most powerful prayer warriors of the infant church; 'his prayer often rose to a sublimity both of ideas and expression which impressed every listener'.

## Scenes from Richmond Court

### Three snapshots

On 25 October 1810, the nation celebrated the fiftieth anniversary of King George III's accession to the throne. As prayer for the rulers of nations is enjoined in 1 Timothy 2:2, and is still regularly offered in the Chapel, it is worth noting how Christopher Anderson marked the jubilee. During the day, he visited Danish prisoners-of-war and distributed 70 Testaments; then he and the congregation met at Richmond Court to pray for the Royal Family: 'I fervently remembered our good King in prayer ... O that he may be found written among the living in Jerusalem!' At the end of the prayer meeting, there was a collection for impoverished members – the first extant reference to the Fellowship Fund – because Christopher Anderson would not allow them to accept help from the parish or from outside charities. On the following Sunday, he preached twice more on the theme of jubilee, in the afternoon from Psalm 21:4 and in the evening from Psalm 57:15, although he focussed on 'such a king as Jesus', not on the House of Hanover.

A second snapshot of Richmond Court is recorded in September 1812, when news arrived that fire had destroyed the printing press at Serampore, India. Christopher Anderson preached on the Sunday evening from Romans 11:33-5: 'O the depth of the riches... ', and invited contributions to repair the damage; £55 was given that night, and a further collection was taken a week later. On the Monday evening, Anderson attended a committee meeting of the Edinburgh Bible Society, of which he was joint-secretary. They had £279 in the bank, but voted to send £300 to get the press running again as quickly as possible – and later that evening £43 was handed in. To put the donation of £300 into perspective for today, it should be remembered that £365 had purchased not only the 400-seater Richmond Court meeting-house but also the dwelling-house on the ground floor, when Christopher Anderson bought them as a unit in 1806.

The third snapshot focuses on an incident in March 1813. The British East India Company, supported by the British Government, imposed restrictions on preaching the gospel to the natives in Bengal, in case it interfered with trade. Christopher Anderson, at Andrew Fuller's suggestion, prepared a petition to both Houses of Parliament; he had considerable success in getting ministers and lay people from all denominations in Edinburgh to sign it. However, he was alarmed to discover that Fuller had sent copies of the petition to all the mission's supporters. He wrote urgently, reminding Andrew Fuller that if 'petitioners express their wishes in nearly the same language', opponents can undermine the effect by claiming that 'all the petitions must have been fabricated in the same mint'. He urged Fuller to suggest different phraseology for different parts of the country and for different individuals.

The Evangelical Alliance gave similar advice in the year 2000, when the Scottish Government introduced legislation about homosexual relationships. Christian organisations circulated a style of letter of protest, for individuals to copy; the Alliance urged Christians to let their Members of the Scottish Parliament know their views in their own words, making the letters individual rather than stereotyped.

### The seats and the passages are full

By December 1813, at the age of 31, Christopher Anderson's preaching was attracting larger numbers than ever. 'On a Lord's-day evening we are occasionally quite crowded', he wrote, and a year later that: 'Richmond Court was never so attended. I am sorry that people have to go away every Lord's Day evening. Had we a place double the size it would, I imagine, soon fill.... Not only do all denominations attend us in the evenings, but people of the best rank in society, which, considering the place and situation, is the more remarkable. Many go away after the seats and passages are full.'

This was indeed remarkable, to pick up his own phrase, because Christopher Anderson's outside interests took him away from Edinburgh for several months in most of his years in Richmond Court. It had been a condition of his accepting the pastorate that 'for the spread of the Gospel ... I must occasionally go out and leave you.' When he was away, he paid for the pulpit supply and he told his brother, Charles: 'Let all the supplies be paid for as they ought, that is,

travelling expenses, which you can ascertain, then add so much for each Sabbath, I can settle all when I return.' He appreciated 'the danger of neglecting one's own vineyard, nay, and one's own soul, amid various other engagements, all good and beautiful in their season', but his times away were so substantial that even his biographer commented they were too many for the good of the church. To take as samples the first and the middle years of his pastorate in Richmond Court, he was away in:

1808
March –
Evangelistic tour of Perthshire
April –
Evangelistic tour of Ayrshire
August, September –
Five weeks evangelising in Ireland and collecting for BMS
October –
BMS deputation up the East Coast of Scotland

1812
January to March –
Extended preaching in Liverpool
July –
Another month in Liverpool, setting up a
Society for Translations
October –
Annual visit to the Gaelic schools in the Highlands

By the spring of 1815, Christopher Anderson, aged 33, was run down in health, partly by his workload and partly by the deficient ventilation in Richmond Court. When the building was crowded to overflowing, as it regularly was on Sunday evening, the ventilation system could not cope. The death of his friend Andrew Fuller in May 1815 and the anxious correspondence which followed, about whether he should become the secretary of the Baptist Missionary Society, added to the stress. His friends persuaded him to take a complete break on the coast of Devon and Cornwall from July until the end of September. He returned to Edinburgh considerably improved in health.

### Marriage

In July 1816, Christopher Anderson married at the age of 34. He was so happy that he wondered why he had not done so sooner. Writing to a friend six months later, he said: 'Daily I have occasion to bless God for the partner in life he has given me, one so suited and fitted to aid me as a minister, whose mind is so congenial with my own, and who enters with so much interest into the concerns of the cause of Immanuel.'

> Married at Paisley, on the 2d inst. by the reverend Robert Burns, the reverend CHRISTOPHER ANDERSON, of Edinburgh, to ESTHER, daughter of the honourable James Athill, of Antigua.

*Newspaper notice of the wedding. Esther Athill was the eldest of the four daughters of the Chief Justice of the island of Antigua in the West Indies. The link with Paisley is difficult to establish, except that Mrs Athill was living there at the time.*

The next few years were the most fruitful, and certainly the happiest, of Christopher Anderson's life. There was much in the church to encourage him, and his various outside interests were flourishing. A phrase crops up frequently in his diary at this time, that he 'might have been useful' to someone or other. The phrase is not commonly used today, but as Christopher Anderson was getting married, some Edinburgh businessmen were putting together a prospectus for a new newspaper, to be called *The Scotsman*, and 'their first desire was to be honest, the second to be useful.' It began publication on Saturday 25 January 1817 and one of its enduring traits, contrasting with the *Glasgow Herald*, was to include *'The'* (capital T) in its title.

## Plans to move

Shortly after his marriage, Christopher Anderson felt that the time had come to move the congregation from Richmond Court. He told friends that although outside financial help would be required: 'My heart is set on a place of worship worthy of the city and of our denomination.... There never was an opportunity at all like this for the denomination having a chapel such as they might look to as a permanent interest when I am no more.' In 1818, aged 36, he found his 'worthy' building at the west end of Rose Street, one of the two service roads in the New Town – the other was Thistle Street. Charlotte Chapel had been built as an Episcopal church in 1796 and opened in May 1797. It was so well supported that the Episcopalians decided, in 1814, to move to a more prestigious site and to erect a new and enlarged place of worship on the southwest corner of Princes Street, the Church of St John the Evangelist.

The Princes Street proprietors vigorously opposed the Episcopalians' plan to put a tall building on Peter Lawson's nursery garden – they wanted to keep their view of the Castle. A mutually acceptable compromise was reached in 1816, which permitted the building of St. John's and its graveyard on the basis that there would be no further development on the south side of Princes Street west of the Mound. The fine Gothic building, which is still one of the architectural features of the west end of Princes Street, was based on St George's Chapel, Windsor, and Westminster Abbey, London.

*The original congregation of Charlotte Chapel moved in 1818 to the newly built Church of St John the Evangelist. To the right of the picture is St Cuthbert's Church, with Edinburgh Castle in the background.*

## Charlotte Chapel

The building vacated by the Episcopalians was ideal for Christopher Anderson's purpose, but the asking price was £1,550 and the cost of repairs and alterations was formidable. There was no one, or indeed no group, at Richmond Court who could raise that kind of money. Some gifts were promised, but Christopher Anderson remarked: 'they bore a small proportion to the sum required, and money was at that time bearing, even on the most unexceptionable security, interest of five per cent, and difficult to be had.' After serious consideration, he resolved to proceed anyway. He raised £416 by approaching friends in Liverpool, London, Glasgow and Edinburgh, donated £525 himself, and obtained a loan of £1,400, leaving the congregation to raise only £105 to meet the total cost of £2,446 for buying and altering the building. He got occupation of Charlotte Chapel early in 1818 and kept the original name. To those who had been meeting for 12 years in the close confines of Richmond Court, it was indeed the answer to their prayers.

## St Paul's and St George's

The excellent relationship that Charlotte Chapel enjoys today with St Paul's and St George's Episcopal Church in York Place, justifies a mention about its origin, and how it might have been the Chapel's nearest neighbour. When the office-bearers of the Episcopal Charlotte Chapel thought of moving to Princes Street, they approached the Episcopal congregation in the Cowgate, which was also thinking of moving. They proposed uniting, to form one large congregation, in one new building. However, the Cowgate church felt it was better to have two new purpose-built 'cathedrals', one at each end of the New Town. They bought a site in York Place and built St Paul's, a scaled-down copy of King's College Chapel in Cambridge. Both it and St John's were completed and consecrated in 1818. When the rector of the nearby St George's Church died in 1932, its congregation joined with St Paul's, to become St Paul's and St George's.

Additional information on the following topics, mentioned in this chapter, is available on the CD.

Andrew Fuller
Charlotte Chapel as an Episcopal Church
Christopher Anderson's advice to enquirers
Christopher Anderson's 'call' to form a church
Christopher Anderson's ordination
Christopher Anderson's evangelising in the Highlands
Christopher Anderson's preaching
Christopher Anderson's review of his ministry
Christopher Anderson's wife and children
Church discipline
Church register of baptised believers
Committee structure, 1808-1958
Fellowship Fund
Membership patterns, 1808-1875
Open-air meetings
Richmond Court
Why are women more religious than men?

# Chapter 4
# Rose Street – the early years (1818–1823)

## A typical week in Charlotte Chapel

### Five services a week

In August 1818, Christopher Anderson started holding three Sunday services in Charlotte Chapel – morning, afternoon and evening – together with a members' meeting on Tuesday and a public Bible School on Thursday; on Monday evening he was 'at home' to enquirers. The pattern, which he had begun in Richmond Court, continued in Charlotte Chapel for the next 33 years, as he reminisced to a friend in 1851: 'In August it will be forty-five years since I began to preach in Edinburgh. During forty-three years of that time, I have had five services weekly; three on Lord's-day and two on week-days'; he commented from time to time about the commitment required to prepare for five services a week.

Christopher Anderson's 'place of worship worthy of the city and of our denomination' was a two-storey building, which seated 750 (area and gallery), with housing for the caretaker underneath. His nephew Hugh, who attended regularly, commented that although it 'was considerably more than double the size of that he had left' [not quite true – Richmond Court held four hundred], the new building was soon filled to capacity, especially on Sunday evening.

The 1906 pictures (right) are not substantially different from descriptions of the building in 1818, except that the electric lights above the front doors and the large notice board, prominent on the left hand railing, were not added until 1906.

### Sunday morning

Christopher Anderson was both a Bible expositor and an evangelist; he structured his services to meet both needs. The Sunday morning service was open to all, but it was intended primarily for believers, to instruct and to edify, although he rarely closed any meeting without some appeal to the unconverted, drawn naturally from the subject of the sermon. 'A morning service attended was not an occasion to pass from memory – so punctual, so orderly, so thoughtful, so searching that the heart-cry, "Surely the Lord is in this place" was a common experience.' Christopher Anderson usually expounded a passage of Scripture over a series of Sunday mornings, every one following naturally from the last; sometimes he covered only a single phrase from the

*The first Charlotte Chapel, built in 1796 and home to a Baptist congregation for 93 years, from 1818 to 1911.*

*He first laid open the whole passage in its connexion to full view, in few words, and then at greater length drew out the spirit of the writer, or rather 'the mind of the Spirit', from the various clauses, applying the whole to the circumstances of the believer at the present time....*
*His preference for exposition, and the textual mode of preaching in general, arose naturally out of his love for the letter of the Bible, from which he drew the spirit.*

1 Anderson, *Life and Letters*, p. 369.

He refused to wear a Geneva gown in the pulpit. A colleague, who did this during a visit to Liverpool, because it was the custom there, was admonished on his return because of 'the Scotch dread of everything which comes from Rome'. Christopher Anderson was also averse to religious titles for ministers of the gospel: 'Oh, don't address me Reverend,' he wrote in 1807, 'I assure you it does me no good.' To another in the ministry he said: 'I would rather affix Esq. than prefix Rev. to your name.' However, as secretary of the Edinburgh

Bible Society, he found that his refusal to be called Reverend led to misunderstandings with those who did not have his scruples, and he acquiesced even if he did not approve.

### Sunday afternoon

There were two activities on Sunday afternoon. One was a weekly communion service, open to baptized believers only. The custom of holding the Lord's Supper weekly, as opposed to fortnightly as in England, was the only visible difference between English Baptist Churches on the two sides of the border. After conducting communion, Christopher Anderson exercised his main pastoral ministry for the membership. He left the table seat and went from pew to pew, talking, advising, consoling and giving counsel and encouragement. Although not slow to visit the sick if requested to do so, he had an aversion to calling at people's homes on a regular basis, partly because of the scattered membership, which would have involved much travelling, but partly from a dislike of gossiping talk, which, he feared, took place on many of these visits. His biographer, himself a Baptist pastor, felt that his uncle carried this reluctance too far, and commented:

*It would have been well had the more retiring members of the Church had more frequent opportunities of intercourse with him ... to conciliate the affections of the people, to encourage the more timid and distressed to express their difficulties, to secure the attachment of the young, and to help all by advice which would not elsewhere be asked.... Many lamented the want, to whom a sight of one they loved so well, at their own firesides, and a few kind words from him there, would have yielded encouragement and comfort.*

2 Anderson, *Life and Letters*, p. 374.

The other activity on Sunday afternoon was a Sunday School for 'the children connected with the congregation, conducted by two members of the church'. This was presumably for the children of members attending the communion service, as the children would not be admitted to it; if two teachers were sufficient, it implies a small number attending, rather than outreach to the community. If it was held during communion, it was 175 years ahead of its time, because it was 1994 (Chapter 53) before the elders, concerned at teachers missing a service to teach children, agreed to have Sunday School during a worship service.

*These 1906 photographs show the area and the gallery substantially as they were in 1818, with two exceptions. The original pulpit was barrel-shaped and sited high on the wall, until modified at the end of the nineteenth century, and lighting was by gas, not electricity, until 1906.*

### Sunday evening

Sunday evening drew the largest congregation. Christopher Anderson's preaching was solemn and searching, and yet it must have been attractive because the Chapel was regularly filled to overflowing – often before the service started, with every foot of standing room taken. There were thousands of servants in the New Town, working as domestics in the large houses or looking after the horses in the mews. They formed an important part of the Sunday evening congregation. Well-to-do employers had their main meal at midday on Sunday, so their staff spent the morning preparing and cooking and then, after serving a high tea in the late afternoon, they were free to attend evening church services. The introduction of gas street lighting to Edinburgh, from 1817 onward, assisted evening attendance in the winter months.

*This boy had been finding his way through non-lit streets by torchlight and, on entering gas-lit Charlotte Square, he extinguished his torch in a link horn – they are still there.*

The evening sermon was almost invariably addressed to the unconverted, with a view to bringing conviction of sin and conversion.

*Of it, in his own quaint way, Mr. Anderson was wont to say to his members, 'I go a fishing, and it is for you to support me by your sympathy and prayers.' With such a spirit pervading the service, it is not surprising that the word spoken was often 'the power of God unto salvation'.*

3 *SBM*, 1896, p. 158.

Christopher Anderson invited any who were spiritually awakened to come to the vestry after the service, where he tried to lead them to knowledge of Christ as Saviour and Lord. He remained for a considerable time, talking, answering enquiries, and sometimes, when asked, expanding on the subject of the evening sermon. Not many other churches had an evening service in those days, so quite a few Edinburgh clergymen attended regularly and spoke appreciatively of the benefits they received. Anderson's nephew picked up a card, left in the pew where he was sitting: 'Rev. F- B-, rector of F-, has listened with delight to the very faithful preaching of the Gospel this evening. May the Lord be with you.' During the General Assembly of the Church of Scotland, some of its ministers attended the Chapel's evening service.

There was no organ in the Chapel in Christopher Anderson's time. Baptists, like Presbyterians, preferred singing in church to be led by a precentor. The Episcopalians who built the Chapel had an organ, but Christopher Anderson did not want it, so they gave it to St Peter's Episcopal Church in Peebles.

## Baptist ministry

Many university students came to the Chapel; under Christopher Anderson's guidance, 16 of them went into Baptist ministry, and others were ordained into Presbyterian and Anglican churches. It gave him great pleasure to comment, toward the close of his own ministry: 'as there were sixteen of us on sitting down at first at His table, so about sixteen have been called from ourselves to the work of the ministry.' The first two were Thomas Swan, a native of Edinburgh, and John Leechman, who had come to Edinburgh from the west of Scotland; both were valedicted by Christopher Anderson to the Serampore Mission in India where, supported by the Chapel, they taught for some years and then returned to pastorates in Britain.

Others, lay people, including students from England, acknowledged Christopher Anderson as their spiritual father and went into their chosen secular careers with a Christian commitment learned in the Rose Street building. A medical student from Bristol, not a believer when he came to Edinburgh, was impressed with the preacher's grasp of his subject. He amused himself by sending an anonymous note to Christopher Anderson, asking him to explain the difference between Calvinists and Arminians on the following Sunday evening. Anderson rightly read into the note that the student needed more basic teaching than that, and anticipating at least one attentive hearer, he preached on: 'What shall it profit a man if he gain the whole world and lose his own soul?' The questioner was duly convicted, came for counsel, was persuaded, converted and joined the church.

Charles Darwin, who at this stage was considering the church as a career, studied at Edinburgh University from 1825 to 1827. There is no indication in his biography that he ever attended Charlotte Chapel, but it illustrates the potential for student-churches like the Chapel, then as now, to influence future leaders in many fields of human enterprise. If he had been brought to the Chapel, and if Christopher Anderson's

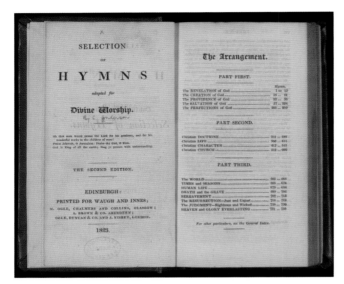

*The frontispiece of Christopher Anderson's collection of 769 hymns, which the congregation used regularly from 1818 onward.*

preaching had convinced him to continue in the church and to travel the world preaching the gospel instead of looking for the origin of its species, would the theory for which he is best known have evolved as it has?

## Monday

During his evangelistic sermon on Sunday evening, Christopher Anderson invited enquirers to call at his home on the following day, for counselling on a one-to-one basis. As noted in Chapter 3, there were two subjects that he would not discuss with initial enquirers – baptism and church government. There was wisdom in this self-imposed embargo, because they were potentially divisive subjects, even among those who practised believers' baptism by immersion, and his first concern was to establish the enquirers' right relationship with the Saviour.

## Tuesday

On Tuesday evening, there was a singing class. Anderson was coy, when the Parliamentary Commissioners probed him in 1836 (aged 54) about it. All they could put in their report – which was extremely detailed on other aspects – was that the Tuesday evening meeting was for members, not for the public, and that it was 'of a more select character' than the Thursday evening Bible School. It included a time of prayer, with a missionary emphasis on the first Tuesday of the

month. Since Anderson had to prepare for five services every week, he must have given a word from the Scriptures on Tuesday.

As he called it a singing class, it presumably included rehearsal of the hymns to be sung on Sunday. Hymnbooks were still a novelty in Scotland; the first was published in 1786, but hymn singing did not become a significant part of most church services until after the evangelistic campaign of Moody and Sankey in Edinburgh in 1873-4 (Chapter 9). Christopher Anderson had, by 1818, produced his own hymnbook, entitled *Selection of Hymns*; it contained 769 hymns for all types of services. He used it regularly in the Chapel, to complement the metrical psalms and paraphrases; it must have been popular, because he brought out a second edition in 1823, with larger type.

## Thursday

The Thursday evening Bible School was open to the public and was more 'experimental' than the sermon on Sunday morning. It was prized by Christians of various denominations, who had their church membership elsewhere but who came on Thursday evening, to hear Bible truths applied in a practical way.

## Church government

English Baptist churches, including Charlotte Chapel, appointed a plurality of deacons. (Scotch Baptists did likewise, but they insisted on a plurality of pastors/elders as well.) The Chapel deacons prepared and distributed the elements at the weekly communion service, and assisted the minister in caring for the poor, but Christopher Anderson ran the church. It was his building; he let out the seats, he led the services, he precented the hymns, he prayed, he preached, and he compiled the hymnbook. He once said to his friend Andrew Fuller: 'I know what committees are – many men, many minds, and, after all, one or two direct. You had better choose that one or two without their appendages.' No records of church meetings or deacons' meetings have survived, but none may have been taken. No business could be introduced by motion or decided by a majority. Every member was at liberty to express his or her mind on any matter, but if there was a difference of opinion, the church waited on the Lord in prayer until his will became clear. This strengthened their respect for each other, and the young church enjoyed a great spirit of unity.

*Christopher Anderson's portrait in the vestry in Charlotte Chapel depicts him about age 41, in 1823.*

## Membership

### Paucity of records

No membership statistics are available for the 27 years between 1809 (when there were 40 members) and 1836 (when there were 110). Christopher Anderson's outside interests are better documented than his work as pastor of his own church, because other bodies published their correspondence with him, whereas he destroyed almost all his papers shortly before his death. The first extant membership register was started by Christopher Anderson's successor in 1851. It lists 79 men and women who had joined during Christopher Anderson's time and who were still in membership; there is no record of those who had both come and gone during Anderson's 43 years.

The early years of Charlotte Chapel as a Baptist church show a small but stable membership of committed people, who formed the nucleus of the church, together with a much larger number of 'hearers', four or five hundred, who regularly came to the Sunday services, but who did not join. Anderson's aim was to win men and women to Jesus Christ and to gather the converts into a spiritual family, of whom he was the spiritual father.

He would not on principle receive members of other local congregations; he aimed to build a closely-knit and well-instructed people, who had come to faith under his ministry, and to hold them together in one church order and one faith. He was conscious of the need to guard against splitting tendencies, which he saw in other churches, particularly in the offshoots of the Haldanes' Tabernacle. He spoke with sorrow about 'the multitudinous divisions of evangelical Christianity'. The first documented transfers into Charlotte Chapel from other churches were not until 1838 – 30 years after the church was founded – and they were from Baptist congregations in Glasgow and Leamington, people coming to Edinburgh and not simply moving their allegiance within the city. There must, however, have been quite a few transfers over the next decade, because in 1851 'the younger members, and those who had come to us from other churches' formed a three-fifth majority of the 132 members (Chapter 7).

### Loyalty and generosity

Christopher Anderson's success in building a stable family of believers is illustrated by mentioning three of the early converts. Miss Martha Ketchen, one of the 13 who signed the 'call' in 1807, had a small business in 174 Rose Street, near the Chapel. She continued actively in membership for 62 years, becoming the senior member and outliving her first pastor by nearly 20 years. She 'died in great peace, aged 88 years, on 17th March 1870'. Mrs John Smith – married women were described by the first name of their husband – was baptized in January 1822. She was the wife of the governor of Edinburgh's prison on Calton Hill. When she died in 1871, the minister of the day wrote: 'After 49 years of most consistent, exemplary, useful and lovable walking, she died of gastric fever after 11 months' illness. No words can describe the general sorrow of pastor and people at her loss.' George Sleigh joined the Chapel in 1825 and when he died 52 years later, still in active membership, he left his whole estate to the Chapel (Chapter 11).

*The Governor's House (the round turret towards the left of the photograph) was retained as a landmark when the Edinburgh Prison on Calton Hill was demolished in 1936. The governor's wife was baptized in the Chapel in 1822 and was a 'consistent, exemplary, useful and lovable' member for 49 years.*

The congregation was never wealthy. In May 1835, Christopher Anderson proudly drew a friend's attention to an entry in the *Periodical Accounts of the Serampore Mission*, where 'you find about £100 contributed by our little Church here, containing not one opulent member'. As mentioned at the end of the previous chapter, the purchase of the Chapel was possible only because Anderson donated £525 of his own money and borrowed £1,400 more on his own security. In 1835, the lender wanted the outstanding balance of £1,000 repaid, which led Christopher Anderson to comment to a colleague:

*Among other things I have to look out for £1000 at 4 per cent. on my chapel. The person from whom I have had it for years wishes to invest it otherwise. This burden I have sustained personally for seventeen years, and I hope at last the cause may stand. There is more prospect. But as none of them can aid me here, I must do as I have done before - try to procure it elsewhere.*

4 Anderson, *Life and Letters*, p. 312.

### What happened to the trustees?

Although the membership was generally stable, illustrated by the faithfulness of Martha Ketchen, Mrs John Smith and George Sleigh, there was a surprisingly high turnover in the men whom Christopher Anderson appointed as trustees for the legal ownership of the building. He had bought it in his own name in 1818, and then decided, in 1824, to transfer it to trustees. He appointed seven members – they had to be members to be trustees – whose occupations were: accountant, brewer, cabinetmaker, leather factor, plumber, shoemaker, and upholsterer. They operated conscientiously for two years, but over the next decade, three of them left the church (the brewer went to the Clyde Street Scotch Baptist Church in 1828), two others withdrew their consent to be trustees, the upholsterer was housebound through incurable illness and the accountant 'resigned all interest'. There is a poignant handwritten comment by Anderson himself in the margin of the 1824 Trust Deed: 'because all had withdrawn … this deed is null & void and the whole again devolves on the shoulders of Christopher Anderson as before. Still it is well – Man proposes – God disposes – Man appoints – God dis-appoints.'

In 1837, Christopher Anderson asked another seven men to become trustees – a baker, a cabinetmaker, a clerk, a clothier, a doctor of medicine, a shawl manufacturer, and a shoemaker. Within a decade, the baker and the doctor were no longer in membership and the clerk and the shoemaker were dead; the remaining trustees assumed four new ones, to bring the number back up to seven. The occupation of one is not given, but the others were a clerk to her majesty's printers, an engraver, and a powder manufacturer. Five of these seven left the church in 1851, in the unhappy circumstances described in Chapter 7, and five new trustees were assumed – a bank manager, a boot maker, a doctor of medicine, a printer and a type founder. Five years later, three of them had left the Chapel and an accountant, an edge tool maker and an upholsterer were appointed in their places.

So the men were there, and apparently in plenty, but they did not have the same commitment to the work in the Chapel as the women. Stewardship of money was a recurring problem in the Chapel's first hundred years. As men usually controlled family wealth in those days, Christopher Anderson's comment in 1835 (above) that there was 'not one opulent member', and that 'none of them can aid me here', is a sad reflection on the commitment of the businessmen in the church. Fortunately there was at least one exception. George Sleigh, who, as mentioned, joined the Chapel in 1825, made a Will 50 years later, when he was still in active membership, leaving his estate to the Chapel. It was an opportune move, because the congregation was in a precarious financial position when he died in 1877. His legacy cleared the outstanding loan of £700 on the building, leaving the members with only current expenses to meet, but they struggled to do even that (Chapter 11).

### Royal visitors in Edinburgh

King George IV, who had succeeded to the throne in 1820, visited Edinburgh in August 1822, in the sixtieth year of his life, dressed in full Highland regalia. It was an occasion of great excitement – no reigning monarch had been in Scotland since Charles II left in 1651. In the streets between Charlotte Square and Christopher Anderson's manse, now at 3 Frederick Street: 'Every building and every house had its illuminations ... with such a multitude of candles, transparencies, lamps and gas-jets it was a miracle that no serious fire occurred.' Charlotte Square received particular attention as the royal procession set off from there on 29 August to visit Lord Rosebery's Dalmeny estate, just past South Queensferry.

Christopher Anderson's brother, Charles, with whom he had spent his early years in the country, felt his feet tapping as he passed the king's ball in the Assembly Rooms in George Street, and said: 'the sound called up a long repressed passion which nothing but the Cross of Christ enabled him to mortify' – for ballroom dancing was worldliness to Baptists in those days, as it was to many of the older readers of this book in their youth.

### The shadow of death

In 1823, Christopher Anderson (aged 41) and his wife Esther and their five children were living at 3 Frederick Street. He was happily married, doted on his children, and there was much in the church to encourage him. However, in the summer of that year, one of the children, called Esther after her mother, died of tuberculosis. Over the next five years, Christopher Anderson lost his wife and the other four children and two of his wife's three sisters, all through the same disease. In the twenty-first century, reasonable health in childhood and adolescence is the norm, although there are tragic exceptions; in the nineteenth century, tuberculosis broke up home after home. Against such a background, the character of many in the Chapel, as elsewhere, was formed, maturing the Christian qualities of constancy and trust in their Heavenly Father despite their earthly tribulations. The next chapter describes how Christopher Anderson's

lifestyle and ministry, and consequently the pattern of life in Charlotte Chapel, changed first in response to his domestic tragedy and then in response to the situation in Serampore.

Additional information on the following topics, mentioned in this chapter, is available on the CD.

Andrew Leslie
Charlotte Chapel – purchase of building in 1818
Christopher Anderson's advice to enquirers
Christopher Anderson's doctrinal position
Christopher Anderson's hymnbook
Christopher Anderson's outside interests
Christopher Anderson's portraits
Christopher Anderson's preaching
Church register of baptised believers
Edinburgh Bible Society
John Leechman
Membership patterns, 1808-1875
Overseas mission
Temperance
Thomas Swan
Trust Deed of 1837
Trust Deeds generally

# Chapter 5
# Sorrow and stress (1823–1838)

## The scourge of tuberculosis

### The two Esthers succumb

There was no equivalent, in Christopher Anderson's ministry, of the rich partnership between pastor and lay people, which is such a feature of Chapel life today. The next 15 years in the Chapel's history are the story of how the pastor coped with the domestic tragedy of losing his wife and all five of their children, followed by the burden of supporting his beloved mission in Bengal, when it was estranged from its parent body for ten long years.

When little Esther died in March 1823, the other four children seemed healthy, but the situation preyed on Mrs Anderson's mind. Medical science did not know, in those days, whether tuberculosis was hereditary or contagious. The question was much debated until 1882, when the German bacteriologist, Robert Koch, identified the bacillus, proving that the disease was infectious, not hereditary. Most people in Christopher Anderson's day believed that it was inherited – not unreasonably, because it was within households, where frequent contact increased the risk of infection, that the highest incidence arose. Mrs Anderson was, unknown to anyone, already in the early stage of tuberculosis when Esther died.

As soon as it was diagnosed in Mrs Anderson, everything possible was done to arrest the disease, but in vain. Christopher was due to preach the annual sermon for the Baptist Missionary Society in London on 26 June 1824. He was reluctant to leave his wife for a single day, but she wanted him to fulfil his engagement. Those who heard him commented on the solemn and tender manner in which the sermon was delivered. He hurried back from London, and the change that had taken place in his wife, even in his short time away, made him realize how serious her condition had become. He got back on a Saturday, and his nephew Hugh was in the congregation in Charlotte Chapel on the following day.

*Next morning he entered his pulpit at the usual hour, but the change which grief had made on him was so apparent as to move the audience deeply. The hair on his cheeks had been suddenly blanched, and the deep furrows on his brow were those which care, not time, had ploughed. Never will the writer forget the subject or the sermon of that morning, or the tone in which the text was read, 'I am the true Vine, and my Father is the husbandman; ... every branch that beareth fruit He purgeth it, that it may bring forth more fruit.' No allusion to his own trouble was made, but all felt that to himself as much as to any, he addressed the word of 'strong consolation.'*

---

1 Anderson, *Life and Letters*, p. 166.

He took her to Blairlogie, near the present Bridge of Allan in Stirlingshire, two days journey, and wrote to his brother, Charles, on 23 July: 'Yesterday forenoon we got to the farmhouse. Here we are in as favourable circumstances as we could wish. Considering the distance and fatigue of these two days, it is to me a matter of gratitude that she seems so little exhausted.' The fine air gave her some relief for a while, and on 12 August Christopher reported: 'Dear Esther's case is one that requires both faith and patience, and therefore we shall try to exercise both. We can as yet say nothing certain. The air and milk seem to agree with her, but to the power and blessing of God I must try to keep my mind directed.' His severest trial over the next few weeks was the uncertainty of her condition. In September, she returned home to die. On the morning of Sunday 3 October 1824, Charles received a note: 'Dear Brother, She entered into glory without a struggle at five this morning. Send to Mr. Swan to engage the whole day, and God will be with him. Ever yours.'

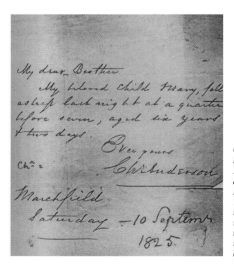

*Christopher Anderson's letter to his brother, Robert, notifying the death of his daughter, Mary, on 9 September 1825. He wrote from the home of friends in Davidsons Mains, who had invited him to stay after the bereavement.*

*Six times in the five years between 1823 and 1828, Christopher Anderson had to lead a cortege up Waterloo Place (drawing, above, upper) to the Old Calton Cemetery (photo, above, lower), to bury his wife and all five of their children.*

## The rest of the family succumb

Within 18 months, the other two daughters joined their mother and sister in heaven; by July 1826, the elder boy, Christopher, was also dead. All are buried in the family grave in the Old Calton Cemetery.

Christopher Anderson's health was so impaired by these harrowing bereavements that he withdrew from public life and from his many outside interests. He devolved his duties in the Edinburgh Bible Society and the Edinburgh Gaelic School Society to the junior secretaries for a while, and then resigned altogether. He found his study more congenial than the committee-room. On 12 August 1826 (aged 44), he wrote to one of the Chapel missionaries, John Mack, in Serampore:

*Of late I have passed through such scenes of sorrow and uninterrupted anxiety, that I am astonished I am on this side the grave. About seven or eight weeks ago, on rising*

*one morning, without one moment's previous intimation, I dropped down in a dead faint, I imagine through constant anxiety. In falling, my forehead had come in contact with a piece of furniture, which hurt me not a little.*

2 Anderson, *Life and Letters*, p. 269.

During these 'long dark days of waiting on a sick chamber', he wrote his first major book *The Domestic Constitution* focussing on the Christian family as the source of national stability. Sending a copy of it to John Mack, he wrote:

*I question whether a book ever left the press, during the writing of which more tears have been shed ... it was resorted to to prevent excess of grief, and it served its purpose. When I lost my boy, being the last intelligent companion at home, no wonder than it proved a heavy trial. Dear little William Ward, a very quick and promising child, is but delicate, but perhaps in mercy to me he may be spared.*

3 Anderson, *Life and Letters*, p. 270.

Sadly this was not to be, and William, the last of the Anderson's five children, died from tuberculosis on 8 May 1828.

## Wider visions

### The first Baptist Union of Scotland

Mention was made, in the Preface to this book, that lay people have contributed significantly to the history of Charlotte Chapel. There has been little recognition of this so far, and the section 'What happened to the trustees?' (Chapter 4) showed only intermittent lay support. Events in the spring and summer of 1827 present a more positive picture. While Christopher Anderson was looking after his one remaining child, and supporting the mission in Bengal (below), five or more of his members (probably more, but five are named) were meeting every Wednesday at 7.30pm. They spent an hour in prayer for better co-operation among the three streams of Baptist life in Scotland – English Baptists (like the Chapel), Scotch Baptists and Haldaneite Baptists. (Many of the churches founded by the Haldane brothers became Baptist churches after the Haldanes adopted Baptist

32

principles in 1808.) The three groups had been working ever more closely together in evangelism, but the lay members of Charlotte Chapel had a burden for greater association, if not unity, in other aspects of church life.

In March 1827, they judged that the time was ripe to send a circular letter to all 62 Baptist churches in Scotland, suggesting a meeting in the Elder Street (Scotch Baptist) Church in Edinburgh on 19 April. Its pastor, William Innes, was known to be keen to unite Baptists in Scotland, so Elder Street was an obvious venue for such a meeting. Pastors and deacons attended from Baptist churches all over Scotland, and agreed to set up a steering committee of three, namely two of the five Chapel men and William Innes.

Moving with astonishing rapidity, which indicates that the Chapel had correctly discerned a need in Scottish Baptist life, the committee issued a circular on 4 May, calling a further meeting of all churches for 13 June. At it, 28 of the Baptist churches in Scotland (45 per cent) agreed to form a Union. All three strands were represented, and there was also a good geographical spread, from Grantown-on-Spey to Hawick, from Aberdeen to Tiree; both urban and rural churches were involved. All five Chapel men behind the original proposal, together with nine others, were elected to take the vision forward. By providing 35 per cent of the first full committee, the laity of Charlotte Chapel emerged from obscurity to take on a pivotal role in the establishment of the first Baptist Union of Scotland.

Furthermore, by selecting and setting out, in their original (March) letter, 'what are generally considered the essential doctrines of the Word of God', they displayed a theological maturity that did credit to the teaching they had received under Christopher Anderson. Their circular letter included:

*With regard to what are generally considered the essential doctrines of the Word of God, such as the Unity and Trinity of the Godhead, the essential Deity, Incarnation and Atonement of the Son of God – the necessity of the influence of the Holy Spirit – justification by faith – the sanctifying power of the belief of the truth as it is in Jesus – we are persuaded that the views of most of these Churches are the same; and they are known to be of one mind as to the independency of the Churches of Christ.*

4 Brian R. Talbot, *The Search for a Common Identity: The Origins of the Baptist Union of Scotland 1800-1870* (Paternoster Press, Carlisle, 2003), pp. 202-3.

This was a thoughtful modification of the Chapel's doctrinal position, because they discerned – and remember they were laymen – what was the common heritage of the various churches to which the circular was sent; it was important neither to include anything which would be a problem to congregations with other traditions, nor to omit anything which the others would expect to see mentioned. The independency of the local church was crucial for all to whom they wrote, so it was italicised, to emphasize that the Union would not jeopardize it.

Sadly, early unity was followed by unwillingness on the part of some delegates from stricter churches to tolerate even minor differences in theology and practice in others. By 1830 the first Union had disbanded. The disappointment felt by the visionary leaders from Charlotte Chapel may explain their standing aloof from the next attempt to unite Scottish Baptists in a national body, which took place between 1835 and 1843 (Chapter 6).

## Serampore

While Chapel laymen were, with Christopher Anderson's encouragement, seeking greater interdependence among Scottish Baptists, Anderson himself was promoting another important aspect of Baptist witness – the missionaries at Serampore in Bengal, India. He had supported the work there ever since the Baptist Missionary Society's secretary, Andrew Fuller, preached in the Circus two months after Anderson's conversion. Unfortunately, relationships deteriorated after Fuller's death in 1815. The Society had been formed in Northamptonshire, where it still had many loyal followers, and all three streams of Scottish Baptists were generous in supporting it. Northamptonshire and Scotland wanted to continue the existing arrangement with Serampore, but some London Baptists were determined to control the society through a committee in the metropolis. In 1817, William Carey himself warned them not 'to attempt to exercise a power over us to which we shall never submit'. For the 11 years after Fuller's death, the situation became increasingly fraught.

## Visit to Copenhagen

In June 1826, Dr John Marshman came home for his first furlough from India in 27 years. He sought Anderson's co-operation in obtaining a charter from the King of Denmark for the college at Serampore. Marshman arrived in Edinburgh as Anderson was watching over the dying-bed of his son Christopher. 'On the passing of that cherished child, he allowed himself to be persuaded, both by his friends in Edinburgh, and by Dr Marshman, to accompany the latter to Copenhagen, a journey which would serve the double purpose of invigorating his spirits, depressed by long watching and sorrow, and of rendering essential service to the College interest.'

This was the longest single journey that Christopher Anderson ever made – over three thousand miles through France, Belgium, Holland and Germany. Its purpose was to seek a personal interview with the King of Denmark, because mission work in Bengal had to be conducted on Danish territory – the British East India Company would not allow evangelisation of natives on British territory. Marshman and Anderson persuaded King Frederick VI of Denmark to grant a university charter to the college at Serampore, putting it on a par with the universities of Copenhagen and Kiel, and giving it authority to grant degrees in all faculties, including divinity, the first of its kind in India. The king also made a generous gift to the funds of the Baptist Missionary Society, so Christopher Anderson's gruelling travel was well rewarded.

He was away from the beginning of August 1826 until October, and he then undertook deputation with Marshman in the north of Scotland, England and Ireland. If John Marshman had gone as planned to America, he would have accompanied him there as well. Slowly, therefore, Christopher Anderson put the pain of bereavement behind him in exacting Christian service. The importance of this for Charlotte Chapel is that for months on end, local or itinerant preachers supplied the pulpit, paid for by Christopher Anderson via his brother, Charles (Chapter 3).

## Two heads and four hands

While the granting of the Danish charter opened the way for Serampore to withdraw from the Baptist Missionary Society, which it did in 1827, the mission still had to be financed from the United Kingdom. For the next ten years, the burden of raising funds for Serampore fell on the shoulders of Christopher Anderson and George Barclay in Scotland and a philanthropic Liverpool banker in England. It became Anderson's passion, to the extent that his conscience troubled him, and he wrote in May 1832:

*Things with us in the Church have been in a very pleasing state. Additions already, and more expected. The truth is, my dear friend, that the cause here would justify my giving to it my undivided strength. I have reproached myself for its being allowed to wait on Serampore … had I two heads and four hands, they should be equally divided between home and abroad, but as it is, what can I do but get on as well as I can.*

5 Anderson, *Life and Letters*, pp. 311-2.

Christopher Anderson's journeys over the ten years of Serampore's independence included first biennial and then annual visits to Ireland, and many tours of Scotland and the north of England, to collect funds and to communicate information. His correspondence was voluminous and his house doubled up as the mission office in this country. The history of a church should be wider than the story of its individual ministers, but when a pastor writes, as Christopher Anderson did on 29 December 1835: 'I have generally been at my desk by seven in the morning, and incessantly occupied till ten at night', it says something about the situation in the pews. It was a labour of love, and while he never complained, it took a tremendous toll on his health and energy. When at home, he still had five services every week.

One service in the Chapel at this time had unusually wide repercussions, and also gives insight into the character of Christopher Anderson. William Carey died at Serampore on 9 June 1834; on Sunday evening 30 November, Anderson preached a memorial sermon on his life and character. His hearers were so impressed that they urged him to publish it. Christopher Anderson felt that the sermon was only a 'hasty outline', so he worked at it and the resulting *Discourse, occasioned by the death of the Rev. William Carey, D.D.* was the first of many biographies of the first missionary of modern times.

## Parliamentary Commission of 1838

### Pastoral care in 1836

In 1836, Christopher Anderson gave evidence to a Parliamentary Commission, investigating the state of churches throughout Scotland. He told them, on 15 January, that membership was 110, recently diminished by the removal of many to parts of England and Scotland and overseas – emigration was a significant factor – but now increasing. Average attendance on Sunday morning, which was specifically for believers, was 300 to 350. The average attendance on Sunday evening was 400 to 500. In all 625 people 'were in the habit of attending' the services. Considering that the seating capacity was 750, this was a drop from the days when there was standing room only. He did not give figures for the Sunday afternoon communion service, but since it was open to baptized believers only, and since the membership was 110, it is unlikely that attendance exceeded that number.

ROYAL COMMISSION for inquiring into the Opportunities of Public Religious Worship, and Means of Religious Instruction, and the Pastoral Superintendence, afforded to the People of Scotland.

FIRST REPORT

OF

THE COMMISSIONERS

OF

RELIGIOUS INSTRUCTION.

SCOTLAND.

*During 1836, a Parliamentary Commission took evidence, both orally and in writing, from congregations throughout Scotland, about seating accommodation, stipend, means of finance and services provided.*

The members of the Chapel lived in various parts of the city – it was, as it is now, a gathered congregation – but none of the city-residents travelled more then two miles. Three others came into the city from the country, which in those days included villages like Davidsons Mains. The majority of the members were working-class, but 'much less than half' of those attending were poor. No member was permitted to receive assistance from any public charity and the number requiring aid from the church was two or three – a phrase that Christopher Anderson, who was obviously not happy at the Commissioners' probing on financial matters, used several times to avoid being more specific. When he was questioned about the outstanding balance on the purchase price – which he had procured almost entirely by himself – he said: 'I decline answering further'. Collections were made from the members for the Fellowship Fund, which was distributed in confidence to members in need. The Commission noted:

*The pastoral superintendence of the minister only extends to the members (110) of the church. He has no connexion with the hearers further than their attending the church. He has been ready at all times to visit any who attend only as hearers, and has done so when they were sick or dying; but the pastoral superintendence, properly speaking, belongs to the church (the members). He does not readily extend his pastoral superintendence beyond the individuals belonging to the congregation, but he goes when invited.*

6 *Report of the Commission of Enquiry into the Opportunities of Public Religious Worship, and Means of Religious Instruction, and the Pastoral Superintendence afforded to the People of Scotland 1837-8* (House of Commons, London, 1838), 9 vols; vol. 1, p. 135.

### Chapel finances in 1836

Seat-rents, which were almost universally levied in those days, were used in the Chapel to pay for 'what is regarded to be the rent of the church'. Christopher Anderson made clear to the Commissioners that although figures were quoted for seat-rents, different rates for different parts of the building, payment was not demanded for them, even if the seats were occupied; it was for the individual to volunteer payment. Of the 750 seats in the Chapel, 150 were paid for in this way, leaving 600 seats for others. Those paying seat-rent had to leave one space free in every pew for a stranger to occupy; this was unique among Edinburgh churches of all denominations, and was commented on by the

Commissioners. Twice a year, Anderson told them, when seat-rents came up for renewal, he stressed to the congregation that putting one's name down for a seat was not imperative and that all who wished to attend were welcome to do so. This was typical of all Baptist churches in Scotland at the time.

Anderson would not tell the Commissioners the amount of the weekly offering, although he was willing to answer questions about donations to outside bodies. Over the five years ending 1835, the Chapel sent £445 to various home and foreign mission societies. Anderson's stipend was £105 a year; Hope Street in Glasgow, a large city-centre Baptist church, paid its minister £200, but the ministers in Cupar and Stirling received only £50 and £48 a year. Comparison with other Baptist churches in Edinburgh is not possible because, being Scotch Baptists, they had lay pastors who did not receive any payment. The average stipend across the 39 Protestant churches in Edinburgh (Chapter 2) was £225.

The Commissioners noted that while most churches saw preaching and evangelism as the prerogative of the salaried clergy, the members of the Chapel, who had obviously taken to heart their founder's passion for outreach, 'have visited the poor in the city, have given them tracts, and spoken with them; and students connected with the church have on Sabbath preached in the vicinity of the city, and in various places' – a comment which the writer has not found anywhere else in the Report.

As mentioned, membership in 1836 was 110. The next reliable figure, in 1843, was still 110 and in 1851 it was 132. Charlotte Chapel's membership throughout Christopher Anderson's years in Rose Street seems to have been consistently a little over a hundred committed people, who formed the nucleus of the church, supplemented by a larger number who came regularly to hear the Word but who did not join.

## Three other churches

### Pleasance Baptist Church

As there are no extant details of Sunday services in Charlotte Chapel at this time, it may be helpful to look at what was happening, week in and week out, in two other Baptist congregations in Edinburgh, starting with the one that sold Richmond Court to Christopher Anderson. He had attended it for a while as a teenager, and weekly communion in Charlotte Chapel came from the Scotch Baptists – English practice was fortnightly. Apart from the love-feast (which was held after the morning service) Anderson's two objections to the Scotch Baptists were: (1) lay pastors and (2) mutual exhortation; if they (alone) were the differences, the Chapel's Sunday morning service may not have differed greatly from theirs, except that since Anderson alone spoke, there may not have been so many hymns and prayers.

The Sunday morning service in the Pleasance church began at 10 a.m. and went on for nearly three hours. After a break for lunch, during which the members ate together (the love-feast), the afternoon service, which included communion, started at 2 p.m. The shortness of the break was for the benefit of those who had come from a distance and who had nothing else to do between services. The love-feast was not part of the English Baptist order, and was never practised in Charlotte Chapel.

10 a.m.
First psalm or hymn. First prayer. Second psalm or hymn. Second prayer. Third psalm or hymn. Old Testament reading. New Testament reading. Third prayer. Two or three 'exhortations' by members. (There was no equivalent in the Chapel.) Fourth psalm or hymn. Short prayer. Sermon by one of the pastors. Hymn. Benediction.

2 p.m.
First psalm or hymn. First prayer. Second psalm or hymn. Second prayer. Readings from the Prophets and Epistles. Hymn. Sermon. Hymn. Institution of the Lord's Supper by reading from one of the three Gospels or from 1 Corinthians. Prayer. Bread was broken and passed around. Prayer. Cup was passed around. Prayer. Fellowship Collection, 'and when they had sung an hymn, they went out.'

There was no Sunday evening service in the Pleasance church, but they met during the week, on Tuesday evening and Friday evening. Glancing over the orders of service, one can understand why Christopher Anderson described the

Scotch Baptists as good people in themselves, but lacking any active concern for those outside the faith.

### Clyde Street Baptist Church

The nearest Baptist church to the Chapel, geographically, was the Scotch Baptist congregation in Clyde Street (where Harvey Nichols now stands). The Sunday morning service began at 10.30 a.m. and included communion. The members, who numbered between 60 and 80, sat together; non-members, who did not take communion, sat at the back. The order of service was the singing of a psalm (with a precentor), a prayer, a reading from Scripture, another psalm or hymn, and then one of the deacons prepared the table for the Lord's Supper. That done, a passage of institution was read, without comment, thanks were given by the elders and communion was taken round. After another hymn, boxes were passed round 'for the support of the poor and for other necessary expenses'. Thus far, it may have been similar to the afternoon service in Charlotte Chapel, but the Clyde Street meeting was then open for mutual exhortation – any of the men were at liberty to contribute. This was followed by a time of prayer and praise before the morning gathering ended. The doorkeeper kept up the Scotch Baptist custom of the kiss of charity.

Little is known about the afternoon and evening services, except that psalms were preferred to hymns; the evening service was the worst attended of the three. The idea of a Sunday School was never entertained. There is no mention of meetings during the week, other than social gatherings in the houses of the members. Thus, again, one can appreciate Christopher Anderson's concern about this Scotch Baptist church – the absence of consecutive teaching by a qualified person, and the absence of any outreach to the community.

### The Church of Scotland

Sunday worship in the National Church was equally austere at this time. The structure was, as it had been for the previous hundred years or more, a psalm, an extempore prayer, Scripture reading with running commentary, a second psalm, a sermon, a second extempore prayer, and a closing psalm or paraphrase. This lasted for two hours and was conducted entirely by the minister, except that precentors led the singing. The sermon was all-important, but even the prayers had a didactic and doctrinal character.

*As the town clock struck eleven the beadle climbed the pulpit steps with the Bible and Psalter under his arm and stood waiting at the foot of the stair while the minister entered, no sound breaking the silence save the creaking of his boots. Cairns [the minister] bowed his head and prayed. After the opening psalm came a prayer lasting fifteen or twenty minutes, a reading of Scripture, another psalm, a sermon lasting fifty minutes and delivered without notes, a second long prayer, another psalm, and the blessing.*

7 A service in 1850 – Andrew L. Drummond & James Bulloch, *The Church in Victorian Scotland, 1843-1874* (The Saint Andrew Press, Edinburgh, 1975), pp. 181-2.

### Christopher Anderson's breadth of vision

Lest it be thought that Anderson's reservations over the policies of the Scotch Baptists imply a rigidity of view, his entry in Oliver and Boyd's Edinburgh Almanack for 1835 shows his breadth of interest. He was a director of the Irish Society and of the Society for Promoting Christianity among the Jews, a Director for Life of the Edinburgh Society for the Support of Gaelic Schools, a committee member of the Edinburgh Society for the Abolition of Negro Slavery and the Voluntary Church Association and the Edinburgh Association in Aid of Moravian Missions. He was also a committee member of the Edinburgh Subscription Library and an Examinator for the Edinburgh City Mission.

Paradoxically, however, while the Scotch Baptist congregation in the Pleasance had to expand its premises four times in 50 years, Christopher Anderson's ministry peaked in attendance less than 20 years after his move to Rose Street. Although the membership increased and his preaching matured over the years from 1838 to 1851, the number of 'hearers' gradually went down. The next chapter looks at the reasons for this decline.

Additional information on the following topics, mentioned in this chapter, is available on the CD.

Christopher Anderson, lecture for BMS Ter-Jubilee, 1942
Christopher Anderson's doctrinal position
Christopher Anderson's evangelising in Ireland
Christopher Anderson's health
Christopher Anderson, *The Domestic Constitution*
Fellowship Fund
Gaelic Schools Society
John Mack
Old Calton Cemetery
Serampore

# Chapter 6
# An ebb tide (1838–1846)

## Christopher Anderson's preaching and writing

### Diminishing numbers

By 1838, that is 20 years after Christopher Anderson's move to Charlotte Chapel, attendance at the Sunday services was dropping, particularly in the evening, and the ebb tide continued over the next decade. This was partly because Presbyterian churches were starting to hold their own evening services, diminishing the Chapel's congregation, partly though Christopher Anderson's frequent absences from his pulpit on Serampore business and partly through his declining health. His letter to a friend in May 1835 (aged 56) is revealing:

*The state of my health has been lately indifferent.... I lost my voice while preaching seven or eight weeks ago, and have only lately recovered it. My friends say I have too much to do ... [but the same letter ends] ... Now as to this Irish journey, I go to Belfast first and collect there next Lord's-day, then into the heart of the Native Irish for a few days, then to Dublin, and home by Liverpool.*

---

1 Anderson, *Life and Letters*, p. 315.

Even when Serampore reunited with the Baptist Missionary Society in 1838, and Anderson's official duties on its behalf were over, he did not devote his additional time to the Chapel, but looked for some other external stimulus to stretch his mind:

*When the game with Serampore seemed to be up, a mind such as this had to cast about for some object sufficient to hold it again, and sustain those spirits which would certainly flag without one.... I have thought, as I proceeded, that I must have been influenced from above, and having found no small enjoyment in my work [The Annals of the English Bible], have persevered.*

---

2 Anderson, *Life and Letters*, p. 326.

### The Achill Mission

Before looking at Christopher Anderson's best-known book, *The Annals of the English Bible*, it is worth noting how his earlier writings continued to influence people far and wide; one example will suffice, the formation of the Achill Mission on the west coast of Ireland. As a direct result of the interest aroused by his *Historical Sketches of the Native Irish*, a Protestant mission was established in the village of Dugort (see photograph). In addition to teaching, it introduced major landscape improvements on the island and new farming methods. By 1842, the mission had its own church and school, corn-mill, grain stores, hardware shop, hospital, orphanage, hotel and houses. Its newspaper, *The Achill Missionary Herald and Western Witness*, acknowledged its continuing indebtedness to Christopher Anderson.

*Achill Island, off the west coast of County Mayo, Ireland, is among the most westerly inhabited areas in Europe. As a direct result of Christopher Anderson's writings, a Protestant mission was established in the village of Dugort (in the photograph), underneath Slievemore mountain.*

### The Annals of the English Bible

Sunday 4 October 1835 was celebrated throughout Great Britain as the tercentenary of the first complete translation of the Bible into English – Miles Coverdale's translation, which he finished on 4 October 1535. Christopher Anderson preached a sermon in Charlotte Chapel from 2 Timothy 3:15-17, which was published in book form in January 1836 by public demand. This led to requests for a fuller version. He took up the challenge, because at that time there was no complete history of the English Bible; apart from preaching in the Chapel, he seldom appeared in public for the next eight years. His study became his den, where he worked on the notebooks that he filled during visits, in every one of these eight years, to the British Museum Library, and he also carried out research in the Bodleian at Oxford, the Cambridge University Library, the Baptist Museum at Bristol, and various private libraries.

This intensive study, on top of his regular preaching duties, seriously affected Christopher Anderson's health. He told a friend, concerned about his condition, that the *Annals* were written 'amidst a thousand interruptions'. He did not suffer any specific pain, but he simply over-taxed his natural strength over a prolonged period. When the book was nearly ready to go into print, he set off in 1844 (aged 62) on a second journey to the Continent, partly to verify his facts, partly as a break to restore his health. He visited Antwerp, Brussels, Cologne, Strasbourg, Basel, Berne, Zurich, and Geneva. On his return, he felt so much better that he worked harder than ever, correcting the sheets as they passed through the press and hoping that the publication of the book would give him more free time. He published the *Annals* on his sixty-third birthday, 19 February 1845. He then took an extended holiday in England to build up his reserves of strength, and spent July and August, as was his custom, visiting mission stations in the Highlands. Publication of this monumental two-volume work 'brought its author into contact with many new friends, and gave him a leading position in this branch of literature'.

From the early days of Christopher Anderson's publications, several American periodicals added the letters DD to his name, leading people to assume that he had received an honorary Doctorate of Divinity from some American college. This was not so, nor did he accept it when the University of New York offered to confer one on him in 1844, on condition that he would use it; he declined, feeling that such recognition was of only earthly value. Nevertheless, some people in this country and in America, knowing that the offer had been made and assuming that he would accept it, affixed DD to his name in their reviews of his *Annals* and addressed him as Dr Anderson – in the same way as earlier writers had done with Andrew Fuller, although he too had declined the degree and strongly disapproved of its use.

### Glimpses into Charlotte Chapel

Christopher Anderson's diary, as he worked on the *Annals*, was recorded in notebooks that he destroyed before his death. There are, therefore, only occasional glimpses of what was happening in Rose Street between 1838 and 1846. Anderson's preaching matured with the passing of the years, and the membership remained steady at 110, but fewer and fewer 'hearers' attended. His biographer noted: 'If his evening discourses were less exciting, they were richer and mellower

than in the earlier part of his ministry; and if his stated hearers were asked when they profited most by his instructions, they would point to later and maturer years than those in which the multitude crowded to hear him.' A journalist reported in 1845:

*We have several times in the evening attended the little chapel in Rose Street, and ever, we must say, with renewed satisfaction. It belongs to the Baptist persuasion. It is one of those solitary, quiet nooks, in which ambition finds no room to play vagaries, and whose pastor and flock, with evidently reciprocal regard, are content to meet, apart from all worldly stimulants, to fit themselves for eternity. The preacher speaks under felt responsibility, with solemnity; and the people listen as those who feel the deep privilege of such instruction. The place itself seems almost hallowed.... During the service the silence maintained is of a nature so striking, as to make the rustle from the turning over of the leaves of the Bible itself impressive.... All this too, we must add, is of a piece with the decorum, almost reluctance, with which the congregation separate, so very unlike what we are accustomed to witness in most cases. We are no Baptist; but to those of our own brotherhood, in all kindness we would say, – Go and see; there is much there to be learned.*

---

3 Anderson, *Life and Letters*, pp. 390-1.

Another visitor, vexed with the lack of reverence in other churches, wrote: 'Mr. Anderson's congregation is a striking exception. Here was such a stillness, a quiet solemnity. This congregation wore a Christ-like dress.'

*A quarter of the members of the Chapel in Christopher Anderson's time may have been domestic servants in the New Town. This is a typical 'upstairs' dining room and 'downstairs' kitchen in Charlotte Square at the time.*

Mary Melville, a member of the Chapel, was 44 years in service with one family at 72 George Street. She saved enough to leave a legacy of £6 to the Chapel when she died in 1869. One in four of the members of the Chapel may have been domestic servants in the New Town – that was the ratio in the nearby Baptist church at Elder Street in 1843 (below).

Students from Baptist churches south of the border, who had come to Edinburgh for a university degree, continued to be attracted by the English order in Charlotte Chapel, as there was still no other English Baptist church in the east of Scotland. Rev. Dr F.B. Meyer, a Keswick speaker, wrote to the Chapel during its centenary celebrations in 1908, to say how much his father had appreciated Christopher Anderson's ministry in the Chapel while he was studying here.

### Demography of a neighbouring church

There are no membership figures for the Chapel between the Parliamentary Commission in 1836 and a census carried out by the Baptist Union of Scotland in 1843. As mentioned, both of these give the membership as 110 but the latter, unlike the former, does not give any detail. It is therefore worth glancing at the 1843 roll of a Scotch Baptist church near to the Chapel, the Elder Street Church. It was constituted in 1810 and the founding pastor, like Christopher Anderson, preached there for the rest of his life – 45 years. Like the Chapel, it was located in the New Town, where many servants were required to staff the homes of the well-to-do. Of the 243 women members at Elder Street in 1843, 57 were domestic servants, 67 were wives (usually described by their husband's job, e.g. draper's wife), 88 had no vocational designation and 31 were recorded as daughters.

Among the 139 men, there were more than 20 shopkeepers, selling a variety of goods, more than 20 in manual occupations, including shoemakers, brushmakers, slaters, boat builders, cabinetmakers and upholsterers; six were in the printing trade. There were 16 professional men, including physicians, teachers, a stockbroker, an accountant and an inspector of prisons. Between 1841 and 1846, the Elder Street church received 232 new members and lost only 96, including those who died. There was therefore considerable increase, at a time when the Chapel was static in membership and the number of 'hearers' was declining. The social mix of the 110 members of Charlotte Chapel may not have been all that different from Elder Street, because the Parliamentary Commission noted that 'much less than half' of those attending both churches were poor and working-class. One significant difference, which may account for the growth in Elder Street, is that it had (and its successor, the Canonmills Baptist Church, still has) open membership and open communion; the Chapel at that stage restricted both membership and admission to the Lord's Table to baptized believers. As the Chapel discovered the hard way, when Christopher Anderson's successor arrived in 1851, opinion was shifting in favour of allowing all who loved the Lord to attend the communion service.

## Division and co-operation

### Thomas Chalmers

While Christopher Anderson was working on his *Annals*, the Rev. Dr Thomas Chalmers was leading a growing movement for spiritual independence within the Church of Scotland. The problem was that patrons had the power to appoint ministers, without consulting the congregation. Chalmers led an evangelical party within the church, which wanted to be free to run its affairs without state or other interference.

Christopher Anderson met and corresponded with Thomas Chalmers about their common interest in missionary work in India and the emancipation of American Negro slaves and their mutual dislike of committees in Christian work – the main reason why Serampore had parted for ten years from the BMS. Chalmers wrote about his own denominational structure:

*Some people are extremely fond of deliberative meetings. They have a greater taste, and are more qualified for the field of deliberation than for the field of action, in which former field they act as penmen, as spokesmen, as framers and movers of resolutions, and have withal a marvellous faculty of threading their way through a cumbrous and elaborate mechanism of committees and sub-committees, so interwoven with each other, that the whole becomes a very complicated affair. And then they go on consulting and deliberating, and treading upon each other, and no one going forward.*

---

4 Anderson, *Life and Letters*, p. 333.

The church-state issue came to a head during the annual

41

General Assembly of the Church of Scotland in May 1843, in St Andrew's Church in George Street, not far from Charlotte Chapel. Over one-third of the twelve hundred ministers of the Church of Scotland walked out and formed themselves into the Free Church of Scotland, electing Chalmers as their first Moderator. The Disruption (as it is known) puts into perspective the Chapel's own problems eight years later, when over one-third of the Chapel members resigned in protest over the policies of Christopher Anderson's successor. They were reconciled and rejoined the Chapel nine years later, but it was 1929 before the descendants of those who had left the Church of Scotland in 1843 were reunited with the parent body.

*St Andrew's Church, George Street (now the Church of St Andrew and St George), where the Disruption, which divided the Church of Scotland for 86 years, began in May 1843.*

### The Assembly Hall

Two legacies of the Disruption benefit Edinburgh today. One is the Assembly Hall, built in 1859 by the Free Church of Scotland; many inter-denominational evangelistic rallies have been held in it over the years, and the Chapel has hired it three times – for Graham Scroggie's farewell meetings in 1933, for seven weeks in 1936 while the building in Rose Street was being redecorated, and for another four weeks in 1970 for the same reason. The second is the library, which the Free Church of Scotland opened in 1850, and which, as part of New College, contains the largest separate theological collection in the United Kingdom. However, the immediate aftermath of the Disruption was not beneficial to the Chapel; the increased number of congregations and the rivalry between them diminished further the number of regular

'hearers' at Charlotte Chapel.

Thomas Chalmers did not survive for long after 1843. On his death in June 1847, Christopher Anderson made one of his very few negative comments about a fellow evangelical. Support was growing in Scotland for emancipation of American Negro slaves, and Anderson was disappointed that Chalmers had not been as forthright as he himself had been on the evils of slavery. He wrote:

*Would that he [Chalmers] had not blinked the subject of slavery in his latter days! I, too, wish he had not, but he is now among the spirits made perfect; and if the departed were allowed to have any influence at all upon mundane things, I am sure he would gladly employ it now to neutralize the evil and let the oppressed go free.*

5 Anderson, *Life and Letters*, p. 332.

This contrasts strangely with Christopher Anderson's words in 1852, about his own immediate future after death, which will be discussed at the end of Chapter 7.

### The first commercial Christmas card

One other event in the summer of 1843, not directly involving the Chapel at the time, is worth recording. Henry Cole (later Sir Henry Cole) was a very busy man, working in the Public Records Office in London. He was so busy that he had no time to hand-write personal greetings to his family and friends at Christmas, as was the custom at the time. In the summer of 1843, he asked an artist-friend, John Horsley, to design and print a batch of cards with the message 'A Merry Christmas and a Happy New Year', which he could send to his acquaintances.

Horsley printed a thousand cards; Cole used as many as he needed, and sold the rest. The two side panels on Horsley's card (next page) depicted the feeding and clothing of the poor, a reminder of the spirit of Christmas, with sprigs of holly, the symbol of chastity, and ivy, symbolic of places where God had walked. The centre panel featured a party of adults and children, with plentiful food and wine glasses raised in a toast – the British Temperance Movement severely criticised the latter. The concept of Christmas cards caught on quickly and the custom spread – publicised, as so often happens, by valid criticism from a well-meaning body.

*The earliest-known printed Christmas card was sent out in 1843. Panels depicted a typical family enjoying the holiday, and people performing acts of charity.*

## The second Baptist Union of Scotland

The contribution of Charlotte Chapel to the first Union, in 1827, was mentioned in Chapter 5. The next attempt to unite Scottish Baptists in a national body took place quietly between 1835 and 1843, using the word Association rather than Union. Initially it attracted support from only 15 of the 94 Baptist churches in Scotland (16 per cent), mostly rural and none in Edinburgh or Glasgow. However, when the visionary and dynamic Francis Johnston, whose father had been an office-bearer in Charlotte Chapel, became its secretary in 1842, another 23 congregations joined the Scottish Baptist Association, raising its membership to 39 per cent of the Scottish churches.

In 1843, the name was changed to the Baptist Union of Scotland. Those ministers not yet involved, including Christopher Anderson, proposed in 1845 that the Union should merge with the Baptist Home Missionary Society for Scotland, which they had supported for years. This would have secured a Union of most of the Baptist churches in Scotland. Sadly, the fledgling Union, which had a different strategy for evangelising Scotland, rejected the proposal. Those who had proposed the merger, including Christopher Anderson, were outraged when the minority body, which excluded the majority of Scottish Baptists, continued to call itself the Baptist Union of Scotland.

The depth of feeling became evident in February 1846. The Union had circulated a tract, entitled 'The Origin, Antiquity and Claims of the Baptists'. In January 1846, the editor of the *Free Church Magazine*, a man of great influence among evangelicals, denounced the tract from a paedobaptist point of view. The next issue of the *Free Church Magazine*, in February, carried a letter signed by nine of the established Baptist leaders, from all three streams of Baptist ecclesiology, including Christopher Anderson. They did not comment on the tract, but objected to the Union claiming to speak for Scottish Baptists when it was a 'mere fragment claiming a lofty name to deceive the ignorant'.

*Now we have no knowledge of the tract in question, neither have we any connection with the said 'Union', but we owe it in justice to the older established Baptist Churches in Scotland to say, that it is but a mere fraction of their membership which has lately shot up into an association assuming this lofty appellation, calculated to lead the ignorant to conclude that the Baptists in Scotland have marshalled themselves under its banner, whereas the great body stand aloof from it, altogether disapproving of its proceedings. We are, &c. J. A. Haldane, William Innes, H. D. Dickie, Christopher Anderson, Jonathan Watson, Andrew Arthur, John Leechman, Irvine, Alex. McLeod, Glasgow, James Paterson, Glasgow.*

6 The *Free Church Magazine*, No. XXVI, February 1846, pp. 60-1.

Francis Johnston defended his right to speak for Scottish Baptists, and went on with his work for a few more years. However, the lack of support, especially financial support from the stronger churches in the central belt, left the Union impoverished; the wrangle about the article did not help. In 1853 the Union reverted to being an Association of individuals, and in 1856 it dissolved. It took time for Baptist leaders to recover from the hurts inflicted during these years. The third and successful move to unite the Baptist churches in Scotland took place in 1869, after Anderson's death, and it endures to this day (Chapter 9).

A shopkeeper by name of George Boyd, who sold tartan in the Lawnmarket, persuaded a builder to dump some rubble into the half-drained Nor' Loch, to make a foot-path for him to visit the New Town. It became known as Geordie Boyd's Mud Brig. Other builders saw this as a convenient way to dispose of their rubbish, so the Mound grew rapidly, at no cost to the community. When it reached the level of the High Street in 1830, there was no way through, so Boyd suffered the indignity of seeing his shop pulled down by the magistrates in order to link the Mound to the Lawnmarket. The present layout of the Mound dates from 1850.

*Construction of the Mound made Charlotte Chapel more accessible to members living in the Old Town and also to university students.*

### The Evangelical Alliance

Because of the historic tension between the Church of England and the various nonconformist bodies there, it was felt politic for Scotland to take the initiative in 1846, to bring evangelical Christians together from all the Protestant denominations in Great Britain. This led to the formation of the Evangelical Alliance, and Scotland's role in the process was recognized by the Alliance coming to Edinburgh for its first annual conference in June 1847. Christopher Anderson's name is not on the list of delegates, but with his pan-denominational sympathy for all things evangelical, it is inconceivable that he was not supportive behind the scenes. For its first 115 years, membership of the Alliance was for individuals, not for churches; as soon as corporate membership was possible, Charlotte Chapel joined and was represented at the significant Assembly in London in 1966, as described in Chapter 44.

### Affection for the Chapel

For the last 27 years of his life, Christopher Anderson lived at 5 North Charlotte Street, on the corner of Albyn Place, about three hundred yards from Charlotte Chapel. It was a large flat in the New Town, with a living room and four bedrooms, and it housed his library. Thomas Constable, the publisher, occupied one of the other flats in the stair.

*Christopher Anderson lived from 1825 to 1852 at 5 North Charlotte Street, in the flat immediately above the For Sale board in this 1999 picture.*

Over the years, Anderson received many invitations to go elsewhere, but he declined them all – he loved his first charge with the fervour known only to those who, like him, have watched the birth and tended the infancy of a work which was peculiarly his own. Its interests were his interests and its prosperity was his happiness. Someone who knew both the Chapel and Christopher Anderson commented that it had become his idol. While the description is hardly complimentary, both he, and also the colleague who took his funeral in 1852, acknowledged its truth. In the oration at the memorial service, the speaker referred to the word 'idol' and said: 'He himself, assenting to the strong term used by a highly esteemed Christian friend, admitted it was his idol, there being hardly any thing he would not have done or have borne for the promotion of its interests.'

By 1846 (aged 64), Christopher Anderson's thoughts were turning to partial retirement and to seeking an assistant, who would initially share responsibility with him and who would ultimately take over the pastorate. As mentioned, his ministry had matured with the passing of the years, and Christians of deep spiritual experience found enrichment from his lucid exposition of Scripture. Nevertheless, he was beginning to feel the combined effects of age and arduous Christian service; he realized that for the good of the church, he should seek a successor. Only one of the original 16 who had constituted the church in Richmond Court – Martha Ketchen – was left.

## Christopher Anderson's review of his ministry

He therefore called a meeting of members, to remind them about the principles for which the church had been founded. He explained why this particular congregation had been started in November 1806, when there were already other Baptist churches in Edinburgh. He focussed on the differences between the English and Scotch Baptists – comparison of his letters in 1806 with his formal address in 1846 shows that he maintained, for all of these 40 years, the same two basic objections to Scotch Baptist churches:

Their understanding of ministry: he believed it was the privilege and duty of every church to support its own pastor, who ought not to engage in business except for study and prayer and the ministry of the Word.

Their understanding of a local church: he saw no warrant in the New Testament for ordinances other than baptism and the Lord's Supper.

Christopher Anderson had also been concerned, in 1806, at the Edinburgh Scotch Baptists' lack of evangelistic zeal, but that was a local matter, not a principle of the denomination, and it did not feature in his 1846 survey. He went on to remind his members how God had led them down the years, and he called on them to join with him in prayer, for someone to follow him in the pastorate. Having delivered that address, he began to look for a successor; the sad and unexpected outcome of his five-year search will be explored in the next chapter.

## Church attendance

As noted at the beginning of this chapter, attendance at the Sunday services in Charlotte Chapel decreased during the 1840s, particularly in the evening. How was it in other churches? Once and once only, in 1851, the government's

ten-yearly census asked about attendance at public worship. The average Scottish church was about half full for the morning service on Sunday 30 March of that year, one third full for the afternoon service and one tenth full for the evening service. There was, following the Disruption of 1843, a lot of extra accommodation in Scotland's churches, and the Chapel seems to have fared better than the average, even in the last decade of Christopher Anderson's ministry.

Additional information on the following topics, mentioned in this chapter, is available on the CD.

Achill Mission
Christopher Anderson's doctrinal position
Christopher Anderson's entry in the Dictionary
of National Biography
Christopher Anderson's library
Christopher Anderson's preaching
Christopher Anderson's publications
Christopher Anderson's review of his ministry
Christopher Anderson, *The Annals of the English Bible*

# Chapter 7
# Search for a successor (1846–1851)

## Introducing Alfred Thomas

### Christopher Anderson's initiative

Contrary to the guidelines issued to search committees in Baptist churches in the twenty-first century, it was acceptable in 1846 for a minister to nominate his successor. As there were no Baptist theological colleges in Scotland at the time, Christopher Anderson made enquiries among English churches and colleges. No one suitable was suggested to him, either in 1846 or in 1847. The urgency was taken out of the search when generous holidays in Wales, Southampton, Jersey and Guernsey in July and August 1848 did wonders for Anderson's health. Although 'his natural force was somewhat abated, and his fine voice was never again to be what it had been', he was able to preach at least twice a week during the following winter.

*Christopher Anderson travelled from the North Bridge (later, Waverley) station and its rival, the Lothian Road (later, Caledonian) station, one at each end of Princes Street.*

When Christopher Anderson went on holiday in July 1848, he had, for the first time, a choice of railway routes to England. Trains left the North Bridge (later, Waverley) station via Newcastle, and still do. The rival line via Carstairs and Carlisle operated from the Lothian Road (later, Caledonian) station from 1848 until the Beeching axe of 1965. The editor of the *Scottish Baptist Magazine* commented on the cutthroat rivalry between the two railways: 'The world admonishes Christians by the energy and resoluteness with which it pursues its aims.'

In 1849, Christopher Anderson visited the north and south of France, distributing copies of the Gospel of John and the Letter to the Romans in French, to test his theory that unbound single books of the Bible would not be easily detected by the priests and would stimulate readers to obtain other Scriptures. He encountered no difficulty in giving them out all over the country.

In 1850, Anderson became increasingly drawn to Alfred Thomas, a student of the Bristol Baptist College, who attended the Chapel while taking classes at Edinburgh University from 1849 to 1851. Christopher Anderson invited him to supply the pulpit for two months during the summer of 1850, which he did with much acceptance. Accordingly, the Chapel sent him a 'call' in April 1851, with a covering letter written personally by Anderson, who offered to relinquish his own salary (a word he greatly disliked) so that the church could pay £200 a year to Thomas. Anderson also wrote: 'Never have I had the opportunity of conversing with any Christian brother as I have done with you again and again.' Present-day historians have opined that for Christopher Anderson to seek his successor in the pastorate was a mistake, but he regarded it as part of his duty to his congregation.

### June and July 1851

With happy anticipation, the Chapel awaited an answer to the 'call'. What they did not know was that Thomas was also negotiating with the New Park Street Church in London, to which C.H. Spurgeon was 'called' five years later. Thomas did not reply to Charlotte Chapel for ten weeks and then, when he seemed unlikely to be offered the pastorate of the London church, he sent two separate letters to Edinburgh in June 1851. One purported to be an unconditional acceptance of the invitation but the other, addressed to the deacons, demanded that various changes should be made, including opening the Lord's Supper to all believers, not just to baptized Christians. Furthermore, he wished to discontinue the Sunday afternoon service and to incorporate communion into the morning service.

This letter was like a bombshell; it showed a complete misunderstanding about what he had been offered. He had been invited to assist Christopher Anderson, but he never once mentioned his name and assumed, erroneously, that Anderson was going to retire right away. He also requested six weeks' holiday every year and the highest possible salary. Thomas' attitude becomes explicable – although not excusable – when one reads the *Statement of the Circumstances* prepared by the two-fifths of the congregation who supported their lifelong pastor in the ensuing debate; Thomas had been put up to it by some members who wanted rid of Christopher Anderson, but it remains inexcusable that Thomas had given no inkling of his views when he conversed with Anderson 'again and again' (above).

Christopher Anderson was deeply grieved by Thomas' second letter, which he read to the church on 24 June without comment. The deacons wrote to Thomas, concerned at the changes proposed, and implied that the 'call' was cancelled. Christopher Anderson put it even more bluntly in a personal letter to Thomas on the same day: 'in my deliberate judgement, it would prove neither for their comfort nor your own happiness that you should come together. You will easily find some other sphere of usefulness.' Instead of accepting the position, Thomas hurried north from Bristol and started to canvass the members, as for a political election. Sides were taken, as they always are in such situations, and orderly, calm discussion became impossible. At a church meeting on Wednesday 30 July 1851, Thomas claimed that he had accepted the 'call' and that he was the rightful pastor. Others maintained that his acceptance had been so hedged about with conditions that it was not an acceptance at all.

Christopher Anderson remained calm and dignified, even when a vote was taken and three-fifths of the members supported a motion that Alfred Thomas should take over the pastorate right away. The rude and bitter expressions used by Thomas' supporters at the meeting were intended to provoke Christopher Anderson into resigning and retiring in disgust from the scene. Thomas himself demanded: 'Won't you resign now, sir? Won't you resign now?' Thomas pointed to the pulpit and announced his intention to preach there at the Thursday Bible School on the next night – which he did. He achieved this by taking physical possession of the building:

*Mr. Thomas and his party, including most of the younger members, and of those who had come to us from other churches – a majority, we admit – took possession of the chapel the same evening, some time before the usual hour of meeting and they have since retained it. Great efforts were previously made by them to collect a congregation on that occasion: the leader had been again canvassing for this, and to one person on whom he called, he expressed the hope that they would 'get Mr. Anderson out and Mr. Thomas in'.*

1 *Statement of the Circumstances Relative to the Church lately under the pastoral care of the Rev. Christopher Anderson* (Edinburgh, 1852), p. 26.

Most of the members who had been converted through Christopher Anderson's ministry up to the year 1841 sided with him, but nearly all of those who had come into membership since then favoured Alfred Thomas.

## Two views of ministry

Christopher Anderson was never again in the pulpit of Charlotte Chapel. It was more than a generation gap – it encompassed two different views of ministry and two different cultures. The booklet *Statement of the Circumstances* shows on the one hand a patriarchal figure, the father of a church built up by a single pastor over half a century, who believed in lifelong ministry, and on the other hand a young man trained in a new world of ministerial professionalism, choosing between churches, moving on after a few years and questioning traditional practices like closed communion. Why the latter was such an emotive issue is explored in Chapter 8. Thomas' ideas, although gaining favour elsewhere, were incompatible with Anderson's; he should have disclosed his position before accepting the 'call' and then riding roughshod over existing ways.

Again, on the question of stipend, the older and younger generations held diametrically opposite views. Christopher Anderson was never slow to ask for money for mission or any other form of outreach, but he hated discussing his own support; with his private means, he did not need to. Alfred Thomas went to the other extreme and wrote to the deacons: 'I hold it as a principle that no church has a right either to engage or retain the services of any man in the Pastoral Office without the highest remuneration possible in their circumstances, consistent with the other claims of the church and the world.' This seems to imply that after the expenses of running the church had been met, the remainder should be made over to the minister.

*Christopher Anderson photographed by daguerreotype process, probably about 1846, aged 65.*

## Christopher Anderson's last six months

### August 1851–February 1852

This chapter would not be complete without an account of Christopher Anderson's remaining life. He continued to be pastor to the two-fifths of the congregation who had voted against Alfred Thomas. He spent the following Sunday at the home of friends near Roslin, partly to avoid callers who, although kindly intentioned, troubled him at that sensitive time, and partly to avoid giving any impression that he was holding rival services. He conducted Sunday worship privately in his friends' drawing room, preaching from 1 John 3:16: 'Hereby perceive we the love of God, because He laid down His life for us; and we ought to lay down our lives for the brethren.'

The next Sunday he was with other friends in Newcastle. He returned to Edinburgh on 21 August; on the following day, his sister-in-law and housekeeper, Mrs Margaret Anderson, took ill. She had long been subject to a medical condition,

which, to prevent fatal illness, required composure of mind and freedom from stress. She was a member of the Chapel, and she felt the insults heaped on her brother-in-law even more acutely than he did. As they talked on his return from Newcastle, she expressed her convictions in strong language and in consequence suffered a stroke. She realized that she would not survive for long and, looking at her distressed brother-in-law, she said: 'They have put us both in our graves, but me first.'

Christopher's niece, Euphemia Anderson, nursed her aunt until she died two weeks later, on 5 September 1851. During her illness, Christopher Anderson scarcely left the house, but after her funeral, where he took the service at the grave in his usual solemn and pointed manner, he resumed his pastoral care of those members of the church who adhered to him. They met in the home of one of the members on Wednesday evening, but, except for a prayer meeting, they had no public worship. He refused to hold rival Sunday services.

### Despicable conduct

The majority of the seven trustees of Charlotte Chapel – the trustees were and still are the legal owners of the building – supported Christopher Anderson. In a letter to Alfred Thomas on 31 July 1851, they called on him and those who adhered to him to vacate the Chapel premises. Thomas replied that his supporters formed the majority of the congregation and so they had sole right to the building. There was heated correspondence between the trustees and Thomas over several months, without result. On 23 December 1851, Thomas and his friends resorted to a despicable way of legalizing their possession of the Chapel building. The trust deed of 1837 provided that the trustees had to be members of the Chapel; Thomas called a church meeting and proposed that those who had left with Christopher Anderson were no longer members. Since expulsion from membership disqualified them from being trustees, Thomas replaced them with his men.

Christopher Anderson bore it all with grace and meekness. Although he had been excommunicated from the church that he had built up from nothing and from the Chapel that he had bought largely with his own money, he spoke no words of anger. His strongest comment to a sympathising friend was: 'Oh, to be delivered from unreasonable men!'

## Christopher Anderson's death

Just eight weeks later, he was dead. He suffered a stroke on 18 January 1852 and never recovered. Today's readers may find his last words strange, and they deserve explanation. A week before he died, he rallied and said to those attending him: 'Don't be alarmed about me, I shall fall asleep in Jesus, and wake at the resurrection.' He then went into a comatose state and did not regain consciousness. He died at two o'clock in the afternoon of 18 February, the eve of his seventieth birthday. He was by then the oldest minister, both in years and in length of time in the pastorate, in Edinburgh.

It is common nowadays to say, on the death of Christians, that they are now in the presence of the Lord Jesus Christ – based on the Scripture quoted below. A typical notice in *The Scotsman* reads:

*Sheila Masterton (Edinburgh/India) … went into the presence of her Lord on Sunday, March 5, 2006 … a Thanksgiving service will take place at Charlotte Baptist Chapel, West Rose Street, Edinburgh, at 11 am on Saturday, March 18*

2 *The Scotsman*, 13 March 2006, p. 42.

Christopher Anderson's belief – at least on his deathbed – that Christians sleep without consciousness until the resurrection, is known as soul-sleep. It was common among the early church fathers, and has been heard among Evangelicals in the last 50 years, but the preacher at Christopher Anderson's memorial sermon, on Sunday evening 29 February, took the opportunity of stating the more usual view:

*But a question of no little interest here suggests itself: Are we never to be with the Lord till then [the resurrection]? Is he never to 'receive us to himself' till then? So some think; conceiving, according to one view, that till the resurrection the soul sleeps, with the body, in a state of entire unconsciousness.... I cannot, however, bring myself to believe, that Paul, who 'desired to depart and to be with Christ', as being, in his estimation, 'far better' than to 'continue in the flesh' is not with Christ yet!... The Apostle settles the point, in 2 Cor. v. 6–8 [quoted]. Jesus is 'gone into heaven': believers, when they die, 'are absent from the body, and at home with the Lord.' They are*

*therefore, in heaven. This is a partial fulfilment of their hopes: and it is a very cheering one.*

3 Rev. Dr Ralph Wardlaw, *A Sermon preached in Albany Street Chapel, Edinburgh, on Lord's Day evening, February 29th, on the occasion of the death of the Rev. Christopher Anderson*, (London, 1852).

That was the settled teaching in Charlotte Chapel throughout the twentieth century. Joseph Kemp, preaching on 1 Thessalonians 4:13, said: 'Our loved ones are consciously happy in the Lord's presence. They are "at home" with the Lord. I say consciously happy. I do not believe they are in an unconscious state.' Sidlow Baxter's last recorded sermon, at the age of 88 in 1991, emphasized what he had taught while pastor of the Chapel from 1935 to 1953, that the believer is in the conscious presence of Jesus from the moment of death. A testimonial with the same message by Derek Prime, at a thanksgiving service in 2000, is quoted in chapter 45.

*Christopher Anderson's grave and headstone in the Old Calton Cemetery; the smaller stone on the left is for his nephew and biographer, Hugh Anderson.*

Christopher Anderson was buried beside his wife and their five children in the Old Calton Cemetery, where a stone on the wall marks the grave. (Do not look for it on your own, because the cemetery is walled and undesirable characters now frequent the area.) His memorial service was held in Albany Street Chapel, not in Charlotte Chapel. Christopher Anderson had set out to build a congregation on very definite lines, to ensure its continuance and unity. Until seven months before his death, the church did indeed resemble a family, of which he was the spiritual father. He had built a stable church, but the problem of succession split the congregation.

## Christopher Anderson's legacy

The enduring foundations that Christopher Anderson laid for the Chapel include:

Evangelism: he was an evangelist, seeking souls for Christ; this has been the constant thrust of Chapel activity.

Teaching: he was a doctrinal preacher, who knew his Bible well, and his ministry was grounded in Christian doctrine; successive pastors have stood in this succession.

Mission: he had a passion for home and overseas mission; this has grown rather than diminished over the intervening years.

Co-operation: he had wide Christian sympathies, evidenced by the list of committees on which he served; the Chapel still co-operates with evangelical Christians of all denominations in areas of mutual concern.

There have been 17 other pastors of Charlotte Chapel over the two hundred years. Two of them were Welsh and 15 were English. Various assistants and members of the pastoral team have been Scots, but Christopher Anderson is, so far, the only native Scot to be the senior pastor.

*The only extant personal item from Christopher Anderson's long life, apart from some letters, is a map of Europe, drawn when he was 16; map-making was one of his favourite subjects at school.*

## Events in Queen Street

### The true Charlotte Chapel

The two-fifths who supported Christopher Anderson, 53 in number, regarded themselves as the true Charlotte Chapel, although they met in the Theological Hall at 5 Queen Street (until recently, the studios of BBC Scotland). Both they and the congregation in Rose Street increased in number over the next few years. In December 1853, the Queen Street congregation called a pastor of their own; until then:

*the dispensation of ordinances [are] conducted by ministers whose services are secured and the affairs of the Church are conducted by the Deacons and members in the same way as they were conducted before any invitation was sent to Mr. Thomas and when the Church assembled in Charlotte Chapel.*

4 'Memorial for the Opinion of Counsel' by Anderson's supporters.

In other words, they had a Sunday afternoon communion service and admitted only baptized believers to it. Alfred Thomas left Edinburgh in 1855 through ill-health, but 'the Deacons and Members who adhered to Mr. Anderson and other Deacons elected and members admitted subsequently to the rupture, continue to assemble together as a church for the purposes of Divine Worship.' About six years later, probably in 1861, the two congregations were reconciled and the excluded members returned to Rose Street (Chapter 9).

### Another debate

When Christopher Anderson's followers moved to 5 Queen Street in 1852, another debate was taking place along the road, in number 52, scientific rather than theological in character – although the meaning of Genesis 3:16 came into it. James Young Simpson, whose home and surgery was at 52 Queen Street, had discovered the anaesthetic properties of chloroform as a substitute for ether in surgical operations. Simpson's work was strongly debated and there was much opposition to it from the medical profession, and from some clergy (based on Genesis). Simpson was an evangelical Christian; his nephew, also an evangelical and a supporter (although not a member) of the Chapel, entertained visiting Chapel preachers at the actual table where Sir James and his two assistants, Keith and Duncan, made their initial experiments.

*In the experiment depicted in this sketch, James Young Simpson and his assistants have dramatically put themselves to sleep with a small phial of the anaesthetic chloroform.*

Additional information on the following topics, mentioned in this chapter, is available on the CD.

Authority of Scripture
Christopher Anderson remembered
Christopher Anderson in the *Biographical Dictionary of Eminent Scotsmen*
Christopher Anderson's early years
Christopher Anderson's entry in the *Dictionary of National Biography*
Christopher Anderson's entry in www.electricscotland
Christopher Anderson's last six months
Christopher Anderson's Memorial Sermon
Christopher Anderson's obituary
Christopher Anderson's profile
Christopher Anderson's search for a successor
Old Calton Cemetery
*Statement of the Circumstances*
Trust Deed of 1837

# Chapter 8
## Two congregations (1851–1860)

### 1851–1855: Rev. Alfred C. Thomas

#### Ichabod?
Two recent Baptist writers have described the second half of the nineteenth century in Charlotte Chapel as:

*for fifty years the church became a backwater,*

and

*a cloud settled on Charlotte Chapel after 1852 and … it was not until 1904-5 that Charlotte Chapel rose from the ashes of comparative obscurity.*

1.1 Rev. Dr Derek B. Murray, in Donald E. Meek (ed.), *A Mind for Mission: Essays in appreciation of the Rev. Christopher Anderson* (Scottish Baptist History Project, Edinburgh, 1992), p. 5; 1.2 Meek, *Mind for Mission*, p. 2.

William Whyte was even more severe. He gave the title 'Ichabod' to his chapter on this period – a reference to 1 Samuel 4:21 where, after a calamitous incident in Israel's history, the priest's grandson was named 'Ichabod', meaning 'The glory has departed'. The writer has added a question mark to Mr Whyte's description; apart from one disastrous pastorate at the end of the century, 'Immanuel' (God with us) might be a better summary of the fifty years. Although there were ten comparatively short pastorates, there were more encouragements than discouragements during them, as the next four chapters will show.

#### The new pastor
Alfred Thomas was a Welshman, a son of the manse, who had started off in business with his uncle – as had Christopher Anderson – and who had been converted at the age of 17 – as had Anderson. He continued in business until he was 22, when he felt drawn to Baptist ministry. He went to the Bristol Academy for four years, and completed his studies in Edinburgh from 1849 to 1851. As he was finishing at the university here, the Chapel issued a 'call' to him, which, at the age of 29, he accepted. Although occupying the pulpit of Charlotte Chapel from August 1851 onward, Thomas was not formally inducted as pastor until after Christopher Anderson's death in February 1852.

Chapter 7 gave the impression that Alfred Thomas was a cad, whose tactless and tasteless conduct split the church and hastened the death of its founder. The 53 dissenting members of the Chapel would have agreed, but on his premature death at the age of 44, his obituary gave a different picture:

*In 1851 he accepted the pastorate of the church at Charlotte Chapel, Edinburgh, where he laboured with great success for four years, at the end of which time, having repeatedly suffered haemorrage from the lungs, and his physicians reiterating their conviction that owing to the keenness of the atmosphere, he could not live and work in Edinburgh, he removed to London, in July, 1855, to become the pastor of the church at Cross-street Chapel, Islington…. His sole aim and purpose was to win souls for Christ, and to that end he devoted himself with a zeal and love almost impossible to understand.*

2 *The Baptist Handbook*, 1867, Obituaries, p. 137.

There is no record of how many 'hearers' attended the Chapel without joining between 1851 and 1855, but in Thomas' first year, 27 new members were received by baptism, 8 more by transfer and 1 by restoration – a net gain, after deaths and resignations, of 31. In his final year, 19 were baptized and 7 joined by transfer, bringing the membership back up to 132, the number before the split. If 'the glory had departed', there was still evidence of grace at work.

Among the four baptized and received into membership on 16 October 1851, at the height of the unpleasantness, was James Cumming Brown. Under Thomas' guidance, he heard the 'call' to Baptist ministry; after training at Regent's Park College, he was the pastor of the Anstruther Baptist Church from 1859 to 1862. After other pastorates, during one of which he was the president of the Baptist Union of Scotland in 1878-9, he founded the Morningside Baptist Church in Edinburgh in 1894.

#### Chapel membership
The first extant church register shows a congregation gathered from around the city. The 79 who remained in membership with Alfred Thomas in August 1851 – that is after the other 53 had left in protest – lived in:

Central Edinburgh: Castle Street, Duke Street, Newport Street, Princes Street, Rose Street (five from here) and South Charlotte Street.

East of Princes Street: Broughton Street, London Street and Regent Road.

North of Princes Street: Abercromby Place, Clarence Street, Cumberland Street, Mackenzie Place, Royal Circus, Raeburn Place and St Vincent Street.

West of Princes Street: Coates Crescent, Dalry Road, William Street and Davidsons Mains (then a separate village).

South of Princes Street: Bread Street, Brighton Street, Buccleuch Place and Street, Charles Street, Earl Gray Street, Findhorn Place, Fountainbridge, George IV Bridge, George Square, Gilmore Place, Grindlay Street, Hope Park Crescent, Lothian Road and Street, Morningside Bank, Nicolson Street, Tarvit Street, Teviot Row, West Bow and West Nicolson Street.

Every nineteenth-century minister in the Chapel had to make his own arrangement for a manse. Alfred Thomas chose 2 Atholl Place. His wife, Eliza, joined the Chapel by transfer from Haverford West – Thomas was from Pembrokeshire, so perhaps they had just got married – but there is no record of any family. Thomas 'possessed the fervour and eloquence of his native land – dear little Wales'.

Despite Alfred Thomas' discourteous treatment of Christopher Anderson in July 1851, Anderson would surely have been gracious enough to applaud Thomas' immediate involvement with the Baptist Home Missionary Society for Scotland, a work dear to Anderson's heart. At its annual meeting, held in Glasgow on 22 April 1852, Thomas spoke after the annual report had been given, and urged greater effort on the part of the Society 'to diffuse the knowledge of salvation more extensively in the field which the Society occupies'. Far from resenting this intervention by a newcomer to Scotland, the Society accepted Thomas' proposals – he must have been eloquent indeed. He also added his name to the list of ministers of all denominations who refused to counter-sign applications for the licensing of public houses, urging 'the Servants of Him whose mission on earth was fraught with love, to discontinue signing such Certificates in future'.

## Open or closed communion?

Alfred Thomas' major change in the Chapel involved the communion service. Until he came, the Lord's Supper had been the focal point of a separate service every Sunday afternoon. Because many 'hearers' came to the Sunday morning service, and because the Lord's Table was open only to baptized believers under Christopher Anderson, a separate communion service was essential. Thomas wanted all believers, baptized or not, to attend communion, so he incorporated it into the Sunday morning worship. One of his critics described it as 'tacked on', so it must have come at the end of the service. At that time there were no elders, so the deacons assisted the minister by preparing and distributing the bread and the wine.

Thomas discontinued the Sunday afternoon service. He could have continued it and invited all Christians to come, but he felt – this aspect was not so divisive – that three services in one day were too much, not least for him. At this time, English Baptist churches were debating whether communion should be held irregularly or monthly or fortnightly or weekly, and whether only non-alcoholic wine should be used, but these were not issues in Charlotte Chapel.

Without excusing Alfred Thomas' rudeness toward Christopher Anderson, which was inexcusable, it is worth asking why he felt so strongly about opening the Lord's Table to all believers? At the beginning of the nineteenth century, when Christopher Anderson visited England and then started his ministry in Edinburgh, the vast majority of Particular Baptists (among whom he moved) held that only those who had been baptized as believers could participate in the Lord's Supper in a Baptist church (closed communion). However, a Leicester minister, Robert Hall, published *On Terms of Communion* in 1815, in which he advocated opening the table to all believers. Others responded, saying that communion in a Baptist church should be served only to those who had been baptized. Thomas had grown up during this debate, and the issue was a live one in the 1850s, not least because open-communionist preachers were attracting many who felt excluded from church life by the older, restrictive view.

The strength of feeling on both sides is illustrated by the experience of one of Alfred Thomas' successors in the Chapel, John Dovey, pastor from 1862. He came from a congregation that had wrestled with, and divided over, the issue. He was so much in favour of open communion in his church in Lowestoft, that he resigned the pastorate in 1860 because they would not accept it. The church then adopted open communion in order to secure his continuing with them, but that led to 30 members seceding and forming a Strict Baptist church nearby.

Much the same happened in Newington, in the southern suburbs of Edinburgh, as late as 1877. After James and Robert Haldane became Baptists in 1808, the Tabernacle at the top of Leith Walk functioned as a Baptist church and had a closed table. The Tabernacle congregation moved to Duncan Street in 1864, still with the same policy. At Duncan Street's anniversary weekend in April 1877, the minister 'in the course of his interesting remarks, referred to the recent defection of a considerable number of members in consequence of the resolution of the majority to become an open communion church; but he declared that, discouraging as that falling-away had been, he felt that they had right on their side.'

### Who owned the Rose Street building?

The deposed trustees of Charlotte Chapel and the supporters of Alfred Thomas both took legal advice about ownership of the building; they argued their respective positions for several years. Was Alfred Thomas the pastor of Charlotte Chapel or was Christopher Anderson the pastor in exile until his death; were his followers the true Chapel? The debate hinged on whether Thomas had, in responding to the 'call' to Charlotte Chapel, inserted conditions about communion; if so, he had not accepted the invitation sent to him, and therefore he had no right to occupy the building. Thomas' view was that he had cordially and unconditionally accepted the 'call' and had then gone on, as a separate matter, to express certain views.

As long as there were two congregations, one meeting in Charlotte Chapel and the other in Queen Street, both claiming to have exclusive right to the building in Rose Street,

the issue would not go away. In November 1853, a medical doctor, one of the new trustees of the Chapel, left the church along with nine others 'in consequence of a change of sentiment regarding the division in the church at the time of the present pastor's settlement in July 1851'. Over the next year, another seven resigned, some of who had been in membership since Richmond Court days. It was all very sad.

The issue was still unresolved when Thomas' medical advisers told him in 1855 that Edinburgh's climate was undermining his health, and that he should return to the south. He went to a church in London, and he must have left with mixed feelings. On the one hand, 56 had been converted and joined the Chapel during his four years in Edinburgh and another 34 had come into membership by transfer. Of these, 21 were men, 16 were married women and 53 joined as single women, five of whom subsequently married in the Chapel. One of the most encouraging features of Alfred Thomas' early ministry in the Chapel was the number of husbands and wives who joined the Chapel together – there were very few couples toward the end of Christopher Anderson's years.

On the other hand, 17 of the oldest members resigned during Alfred Thomas' ministry, specifically over his policy about communion, in addition to the 53 who had walked out in protest as he arrived. When he left, only 35 of the 79 who had supported his 'call' (less than half) were still worshipping in Charlotte Chapel. In addition to those who left through disagreement, emigration was a major factor in the mid-nineteenth century. Who could blame those who accepted the government's offer of transport by ship to Natal, with full provisions on the way and 20 acres of land when they arrived, all for £10, and with no opposition at that time from Zulus or Boers.

### Losses to Christian Brethren

Three adjoining entries in the church register are eloquent of the turnover. Three single women were baptized and joined on 23 December 1851, almost the firstfruits of Alfred Thomas' ministry in the Chapel. Within five years, the one who lived just round the corner, in North Charlotte Street, had sailed for Australia, the one who lived in George Square had transferred to the nearby Bristo Street Baptist church, and the third, from Scotland Street, 'united with the Plymouth Brethren'. Over subsequent years, many came to the Chapel from the Christian Brethren, but in the 1850s and 60s, the movement was entirely the other way, ten in all; the first to transfer to the Chapel from the Brethren was in 1870. The church register pointedly comments that they joined the Brethren 'in this city' and once, perhaps in exasperation, simply a terse 'To PB's' (Plymouth Brethren). Not only the Chapel was losing members to Assemblies at this time, because over Scotland as a whole:

*Around this time there began to be a great troubling in many of these churches over the appearance of Plymouth Brethrenism. As Brethren Assemblies began to rise up in many areas, so a good many Baptists moved their allegiance and united with them. The new teaching of dispensationalism was an attraction to some, and the Brethren view of the ministry was very much akin to that already held by some of the Scotch Baptist order of churches.*

---

3 W.J. Seaton, *A short history of Baptists in Scotland* (Fauconberg, Dunstable, 1983), p. 10.

## 1856–1858: Rev. James Martin, BA

### A scholarly pastor

To twenty-first-century eyes, the Chapel's choice of successor to Alfred Thomas was a strange one. James Martin was not a preacher – he was a quiet and introspective man, who spent his spare time translating German theological works into English. He had been born and brought up in London and, like both Christopher Anderson and Alfred Thomas, had started life in a merchant's office. At the age of 20, he felt 'called' to the Christian ministry and studied at the Baptist College and the University of London. He then received a scholarship to spend a year in Bonn, after which he was called to a pastorate in Lymington in 1848. He worked systematically and conscientiously there until 1855, when he went to Stockport, but his quiet, scholarly ways were not appreciated in that bustling Lancashire town. On the recommendation of a mutual friend in Liverpool, the Chapel sent him a 'call'; at the age of 35, he came to Edinburgh in January 1856, after a vacancy of seven months. He and his wife lived at 1 Danube Street; nothing is known about any children.

Like his two predecessors, James Martin actively promoted the work of the Baptist Missionary Society, welcoming

54

*As Alfred Thomas left Edinburgh, the finishing touches were being put on the New Town. This 1999 picture illustrates the strategic position of Charlotte Chapel. On the left hand margin of the photograph, Charlotte Square (nearer camera) and Moray Place (beyond it) were the two jewels of the Georgian New Town.*

missionaries on deputation, addressing rallies and holding a meeting in the Chapel 'for the benefit of the young'. One of his deacons in Edinburgh said that although his preaching was good and instructive, he was very quiet and 'people who like excitement were disappointed. While pastor of Charlotte Chapel he translated many theological works from the German for T. & T. Clark's Foreign Theological Library'. To what extent that commended him to his people is not recorded, but there was growing concern among Evangelicals in Britain about the influence of liberal teaching by German theologians. When Christopher Anderson sent some books to his nephew Hugh in March 1836, he wrote a covering note:

*I have not sent you these critical books from any high opinion I entertain of the German School. Very far from it. In these verbal critics there is frequently not only an ignorance displayed of the scope of the passage, but they pass away over it without catching any degree of its fine and exalting spirit.*

4 Anderson, *Life and Letters*, p. 386.

In September 1858, that is after two years and nine months in Edinburgh, James Martin received a 'call' to Derby Road Baptist Church, Nottingham. 'He left us,' said the same deacon who had commented on his preaching, 'to the great regret of the church and with the warmest feelings of regard for him and of desire for his success.' He seems to have flourished in Nottingham, because they were sorry when he accepted a call to Melbourne, Australia, in l869. He had an outstanding ministry there.

During his pastorate in the Chapel, 13 were baptized, another joined by transfer and two were received on confession of faith, 'baptism omitted on account of health'. This is the first reference to a concession that has been made over the years, and is still made, where a person accepts the principle of believers' baptism but where it is inadvisable on medical grounds to carry out the physical immersion. Rather than have baptism by affusion, on confession of faith, it is preferred to excuse the water altogether. The next instance is in 1871, where the entry reads: 'In consequence of heart disease, was not baptised, but yet received as a baptised believer'. It was well expressed in a church minute in 1892, regarding:

*a woman of upward of 60 years of age and afflicted with asthma and heart complaint to such an extent as to render it dangerous for her to be baptised. If she could be baptised she would be perfectly willing. Under the circumstances the Church accepted the will for the deed.*

5 Church Minute Book 1891, 18 December1892.

The membership had gone down from 132 to 129 during the vacancy before James Martin came, and remained at that figure for his first year. However, only five dropped off the roll in his second year (one death, two moving away, one resignation and one exclusion) so 11 new arrivals that year brought the membership up to 135, the highest figure recorded so far. Of the 34 who joined during James Martin's ministry, there was a better gender balance than previously, although the 15 men were still outnumbered by 19 women, 8 married and 11 single; of the 8, only 3 joined along with husbands. More significantly, for the first time in the Chapel's history, growth by transfer exceeded growth by conversion; 10 of the transfers were from nearby Edinburgh Baptist churches. Christopher Anderson would not have approved; at a later date, the Chapel required all transfer applications from other Edinburgh Baptist churches to lie on the table for six months – to discourage hasty decisions.

## Foundations for an enduring Union

Charlotte Chapel had taken the initiative in the first attempt to bring the Baptist churches of Scotland together in 1827; it had been rebuffed in the second attempt in 1845 (Chapters 5 and 6). In 1856, James Martin renewed the Chapel's concern for good inter-church relations. Wisely, in view of the demise of the previous two Unions, he first of all encouraged the formation of an association of individuals, not churches. Known initially as the Scottish Baptist Association, and then, from 1859, as the Baptist Association of Scotland, it embarked on the excellent strategy of getting as many people as possible involved, by meeting in different churches around Scotland, by inviting a wide variety of speakers and by having fellowship dinners afterward. The Chapel was host in 1861.

James Martin was one of the speakers at the Association's first annual meeting. It adopted a basis of faith that was basically evangelical Calvinistic, but which was wide enough to accommodate evangelical Arminians as well. This was important, because more and more of the younger ministers were adopting a moderate Arminian theology in place of the traditional Calvinistic view of election and redemption. Clearly no formal Union of churches could be set up (which was the long-term goal of the Association) until sufficient bridge-building had taken place among ministers with different theological perspectives. The following three Chapel ministers were actively involved, and by 1869 there was sufficient mutual forbearance for the goal to be achieved (Chapter 9).

## 1859–1860: Rev. William Stacey Chapman

### The Chapel's shortest pastorate
'Mr. Chapman's pastorate was so brief that slight opportunity was afforded for displaying his ability and knowledge.' After a ministry of one year, he resigned on account of ill health; where he came from, or where he went to, is a mystery to the writer. He was one of three ministers to represent Edinburgh on the Baptist Home Missionary Society in 1860, but apart from that, he does not appear on any list of Baptist ministers. He lived at 11 West Maitland Street, but he did not remain in Edinburgh after his resignation. In 1896, it was said that Chapman and four other previous ministers of the Chapel 'remained on earth doing the will of Christ in His churches', but he is not listed as a Baptist minister then, either in Great Britain or abroad, and there is no obituary for him in any of the usual places. This is a pity, because 1859-60 were years of religious revival in Scotland and it would have been fascinating to know how Chapman prepared the Chapel to share in it, because share it did, as described below.

The Moderator of the General Assembly of the Free Church of Scotland spoke in May 1860 about 'the pregnant cloud' sweeping over America and Ireland, and 'this year, the same precious showers have been and are falling within the limits of our own beloved land.... Whole congregations have been seen bending before it like a mighty, rushing wind.' At the same time, the General Assembly of the Church of Scotland, 'taking into consideration the gratifying evidence manifested in many countries and in various districts of our own land, of an increased anxiety about salvation and deepening interest in religious ordinances, followed in so many cases by fruits of holy living, desires to record its gratitude to God'.

During William Chapman's brief pastorate, ten were baptized and six more joined by transfer; of the eight men among them, six were married and four of them joined along with their wives; there were two other married women and two single. What else happened is not now known, but Chapman must have laid a foundation for the Chapel to receive the fruits of the revival, because in the calendar year 1861, while the pulpit was vacant, there were baptismal services in January, March, April, July, August, September, November and December. A total of 15 were baptized, another joined by transfer, and a woman who had drifted away was restored. Three were men, three were married women (no couples) and eleven were unmarried women, and nearly all lived locally – Atholl Crescent, Castle Street, George Street, Jamaica Street, Moray Place, Princes Street, Queen Street and Rose Street. Three of them went on to full-time Christian service, one as the founding minister of the Broughty Ferry Baptist Church and two to head up the Seamen's Mission in Thurso.

### Inter-denominational co-operation
The first recorded inter-denominational activity on the Chapel premises started during the 1860–61 vacancy. The elders of the Presbyterian St George's church (then in Lothian Road, now in Shandwick Place) were concerned about Presbyterians living in Rose Street 'who neglect attendance on the means of grace'. In January 1861, they asked for (and were granted) the use of the Chapel building every Wednesday and Friday, for prayer and Scripture reading, in which they were 'assisted by office bearers of other denominations'.

### The one o'clock gun
During the vacancy of 1861, while the deacons of Charlotte Chapel were looking for a new pastor, scientists in the Royal Observatory on Calton Hill were trying to solve another problem – how to get the city's church clocks to chime the hours and the quarter hours at more or less the same time. After the Disruption of 1843, there were dozens of church towers with chiming clocks around Edinburgh, but which of them was right if neighbouring clocks disagreed?

The problem had been partially tackled a decade previously, when a visiting sea captain, who had moored his ship off Leith, complained that no one could give him the correct time of day. To meet his criticism, a time signal was inaugurated in 1853. A large canvas-covered ball was added to the mast on the top of the monument to Lord Horatio Nelson on Calton Hill; known as Nelson's Column, it was built in the shape of an inverted telescope. (The Council still decks the monument with flags annually on Trafalgar Day.) Every weekday, at ten minutes to noon (in those days; the signal was later moved to one o'clock), a boy from James Ritchie and Son, Edinburgh watch and clock makers, cranked the ball up the pole to the top of the mast. Exactly at twelve, it was dropped by an electrical connection running from the Royal Observatory. Sea captains anchored in the Firth of Forth could watch the signal through their spyglasses and check their ship's chronometers.

*The one o'clock gun is not usually fired on Sunday, but its dull boom echoes around the Chapel at the beginning and end of the two-minutes' silence on Remembrance Day.*

The gun marks the beginning and end of the two-minute silence on the Sunday nearest to 11 November every year. The Chapel's Remembrance Day service starts at ten minutes to eleven, aiming to observe the silence along with the rest of the country. Until 2001, it was difficult for the preacher to time the preliminaries to end at exactly 11 a.m; if he was early in inviting the congregation to stand in silence, or late in re-commencing the service, a very audible boom echoed around the church. On 11 November 2001, the Chapel was linked for the first time by television and PowerPoint to the Cenotaph service in London, projected onto a screen in the choir-stalls, and Big Ben drowned out the local time signal from the Castle. This is now a regular feature of Remembrance Sunday.

*The large canvas-covered ball on the top of Nelson's Column was (and still is) cranked to the top of the mast shortly before 12 noon (now one o'clock) and dropped on the hour, to allow observers to check their clocks and watches.*

That was all very well for those who could see Calton Hill, but what about the rest of Edinburgh? In 1861, the Observatory men learned that the Parisians fired a cannon every day at 1 p.m; they wanted a similar time signal from the Castle on every hour of the 24, but fortunately they were persuaded to restrict it to 12 noon daily except Sunday (later moved to 1 p.m). A copper wire was laid between the Observatory and Edinburgh Castle – a similar wire already connected Nelson's Monument to the Observatory – sending a signal to set off the gun, loaded with powder. Pigeons took off in flocks, as they still do today, and people set their watches and their clocks, as they still do today.

Additional information on the following topics, mentioned in this chapter, is available on the CD.

Alfred Thomas
Communion – open, closed, frequency
James Martin
Membership patterns, 1808-1875

# Chapter 9
# Steady growth and mission (1861–1875)

## The highest membership so far

### Reunion

During the vacancy of 1861-2, those who had left in protest at the actions of Alfred Thomas in 1851, and who had been worshipping at 5 Queen Street, were reconciled and rejoined the Chapel. Among the 51 names added to the church register was Martha Ketchen, the only surviving signatory of the original 'call' to Christopher Anderson in 1807. Her address was 174 Rose Street, and since the Chapel's postal number is 204, it must have been a particular pleasure for her to rejoin her local church. Despite the turnover in membership during the decade of separation, both in Rose Street and in Queen Street, 25 of the 53 who had left with Christopher Anderson and 26 of the 79 who had remained with Alfred Thomas were among the 169 members who greeted the next pastor. Seventeen joined the church during the vacancy, including those from Queen Street who had not previously been Chapel members; encouraged by reports of the revival throughout the land (Chapter 8), the Chapel was in excellent heart.

### 1862-1866: Rev. John Edward Dovey

John Dovey was another Londoner and another son of the manse, born in 1823. His first pastorate at Lowestoft lasted for 17 years and he was a successful preacher. In 1862, at the age of 39, he accepted a unanimous invitation to the pastorate of Charlotte Chapel, where he stayed for five years. From 1864 to 1866, his manse was a flat at 2 Great Stuart Street. In a pastoral letter to the church on his arrival in 1862, Mr Dovey wrote about church meetings and he named five men who were deacons. This is the first extant reference to deacons in the Chapel since 1851, and it is clear that they were still fulfilling the office of elder as well as deacon. As noted earlier, open or closed communion had been a divisive issue in the Lowestoft church in 1860, with Mr Dovey being strongly in favour of the former. The opening of the Lord's Table to all believers, introduced by Alfred Thomas in 1851, must have continued, or Dovey would not have come.

John Dovey published a 12-page 'Church Manual' in January 1863; it gave details of Chapel activities and particulars about the deacons, and it listed all the members by name. Sunday started with a prayer meeting at 10 a.m., followed by services at 11 a.m. and 2.15 p.m. (incorporating communion). On the second Sunday of the month, there was an evening sermon at 6.30 p.m. 'Public worship' (undefined, except that on the second Tuesday of the month it was a missionary prayer meeting) was held weekly on Tuesday at 7 p.m.; there were prayer meetings on Thursday at 7 p.m. and Saturday at 8 p.m. Four different sections of the Sabbath School met weekly (details are given in Chapter 10) and there was a Bible class for young men on Wednesday evening. The Dorcas Society met in the vestry on the second Monday evening of the month.

John Dovey baptized 18 during his first year in Edinburgh and another 23 in his second. When the congregation of Haldane's Tabernacle moved to Duncan Street in the south of Edinburgh in 1864, 14 Tabernacle members in the New Town transferred to the Chapel rather than travel out to Newington. During John Dovey's five years as pastor, 112 joined the church (31 men and 81 women), bringing the membership when he left in 1866 to 170, the highest so far. He was 'a devoted pastor, and a faithful preacher. He possessed a fine sense of the "proportion of faith", which made his sermons instructive and useful.' He must also have encouraged evangelism in the open air, because during a visit to Newcastle in 1914, Joseph Kemp (pastor, 1902-15) met an old man who had been converted in 1862 at a Chapel meeting at the corner of South Charlotte Street and Princes Street, and who still retained the freshness of the early days of his Christian life.

### Sunday observance

When the railway line between Edinburgh and Glasgow was opened in February 1842, a morning and evening train was run each way on Sunday until the Sabbath observance members of the railway board were strong enough to have them stopped in 1846. The issue was then debated endlessly at Presbyteries and General Assembly meetings and on Town Councils. There were strong commercial pressures to restart Sunday trains; when the board gave in, in September 1865, they salved their consciences by charging double fares for Sunday travel.

*A Sunday train service between Edinburgh and Glasgow was resumed in 1865, despite opposition from churches of all denominations. The number of carriages at the east end of Waverley station in this 1860 photograph shows the popularity of railways.*

In 1866, John Dovey had health problems and moved south, but two years later he returned to Scotland. After brief ministries in Anstruther and Grantown-on-Spey, he retired and preached occasionally as opportunity offered. He died in 1893. His son stayed in Edinburgh and gave long and faithful service as an office-bearer in the Chapel. His granddaughter, Eleanor, was one of the Chapel missionaries from 1913 to 1925.

### Ministers' families

Between Christopher Anderson's warm appreciation of his bride in 1816 (Chapter 3) and the tribute of John Dovey's eldest son after his father's death in 1893, there is no extant recognition of the role of Chapel ministers' wives. Dovey, Junior, wrote:

*No notice of my father, however brief, would be complete without some allusion to my dear sainted mother, who predeceased him a little more than two years ago. Words fail me to say all she was to him and to us, especially during those many anxious years when my father's health having broken down we never knew how ends were to meet year in and year out.*

---

1 *Baptist Handbook*, 1894, Obituaries, p.153.

---

While larger Baptist churches like Charlotte Chapel looked after impoverished members through their Fellowship Fund, and did not let them go 'on the parish', if a man had to give up his pastorate through disability, he was in a very precarious position. A national Poor Law, introduced in

1854, did something to relieve the destitution of the sick and unemployed, but one of the first tasks of the Baptist Union of Scotland of 1869 (below) was to set up a scheme for retired ministers, because the State provision was inadequate. All it could offer, in its early stages, was an annuity of £40 to those who were by age or infirmity unfit to carry out ministerial duties, or an annuity of £20 to their widows.

## 1867–1872: Rev. William Christopher Bunning

### A burning and a shining light

Christopher Bunning (he was known by his middle name) came to the Chapel on the personal recommendation of Charles Haddon Spurgeon, at whose college he had trained. He exercised a popular ministry, and the *Scottish Baptist Magazine* commented: 'Mr. Bunning was a burning and a shining light, and possessed the enviable power of crystallising and enforcing his thoughts in good Saxon words.' However, that glowing testimony masks continuing problems with both his physical and nervous strength, which forced him to resign from the Chapel after five years, to take up work in Australia, and which ultimately led to his untimely death.

Christopher Bunning was born in Bermondsey, South London, on 13 December 1838. He attended the Sunday School of the Maze Pond Baptist Church, Southwark, but he was 18 before he made a personal commitment to Christ, in a Bible class for young men conducted in his father's house. He was baptized and took over an infant class of 50 or 60 in the Sunday School. He later became superintendent of the Sunday School and was one of the first to establish Sunday evening religious services for the young in London. This outreach was so blessed by God that he felt called to ministry or missionary work.

*A sketch and two photographs of Christopher Bunning after he emigrated to Australia.*

He was accepted by the Baptist Missionary Society to go to China, but as with Christopher Anderson before him, it was decided, as his studies progressed, that his health would not stand the climate. Encouraged by the church at Maze Pond, as well as by some of Mr Spurgeon's deacons, who were his personal friends, he left his job as a compositor and reader for the press, and entered the Metropolitan Tabernacle College in 1861. He married Hannah Elizabeth, who was an organist and who loved to encourage the young people to sing hymns. There is no record of children.

Christopher Bunning came to the Chapel, his first pastorate, directly from College at the age of 29. He was inducted on 17 February 1867. Both he and his wife transferred their membership to the Chapel from the Maze Pond Church in London. His manse was initially at 2 South West Circus Place and then at 12 Clifton Terrace, Haymarket. He threw himself enthusiastically into the work of the Chapel, and 31 new members were received in his first year, 15 by baptism and 16 by confession or transfer.

In those days, and until the 1960s, the preacher read and spoke from a large Pulpit Bible, which lay permanently on the lectern. In 1867, 'a few ladies in the Congregation' were concerned at its poor condition, and welcomed Christopher Bunning by presenting the church with a new one. This one lasted for 51 years, until one of the office-bearers thought that it too needed replacement; late in 1918 he donated a new one as a thank-offering for the preservation of his son in the War.

## Jubilee in Rose Street

The Chapel invited C.H. Spurgeon to Edinburgh in 1868, to celebrate the fiftieth anniversary in the Rose Street building:

*Mr. Spurgeon took more than a passing interest at the end of the year 1868 in the celebration of the jubilee of Charlotte Chapel, Rose Street, by the Baptists of Edinburgh. He was not able to attend himself, on account of time and distance, but the heartiness with which the work was carried on in the Scottish Capital gave him genuine satisfaction.*

2 Godfrey Holden Pike, *Seven portraits of the Rev C.H. Spurgeon* (London, 1879), p. 301; *Record*, 1913, p. 50.

Christopher Bunning was actively involved in setting up the third (and enduring) Baptist Union of Scotland, as described below. Two months later, in December 1869, he suffered his first nervous breakdown, which lasted for five months. The elders today interview and receive new members during the absence of the pastor, but the church register noted laconically: 'Between December 1869 and May 1870 the Pastor was ill and so no additions [of new members] were made'.

## Emigration

Christopher Bunning recovered and God again blessed his work. Over his five-year pastorate, he received 120 women and 34 men into membership, bringing the roll to 218, the highest so far. However, emigration from the Chapel was a microcosm of Scotland as a whole – huge numbers left every year to make a new life in Canada, the United States, Australia or New Zealand. It is sad how many entries in the membership register conclude: 'left Edinburgh'. The elders today try to keep in touch with people who move away, and encourage them to link up with their nearest evangelical church, with a view to transfer of membership, so that there is no time when they do not have a church taking an active interest in them.

In the increasingly mobile society of the 1870s, the turnover in membership was so substantial that of the 154 new members during Bunning's ministry, he or his successors had to remove the names of 44 with whom they had lost touch. Fifteen died while still in membership, 36 were transferred to other churches and another 20 withdrew without another place of worship being recorded. A decade later, only 31 of the 154 were still worshipping in the Chapel.

The Bunnings were among those who emigrated to Australia. By the spring of 1872, Christopher Bunning's 'brain and nervous system being unstrung with, perhaps, overstudy and anxiety, Mr Spurgeon advised him to respond to a letter he had received from Geelong [Victoria, Australia], desiring him to send out a suitable pastor.' It was common for churches in the colonies to write to Spurgeon in this way, and he obliged them whenever possible. The Bunnings left Edinburgh on 15 May 1872, sailed from London on 4 June and arrived in Geelong on 20 August. In November 1880, Mr Bunning's 'health was very unsatisfactory, and his medical advisor recommended change and rest.' A trip to New Zealand restored him to 'almost unbroken health, and he was able to conduct all the work with full energy'. However, in the autumn of 1893, his health broke down completely, leading to his untimely death.

## The Baptist Union of Scotland

The Scottish Baptist Association, set up in 1856 by individuals who wanted to see Scottish Baptist churches linked together for their mutual benefit (Chapter 8), gained two enthusiastic supporters in 1867. One was the Chapel's new minister, Christopher Bunning, and the other was a layman, John Walcot, who returned to the Chapel from England. When it was apparent that 51 congregations, from all parts of Scotland, were now in favour of establishing a Baptist Union of Scotland, a founding meeting was held in October 1869. Bunning's presence on the Union's executive committee, and also on its education committee, demonstrated his commitment to the cause, although over-commitment was a factor in his nervous breakdown two months later. He was a lively figure; the *Glasgow Herald* reported his jokes at the inaugural meeting of the Union.

When the Union had its second annual assembly in Edinburgh in October 1870 – it alternated for many years between the two largest cities – the Chapel was host to an evening 'for prayer and free fraternal conference, relative to the state of religion in the associated churches.' The 1869 Union welcomed all evangelical Baptists, whether Calvinist or Arminian; the ascendancy of Calvinism was over, and evangelical Arminianism increasingly dominated the Scottish Baptist scene for the remainder of the nineteenth century.

*In November 1871, horse-drawn trams were introduced to Edinburgh. Advertisers realized the potential and tramcar destinations became difficult to spot among hoardings for Bovril, Rising Sun floor polish, Suchard's Cocoa and Sanitas disinfectant.*

The first annual *Yearbook* of the Union contained the last extant reference to Mrs John Smith, the wife of the governor of Edinburgh Prison on Calton Hill, who, as mentioned earlier, was baptized in the Chapel in 1822 and who remained active in membership until her death in 1871. It was the practice in those days to list the names of all donors to the Union and the amount of the donation; of the 14 members of the Chapel who subscribed in that first year, her gift of £1 was among the largest – most gave either five shillings or ten shillings (25 or 50 pence).

## Education Act 1872

As Christopher Bunning left Edinburgh for Australia, control of education in Scotland passed from the church to secular school boards. The significance of this can hardly be exaggerated. For example, the Free Church of Scotland had maintained, and staffed, 548 schools; control of 139 of them was taken over by school boards and 282 others were closed. Until 1872, teachers were officers of the church, and the purpose of education was not just to impart information but also to teach moral standards in conformity with the Christian faith. After 1872, learning and social behaviour no longer needed to be related to belief. When A.E. Taylor saw the consequences of this working through, he wrote:

*It may quite well be that the future philosophical students of history will yet find the most significant and disquieting of all the social changes of the "Victorian age" to be the combination of universal state-enforced primary education with the transference of the work of the teacher to the hands of laymen under no effective ecclesiastical or theological control.*

3 A.E. Taylor, *The Faith of a Moralist*, (Macmillan, London, 1930), vol. i, p. 11.

One illustration will make the point. D.L. Moody (mentioned below) was addressing a children's meeting during his crusade in Edinburgh in 1873; rhetorically, he asked the question: 'What is prayer?' Not knowing (as an American) that generations of Scottish children had been schooled in the Shorter Catechism, he was astounded when hundreds of young voices responded in unison: 'Prayer is an offering up of our desires unto God, for things agreeable to His will, in the name of Christ, with confession of our sins, and thankful acknowledgement of His mercies.'

## 1872–1875: Rev. Lawrence George Carter

### Moody and Sankey

The next pastor, Lawrence Carter, was born in Southampton in 1837. After training at Rawdon College, Leeds, and after pastorates in Birmingham and Banbury, Oxfordshire, he was 'called' to the Chapel in 1872 at the age of 35. He began on 3 November after a vacancy of only six months. Carter was widely read and scholarly, and his sermons were characterized by deep, earnest thought and careful, exact exegesis. His preaching was powerful and although his ministry was comparatively brief, it was a happy one.

Lawrence Carter came to the Chapel as a bachelor and on 4 August 1874 he married one of the members, Miss Ellen Annie Smith, who had joined by baptism, presumably by her fiancé, on 25 February of that year. As mentioned below, the spring of 1874 was a time of reaping the rewards of the first Moody and Sankey mission in Edinburgh, and it seems that Annie Smith, then living in Regent Road, was converted during the crusade. The daughter of the Chapel stalwart, John Walcot (Chapter 10), who was baptized on the same day as Annie Smith, certainly was.

*Until 1954, the Chapel did not provide a manse; ministers rented or purchased their own accommodation. Lawrence Carter chose 20 Ann Street, one of the few places in the New Town where every house had its own front garden. This was the home of two elderly single women, members of the Chapel, so Carter lodged with them until his marriage. This recent photograph was taken from the drawing room of number 20.*

Lawrence Carter took a prominent part in Dwight L. Moody's and Ira D. Sankey's first visit to Edinburgh in 1873. From the end of November until late January 1874, the Assembly Hall on the Mound, then the largest public building in Edinburgh, was crowded nightly.

*Dwight L. Moody (preaching, left of picture) and Ira D. Sankey (sitting at the harmonium) came to Edinburgh in 1873; their evangelistic crusade altered the Chapel's attitude to music and to lay involvement in church life. The sketch is of a similar campaign in New York.*

### The kist o' whistles

There were four innovations, all of which took Edinburgh by surprise, but people soon warmed to them. The first was the advertisement: 'Mr. Moody will (D.V.) [God willing] preach the gospel, and Mr. Sankey will sing the gospel'. Singing was not new in revival work, but for the first time Sankey made solo singing an integral part of the mission. He accompanied himself on a small American organ – the Scots called it a 'kist o' whistles' – and his gospel solos 'struck home to hearers left unmoved by Moody's preaching'. When the first edition of *Sankey's Sacred Songs and Solos* came out – one penny for the words, sixpence for the music edition – his lyrics were sung in homes, although not yet in church services, all over the country.

The second innovation was that Moody stressed the joys of heaven and the love of God, demonstrated at Calvary; many contemporary evangelists preached only on hell and judgement. This trend towards a moderated Calvinism had been gradually adopted by Scottish Baptists, and led to the end of the Calvinist ascendancy and the beginning of an era in which evangelical Arminianism would predominate.

The third new idea was requests for public prayer, either by people themselves or by relatives and friends. Written requests were read out by the preacher, and others prayed for them; those who became 'anxious' during the meetings were asked to indicate this publicly, and concerted prayer was offered for them. The fourth novelty was the enquiry meeting at the end of the service, for those whose conscience had been awakened by the message. Experienced Christians

63

counselled them personally, and 'Decisions for Christ' became the watchword of the campaign.

The impact of Moody and Sankey's first visit to Edinburgh was greater among Presbyterian churches rather than among Baptists, but 32 were baptized at nine baptismal services in the Chapel in the six months after the mission. Scarcely any congregation in Edinburgh was untouched; 46 were baptized at Dublin Street (now Canonmills) Baptist Church; in Baptist churches throughout Scotland, 788 baptisms took place in 1874.

Two other results of the mission were that Sunday services became user-friendlier, and lay-people realized that they, as well as the ordained ministry, could reach their neighbours for Christ. Moody's afternoon Bible readings led to renewed interest in the Scriptures, and Bible classes became a regular feature of church life. Sankey's hymns remained popular in the Chapel, and his hymnbook *Sacred Songs and Solos* was used at the Chapel's evening service until 1971.

### BAPTIST CHURCH DIRECTORY.
*Divine Service is conducted in the undermentioned Places of Worship, as noted below :—*

| PLACE OF WORSHIP. | PASTOR. | HOURS OF SERVICE. | |
|---|---|---|---|
| | | SABBATH | WEEK-DAY. |
| Dundee—<br>Long Wynd,<br>Nethergate | J. C. BROWN | 11 and 6.30 | Thurs. 8 |
| Edinburgh—<br>Charlotte Chapel | LAWRENCE G. CARTER | 11 and 6.30 | Wed. 7.30. |
| Dublin Street | J. WATSON, and<br>S. NEWNAM | 11 and 6.45 | Thurs. 8 |
| Glasgow—<br>Blackfriars Street | HARVEY PHILLIPS, B.A. | 11 and 2 | Wed. 8.15 |
| N. Frederick St. | J. W. ASHWORTH | 11 and 2 | Wed. 8 |
| Greenock—<br>Westburn Street | EBEN. MACLEAN | 11 and 2.15 | Wed. 8 |
| Govan, . . | JERVIS COATS, M.A. | 11 and 6.30 | Thurs. 8 |
| Leith—Whitfield Hall | W. H. WRIGHT | 11, 2.15, 6.30 | Wed. 8 |
| Lochgilphead—<br>Baptist Chapel | C. W. GREGORY | 11, 2, 6.30 | Monday 8 |
| Paisley—Storie St. | OLIVER FLETT | 11 and 2 | Wed. 8.15 |

THE MONTHLY UNITED PRAYER MEETING of the BAPTIST CHURCHES in EDINBURGH and LEITH, for the spread of the Gospel, especially in connection with the Home Missionary Society for Scotland, will be held on *Monday Evening, the 1st February*, at Eight o'clock, in DUBLIN STREET CHAPEL.
*Interesting Intelligence from Mission Stations will be communicated.*

*There were 83 Baptist churches in Scotland at this time, but only ten of them (including the Chapel) advertised their services in the monthly* Scottish Baptist Magazine.

### Anniversary services
Anniversaries in the Chapel were still held on the Sunday nearest to the foundation of the church on 24 January 1808. On 25 January 1875, a guest preacher spoke in the morning

and in the evening, the pastor delivered a forceful sermon; the day concluded with a well-attended prayer meeting. Later that year, Lawrence Carter accepted a call to Australia, leaving Edinburgh on 28 December. The *Scottish Baptist Magazine* commiserated with the Chapel on losing two successive ministers by emigration to Australia:

*The Rev. L. G. Carter, pastor of the church meeting in Charlotte Chapel, has received a very cordial invitation to the pastorate of the Tynte Street Church, North Adelaide, South Australia. which he has seen fit to accept. In leaving Edinburgh, he leaves a deeply and growingly attached church and congregation. He will be missed also by many outside the church and outside the denomination, having all along been on the most friendly footing with ministers of other churches, and taken a warm interest in the noon prayer-meetings and other services in connection with the recent religious awakening.... It is only some three or four years since their last pastor, the Rev. W. C. Bunning, emigrated to Victoria.*

4 *SBM*, 1875, pp. 183-4.

During Lawrence Carter's ministry, 41 were baptized (26 women and 15 men, including two married couples) and 19 joined by transfer. There were therefore 60 new members in his three years, during which the membership increased from 170 to 200 and then dropped to 186.

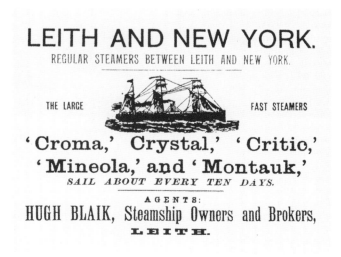

*Many Chapel members emigrated to America about the same time as Christopher Bunning and Lawrence Carter sailed to Australia; there was a scheduled service from Leith to New York every ten days, as this poster advertises.*

Reflecting on Lawrence Carter's pastorate, one of his office-bearers wrote:

*He had good understanding of the word of life, and presented its great truths in harmonious setting and carefully selected terms. His power of suddenly making a sentence instinct with power, and sending it on to the heart as with lightning speed, proved how apt a learner he had been in listening to his honoured pastor. He rendered to Mr. Moody earnest aid, and this reacted with much blessing on his own work in Charlotte Chapel.'*

5 *SBM*, 1896, p. 159.

He spent five happy years in North Adelaide, after which he returned to England. His last pastorate was in Chesham, where he died in 1913.

*In the church register, the address of several Chapel members was given as 'Jenners, Princes Street'; staff lived in dormitories above the shop until it was destroyed by fire in 1892 and replaced by the present building.*

Jenners, the world's oldest independent department store, has been a feature of Princes Street since 1838, when two young men, Charles Kennington and Charles Jenner, rented a shop at the corner of St. David's Street for £150 a year. They had been dismissed by their employer, a draper in Waterloo Place, for taking a day off work to go to the Musselburgh Races. They rapidly expanded the business into adjoining premises, and several Chapel members gave 'Jenners' as their address in the church register; 120 employees lived in dormitories above the shop. The original building was destroyed by fire in November 1892 and replaced by the pink sandstone building shown in the photograph. Jenners remained independent until March 2005, when the family sold it to the House of Fraser.

Additional information on the following topics, mentioned in this chapter, is available on the CD.

Committee structure, 1808-1958
John Edward Dovey
John Walcot
Lawrence Carter
Manses
Membership list, 1862
Membership patterns, 1808-1875
Why are women more religious than men?
William Christopher Bunning

# Chapter 10
## Emergence of lay leadership (1876–1877)

### Innovative years

#### Victoria, Empress of India

Queen Victoria, who had been a recluse for a decade following the death of Prince Albert in 1861, came out of her shell in the 1870s. To mark this, she was given the title Empress of India; the resulting spirit of adventure in the country at large was mirrored by experiment and innovation in Charlotte Chapel – new structures, new music, new outreach and a new style of Bible School.

These will be taken up in the next chapter, but first it is necessary to introduce three laymen who, humanly speaking, saved the Chapel from extinction at the end of the century – a town councillor, an accountant and a lawyer. Christopher Anderson said there were none with whom he could share the burden of leadership (although he did have reservations about involving lay people, as he saw the fortunes of the Scotch Baptists in Edinburgh, where laity was meant to be their strength, steadily decline). When the Chapel needed stability and wise administration in the late nineteenth century, God put John Walcot, John Dovey and Andrew Urquhart, not in the pulpit, but in the pew.

*Queen Victoria's visits to Edinburgh were commemorated by this 1876 equestrian bronze statue of Prince Albert, her consort, in Charlotte Square Gardens, near the Chapel. The railings were removed to provide metal to help the war-effort in 1941.*

#### Baillie John Walcot, JP

John Walcot was the only link between Christopher Anderson, under whose ministry the church was founded, and Joseph Kemp, under whose ministry it was revived. Born in Wiltshire in 1823, he was baptized as a young man in Bristol. When his business brought him to Edinburgh in 1846, he joined the Chapel. Christopher Anderson, of whom he spoke with gratitude, affection and joy, made such an impression on him that he resigned from his business career and trained for the ministry. He began at the University of Edinburgh and then went, like many others connected with the Chapel at that time, to Rawdon College in Leeds. He studied there from 1847 to 1850, and then served as the pastor of two Baptist churches in England.

*In 1881, John Walcot was elected to Edinburgh Town Council. The other photograph was taken in 1908, when he was aged 86.*

In 1864, ill health forced him to return to Edinburgh and to resume his secular career. He rejoined Charlotte Chapel, and regularly preached in Baptist pulpits. He took a prominent part in the founding of the Baptist Union of Scotland in 1869, where he was convener of the loan and building fund; in 1881 he was elected president of the Union for a year. As mentioned in the last chapter, it was the practice in those days to list the names of donors and the amount of all donations to the Union. John Walcot's gifts of one guinea (one pound and five new pence) in 1871 and £2 in 1872 were among the most generous in the entire list.

John Walcot was a manager of the Edinburgh Royal Infirmary and chairman of its house committee. He was appointed a magistrate in 1885; the Police Court gave him opportunity to show the spirit of Christ towards the weak and the helpless. He exemplified his own words: 'Kindness in the Christian worker is a priceless treasure; let us be kind always in all things and to all persons'. He lived to see the Revival in the Chapel, and to hear talk of a new building before he died in 1909 at the age of 86.

## John Edward Dovey, CA

John Edward Dovey, Junior, was a son of the fifth minister, John Edward Dovey (1862-6). He grew up in the Chapel and made his own profession of faith in his early teens. He joined in 1868, and took a special interest in work among the young. He became a Sunday School teacher and then the superintendent for over 20 years. He married Eleanor, the daughter of John Walcot, who warmly supported his work among youth.

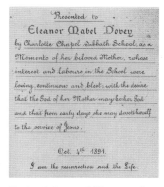

The inscription on a Bible presented to the daughter of Eleanor Dovey, also called Eleanor. Young Eleanor (later Mrs Mackenzie) referred to it at her valedictory service as she left for China as a Chapel missionary in 1913.

John Dovey used his professional skill as a chartered accountant while treasurer of the church from 1880 to 1918, with only a short gap from 1899 to 1902. He too lived to see the revival of the church he loved so well, during the ministry of Joseph Kemp, and later he welcomed Graham Scroggie to Charlotte Chapel in 1916.

John Dovey's wife died in 1891 and he remarried a year later. His second wife, Miss Agnes Campbell, was a member of the Free Church of Scotland in Glasgow, but was baptized in the Chapel before her marriage – the first recorded example of an issue that the Chapel elders have debated from time to time, namely what should happen when someone christened in infancy wishes to become a full member of a Baptist church? (Chapter 46).

## Andrew Urquhart

Andrew Urquhart was born in 1852 in Aberdeen, where his father was a shipmaster. It was not until he came to Edinburgh in 1873, as a young solicitor, that he became a committed Christian at the age of 22. He initially attended the Broughton Place United Presbyterian church and wrote a grateful letter of thanks to its minister: 'Partly … through your preaching then I owe the decision I came to on the afternoon of the 16th January, 1874, to become a Christian and a follower of the Lord Jesus.' Andrew Urquhart made that decision because he wanted to hear D.L. Moody preach. He went to the Assembly Hall on the Mound, but he was refused admission, because Moody was about to address a meeting for fourteen hundred converts by invitation only and Urquhart was not on the list. Two days later he tried again, with the same result. Half way across the quadrangle outside the Assembly Hall, where the statue of John Knox stands, he stopped and said to himself: 'I will step over the line'. He accepted Jesus as Saviour, went back up the steps, and on his profession of faith he was allowed in to Moody's last meeting of the Edinburgh campaign.

John Knox's statue in the quadrangle of New College. Many and varied are the ways in which members of Charlotte Chapel have come to faith in Jesus Christ; one of the more unusual was Andrew Urquhart's decision at this spot in January 1874.

Andrew Urquhart's study of the Bible then convinced him of the rightness of believers' baptism. Three years later, in January 1877, he applied to John Walcot (during the vacancy) for baptism in Charlotte Chapel. He was the first new member to be baptized and received into membership when Owen Campbell commenced his ministry in the Chapel later that year. Almost at once he helped John Dovey with Sunday School work and succeeded him as

67

*Andrew Urquhart, like John Walcot before him, was elected as president of the Baptist Union of Scotland, in his case in 1911. He served as church secretary for 31 years, until his death in 1917. In all those years, he never failed to bow in prayer with the minister in the vestry before the commencement of a service.*

started at Gloucester in England in 1780, coming to Scotland in 1789. The school in the Chapel met four times every Sunday, for young men (at 9 a.m.), for children (at 10 a.m. and 4.15 p.m.) and for young women (at 7 p.m.). Once a quarter, they came together, but it is not clear whether this was to join the normal morning service, or whether it was a special service at another time. There was also an anniversary Sunday, when the morning and evening offerings went to the work of the School – as still happens. Another part of the Sunday School met in a teacher's house at 29 Hamilton Place, Stockbridge.

The Moody and Sankey mission, starting in November 1873, had a huge impact on 'young men and women of all social grades, but mainly belonging … to the families of Christian professors.' As mentioned earlier, more Presbyterians than Baptists made a decision for Christ during the crusade, but the Chapel's Sunday School was revolutionized by it. The number of scholars on the roll had fallen from 60 to 50 to 30 in the preceding three years, but during the mission, there were 130 and this rose, over the next few years, to 226:

| | Bible Class | Sunday School | Teachers |
|---|---|---|---|
| 1869 | 10 | 50 | — |
| 1870 | 100 | 60 | — |
| 1871 | 100 | 50 | — |
| 1872 | 98 | 30 | not given |
| 1873 | 30 | 130 | until 1874 |
| 1874 | 25 | 153 | 24 |
| 1875 | 25 | 153 | 27 |
| 1876 | 20 | 173 | 28 |
| 1877 | 20 | 186 | 27 |
| 1878 | 35 | 226 | 31 |
| 1879 | 65 | 226 | 31 |
| 1880 | 65 | 226 | 31 |
| 1881 | 36 | 217 | 26 |

1 'Sunday School statistics' on the CD.

This section concludes with a look at the summer excursions of 1875 and 1878, and what little is known about the regular Sunday School activities.

superintendent. He was leader of a young men's Bible Class, which was formed in 1880. He married in 1881, the same year as he set up his own legal firm in Edinburgh. In the office-bearers' election of 1884, he moved from the diaconate to the eldership and was appointed church secretary. During the vacancies in the last part of the century, his was the faith that gave clear and far-sighted leadership. As will be seen in Chapter 13, he refused to close the Chapel when many in the congregation were in favour of selling it and dissolving the church.

## Sunday School

### The first known scholar
The earliest named Sabbath School scholar (as those attending were known) in Charlotte Chapel is James Watson, who joined in 1864 at the age of 5 or 6. It is clear that he joined a well-established school, which is not surprising, as the Sunday School movement had grown rapidly since it was

*Barnbougle Castle, on the public walk from South Queensferry to Cramond, is in the Dalmeny Estate and on the shore of the River Forth. The Chapel's Sunday School spent a Saturday in its grounds in 1875.*

## Sunday School picnics

The outing on Saturday 26 June 1875 was a joint effort with the Dublin Street Baptist Church. They met at 8 a.m. in East Princes Street Gardens and marched, with flags and banners flying, to the Waverley Station. At 8.40 a.m., a special train for the 450 scholars, teachers and friends set off for Dalmeny. They then walked to the grounds of Barnbougle Castle, which took about 45 minutes. Hymns were sung and prayer was offered for the day. 'Lunch' (a morning snack) was then served to the children, with a plentiful supply of buttermilk. Cricket and football matches and turns on the park swings occupied the children until 'dinner' (lunch) at 1 p.m.

*The combined Sunday Schools of the Chapel and the Dublin Street Baptist Church, 450 people in all, gathered in Princes Street Gardens (bottom of picture) and marched, with flags and banners, along an otherwise quiet Princes Street, to the Waverley station.*

In the afternoon, there were races for boys and girls according to their ages and also for teachers, with prizes of framed picture cards and texts, books, balls and penknives. Tea was served at 4.30 p.m., with the teachers and their friends sitting around tablecloths on the grass. A local band, which had played throughout the day, led the procession back to Dalmeny – the last stage, up the steep hill to the railway station, must have seemed endless to the youngsters. They arrived back in the centre of Edinburgh at 9 p.m., after 13 hours of non-stop activity.

The corresponding outing, three years later, was described in note form in the superintendent's diary:

*Saturday, 6th July [1878] – Trip to Dalmeny – great success. Notes for next year – No sweets, but if any, get boiled sugar at 8d. per lb. from Pillans. If possible, make each teacher come to tent and supply own class. On previous Sunday speak about regularity in marching and issue orders for the day. Dinner – Gooseberry tart and mutton pie, in bags. Tea – 1/2d. currant brick, 1/2d. rye roll, 1/2d.German bun, 1/2d. worth of mixed biscuits at 8d. per lb., Total 2d. Infant classes, same as above, but for dinner, bun instead of pie and for tea, omit currant brick.*

2 Manuscript by George Rae in the Chapel archives.

## Sunday School teaching

The agenda for the Sunday School teachers' meeting on 5 November 1878, when all 31 teachers were present, included: missionary interest, temperance, Christian instruction class, teachers' prayer meeting, systematic class teaching and special topic Sunday (subjects suggested were: Telling Tales, Speaking the Truth, Keeping the Sabbath and Kindness to Animals). The superintendent's aims were listed in his notes for another teachers' meeting in the following year:

*How to get our senior classes interested. How to improve the Teachers' Prayer Meeting. Articles on helping children to Christian decision. 'God is able to save to the uttermost', therefore we ought not to exclude even the worst from our Schools. We have no right to despair of any. The words afford no excuse for those who do not expect the conversion of children.*

3 George Rae's manuscript.

Between 1879 and 1907, there are few references to the Sunday School in the Chapel records. A Band of Hope was started in 1878, and met on alternate Wednesday evenings in 1879 and 1880, but no details are available. The Sunday School outing in June 1888 was again to Dalmeny, with 250 attending, and in July 1889, 300 went to Colinton. In January 1886, the school rented the building opposite the Chapel, on the other side of Rose Street, for £15 a year and met there in what they called the Schoolroom. Other snippets include:

*On 17th March [1896], a cantata entitled 'Biddy', illustrated with lantern views, was given in the chapel by a specially trained choir, numbering some twenty-four children, from the Sunday school, under the leadership of Miss Dunne. The children acquitted themselves well, the piece in all its parts being admirably rendered, and they earned the generous applause of an appreciative audience, which numbered upwards of 300. The reading was given by the superintendent of the school, Mr. Geo. C. Walcot. As a result of the effort, over £2 has been added to the Sunday-school funds.*

4 *SBM*, 1896, p. 89.

*On 5th January [1898] the children's annual tea and entertainment was held in the church, and went off satisfactorily. The cantata entitled 'Won by a Child', which, under Miss Dunne's leadership, had been in preparation for some time, was rendered by a choir of the school children. It was illustrated by lantern views, exhibited by a kind friend. … Mr Urquhart read the story, which was very touching and impressive in some of its details. A happy and profitable evening was spent.*

5 *SBM*, 1898, p. 30.

The lack of information about the Sunday School in the last quarter of the nineteenth century contrasts with the full records of other activities that were kept by the office-bearers from 1877 onward. Until then, no one took minutes of the meetings of the deacons or of the members. It is not that records have been lost – they were simply not taken. A breath of fresh air blew through the Chapel's administration with the arrival of a new minister in 1877, and the next chapter draws on his detailed accounts of pastoral oversight.

**Exclusion**

One of the ruled columns in the church register was, regrettably but realistically, for those who were excluded, as opposed to resigning or transferring elsewhere. Among the six hundred entries from 1851 to 1876, nineteen were put out of fellowship in this way, but only seven had to be excluded in the remaining quarter of the nineteenth century. The commonest reasons were theft, dishonesty or drunkenness, and there was always opportunity for repentance. A married couple were excluded in November 1871, after eight years in membership, 'for imprudent conduct on his part and for drink on hers. O Lord, restore them!'

Two women, who joined separately in 1852, were excluded, one in 1857 'according to a rule of the church, for marrying a young man who was not thought to be a decided Christian'; she was 'restored in 1868 on confession' but no more is heard of the other, who was excluded in 1853 for the same reason 'after reasonable warning of the consequences, see 1 Cor: 7:39 and 2 Cor: 6:14-18'. Considering the frequency with which kirk sessions in the National Church had to deal with immorality, it is a testimony to the high standards adopted by Chapel members that only one person, a woman who joined in 1861, was ever excluded for that reason.

**On the move**

Although few had to be excluded, the turnover of members through mobility of labour was a constant concern to pastors of the Chapel in the later nineteenth century. Two examples will suffice. In the seven years between 1855 and 1862, 88 new members joined the Chapel; only six of them were still in membership in 1881. Secondly, membership in 1862 totalled 169; two decades later, only three of them were at the same postal address; at least 136 of the 169, and possibly as many as 156, had left Edinburgh in 20 years.

Additional information on the following topics, mentioned in this chapter, is available on the CD.

Church discipline
Eleanor Dovey
John Walcot
Sunday School statistics

# Chapter 11
# Owen Dean Campbell (1877–1884)

## A whirlwind of new ideas

### Induction or endurance test?

Owen Campbell was another son of the manse, born at Towcester in 1853 and baptized by his father in 1864. Like his predecessor in the Chapel, he attended Rawdon College, Leeds, from which he won a scholarship to St John's College, Cambridge. While in Edinburgh for a holiday in the summer of 1876, he was invited to preach in the Chapel; this led to a very cordial and unanimous invitation to return as the pastor after he graduated in the following year. He duly gained his BA and was ordained and inducted on 5 July 1877, at the age of 24.

Members had stamina in those days – one minister gave the ordination prayer, his father preached a sermon, and then a third minister gave charges to the minister and to the congregation. Owen Campbell responded, giving an account of his conversion and his views on the doctrines of the Bible. After a break for tea, addresses were delivered by [nine men are named] and others, interspersed with pieces from the choir. The length of that induction service was not exceptional, as the programme for a social evening on Tuesday 13 March 1883 discloses. It started with a review of the year by the pastor – a forerunner of the annual report – after which five different addresses were delivered by five different speakers on 'subjects appropriate to the occasion – Fidelity, Kindness, The duty of seeking for the salvation of men, the Sabbath, and Sunshine.' The pastor then preached a closing sermon.

Campbell came to Edinburgh as a bachelor, but married Mary Annie in Cambridge, where he had studied, at Christmas 1877. Nineteenth-century records are frustratingly devoid of details about the pastor's wife and family.

### Elders and deacons

Charlotte Chapel was Owen Campbell's first pastorate, and he prepared assiduously for the pulpit, beginning study every day at 6 a.m. He also edited the *Scottish Baptist Magazine* for three years. However, his lasting impact on the Chapel was to recommend the appointment of elders as well as deacons. He set up and chaired a committee, composed of deacons and other members (which included a bank manager, a chartered accountant and a business man), to overhaul the organisation of the church. In November they recommended:

*That it is desirable that arrangements should be made for securing the active co-operation of some of the younger members in the care and direction of the temporal concerns of the church; and that this co-operation would be most effectually secured by creating an organisation which would embrace both Elders and Deacons – the Elders to be appointed primarily to assist the pastor in the spiritual oversight of the church and the Deacons to co-operate with the pastor and Elders in the charge of temporal matters only.*

1 Minute of 23 November 1877.

This was based on reforms that Charles Haddon Spurgeon had introduced to the Metropolitan Tabernacle in London in 1859. The Baptist principle of congregational government was safeguarded in both situations, because an undertaking was given that 'the ultimate control over the affairs of the church lay with the members, and the pastor, elders and deacons were directly responsible to the church for all their actions.' Campbell's recommendation, which included a timetable for elections, was accepted by the church and put into effect right away – the new courts met on 13 December 1877, just five months after his induction.

*Owen Campbell and his five elders in 1883. Left to right: John E. Dovey (treasurer), John Anderson (secretary), R. A. Roberts, Alexander Picken, Campbell and John Walcot.*

The forward policies adopted by Owen Campbell bore fruit, and with increased evangelistic effort, membership went up from 164 when he arrived to 183, 212 and 232 (the peak for the nineteenth century) over the next three years. The 1881 roll, with names and addresses, is on the CD under 'Membership list, 1881'. His structure for elders and deacons lasted almost without alteration for 120 years. In preparation for the quinquennial election in the year 2000, it was felt that although both offices should be retained, a new millennium required a new structure for them. That was the first major change in the Chapel's constitution since 1877.

## Congregational government

There were no regular quarterly or half-yearly business meetings of members at that time. As mentioned elsewhere, the members stayed behind after communion, when required, to consider membership matters. When the deacons felt that a formal meeting was required – usually when there was a crisis in the church finances – they called one. The agenda for such a meeting on 19 June 1878 is revealing. At the deacons' regular bi-monthly meeting on 25 May, there was so much concern about the deficit over the first four months of the year that they considered sending a circular letter to all members, 'regarding the desirableness of more liberal giving towards the maintenance of the "cause"'. After discussion, they decided that a personal challenge would be more effective and called the meeting mentioned. The agenda was: 'Reports should be given on the various branches of church work and at which an opportunity would be taken to make some remarks upon the condition of the finances.' There was, therefore, some reporting and accountability, as one would expect in a Baptist church.

## Duties of elders and deacons

Under the guidance of Owen Campbell, minutes were taken for the first time in the history of the Chapel. These provide a valuable insight into the work of the elders' and deacons' courts and the relationship between them. Although:

*in Mr. Spurgeon's Church the Deacons are entirely independent of the Elders, in the circumstances of Charlotte Chapel, the Committee ... recommend that the Deacons ... should act only in co-operation with the Pastor and Elders. As a practical means of securing this result ... no meeting of the ... Deacon's court [sic] should be regular unless the Pastor and Elders receive a simultaneous invitation with the Deacons to be present – in short that the Pastor and Elders shall ex officio be members of the Deacons' Court.*

---

2 Minute of 23 November 1877.

As far as the writer can trace, this arrangement was unique in Scotland at the time and remained unique until it ended when the two bodies began to hold separate meetings in 1995. Owen Campbell must have been a man of action as well as ideas, because the new groups hit the ground running, as it is now put.

The duties of the 'Pastor and Elders, or Church Session' – the phrase 'Church Session' was regularly used to describe elders as distinct from deacons – were the maintenance of public worship, baptism and the Lord's Supper, custody of the roll of members, systematic visitation of members and especially the sick, 'to edify and comfort believers – to arouse the careless – to encourage enquiries and generally to aid the Pastor in seeking after the Fruits of the Ministry'. The pastor and elders were 'to appoint one of their number to act as Secretary and the Elder so appointed shall be considered the Secretary of the Church' – which remained the position until the radical reorganization of 2005, when no church secretary was appointed, but a church administrator (not an elder) took over many of the duties.

From the beginning, the elders (in the words of the minutes) 'proceeded to the meeting of the Deacons' Court' after they had met on their own, and they contributed actively to it. One early minute records a plea from the minister, in the chair, that they should try to finish the combined meeting by 10 p.m. The deacons were to manage the property and all finance except the Fellowship Fund, to appoint the church treasurer, precentor, chapel keeper (church officer, caretaker) and to fix their salaries. The precentor and the chapel keeper were each paid £10 a year; the chapel keeper received free accommodation under the Chapel, together with free coal and gas.

The phrases 'church session' and 'deacons' court', used in Owen Campbell's constitution, grated in the minds of some Baptists, who regarded them as unacceptable parallels with the Presbyterian churches by which they were surrounded. Presbyterians, they pointed out, have a graded hierarchy of courts and sessions; Baptists have diaconates, not 'deacons' courts'.

Incidentally, the invention of the telephone in 1876 (next page), was used to illustrate many talks on prayer – God was never engaged, never unobtainable, etc.

*Alexander Graham Bell, the inventor of the telephone, was born at 16 South Charlotte Street on 3 March 1847. His house, marked by a plaque, looks directly onto Charlotte Chapel. This 1999 photograph shows the evening sun on the Chapel, with Bell's house, facing the camera, at the end of Rose Street.*

By the end of November, an organ was installed. The precentor was renamed 'the leader of psalmody', which is how *Chambers Dictionary* defined him already; at the beginning of the twentieth century, the Chapel changed his title to 'choirmaster'. The 1879 organ served the church for 50 years, until a new one was purchased, after much discussion, in 1929 (Chapter 25).

## A manse in the Grange

Owen Campbell's first manse was on the south side of the Meadows, at 19 St Catherine's Place. Although Edinburgh had its share of the chronic overcrowding in working-class areas of nineteenth-century British cities, the overall picture in Edinburgh was of a confident, prosperous and growing middle class. Campbell, and many others like him, wanted to live in the suburbs; by 1875, almost the whole of Princes Street, previously residential, was taken over by shops. However, travel from the Grange was too much for Owen Campbell, especially on Sunday when there was no public transport; he moved the manse to 4 Comely Bank, which was a shorter walk from the Chapel.

Edinburgh was revolutionized at this time in two other ways. From the mid-1870s, water was piped directly into houses, transforming food preparation, laundry and toilet arrangements. Women no longer had to queue up at pumps and carry water over long distances – and tap water did not need to be boiled before use. So too with gas. Coal fires and ranges had been used for cooking since Edinburgh began, but gas, which had been laid on for street and factory lighting from 1820, was available for domestic illumination and cooking in the 1870s.

The other transforming factor was the abundant supply of cheap imported wheat and meat. The end of the American Civil War in 1865 opened the way for American railways to transport grain quickly from the prairies to steam-ships, which had been purpose-built to open up the European market. The price of wheat halved and the standard of living here rose accordingly. The importation of refrigerated Australian beef from 1878 and New Zealand lamb from 1882 brought similar benefits.

## Baptism and membership

Owen Campbell divided Edinburgh into three geographical districts, and allocated an elder to every district 'for the

## The first church organ

Until Moody and Sankey's visit to Edinburgh in 1873 (Chapter 9), singing in the Chapel was led by a precentor – 'the leader of the psalmody in Scotch churches'. The congregation then decided to install an organ. The procedure for purchasing it illustrates how the elders, deacons and the congregation related to one other. In the spring of 1879, the elders, having responsibility for the conduct of worship, 'agreed that the Sunday School harmonium should be used at both services on the Lord's day'. Six months later, the deacons decided that 'the present harmonium was quite insufficient to lead the singing of the congregation and that many members [dissatisfied with the harmonium] had promised liberal subscriptions if the deacons' court sanctioned the purchase of a suitable instrument'. The court appointed a group to collect funds, with authority, as soon as they had £30 in hand and the expectation of the balance, to select and purchase an organ at a price not exceeding seventy guineas (just over £73). In other words, the elders saw the need for a change in the pattern of worship; the deacons took on board the practical implications; the congregation supported the project.

purpose of systematic visitation of the members'. When five elders were elected, a year later, he was able to extend this to five districts and later, in 1881, to six. He also formed a ladies visiting committee, primarily 'for the visitation of sick Female Members', but they also interviewed female candidates for membership. On the third Sunday of every month, the elders, deacons and the members of this committee met at 10.15 a.m. for a combined time of prayer.

Applications for baptism and membership came to the elders before interview, and then back to the elders after interview, before going to the church. Great care was taken. In an application by 'a young man engaged to Miss ...', it was decided to make enquiries about his character before proposing him as a Candidate for Baptism.... After enquiries had been made, he was proposed for Church fellowship, but the Visitors appointed were not satisfied, and the case was stopped'.

Even after the elders were satisfied, the congregation had an important part to play. No decision was made when the information was first laid before the members. In every instance between 1891 and 1896, the interviewing pair (two elders or two members of the ladies visiting committee, or one of each) reported fully to the church one Sunday and the vote was taken on the following Sunday. If, however, the application was to receive a member by transfer from another Baptist church, the vote was taken immediately after the letter of transfer from the other church had been read to the meeting.

Owen Campbell also had a pastoral concern for those who regularly attended the Chapel but who were not members. He drew up a supplementary list – there has never been a formal roll of adherents (Chapter 25) – to ensure that they were looked after. He also arranged one meeting a month in a home, working through the different districts in rotation, so that he could personally meet the members in an informal way.

## Prayer meetings

One of Owen Campbell's first pleas to the congregation was to improve the attendance at the prayer meeting before the Sunday morning service; sadly, his plea went unheeded and the meeting was discontinued. Eight years later, 'the former practice of the Church to hold a short Prayer Meeting before

the morning service' was resumed, with the elders taking turns to lead it.

In 1878, Owen Campbell secured the approval of the elders to move the mid-week prayer meeting from Wednesday to Thursday at 7 p.m. It is hard to gauge how well it was supported, but three years later, it went back to Wednesday. Once a month, it was designated a missionary prayer meeting. Just occasionally, if there was important (usually financial) business too lengthy to be dealt with at the conclusion of a Sunday morning service, due pulpit intimation was given of business to be discussed at the mid-week meeting.

## A typical week

The Chapel's Handbook for 1881 shows a rather different week from the Manual of 1863, quoted in Chapter 9. As mentioned above, there was no longer a prayer meeting before the Sunday morning service, but the Young Men's Fellowship (below) met at 10 a.m. The Lord's Supper was observed at 12.30 p.m every Sunday, after the 11 a.m. service, and the Sabbath School met at 2.15 p.m. After the 6.30 p.m. service, there was a prayer meeting every Sunday at 8 p.m. The minister's Bible Class was held on Tuesday evening at 8 p.m. On Wednesday, there was an enquirers' meeting at 7 p.m, for pastoral issues and for those considering baptism or membership, followed by the mid-week prayer meeting at 8 p.m. The elders met at 8 p.m on the first Monday of the month and the deacons (including the elders) met at the same time on the second Monday in March, June, September and December.

*During the vacancy after Owen Campbell left, the faithful were concerned about winter draughts, so the deacons fixed 'iron standards with Curtains across the centre of the Chapel for use at the Weekly Evening Prayer Meeting.' At this time, the interior of the church was dull and poorly lit, and had boxed-in family pews which discouraged visitors. This photograph shows its new look in 1906.*

## Snapshots of Chapel life in 1877

### Hymnbooks

Little nuggets of information drop out of the early minutes. Within a month of his arrival, Owen Campbell persuaded the church to change to a new hymnbook, *Psalms and Hymns*. This had been produced in 1858 for the English Particular Baptists, and it was the most popular hymnbook in Scottish Baptist churches. Changing hymnbooks can be divisive, but by the end of the year, 153 Chapel members had purchased personal copies – the deacons astutely offered a discount for a short period. Owen Campbell was a stickler for detail, and displayed the tunes, to which hymns were to be sung, in a conspicuous position beside the numbers of the hymns. The new book proved popular and in 1885 a supply of the supplement to it was purchased.

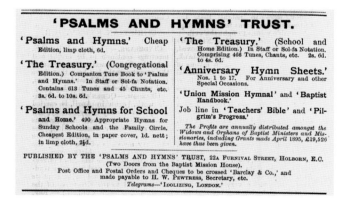

*In 1877, the congregation took enthusiastically to a new hymnbook,* Psalms and Hymns.

### Tithes and offerings

A year after Owen Campbell arrived, the deacons reviewed the church finances. No offering bags were passed round during the service at that time – there was a plate at the door on Sunday – so the deacons decided: 'to have the box, which was formerly used in the time of Christopher Anderson, placed on the wall of the front lobby of the Church, lettered with the words "Visitors Offertory"'. They also prepared a sheet, to go inside the cover of the hymnbooks used by visitors, listing the times of the services and drawing attention to the box in the lobby. Seat letting arrangements were also detailed.

As mentioned earlier, payment of seat rent was not essential in the Chapel, but it was an important source of revenue from those willing to contribute. It illustrates, incidentally, where it was popular to sit – in 1880, the back seats downstairs cost 10s (50 new pence) per half-year, the area 8s (40 p.), the side seats 6s (30 p.), the front gallery 7s (35 p.) and the remainder of the gallery 5s (25 p.). Seat rental had been abolished in the Chapel before the present pews were installed in 1912, so the pews do not have the brass holders, still seen in many older churches, for holding the cards with the names of the seat-renters.

### Social evenings

Soirées (social evenings) were important in the life of the Chapel in the 1870s and 80s. All manner of reasons were found to have them – autumn, Christmas, spring, summer, welcoming a new minister, the anniversary of his arrival, saying farewell on his departure, etc. There were always several speakers, in addition to tea and musical items. Substantial decorations were put up, even out of the Christmas season; one deacon stewarded, two others arranged the music, two women prepared the tea, but four deacons were needed for the decorations. Tickets were sold, sometimes to outsiders also, at 9d (3 new pence) or 1s (5 new pence); soirées made a small profit for the general funds of the church. On one occasion, the invitation specifically mentioned 'members of the church and other seat-holders', so people could rent seats and attend regularly without joining – permanent 'hearers', to use Christopher Anderson's word.

Owen Campbell preferred to baptize on Sunday, not on a weekday. Accordingly, 'the Elders officiating the Sabbath before' had to assist, because the duty elders for that Sunday could not be in two places at once. However, Campbell had to be flexible to suit the off-duty of candidates in service, and every single day of the week is mentioned in the church register.

The baptistry was under the platform at the front of the church, as it is in the present building. When the harmonium began to be used at Sunday services (above), it had to be lifted off the platform every time there was a baptism. The harmoniumist protested, so the deacons 'authorised that a space sufficiently large to admit the Harmonium and provide for a passage to the seat be made by cutting the two front pews'. They revoked this at their next meeting, because they had, in the meantime, authorized the purchase of an organ, which had its own permanent location.

```
BRISTO  PLACE  BAPTIST  CHAPEL.—MR
      GRANT will Preach TO-MORROW EVENING, at 7.
CHARLOTTE      BAPTIST      CHAPEL,
      West Rose Street (Corner of South Charlotte Street).
   TO-MORROW—REV. OWEN D. CAMPBELL, B.A.
   MORNING SERVICE, at 11.   EVENING, at 6.30.
DUBLIN  STREET  BAPTIST  CHURCH.—
      The Rev. SAMUEL NEWNAM, TO-MORROW—
Forenoon, 11 A.M. ; Evening, 6.30.
DUNCAN  STREET  BAPTIST  CHAPEL.—
      REV. J. M'LELLAN, TO-MORROW, at 11 and 6.30.
```

*Despite constant worry about balancing the books, the Chapel advertised its Sunday services in the* Edinburgh Daily Review.

### Press advertising
The first edition of the *Edinburgh Evening News*, in May 1873, bore no resemblance to its popular tabloid form of today. Four tightly packed large sheets, with no photographs or illustrations, did not commend it to the Chapel for advertising church services, but they took space every week in the rival *Daily Review*.

## More new ideas

### Young Men's Fellowship
In 1879, the young men in the Chapel asked for a meeting of their own. The elders encouraged Andrew Urquhart to start a Young Men's Christian Fellowship Association, to meet at ten o'clock on Sunday morning from January 1880. They were delighted at its progress, but dismayed to learn in October 1882 that the Association had admitted young women to its meetings. 'Whilst all the Elders regretted that this step had been taken, it was thought that it would be unwise to interfere in the matter.' The same elders took a similarly common-sense approach to a letter from an irate member who had been 'turned out of his pew by the Choir on a recent Sunday evening when a baptismal service was being held.' They replied that he should take some other pew in future. That shows, incidentally, that a choir was functioning in 1880, a year after the first organ was installed.

By 1881, and possibly earlier, Owen Campbell held a service in the Chapel at 11 a.m. on New Year's Day, even when it was not a Sunday. In those days, and until the mid-1960s, New Year was the main public holiday in Scotland, with many people working normally on Christmas Day; it was an opportunity for the church to come together, for a time of dedication for the new year. This grew into the New Year conference, about which some older members of the Chapel still speak nostalgically, although it was discontinued in 1971, as described in Chapter 47.

### The poetry of Elizabeth Barrett Browning
Tuesday evening, about which Christopher Anderson was reluctant to give details to the Parliamentary Commissioners, is not mentioned again in any extant document until a well-publicized series of monthly lectures in the winter of 1879-80. These were held under the auspices of the minister's Bible Class (listed above), and were open to all. The minister of the Govan Baptist Church gave the December lecture, on 'Christian Pictures in the Catacombs at Rome', with illustrations; it 'was listened to with much interest by a good audience'. The subject in January was 'Jewish parties in the time of Christ'. The first lecture in the 1880-81 series was entitled 'Alfred Tennyson', and the second was on 'The Poetry of Elizabeth Barrett Browning'.

The lectures were not just on poetry. Alexander Whyte, who occupied the pulpit of Free St George's (now, St George's West, along the road from the Chapel in Shandwick Place), also gave poetic titles to introduce his Bible studies; Oswald Chambers advertised lectures on Egypt or Babylon – it was their way of getting Bible truths across in popular form. Chapel members were challenged, at the end of the twentieth century, to learn from the user-friendly approach of the Willow Creek church in Illinois; to give such titles to Bible studies was a nineteenth-century way of getting alongside people. The lectures in the Chapel were well received, and at the close of the 1882-3 session, the Bible Class presented Owen Campbell with a walnut writing case, in appreciation of his leadership throughout the series; he responded by giving a lecture on the life and works of the hymn writer, Frances Ridley Havergal, who had just died.

*Many who attended the Chapel were employed in domestic service in the New Town. The Edinburgh School of Cookery, opened in 1875, became a near neighbour of the Chapel when it moved to the Albert Buildings in Shandwick Place in 1877.*

The Edinburgh School of Cookery expanded in 1891 from Shandwick Place to Atholl Crescent. Many students from its residences attended the Chapel on Sunday; some were converted and baptized. In 1930, it was renamed the Edinburgh College of Domestic Science, but it was still popularly known as 'Atholl Crescent' until it moved in 1970 to become part of Queen Margaret College (now University) at Clermiston. Numbers of students continued to attend the Chapel services, even after the move to Clermiston.

### Election of elders and deacons, 1878

When Charlotte Chapel adopted the Metropolitan Tabernacle's way of electing elders and deacons, it either did not know about, or did not give much weight to, the views of C.H. Spurgeon on the method of selection:

*In my opinion, the very worst mode of selection is to print the names of all the male members, and then vote for a certain number by ballot. I know of one case in which a very old man was within two or three votes of being elected simply because his name began with A, and therefore was put at the top of the list of candidates.*

3 C.H. Spurgeon, *Autobiography, vol 2: The Full Harvest 1860–1892,* revised edition (Banner of Truth, Edinburgh, 1973), p. 75.

The validity of Spurgeon's concern is illustrated by the 1878 election in the Chapel. There was no problem with the elders, because five names were proposed for five places. However, eight names were put to the congregation, in

alphabetical order, for six places on the diaconate. Considering that the members had prayed about the election, it may be irreverent to suggest that the layout of the ballot paper influenced the result, but the fact is that Messrs Cairns, Coutts, Davis, Dovey, Johnston, and Urquhart were elected and Messrs Weddell and Young were not.

After two annual elections, the Chapel elders decided that one year was too short for the good of the church and proposed elections every five years. The pastor gave notice to the congregation on the first Sunday in December 1879: 'that on the following Sunday he would propose the re-election of all the present office-bearers for a term of five years (until December 1884)'. The congregation agreed and the phrase 'quinquennial election', which still mystifies some newcomers to the Chapel, came into being.

### University students in the Chapel

The *Scottish Baptist Magazine* commented: 'Mr. Campbell possessed rich scholarship, exquisite style, fervent convictions, and a chaste imagination. His ministry attracted many university students, and the lives of several of them were influenced for good. He was not blessed with robust health of body, but he was vigorous in thought, and devoted to his work.'

Over the two centuries covered by this book, advice to students attending the Chapel has varied, as to whether they should evangelise and learn through student Christian Unions or through a local church. When the writer was a student in the early 1950s, it was strongly recommended that evangelical Christians should give all available time to their university Christian Union, on the basis that it was the best place to witness to, and to learn from, their fellow students; after graduating, they could devote their energies to their local church for, hopefully, the rest of the lives. The recommendation, now, is exactly the opposite, namely that students should mature in the Christian faith through attending an evangelical church in their university city, and bring non-Christian friends to it. Student leaders now urge city churches to provide appropriate training programmes.

In the second half of the nineteenth century, the former policy prevailed. When James Balfour (a distant relation of the writer) finished his studies in Edinburgh in 1881, it was noted that: 'unlike many students, [he] had been regular in his attendance at the services of the sanctuary, and had ever been ready to co-operate in various branches of the Chapel's Christian work.' He came to the Chapel from the Orkney island of Westray. His interest in overseas mission was awakened in childhood, by reading the *Juvenile Baptist Missionary Herald*. He attended the university here to equip himself for missionary service and, on graduating MA, he was appointed tutor at the Calabar Missionary College in Kingston, Jamaica. He was ordained and valedicted from the Chapel on Wednesday 12 September 1881.

Four years earlier, another Edinburgh graduate, Kate Elder, went to China, but not as a Chapel missionary. She joined the Chapel from the Penge Tabernacle in August 1870, and rejoined the Penge church on completion of her studies here in 1873; after further training, she sailed to the mission field in 1877. About the same time, two other Chapel members went to China – Christina Anderson (Mrs Howells) and Mary Brock – but the church register does not say whether they went as missionaries; the entry implies termination of membership, as does a similar note when J. Lomber went to Congo at the same time as James Balfour came to Edinburgh. Several other students, who had become Chapel members during their time in Edinburgh, left as pastors or missioners, transferring their membership to their new church or mission as they left.

### Second Moody and Sankey mission
Dwight L. Moody and Ira D. Sankey returned to Edinburgh by invitation in 1881, for a campaign that lasted six weeks. This time it was centred on the Corn Exchange. Many came to the Saviour, but not on the scale of the 1873-4 visit. Although Moody 'was just as earnest, as vigorous and as impressive as before', there was a change of emphasis in his message. Moody had previously 'exulted in the free grace of God', and 'men leaped out of darkness into light'; in 1881, 'he insisted very much on Repentance'. People were as deeply moved, and hundreds went into the enquiry room every night, but the impact of the Corn Exchange crusade was mostly among Presbyterian churches, and it is not possible to say how far the Chapel shared in its blessing.

There was, however, one outcome that has been a feature of Edinburgh evangelical life ever since. During the campaign, Moody heard that Carrubber's Close Mission, off the High Street, held an open-air meeting every evening of the year. He paid a surprise visit to one of these meetings and was greatly impressed. He was told that more suitable premises would expand the work, so he set about collecting £10,000 for the purchase of a site and the building of a new mission. He succeeded, and he personally laid the foundation stone of the present building at 65 High Street on 24 April 1883 – the mark can still be seen on the left of the door. A year later, on 4 March 1884, the premises were opened. Moody preached with great power at the opening of the building, basing his message on the text: 'Come unto me all ye that labour and are heavy laden and I will give you rest.' The present internal layout dates from the late twentieth century, and the name is now Carrubbers Christian Centre.

## Financial struggles

### Don't report the overdraft
Although the Chapel membership reached its nineteenth-century peak in 1880, at 232, financial giving did not, unfortunately, keep pace. It was just as well that the proposition put forward by Alfred Thomas, that the minister should receive whatever was left over after general expenses had been met, was not operating, because the deacons relied on a bank overdraft to pay Owen Campbell's salary of £250 a year. Five months after he arrived, the overdraft was fluctuating so much that the church treasurer was told to report to the deacons only when it exceeded £100. They must have grown weary even of these reports, because the figure was soon raised to £130 and then to £150. The 1878 accounts (below) had an opening and closing credit balance, but the 1881 accounts started with a deficit of £29 and were balanced only by of a legacy of £16.

While commendably honouring their obligations to the minister, the deacons put a moratorium on essential repairs. There were concerns about the ventilation of the church, so an architect recommended installing four airshafts, two at the vestry door and two in the gallery, at £5 per pair, with extractors on the roof costing £13. The deacons approved the report but decided 'that in view of the state of the funds no action would be taken meantime'. This was not a healthy situation, in any sense of the word, and the congregation was jolted into increased giving. By the end of the following year, they were able to install the ventilators, which improved the atmosphere but wiped out the reserves. The experience of a certain church treasurer is worth repeating, because it illustrates the position of the Chapel throughout the 1880s. The church (in the story) had a deficit on its accounts year after year, which the treasurer recorded in traditional red ink. One year, to his delight, he found that he had a small surplus, so he bought a bottle of black ink – and that put the account back into the red.

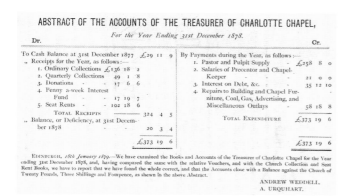

How simple (even if precarious) the Chapel finances were in 1878. This abstract of accounts for the year to 31 December was issued to the members on 18 January 1879, audited by two members; nowadays, it takes five months to get professionally audited statements into the hands of the members.

## Continuing deficits

The Chapel's finances really were on a knife-edge. Deficits of £40, £31, £10 and £17 in the Chapel accounts for the years 1882 to 1885 may not seem much today, but £30 was a year's salary for a male secretary in a New Town business; a good cook earned £28, and a strong early-rising kitchen maid £14 a year. Such people made up the majority of the Chapel members at the time; they were genuinely devout and spiritual, concerned to reach the district for Christ, but their meagre wages were not enough to meet the church's running costs. The deacons constantly had to make personal and direct approaches to wealthier members, to balance the books at the end of these years. The Chapel was quite open about its needs – the press advertisement in the Edinburgh *Daily Review* for Saturday 1 January 1881 gave details of the services for the next day, and gave advance notice that on the following Sunday there would be a Special Quarterly Collection for Church Expenses.

Men came from all over the country to work on the Forth railway bridge between 1882 and 1890, attracted by average earnings of £2 a week, even although it was dangerous and arduous work – 57 were killed.

Owen Campbell's ministry was so greatly appreciated that a special and successful appeal was made to the congregation in 1881 to raise his salary of £250 by £25. Their generosity was not, unfortunately, sustained and the two remaining years of his ministry closed with deficits. The deacons ungraciously commented that this was due to the addition made to the pastor's salary. Had it not been for a generous legacy from George Sleigh, the church treasurer, the Chapel might have become bankrupt in these lean years. As mentioned earlier, Sleigh joined the Chapel in 1825, and 50 years later, when he was the treasurer, he made a Will leaving his estate, after the death of his two sisters, to pay off 'the whole of the debt that may exist on the Chapel' – which he knew was £700, with interest of £35 a year running on the loan. George Sleigh died in 1877 and the legacy became available on the termination of the liferent to his sisters in 1881. Even then, current expenses could not be met; as mentioned, 1882 ended with a deficit of £40.

### *Scottish Baptist Magazine*

For more than a hundred years after the formation of the Baptist Union of Scotland in 1869, ministers in pastoral charges edited its monthly *Scottish Baptist Magazine*. Owen Campbell did this from January 1881 to December 1883. His editorial policy, not avoiding controversial issues, increased circulation steadily during these three years – until he increased its size by 50 per cent and put up the price. His final editorial, as he left Edinburgh, defended his policy of increasing its size (and so its cost), even although every increase in price led to the cancellation of some subscriptions.

### Men and women

During Owen Campbell's ministry, the gender imbalance mentioned earlier was in part corrected. There were still more women received into membership than men during his seven years – 87 women (49 baptized and 38 transferred) and 64 men (37 baptized and 27 transferred) – but nearly all the transfers were of people coming to Edinburgh from north, south and west; transfer from other Edinburgh churches was minimal. While many came to Edinburgh, almost as many others went south or emigrated. Owen Campbell himself left in May 1884, first to Nottingham, then to Newport in Monmouthshire and finally to Haverfordwest.

Of all the nineteenth-century ministers, Owen Campbell was the best at keeping in touch; when on holiday in Scotland, he made time to visit the Chapel and he named his first daughter, born after he left Edinburgh, Charlotte; 'the dear old church will always have a warm place in my heart and in my prayers'. He attended the centenary celebrations in 1908.

Additional information on the following topics, mentioned in this chapter, is available on the CD.

Albert Hall
Anniversaries and Thankofferings
Annual report
Choir
Church officers to 1911
Church register of baptised believers
Committee structure, 1808-1958
Constitution
Deacons before 1877
Elders and deacons – history
Elders and deacons – names
James Balfour
Membership
Membership list, 1881
Minutes of Meetings
Overseas mission
Owen Campbell

*The West End of Princes Street – parasols and the horse-drawn trams – as Owen Campbell left Edinburgh in 1884. The Chapel is just behind the shop with awnings going round the corner into South Charlotte Street. Princes Street was still lit by gas – electric street lighting was not installed until 1895.*

# Chapter 12
# The late nineteenth century (1885–1901)

## 1885–1888: Rev. Samuel George Woodrow

### Social concerns

Scottish society was in a state of flux in the late nineteenth century. Expansion of the iron and steel industry, with its seemingly insatiable demand for coal, attracted people from all over the country into degrading urban living conditions – many of them ghettos. The Assembly of the Baptist Union of Scotland deplored: 'the unblest poverty that is growing side-by-side with enormous wealth.... Christ's churches cannot fold their hands and say: "we knew it not". You are not your brother's keeper; you are your brother's brother ... you are bound to care for him.' Baptists were realising the social implications of the gospel they preached, and the next minister of the Chapel was more involved than most in its practical outworking.

After 14 months, one of the longer vacancies of the nineteenth century, Samuel Woodrow settled in the Chapel in July 1885. Born in Wiltshire in 1841, and trained for ministry at Regent's Park College, Oxford, he had a six-year pastorate in England, and then went to the USA for eight years. While there, he and his wife, Olive, lost two of their four daughters and one of their sons became a deaf mute. They returned to England and settled at Wokingham, where his father and grandfather had been ministers before him. After five years there, they came to the Chapel; he was aged 44.

The building urgently needed painting and cleaning, but the members were not in a position to do more than meet immediate expenditure. The deacons adopted a psychological ploy, which was partially successful. They suggested: 'the best time would be between the call of the Pastor and his coming'. Who would not respond to an appeal to redecorate the building at such an exciting time? However, as successive church treasurers have discovered, there is only so much money available; to stress one special offering reduces the giving to others, and to the general fund. Despite several pulpit appeals and an emergency collection in June 1885, toward the removal expenses of the Woodrow family from Wokingham – the Chapel had called them in April and they were due in July – the removal fund was still £16 short of the actual costs, three months after the new minister arrived.

There was a legacy fund, which the deacons were meant to keep as a capital reserve, but they had to draw on it in September 1886 to pay the pastor's salary, because they were at the limit of their bank overdraft. The deficit on the general fund at the end of 1886 was the largest ever – £62, leading to yet another personal approach by the treasurer to the wealthier members. They had to borrow another £63 from the legacy fund at the end of 1887, to meet the deficit on the general revenue account, and yet another £70 at the end of 1888, for the same purpose. The Chapel was living dangerously.

*Rev. Samuel G. Woodrow, pastor of Charlotte Chapel from 1885 to 1888 – this photograph was taken in 1901, to commemorate his sixtieth birthday.*

### Samuel Woodrow's induction

Mr Woodrow began his ministry on Sunday 5 July 1885, when he conducted the morning and evening services; a guest preacher led a Sunday afternoon service, and there were large attendances at all three. The social on the Tuesday evening followed the extended pattern remarked on in Chapter 11. There were two substantial speeches of welcome, one on behalf of the Chapel and the other on behalf of the other Edinburgh churches, to which Mr Woodrow responded; that was followed by five addresses from distinguished guests, and then three votes of thanks, all interspersed by hymn-singing and the choir.

### Rose Street mission

In 1882, house-to-house visitation was started in Rose Street, apparently the first such outreach; it led to the formation of the Rose Street mission in 1883. Under Samuel Woodrow, a superintendent was appointed in 1886, with all expenses met by the church. As mentioned in Chapter 10, a hall opposite the Chapel (where the leisure club of the Roxburghe Hotel now stands) was rented for £15 a year, for Sunday School work and for evangelism on three evenings during the week. In it, the Chapel ran: (1) a Mutual Improvement Association, for younger people connected with the church, (2) a Temperance Association and Band of Hope, and (3) an Evangelistic Association, 'to conduct in the Hall a weekly Evangelistic Meeting, to carry on House-to-House visitation and Kitchen Meetings, and to take over the new Tract Mission as a Branch of its operations'. The start of the evangelistic meeting on Sunday evening was put back to 8.30 p.m., so that members attending the Chapel's evening service could be present at it.

Through this activity, the church membership, which had declined to 176 by 1885, grew again over the next few years to 212. In May 1889, the landlord of the hall wanted it back for his own use, so the Chapel tried unsuccessfully to lease part of an old school building; the owners were not prepared to make it available for only three nights a week and Sunday afternoon. The Sunday School therefore met on the Chapel premises until another hall could be found. The Chapel was also involved in an outreach known as the Stockbridge Mission, which led to the formation of a Baptist church in the working-class district there in 1899. Sadly, it lasted for only six years.

*The foundations of the Edinburgh Central Library are in Merchant Street, which was Christopher Anderson's home for the first three years of his married life (1816-19). Andrew Carnegie laid the foundation stone for the library in 1887, and donated £50,000 to build it.*

## Members' meetings

Samuel Woodrow proposed, shortly after he arrived in 1885, occasional social evenings for members only, where they could discuss questions affecting the church in an informal context, and get to know each other better; they were self-financing, by taking up a collection. They were held three times a year during his pastorate, in addition to the public social gatherings, which continued as before.

On leaving Edinburgh in 1888, Mr Woodrow went for a couple of years to Fuller Chapel, Kettering, named after Andrew Fuller, the first BMS secretary, who had greatly influenced Christopher Anderson (Chapter 2). Samuel Woodrow's final move was to Aberdeen in 1893, where he was the first minister of the Union Grove church. He was surprised to find that there was no society in Aberdeen to care for the deaf and dumb, so he founded one and acted as its secretary for more than 30 years. He was a frequent visitor back to the Chapel, both as a guest preacher and in connection with Baptist Union of Scotland activities.

Travel from Aberdeen to Edinburgh was much easier after the Forth railway bridge opened on 4 March 1890. Before that, trains from the Waverley Station went through a long tunnel running northward under Princes Street and Queen Street, to emerge at the foot of Scotland Street; the line went on to Granton harbour, where train and passengers embarked on a ferry to Burntisland in Fife – the first train ferry in the world. After 1890, the disused tunnel was used for growing mushrooms. Although that enterprise has also been abandoned, the two ends of the tunnel are still visible, one at the northwest of Waverley Station and the other in the King George V Park at the foot of Scotland Street.

## Detected by a duster

Nothing has been said so far about the Chapel's residential caretakers, or Chapel keepers as they were known. The tied accommodation below the sanctuary was damp and gloomy and the position was often difficult to fill. In November 1881, it had been vacant for five months, despite public advertising and canvassing members of other Baptist churches. When the church treasurer, John Dovey, recommended the woman who cleaned his office premises, Mrs McNab was interviewed by two deacons, and appointed at a wage of £10 per annum, use of the house and free coal and gas. Her husband, Robert, who was a coachman, took up residence with her below the Chapel.

The entire Chapel diaconate of 12 men and the pastor was summoned to an urgent special meeting on 7 January 1882. The pastor asked Mr Dovey why he had 'omitted to state what he knew of the antecedents of Mrs McNab's husband'? The two interviewing deacons were furious that they had not been informed that Robert was a returned convict from Australia. The treasurer's explanation, that he had not known, was accepted, and the pastor proposed: 'it is unnecessary to disturb the appointment of his wife as Chapel Keeper'; this was unanimously approved.

All went well for nearly four years, but when Mr Dovey returned to his home in Eildon Street on 17 December 1885, after attending a children's party in the Chapel, he found his house in disorder and a number of valuable items missing. At first there was no clue as to responsibility, but then he noticed a duster in the house, identical to the dusters used in his office. The police searched the caretaker's flat under the Chapel and found the missing items. Mr McNab admitted reset, but blamed his brother and his son for the burglary. A High Court jury found him guilty of theft, and he was sentenced to ten years' penal servitude. The headline in *The Scotsman*'s report of the trial was: 'Detected by a duster.'

The deacons met on 30 December 1885 and 'unanimously agreed to record their sympathy with Mrs McNab, Chapel Keeper, in her present painful position and regret that in the interests of the Church they consider it necessary to advise that she tender her resignation to the Deacons.' The secretary was asked 'to communicate this decision in a fitting manner to Mrs McNab', and to look for a successor.

### Eligibility for the choir

In 1886, a question arose about membership of the Chapel choir. Everyone agreed that those who sing redemption songs should have redemption grace in their hearts, but opinion was divided as to whether this included membership of the church. In a referendum, 61 members of the church, a majority, voted for the choir to become 'open to all who possessed musical gifts and who desire or may be willing to assist in the service of praise', on the understanding that they were Christians. However, 40 others voted that the choir should be restricted to members of the church. This is a useful record of how many voted on such occasions – 101 out of a membership of 186. The question came up again in 1917 (Chapter 26), and open membership was confirmed.

## 1888–1896: Rev. Thomas Wreford Way

### A quiet, stable ministry

Thomas Way had the longest pastorate in the second half of the nineteenth century – seven and a half years. He was born in Devon in 1858 and while in London, he heard the 'call' to missionary work in China. He trained at Regent's Park College, but toward the end of his course he was told, as Christopher Anderson had been told in 1805, that his health was not robust enough for a tropical climate. He therefore sought a home pastorate, as Anderson had done, and the Chapel was his first charge. He came in November 1888, at the age of 30; his stipend as a bachelor was £150 a year, compared with the £275 that his predecessor had received as a married man. It was widely and uncritically accepted until the 1960s that single men in the professions should be paid less than married men, because wives were expected to give up their employment on marriage.

*Thomas Way, during his pastorate in Charlotte Chapel from 1888 to 1896.*

Thomas Way was a diligent student, a devoted pastor and a thoughtful and able expositor. Tall and slimly built, he had a gracious personality and a spiritual ministry, which endeared him to his hearers. Many came long distances to the church, which, in the absence of Sunday transport, meant walking both ways – often twice every Sunday. His visits to the homes of the people were greatly appreciated. However, the gender imbalance that has been noted from time to time grew, as his ministry progressed. There was not a married couple among the 28 who joined the church in 1891, 9 women and 4 men by baptism and another 11 women and 4 men by transfer; for 1892, the corresponding figures were 12 and 3 baptized, and 6 and 4 transferring in.

83

While transfers, especially from the Shetlands and the Borders at this time, added substantially to the membership, many left Edinburgh for London or for America. Wherever possible, the Chapel formally transferred them to a church of their choosing in their new location, but some did not communicate after they left and Thomas Way had regularly to purge the roll – a church meeting on 30 June 1895 removed 26 names. Reasons ranged from joining other churches – Brethren, Presbyterian, Episcopal – to non-attendance, lost touch or disciplinary action. A curious reason was given for two separate men, who had transferred to the Chapel from their home churches; their transfers had been approved at a Chapel members' meeting, but they 'never came forward to receive the right hand of fellowship after transfer received.'

Despite these comings and goings, the membership total stood practically unchanged throughout Thomas Way's years in the Chapel – 212 when he came to Edinburgh and 213 when he left. For some, who had joined the Chapel in Christopher Anderson's day, Thomas Way was their tenth pastor:

*The death of Mr. and Mrs. John Anderson, at their residence, 54 Findhorn Place, Edinburgh, is deeply regretted by all who enjoyed their friendship. Both were called away after a brief illness, and within a fortnight.... On [Mr. Anderson's] removal to Edinburgh, more than 40 years ago [1847], he identified himself with Charlotte Chapel, then under the care of the Rev. Christopher Anderson, and to the end of his life was its steadfast friend and helper.... Mrs. Anderson had been a member of the church for nearly 50 years [1840].*

---

1 *SBM*, 1889, p. 74.

### Election of elders and deacons, 1889

Those who have been involved in the paper chase of recent quinquennial elections of office-bearers will be impressed by the speed of the 1889 election. The deacons decided on 31 October 1889 that voting papers for elders should be sent out by 6 November to be returned by 17 November. The result of the vote was sent to the members by post, together with voting papers for deacons, 'returnable on 1st December, the new Office bearers to be inducted on 8th December'. In other words, it took 38 days from initiation to completion.

A year later, the church unanimously resolved to raise Thomas Way's stipend to £175 (he was still a single man), and to present him with a New Year gift of £25 – partly to express appreciation of his ministry, but also 'in view of the gratifying result of our financial year 1890'. The gift was handed over during the New Year's Day service and the church secretary's covering letter included:

*We would take this opportunity of expressing to you our deep indebtedness for the spiritual help and encouragement which we have received from your weekly ministrations of Divine Truth, for the kindness and sympathy which as our Pastor you have always shown in your going in and out amongst us, for the tender interest you have taken in our families and our homes and for the affectionate ministry you have exercised in the sick room and by the bed of death.*

---

2 Church Minute Book, 1891, p.1.

### Ward services

In 1890, the Chapel started to hold Sunday afternoon services in the wards of Edinburgh Royal Infirmary. At first, volunteers were few and teams had to move from ward to ward, repeating a short service. As numbers grew, a full half-hour of singing, Scripture reading and a message was possible in every ward. All went smoothly until 1913, when the infirmary chaplain withdrew permission; he had difficulty in attracting a congregation for his service in the infirmary chapel, and blamed the competition.

*The Chapel's links with Edinburgh Royal Infirmary are mentioned at various places in this book. Sunday services were held on the wards from 1890 to 1978. This Infirmary was opened in Lauriston Place in 1879 and moved to its present site at Little France in 2001-3.*

The Chapel workers and others formed themselves into the Sacred Song Union, and pointed out to the infirmary managers that the chaplain never got more than 70 to the chapel, while the teams could take hymns and a message to all 850 patients. Ward services resumed in November 1913, and by 1921, there were sufficient volunteers to cover the adjoining Simpson Maternity Pavilion as well; services were later held in Leith Hospital also. The Sacred Song Union organized the volunteers, from many churches, and held its annual meeting in the Chapel; except for the years of the Second World War, it continued until 1978, when ward services were discontinued (Chapter 27).

## Church minute book, 1891

Thomas Way started the first-ever extant church minute book, recording meetings of members (as opposed to meetings of office-bearers). He wrote it himself, conscientiously, until he left Edinburgh in May 1896 and it gives fascinating glimpses into Chapel life, particularly membership, baptism and church discipline. Mr Way added his personal comments to the formal records of business. For example, he himself proposed, at a meeting of members on 9 June 1895, that the church should petition Parliament in favour of a Liquor Control Bill. Three members opposed the motion, on the ground that the church should not get involved in politics. The motion was carried, but in writing up the minutes, the gracious Mr Way added: 'I think that the opposition was not against a move in favour of temperance but a difference of opinion on the effect of the measure.'

Members met as and when required, averaging twice a month, after the Sunday morning communion service. Applications for baptism and membership, normally two parts of one process, were reported on by the office-bearers who had interviewed the applicants. The members also considered requests for transfer to and from the Chapel. One woman, who had been baptized by Mr Way on 29 March, subsequently applied for membership and was received on 26 April, so he baptized believers even where membership of the Chapel had not been (initially) sought.

As mentioned in Chapter 6, the Chapel accepted into membership, in December 1892, a woman of over 60 who had asthma and heart problems, and who would have been baptized if it had not been dangerous for her health. The church accepted the will for the deed. A meeting on 2 December 1894 approved the transfer of a member to the Dublin Street Baptist Church, because his wife, not having been baptized, could not be a member of the Chapel. The Dublin Street Church had open membership, and so the couple could both be members there.

When the Chapel heard of the death of Charles Haddon Spurgeon in February 1892, the members sent two formal Resolutions (as was the practice at the time), one expressing sympathy to his widow and the other commiserating with the Tabernacle in their loss. The latter commences, 'To the Church of Christ worshipping in the Metropolitan Tabernacle, London, We, the Church of Christ worshipping in Charlotte Baptist Chapel, Edinburgh, desire to express our deep sympathy.' They received an immediate acknowledgement, reproduced below.

*On the death of Charles Haddon Spurgeon, the Chapel expressed sympathy to his widow and to his church; they received this immediate acknowledgement.*

## Anniversary weekends

Thomas Way restructured the traditional anniversary service in January, which commemorated the founding of the church in January 1808; he moved it to the anniversary of his own coming to Edinburgh. He had been inducted on 21 November 1888, and so on the nearest Thursday in November 1889, there was a social occasion, at which he presided. Reports were given of work done and progress made, followed by four addresses. It must have been a success, because it was repeated in 1890, when there were five invited speakers. On Sunday 20 and Monday 21 November 1891, he began a pattern that lasted for 85 years – to make a weekend of it. A guest preacher spoke twice on the Sunday and stayed for a social occasion on the Monday evening. Clearly this was popular – the social on Monday 21 November 1892 was the largest and most enthusiastic ever held in Charlotte Chapel on such an occasion. At a later date, Saturday evening was included as well. This pattern lasted until 1977, by which time attendance on Monday evening no longer justified the guest preacher staying on.

Until 1954, the anniversary weekend marked the commencement of the current ministry. It so happened that both Graham Scroggie (1916) and Sidlow Baxter (1935) were inducted in October; anniversary services were found to be a good way to launch the winter's work, so although the next minister was inducted in June, the church anniversary is now (usually) celebrated over the first weekend in October, without regard to the starting date of pastor.

### Polishing the Chapel's image

In the autumn of 1892, the inside of the Chapel was repainted and re-cushioned, in preparation for a fortnight of special services held in January 1893, with visiting preachers from Glasgow and Dundee. The meetings were well attended and a number, both young and old, professed conversion. One woman, who joined in 1893, remained a loyal and interested member of the Chapel for the next 65 years, ending only when she died after fracturing her hip in 1958, at the age of 96.

As will be seen in Chapter 13, Joseph Kemp, who was the minister a decade later, did not like the 1892 colour scheme, and one of his first actions was to redecorate the interior of the Chapel. He also installed electricity, which the deacons might have considered (but did not) in 1892. Nowadays, candlelit dinners are *chic*, but in the 1890s there was no more stylish invitation than to dine at a table lit by electricity. Shops were beginning to choose it in preference to gas, and in 1895, electric street lighting was installed permanently in Edinburgh for the first time. The power station in Dewar Place asked a butcher, who had an electric mincing machine, not to use it during the hours of darkness, because it was dimming the streetlights.

*The Chapel was spruced up in the autumn of 1892, in preparation for an evangelistic mission. This is the only extant photograph of the building before electric lighting was installed in 1905 – both the street lighting and the Chapel's own lights are gas globes.*

### The pastor's wife

Thomas Way arranged for a friend to supply the pulpit at Christmas 1893, while he visited Devizes, Wiltshire, to finalize his wedding plans with Charlotte Elizabeth Gillman. They were married on 25 April 1894, and he took half of his annual holiday for the honeymoon. The elders brought the June social meeting forward to 10 May, in order to welcome them. They presented Mr Way with a marble clock and a purse containing 24 sovereigns (£1 gold coins), and Mrs Way with an afternoon tea service; these came from congregational subscriptions, which shows the high regard in which Thomas Way was held.

### Baptist church services

As will be seen from the advertisement below, Dublin Street, Duncan Street and the Chapel had Sunday services at 11 a.m. and 6.30 p.m. and a Thursday meeting at 8 p.m. Bristo Place had similar Sunday and midweek services and also an afternoon communion at 2.15 p.m. Marshall Street had services at 11 a.m. and 2.15 p.m. (communion) and a Wednesday meeting. There was a limit to how much the Union could charge churches for such advertising, so the cost of producing the monthly *Scottish Baptist Magazine* was offset by advertisements, not only from Christian organisations but also from anyone (other than drink or tobacco companies) prepared to buy space. Early editions of the Chapel *Record*, which commenced publication 12 years later, also depended heavily on advertising revenue, not, as the editor made plain, from choice but from economic necessity.

### CHURCH NOTICES.

| CHURCH. | MINISTER. | HOURS OF SERVICE. | |
|---|---|---|---|
| | | SABBATH. | WEEK-DAY. |
| **Dundee—** | | | |
| St. Enoch's, Long Wynd | DAVID CLARK | 11 and 6.30 | Wed. 8. |
| **Edinburgh—** | | | |
| Dublin Street | Vacant | 11 and 6.30 | Thur. 8. |
| Duncan Street, Newington | PETER FLEMING | 11 and 6.30 | Thur. 8. |
| Charlotte Chapel, Rose Street | T. W. WAY | 11 and 6.30 | Thur. 8. |
| Bristo Place | WM. GRANT and A. CROMAR | 11, 2.15, & 7 | Thur. 8. |
| Marshall Street | ALEXANDER WYLIE, M.A. | 11 and 2.15 | Wed. 8. |

*Although there were nine Baptist churches in the Edinburgh area during Mr Way's ministry, only five of them thought it worth the cost of advertising their services in the monthly Scottish Baptist Magazine; the others were Abbeyhill (founded in 1895), Leith (1849), Ratho (1892) and South Leith (1891).*

## A mid-week meeting for young people

The Young Men's Christian Fellowship Association, which Andrew Urquhart had started on Sunday morning in 1880, and which admitted young women to its meetings two years later, continued to flourish. In 1888, it began to hold open meetings on weekday evenings as well, also on the Chapel premises. In the same way as Owen Campbell had used secular titles to publicize the Bible School (Chapter 11), the young people gave popular titles to the subjects for their mid-week meetings. The evening of 28 February 1896 'was devoted to the poet Robert Burns. Selections from his works were read and sung, and two very interesting papers were contributed.' The meeting went on, of course, to apply Christian lessons to the secular subject. The Association discontinued toward 1900, and re-started, with the name Young Peoples Meeting, in 1908 (Chapter 16).

## Edinburgh Baptist Churches Association

Toward the end of Thomas Way's ministry here, he took a leading part in inaugurating the first ever link-up of local Baptist churches 'for mutual helpfulness'. In December 1894, the Association of the Baptist Churches of Edinburgh, Leith and District was formed. Conferences were held quarterly, the first on 11 March 1895. The Chapel hosted the third, in October, when 'the body of the Chapel was well filled and the audience included a considerable number of ladies.' In 1952, the Association changed its name to the Edinburgh

and Lothians Baptist Association (Elba). The Chapel continued to be supportive (although not in membership for the years 1955-90, Chapter 39) until Elba was dissolved in 2002; by then, the usefulness of district associations had disappeared from Scottish Baptist life.

There was no universal right to vote in Westminster parliamentary elections at this time, but those Baptists who had the franchise were overwhelmingly Liberal in their allegiance – because of the Liberal Party's stand for moral principle and because it supported non-conformist concerns. The *Scottish Baptist Magazine* of August 1895 recorded the rout of the Liberals at the polls, and the magazine became politically neutral until the 1980s.

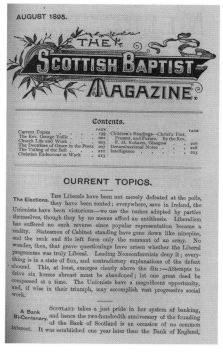

*The Scottish Baptist Magazine commented, with regret, on the rout of the Liberal Party at the 1895 general election.*

## Farewell to Thomas Way

In 1896, Thomas Way decided to leave Edinburgh and 'after a short rest … to seek a pastorate in the south of England'. He soon accepted a 'call' to a church in Fleet, in Hampshire.

*A social meeting was held on the evening of Monday, the 25th May, to bid farewell to the pastor, the Rev. T. W. Way, who was leaving for England after a pastorate of seven and a half years. Ex-Bailie Walcot presided. The chairman expressed the deep regret of the church at Mr. Way's resignation, bore hearty testimony to the excellent services he had rendered to the church during his pastorate, and wished him hearty God-speed in his future ministry.*

3 *SBM*, 1896, p. 131.

The *Scottish Baptist Magazine* recorded that: 'Mr. Way, by his kindness and careful work, always commanded respect, and accomplished good.'

## 1896–1901: Rev. Foster Henry Bardwell, MA

### Hopes for blessing and prosperity

After only two months of vacancy, the same magazine reported:

*The Rev. Foster H. Bardwell, M.A. of Glasgow University and Rawdon College, has received and accepted an invitation to the pastorate of Charlotte Chapel, Edinburgh. Mr. Bardwell is a son of a Baptist minister in Chippenham, Wiltshire. He went to Glasgow about seven years ago, took the full University course there, and duly graduated M.A. Simultaneously he studied theological subjects at the Baptist Union Summer Classes for four sessions, and thereafter he went to Rawdon College, where he completed his theological studies.... it is sincerely to be hoped that times of blessing and prosperity may be in store for pastor and people. It is expected that Mr. Bardwell will begin his ministry in the beginning of October.*

4 *SBM*, 1896, p. 163.

The hopes for blessing and prosperity were sadly disappointed. One Sunday evening, there were only 19 present, including the preacher; during the summer months, from 1899, there was no evening service. Shortly before Foster Bardwell left in 1901, the congregational prayer meeting was held in the vestry instead of the church, because only three were attending.

What had gone wrong? There are five clues, some of them contradictory. A Chapel member reminisced, 20 years later:

*we remember, as a lad, craning our neck over the ledge of the side gallery of the old Chapel, as he [the chairman] introduced a nervous and somewhat apprehensive minister to the pulpit of Rose Street. And we also remember condemning this new minister in our own boyish mind as a complete failure – so slow and halting were his utterances that a 'Scotsman' reporter might have made a complete meal in between each sentence.*

5 *Record*, 1923, p. 83.

It is hard to reconcile that negative comment with the second clue, the memoirs of another member, written 60 years later. He recollected that although Bardwell was:

*of a quiet and retiring disposition, and his preaching was in a quiet strain, without any ostentation, or attempts at oratory, yet his scholarly mind enabled him to expound the truths of the Gospel in simplicity and clearness, which commanded the rapt attention of his hearers. The membership of the church was about the same as in the time of his predecessor, and those who lived at a distance were most loyal in attendance.*

6 James Scott, at the Ter-jubilee in 1958.

Foster Bardwell's preaching had been warmly appreciated during his two visits while the church was vacant, so perhaps the second reminiscence is the more accurate. However, the third clue is less subjective. At the ten elders' meetings between October 1896 and November 1898, only two applications for baptism and membership were received – loyalty is all very well, but new blood is required. Paradoxically, at the last recorded meeting, in December 1898, there were five new applications; the minute book then went blank, and nothing further is known about Foster Bardwell's last two years.

Support for the Sunday School and Bible Class provides the fourth clue. When Foster Bardwell came, average weekly attendance was 95, with 17 teachers; when he left, the average was 32 and 8, so there was malaise there as well. The fifth clue gives the best insight into the problem; one member said, later, that Bardwell 'never really fitted into the ways of Charlotte Chapel, although a cultured and kindly gentleman. Many had drifted away from the Chapel prior to Mr Kemp's call in 1902'.

Foster Bardwell moved the manse three times during his five years at the Chapel; between 1896 and 1899, he lived at 8 Brandon Terrace, then in 1900 at 7 Frederick Street, and from 1901 onward at 90 Morningside Road. Early in 1901, he applied to the United Free Church of Scotland, for admission to its ministry; he left the Chapel in April 1901, to become a Presbyterian minister in the Colonies, but he is not listed anywhere in the records of the United Free Church or the Church of Scotland. His name appears in the *Scottish Baptist Yearbook* at the Morningside address until 1904; if it was his own house – and the Chapel did not provide a manse at any time in the nineteenth century – he would naturally stay there until he was called to a new charge.

### Christian Endeavour

During Foster Bardwell's pastorate, a Christian Endeavour Society was started in the Chapel. Such societies were popular in Scotland at the time, with their emphasis on meetings during the week, conducted exclusively by and for young people, encouraging open confession of Christ, active service for him, loyalty to his church and fellowship with his people. Three months after its launch in the Chapel in the autumn of 1896, with an initial membership of 15, there were 24 regular members. It disappeared from the Chapel records in 1902.

### Quietly into the twentieth century

Compared with the worldwide celebrations for the millennium on 31 December 1999-1 January 2000, the transition from the nineteenth to the twentieth century was quiet – almost unnoticed. The *Scottish Baptist Magazine* did not even mention it, saying only: 'With sincere cordiality do we wish our readers and our churches a Happy New Year. It is true the war-cloud hangs threateningly over the nation, darkening the prospect and oppressing the heart, yet faith and courage have here their opportunity.' The reference was to the war against the Boer Republics in South Africa.

Although the Chapel was at its lowest ebb during the Boer War, as described below, one incident in February 1901 deserves mention. *The Scotsman* newspaper championed a Shilling Fund (5 new pence), to provide relief for the widows and orphans of British soldiers killed in South Africa. Among

the 800,000 shillings (£40,000) donated by February 1901, was 80 shillings received 'as a result of a cinematograph entertainment on Wednesday evening [20 February 1901] in Charlotte Baptist Chapel, West Rose Street, Edinburgh. Messrs Fraser and Elrich provided a capital selection of views, which were greatly appreciated by a crowded attendance.' The Borders town of Hawick – 'a town which has been as generous to the Fund as almost any Border district' – sent 40 shillings in the same week as the Chapel sent 80. The Chapel's use of the new phenomenon of cinematography is taken up in Chapter 16.

### Sunday transport

As mentioned earlier, horse-drawn trams were introduced into Edinburgh in November 1871. By 1887 there was a huge network, covering the city and its suburbs, some drawn by horses but many, by that time, by cable. Until December 1901, both staff and horses enjoyed the traditional Sabbath rest, and the public walked to church. However, in the autumn of 1901, the Edinburgh Street Tramway Company wanted to increase its revenue. Commercial pressure, which over the years has made so many inroads into the Christian Sunday as a different and special day, prevailed. On Sunday 1 December 1901, 82 cable-cars operated from 10 a.m. to 10 p.m. The horses were still given a rest, someone remarking that even if the drivers and conductors wanted to work on Sunday, the animals needed a day off. For reasons set out in Chapter 20, many devout Christians would not use tramcars on Sunday.

*From the dress of the pedestrians in this picture of Waterloo Place in 1901, and from the number walking when trams were available, it looks like a Sunday. Many devout Christians would not use tramcars on Sunday, because they disapproved of Sunday employment.*

## The Chapel's lowest ebb

By the summer of 1901, Charlotte Chapel had sunk to its lowest ebb. The pastorate was vacant, and although the membership on paper was 108, less than half of them attended. William MacDuff Urquhart, the ten-year-old son of the church secretary (William, then; later, the middle name), passed the time by marking attendances on his hymn book, checking it to see whether there were more or less than the previous Sunday. 'I can assure you', he told the writer, 'average attendance was in the vicinity of 40 to 50.' As mentioned, the number of Sunday School teachers had fallen to 8, and less than half of the scholars on the roll turned up. No evening services were held during the summer months of 1901.

**CHARLOTTE BAPTIST CHAPEL**
(West Rose Street, corner of South Charlotte Street.)
Morning 11—Mr ALEX. M'KENZIE. No Evening Service.

*In September 1901, the Chapel's advertisement in* The Scotsman *concluded with a terse 'No Evening Service'.*

A spirit of despondency prevailed, and the future was wrapped in uncertainty and gloom. The building was in a poor state, unsanitary and in need of repair. It had a Victorian unattractiveness both inside and out, and did not offer much inducement to the outsider. Its boxed-in family pews discouraged visitors. It was a place of holy memories, but with the exception of three or four loyal and devoted families, strong in faith and confident in prayer, the place was empty. A handsome financial offer for the building came from a business firm requiring a warehouse. What should the Chapel do? No minister – scarcely a congregation – no vision – should the church close its doors?

Additional information on the following topics, mentioned in this chapter, is available on the CD.

Anniversaries and Thankofferings
Choir
Christian Endeavour Society
Christopher Anderson's home
Church Meetings
Church officers to 1911
Church register of baptised believers
Samuel George Woodrow
Stockbridge Mission
Sunday School Statistics
Thomas Way

# Chapter 13
## Prelude to Revival (1902–1904)

### A lost cause?

#### A faithful few

The last chapter closed with a financial offer on the table, from a company looking for a warehouse. Many would have taken it, but the church secretary, Andrew Urquhart, had no hesitation in rejecting the offer:

*I, for one, am not going to believe that the light which has burned for so long in this place is going to be put out; that the people who so long laboured for the advancement of the Redeemer's cause are to retire from the work in despair; that the door of this dear old Chapel, hallowed by many blessed and holy memories, is to be closed, and the building itself turned into a music hall or a grocery store. No, brethren, I don't believe it, and in your hearts neither do you. I believe the crisis is of God, and He will bring us through it.*

---

1 Winnie Kemp, *Joseph W. Kemp, by his wife* (Marshall, Morgan and Scott, London, 1936), p. 23.

Andrew Urquhart was a man of faith, tenacity and vision. His son William who, as mentioned in the previous chapter, recorded the number attending the morning service, recalled how his father sometimes said, as the family turned into Rose Street towards the Chapel on Sunday morning: 'Look at the crowds waiting to get in', when the street was empty and the church, they knew, would be nearly so. Andrew Urquhart lived to see the crowds queuing in Rose Street to worship God in Charlotte Chapel for the last ten years of his life. His remarks to his family on these Sunday mornings in 1901 were visions of faith from a man of prayer, confident of the future when all around seemed hopeless. He believed that God still had a work to do in the Chapel.

*In 1901, Charlotte Chapel was unattractive both outside and in. This photograph was taken in 1906, after Joseph Kemp had cleaned it and installed electric lights. Someone has put a disapproving 'x' over the 19 licensed premises in Rose Street. This building was pulled down in 1911 and the present Chapel was built on the site.*

At the social meeting to say farewell to Foster Bardwell in April 1901, he advised:

*We are few in numbers and inclined to be downhearted and despondent. We know not what is before us, but 'Jesus we know and He is on the throne', and that is enough. There is no reason why we should not, under an earnest and consecrated leader, even although we have an old and dilapidated building, hidden in a back street, retrieve our position and yet do a work for Christ, which shall shame all our fears. But how? In one way, by earnest and believing prayer. I appeal to all of you to meet in the vestry next Wednesday. We shall not dare to meet in the Church, for there were only three at the last meeting.*

---

2 *Record*, 1912, pp. 168–9.

As a result of this appeal, 12 met, and the prayer meeting increased in power week by week. However, the building was still terribly depressing and the pastorless congregation was in a pitiful condition; some did not hesitate to say openly that it was a lost cause. One of the most negative comments, quoted below, came from the man whom God later used to revive the church.

#### 'Call' to Joseph Kemp

Joseph William Kemp was enjoying a happy and successful pastorate at Hawick Baptist Church. When he attended a meeting in the Chapel in early October 1901, he remarked to a colleague: 'God pity the man who comes here'. Kemp had introduced several new features into the Hawick church since becoming its pastor in July 1898 and it now had a membership of 150; he conducted gospel services in the local theatre, which attracted large congregations.

Orphaned at an early age, Joseph Kemp grew up in Hull. When he was aged 20, in 1892, a generous friend funded his training for two years at the Bible Training Institute (now the International Christian College) in Glasgow. After graduating and (on the same day) being baptized as a believer, Joseph Kemp worked for a time as an evangelist in the west of Scotland. He was then 'called' in April 1897 to the Baptist church in Kelso. He married a local girl, Winnie, whose mother, Mary Ann Binnie, had been a member of Charlotte Chapel until her husband's business took them away from Edinburgh in 1874.

A Chapel member, who knew about Joseph Kemp's effective ministry in Hawick, suggested to Andrew Urquhart that he might persuade Kemp to come to the Chapel. Urquhart approached him, on the basis that he was needed more in Edinburgh than in the Scottish Borders. 'The Hawick church is enjoying a happy prosperity, and the Edinburgh church is in direst need – almost in peril of dissolution. Can there be room for doubt as to which way the Master's finger points?' His letters breathed optimism and prophetic insight: 'I would ask you to believe', he wrote, 'that the Master is pointing you to us. One should never venture to prophesy, but I feel almost inclined to do so and to say that you will, by God's help, fill Charlotte Chapel inside of eighteen months and that it will be, after the first month or two, a centre of evangelical life in Edinburgh and increasingly a birthplace of precious souls'.

Andrew Urquhart was careful to point out the unfavourable conditions that any new man would face. Many would have shrunk from the task, but Kemp gave it prayerful consideration. The more he prayed, the more he realized that the 'call' was from God. His friends said: 'Don't go' – all, that is, except his wife and his wife's mother, who were sure it was God's purpose. In an interview between the two men, Joseph Kemp said: 'If I come, I must have an absolutely free hand'. Andrew Urquhart replied that he could have a free hand on one condition. Kemp asked: 'What is that condition?' and Urquhart replied: 'That you preach the gospel'.

*Joseph Kemp and his wife Winnie, as they arrived in Edinburgh in 1902. He was aged 30. Older men still wore Victorian beards and side-whiskers (see the pictures of John Walcot and Thomas Way in Chapters 10 and 12), but by 1902 younger men preferred the moustache, clipped neatly in military fashion. Only a minority of men went completely clean-shaven.*

A month before the Kemps left Hawick in January 1902, a notice in the Hawick paper announced: 'Births. At 7 Wilton Hill Terrace, Hawick, on the 30th ultimo, the wife of Rev. Joseph W. Kemp, of a son.' They left with deep regret but with delightful anticipation of God's favour and blessing for the future – a new city, a new church, a new home, and a new baby. From a financial point of view, the salary was less than at Hawick, but they believed 'that the barrel of meal and the cruse of oil in His hands never fail.' Mr Kemp was happy in the knowledge that God wanted him in the city and there was a great urge on his soul as he took up the work in Charlotte Chapel.

*As the Kemps arrived in Edinburgh, horse-drawn taxis were giving way to motorized ones. This motor-taxi was photographed in Charlotte Square in 1900.*

## Joseph Kemp's induction

Mrs Kemp's biography of her husband painted a dismal and depressing picture of his induction to Charlotte Chapel on Sunday 2 February 1902. She wrote:

*On the Sunday morning of his induction the congregation numbered thirty-five, out of a nominal membership of one hundred. The thirty-five represented the strength of the church.... Gradually others joined them, and their perseverance and fervour soon told upon the work. To begin with, the growth was slow; but an intensity of longing soon revealed itself amongst the members, and the prayer meeting became a place of power.*

3 Kemp, *Joseph W. Kemp*, p. 20.

However, Mrs Kemp was not at the induction, because she was looking after their infant son. Her recollection was written 30 years later, and she may have been thinking of the Sunday morning when her husband preached 'with a view', when the congregation did indeed total 35. The *Scottish Baptist Magazine* reported encouragingly on large congregations at all three services over the induction weekend:

*Edinburgh – Charlotte Chapel – Friends in all the Churches will rejoice that a break has at last appeared in the clouds which have unhappily for some time overshadowed this old Church, and that a period of prosperity has begun with the advent of its new pastor – the Rev. J. W. Kemp, formerly of Hawick. Mr. Kemp began his ministry on the first Sunday of February. The Rev. T. W. Lister of Glasgow preached in the morning, and introduced Mr. Kemp, and the pastor himself preached in the evening. At both services the congregations were large, and a spirit of gratitude and hopefulness filled all hearts. A social meeting was held on the following evening, which was largely attended, about 400 being present. … Mrs. Kemp was unable to be at the induction services, but a deputation of ladies have since waited upon her, and presented her with a purse containing £7 as a gift of welcome from the Church.*

4 *SBM*, 1902, p. 48.

It was the Presbyterian practice at the time for a neighbouring minister to preach an 'introduction sermon'. Why and when this took place in the Chapel in February 1902 is not clear – it cannot have been Sunday 2 February, because the preacher, Alexander Whyte, is not named in the report of that day – but it deeply impressed one Chapel member:

*Dr. Whyte, of Free St. George's, preached the introduction sermon – and such a sermon! But Mr. Kemp was not the man to leave us long on those heights of Parnassus, whither Dr. Whyte's ecstatic imagination had attracted us. No sooner had the saintly prophet of God concluded his discourse than the new pastor stepped to the front of the platform and announced that 'the workers will meet for prayer this evening, before going out to the corner of South Charlotte Street.' It was like a shot out of a gun, and climax at once gave place to anti-climax. But a new note was struck in C.C. that morning.*

5 *Record*, 1923, p. 83.

## Strategy for revival

### Prayer

Joseph Kemp put three strategies in place. The first was prayer – he impressed on the faithful nucleus of the church how he needed their co-operation in the great work of prayer. In his

first sermon, he called his people to prayer, intensive, fervent and continuous prayer. To this end, he started three new prayer meetings on Sunday in the summer of 1903; one was at seven in the morning, which he himself always attended, the next was at 10 a.m., especially to pray for the morning service, and the third was at 5.45 p.m., to pray for the evening service.

Growth was slow at first, but their fervour inspired and encouraged each other and gradually others joined them. People came in all weathers and from all parts of the city; soon there were between 30 and 40, and sometimes more, at the 7 a.m. meeting. As the prayer meetings became places of power, numbers increased and hope grew. More often than not, Sunday evening was concluded with an impromptu prayer and testimony meeting. In 1906, the church secretary reported:

*For four years, fine day and foul, the Pastor and a company of thirty to forty of God's people have met in the Upper Vestry every Sunday morning, at 7 o'clock, and waited upon God. Later, at 10 o'clock, in the same place, a band of praying men and women meet for a similar purpose, and to plead for blessing on the work of the day. But not in this place, or on this day only, do the people meet for prayer, for there is a season of prayer before every service, weekday and Sunday. To this Upper Room and the praying friends who meet there week by week, we may fitly point as the source and spring of the spiritual prosperity which the Church has been so privileged to enjoy.*

6 'Charlotte Chapel Handbook', 1906, pp. 9-10.

*The upper vestry (or prayer meeting room, as it was popularly known), where Joseph Kemp held three prayer meetings every Sunday. The harmonium is in the corner because the choir practiced in this room on Friday evening.*

Geographically, the upper vestry was roughly where the enquiry room and vestry are now but, as the picture shows, it ran for the whole width of the building; the windows on the left of the photograph (taken in 1906 or later, as electricity was not installed until late December 1905) looked onto open ground to the south.

Why the emphasis on prayer? Joseph Kemp delighted to recall an incident while he was a student in Glasgow; he went to a convention on Keswick lines, where the speaker was Rev. Andrew Murray of South Africa. Murray, a slim, solemn and stern figure, raised his index finger and called out: 'Wanted – men who can pray!' The effect on Joseph Kemp was overpowering and, he said, influenced the remainder of his life and ministry.

## Open-air meetings

The second prong of Joseph Kemp's strategy for Charlotte Chapel was open-air preaching. If people would not come into the church, then the church would go out to them. The corner of South Charlotte Street and Princes Street became the pulpit and the open air the sanctuary.

*The preferred venue for open-air preaching was the corner of South Charlotte Street and Princes Street – the wide pavement toward the left of this photograph. During Joseph Kemp's ministry, this site was the birthplace of many souls.*

Mr Kemp was an evangelist, with a consuming passion for conversions. If there were not enough outsiders in the church when the evening service started, the members would sometimes go out to their usual open-air stance, or march along Princes Street, collect a crowd and bring a congregation back in with them. The messages in the open air reached and arrested hundreds of people, of whom Annie Wighton was

one. As a girl of 13, from a non-Christian home in a mining village in Lanarkshire, she stopped to listen to the singing and followed the crowd back into the Chapel.

*Annie Wighton was converted after stopping to listen to an open-air meeting. This 1936 photograph was taken during a furlough from Nigeria, where she was a missionary-nurse supported by the Chapel.*

She continued to attend and a few weeks later responded to an appeal to make a decision for Christ. She became a domestic servant in the Kemps' household for seven years, first in Edinburgh and then in New York. When Mr Kemp left New York, she took nursing and Bible College training, and then served for 44 years with the Sudan Interior Mission in Nigeria. Furthermore, she set herself from the beginning to pray earnestly for her father and mother, five sisters and three brothers. Not only did she have the joy of seeing all of them converted, but one brother became the minister of the Coatbridge Baptist Church, one sister married a minister in Canada and her youngest sister became a missionary in the New Hebrides with her husband, Adam Wilson, a member of Charlotte Chapel.

## Improving the building

The third prong of Joseph Kemp's strategy was to renovate the Chapel building. It 'presented no outward beauty to charm the eye, and the interior, with its dark-stained walls, boxed-in pews, dim religious light, and unattractive entrances, did not offer much inducement to the outsider to enter.' While priority was given to prayer and evangelism, Mr Kemp also made the building more attractive. Every pew had a door with a catch, so that worshippers could shut themselves in. The doors were the first things to go, so that strangers could slip in without difficulty – all seating was made free – and so that a personal worker could easily get in to speak to them.

Joseph Kemp looked not only for conversions; he wanted children to be baptized and to join the church. Andrew Urquhart's son, William, did so in 1903, before he was in his teens. Kemp had the pleasure of baptizing his own son and receiving him into membership at the age of 11. Everyone was encouraged to make a public confession in baptism as soon as they had come to faith – a man who went to the vestry on 25 May 1905, under conviction of sin, believed the words of John 3:16 that evening and Joseph Kemp baptized him on 15 June.

## Revival

### Seven nights a week

Joseph Kemp's profound belief in the truths he preached, and his passion for souls, gave his people growing hope, inspiration and encouragement; this led to prolonged waiting on God in prayer. Throughout 1904, there were prayer meetings night after night, steadily increasing in numbers and intensity and deepening in interest. Joseph Kemp commented: 'Much has been done to beautify our little sanctuary and make it more pleasing and attractive, but nothing has made the place so beautiful to hundreds as the fact that "they were born there"'. As mentioned above, a good work was underway before Revival came in January 1905.

### Three meanings of 'revival'

Over the next few years, the office-bearers of Charlotte Chapel used the word 'revival' in three different senses. At the opening of the new building in October 1912, the church secretary, reflecting on Joseph Kemp's ten years in Edinburgh, said: 'this one-time little congregation has seen hundreds born into the Kingdom, enjoyed an almost continual revival, witnessed almost continually men and women far down in sin being gloriously rescued and blessedly converted to God.' That is a common use of the word 'revival', describing God's blessing over a period of time in vibrant church life.

Kemp and his office-bearers used the same word in a more restricted sense, for two particular, spontaneous, fairly brief, outpourings of God's Spirit, one starting in January 1905 and the other in December 1906. They described these two as 'Revivals' with a capital letter, and this book will do the same. Thirdly, they used the word 'revival' for a planned evangelistic event. It is still used in that sense in America,

where church notices may say: 'There will be a revival here, next Sunday at 11 a.m.', meaning a gospel meeting culminating in an appeal. The Chapel held a week of 'revivals', in that sense, in December 1904, just three weeks before the first Revival. In this book, such 'revivals' are described as 'missions'. A guest evangelist led that week of mission, but nothing out of the ordinary happened. The Chapel office-bearers advised the church to continue in prayer, until Revival came. This chapter closes with an explanation of how, humanly speaking, Revival came to Charlotte Chapel.

CHARLOTTE BAPTIST CHAPEL, W. Rose St.
7 and 10 A.M.—PRAYER MEETINGS.
11 and 6.30—Rev. JOSEPH W. KEMP, Pastor.
3.15—School for Bible Study.
REVIVAL MEETING TO-NIGHT at 8.
THURSDAY—REVIVAL and BAPTISMAL SERVICE at 8.
Rev. JOHN M'NEILL, Sunday, 1st October, at 11.

*Joseph Kemp used the word 'revival' in three ways, one of which was for a planned future event with a gospel message, culminating in an appeal, as in this advertisement in* The Scotsman.

### Revival in Wales

Edinburgh's climate badly affected Mr Kemp's health; every winter, he suffered from asthma and nasal catarrh. After a sleepless Saturday night, when his asthma had been particularly trying, he still attended the Chapel's 7 a.m. prayer meeting, even if this meant wading through slush and snow. He dreaded lest he or his people should lack intensity and urgency in intercession for the lost. He was sensitive to the disapproval of many Christians about using public transport on Sunday, although he himself did not feel strongly about it. To avoid giving offence, he walked the mile from the manse at 92 Gilmore Place to the Chapel, for the 7 a.m. prayer meeting, then back home to prepare for the morning service. In all, he walked this mile eight times every Sunday.

When rebuked for preaching when he seemed unfit, he answered brightly: 'There is nothing like preaching to cure all ills'. He had a vision of what God wanted him to do, and in humble dependence he went forward with serenity under difficulties arising from these maladies. The family doctor, who was also a friend and thoughtful helper, found him incorrigible.

*The West End of Princes Street on a snowy morning in 1904. Joseph Kemp waded through slush and snow to get to the 7 a.m. prayer meeting via Lothian Road – many Christians would not on principle use tramcars on Sunday. Other Chapel members converged on this junction via Shandwick Place from the west or Queensferry Street from the north-west.*

There was a regular afternoon conference in the Chapel, on the fourth Saturday of every month. The one in January 1905 had started when Joseph Kemp and a Welshman, whom he had brought with him, walked down the aisle. They and others from Wales told what they had seen and experienced in the Welsh Revival; what followed is described in the next chapter.

Additional information on the following topics, mentioned in this chapter, is available on the CD.

Adam Wilson
Annie Wighton
Anniversaries and Thankofferings
'God pity the man who comes here'
Jamaica Street mission
Jean Scott
Joseph Kemp before Charlotte Chapel
Joseph Kemp's family
Joseph Kemp's School of Bible Study
Mary Ann Binnie
Preaching styles
Tract Society

However, early in January 1905, just after the mission mentioned above, the Chapel office-bearers persuaded Mr Kemp to take a holiday in Bournemouth, on the south coast of England. The sight of so many invalids in wheelchairs made him feel worse, so after only one day at the seaside, he went on to Wales, to see the Revival that had broken out there. He had heard that thousands had been converted, pugilists, drunkards, gamblers, public house owners and men and women from all strata of society. What he found is best described in his own words:

*I spent two weeks watching, experiencing, drinking in, having my own heart searched, comparing my methods with those of the Holy Ghost; and then I returned to my people in Edinburgh to tell what I had seen. In Wales I saw the people had learned to sing in a way which was new to me. I never heard such singing as theirs. They sang such old familiar hymns as 'When I survey the wondrous Cross,' and 'There is a fountain filled with Blood,' and 'I need Thee, oh, I need Thee.' They needed no organist or choir or leader. Their singing was natural. The Holy Ghost was in their singing as much as in any other exercise. They had the New Song.... The world knows nothing of it. Do not tell me that the sporting clubs, the dance halls, the movies, and operas can give you joy. They can for the moment give you some fun, but that is not joy. Joy is the gift of God. When a revival from God visits a congregation it brings with it joy.*

---

10 Kemp, *Joseph W. Kemp*, pp. 29-30.

# Chapter 14
## The 1905 Revival (1905–1906)

### Early 1905

#### Saturday 22 January 1905

As mentioned at the end of the last chapter, Joseph Kemp and colleagues from Wales told the Chapel's monthly conference, in January 1905, what they had experienced in the Revival there, and its effect on their own souls. Kemp then asked if anyone present wanted to be saved. About five seats from the front a man rose, saying: 'I want you to pray for me.' He was the first of hundreds to be converted over the next few months, as Revival came to Charlotte Chapel, starting on Saturday 22 January 1905. The conference lasted from 3.30 p.m. until after midnight; the fire of God fell – the prayers of many months were answered.

#### One continuous prayer meeting

That was the first of innumerably prolonged meetings over the next few weeks and months. Night after night, week after week, month after month during the year 1905, prayer meetings went on increasing in numbers and intensity – it was almost as if the year was one continuous prayer meeting. Kemp wrote in March 1906: 'the Chapel has been open every night, for 455 nights [that is since January 1905] without one solitary break, and during the whole of that period, there have been but few nights when there have not been anxious souls seeking the way of life.' People poured out their hearts, and a mighty flood of blessing swept through the church; services often began long before the appointed time, with spontaneous prayer and praise.

On Sunday morning, which was for the exposition of the Word, the area of the church was filled and the gallery nearly so. In the evening, the Chapel's 750 seats were always crowded and many were unable to get a seat – the aisles and pulpit steps and every nook and cranny were occupied. The Revival not only filled the church, but conversions took place at every meeting. When the treasurer's wife, Mrs John Dovey, told the story of her own conversion one Sunday evening, over 30 accepted the Saviour. About one thousand were born again in 1905. At one communion service, 66 new Christians were received into membership.

Giving his mature reflection on these events, ten years later, Joseph Kemp sub-titled his article: 'The amazing story of Charlotte Chapel, where for two years [1905–7] there was

practically no preaching'. He was referring to the ordinary activities of the church, apart from the Sunday services. At the time, he wrote: 'Beyond our ordinary services on the Lord's Day, there has been very little or no preaching'; Joseph Kemp normally occupied the pulpit at the morning and evening services on Sunday, but there were times when the congregation was so caught up in an outpouring of prayer, that preaching was out of the question. An example is given in the next chapter.

*Joseph Kemp at the time of the Revival of 1905.*

### Restoration

Many who were following Christ afar off were brought face to face with the Saviour anew, seeking forgiveness and cleansing. The Revival restored many who had grown cold: it purified lives, changed hearts and homes and blessed hundreds of souls. The spiritual experience of such a visitation of the Holy Spirit could not be expressed in human terms – there was a holy abandon, a spiritual glow, and a deep, overwhelming sense of the presence of God. There was uninhibited liberty, abounding unspeakable joy and an outflowing of Christian love. There was heart-warming fellowship and radiant communion with the Lord. At the same time, there was a keen sensitiveness to the awfulness of sin and worldliness, and a deep desire to be right with God and with one another.

There was also an overwhelming longing for the salvation of others. It was essentially a prayer movement. The clock did not govern the meetings. Although there were half-nights and whole nights of prayer, the meetings were not organized.

Prayer was spontaneous, with many praying at one time and sometimes it seemed as if the whole gathering was praying together, but there was no confusion. All was in the Spirit. There were outbursts of song, which were truly joy unspeakable and full of glory. The effect of the Revival was seen, not only in hundreds of conversions but in a quickening of spiritual life and holiness of character, a deeper urge to evangelise, a keen desire for Bible study and an enlarged spirit of giving. Joseph Kemp wrote:

*I have yet to witness a movement that has produced more permanent results in the lives of men, women and children. There were irregularities no doubt; even some commotion.... The people poured out their hearts in importunate prayer. Such a movement with all its irregularities is to be preferred far above the dull, dreary, monotonous decorum of many churches. Under these influences the crowds thronged the Chapel, which only three years before maintained a 'sombre vacuum'. After the first year of this work we had personally dealt with no fewer than one thousand souls. Who had brought it? God during the prayer meetings.'*

1 Kemp, *Joseph W. Kemp*, p. 30.

Children, too, shared in the blessing. One Sunday School teacher found that 12 of the 14 in her class had openly decided for Christ; at a meeting for young people, a number of the older children were brought to the Lord. The children were so keen that they started a prayer meeting of their own, and a sympathetic leader was appointed to guide them. Ten children were baptized at one baptismal service on profession of their faith in Christ.

## Thursday 16 March 1905

Not only was God's Spirit moving in Revival in Wales and in Charlotte Chapel in 1905, but reports from all around Scotland prompted the Baptist Union of Scotland to ask 50 ministers to respond if they had 'anything special to communicate'. Replies came immediately from all over Scotland – from Arbroath, Bellshill, Bowhill (Fife), Bridgeton (Glasgow), Bristo Place (Edinburgh), Clydebank, Coatbridge, Cowdenbeath, Denny, Elgin, Forfar, Galashiels, George Street (Paisley), Gilcomston Park (Aberdeen), Hawick, Inverkeithing, Kelvinside (Glasgow), Maxwelltown (Dundee), Maybole, Motherwell, Orangefield (Greenock), Paisley Road (Glasgow), Partick (Glasgow), Port-Ellen

(Islay), South Leith, Victoria Place (Glasgow), Stirling and Wishaw. Typical of the replies was the postcard from the Chapel to the Union:

*Revival services have been held nightly since 1st January, and a large number have professed faith in Christ. The attendances have been large, especially on Sunday evenings when the church has been filled – every available place, including the pulpit steps, being occupied. Great things had been done; but greater are to follow. On Thursday, 16th March, a combined revival meeting and baptismal service was held. Ten were baptised. After his address, the pastor made an appeal to the Christians present who had not been baptised, to signify their decision to follow Christ in baptism, by rising; and over 50 stood up. In addition to this there were several cases of conversion. The whole service was one of the most impressive ever held in the Chapel.*

2 *SBM*, 1905, p. 67.

The minister of the Paisley Road Baptist Church in Govan, Glasgow, John Harper (who was drowned when the Titanic went down, as described in Chapter 19) reported over seven hundred conversions by April 1905, of whom more than one hundred had joined the church. That chimes with the report from the Chapel, quoted above. Asked if he had 'anything special to communicate', the author of the postcard did not describe the intense prayer meetings, nor the restorations, nor the turning from sin and worldliness in the lives of believers (all of which were happening), but concentrated on conversions and baptisms.

## Princes Street marches

One outworking of the Revival was the decision by Mr Kemp, when prompted by the Spirit, to lead the whole congregation in a march of witness along Princes Street. They formed up in two companies, those in the gallery going first and then a few minutes later those in the area. Mr Kemp and the elders in their frock coats and silk tile hats led them. They sang gospel hymns and choruses. They marched as far as the Mound, where the policeman on point duty halted the traffic to let them turn and come back on the opposite side of the street. Some who followed the marchers back to the Chapel were converted. The *Edinburgh Citizen* newspaper reported on one such march on 16 June 1905:

*On Sunday night we witnessed two big marches in Princes Street within a few minutes of each other, the one led by an office-bearer and the other by the pastor of Charlotte Chapel. In front of each company there was a young man carrying boards announcing the Sunday and week-night meetings, while there could not be less than 400 to 500 persons taking part in the marches, many of whom but a short time before were slaves to sin. The hymn-singing was simple, easily understood, effective, and well calculated to arrest the passers-by.*

3 Kemp, *Joseph W. Kemp*, p. 40.

A Chapel member explained another reason for the marches – to make room for unconverted people to get into the building:

*I remember one Sunday evening when the church was packed upstairs and downstairs, and crowds were still waiting to get in. Mr. Kemp called upon the saints present to get outside and make room for sinners; whereupon a good company of saintly men and women and a larger company of 'lesser lights' got out; and some of them donned sandwich-boards with texts – for example, 'Christ died for the ungodly', in front, and 'Repent ye therefore, and be converted', behind. They sang the Gospel as they marched along Princes Street and back to Charlotte Street, when they held a glorious open-air, and then back to the chapel for a prayer and praise meeting.*

4 Kemp, *Joseph W. Kemp*, p. 26.

*Sandwich boards were a popular means of advertising. No photograph is available of a Chapel march or of a sandwich board with texts, but this picture of the West End of Princes Street in 1900 shows their potential for publicity.*

This reminded some members of an evening during the Torrey mission in 1903, when the building was full to capacity. The evangelist came to the platform, before the meeting started, and asked all who were 'saved' to stand up. A large number did so; he asked them to vacate their places, to make room for the 'unsaved' who were waiting outside.

## Consequences of the Revival

### Increased membership

In his annual report for 1905, the church secretary recalled his corresponding report to the church only four years earlier, where he had said: 'we are passing through a crisis in the history of this Church. We are without a pastor. Our membership is not what it was, nor our finances, nor our activity in Christian work. A spirit of despondency prevails, and our future is wrapped in uncertainty and clouded with gloom.' He now reported:

*During the past twelve months, 203 new members have been received, 142 by baptism and 61 by transfer; deducting 28 losses by death, transfer, etc., we have a net gain for the year of 175.... Four years ago the membership was about 100, now it is 520. The attendances at all the services have shown a gratifying increase week by week. At the morning services on Lord's Day, the area of the Church has been filled, while the gallery has been nearly full. At the evening services the Church has been invariably crowded. The School of Bible Study conducted by the Pastor on Sunday afternoons, has an average attendance of about 200. The numbers attending the week-night services on Thursday evenings have risen from 100 to 270. It is worthy of note that the Church has been open for Gospel work from the 1st of January 1905 to the present date – March 1906 – and the meetings still go on.*

5 'Handbook', 1906, p. 8.

### Increased activity

One of the marks of evangelicals is activity – doing things. Even at the height of the Revival, the ward services in Edinburgh Royal Infirmary, the Sunday School, Joseph Kemp's Sunday afternoon School of Bible Study, the Young Men's Wednesday meeting, the Thursday evening Bible School, and many more, were well supported – although perhaps there was less speaking and more praying. Joseph

Kemp wrote in February 1906: 'For more than a year, open-air services have been held at Charlotte Street corner every night, very often twice during the same evening.... nobly supported by the bravest band of workers any Church could desire.' How could regular, routine meetings be maintained during the Revival? As just mentioned, the membership was over five hundred in 1905, and the largest of the Revival prayer meetings was attended by about two hundred, so (perhaps) several hundred made prayer their priority and several hundred others responded to the Revival with increased activity.

*The Chapel had a lending library, containing over four hundred missionary and theological works, housed in these bookcases. Through the open door of the bookroom (left picture) is a glimpse of the librarian's room (right picture).*

## Increased giving

Not only was there spiritual blessing throughout 1905, but Joseph Kemp's teaching on the importance of giving a tithe (one tenth of one's income) to the Lord's work resulted in a healthy surplus on all the Church accounts. Regular offerings (weekly, monthly and half-yearly) totalled £484 for 1905, while expenditure (rounded to the nearest pound) was £250 for the pastor's stipend, £4 for pulpit supply, £36 for repairs to the building, £24 for new furnishings, £40 for the chapel keeper's salary, £36 for coal and gas, £14 for advertising, £7 for insurance, £2 for stationery, £8 for hymn books for visitors and for the choir, £10 for the painting reserve and £17 for miscellaneous items, which totalled £448 and gave a surplus of £36 for the year. These figures seem modest now, but railway workers earned £69 a year, and road menders £45. Women earned rather less than half the average male wage.

## Special funds

In addition to the regular offerings, there were three special funds: (1) The annual Thankoffering for the upkeep of the premises brought in £54 in 1905; it was spent on new pew cushions, repairs to the chapel-keeper's house and the purchase of a new electric lantern. (2) The Fellowship offering, after the weekly communion service, had two purposes; £51 was given in 1905, of which £12 met the cost of the communion elements and the balance was distributed in confidence among members in financial need. (3) The Special Services Fund attracted £133 in 1905, through free-will offerings, and covered the cost of employing evangelists (£47), the rent of the Grand Theatre (£20), advertising, including making a new sandwich board (£32), printing and publications (£13) and 'help to needy cases and cost of social meetings' (£14).

A further £100 was divided among six overseas missionary societies and three home missions, and £6 was sent to the Edinburgh Royal Infirmary. The weekly offerings at the School of Bible Study (total, £11) were disbursed in the same proportions, but the Sunday School sent all their collections, totalling £6, overseas.

## Baptism and the Lord's Supper

*The ordinance of Believers' Baptism is administered the last Lord's Day of each month, to those who desire it, on a credible profession of their faith in our Lord Jesus Christ. Friends desiring baptism can see the Pastor at the close of any of the evening meetings, or on Monday evening in the vestry from 6 to 8 o'clock.*

6 'Handbook', 1906, pp. 23-4.

From 1908 onward, baptisms were held monthly on Thursday evening, not Sunday evening.

*The Lord's Supper is observed every Lord's Day, after the morning service, and is open to all believers. Non-attendance at the Lord's Table for a period of six months consecutively, without sufficient reason, is regarded as an actual departure from fellowship, and involves the absentee's liability to have his or her name removed from the Roll of the Church.*

7 'Handbook', 1906, pp. 23-4.

## Three assistant ministers

James Johnstone was one of the young Chapel men deeply influenced by the Revival of 1905. The work had grown so rapidly that the annual meeting in February 1906 invited him to become the assistant to the pastor – with the title Congregational/Chapel Missionary. He began right away and proved a valued helper until he left in September 1906, to study at the Bible Training Institute in Glasgow. On completion of his course, in the summer of 1908, he accepted a 'call' to a Presbyterian church in Queensland, Australia.

*James Johnstone was the first assistant to Joseph Kemp, from February to September 1906, with the title Congregational or Chapel Missionary.*

Another young Chapel man, James Scott, who had also matured in the 1905 Revival, took his place. He was already a deacon, and had trained for full-time service at the Moody Bible Institute in Chicago. He served as assistant to the pastor from 1906 and more will be said about him later. When he went to be the pastor of the New Prestwick Baptist Church in 1912, a third Chapel member, Archibald Jack, who had also been involved in the 1905 Revival, was appointed in his place.

*James Scott and Archibald Jack who, together with James Johnstone, matured in the Christian faith during the 1905 Revival. They served successively as assistants to the pastor – Johnstone in 1906, Scott from November 1906 to 1912 and Jack from 1912 to 1913.*

Although Joseph Kemp was fully committed to Charlotte Chapel, he found time to contribute to the wider Baptist scene. He travelled throughout Scotland, giving talks on the Welsh Revival, illustrated by lanternslides, and got as far as Woolwich, in London:

*Rev. Joseph W. Kemp, of Charlotte Chapel, Edinburgh, has been with us for a week. He came to preach our Mission Sermons, and knowing his love for work we provided him with full opportunity for the use of his gifts. He preached four times on Sunday, and taught us to sing, 'Step by Step to the Glory Land': and commencing on the Saturday night he gave us lantern lectures on the following subjects: – 'The Welsh Revival', 'Delia, or Transformation by Grace', 'Down in Water Street' and 'D. L. Moody'.*

8 *Record*, 1908, p. 74.

## 1906

### Generally accepted Church lines

'By the end of the year 1905' (Kemp's phrase), the Revival was over; it is difficult to be more precise, but in December Joseph Kemp was 're-organizing the work in the Chapel on generally accepted Church lines.' One of Scotland's best-known evangelists conducted a traditional mission in the Chapel. On Sunday, the church was crowded at night, but numbers during the week were not large; nevertheless, some men and women accepted the Saviour. Joseph Kemp commented that while 1906 was a year of advance, it was not like the blessings of 1905.

Nor was there the same enthusiasm. Andrew Urquhart drew attention in his 1906 annual report to those 'whose clocks or whose movements are somehow generally on the slow side, and who come in late' on Sunday morning. In December of the same year, Joseph Kemp wrote the editorial for the first edition of the Chapel magazine, the *Record*, due out on 1 January 1907: 'It would be an excellent thing if this New Year's resolutions included this one … "not to be late to the Forenoon Service on the Lord' Day".… On a recent Lord's Day, some of our members were coming in at 11.20.… To the Evening Service, let friends come when they can, and be sure to bring some one with them.'

Before these words appeared in print, a second Revival had come to the Chapel, as described in the next chapter, disrupting all 'generally accepted' plans for January. Nevertheless, that public rebuke is worth noting for two reasons. First, the choice of the word 'members' for the morning and 'friends' for the evening is a reminder of the different emphases in the two services. Secondly, it illustrates Joseph Kemp's blunt, direct, and sometimes abrasive, way of speaking his mind; part of his wife's ministry was to smooth ruffled feathers.

## A typical week

Although Joseph Kemp described 1906 as back to normal, his definition of normality was: 'the Chapel is open every night and Gospel work, both indoors and outdoors, is engaged in without so much as a solitary break for one night.' A typical week in the Chapel in 1906 was:

SUNDAY

| | |
|---|---|
| 7 a.m. | prayer meeting |
| 10 a.m. | prayer meeting |
| 11 a.m. | morning service: Exposition of the Word |
| 2:15 p.m. | Sunday School |
| 2:45 p.m. | open-air meeting |
| 3:15 p.m. | Lads Bible Class |
| 3:15 p.m. | School of Bible Study |
| 5:45 p.m. | prayer meeting |
| 6 p.m. | prayer meeting for children |
| 6 p.m. | open-air meeting |
| 6:30 p.m. | evening service: Evangelistic Meeting |
| 8 p.m. | open-air meeting |
| 9 p.m. | meeting following open-air |

MONDAY

| | |
|---|---|
| 6-8 p.m. | pastor in vestry |
| 8 p.m. | prayer and testimony (winter) |
| 8 p.m. | open-air meeting (summer) |

TUESDAY

| | |
|---|---|
| 7 p.m. | Children's meeting |
| 8 p.m. | open-air (summer) |
| 7-9 p.m. | Girls Missionary Auxiliary |
| 8 p.m. | open-air meeting (summer) |

WEDNESDAY

| | |
|---|---|
| 3 p.m. | Women's Prayer Meeting |
| 7 p.m. | prayer meeting – half-hour |
| 8 p.m. | Young Men's Bible and Missionary Training Class (winter) |
| 8 p.m. | open-air meeting (summer) |

THURSDAY

| | |
|---|---|
| 7 p.m. | prayer meeting – half-hour |
| 8 p.m. | Bible lecture by pastor |

FRIDAY

| | |
|---|---|
| 8 p.m. | prayer, praise and testimony meeting |
| 8 p.m. | choir practice |
| 8 p.m. | open-air meeting (summer) |
| 8 p.m. | Lads Class |

SATURDAY

| | |
|---|---|
| 3:30 p.m. | Monthly conference |
| 7 p.m. | prayer meeting – half-hour |
| 8 p.m. | Song, Scene and Story (evangelistic) |
| 8 p.m. | open-air meeting (summer) |

*Princes Street after a snowfall in 1906 (painting). Chapel members on the east of the city walked or rode along it seven days a week, sometimes more than once a day, to get to the Chapel services.*

## Membership

The church roll in April 1906, that is a year after the combined revival meeting and baptismal service on 16 March 1905, mentioned above, was 519. Discounting 32 (27 women and 5 men), who lived too far away from Edinburgh to attend regularly, the membership consisted of 359 women and 128 men. Of these, 59 were married to another member and 18 of the couples had one or more children, living at home, also in membership. There were 21 single-parent families, widows with children in membership living at home – in one case, three boys and two daughters. There were 84 women and 9 men in service, several to families in membership of the Chapel.

## Girls Missionary Auxiliary

Women of prayer are generally women of action; prayer guides them towards many ways of loving and helping others. In October 1905, under the leadership of Mrs Kemp, a meeting was held in the home of Mrs Christian Urquhart (Andrew's wife), to pray and work for Foreign Missions. Two years later, Mrs Urquhart reported: 'The Girls Missionary Auxiliary meets for two hours weekly on Tuesdays and a busier and more attractive hive of industry you could not wish to see. Their chief business is the making of garments for women and children in some corner of the mission field.' Before long, they were supplying missionaries all over the world.

As the girls grew older, and younger ones joined, a Women's Missionary Auxiliary was formed as well, and then, in 1916, a Junior Girls Missionary Auxiliary, which met every other Saturday, with 30 girls from 10 to 17 years of age. More will be said about all three in Chapters 28, 37 and 49, as they formed a significant base for the Chapel's missionary interest.

## Further reviving

Towards the close of 1906, there were indications that the Lord was about to move again in Revival. Joseph Kemp was surprised, but delighted:

*Thinking that the movement had found its level, arrangements were made [in 1906] to reorganize the work on generally accepted church lines. But again the revival fires blazed forth, and the meetings became marked by a deeper outgoing of the soul to God in prayer than ever, and a passionately expressed desire for the salvation of men was a dominant feature of it.*

9 *Sunday School Times*, 19 June 1915, p. 363.

The burden for prayer became heavy and the 7 a.m. prayer meeting on Sunday morning often started an hour earlier, despite most people having to come from some distance on foot. Not only did attendance at this meeting increase, but also a deepening spirit of prayer. This was evident in the weeknight meetings also, with (as Kemp put it in the quotation above) a passionately expressed desire for the salvation of outsiders as a dominant feature. The church secretary commented:

*What am I to report about our wonderful Prayer Meetings? Did ever any one see such meetings? They used to begin at seven o'clock on Sunday mornings, but that was felt to be far too late in the day for the great business that had to be transacted before the Throne of the Heavenly Grace! The meetings now begin at six o'clock and go on for almost seven days a week, with occasional intervals to attend to business, household duties, and bodily sustenance! Some of you who are strangers may smile – many of us did – but we don't now. It is that continuous, persevering, God-honouring weekly campaign of prayer that has moved the mighty hand of God to pour upon this favoured people the blessings of His grace in such rich abundance; and if ever you should be asked the secret of this church's great spiritual prosperity, you can tell them of the prayer meetings, and especially of the gatherings of God's people – forty to sixty strong – in the Upper Vestry every Sunday morning at six or seven o'clock – summer and winter, wet day and fine – to pray. Yes, that is the secret – the secret of our church's success and prosperity.*

10 *Record*, 1907, p. 55.

On Saturday 20 December 1906, the Chapel's monthly afternoon and evening conference was addressed by a deputation of students from Joseph Kemp's former college, the Bible Training Institute in Glasgow. After hearing about Revival at the Moody Bible Institute in Chicago, they had experienced a quickening in their own hearts, and they spoke about Revival. This awakened memories for many at the conference. Some could not sleep on that Saturday night for thinking about it and others, who had not been at the Saturday meetings, also felt, as Sunday approached, that the Lord was about to work again. Before Sunday was over, Revival had come for a second time to Rose Street.

## Chapter 14
The 1905 Revival (1905–1906)

107      Additional information on the following topics,
mentioned in this chapter, is available on the CD.

Anniversaries and Thankofferings
Archibald B. Jack
Children's meetings under Joseph Kemp
Choir
Girls Missionary Auxiliary
James Johnstone
James Scott
Joseph Kemp after Charlotte Chapel
Joseph Kemp's writings on Revival (collected) (for article in
the *Sunday School Times*)
Joseph Kemp's School of Bible Study
Lads' Bible Class
Membership
Monthly conference
Overseas mission
Song, Scene and Story
Sources of Income for Maintenance of Public Worship
(1906).
Women's Prayer Meeting
Women's Missionary Auxiliary
Worldliness
Young Peoples Meeting

# Chapter 15
# The 1907 Revival

## Start of the second Revival

### Sunday 21 December 1906

Earnest prayer, and a passionate desire for the salvation of outsiders, characterized the services on Sunday 21 December; many were also aware of personal dealings – Jacob-like – with God alone. At the late prayer meeting, held that evening at 9.30 p.m, the fire of God again fell. There was nothing, humanly speaking, to account for what happened. Quite suddenly, an overwhelming sense of God's presence came on one and another. Prayer was spontaneous and gained in intensity. People sang on their knees and prayed, oblivious of one another, then sang together, then prayer broke out again, waves and waves of prayer. In no time it was midnight – the hours had passed like minutes. One who was present said:

*I cannot tell you what Christ was to me last night in the late meeting. My heart was full to overflowing. If ever my Lord was near to me, it was last night. It is useless being a spectator looking on, or praying for it, in order to catch its spirit and breath. It is necessary to be in it, praying in it, part of it, caught by the same power, swept by the same wind.*

1 Kemp, *Joseph W. Kemp*, p. 32.

### Hogmanay

Early on the last night of 1906, a large congregation gathered for prayer, and continued in prayer until the Watchnight service started at 10.30 p.m. Joseph Kemp wrote:

*At that meeting, the power of the Lord was again manifest. What the closing hours of 1906 meant to many, only the Eternal Day will reveal. Crushed, broken, and penitent on account of the defeated past, many of us again knelt at the Cross; and as the bells rang in the New Year, we vowed by God's grace to press into our lives more service for Him, to be more like Him in spirit and walk, and win to Him our fellowmen.*

2 Kemp, *Joseph W. Kemp*, p. 32.

Kemp's three vows sum up the priorities of these Revival meetings – (1) to do more (activism), (2) to be more like Christ (devotion) and (3) to win more (evangelism).

### New Year's Day 1907

The Chapel was open all day on Thursday 1 January 1907; meetings were held at 11 a.m., 3 p.m. and 6.30 p.m. Then, as now, the pastor chose a Verse for the Year and preached on it at the first service in the new year. For 1907, it was: 'My presence shall go with thee, and I will give thee rest' (Exodus 33:14), which was felt to be particularly appropriate. The afternoon meeting departed from the planned programme and became a time of prayer, confession, testimony and praise. The evening meeting went on without the guidance of any human hand; although speakers had been invited to address it, no address could be given. The congregation bowed in prayer, heart-searching and contrition, and God's presence was very real to all present. A number of unconverted people decided for Christ, but the burden of the meeting was that judgement must begin at the house of God.

One Sunday morning in January 1907, Mr Kemp said: 'I cannot preach this morning; the Holy Spirit has said I am not to preach this morning.' One of the elders rose and led in prayer; others followed, and the prayers went on and on. When they stopped, 30 people testified that they had been born again that morning.

### Simultaneous prayer

A half-night of prayer was held on Sunday 13 January. Mr Kemp reported:

*to the curious the meetings appear disorderly; but to those who are in them and of them, there is order in the midst of disorder. The confusion never gets confused; the meetings are held by invisible hands. Believers have been awakened to a sense of having lived defeated lives ... Over all these things victory has been claimed. Brethren have been reconciled to one another; differences which kept sisters apart have been destroyed.... While the work has been chiefly confined to the saints of God, purifying, humbling, purging, cleansing, there have been numerous conversions.*

2 *Record*, February 1907, pp. 20-4.

He went on to explain how so many could pray at the same time at these meetings:

*One does not readily take in the meaning of simultaneous praying, in a meeting of from 100 to 200 people, full to overflowing of a strong desire to pour out their hearts before the Lord. How would there possibly be time for each to pray separately? After all what need is there to wait? As Evan Roberts used to say in Wales, 'If we pray to one another, then only one at a time; but if we pray to God, what does it matter how many pray at once?' His ear finds no difficulty in dealing with the simultaneous prayer of a revival meeting.*

_____

3 *Record*, February 1907, pp. 20-4.

If there was simultaneous praying, in a meeting of from 100 to 200 people, it must have been in the church itself, because there was nowhere else in the building for such a number to meet. On other occasions, several rooms were used at the same time:

*The 5.45 p.m. prayer meeting starts at 5.30, and such has been the power of God in the meetings that it has been impossible to get to the open air at the usual hour, the Upper Vestry and the Pastor's Vestry and the Library all crowded with praying people.*

_____

4 *Record*, 1907, p. 35.

### Features of the Revivals

In 1905, the emphasis (certainly in the reporting) was on packed public meetings and many conversions, starting with the conference on Saturday 22 January 1905 and including marches along Princes Street. The emphasis in 1907 (at least in the reporting) was on the prayer meetings, starting with the evening of Sunday 21 December 1906. Joseph Kemp noted three features of the eight weeks of the 1907 movement – there were only eight weeks, as explained below. He wrote that the features of the 1907 Revival were:

(1) A deep conviction of sin, even where the outward life appeared blameless.

(2) Prolonged intercession. The Sunday prayer meeting started at 6 a.m. instead of 7 a.m. and continued until 8 a.m.. At 9.30 p.m., after the Sunday services were over, about 60 met again for prayer and continued until after midnight.

*Not only have lengthened meetings been a feature of the work, but the gift of prolonged intercession has been given to*

*several brethren. Losing all consciousness of another's presence, the soul has poured itself out, often audibly, for over an hour. One brother, unknown to any of us, prayed in an agony for the people of his own town for fully an hour and a half. The perspiration was standing on his brow like beads. He was almost too weak to stand when the hour came for closing the chapel, and was literally lifted from his position.*

_____

5 *Record*, 1907, p. 3.

(3) Many who never prayed in public before found it easy to do so. 'Prayer at such meetings is not a mere perfunctory exercise, cold and meaningless, but a living vital reality.'

Did the Charlotte Chapel Revivals included 'speaking in tongues'? The records give no indication of it, and disapproval of *glossolalia* clearly comes through a report in the 1907 *Record* about a contemporary awakening in Norway: 'much "speaking with tongues" (so-called) and much disorder.'

The Revivals in the Chapel were therefore different from the near-contemporary movements in America, now called Pentecostalism, starting in Topeka, Kansas, in 1901 and in Azuza Street, Los Angeles, in 1906. Speaking in tongues was there identified as evidence of baptism in the Holy Spirit, which was generally rejected by the established churches at that stage, resulting in the formation of distinctive Pentecostal denominations like the Church of the Nazarene and the Assemblies of God. The Pentecostal movement first came to the United Kingdom in the second half of 1907, at All Saints Anglican Church, Monkwearmouth, near Sunderland; between September 1907 and April 1908, about five hundred people were 'baptized in the Holy Spirit' in that church. Pentecostalism then spread rapidly round the world – Pentecostals were, and still are, remarkably successful at rural and urban evangelism.

## End of the second Revival

### Sunday 24 February 1907

The last special movement of God's Spirit in Revival in the Chapel seems to have been on Sunday evening, 24 February, although conversions and deepening of spiritual life went on throughout 1907 and beyond – 'revival' in the broader sense of the word.

A whole night of prayer had been arranged for Saturday/Sunday, 16/17 February. Beginning at ten o'clock at night, the meeting continued until eight o'clock the next morning. The only break was at 2 a.m., when tea was served. Over two hundred were present until then, and more than 150 remained for the whole night:

*From the beginning to the close the prayers ascended in one unbroken continuity. At times the prayers rose and fell like the waves of the sea. At half-past three in the morning the scenes were bewildering to behold. It seemed as though everybody in the meeting was praying at once. There was no confusion, nothing unseemly. The passion of prayer had caught the people, and we felt we must pray. We entered upon our work on Lord's Day morning with high hopes and expectancy, but as is often the case, our faith was put to the test, for the Lord's Day passed without any seeming blessing. We had looked for a great ingathering of souls, which did not come. But our prayers were not lost. We had complied with the conditions, and we felt justified in continuing to wait. The Lord's Day following [Sunday 24 February], over a score of souls professed faith in Christ.*

---

6 *Record*, 1907, p. 51.

So, they expected a harvest of souls on Sunday 17 February – but nothing happened. The phrase 'We had complied with the conditions' explains their perplexity, after praying through the previous night. The following Sunday, 24 February, was the fifth anniversary of Joseph Kemp's coming to the Chapel. (In fact, he started on 2 February 1902, but anniversaries were flexible). There were more than 20 conversions. The people who had been disappointed on the previous Sunday said, in effect: 'the good Lord simply kept us waiting for a week, and then answered our prayers.'

### Why select 24 February?

Five scattered events seem to point, collectively, to Sunday evening, 24 February 1907, as the last Revival in Charlotte Chapel.

(1) Joseph Kemp continued to plead for 'blessing'. The first recorded answer to his prayers came over a weekend in February 1908, which he described in the March *Record*:

'Much warmth has been felt in some of our prayer meetings recently, reminding us of the gracious seasons enjoyed a little over a year ago.' A little over a year back from early March 1908 is late February 1907.

(2) In April 1907, Kemp gave a lecture on the Welsh Revival in the Tent Hall, Glasgow, and commented: 'the recital made us long for a return of the movement' – implying that there was no current 'movement' in the Chapel.

(3) In December 1908, a missionary on furlough spoke about revival in China. Joseph Kemp, as editor of the *Record*, commented on it in January 1909, and added: 'it reminded us of the Revival season of two years ago, when God visited us in the Chapel. Oh Lord, wilt thou not revive us again.' In other words, there had been no Revival since 'two years ago', i.e. early 1907.

(4) It is an argument from silence, but there are no further records of nights of prayer or of experiences like those in the first eight weeks of 1907.

(5) The church secretary, in preparing his annual report in early February 1907, said: 'meetings … go on for almost seven days a week, with occasional intervals to attend to business, household duties, and bodily sustenance!' After eight weeks, were they simply too exhausted to carry on?

**About the Calendar.**

PASTOR'S
**FIFTH ANNIVERSARY,**
*On February 24th and 25th.*

Mr KEMP will preach on LORD'S DAY, 24TH, at 11 and 6.30.

*MONDAY.* Tea from 7 to 7.45.
Addresses will be given by
**Rev. EDWARD LAST,** Ayr.
**Mr T. F. ARTHUR,**
Tutor, B. J. T., Glasgow.
**THOMAS RAMSAY,** Esq., Maybole.
———
Rev. JOSEPH W. KEMP, presiding.

*The Sunday evening of Joseph Kemp's fifth anniversary seems to have been the last night of Revival in the Chapel, although the Spirit's working continued throughout his ministry in Edinburgh.*

## Marches of witness

There may not have been Revival after February 1907, but the consequences of it continued through the spring of that year. The time between the afternoon and evening meetings of the monthly conference was used for marches of witness.

*At the close of the Saturday monthly conference, we formed ourselves into rank at the Chapel door, and marched along Princes Street – headed by the Hallelujah Army Silver Band – and back, proceeding to Lothian Road, round by Castle Terrace and the Lyceum Theatre, at which place we sang, 'Now none but Christ can satisfy', hoping thereby to strike some heart that is weary of life's pleasures. Returning to Charlotte Street corner a monster open-air meeting was held, after which the usual meeting at eight o'clock.*

---

7 *Record*, 1907, p. 67.

The editor of the *Edinburgh Citizen* newspaper was impressed:

*On Saturday night, May 4th [1907], the workers in connection with Charlotte Chapel held a late march. Leaving Rose Street they marched along Princes Street as far as the Scott Monument, then back to the west end and up Lothian Road. An open-air service was held in the Square at Grindlay Street. Mr R. Aitken gave a short address, after which the demonstration marched back to Charlotte Chapel, where they held an indoor meeting. The body of the chapel was well filled, many drunks having been induced to attend, the service was somewhat lively. The Redeemed Drunkards' Band gave short, pointed testimonies. The life-story of some of these men is simply marvellous, and is proof positive that the day of miracles is not yet past. A religion that can change such men and make them loving husbands and respectable citizens is a religion worth having.*

---

8 *Record*, 1907, p. 84.

## A time of (comparative) declension

Joseph Kemp was aware from the beginning, and warned the Chapel, that:

*All who know anything at all of Revivals know that periods of declension almost invariably follow.... By and by a cooling process begins, the exuberance of feeling is dulled, activity slackens, and meetings lose their freshness and power, the blessing ebbs, conversions are less and less frequent, rivalries appear, and in the end many fall back into apathy and some into sin.*

---

9 *Record*, 1908, p. 91.

By the end of 1907, people spoke nostalgically about Revival in the Chapel as a historical event. The Saturday conference in December 1907 was addressed by students of the Bible Training Institute, whose visit in December 1906 was the prelude to the Revival described above. However, the 1907 conference was much smaller than usual, and was laconically reported in the *Record*: 'The different brethren spoke words suitable to the time of the year, and we trust not without some blessing to the hearers.'

On the same theme, Joseph Kemp had this message for the readers of the *Record* in January 1908:

*It is to be feared that at present the holy fire is burning very low with some of us. Can we not at the opening of another year seek to add on more fuel? Fire is what we need. We want a great many things in our churches to-day, do we not? Some want new pews, some new organs, some new pulpits, and some a different order of service. But we think what is wanted is new fire, fire everywhere, fire in our hearts, fire in our Sabbath Schools, fire in our open air, fire in our services.*

---

10 *Record*, 1908, p. 2.

As Kemp's heartfelt pleas for Revival continued, there were some 'raindrops' of blessing in 1908, although he could not described them as 'showers' (his phraseology). On Friday 14 February, 'the spirit of prayer came upon the few who were gathered, in uncontrollable power, so that for nearly two hours we continued bowed and broken before God. Experiences, all too sacred to put into cold print, were given to many.' On Sunday 1 November, a large group prayed from 9.30 p.m. until midnight: 'God's power was manifested amongst us. Many entered into blessing, and habits which had been hindering Christian progress were, by God's grace, broken off.'

Although the church continued to prosper and to grow (revival), neither in Charlotte Chapel, nor during a fruitful ministry in Auckland, New Zealand, did Joseph Kemp ever again experience Revival. He wrote in 1930:

*We often wonder why revival tarries. For over eighteen months a daily prayer meeting has been held in the Tabernacle, in addition to two or three prayer meetings of the regular order – the burden of all of which has been, 'Wilt Thou not revive us again?' Still the revival tarries. People do not respond so readily now to the appeal as they did twenty-five years ago.*

11 Kemp, *Joseph W. Kemp*, p. 96.

## Follow up

To look after those who had been converted in the spring of 1907, the city was divided into 34 districts, and new believers were assigned to them. Leaders visited the converts, in their homes if possible, to follow up their progress and to offer help in spiritual life. They soon learned the importance of this – where it was not done, some were lost to the church. 'It also brought to light the sad fact that some of those visited had never been truly saved, which gave the visitors a great opportunity for personal evangelism. By far the larger percentage of those visited were found to be genuinely saved'. The new system of visiting young converts in their homes proved very satisfactory throughout 1907, and the visitors found the contacts were a blessing to themselves.

**CHURCH REGISTER.**

| No. at beginning of month | ADDITIONS. | | | | REMOVALS. | | | | | De-crease. | In-crease. | Present Member-ship. |
|---|---|---|---|---|---|---|---|---|---|---|---|---|
| | Bap-tism. | Trans-fer. | Depu-tation. | Tl. | Trans-fer. | Revi-sion. | Resig-nation. | Death. | Tl. | | | |
| 601 | 18 | 5 | | 23 | 3 | 8 | | 1 | 12 | | 11 | 612 |

*The* Record *gave statistics, but not names, on a monthly basis; this is the entry for June 1907.*

Sixty-seven of those welcomed into membership at the monthly communion services during the year 1907 came by baptism, and 42 in the year 1908. However, figures from later in Joseph Kemp's ministry in Edinburgh (below) suggest that less than one in four of the converts in the 1907 Revival settled in this particular church. Joseph Kemp gave details of those who joined, but he refused to say how many were converted. He explained, in an editorial in the *Record*: 'if we yielded to the temptation to publish statistics of those who have professed faith in Christ in our midst, we might be able to make a gratifying report, but we are content that "wonders have been wrought through the name of His Holy Child, Jesus." The praise be to Himself alone.' Statistics are available for the last three years of Mr Kemp's ministry, and they were:

1913 – 170 converted,
of whom joined 43 joined Charlotte Chapel

1914 – 131,
of whom 40 joined

1915 – over 100,
of whom 20 joined

## Joseph Kemp's antidote to Modernism

Joseph Kemp knew that when Revival brought life to a church, theological Modernism in that same church could rapidly undo the Spirit's work. In 1907 and again in 1908, he invited a proto-fundamentalist, James Gray, Dean of Moody Bible Institute in Chicago, to conduct a Summer School of Bible Study in the Chapel, with teaching on: 'Is Jesus God or Man?' and 'Is the Bible the Word of God?' He described these lectures as 'a tremendous counterblast to the New Theology'. Kemp himself denounced Modernism from the pulpit, condemning those who impugned the deity of Christ and questioned the integrity of Scripture. He vigorously defended biblical literalism, pre-millennial dispensationalism and the Keswick holiness movement. When statistics indicated that 'the numbers attending our churches are growing less and less,' he said that the remedy was for the 'pew and the pulpit':

*to return to the old truths ... the old words of scripture ... the ancient doctrines ... we must get back to the words of 'the cross', 'the Blood' ... we must emphasise 'sin' its heinousness, deceitfulness, and the awful judgement God has pronounced over it. There must be no two opinions regarding heaven and hell ... there is no need for us to depart from our doctrinal basis ... we shall hold forth the Atonement of Christ as the only hope for precious souls.*

12 *Record*, November 1908.

## Three enduring innovations

### The *Record*

In January 1907, the Chapel began a monthly magazine, the *Record*. It not only reported 'the doings of the Church' (hence its title), but it also promoted 'those things which are most surely believed among us'. This was achieved by printing full notes from the Sunday afternoon School of Bible Study and extended notes of the Thursday evening Bible lectures. The initial price was one penny per copy. Although it was (and still is) greatly appreciated, it has nearly always needed a large subsidy. At the end of the first year, the price was held at one penny, although there was a deficit of over £17; donations were invited, but only three were received and they totalled less than £1.

After three years, the editor reported that circulation was steady, but unless it could be increased, the *Record* would be a constant strain on church funds; he questioned whether it could continue. (It is still going, still subsidized.) He apologized for the number of advertisements, and said that he wanted to dispense with them, 'but this our means will not allow.' The *Scottish Baptist Magazine* had the same problem, and adopted the same remedy.

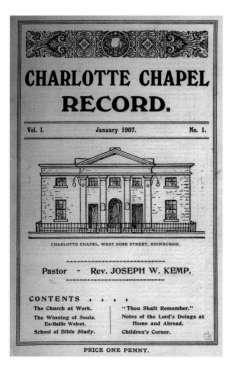

*The* Charlotte Chapel Record *began publication in January 1907, as this first cover shows. It has proved its worth over the years, and still has a worldwide circulation.*

### Deaconess

In 1907, the Chapel gratefully accepted an offer partially to support a deaconess – the church undertook to meet the balance of her salary. Miss Elizabeth Boyle was appointed. She was an Edinburgh businesswoman, a member of the Chapel, already active as a worker and a soul-winner. Apart from a year in New York with the Kemps, in 1916-17, and two short appointments elsewhere on her return to Britain, she served the Chapel in this office for 36 years. Her duties snowballed – visiting the sick and needy members of the congregation, and going round the houses in Rose Street. Every year, as she gave her report, the listeners' minds reeled with the statistics of hundreds of visits made, scores of garments distributed, and meetings addressed. In addition, she dealt with the Chapel's clerical work, kept the membership roll, and typed and produced the monthly *Record*.

*Miss Elizabeth Boyle, the first Chapel deaconess. Her hat may seem substantial, but compare it to the one worn by the lady beside the taxi with Joseph Kemp. Another photograph of her, in 1922, when she was reappointed as deaconess (Chapter 25), is much more relaxed.*

Two meetings grew out of her work, and both outlived her leadership of them. The pathos of many Rose Street homes captured her heart, so she started a weekly kitchen meeting on Tuesday evening, in the home of two Chapel members who lived in Rose Street. It was known officially as the District Women's Meeting, and attracted between 30 and 40. Lizzie (as everyone called her) had a vital ministry among young women caught up in sordid haunts of sin, from which, by the grace of God, she was able to rescue some.

Secondly, she started a Girls Own Fellowship, on Sunday afternoon. This was for girls who had come to Edinburgh for domestic service in the houses of the New Town. Many were from the Highlands and Islands and the Borders, and most of them had nowhere to go on their Sunday afternoon off. They welcomed the opportunity of friendship and company in the Chapel and a large number were converted. Until the 1970s, a similar meeting, the successor of the Girls Own Fellowship, was held in the Chapel, attended by women who had started coming in their teens. Some of them told the writer that until they heard about the Fellowship, they used to sit in the waiting rooms of the railway stations, as they had nowhere else to pass their free time.

### Monday evening prayer meeting

On 28 September 1907, the deacons decided to begin a meeting on Monday evening, devoted exclusively to prayer, and that there should be no collection at it. This soon became one of the most significant focal points in the life of the church, and remained so for 90 years. Everything else was subordinated to it, and successive church secretaries refused to publicize any outside activity planned for a Monday evening. The pastor's day off, and the caretaker's day off, was Tuesday. Graham Scroggie built on this foundation by extending the meeting for 15 minutes, and giving a short Bible study.

The writer was both amused and impressed when attending a parents' evening one Tuesday in 1977, to have a chat with ten-year-old Jeremy's schoolteacher. Noticing that all the other parents had surnames in the second half of the alphabet, he asked whether he had come on the wrong night. The teacher, equally amused and impressed, replied that when she told the class that parents with surnames from A to L were to come on Monday, Jeremy replied in alarm: 'but that's the night of the church prayer meeting'; she changed his evening to Tuesday.

## Wider concerns

### Pastoral work

Joseph Kemp was determined, among all the other claims on his time, to visit promptly everyone in the congregation who was ill. He kept a book in the vestibule of the Chapel, and exhorted members to notify him, through it, about all cases of sickness. Mrs Kemp's health was very poor during the winter of 1906-7, and this must have been especially worrying to the pastor at the time of the Revival. She was confined to bed for six months, and at one stage there was serious concern for her. By the late spring, she was able to leave the house briefly, and after a time of recuperation in her native Kelso, she was fit to join her husband on their first visit to Canada and the United States in July (below).

In February 1907, the deacons recognized 'the exceptional amount of correspondence and other writing which the Pastor has to undertake in connection with the work of the congregation', and bought him a typewriter. Moving equally rapidly with new technology, they obtained a 'telephone installation' for the manse in September 1908. Choosing the best package for a phone was a problem even then – they debated whether to have three hundred calls per year for £5 3s (£5.15), or to go for an 'unlimited service system'.

The hard-of-hearing in the congregation learned about 'the accousticant telephone package for the deaf', installed in Westminster Chapel, London, and asked if they could have one too, to help them hear the preacher. The deacons were enthusiastic until they discovered that the cost was £50, and no further action was taken. They did, however, buy a bicycle for the pastor's assistant, as 'it would be a considerable aid to him in visitation'.

### Joseph Kemp's first visit to America

During July and August 1907, Mr and Mrs Kemp made their first visit to Canada and the United States of America. They sailed from Liverpool on 21 June, for preaching and lecturing engagements in Montreal, Toronto, Niagara Falls, Chicago, New York and Boston, returning home on 5 September. They found that 'the news of God's goodness to the Chapel had travelled across the Atlantic', and they were asked many questions about the Revivals in Edinburgh.

How did the Chapel fare during the first extended absence of Joseph Kemp? Surprisingly well. Attendance at the Sunday early-morning prayer meeting was less during the month of August, but that was attributed to the holiday season. Numbers at the Sunday services, conducted by visiting ministers, remained high throughout July and August, and the evening attendances were exceedingly good. The Thursday evening Bible School, normally taken by Mr Kemp, was exceptionally good throughout the summer. Several professed faith in Christ at the open-air meetings, which were carried on nightly throughout the summer, and began to attend the Chapel services. Open-airs were also held at Portobello on Saturday afternoon, when attendance and attention was good.

*In June 1907, the Chapel 'recommenced the sand services at Portobello every Saturday afternoon' and continued them throughout the summer. The upper photograph was taken in 1907; present readers may find it incredible that the lower picture was taken in July 1952.*

Visitors from England are sometimes surprised, to this day, that Scottish Sunday Schools, and many other church activities, close for the summer. In 1907, the Sunday School did not resume until the last Sunday in September, and the monthly conference re-convened on the last Saturday in October. Joseph Kemp instituted a Bible conference for the whole of the first week of October every year, saying: 'October is the month that can give the tone to all our winter's work.'

## The New Building Scheme

### Need for a new building

With so much activity, there was no doubt that the centenary of the first meeting in Richmond Court on 24 January 1808 would be worthily celebrated. There was only one complaint – that the building was inadequate for the crowds now attending the Chapel. Not only was it too small, but it was unsanitary and in need of constant repair. On Monday 17 June 1907, the half-yearly church meeting accepted the deacons' recommendation that a New Building Scheme should be launched. 'We must expand or go back', said Mr Urquhart. 'Certain meetings have outgrown the accommodation and others cannot be held for lack of proper room. The Sabbath School has been in difficulty for years, having to meet in the church when it ought to have a proper suite of rooms.'

It was estimated that a new building on the same site would cost £10,000. The office-bearers prayerfully considered how to raise this. They immediately decided that there should be no bazaars or sales of work; the project was to be committed to the Lord in prayer, and his people informed of the need. Differing in this respect from Christopher Anderson, Mr Kemp was emphatic that the new building should open free of debt. The church meeting went further, and resolved that work should not start until the money for the new building was in the bank. Later in the meeting, the Kemps were presented with a love-gift of £25, as they were about to visit North America; Mr Kemp handed the gift back to the church, as the first donation for the New Building Scheme.

Others were not so quick to respond; contributions came in painfully slowly. The church treasurer kept reminding the congregation that work could not commence until the money was in hand, but the New Building Scheme scarcely moved. After six months of appeals, the total was £152. The project seemed to be dead. The congregation had no option but to celebrate the centenary in the old premises. The centenary deserves a chapter to itself, and then, after a look at the years 1909 and 1910, the progress of the building fund will be taken up in Chapter 18.

*Christopher Anderson added an extension to the back of the Chapel, when he purchased it in 1818, with a vestry, parlour, prayer room and bookroom. By 1907, they were too small for the crowds now attending, and also in need of constant repair. The photograph on the back wall of this (typical) room is of Thomas Way, minister from 1888-96.*

## Autumn 1907

It is difficult to make a balanced assessment of the spiritual state of the Chapel in the autumn of 1907. Editorials in the *Record*, written by Joseph Kemp himself, contain both chiding and praise in equal measure. The lack of support for the building project was mirrored by apparent apathy during a fortnight of special meetings in October. Kemp, who was never slow to speak his mind, challenged the congregation in the November *Record*:

*Our brother has been with us for fully two weeks and conducted meetings every night; he also gave Bible readings each afternoon, Saturdays excepted. The afternoon meetings were not very large, but many of those who came testified to the timeliness of our brother's messages. The evening meetings in point of attendances were much below what we desired.... We have never had a mission when so few unconverted people have been gathered in.*

13 *Record*, 1907, p. 163.

This may have been a wake-up call to the Chapel, as Joseph Kemp was back to his more optimistic self by December:

*Very encouraging meetings have been held on Sunday nights at 9 o'clock. Altho' the hour is late, it has not been too late for several hundreds to meet. After the 8 o'clock open-air service, the march chapelwards brings many unconverted to this late meeting.... If home duties or kindred ties claim your attention*

*at this late hour, as doubtless is the case with many, then lift your heart to God for those of us who, 'in season and out of season' are seeking to rescue the perishing.*

14 *Record*, 1907, p. 179.

In addition to the Chapel's outreach to adults, there was a commendable concern for children, both in the weekly Sunday School, which had record attendances in the autumn of 1907, and in children's meetings on Tuesday evening. However, following Joseph Kemp's praise and thanks for these gatherings, he concluded the next editorial with his severest-ever indictment of some Chapel members:

*In many departments our workers are thinning out. Many have recently been transferred to distant places, some have grown weary and have fallen out, while not a few have made over their energies to outside causes. All this is weakening to the church. To find office-bearers and church members sitting in other churches while their seats in their own church are vacant is, to say the least, disquieting and discouraging. On a recent Lord's Day evening [January 1908], workers from the Chapel were to be found at nearly a dozen places, some serving, others seeing.... matters are serious when the church work is undermanned.*

15 *Record*, 1908, p. 16

With this mixture of 'well done' and 'not good enough', the Chapel entered its centenary year.

Additional information on the following topics, mentioned in this chapter, is available on the CD.

Bible Conference
Charlotte Chapel as an Episcopal church
Deaconess
Joseph Kemp's appreciation of Ira D. Sankey
Joseph Kemp's seven visits to America
Joseph Kemp's writings on Revival (collected)
Kitchen meetings
New Building Scheme
Summer School of Bible Study
Sunday School statistics

# Chapter 16
## Centenary year (1908)

### January and February

#### Crowded services

Despite Joseph Kemp's anxiety over the state of the church (end of the last chapter), many in the Chapel were excited by the closing days of 1907 and the opening hours of 1908. At the morning service on Sunday 28 December, a number spoke about blessing they had experienced during the old year; one said: 'This has been the crowning year of my life.' Another said: 'This has been the most wonderful year in my experience. I have been a Christian for twenty-five years, but more joy has come into my life this year than all the previous years.' A half-night of prayer, commencing at 9.30 p.m. on that Sunday evening, reminded many of the memorable corresponding night in 1906. Over four hundred gathered for a Watchnight service on Wednesday 31 December. As was the custom, they went to the corner of Princes Street and South Charlotte Street shortly after midnight and held an open-air service for an hour. All three meetings in the Chapel on New Year's Day were well attended, and all three were preceded by an open-air outreach at the street corner.

#### Social action

For five days, and for eight hours every day during the New Year holiday of 1907-8, a team headed by Dr Maxwell Williamson, an elder in the Chapel, provided accommodation and hospitality for two thousand men and women who usually lived rough in the Grassmarket and Cowgate areas of Edinburgh. They took the Corn Exchange, and repeated the outreach in the first week of January 1909, when thousands of men, women and children received free meals and were entertained in various ways. On the closing night the Chapel choir sang and gave brief messages. No response was recorded to the gospel message, but the organisers remained hopeful. Joseph Kemp carefully distinguished this social concern from the prevalent 'social gospel' – 'a danger that must not be treated lightly'.

In March 1908, the Chapel membership was 603, of whom 519 lived in Edinburgh – the other 84 lived elsewhere in Scotland (45) or in England (10) or overseas (21) or no address was known (8). Of the 603, 157 were men and 446 were women; nearly one in seven of the Edinburgh-based men (22), and nearly one in six of the women (68) lived in their employers' homes.

#### Missionaries

On 6 January 1908, Miss Jean Scott sailed for China with the China Inland Mission, the second young woman to be valedicted within two months – the Chapel had bid Godspeed to Laura Gray on Thursday 7 November 1907, as she left for India with the Poona and Indian Village Mission.

*Miss Laura Gray, SRN, a Chapel missionary for nearly 20 years, photographed as she went to India in 1907 (left) and, rather more casually dressed, when she retired in 1936 (right).*

Both had been members of the Chapel's School of Bible Study, and both had studied at the Bible Training Institute in Glasgow. Mr Kemp was extremely happy when God called out missionaries from among his own young people, especially those who, like Jean Scott, had been converted under his ministry. They were the first overseas missionaries from the Chapel for 25 years – the previous one was James Balfour in 1883. There were two more in 1912 (Chapter 17).

*No photographs are available of Chapel missionary farewells on railway platforms, when hymns were sung and prayer was offered, but this is Waverley station, Edinburgh, in 1908, when Jean Scott left for India.*

In addition to the valedictory service in the Chapel, a crowd gathered on the railway platform on these occasions to say farewell; hymns were sung and prayer was offered as the missionary embarked. Over a hundred were at the station for a final handshake for Jean Scott. Donald Fleming, who left Edinburgh for Malaya in 1952, and Ian and Sheila Finlayson, who went to Nigeria in 1965, have all told the writer how they still remember the thrill of having Chapel members doing this, as they set off for the first time.

## Missionary interest

The Chapel's emphasis on overseas (foreign, as it was called then) missionary work was immense in 1908, almost overpowering. Missionaries on furlough addressed meeting after meeting, and the monthly *Record*, in addition to a page of missionary notes (about events elsewhere), reported in detail what they had said. For example, one Saturday conference had three speakers at the afternoon session; the first made an impassioned plea that foreign mission was the highest form of Christian service, after which the second and third speakers described their own situations in China and South America. That same evening, there was a lime-light (lantern) lecture on work among lepers in India and China. Two weeks later, the guest preacher on the Sunday morning spoke about mission work in the Congo; three days after that, another missionary on furlough gave an illustrated lecture on 'The Conquests of the Cross in dark Congoland'.

## Joseph Kemp's sixth anniversary

The sixth anniversary of Joseph Kemp's arrival in Edinburgh was remembered over the weekend of 23-24 February 1908. The actual anniversary was 2 February, but dates were flexible to suit guest preachers. As on all his anniversary weekends, Joseph Kemp sat in the vestry on the Monday, from 12 noon until the public social meeting began at 8 p.m., to receive gifts for the annual Thankoffering. He described 'the charm of this method of Thanksgiving', as members placed their gifts in a box in the vestry, without anyone else knowing the value of the gift – it was 'distinctly a gift unto the Lord'. Two-thirds of the membership 'took part with a cheerful heart' on these occasions, so more than four hundred people came to the vestry. Others sent gifts by post, and the Thankoffering raised about £100 annually. The Christian newspaper, *The British Weekly*, reported on 'Remarkable Progress of a Baptist Church':

*The sixth anniversary of the settlement of the Rev. Joseph W. Kemp as pastor of Charlotte Baptist Chapel, Edinburgh, was held on Monday February 24. The chapel was crowded with an audience of over 600.* [The April *Scottish Baptist Magazine* lifted this report, word for word, but increased the audience to 'over 700' – perhaps the editor was present?] *Reports of the finance and general work of the church were highly satisfactory. There has been a net increase in the membership of forty-five for the year, and that notwithstanding the pastor's three months absence in America last summer, and the membership now stands at 631, an increase of over 500 since the pastor's settlement. The contributions to Foreign Missions have been more than double the contributions of the previous year.*

1 *The British Weekly*, 5 March 1908.

## The White House

### The need

The Chapel began a number of new ventures during its centennial year, starting with a rescue centre called the White House. Many girls came to Edinburgh, looking for work; if they were unable to find it, and if they had nothing to eat and nowhere to sleep, some sought an easy way of making a living. Chapel women, coming out of evening meetings where they had thought about the light of heaven, were confronted with the spiritual darkness of Rose Street and its 19 public houses. What could the Chapel do? It was not enough just to lead the girls to Christ – what was their future? The Kemps took some of them into their own home and cared for them, but the need of a permanent home, where they could find shelter and love, was pressing.

On Saturday 4 January 1908, Joseph Kemp gave a lantern lecture to a full church on 'Delia – a story of grace triumphing over sin'. During the meeting, he said that a friend had offered to bear one seventh of the cost of a home for the rescue of fallen girls, if the church would meet the remainder. Dr Maxwell Williamson, soon to be appointed Chief Medical Officer of Health for Edinburgh, led the search for premises. A deacon in the Portobello Baptist Church offered a house in Fettes Row, rent-free for three years. The half-yearly meeting of the church, on Thursday 11 June 1908, accepted the offer and decided to support a 'Door of Hope', to accommodate young women who had been reclaimed from a life of sin on the streets. It was to be called the White House.

## Matron and deaconess

Gifts poured in; some of the most touching were from women who had already been helped. One, saved at the open-air, offered a month's free work to help prepare the new home for occupancy. Miss Bolton, a member of the Chapel, was appointed matron and the White House opened in October 1908.

*Miss Bolton, first matron of the White House, and a group of residents in 1909. In the language of the day, the caption on the photograph is 'The Inmates of the Home'.*

The White House could accommodate 20 girls at a time, and usually had about 16, from the age of 14 upward. Not only were they fed and clothed, but attempts were made either to place them in good situations or else to persuade them to return to their own homes. Above all, the power and claims of Christ were pressed upon them. A member of the congregation, Miss Lizzie Stevenson, was appointed in December 1908 as the Institute deaconess. She went out into the highways and into the lanes and streets of the city, looking for girls whom the Institute might help.

There were some triumphs of grace, but some disappointments as well. Many admitted to using the House only as a temporary lodging place, without any intention of reforming their ways. Many of the girls were Roman Catholics, and were not prepared to stay when they found that they had to attend the Chapel services twice on Sunday and once during the week, as well as a Bible Class held every Sunday afternoon in the Institute. There was therefore a fairly high turnover – in the first seven months, 78 girls came and 62 went.

Things then stabilized a little, and the statistics at the end of the first year were:

| | |
|---|---:|
| *The number of girls at present in the Home* | *16* |
| *Left on their own account, some, alas, to return to their old life, others to various kinds of employment* | *44* |
| *Situations provided* | *11* |
| *Restored to friends* | *10* |
| *Expelled* | *8* |
| *Removed to an asylum* | *1* |
| *Total during the year October 1908 to September 1909* | *90* |

The White House was maintained for nearly two years, but the running costs proved to be more than the Chapel could fund.

*We had hoped that outside friends, realising that the work was really Christ's and not that of a single Church, would add their material help to our own, but we were disappointed. And so after mature consideration, with great sorrow and many regrets, we closed the door [July 1910], having secured situations or homes for every one of the girls.*

2 *Record*, 1910, pp. 36, 113.

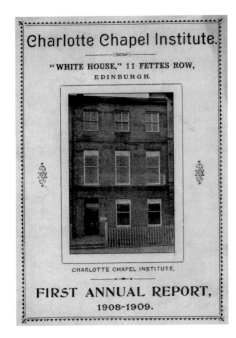

*11 Fettes Row was offered to the Chapel, rent-free, to establish its White House.*

## Midnight outreach

As soon as the Chapel had a suitable hall (next paragraph), the White House workers began a Friday night meeting in it, from 10.30 p.m. until midnight during the winter months.

Lizzie Stevenson gave out invitations throughout the week, to come for supper; after it, there were several brief addresses or testimonies, followed by an opportunity of personal counselling. Up to 75 girls and women came from the surrounding streets, with an average attendance of between 30 and 40. 'Not a few' were converted and attended the Sunday and weeknight services in the Chapel. At an open meeting before the Friday enterprise closed for the summer in May 1909, the workers were encouraged by the number of girls who gave clear testimonies of conversion.

## Other new ventures

### The first church hall

In January 1908, Dr Williamson advised that the chapel-keeper's house, below the sanctuary, was no longer suitable for habitation, and that future caretakers should live elsewhere. The deacons considered transforming the area into halls for meetings and also making more lavatories – there had always been space under the Chapel, but the only access to it was through the caretaker's house. As plans were under way for a whole new building, they decided to make just one hall, for which they ordered linoleum, one hundred new chairs and a harmonium.

Requests to use it came flooding in. The Young Men's Bible Class met at 10 a.m on Sunday morning 'in the hall below the Chapel', with an average attendance of 18. The Sunday School moved their infant department to it, but had to leave by 3.15 p.m. to let others in. The Friday evening outreach to girls and women, mentioned above, was held in 'the hall below the church'. The kitchen meetings in Rose Street, which had been carried on with conspicuous success over the winter of 1909-10, closed for the summer with a social meeting there on Tuesday 26 April 1910.

### Bible Correspondence Course

Early in 1908, those who could no longer attend Joseph Kemp's Sunday afternoon School of Bible Study, told him how much they missed his typewritten notes of the weekly lesson. He provided an outline in the *Record*, but there was no space for the full notes. With true spiritual vision, Joseph Kemp realized how useful a Bible Correspondence Course could be to those who had been converted in the Chapel but who had moved to places where no systematic Bible teaching was available. He therefore devised a three-year course:

Year 1 – Bible introduction, including the Names, Titles, Canon, Inspiration, Claims, Interpretation and Preservation of Scripture.

Year 2 – Going through the Bible, book by book.

Year 3 – Twelve great doctrines, namely God, Christ, Holy Spirit, Man, Sin, Immortality, Justification, Faith, Repentance, Regeneration, Sanctification, Things to come.

The course started in March 1908. Initially, it attracted people from the Edinburgh area only, but soon enrolments were received from all over Scotland and England, and some from America. This was a precursor for Mr Kemp's Bible Correspondence Course in *The Life of Faith*, which he started in 1912, and which he maintained for the rest of his life. The Chapel course ceased when he left Edinburgh in 1915.

### Sunday evening in the Synod Hall

The Chapel held a mission, with a guest preacher, from Sunday 10 to Sunday 17 May 1908. The meetings were at 8 p.m. every night except Saturday, and were held in the Chapel on weeknights. For the two Sunday evenings, Joseph Kemp hired the Synod Hall in Castle Terrace. On the concluding evening, over 20 accepted Christ. At the beginning of June, Mr Kemp invited everyone who had been converted since 1 January of that year, either in the Chapel or in the Synod Hall, to meet with him. He spoke to them about the necessity of confessing Christ, reading the Bible and unceasing prayerfulness as means of growing in grace; Andrew Urquhart gave some wise and practical counsel to these young Christians. Afterwards, Kemp wrote:

*In these days of lament over the dearth of conversions, it was an unbounded joy to meet so many who are so young in the faith. Every one present testified to having been saved and gave the time so far as this was possible. Some six months, others three months, two months, one month, a fortnight, and one saved only two days.*

3 *Record*, 1908, p. 91.

The Synod Hall had a key place in the life of the congregation over the next four years, partly because the Chapel hired it for any significant occasion in 1908-11, and partly because it 'was' the church for 16 months in 1911-12 while the building in Rose Street was demolished and rebuilt.

Encouraged by the two Sundays in May, and having regard to the overcrowding in the church every Sunday evening, the Chapel booked the Synod Hall for all the Sunday evenings of July and August 1908, and provisionally for every Sunday, morning and evening, in 1909. They still hoped that the rebuilding programme would start early in the new year. The Synod Hall meetings were preceded by a prayer meeting in the Chapel and then an open-air march, in addition to the usual summer open-air campaign, which was carried on nightly without a break. Sunday night congregations averaged twelve hundred, but in April 1909, the deacons reluctantly accepted: (1) that the new building programme was still some time away, and (2) that the church could not afford the rental for the Synod Hall, at £4 a night, over an indefinite period. The Sunday evening service had to revert to the old Chapel, but continued to be blessed by many conversions.

*Poole's Synod Hall, in Castle Terrace, which Charlotte Chapel hired for occasions when more people were expected than would fit into the Chapel, and then for 16 months while the Rose Street building was demolished and rebuilt. The complex was pulled down in 1965.*

## Cine films in the Chapel

Motion pictures or cinematograph (as it was then called) came to Edinburgh in 1896. The pictures may have been flickering, soundless, disjointed and frequently breaking down, but they were compulsive viewing. Those early films were silent and were all in black and white until 1927; sound track came even later. As mentioned in Chapter 12, the Chapel laid on a very successful 'cinematograph entertainment' in February 1901. Evangelicals were not slow, on the one hand, to realize the potential of cine film; the Chapel had a magnificent cinematograph display at the 1907 Sunday School Christmas party, and, in the following year, the Young Peoples Meeting used cinematograph to illustrate missionary work in India. On the other hand, those same evangelicals saw the emerging film industry as worldliness personified. Attendance at picture houses was absolutely taboo for keen Christians, until the increasing number of television sets in Christian homes in the 1960s led the younger generation to ask why it was wrong to visit a cinema when the same films could be, and sometimes were, watched in the parents' home.

## October to December

### Centenary services

As mentioned, the annual celebration of the pastor's settlement was flexible in date, to suit guest preachers and other factors. Similarly, the Chapel did not focus on 24 January 1908 for its centenary, but arranged a fortnight of special meetings in October. Many activities closed down from July to September, so there was always something special in October, to launch the winter's work; so it was for the centenary. Former ministers of the church were invited and Lawrence Carter, Owen Campbell, Samuel Woodrow and Thomas Way accepted. A souvenir booklet, with many photographs, was sold for threepence. The major celebrations were held in the Synod Hall, but to encourage greater praise and thanksgiving at services held in the Chapel, a piano was leased, to accompany the organ.

October 1908

Sunday 4
11 a.m. and 6.30 p.m., Joseph Kemp preached.

**Monday 5**
3 p.m., opening of the White House at 11 Fettes Row.
8 p.m., special service in the Chapel, conducted by the pastor.

**Tuesday 6**
3 p.m., sermon by Dr Len G. Broughton, in the Chapel.
8 p.m., lecture by Dr Broughton, in the Synod Hall.

**Wednesday 7 to Saturday 10**
8 p.m., special meetings in the Chapel.

**Sunday 11**
11 a.m., Rev. Thomas Way; 6.30 p.m. (speaker not named).

**Monday 12**
7.30 p.m., centenary celebrations, in the Synod Hall.

**Tuesday 13 to Saturday 17**
Special meetings in the Chapel, with guest preachers.

One of the speakers in the Synod Hall opened his address with words that showed the sympathies of the Chapel leadership were as wide at its centenary as they had been at the founding of the church:

*It gives me great joy to be present on this occasion – on the Centenary of a Church which has been doing Christ's work so splendidly under such difficult conditions. It matters very little to me whether a man is a Baptist or an Episcopalian, so long as he is on fire with love to Jesus Christ. That is the reason above all other reasons, why I love Charlotte Chapel.*

4 *Record*, December 1908.

### Young Peoples Meeting
It is sometimes said that the Chapel's vibrant Young Peoples Meeting (YPM) first met in November 1918. That is correct, as far as its present constitution is concerned, but a Young Men's Bible and Missionary Training Class met in the upper vestry on Wednesday evening from 1906 (October to May), led by Joseph Kemp, and a Young Women's Bible and Missionary Training Class met at the same time, led by Andrew Urquhart in the church. Their 1907-8 sessions closed with a joint meeting on Wednesday 15 April 1908. When they resumed in the autumn of 1908, it was as a combined

Young Peoples Meeting – the first time that name was used. They modelled it 'on the lines of the Christian Endeavour Society, in which there would be greater opportunity for all to take part'.

*The syllabus contains an interesting variety of subjects. The first Wednesday of each month is to be devoted to the study of one of the great mission fields; on the second Wednesday some biography will be dealt with; the third, one of the great doctrines of Scripture, and the fourth, general themes.*

5 *Record* 1909, p. 81.

### Joseph Kemp's illness
On Wednesday 11 November 1908, Joseph Kemp became seriously ill with appendicitis, for which surgery was required on the following day. Instead of the Thursday Bible School, which he would have conducted, the evening was spent in prayer for Mr and Mrs Kemp. The operation was completely successful, although recuperation was slow – Chapel members remained anxious until they saw him back in the pulpit on 1 January 1909.

### Watchnight and New Year's Day
A visitor conducted the Watchnight service on 31 December 1908, although Joseph Kemp was able to attend. After the sermon, the congregation waited in prayerful silence until the new year was ushered in. There was then an open-air meeting in the usual way. The service at 11 a.m. on 1 January was well attended, and Mr Kemp preached. The conference was on a theme that became standard for the afternoon of New Year's Day in the Chapel for many years to come – the Second Coming of Christ. The first day of 1909 concluded with an evangelistic meeting in the evening.

### Reflection on the centenary
In his annual report, the church secretary commented on the regular Sunday services during the centennial year:

*The church has [throughout 1908] been nearly full in the morning and invariably crowded at night, passages and pulpit stairs being almost always occupied.... What are we to say of the Pastor's faithful and earnest preaching of the Word? Only this. It has not only increased our knowledge of the Scriptures, but has furnished and equipped us for the Christian life and service as perhaps nothing else has done.... The evening services*

123

*have been specially for the unsaved, and the earnest and winning gospel appeals have been fruitful in many definite decisions for Christ…. hardly a Sunday passes but what one or more publicly acknowledge that God has met them in this Chapel and brought them to Himself.*

6 *Record*, 1909, p. 51.

## West End Brotherhood

Planning for the West End Brotherhood started during 1908. Although its first meeting was not until Sunday 10 January 1909, the Chapel called it the second project of the centenary year – the other being the White House. It was an evangelistic outreach to the crowds of men who walked idly along Edinburgh's west-end streets on Sunday afternoon. The Sunday School needed the whole Chapel building between 3 and 4 p.m., so the men of the congregation invited other men into the Albert Hall in Shandwick Place for three o'clock. Average attendance over the early months was 250.

MANLY TALKS FOR MEN.
West End Brotherhood
AT THE
SYNOD HALL.
President, Dr. A. MAXWELL WILLIAMSON.
Speakers are all the best.
BRIGHT SINGING.
A really profitable 60 minutes.
EVERY SUNDAY AFTERNOON AT 3 O'CLOCK.
YOU ARE VERY HEARTILY INVITED TO COME.

*The West End Brotherhood was as an outreach to men who wandered aimlessly along the west-end streets of Edinburgh on Sunday afternoon. Initially held in the Albert Hall in Shandwick Place, and then in the Synod Hall, the Brotherhood found a permanent home when the new Chapel building was opened in October 1912.*

In October 1909, the Brotherhood had their first annual social and distribution of prizes. The thousand-seater Albert Hall was packed; Mrs Kemp distributed a hundred prizes for regular attendance. 'Nearly fifty per cent of the prizes were Bibles, chosen by the men themselves – the old Authorised Version of the English Bible still holds the field, it is after all the most popular book in existence.' Mr Kemp gave a lantern lecture on his visit to the United States and also projected pictures of the Brotherhood picnic; 'for once many of the brethren were able to see themselves as others see them'.

*Between 1908 and 1911, the West End Brotherhood met in the Albert Hall in Shandwick Place. Prince Albert's coat of arms is still prominent above the door at 22 Shandwick Place.*

The Brotherhood encouraged an enrolled membership, collecting one penny per week, but visitors were welcome as well. Numbers rose during the first year to 328, and the annual excursion, with wives and families and friends, was popular.

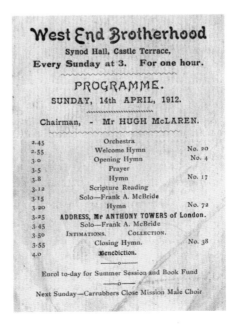

West End Brotherhood
Synod Hall, Castle Terrace,
**Every Sunday at 3. For one hour.**
PROGRAMME.
SUNDAY, 14th APRIL, 1912.
Chairman, - Mr HUGH McLAREN.

| | | |
|---|---|---|
| 2.45 | Orchestra | |
| 2.55 | Welcome Hymn | No. 20 |
| 3.0 | Opening Hymn | No. 4 |
| 3.5 | Prayer | |
| 3.8 | Hymn | No. 17 |
| 3.12 | Scripture Reading | |
| 3.15 | Solo—Frank A. McBride | |
| 3.20 | Hymn | No. 72 |
| 3.25 | ADDRESS, Mr ANTHONY TOWERS of London. | |
| 3.45 | Solo—Frank A. McBride | |
| 3.50 | INTIMATIONS.    COLLECTION. | |
| 3.55 | Closing Hymn. | No. 38 |
| 4.0 | Benediction. | |

Enrol to-day for Summer Session and Book Fund

Next Sunday—Carrubbers Close Mission Male Choir

*A typical West End Brotherhood programme.*

The last Sunday of the month was devoted to testimonies, when the men told the story of their conversion; the emphasis was always on taking the good news to others – 'The land is flooded with "go to meeting societies", and what we are wearying for is "a band of men whose hearts God has touched" and who will "do something"'.

## Picnics

The Chapel auxiliaries had a friendly rivalry, as to which could lay on the best summer picnic. The Brotherhood opened the 1909 season, going to Newhailes, Musselburgh, on Victoria Day – the third Monday in May was a significant holiday in Edinburgh, until overshadowed recently by the first Monday. The Sunday School outing by train to Redhall House, Slateford, on Saturday 12 June, eclipsed all the other organizations, with 650 children and friends taking part in the games and refreshments. The School of Bible Study had its own picnic, on Saturday 3 July, going by train to Niddrie, while the choir chose Bonaly Tower, Colinton. Nowadays people commute from these places to the centre of Edinburgh, but in 1909 they were sufficiently far into the country to make an excursion to them an event to be looked forward to and remembered.

*Joseph Kemp took these snaps with his box camera at the choir picnic at Bonaly Tower, Colinton, in 1909. Long dresses and large hats did not inhibit the most popular game on these occasions, 'The Jolly Miller'.*

Additional information on the following topics, mentioned in this chapter, is available on the CD.

# Chapter 17
# Activity, teaching and prayer (1909–1910)

## A changing and challenging world

### From sedan chairs to aeroplanes

When Dr Henry Littlejohn (1826-1914) retired in 1910, after 52 years as Edinburgh's Medical Officer of Health, he was succeeded by a Chapel elder, Maxwell Williamson. In his leaving speech, Littlejohn commented that when he was appointed, sedan chairs were still used in the city, and only 14 years had passed since railway trains first reached Edinburgh. Until then, no one here had travelled faster than a horse could carry its rider. Now, as he pointed out, Louis Blériot had just flown across the English Channel and explorers had reached the North Pole.

### Emigration

As the world grew smaller in these ways, emigration from Edinburgh (as elsewhere) increased, especially to North America, South Africa and Australasia. The Chapel had always lost members by emigration, but June 1910 affected the church particularly adversely. In one month, George Walcot, the son of Baillie John Walcot, who had been active in the Chapel for 25 years as deacon, elder and superintendent of the Sunday School, emigrated with his wife and three children to Montreal, two women went to Toronto and another to Winnipeg; other members settled in the United States and Johannesburg. This was not untypical. In the corresponding month of the following year, ten members sailed to Chicago, New York, Canada and Australia. At the half-yearly meeting, when membership was reviewed, it was invariably the sad duty of the church to remove the names of those with whom they had lost touch. The ideal was to keep them in membership until they could be transferred to a church in their new country, but many never sent a forwarding address.

On the other hand, some emigrants kept in touch with the church where they had come to faith. Several donations to the New Building Scheme (Chapter 18) came from the colonies, with covering letters of appreciation. One link lasted for 50 years. Robert Gillespie, the last man to be baptized by Christopher Anderson in 1851, went to Melbourne, Australia, in the following year. During his career in banking, and until his death in 1910, he supported the work in the Chapel and distributed news about it to his family in Australia.

## Joseph Kemp's second visit to America

Joseph Kemp's second visit to the United States of America, from early March to late May 1909, had been planned in the autumn of 1908, but, on medical advice, it became part of his recuperation from the appendicitis operation. He presided at his seventh anniversary in the Chapel, over the last weekend of February 1909, and preached to large congregations at both services on the Sunday. His freshness and power was an encouragement to those who had been concerned about his recent health. The Chapel was crowded to capacity for a social gathering on the Monday evening, after which the Kemps left for America.

It was far from a holiday. Joseph Kemp took part in a conference at Atlanta for ten days with several meetings daily, preached and lectured in Pittsburgh, went on to College Point for ten days and visited Brooklyn and New York, before sailing for home on 5 May. He met many former Chapel members, who had emigrated but who had kept in touch. He was back in his own pulpit on the third Sunday in May.

The office-bearers had determined: 'although the Pastor will be absent, all the branches of the work will be maintained and no part of the Church's organisation allowed to suffer.' The prayer meetings continued to be well attended, three times on Sunday and one on every weekday evening. There was also a two-week mission in March, directed specifically to children. A visiting evangelist, known for his work among the young, gave gospel addresses illustrated by lanternslides, such as *Pilgrim's Progress*. 'The attendance of the children was very good throughout, and not a meeting closed without a number remaining behind to give their hearts to the Saviour. It is with joy that we record that there is an evidence of a work of grace in the hearts of many of the young people.'

## Outdoors and Indoors

### Open-air meetings

As the summer of 1909 approached, and indoor evangelism was replaced by open-airs, Joseph Kemp exhorted: 'Even if you cannot sing or speak, your presence and prayers will cheer the speaker and help to gather a crowd.' Open-air meetings continued until the end of October, every night of the week except Monday, which was reserved for the main church prayer meeting. In addition to the gatherings at the corner of South Charlotte Street and Princes Street, the Young Men's Bible Class started an open-air at the corner of Castle Street and Princes Street in July 1909; they wanted to reach young men, who were passing, it was reckoned, at a rate of 150 per minute. Even when November came, and most activities were held indoors, a short outdoor service was held on most evenings, before meetings began in the Chapel itself.

### Expository preaching

Recent pastors of Charlotte Chapel have taken January as an appropriate time to start a new expository series in some book of the Bible, and, as often as not, the morning topic has lasted for the full calendar year. Joseph Kemp preferred to take October as his starting-point – the summer break really was a major break in church activities. Two of his subjects for October 1909 will be familiar to most readers – Colossians on Sunday morning and Ephesians on Thursday evening; however, it is nearly 70 years (below) since the Chapel heard an extended series on the Tabernacle in the wilderness. The minister of the Abbeyhill Baptist Church had lectured on this in the Chapel over four consecutive nights in June 1907, and when a visiting American preacher took the same topic in August 1908, Joseph Kemp remarked: 'We have heard many lectures on the Tabernacle, but we cannot say that ever we saw a lecturer who illustrated his lecture so effectively as did our good friend Mr Allen.'

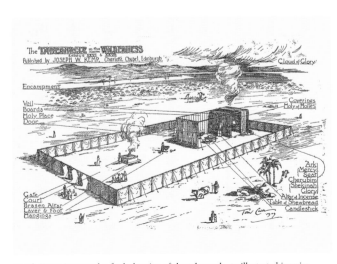

*Joseph Kemp instructed a fresh drawing of the tabernacle, to illustrate his series, as the date of 1909 on this sketch shows.*

Joseph Kemp's own series on the Tabernacle in the wilderness, starting in October 1909 at his Sunday afternoon School of Bible Study, excited considerable interest. Sidlow Baxter used the same drawing for an extended series in 1939. The subject (with appropriate models) was still popular among the Christian Brethren and others in the 1950s, but is rarely taught nowadays.

### Membership

The *Record* for October 1909 gave, for the first time, the address as well as the name of those baptized or received into membership. The details had to be discontinued in December 1912, because salesmen were cold-calling on the people named, trying to sell, among other things, photographs of the pastor. It was June 1958 before the *Record* again gave postal details for people baptized or joining the church. This continued through to 1995; the *Record* then began to give a short biography, and that was deemed to be sufficient identification.

### Deaconess

1909 was again a strenuous and yet encouraging year for Miss Elizabeth Boyle, the recently appointed deaconess. During it, she made 1,100 visits and distributed 232 garments. She was well received everywhere, and those who were in need, materially and spiritually, looked forward to her visits. She introduced many to the services in the Chapel, the School of Bible Study and the Sunday School; she was able to report a number of definite decisions for Christ. Her kitchen meetings in Rose Street continued on Tuesday evening, regularly attended by 35 or 40 who could not, because of family duties, come to the Chapel itself.

### Hogmanay 1909

Encouraged by the response to the hiring of the Synod Hall during the centenary year, the Chapel took it again for the Watchnight service on 31 December 1909. The congregation had distributed thousands of invitations during the previous week, and the huge hall, seating nineteen hundred, was almost filled. There were testimonies about the goodness of God during the past year, followed by an address from a visiting preacher; all this led to a deep sense of solemnity, as the old year ticked away. Several made decisions for Christ,

127

and many others promised that, by God's grace, they would do more for him in the new year than they had in the old.

As in previous years, many went straight from the indoor meeting to the corner of South Charlotte Street, to consecrate the spot again for the service of God and the salvation of souls. A great crowd gathered around the preachers and singers, and several young men accepted Christ as Saviour.

## Balancing activity, teaching and prayer

### The priority of prayer

All this activity, night after night, for month after month, led to over-commitment and something had to give. Joseph Kemp, who personally wrote the editorial for the monthly *Record*, was concerned that it should not be the Chapel's corporate prayer. There were prayer meetings on Sunday at 7 a.m., 10 a.m., and 5.30 p.m., on Monday at 8 p.m. (the main church prayer meeting), and also every Wednesday, Thursday and Saturday at 7 p.m., for half-an-hour, and on Friday at 8 p.m., for 'Prayer, Praise and Testimony'. In three consecutive issues, January, February and March of 1910, Kemp wrote:

*January – We fear the spirit of prayer is waning amongst us. Our meetings, organisations and agencies of one form and another have so crowded in upon us till we are pressed out of measure. Might it not be well to call a halt in our activities and convene meetings for the sole purpose of waiting upon God in united supplications? If the spirit of prayer wanes, spiritual life will assuredly languish and service will become formal and fruitless.*

1 *Record*, 1910, p. 1.

*February – The necessity for calling attention to the condition of our prayer meetings is still very pressing. The fact is, the situation is very acute. One is slow to believe that we are so far reduced in spiritual fervour as to imagine that our organisations and multitudinous efforts can long survive if our prayer meetings deteriorate.*

2 *Record*, 1910, p. 17.

*March – The attendance at the Monday night prayer meeting, which is the recognised weekly prayer meeting of the Church,*

*has not been nearly as large as could have been wished. This may have been partly due to the number of special missions going on in the city during the month.*

3 *Record*, 1910, p. 50.

The congregation responded, and soon he was able to write: 'There has been a welcome increase at the Monday evening prayer meeting. It may not be convenient for friends to come every week, but it would add greatly to the strength of the church if members would come as often as possible.'

### Joseph Kemp's third visit to America

Dr Len Broughton, who had been the main guest preacher at the Chapel's centenary in 1908, was due to open a new church in Atlanta at the beginning of March 1910, six stories high, seating 3,500 and with a salaried staff of 13. On 13 February he sent a telegram to Joseph Kemp, asking him to be a last-minute replacement speaker at the ceremony. This meant sailing on 23 February, but Kemp dropped everything and after a wild and tempestuous crossing, which lasted ten days, he got there just in time. He then conducted a fortnight's mission, but was back in time to resume the Chapel Bible School on Thursday 7 April.

### Children's Decision Day

On the afternoon of Saturday 29 October 1910, a Children's Decision Day service was held in the Chapel, with a visiting evangelist. A number accepted Christ as their personal Saviour, including a lad who had grown up in the Chapel and whose life had been influenced by Christian parents. Exactly 50 years later, the Rev. Walter J. Main returned to the Chapel, from the Moody Bible Institute in Chicago, to recall that Decision Day, to preach at both of the Sunday services and to thank God for his goodness over half a century. He told about the decision he made in October 1910, and the uplift he received during the Chapman-Alexander Mission in 1914.

On the outbreak of war in 1914, he volunteered and served until 1919, when he was demobilized as a pilot in the RAF. He then came under the influence of Graham Scroggie's ministry; an interview with his pastor changed his outlook on life and his ambitions. He studied for three years at the Moody Bible Institute, training to be an evangelist. In 1924, he was invited to join the Chapel's Evangelistic Association, with whom he worked for 12 years. After pastorates in several Baptist churches in Scotland until 1957, he returned to Chicago. It all started with Decision Day on 29 October 1910.

### Hogmanay 1910

1910 ended on a Saturday, so the usual monthly conference was held, with a fine gathering. Following a brief interval after the conference, a prayer meeting was held at 8.30 p.m., then an open-air service and then the Watchnight service – one of the best attended for years. The first half-hour was given over to testimonies, when people spoke from their seats, all over the Chapel, about blessings received during 1910. Of the 44 baptized during the year 1910, 26 had been converted in the Chapel. Mr Kemp then spoke, and a guest preacher led a time of consecration into the new year. The congregation then went to Princes Street, for a half-hour of witness and rededication of the place where open-air meetings were regularly held. The fact that New Year's Day was a Sunday lent solemnity to the whole celebration.

*Joseph Kemp, half way through his 13-year ministry (1902-15) in Charlotte Chapel.*

## Four pan-denominational interests

### World Missionary Conference, June 1910

The Chapel had tried, from Christopher Anderson's day, not to be insular; in the summer of 1909, a good number attended the Keswick Convention, while others went to a student conference in England. However, planning and providing hospitality for the first World Missionary Conference, held in Edinburgh in June 1910, gave the Chapel (along with other congregations involved) an exciting new international dimension. Many attended the meetings, along with the twelve hundred delegates and their wives.

The lead came from Joseph Kemp. He urged the Chapel to take a prayerfully intelligent, personal interest in a conference that promised to be historic, and 'to throw ourselves into the conference, surrounding and flooding it with a spirit of prayer, to issue in a new era in the world's evangelization.' Eight pastors, from different mission fields, occupied the Chapel pulpit during June, and the Chapel hosted a reception for all the Baptist delegates. When the conference was over, Joseph Kemp wrote that it had 'succeeded in exciting an interest in missionary ideals wholly without precedent', and that: 'Not since the Apostolic Council at Jerusalem has there been held a conference more spiritual, or more significant or far-reaching in importance and influence.'

The conference met from Tuesday 14 to Thursday 23 June 1910, in the Assembly Hall on the Mound and in the Synod Hall; 160 missionary societies were represented. Among the greetings read during the opening evening, was one from King George V, which led the delegates spontaneously to stand and sing 'God Save the King'. Speakers that night included the Archbishop of Canterbury, who hoped that some present might not taste death till they saw the Kingdom of God come with power, and a veteran American missionary, who reminded the delegates that no one can follow Christ 'without following Him to the uttermost parts of the earth.' For the next ten days, speeches were interspersed with wide-ranging debate, based on more than one thousand extensive questionnaires, which had been returned by missionaries.

The momentum that began in Edinburgh in 1910 led to the establishment of the Universal Christian Conference on Life and Work in 1925 and to the World Conference on Faith and Order in 1927. These two organisations merged in 1948 to create the World Council of Churches; many see the Edinburgh conference of 1910 as the beginning of the modern ecumenical movement.

### Keswick Convention

Although deeply involved in the World Missionary Conference, Joseph Kemp and a number of Chapel members also made time to attend the thirty-sixth annual Keswick Convention in July. Kemp may have attended before, but he had never previously reported so fully or so enthusiastically about it. He chaired a meeting in the Chapel on Thursday 28 July, where testimonies to blessings received at the

Convention were given. In the following July, 1911, Kemp took his assistant, James Scott, with him for the first time. Both of them enthused about their experiences when they spoke at the Sunday morning service in the Chapel on 30 July, and Kemp preached on the teaching of Keswick. He devoted the entire evening service to 'Life more abundant', and 'many were awakened to their true condition before God, and sought from Him power to live on a higher plane'. Despite all his other commitments, Joseph Kemp was back at Keswick in 1912 and 1913, along with many Chapel members; on both occasions he used the editorial in the *Record* to challenge his own people to greater consecration and prayer. He was not, however, invited to preach at Keswick until July 1926.

### Edinburgh Royal Infirmary

The Chapel had many links with the Edinburgh Royal Infirmary. Chapel members conducted ward services there on Sunday morning and afternoon from 1890 (Chapter 11). Christopher Anderson believed passionately that no Christian in the city could withhold support for the (original) Infirmary without loss of respect. There was no National Health Service or other public funding, so the Infirmary, which never demanded payment for treatment or care, relied on voluntary donations. A Chapel elder, John Walcot, was chairman of its House Committee in the 1880s.

*For 90 years, starting in 1890, Chapel members conducted ward services in the Edinburgh Royal Infirmary on Sunday morning and afternoon; further details are given in Chapter 27.*

Despite the urgent appeals to members to fund the new Chapel building in 1912, there was still an annual collection for the Infirmary, averaging £8; Joseph Kemp commented:

'we might do more for this noble Institution than we are doing. Several of our members have received the benefit of the Infirmary, and we should help to bear some of the burden.' At that time, the daily average number of in-patients was 846; in the year 1911 over 12,600 patients were treated in wards and another 38,800 as outpatients. The cost, per patient per day, was under £5 in 1911.

### Victoria Golf Club

Joseph Kemp spoke his mind frankly about issues on which he felt strongly. The leaders of the Chapel's West End Brotherhood showed considerable restraint when he launched a public attack on their policies in the *Record*. However, the committee of the Victoria Golf Club, where some members were also Chapel members, were not so gracious when Kemp's views on them filtered back to the committee. At a Chapel deacons' meeting in July 1910, Joseph Kemp made five fairly intemperate allegations about the committee. These included: (1) that they deliberately held their meeting on the evening of the Chapel prayer meeting, and (2) that the language used at those meetings was such as he could not repeat in the deacons' court.

The committee, the majority of whom were not Chapel members, demanded an apology. The incident is worth recording for two reasons. First, it illustrates Joseph Kemp's well-known antipathy to football and golf and similar sports, which came under his definition of worldliness. Secondly, it reflects no credit on at least one deacon's sense of confidentiality, because Mr Kemp made the offending remarks at a formal court meeting, where one should be able to speak freely without being quoted to outsiders. The balance between freedom of information and confidential discussion has come up in every generation of elders and deacons.

Joseph Kemp's blunt speaking led to one notable conversion. A Chapel member introduced Kemp to the proprietor of an Edinburgh baker's shop. He was not then a believer, so Kemp told him that 'a fire much hotter than your oven awaits you if you do not repent'. The baker was deeply offended, and ordered Joseph Kemp off the premises. However, as he thought it over, he realized his need of forgiveness, was soundly converted and became a stalwart member of the Chapel for the rest of his life.

## Worldliness

Worldliness (previous paragraph but one) was an important issue for both ministers and laity in Charlotte Chapel in the first half of the twentieth century. It has already been mentioned in Chapter 14 (putting aside worldliness during the 1905 Revival) and in Chapter 16 (the film industry). Graham Scroggie (1916-33) resigned from a previous church in 1905 because of worldliness in the congregation (Chapter 22) and Sidlow Baxter (1935-53) urged applicants for membership 'to avoid all practices and pleasures … of a worldly nature' (Chapter 32).

Worldliness, which every keen Christian was expected to avoid, included smoking, drinking, card playing, dancing, novel reading, theatre and cinema going and, later, the use of make-up. Toward the end of the nineteenth century, partly as a reaction to the rise of Biblical criticism, evangelical Christians retreated behind barricades, both theological and in terms of conduct. Joseph Kemp was the first minister of the Chapel publicly to define worldliness. During the Revival, he reported that 'many have testified to victory over novel reading, dancing, theatre going, etc.', and that 'there are some very good people whose ideas of heaven are all shut out with clouds of tobacco smoke'. He told, with approval, the story of a soldier who was converted at a meeting in London. He immediately destroyed his pipe, tobacco, and betting slips, saying: 'I will go back to my duties a new man'. Kemp went on:

*One thing much to be regretted is the evidence in public of the growth of smoking amongst ministers. There was a day when few men in the garb of ministers were seen smoking openly on the streets. Now it is quite common. We have the conviction that this habit, when indulged in by ministers, office-bearers, and Sunday school teachers, lessens their influence and is a stumbling block. Again and again it has been a hindrance which has kept not a few from entering into the life of full and glad surrender.*

---

1 *Record*, 1919, p. 143

He also reported that Dr Torrey, who had had a mission in Edinburgh, was now having a great time at Omaha, where the work 'has been chiefly amongst the card-playing, dancing, worldly Christians. Hundreds of mothers have withdrawn their children from the dancing schools, and many of the Church card parties have been smashed up, let us hope for ever.' The same issue of the *Record* printed a letter from a member of the Chapel, now living in the United States: 'I have been working in a place called De Whitte. Found a church whose members played cards and danced. I could feel the deadness all around. Very little was done here.'

The 1909 *Record* carried a report from F.B. Meyer, who was visiting Penang, where the church was keen on missions for the heathen, but where 'bridge and fancy dress balls are the rule' in the church itself.

Additional information on the following topics, mentioned in this chapter, is available on the CD.

Children's meetings under Joseph Kemp
Keswick Convention
Preaching styles
Tabernacle in the wilderness
Victoria Golf Club
Walter J. Main
World Missionary Conference 1910
Worldliness

# Chapter 18
## The New Building Scheme (1911)

### The background: 1907–1910

#### A disappointing start

As noted near the end of Chapter 15, the total money received by December 1907, toward the projected cost of £10,000 for a new building, was £152. That was after six months of increasingly urgent pleas from the treasurer, that the work would not begin until the whole £10,000 was in hand. Two months later, when the fund had increased by only another £51, Andrew Urquhart intervened; he concluded his report to the annual business meeting on 17 February 1908, with this challenge:

*Sometime ago I proposed to the Deacons that we might receive promises of gifts towards the fund, but they would have nothing to do with my suggestion. They, it seems, only believe in hard cash put down. So do most of us, but I go further, and believe in promises too – especially the promises made by Christian men and women – because I know they will be redeemed, when the time comes, if they are spared and nothing unforeseen takes place. Accordingly, while clearly giving the first place to hard cash, I am open to receive promises.... You know my address.*

---

1 *Record*, 1908, pp. 47–8.

In consequence of Andrew Urquhart's initiative, it was agreed on 28 February 1908 to submit the plans of a new church and halls, together with an estimate of the probable cost, to the building committee. Mr Urquhart made it even easier from May onward – he went to the vestry for an hour every Thursday evening, before the Bible School at eight o'clock, to receive cash and promises; the first week brought in £70. Even so, the building committee prudently scaled back the original vision for a sanctuary with a double gallery, to seat 1,200. With not even one-fortieth of the required £10,000 in hand, a less ambitious alternative (the present Chapel) was accepted. The design was put out to open competition, and several ideas were received. The winning architects were Edinburgh men, with an office in York Place. Their plans provided for accommodation for about 1000 persons in the main auditorium, 520 in the lower hall and 250 in the upper hall, together with various retiring-rooms, class-rooms, vestries, etc., and caretaker's flat.

Joseph Kemp followed up the church secretary's initiative by including, in the centenary celebrations in October, an appeal to get the building fund into four figures. He pointed out, witheringly, that less than one-third of the members had as yet given anything. 'If the remaining two-thirds contribute within the next month as much as has already been raised, we shall have on hand the four-figure amount.'

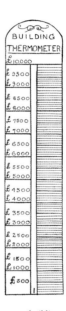

*At this stage, the projected cost for a new building was £10,000. The treasurer commented: 'the rise in the mercury in the thermometer [which he printed monthly in the Record] was so slight as to be hardly perceptible'. Nearly a year after the appeal was started, it stood at £267.*

### Charlotte Baptist Chapel,
*West Rose St., Edinburgh.*

#### SUBSCRIPTION FORM.

*I shall be pleased to give £   :   towards the Building Fund of the New Church. My promise to be redeemed within*

*Name,*

*Address,*

*Date,*

*\*If you wish to give a single donation kindly strike out these words.*

*Joseph Kemp sent a letter, with a subscription form, to all Chapel members. During the centenary programme in October 1908, he sat in the vestry every evening between 6 and 8 p.m. from Monday to Saturday, seeking cash and promises toward the centenary target of £1,000.*

The response was gratifying, but nowhere near the target, even although the urgency was underlined one Sunday in

October 1908 when 'several of our congregation ran great risks of serious personal injury through the falling of huge pieces of plaster, which for the time being stunned the friends.'

## Fresh initiatives, 1909

The Chapel members were 'thrown' by the sudden and serious illness of their pastor on 11 November 1908, his slow recuperation and his absence in America until mid-May 1909. During these six months, the building scheme was hardly mentioned, and the thermometer did not appear in the *Record*.

On Joseph Kemp's return, both he and Andrew Urquhart took fresh initiatives. In July 1909, Kemp wrote a personal letter to every member. He reminded them that on 17 June 1907, the church had unanimously agreed to proceed with a building scheme, on the basis that work would not commence until the money was in the treasurer's hands. That position had now been modified to include promises, but after two years of appealing for £10,000, there was only £950 in the bank. In the meantime:

*We are without the necessary hall accommodation for Sunday School work, Bible Classes, and other work waiting to be undertaken. The present church building is, moreover, too small to accommodate all the people who desire to come to our services, and … many who would come cannot do so because of the over-heated and vitiated atmosphere, caused by this over-crowded condition. The choir, moreover, labours under peculiar disadvantages in having to be partly accommodated on the pulpit stairs. The sanitary arrangements throughout the entire building are antiquated and already condemned.*

---

2 *Record*, 1909, p. 98.

His letter concluded: 'the time has come when our works should accompany our prayers'. He asked every member to give not less than 1s (5 new pence) per week for two years, which would yield £3,120. By the end of 1909, this appeal had produced another £644, so the treasurer now had £1,594 in cash, plus some promises.

## Objections by neighbours

Two neighbours on the west of the Chapel lodged objections to the architects' plans; they were concerned that their amenity would be affected by the height of the proposed structure, which, at 54 feet, was nearly double the height of the existing Chapel. The Dean of Guild Court, which controlled building work in Edinburgh at the time, did not uphold the objections and approved the plans on 14 September 1909.

## Accurate figures

Quantity surveyors could now price the project. So far, everyone had talked vaguely about £10,000 being required, but that was for the original 1,200-seater proposal. The architects' best estimate for a 1,000-seat sanctuary was £7,585, plus £440 for himself and the clerk of works. The deacons asked him what could be pruned from this. He came back a week later, with an absolute minimum of £6,050, which, with professional fees, made £6,490. This was still a huge amount of money for those days, but it was more attainable than the £10,000 that had been talked about so far. There is a strong oral tradition, unsupported by any extant documentation, that the £6,050 was achieved by using cheap wood for the pews, on the understanding that they would be replaced by better quality ones when funds were available. The economy pews are still there.

Meantime, the building committee were running ahead of the principle adopted by the church, to have the money in hand or in promises, before work started. As soon as the building warrant was granted, they 'secured the Albert Hall in Shandwick Place for a period of twelve months from 1st October [1909], during which time we hope to carry on a vigorous evangelistic campaign'. They wanted to start demolition immediately, because there was 'no comfortable sitting room and salubrious air to the crowds who have come', some of whom were 'compelled to leave the Chapel in a fainting condition or have been laid up for weeks with severe chills'. Even so, their proposed move to the Albert Hall could not be endorsed while the treasurer had only £1,500 toward the required £6,490.

Persuaded by the urgent necessity for a new building and by the infectious enthusiasm of the building committee, the office-bearers recommended to the church on 19 January 1910, that the cash in hand principle should be modified to the extent that building could commence when at least half the cost in cash had been secured. Even that must have seemed almost impossible to achieve, because the fund stood at £1,595 (£153 given in 1907, £681 in 1908 and £761

**Marriage.**

YOUNG—URQUHART.—At Dublin Street Baptist Church, Edinburgh, on the 10th instant, by the Rev. Joseph W. Kemp, of Charlotte Baptist Chapel, assisted by the Rev. John Young, D.D., Secretary of the Home Mission, United Free Church, Edinburgh, and the Rev. John Cullen, D.Sc., United Free Church, Greenock, father and uncle of the bridegroom, John Young, M.B., Ch.B., Bearsden, Glasgow, to Annie D. Urquhart, M.B., Ch.B., eldest daughter of Andrew Urquhart, Solicitor Supreme Courts, 9 Inverleith Terrace, Edinburgh.

*Andrew Urquhart had good reason to feel keenly about the dilapidated state of the Chapel building. It had become so unattractive that he held his eldest daughter's wedding, in June 1909, in the Dublin Street Baptist Church.*

in 1909), and half of the most modest estimate for a new building was £3,245.

## No bazaars or sales of work

Joseph Kemp continued to insist that the money should be raised only by direct giving, and that no bazaars or sales of work should be held. It is a sufficiently important point of principle to warrant some comment. The *Scottish Baptist Magazine* carried many advertisements at this time for sales of work for building funds. These churches believed that while men could give money, women, who until recent times were unlikely to have an independent income, could make household goods and donate them for sale at bazaars. One example will explain why this was so popular. The Motherwell Baptist Church (below) needed to raise £800, to clear the debt on their new church hall. Despite a serious trade depression in the surrounding district, their Grand Bazaar in the town hall, over three days in March 1912, brought in £760. Incidentally, Andrew Urquhart, the Chapel secretary, opened it in his capacity as president for the year of the Baptist Union of Scotland.

*While the Chapel relied on direct giving for the new building, the Baptist churches in Bellshill and Motherwell did not object to sales of work and bazaars for their building funds, but would not hold raffles.*

## Direct appeals

The Chapel had no objection to its leaders making direct approaches to fellow-Baptists and others by letters, articles and appeals from the pulpit during visits to other churches. Andrew Urquhart went public, with an appeal to the Baptist denomination in Scotland. Demonstrating remarkable faith, considering the state of the funds, he printed the artist's impression of the new building in the *Scottish Baptist Magazine*, over the caption: 'The above is a view of the new church which is shortly to be erected for the congregation of Charlotte Chapel, Edinburgh, on the site of the existing chapel.' Having outlined the various activities of the church, he asked all friends interested in successful Christian work for help to raise the balance.

*Andrew Urquhart printed this artist's impression of the new building in the* Scottish Baptist Magazine, *as part of his public appeal for donations.*

## Patience and wisdom

Almost immediately after the congregation had decided, in January 1910, to start demolition and building when £3,250 (half of the estimated cost) was in hand, the bad news came that extra costs would push the final price up to £7,000. It was twelve weary months before the new target (£3,500) was in sight. There was so much discouragement at the slow movement on the building thermometer that it was not printed in the *Record* for all of 1910; indeed, there is almost no reference in the monthly magazine to the funds or to the plans, and the new building was not mentioned in the church secretary's annual report. However, Joseph Kemp remained incurably optimistic: 'If the members remain prayerful, united, consecrated and true, "the mountain shall remove"'.

## 'The hour has struck'

### Only £300 more

By January 1911, the treasurer had cash in hand of £2,116 and promises of £1,084, a total of £3,200 – only £300 short of half of £7,000. Mr Urquhart told the members on Monday 30 January 1911: 'The hour has struck. There must be no more delays. We must arise and build.' The deacons recommended and the church accepted: (1) That when not less than the sum of £3,500 is in hand, the Church proceed with the New Building Scheme, and (2) that they would proceed only as far as money was available – there was to be no debt on the new building:

*We shall build the outside walls, put on the roof, and put in the windows. If by that time, say nine months hence, sufficient money has come in to enable us to complete the full scheme, then the full scheme will be completed. If the money required does not come in, sufficient to enable us to get the whole scheme, then we shall complete the Church alone, and wait God's time for the completion of the rest.*

---

3 *Record*, 1911, p. 36.

Even with the inducement of the builders starting, the £300 came in agonisingly slowly. £58 was given in February, £80 in March and £72 in April. The situation was not helped by Joseph Kemp going off to Chicago and Atlanta, from 22 February to early April, as described below. On his return, the fund was still £60 short of the required £300. Then someone noticed that the Chapel had £60 in a painting reserve account; if the building was going to be demolished, there was no need to keep £60 to paint it, and that brought the total up to £3,500. The contractors were instructed and the closing date for the old building was set for 18 May. Cash in hand was £2,525, and the balance of £975 was made up of promises; without Andrew Urquhart's intervention, saying that promises could be counted, it is difficult to say when, if ever, £3,500 would have been reached. Even when

demolition started, and exhortations to pray and to give became more urgent, only £60 was received in the whole of the next month.

Whether, in their enthusiasm to start the work, the office-bearers simply overlooked the known extras, or whether they took the New Building Fund to mean precisely 'building' and no more, the thermometer continued to show the target as £6,000. The office-bearers were aware that £7,000 was needed, because they would not allow the work to start until half of £7,000 was in hand or in promises. However, the thermometer was printed in its original form (below) every month from June 1911 to October 1912, that is, for the 17 months while the congregation was out of Rose Street, creeping up slowly until £6,000 was reached. The congregation would be rudely reminded of the difference between the figures, shortly after the opening ceremony (Chapter 19).

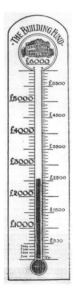

*The thermometer in the* Record, *when the old building closed in May 1911. Cash in hand was ££2,528 and there were promises of another £1,100, but the target of £6,000 was now misleading, because it made no provision for professional fees and extras, which were known to be another £1,000.*

The weeks leading up to the closing of the old building were seen by the members of the Chapel as crucial, but Joseph Kemp accepted an invitation from the Moody church in Chicago and from his friend Len Broughton in Atlanta, to visit them in March 1911. He sailed on 22 February, his fourth visit to America in five years, and after a rather unpleasant voyage caused by stormy weather, he had a week in Chicago and then some time at the Atlanta Convention. He returned in mid-April, to preside over the last month in the old Chapel.

## Closing services

'Memorable' is an apt description for the last four weeks in the old building. Mr Kemp baptized 61 new believers in the last fortnight of April 1911; in a special service on Monday 1 May, he baptized 19 young people from the Sunday School and Bible Classes; on Sunday 7 May, he received 62 into membership, the highest number ever at one time.

*The young people from the Sunday School and Bible Classes, who were baptized on a Monday evening just before the old Chapel was closed for demolition. Mr and Mrs Kemp are in the centre of the photograph.*

Margaret Tullis, second from the right in the front row of the photograph, was aged 11 when she went to the vestry to speak to Mr Kemp about salvation; as soon as she had made a profession, he encouraged her to join the baptismal class. Following baptism, she joined the church, and was a member for 90 years. She reached the age of 101 in 2001, becoming the last survivor of those present at the closing service (not just those in the photo).

There were many conversions in the spring of 1911. Joseph Kemp wrote:

*We never vary the nature of our work on Lord's Day evenings. This is the true 'business meeting' of the church, when business for eternity is done. For years the Sunday evening has been devoted to Evangelism, when Pastor, office-bearers, choir, and church members are on the tiptoe of expectancy for souls; and,*

*thank God, souls are won for Him. If there is anything that can bring us nearer Heaven than such work as this, we have yet to find it.*

4 Kemp, *Joseph W. Kemp*, p. 51.

## The final week

The farewell services extended from Sunday 14 to Thursday 18 May 1911. Mr Kemp preached on the Sunday, and Monday was devoted to prayer; Tuesday night was the final Bible lecture on the book of Revelation. The last baptismal service was held on Wednesday, when nine were baptized, making a total of 70 during the last month in the old building. That brought the membership to 686. The final service was held on Thursday evening. Once more, and for the last time, the old building was packed. Many could not prevent their emotions from getting the better of them, not with tears of sadness, but with the joy unspeakable that people experience only on rare occasions. The meeting ended as a solemn consecration service. With that, the sanctuary was closed, which for years had been filled with the glory of the Lord.

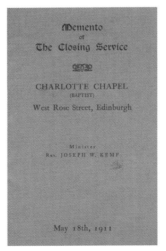

*The brochure for the closing service included a photograph of the building, a photograph of Joseph Kemp, facts and figures about the Chapel, membership statistics, a list of missionaries and a sketch of the new building.*

When demolition began, many were intrigued to know what might be found under the foundation stone of the original building. The vestry (office-bearers) of St John's Episcopal Church, whose predecessors had built the Chapel in 1797, knew that a bottle, containing a print of the minutes of the building committee and some coins, had been placed in the foundation. They asked whether the contents could be returned to them, to be placed in the archives of St John's; when the glass bottle was unearthed, all that remained of its contents was the copy of the Minutes and one old foreign coin. This led Andrew Urquhart to comment, with his usual dry humour: 'We do not intend putting any money into the Stone of the New Church for the very good reason that we have none to spare.'

*A final look at the old building. As it was to be demolished, members were told, at the last service, that they could take away anything that was not being stored for the new building. One popular souvenir was the brass bracket, fixed to the end of every pew, holding the card with the name of the pew-renter.*

## June–December 1911

### One Million Penny Scheme

At a members' meeting on 29 June 1911, the congregation adopted a new scheme, hoping to ensure that the new building would open free of debt. 'The scheme is so simple that every one can have a share in it.' The challenge was for as many as possible to give one penny per week, to be marked on a card and collected at intervals. All donations were translated into pennies, because the target was one million pennies, whether given at a penny a week or in sums of £2 or £5. The first two months brought in 20,038 pennies (over £83); the following month added another 9,802 pennies (nearly £41), and October, with the new building visibly growing before their eyes, topped all records at just under £156, or 25,295 pennies.

Encouraged by visible signs of progress, challenged by the One Million Penny Scheme, and aided by a single gift of £1,000, the building fund went up from £2,584 in June 1911 to £3,640 in July and topped £4,000 in November. Most of the gifts were small; some were from people not in Chapel membership, such as Bible Correspondence Course students from all around the country, visitors to the Synod Hall, those who had emigrated and many more.

*The completed card of one of the many participants in the One Million Penny Scheme; on this card, the receipt of the money is acknowledged by one of the two joint-treasurers.*

### Synod Hall

During the rebuilding, the Chapel met in the Synod Hall in Castle Terrace, seating nineteen hundred. In that big building, even a congregation of seven hundred in the morning and nine hundred to one thousand at night looked small. Joseph Kemp prayed that hundreds might be saved during the temporary residence in the Synod Hall. Nevertheless, and despite their best effort to bring in others, the congregation rattled around the auditorium, and they longed for the day when they would have their own building again. The Thursday Bible School, the prayer meetings and many other activities were held in smaller halls in the Synod Hall complex. One of the notable visitors, during the rebuilding programme, was Dr Scofield, editor of the Bible that bears his name (see end of chapter).

Despite the difficulties, it was a time of blessing. One visitor's impression of a morning service gives a rare outsider comment on Joseph Kemp's preaching.

*Here was a man speaking out of his own experience, not giving us something taken from a book, and we were all brought into living touch with the Christ of whom he spoke. What a touching charm lay in that story of the two little Scots boys. 'Dae ye ken Jesus?' asked the one. 'Ay, I ken Him', was the reply. 'Ah, but dae ye ken Him to speak to?…' Whenever a preacher so holds up Jesus Christ before the gaze of men as to create in them a longing to follow and serve Him, he is fulfilling his ministry.*

5 *Record*, 1911, p.162.

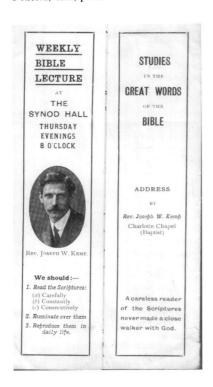

*One of the leaflets publicizing the Thursday Bible School, held in the Synod Hall during the rebuilding in Rose Street.*

The members enthusiastically supported Joseph Kemp's evangelistic ministry. At a social in the Chapel two years later, the guest preacher, a Congregational minister in Edinburgh, told a story against himself. Having a free Sunday in 1911, he went to the Synod Hall, and listened with pleasure to Mr Kemp preaching on Nicodemus. He had been a pastor in Edinburgh for 18 years, and thought that he was reasonably well known in the city, but: 'before I had got out of the doors, I think I had been asked by five people if I was a Christian.'

## Laying the memorial-stone

The old building was rapidly demolished. Five months later, on Saturday 7 October 1911, a large crowd gathered at 3 p.m. for the laying of the memorial stone for the new church. Under ideal weather conditions, and with the crowd filling all the space that the builder could make available, Joseph Kemp, Andrew Urquhart and others ascended a temporary platform near the cavity in the north wall. Next to them were the Chapel office-bearers and the architects of the new building and the builder. The proceedings opened with the singing of the hundredth Psalm, prayer and the reading of passages of Scripture. Mr Kemp made a brief statement about the steps that had led to the decision to build the new church, the method adopted for gathering the money and the plans for the future of the work.

*The brochure for the stone-laying ceremony.*

He then remarked that in the casket, to be placed in the stone, there was a souvenir of the church's centenary, a memento of the closing services of the old building, a complete list of the church members, a photograph of the old Chapel, a sketch of the new one and a copy of *The Scotsman* for 7 October. Andrew Urquhart deposited the casket in the receptacle in the wall and a crane swung the memorial-stone, which was the foundation stone of the old building, carefully preserved by the builder, into place.

*The memorial-stone, inside the front door of the Chapel, was tapped into place by Andrew Urquhart during the stone-laying ceremony on 7 October 1911.*

It covered the cavity, and with a tap of the mallet, Mr Urquhart declared the stone well and truly laid. Mr Kemp presented Mr Urquhart with a silver trowel as a gift from the members of the church, and the builder presented him with the mallet. Andrew Urquhart acknowledged the gift in a happy little speech. It was fitting that he, to whose far-sighted faith the church owed its existence, should be the one to perform the ceremony.

## Reflection on the last five years

Shortly after this, the assistant minister, James Scott, reflected on the five years that he had worked with Mr Kemp:

*The evangelistic note is never absent from his preaching. All the branches of the Church's activities – prayer meetings, tract distribution, Sunday school, open-air meetings, kitchen meetings, advertising, etc. – have one aim in view, and that the salvation of the lost.... During the years 1907 to 1911 inclusive, eight hundred and fifty names of persons have been registered as having accepted Christ, an average of one hundred and seventy per year. We do not suppose this figure represents all who have been saved in our meetings, for we are often hearing of friends being brought to Christ whose names have never been handed in.*

6 *Record*, 1912, p. 55.

Of those 850, only 101 (12%) joined the Chapel – many of the others either went to other churches or trace of them was lost. Scott was not despondent at the low percentage, and explained how hard he and others had worked to establish the converts:

*First, each one who professes to accept Christ is given a small leaflet, 'Guidance to Grace and Glory,' compiled by the Pastor, containing hints as to how to succeed in the Christian life, together with a few helpful suggestions on the study of the Bible. He is earnestly invited to the prayer meetings of the Church, and to the weekly Bible School.*

*Second, we have a loyal body of Guards who watch over the young believers. The city has been divided into Districts, and a Guard placed over each division. These visit the converts in their homes, greet them at the meetings, and seek to give whatever help is needed. Those who leave the city are kept in touch by correspondence. The visitors report on the cases visited, and these reports are full of encouragement.*

7 *Record*, 1912, p. 56.

## Joseph Kemp's autumn ministry

It would be inappropriate to close 1911 without a brief reference to the speaking engagements that Joseph Kemp accepted, on top of his commitment to his home church. In October he preached, not on Sunday, in the Baptist churches in Cambridge Street and in Dennistoun, both in Glasgow, in Hamilton at an all-day conference and in Dundee and Larbert, plus four addresses at a conference in the Tabernacle in Glasgow and the induction of one of the Chapel-boys to the pastorate of the Baptist church in Coatbridge. In November he was at Abbeyhill (Edinburgh), Dalkeith, Hawick, Whiteinch (Glasgow) and Perth. The ministers of Charlotte Chapel have always and automatically been invited to more outside engagements than they could realistically accept, and deciding which to accept has been, and still is, a problem.

*Joseph Kemp at the end of 1911.*

### New Year's activity

From the 10 a.m. prayer meeting in the Synod Hall – 31 December 1911 was a Sunday – until 1 a.m. at the corner of South Charlotte Street and Princes Street, Chapel members were exceedingly busy. Thousands of invitations to the Watchnight service in the Synod Hall had been distributed by the Chapel's young folk over the previous week, and the nineteen-hundred-seater hall was practically filled. As usual, time was given for individual testimonies to the goodness of God during the past year. There was a deep solemnity over the meeting as the last moments of the old year were reached, and many took a solemn review of the past year, and by God's grace promised that the new should be better than the old. Several decisions for Christ were recorded during the meeting, and then the congregation moved to its accustomed open-air site on Princes Street. A huge crowd listened to the singing and preaching, and again there were conversions – in particular, several young men. The congregation reassembled for the New Year's Day service at 11 a.m., followed by open-air meetings at 3 p.m. and 6.30 p.m. The new year continued with meetings every night for a week, in one of the smaller rooms in the Synod Hall. The atmosphere at these meetings reminded some of the revival days of six years before.

### The Scofield Reference Bible

As mentioned, one of the guest preachers at the Synod Hall, while the Chapel was being rebuilt in 1911, was an American, Cyrus I. Scofield, a lawyer who had become a Congregational minister. In 1903, he left his pastorate to concentrate full-time on editing a Bible with extensive dispensational and premillenial headings and footnotes. His chain-referencing scheme picked up the first occurrence of a particular theme, and gave cross-references to all the other passages in the Bible where that theme was addressed. The Oxford University Press published it in 1909, as *The Scofield Reference Bible*, and it became hugely popular among evangelical Christians all over the world. It would be hard to overstate its significance – it sold over two million copies, and some churches automatically presented a copy of it to all new converts. It has to be said that some, including some whom the writer heard preach in his youth, seemed to accept its dispensational divisions, paragraph headings and notes almost as if they were part of the Scriptural text itself.

Scofield divided history into seven distinct periods or dispensations – details are given in Chapter 21 – and taught that God related to humankind differently in each period. To understand passages of Scripture correctly, one must know to which dispensation a passage applied. For example, during the dispensation of law, there was, in Scofield's own words, an emphasis on 'legal obedience as the condition for salvation', but in the dispensation of grace this condition was changed to 'acceptance or rejection of Christ'. Scofield's dispensationalism was also pretribulation rapturist; he taught that believers will be raptured to heaven before the onset of a great tribulation at the end of time, preceding the final (kingdom) dispensation.

Joseph Kemp (Chapter 21), Graham Scroggie (Chapter 29) and Sidlow Baxter (Chapter 32) all interpreted Scripture within this framework, so the Scofield Bible (as it was popularly known) was the Chapel's favourite farewell present to students and missionaries leaving Edinburgh and a regular 'thank-you' to people demitting office. When Kemp's assistant, Archibald Jack, left in December 1913 for a pastorate of his own (Chapter 14), he was given a Scofield Bible and a purse with 20 sovereigns as a mark of appreciation. There were numerous similar presentations of Scofield Bibles, and it was still the preferred gift in 1950, when Robert Aitken retired as Sunday School Superintendent.

Additional information on the following topics, mentioned in this chapter, is available on the CD.

Children's meetings under Joseph Kemp
Joseph Kemp's family
Joseph Kemp's letter about the building fund – July 1909
Lower hall
New Building Scheme
New building, objections lodged
Scofield Bible
Synod Hall

# Chapter 19
## Charlotte Chapel Number Two (1912)

## The office-bearers' dilemma

### Faith and action

By 1 January 1912, the roof of the new building was complete. Although work was two months behind schedule, because of strikes by the builders, there had been no injury to any of the workmen. The office-bearers had a dilemma – they hoped to take occupation at the end of May, but they were committed to open free of debt and that required another £2,400. Should they complete the sanctuary only, and wait for God's timing for the completion of the rest? Nightly prayer meetings were held during February, but only £79 came in. Andrew Urquhart explained in a letter to business colleagues (below) that this was not due to lack of commitment, but because 'our congregation is almost entirely composed of the working-classes'.

At the end of February, the architect called for their final answer – the builders could finish the entire project for £6,519, but if the Chapel wanted partial completion only, that decision would have to be made now. In faith, the deacons said: 'go for it'; Mrs Kemp recruited one hundred women, who promised to try and collect £10 each; an appeal booklet was printed and distributed; Mr Kemp was relieved of some preaching and pastoral duties for the month of April, to visit sympathetic churches in Glasgow, Greenock, Leicester and London, and make the need known.

Andrew Urquhart sent a letter to all Chapel members and friends and called a special congregational meeting for Thursday 21 March, to search for any new ideas. The last week of April was set aside for prayer and self-denial for the building fund. Urquhart also wrote many personal letters to business colleagues, from his office address, explaining the situation and concluding: 'If you are satisfied from what I have said that the cause is worthy I know that you will not withhold your help.'

### The wreck of the *Titanic*

The Chapel's understandable anxiety about paying for the new building was put into perspective when news came through that the liner *Titanic* had sunk in the North Atlantic on 15 April 1912, with the loss of 1635 passengers and crew. Among them was the Rev. John Harper, a Scot who for 13 years had been the minister of a Baptist church in Glasgow. He had recently moved to London, and had preaching engagements in Chicago. In a three-page article in the *Record*, Joseph Kemp paid tribute to Harper's evangelistic zeal, and took the opportunity of warning against worldliness, particularly card-playing. Speaking from experience – he had crossed the Atlantic eight times (four return trips) in the previous six years – he wrote:

*There are few places where the fear of God seems to be less before the eyes of men than on board an ocean-going liner. Gambling, drinking, Sabbath desecration, and kindred sins are in constant evidence, and it would seem that on that fatal Sabbath night, when the Titanic struck the hidden ledge of the monster iceberg, card playing was being indulged in, and it is reported that when the worst was known some men said, 'It is our last game, let us play it out'.*

1 *Record*, 1912, pp. 84–6.

Many stories about the *Titanic* were printed in the *Record* over the ensuing years, of which this is typical:

*I was on the Titanic when she sank. Drifting alone on a spar in the icy water in that awful night, a wave brought John Harper, of Glasgow, near to me. He, too, was holding on to a piece of wreck. 'Man, are you saved?' he shouted. 'No, I am not!' was my reply. He answered, 'Believe on the Lord Jesus Christ, and thou shalt be saved'. The waves bore him away; but a little later he was washed back alongside me. 'Are you saved now?' 'No,' I replied, 'I cannot honestly say that I am'. Once more he repeated the verse, 'Believe on the Lord Jesus Christ, and thou shalt be saved.' Then losing his hold he sank. And there, alone in the night, and with two miles of water under me, I believed. I am John Harper's last convert.*

2 *Record*, 1951, p. 36.

### First foot in the new building

Construction was sufficiently advanced by Sunday 2 June 1912 for the 7 a.m. prayer meeting to be held in a room in the new building, and 74 attended. The remainder of the building was expected to be ready by September. In mid-June, the building thermometer reached £5,000, but another £1,000 was needed to bring the marker to the top – and still (it was emphasized) without resorting to sales of work or anything of that kind.

141

The office-bearers rallied the membership for one final push, offering 'shares' of £2 each in the new building. Joseph Kemp sat in the vestry from 12 noon to 7.30 p.m. from Monday to Wednesday, 29-31 July, and received gifts or promises of £136, £170 and £465. There was no particular significance in a 'share' – it was just another name for a £2 donation. Of the 165 who took 'shares', 136 were Chapel members, leaving Joseph Kemp to comment pointedly that over 500 of the members had not taken part in this final appeal. By mid-August, with the building nearly ready for occupation, the total in gifts and promises was £5,866. A month later, the mercury finally reached the top of the thermometer, and went on to £6,050, but this was now known to be £469 short of the builders' revised estimate. It was confidently hoped that the offerings over the opening weekend would make up the difference.

WEST END BROTHERHOOD.

AFTERNOON
AT
Redhall House Grounds,
SLATEFORD
On SATURDAY, 29th JUNE, 1912.
TEA PROVIDED.          ADULTS TICKET, 9d.

Note—The field will be open from 2 p.m.

*The West End Brotherhood went to Slateford for their 1912 picnic, and then, unlike most of the Chapel auxiliaries, kept going right through the summer.*

The West End Brotherhood was one of the few auxiliaries to keep going through the summer; most closed, after their summer outing, for July, August and September. Although there was a slight falling off in attendance, the Brotherhood attracted sufficiently large numbers to continue. Some Brotherhood members were now attending Chapel services, and from time to time conversions took place. They were delighted to have a permanent home for the Sunday afternoon meeting as soon as the new building was completed.

## Purging the roll

Because of the activity surrounding the building scheme, the Chapel leadership had neglected their regular six-monthly review of the membership. They resolved to catch up before returning to Rose Street, so 26 names were brought to the half-yearly members' meeting on Thursday 4 July 1912, held in the Pillar Hall (part of the Synod Hall complex). The reasons for deleting these names were:

*Several of these were the names of members who had gone abroad and had not kept in touch with the Church for a considerable time.... Other names were resignations of some who have joined other Churches or Missions, while a few decline further fellowship because we will not preach 'sinless perfection'. So far as we know the Scriptures and our own hearts, the chances of our ever doing so are very remote.*

3 *Record*, 1912, p. 114.

Shortly after the new building was opened, the membership (despite the strict purging of the roll) passed the seven hundred mark, exceeding that of any other church in the Baptist Union of Scotland.

## Return to Rose Street

### September 1912

Services were held in Charlotte Chapel Number Two (Kemp's description of the new building) during September, but since some members were still on holiday, the official opening was set for Sunday 6 October. The curiosity of the congregation was such that for the evening service on Sunday 29 September, the Lord's Day before the official opening, people began to take their seats at five o'clock for the 6.30 p.m. service, and the building was packed to capacity by 6 p.m. The new gallery immediately proved popular – it filled up first, as is still the case today. A month after the new building opened, some worshippers were in their seats at 5.30 p.m. on Sunday evening, an hour before the service started, in order to secure their favourite places. When, later, the stewards were instructed not to open the doors until six o'clock, people queued outside from 5.30 p.m., for the same reason.

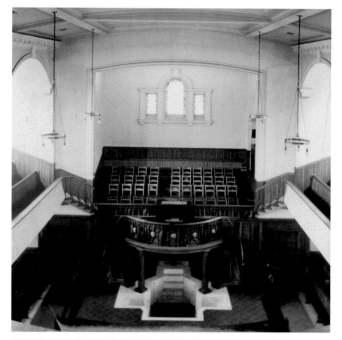

*The new sanctuary, from the gallery (top left) and from the pulpit (top right); the top hall (second left); the lower hall (second right); the committee room (bottom).*

The view from the gallery (top left) is now different in three respects; there are now organ-pipes (installed in 1929), the console and the choir seats have been moved, and there are no longer long chains on the electric lights, so they could be lowered for cleaning. The view from the pulpit (top right) has changed in two ways; in 1989, the dark varnish on the pews was scraped off, to show the natural wood, and the pews in the downstairs 'bed-recess' (as it was known) were removed in 2001, to make room for electronic consoles. The top hall (second left) has been renovated, and the platform is now on the west wall. The lower hall (second right) was completely rebuilt in 1982, and most of the committee room (bottom right), known at that time as the ladies' retiring room, has been taken over by the kitchen.

## Official opening, Sunday-Monday, 6-7 October

Sunday 6 October began with the usual prayer meetings at 7 a.m. and 10 a.m., followed by a morning service that filled the sanctuary. The guest preacher was Rev. Dr Jervis Coats, soon to become the principal of the Baptist Theological College of Scotland. He had led one of the services at the opening of the Baptist church in Paisley to commemorate his cousin, Thomas, another of the well-known family of thread-makers there.

In the afternoon, the Sunday School and Bible Classes and the West End Brotherhood combined for a rally, with two guest preachers and a memorable talk by Tom Curr, well known for his artistic skill with chalk drawings on a

143

blackboard. Over a thousand crowded into the auditorium for the evening service, when Mr Kemp preached. An open-air meeting at the corner of South Charlotte Street and Princes Street concluded a long day, 7 a.m. to 9 p.m., but it was a day to be remembered.

*Jervis Coats, who preached on Sunday 6 October, had led one of the services at the opening of the Thomas Coats Memorial Church in Paisley. Modelled on St Giles' cathedral in Edinburgh, it was (and still is) known as the Baptist cathedral.*

During the afternoon of Monday 7 October, the Chapel was open for visitors. Joseph Kemp sat in his new vestry from 12 noon until the social gathering commenced at 7.45 p.m., and received gifts or promises toward the building fund (details below). Tea was served to six hundred – in relays – in the lower hall. One of the nine guest preachers was Andrew Urquhart, who, although secretary of the Chapel, spoke in his capacity as the vice-president for that year of the Baptist Union of Scotland. After reviewing the Baptist scene in Scotland, he reminisced:

*I can remember as if it were yesterday, although it is nearly twelve years ago, how I made an appeal one evening to the weak and disheartened remnant at the close of a social meeting*

*to bid farewell to the pastor who immediately preceded Mr. Kemp…. What was the cause of the wonderful transformation that had been wrought in this church? Well, the causes were these:*

*1. A firm and unchangeable belief in the power of prayer.*
*2. A pastor and a leader who proclaims, unweariedly and always, the Gospel of God's Grace.*
*3. Hearty co-operation among as loyal and devoted a band of workers as ever any church possessed – all at it, and always at it, outside and inside, ever seeking the sinful and the erring to bring them to the Father's Home.*
*4. An unfaltering faith in the promises of God.*

*Just think of it, this one-time little congregation has seen hundreds born into the Kingdom, enjoyed an almost continual revival, witnessed almost continually men and women far down in sin being gloriously rescued and blessedly converted to God. And then, their crowning act of faith, the erection of this new church and the raising, through their efforts, of over £6000 to pay for it.*

4 *Record* 1912, pp. 168-9.

*The programme for Monday 7 October 1912, part of the opening and dedication of the new building.*

## Other memorable events

### Normal service is restored

On the Thursday evening, 10 October, the first baptismal service in the new Chapel took place, and 17 were baptized. A special children's service was held on the Friday evening at 6.30 p.m., followed by an adult service at eight o'clock. The church was full and everyone was in excellent spirits.

The second week in the new building (Sunday 13 to Friday 18 October) was taken up with the annual Bible conference, which had been in abeyance during the building programme. Sir Robert Anderson, retired chief of the London police CID and a prolific writer on dispensational Bible teaching, preached to capacity congregations at both services on the Sunday. There were meetings every weekday, at 3 p.m. and 8 p.m., with two speakers in the evening and electric lantern slides. The week was well attended, stimulating and strengthening.

Sunday 20 October was a missionary day, with Dan Crawford as preacher at both services. His name may not be familiar to many today, but older readers were brought up on stories of his missionary work in Central Africa. A Scotsman from Gourock, he travelled widely, alone, preaching and teaching individual conversion. He was in the United Kingdom for his first furlough after 22 years, and returned to spend the rest of his days in Africa, until his death in 1926. The crowded Chapel was thrilled and challenged by 'his frank, simple, unpretending manner, and the genuine love that shines through all his talk about the natives.'

## Two remarkable answers to prayer

As mentioned earlier, the building fund stood at £6,050 when the new Chapel opened, and another £469 was needed to pay the contractors' final bill. The members were surprised by joy at the unexpected way in which 'the Lord came to our aid.' While Mr Kemp was in the vestry on Monday 7 October (above), there was a constant stream of visitors and the total in cash and promises was over £250. One of the guest preachers at the social gathering was accompanied by a friend from New Zealand, who handed a card to Joseph Kemp, promising to add ten per cent to whatever was collected or promised at that meeting. On the offer being made known, cash and promises began to pour in to the amount of nearly £100.

However, Joseph Kemp's faith was severely tested over the next fortnight, because he was still convinced that every last penny would be in hand before the opening ceremonies were over; 'we will pray and pray until this liability is met.' His prayer was answered with three days to spare. He had always counted the Baptist Union of Scotland Assembly, to be held in the Chapel from 21 to 24 October, as part of the opening celebrations. On the first day of the Assembly, when

ministers and delegates from churches gathered from all over Scotland, 'a friend who has helped us again and again' met the whole shortfall, to the rejoicing of all assembled. The £6,519, which was the total needed (at that time) to open the building free of debt, had been achieved.

That was the last of the public services, for the opening and dedication of the new Chapel. Mr Kemp called for the closing week of October to be devoted to prayer; every night, expectant people met in the lower hall, to seek for blessing on the winter's activities. Joseph Kemp was never content to mark time. It was his constant aim to keep Charlotte Chapel from becoming simply a well-organized and popular preaching place, with stereotyped methods, but without constant efforts to gather in the outsider.

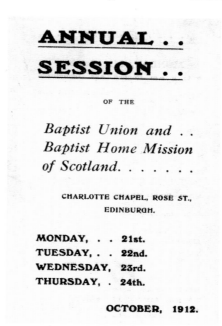

ANNUAL ..
SESSION ..

OF THE

Baptist Union and ..
Baptist Home Mission
of Scotland. . . . . . .

CHARLOTTE CHAPEL, ROSE ST.,
EDINBURGH.

MONDAY, . . 21st.
TUESDAY, . . 22nd.
WEDNESDAY, 23rd.
THURSDAY, . 24th.

OCTOBER, 1912.

*The Baptist Union of Scotland took advantage of the new premises to hold their annual Assembly from Monday 21 to Thursday 24 October 1912, the first time that the Chapel had been able to accommodate it.*

At the 1912 Assembly, held in the Chapel, Andrew Urquhart presented the Union with a large pulpit Bible, which he himself signed as the incoming president. All future presidents, including the writer in 1976, signed it as they assumed office, until the presidency was abolished in 2003.

## The Berean Band

A nation-wide movement, known as the Berean Band, encouraged young people to memorize portions of Scripture (Acts 17:11). A branch was formed in the Chapel in 1912 and, with a girl aged fifteen as its enthusiastic secretary, soon had over one hundred members. The Chapel, along with churches throughout the country, observed Berean Sunday in December. Sidlow Baxter, the pastor of the Chapel from 1935 to 1952, was president of the Band for the year 1941.

## The final costs

The office-bearers had, throughout the building project, been either naïve or blinkered, because they constantly spoke about 'the building work' as if that was the Chapel's only financial commitment. They made no provision, in their budget, for furnishing the new building, for professional fees or for the rent of the Synod Hall. When these were added, there was a shortfall on the New Building Fund of £1,400.

They decided to say nothing about this outside the congregation, but to lay the whole case before the Lord, who knew the end from the beginning. This contrasted with the open canvassing that had gone on previously – they were embarrassed by the shortfall. In consequence, although the need was a regular topic for prayer at church meetings, the low profile meant that little cash came in. It was September 1913, 11 months after the opening, before the redeemed 'shares' and promises brought the cash-in-hand up £6,500. In a typical month, half a dozen small gifts, totalling about £10, came in – otherwise the building fund was static. The creditors were all paid, but nothing active was done to square the books until October 1913.

The members then became more embarrassed than the leadership, and asked the deacons to prepare a scheme, to clear the £1,400. Accordingly, Joseph Kemp wrote a letter to all members, saying that he would sit in the vestry for eight hours, to receive their gifts and promises. This brought in £160 in cash and a further £160 in promises, which he said frankly was 'far below one's expectation, but looking at it from another standpoint, it was magnificent.' This and other efforts brought the deficit down to £1,030 by May 1914.

As successive treasurers have found, there is only so much available; to press the claims of one fund is to reduce the members' capacity to contribute to others. The Sunday School, which met in the new lower hall, asked the deacons for a piano. The sum allocated, £16, was so small that they had to look for a second-hand one. The choir also asked for a piano, to accompany the organ at the Sunday evening

service, and they were told bluntly that there was no money. They then offered to canvass for the money, but were told not to compete with other needs. The honoraria to the choirmaster and the organist (£10 and £15 per annum) were recognized as inadequate but it was all the church was prepared to pay while the debt on the building was outstanding. However, guest preachers at the Chapel, who were many because of Joseph Kemp's wide ministry, were not penalized because of the austerity; the preaching fee was raised from £2 2s to £3 3s in 1914.

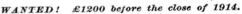

**WANTED!  £1200 before the close of 1914.**

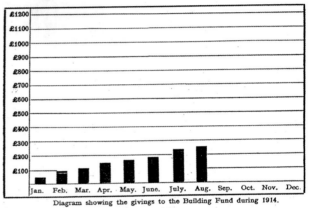

Diagram showing the givings to the Building Fund during 1914.

*Money came in slowly, following the appeal in the autumn of 1913. On the outbreak of the Great War, in August 1914, the deacons ceased appealing for the New Building Fund.*

On the outbreak of the Great War, in August 1914, the deacons invited members to contribute at their convenience. Because of the war, which lasted until 1918, the debt hung over the church until the next minister, Graham Scroggie, gave four lantern lectures in 1918 about his pre-war tour of Palestine. That brought in the last £80, and the liquidated the debt.

Additional information on the following topics, mentioned in this chapter, is available on the CD.

Andrew Urquhart's letter to friends
Berean Band
Bible conference
Lower hall
New building, opening
Worldliness

# Chapter 20
## 'The even tenor of our way' (1913–1914)

## Preaching and teaching

### A typical week in the new building

There was more space in the new building, particularly for the Sunday School and for the crowded Sunday services, but Joseph Kemp made it clear that his mission statement had not changed:

*We pursue the even tenor of our way year after year, and as yet we have found no warrant for departing from the old paths. Any programme drawn up for the days ahead of us is after the old order of things. Praying and preaching are the staple points in our ministry. Let us not forget that a praying church means a victorious church. We conquer on our knees.*

1 *Record*, 1913, p. 145.

If the programme for a typical week in the Chapel in 1913 is laid beside the programme for a typical week in 1906 (Chapter 14), there is little apparent difference. The new items were a Young Men's Bible Class at 10 a.m. and the Brotherhood at 3 p.m. on Sunday, and a Christian Workers' Training Class from 8 to 9.30 p.m. on Wednesday. Otherwise, Joseph Kemp's policy of 'not departing from the old paths' was evident, and appeared to be justified; in October 1913, he wrote:

*When we entered the new Charlotte Chapel our church roll stood at 640. It now stands at 747, with 20 waiting for the right hand of welcome. The net increase for the year is 107. It is not in the numbers that we rejoice, but rather in the fact that the Lord's blessing has continued with us amid our new surroundings. The same spiritual atmosphere which pervaded the old chapel fills the new one, and it has been our constant joy to see almost every week souls deciding for Christ.*

2 *Record*, 1913, p. 146.

### Balancing home and away

Approaches from other churches were not confidential in those days; as far back as July 1909, *The Scotsman* reported: 'The Rev. Joseph W. Kemp, minister of Charlotte Chapel, Edinburgh, has declined for the second time the unanimous call sent to him from the Baptist Tabernacle, Chattanooga, Tennessee, U.S.A.' By the time the new Chapel was opened, and not least because of his travels to raise money for it,

Kemp was even better known, nationally and internationally. It was no secret, and a constant worry to his congregation, that many other churches wanted him to become their pastor. The church secretary tried to reassure the Chapel that although Joseph Kemp had 'received invitations to spheres of wide influence in various parts of the world, [he] has declined them, feeling that his work in Edinburgh has yet to be finished.'

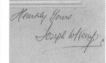

*An autographed picture of Joseph Kemp by the Edinburgh portrait photographer, James Moffat of 125 Princes Street.*

Nevertheless, Kemp, like Christopher Anderson a hundred years before, travelled widely in the interests of the Kingdom. In November 1912, the month after the dedication of the new building, he took services in Hamilton, Glasgow, Dundee, Stirling and London. In April 1913, he led conferences in Motherwell and Falkirk, before leaving on 16 April for two months in America. In September of the same year, he spoke at conferences in Dundee, Perth, Aberdeen and Glasgow; in December, he was the guest preacher at Sunday/Monday events in Glasgow and Irvine, and also visited Kilmarnock. The balance between his wider ministry and his pastoral care for his own people is well illustrated by the twin aspects of his weekly Bible Correspondence Course.

### Bible Correspondence Course

At the invitation of the editor of the Christian periodical, *The Life of Faith*, Joseph Kemp began, on 9 October 1912, a weekly 'Back to the Bible' correspondence course through its pages. Within months, 2,500 people in the United Kingdom and 19 other countries had enrolled for what the editor called 'the religious event of the year'. At the same time, Kemp started, and personally led (whenever possible), a Bible Study Circle at three o'clock on Wednesday afternoon in the lower hall. This was based on the weekly lessons in the periodical, and was open to all 'who desire a knowledge of the Word of God', whether or not they were enrolled with *The Life of Faith*. These afternoon studies were well attended, but by the autumn of 1913, Joseph Kemp found it impossible to prepare for them and his regular Thursday Bible School, so he merged them; the subject on Thursday evening became the Bible lesson that was being studied that week, all over the world, through *The Life of Faith*.

### Sunday in the new building
On both Sunday morning and Sunday evening in the autumn of 1912, Joseph Kemp focused his sermons on Revival, 'first warming his own heart at [Charles C.] Finney's fire, and then seeking to warm others'. A visitor reported in *The Life of Faith*:

*It was the privilege of the writer while in Edinburgh on a recent Sunday to attend some of the prayer meetings held at Charlotte Chapel. The first of these begins as early as seven in the morning … The other prayer meetings at different times throughout the day were equally earnest, and after such pleading with God for the souls of the lost, it was only to be expected that God's mighty power would be manifested. And so it was, for at the evening service there was a complete breakdown, and fully twelve persons sought and found salvation. Attending the services during the day was a young Afghan, a law student at the University, who has just made public acknowledgment of his acceptance of Christ as Saviour and Lord.*

---

3 *Record*, 1913, p. 2.

That student was among those baptized in the Chapel during February 1913. In order to 'acquaint as many as possible … that he had made an open confession of Christ and had renounced Mohammedanism', he put a notice in *The Scotsman* newspaper: 'The undersigned has embraced Christianity, and has no connection with local Islamic Society, or similar bodies in India, Egypt, Turkey. Saghir Baig.' His relatives and friends disowned him; although there was

not one known Christian in Afghanistan at that time, and for him to return to his own country would mean practically instant death, he was anxious to find some way of persuading Afghanistan to open her doors to the gospel.

On Sunday 24 November 1913, two dozen men and women accepted Christ. The total number who professed conversion in the Chapel during the year 1913 was 170, of whom 43 joined as members of the church – although others, being young in the faith, did not join until subsequent years.

### A view from the pulpit steps
Andrew MacBeath, who was converted in the Chapel in 1914, and who went to the Belgian Congo in 1925 with the Baptist Missionary Society, described a typical evening service in the new building. Although it had 25 per cent more seating capacity than the old building, this simply encouraged more people to come and the stewards still had to ask youngsters to vacate their seats beside their parents, and to perch on the pulpit steps. Years later, in 1935, Andrew recollected the impact that this had on him, facing the congregation Sunday after Sunday, as Joseph Kemp drew in the net:

*With great vividness I recall the scenes on a Sunday night when I used as a lad to sit on the pulpit steps, and how wonderingly and yearningly I watched men and women coming through 'the valley of decision'. First I saw faces strained and gloomed with the desire to resist the Saviour, and after a sharp conflict I saw the decision made and a man stand up, yielding to the Saviour…. Mr. Kemp drew in the net, and eager elders and deacons watched for souls as the crowd dispersed.*

---

4 Kemp, *Joseph W. Kemp*, pp. 77-8.

### Joseph Kemp's fifth visit to America
When Joseph Kemp began to write the Bible Correspondence Course for *The Life of Faith*, as mentioned above, he got to know the anonymous author of its weekly 'leader'. He invited the young man, Wilkinson Riddle, minister of a small church in London, to preach at his eleventh anniversary on Sunday 9 February 1913. Wilkinson Riddle and the Chapel struck up such a rapport, that he was invited to take all the services,

Sunday and midweek, during the month of May, while Mr and Mrs Kemp visited America again. Furthermore, when Joseph Kemp left the Chapel in 1915, Mr Riddle was approached to be his successor. He declined, but pointed the church secretary to Graham Scroggie – of which more in Chapter 22.

The Kemps had planned to revisit the Moody Bible Institute in Chicago for the month of May 1913. When they set off a few days earlier than originally intimated, in order to visit the vacant Calvary Baptist Church in New York, and when they spent more time there on their return journey, the Edinburgh congregation openly asked themselves for how much longer they could expect Joseph Kemp to remain their pastor. Nevertheless, they continued, even during his absence, with ventures old and new, as described below. The Chapel's open-air team were greatly encouraged to hear from Joseph Kemp that a young man had approached him at the end of the morning service in the Calvary Baptist Church. This man had previously tried to disrupt the Chapel's evangelistic work in South Charlotte Street, and Mr Kemp had called on him, then, to give his life to Christ. He made no outward response while in Edinburgh, but the challenge remained with him. He introduced himself to Joseph Kemp in New York with the words, 'I have done as you have told me and here I am.'

### Sunday evening prayer meetings

Joseph Kemp was excited and encouraged by a development in the life of the Chapel, all the more pleasing because it was impromptu. Throughout 1913, there were spontaneous gatherings for prayer at 9 p.m. on Sunday, after the other work of the busy day had been completed.

January 1913:

*At a recent Prayer Meeting, held one Sunday night from half-past nine o'clock till midnight, we felt the power and presence of the Lord in a very real manner. From the moment the Prayer Meeting commenced right on to its close there was not a silent moment. The experiences of that late Prayer Meeting were reminiscent of the days when the Church was in the throes of a glorious revival, and it made us long for the times of greater blessing and quickening from the Lord's presence.*

5 *Record*, 1913, pp. 18-19.

December 1913:

*Our hearts are more than cheered by the recent quickened interest in prayer among us. Especially is this the case with late prayer meetings, held on Lord's Day evenings from nine o'clock onwards. These meetings have been held now for several weeks, and continue for about two hours [with about one hundred attending]. Those who were familiar with the workings of the Spirit of God during the revival of seven years ago do not require to have a description of such meetings in print.*

6 *Record*, 1914, pp. 3, 18.

## Mission

### The Gipsy Smith mission

The Chapel, together with other members of the Edinburgh Evangelistic Association, invited a well-known English evangelist, Gipsy Rodney Smith (1860-1947), to conduct a mission in the Assembly Hall on the Mound from Sunday 2 to Wednesday 12 March 1913. Thousands flocked to hear him, and hundreds were unable to get in. As many men were turned away from the Sunday afternoon meetings as would have filled the hall twice over. Afternoon gatherings 'were attended by the more leisured classes, but they filled the Hall some days and at some of these meetings he called for public profession. In the evening, the inquiry room was filled daily with seeking souls.'

The Chapel undertook responsibility for following up many of the converts, and also for continuing the evangelistic momentum. Meetings were held in the Chapel every night; Joseph Kemp preached and the Chapel choir sang. They were fairly well attended, particularly by people from other churches, who were not accustomed to such clear-cut and direct preaching. Many new believers were strengthened and a number of unsaved came to a decision. At a meeting in the Chapel on 22 April, to consolidate the work, 120 were present who had recently been converted. When opportunity was given for personal testimony, many spoke; some had been Christians for only a couple of days. Mature Christians offered advice on how to grow in the faith, under three headings: (1) Good food (Bible study), (2) Good air (prayer) and (3) Good exercise (Christian service). The Chapel *Record* commented, perhaps a little disloyally, that it was regrettable the pastor was not there, as he had left for New York.

### High Street mission

In 1913, two young Chapel men started an outreach in the High Street, an area of the Old Town with many social problems. Initially they had an attendance of two children, but they soon won the hearts of the youngsters and, by contacting the parents, they built up friendship and confidence. It became an active mission, with a Sunday School of 50 to 60 by 1915, a boys club, a girls sewing class and open-air work. It did not come formally under the jurisdiction of the Chapel until 1921, when one of the two founding members entered the ministry and moved away; more will be said about it in Chapter 27. This mission flourished until the outbreak of the Second World War in 1939, and closed in 1943.

### Full-time Christian service

Joseph Kemp was greatly encouraged when members of his congregation were 'called' to full-time Christian work, some in this country and some overseas. During 1913 and 1914, Adam Scott sailed to India with the Ceylon and India General Mission, and Miss Eleanor Dovey joined the China Inland Mission; Beatrice Morrison also sailed to India, to be auntie to the children in the Kalimpong Homes. These three were valedicted as missionaries, and nine others were commissioned for other aspects of full-time Christian service in this country or in North America. Why the Chapel made such a distinction between the three spheres of Christian service – ministry, overseas mission and home mission – is explained in Chapter 28.

*Adam Scott was a missionary in South India for 35 years (1913-46), with the Ceylon and India General Mission, latterly as Field Superintendent. This photograph is from 1932.*

The Chapel supported Adam Scott for 35 years, both prayerfully and financially, as one of its own boys, although he was back in Edinburgh only once (1919-20). His wife, Elsie, was Australian, and they took all their other furloughs there; however, he sent regular reports, which were printed in the *Record*.

Eleanor Dovey's grandfather had been the pastor from 1862 to 1866, and her father was church treasurer from 1880 to 1918. Seven or eight hundred came to her valediction-service on Monday 8 September 1913. She told them how much they had encouraged her:

*When anyone asked me what I was going to be when I grew up I said, 'Be a Missionary'. I was only thirteen, and I had a great longing to be baptised. I used to think that if I died before I was baptised, before I had gone to the Lord's Table, 'this do in remembrance of Me', I did not want to meet Him, I did not want to go before then, but I was so young, and I did not want to be forward, so I had to pray, and a few weeks afterwards Mr Kemp asked me. It was a very great joy, and these ten years' association with this Church have been years of great joy and helpfulness.*

7 *Record* 1913, p. 150.

### A 'gathered' church

The congregation of Charlotte Chapel was 'gathered' from around the city, which meant quite a walk for those who refused on principle to use public transport on the Sabbath. They had two objections: (1) that it was wrong to make (or allow) staff to work on Sundays, and (2) that taking trams or buses would encourage the company to run even more. Some in membership today recollect walking to and from the Chapel, twice every Sunday, until the outbreak of the Second World War in 1939. One man walked in to the morning service, and back, all the way from Balerno until after the war. Between 1913, when the Faith Mission opened its residential college in Ravelston Park, and 1987, when it moved to Gilmerton, all students were required to go on foot to a church of their choice; not least because of the proximity of Rose Street to Ravelston, many regularly chose the Chapel.

### Chapman–Alexander mission

The Chapman-Alexander mission was held in various churches, including the Chapel, from 19 to 23 January 1914, and then in the Assembly Hall until 3 February. This was preparatory to the main mission, which was in the Olympia Palace in Annandale Street, off Leith Walk, from 4 February to 4 March. (A garage for Edinburgh city buses now occupies the site.) Although the Edinburgh Evangelistic Association organized the mission, the idea of inviting Wilbur Chapman to Edinburgh came from Joseph Kemp, in his capacity as one of the vice-presidents of the association. He therefore gave the outreach a high profile in the Chapel, and, as it got under way, he wrote in the *Record*:

*There has been nothing approaching it since the days of Moody, when the city was stirred to its depths (1873)…. Dr Chapman is the sanest of Evangelists. There is nothing sensational. He plays no tricks but relies on the Spirit of God Himself to do what is his own prerogative. Mr Alexander greatly assists by his ministry in song.*

8 *Record*, 1914, p. 35.

and, as it drew to a close:

*What shall we say about the Chapman-Alexander Mission? Unprecedented crowds. 6000 every night, and sometimes as many turned away. Preaching full of convicting power. Hundreds dealt with. All classes and conditions present. Great singing, chorus of 1000. Many, both saints and sinners, blessed. Cannot describe the scenes and the experiences. Wonderful. Prayers answered. Hearts cheered. Homes and lives changed. Glory be to God. And the tide is rising.*

9 *Record*, 1914, p. 47.

*Two motorcars about to convey members of the Fisherwomen's Choir back to Newhaven at the conclusion of one of the afternoon meetings during the Chapman-Alexander mission in February 1914. The first car was owned and driven by the writer's maternal grandfather, Jack Ingram.*

On the first Sunday evening after the close of the mission, the Chapel was filled to capacity, and Joseph Kemp preached on 'Edinburgh's Day of Visitation'. The choir 'sang with distinct utterance, sweetness of expression, and spiritual power. For a while, at least, we shall continue to use Alexander's hymn-book at our evening services [*Alexander's Hymnbook No. 3* had been the mission song-book.]'

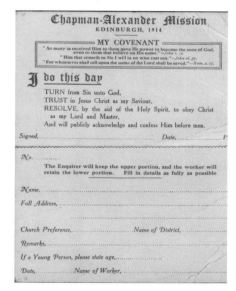

*A covenant card from the 1914 Mission. The bottom part was sent to the church of the enquirer's preference. The Chapel received 71 cards.*

## Ministerial Settlement and Sustentation Scheme

### Starvation salaries

A business meeting of Chapel members, held in October 1913, considered a scheme put forward by the Baptist Union of Scotland. An editorial in the *Scottish Baptist Magazine* of April 1908 had drawn attention to what it called the scandal of starvation salaries to ministers in some Baptist churches – citing one church, with 43 members, which paid its minister £40 a year and three other churches, with memberships of 142, 93 and 54, where the stipend was £60 per annum. The editor reported with approval that the Union had recently refused membership to a church, because it paid its pastor only £68 a year, even although he was satisfied with it because of heavy expenditure on the building.

In 1913, a bold proposal was made by the Union, to appeal for a capital fund of £30,000, to be used to aid ministers

150

**Chapter 20**
'The even tenor of our way' (1913-1914)

whose churches could not afford to pay the minimum stipend, and also to provide more realistic annuities to retired ministers and their widows. This proved contentious, because aid was given only if the Union (who administered the fund) had accredited the pastor. Some felt strongly that this was unwarranted interference with the freedom of a local church to call whom they wished to the pastorate.

## A very cordial agreement

However, the Chapel very cordially approved the scheme, which soon reached £52,000, helped by generous donations from well-known Baptist industrialists, including the Coats family, thread-makers in Paisley, and the Pullars, dye-processors in Perth. With the capital invested, the Union was able to set a minimum stipend at £120 a year for a single man, and £150 for a married man; any church with an accredited minister, which was prepared to contribute the first £70 toward his salary, could apply to have the balance made up from the sustentation scheme. The minimum stipend was gradually raised, to £200 in 1931 and £240 in 1948, and then, as inflation increased, to £420 in 1957, £630 in 1966, £750 in 1968 and £1,500 in 1975.

As mentioned in Chapter 13, Joseph Kemp's initial stipend in Edinburgh was less than it had been in Hawick, but the growing work in the Chapel, and the deacons' optimism about the future, enabled them to raise it from £150 to £175 in 1903, a further £25 in 1904 and another £50 (to £250) on 1 January 1905. There were further increments of £25 per year in 1907, 1908 and again in 1909, bringing the stipend to £325. Another £25 was added on 1 January 1914, and this (£350) was the figure offered to Graham Scroggie when he was invited to the pastorate in 1916.

These figures compare not unfavourably with staff salaries at that time at the nearby Edinburgh School of Cookery in Atholl Crescent. The principal's annual salary was £300; heads of department were paid between £140 and £190; a fully qualified teacher started at £80 and rose by increments of £5 per year to £130; all received two free meals per day. The foreman of the steam laundry was paid £68 and the porter £58, again with free meals.

## Children's work

### 'The Voyage of Life'

Every year, in the week before Christmas, the Sunday School had a soirée in the church. For many, the highlight was stripping the Christmas tree, when Father Christmas selected a present from the tree for every younger scholar. In December 1913, the older children's choir presented 'The Voyage of Life'; a Chapel member photographed the choir and sold copies, with the proceeds going to the building fund.

*'The Voyage of Life', presented in the Chapel by the children's choir at the Sunday School soirée in December 1913.*

### Early conversion

In January 1914, Tom Curr, whose particular gift was to draw with chalk on a blackboard while chatting to children in an arresting way, spoke at the regular Friday evening outreach to children. The seed sown at these meetings came to fruition during the Chapman-Alexander Mission, mentioned above. Sunday 22 February 1914 was designated as another Decision Day throughout Edinburgh churches (Chapter 17). Dr Chapman preached at the morning service in the Chapel, and 30 adults came forward in response to his appeal. In the afternoon, 16 senior scholars over the age of 12 accepted Christ as Saviour, together with a large number of younger scholars. There were also decisions in the Bible Class, and another dozen adults were converted during the evening service. After due instruction on the subject of believers' baptism and the privileges and responsibilities of church membership, 18 young people, all under the age of 15, were baptized at a special young people's baptismal service on Sunday afternoon, 10 May. Mr Kemp described it as 'one of the loveliest baptismal services we have ever had.'

The church was packed and it was a very moving time, reminiscent of the Monday shortly before the old building closed, when Joseph Kemp baptized 19 young people. All 18 on this occasion, together with 26 adults who had recently been baptized, were received into membership at the next communion service. Aware of criticism that the candidates were too young, Joseph Kemp quoted his friend and slightly older contemporary, F.B. Meyer of London, who said: 'No one is too young – I would have no hesitation in proposing a child of nine or ten for membership.' Kemp also pointed his critics to a well-known missionary, who attended his first communion at the age of eight. Joseph Kemp explained: 'We must reach out to the young. They are the hope of the future.'

## Membership

There was only one restriction because of their age. The business meeting in June 1914 decided that, for the first time in the history of the Chapel, there should be a junior membership roll, for those under 17. While enjoying every other privilege of church membership, they were not to attend business meetings. On reaching the age of 17, they automatically transferred to full membership.

As set out in Chapter 11, membership applications were brought to the church at the close of a communion service. Transfers from other Baptist churches were dealt with immediately, but in all other cases, the elders who had interviewed the applicant gave a detailed report and made a recommendation. No decision was asked for then, and a vote was taken on the following Sunday. Joseph Kemp streamlined the procedure in 1913. It was resolved as an experiment to hear reports on Monday evening at the weekly prayer meeting instead of after communion on Lord's Day, and, seven months later, 'With the view of saving time at the meetings when reports on candidates are given, it was arranged that the Secretary should read only such parts of the Reports as he considered necessary.' Since applications (excluding transfers) averaged eight a month over Kemp's years in Edinburgh, the latter must have saved quite a bit of time.

## High days and holidays

### Hogmanay and New Year's Day

As mentioned already, New Year was more significant in Scotland at this time than Christmas – many worked on 25 December as they did on any other day. The Watchnight service on Wednesday 31 December 1913 was attended by about five hundred; most of the time was taken with praise and testimony from the congregation and the choir. There was then the traditional open-air witness at the corner of Princes Street and South Charlotte Street, for the first hour of 1914. On the Thursday (New Year's Day), Joseph Kemp spoke at a well-attended service in the Chapel at 11 a.m. The afternoon conference was (as usual) on the Second Coming of Christ; it was poorly attended – only the lower hall was needed. By contrast, the gospel rally at 7.30 p.m., in place of the usual Thursday Bible lecture, was a great occasion – 'Splendid gathering, fine words and real blessing.'

Two days later, on the first Saturday of January, the annual evangelistic conference was held, with two speakers at 4 p.m. and another in the evening; 'Soul saving is the one business of the Church', said Kemp. There were no concessions when the calendar brought two events together. At the end of 1914, Hogmanay fell on a Thursday. Instead of cancelling the usual Thursday evening meeting at 8 p.m., as would happen now, the intimation read: 'the Watchnight Service will be held on Thursday, December 31st. This will follow the usual week-night service and will begin at 10.30.'

### Anniversaries and Thanksgivings

The twelfth anniversary of Joseph Kemp's induction was celebrated on Sunday-Monday, 8-9 February 1914. All the Chapel auxiliaries came together for a rally on the Sunday afternoon, at which Mr Kemp presided; the choir sang and two addresses were given. In the evening, the pastor led the whole service and seven or eight conversions were recorded. Kemp remarked: 'This is the best Anniversary work.'

On the Monday (Thanksgiving day), Joseph Kemp was in the vestry from 12 noon until the start of the social in the evening. While cheered beyond measure by the number who gave and the amount given, he was taken aback at the small attendance at the social. 'We had honestly expected all our members present at the Anniversary meeting, but the attractions at the Olympia were too great for some, and hence we had huge gaps all over the Church.' Nevertheless, the four guest preachers and the choir were greatly appreciated by those who preferred the Chapel to the Chapman-Alexander mission.

For Joseph Kemp's last anniversary, in February 1915, a prayer meeting was held in the Chapel on the Monday, from 12 noon to one o'clock; about 50 attended, and then the pastor went to the vestry to receive the Thankoffering. He had sent a letter to all members, and got a good response: 'A marked feature of the giving was the number taking part. Almost all the families of the Church being represented'. As usual, the gifts were placed in a box, with no one but the giver knowing the amount. The offering was counted during the evening social and the total was announced at the end of it – to delighted applause.

### Joseph Kemp's sixth visit to America

The pastor of Charlotte Chapel continued (and still continues) to receive invitations to preach in many and distant places. To some extent, this reciprocates the benefits that the Chapel derived (and still derives) from guest preachers to its pulpit. Joseph Kemp spoke at the Newcastle Convention from 3-6 March 1914 and also at the Bristol Convention from 1-2 April. At the end of June, he revisited the east coast of America, preaching at various churches and conferences until the middle of August. While he was there, war was declared and many Americans urged him not to risk either the Atlantic crossing (German submarines) or the consequences of 'the horrible war in which the European nations are involved'. He was determined to return, but hundreds cancelled their bookings; he found the crossing an eerie experience, on a nearly deserted ship, with no lights visible and no wireless communication, lest they gave away the ship's location. The voyage took ten days.

### Invitations

On the morning of his first Sunday back, at the end of August, Joseph Kemp assured the congregation from the pulpit that 'so far as he knew the Lord's will for him at present, he would remain in Edinburgh'. It was known that he had received 'calls' to the Bible Institute of Los Angeles, California, and also to the East London Tabernacle, so the congregation was relieved by this assurance. Such invitations were discussed much more openly than they are now. The *Record* followed with interest the career of its members who went into the ministry; there was often a note that one or another of them had received a 'call' to a named church and that he was considering it; an issue or two later, there was another note, that he had decided to move or to stay where

he was. It was all very public and must have been unsettling for the people in the churches where these men were at the time.

However, the Chapel office-bearers knew, in their heart of hearts, that it was only a matter of time before Joseph Kemp moved on. He was continually troubled by asthma, and felt his strength draining away in the bitterness of Edinburgh's winters. In the summer of 1915, he received and accepted a 'call' to New York; before coming to that, it is important to see how the Chapel responded to the outbreak of the First World War.

Additional information on the following topics, mentioned in this chapter, is available on the CD.

Adam Scott
Anniversaries and Thankofferings
Children's Meetings under Joseph Kemp
Christian Workers' Training Class
Graham Scroggie's 'call' to Charlotte Chapel
Home mission
Joseph Kemp's Bible Course in *The Life of Faith*
Ministry
Missionaries
Overseas mission
Second Coming of Christ
Wilkinson Riddle
Young Men's Bible Class

# Chapter 21
# Joseph Kemp's 'call' to New York (1914–1915)

## The impact of World War

### The caretaker's response

Convinced that France was about to attack its western frontier, Germany declared war on 3 August 1914 and its armies headed for France via Belgium. Germany hoped for British neutrality, but the German violation of Belgian neutrality gave the British government both the reason and the popular support to respond. After some months of rapid advance and counter-advance, stalemate ensued, centred on Ypres; gruelling trench warfare set in along the entire Western Front. For the next three years, the battle line remained virtually stationary.

The Chapel's church officer (caretaker), Robert Hunter, was there for most of those three years. He was a veteran of the Boer Wars in South Africa; although he now had a civilian job and a wife and five young children, he felt that he must do his bit for his country and his family. Immediately on the outbreak of hostilities, he volunteered to rejoin his old regiment, the 2nd Royal Scots. Promoted to sergeant, he was in action throughout 1915 and 1916, and he was awarded the Military Medal for conspicuous bravery. The church nobly helped his wife with the caretaking duties while he was away, and made up his soldier's pay to the usual church officer's salary. Terrible though his experiences were: 'His contention was that although he had no land he had a wife and children, as well as old C.C. to fight for, and he was proud to be a C.C. representative in the firing line.' In his last letter to his wife, he wrote: 'We expect to go into action soon, and if I do not come out alive, I will meet you in the Father's home above.' He was killed on 7 June 1917.

### The Chapel's response

While deploring the evils of war, Scottish Baptists had no doubt about the rightness of the cause. Within weeks, 25 Chapel men volunteered to join the Colours. Seven were already in the Territorial Army, and were mobilized immediately on the declaration of war. Three others volunteered for the Royal Army Medical Corps, but ten chose the Royal Scots; others enlisted in the cavalry, the engineers or the artillery. Within the first two years, over five thousand Scottish Baptists, out of the twenty-one thousand in membership of Scottish Baptist churches, volunteered for the army or navy; many others, including women, were relocated in support of the war effort. Church life, in Rose Street and throughout Scotland, was seriously disrupted.

Joseph Kemp, characteristically, called his people to prayer. The regular Monday evening prayer meeting, and also the Thursday evening Bible School, were both 'devoted entirely to intercession for our Country. The attendances have been good and the spirit of prayer all that could be desired.' As the weeks went by, there was deepened interest and power, although (as always) Joseph Kemp wished that more would attend. What brought out the crowds was a lecture by Joseph Kemp in October 1914, with the title: 'Is this War the Great Armageddon?' His answer, fully reasoned, was 'No', but such was the interest that not only did eight hundred crowd into the Chapel to hear the talk, but notes of it were printed and then reprinted in the *Record*.

As letters began to arrive from Chapel members at the Front or in training, page after page of the monthly *Record* gave a précis of them, and of other war news, so that people might pray intelligently. The first Chapel fatality was Drummer Frederick Bethune, killed in action on 13 October 1914. The year, which had begun with the excitement of the Chapman-Alexander mission, ended with members in the trenches in Flanders. To encourage evangelistic and other activities, when there was so much disruption all around, the Chapel defiantly adopted the slogan: 'Business as usual, only more so'. Details of the Chapel's involvement in the First World War, and its losses through it, will be taken up in Chapter 28.

### Sunday School Christmas party

Anxiety over the war was not allowed to diminish the excitement of either children or adults at the Sunday School soirée on the Tuesday before Christmas 1914. The new Chapel building allowed many more parents and friends to attend than had been possible in the old premises. There were 220 scholars on the roll, with 26 teachers; the pattern was for the children to have tea in the lower hall, and then to join the adults in the church itself. The usual Christmas tree had been set up, with a parcel on it for every child in the junior school. After prayer and singing, the pastor welcomed Father Christmas – this name was preferred to Santa Claus. The Christmas tree was stripped of parcels, and then the children took their places in the gallery for the remainder of the evening. The programme included a lantern display, and the evening closed with the presentation of book prizes to all who had regularly attended the Sunday School. The only reference to the war was when Father Christmas left, not to return to Lapland but to pay an imaginary visit to the children of France and Belgium.

## Review of 1914

After acknowledging the horror of the war in Belgium, Andrew Urquhart's annual report went on: 'War or no war, business goes on as usual in this Church.' The Sunday morning congregation was good, and the Chapel was frequently overcrowded on Sunday evening. There were conversions every week; 79 of the 131 who came to faith during 1914 were baptized and became members. Another 24 joined by transfer, giving a total of 103 new members during the year; 5 members died, 3 resigned, 22 transferred away and another 22 were removed by roll revision. There was therefore a net increase of 51, and the membership stood at 830 at the end of the year. When this report reached Eleanor Dovey, working with the China Inland Mission, she wrote cheerily and cheekily that her church in Hokow had received 77 new members and lost only 25, so their net increase beat the Chapel by one.

## New Year 1915

Hogmanay and New Year's Day, 1915, followed the pattern that Mr Kemp had established over many years – 'closing the Old, and bringing in the New Year in the Lord's House and amongst His people.' The Watchnight service was a testimony meeting for an hour and a half and was well attended. The mood at the open-air service that followed, just after midnight, at the usual corner of South Charlotte Street, was subdued in comparison with the boisterous crowds of previous years; the war 'has chastened the spirits of the most frivolous, and created a desire to learn the abiding joy.' A service at 11 a.m. on Friday 1 January was followed at 3 p.m. by the annual two-hour conference on the Second Coming, with Joseph Kemp and two guest speakers; there was a much better attendance than usual.

New Year's Day ended with a different congregation than the one that had been expected. Hundreds of invitations had been sent out to various barracks, inviting soldiers to tea. The response was meagre, and Joseph Kemp commented, optimistically: 'Probably the men on that night had more invitations then they knew what to do with.' In scenes reminiscent of the Lord's parable of the wedding feast in Matthew's Gospel, Chapel members went to Rose Street and

Princes Street, to invite anyone and everyone in khaki to come to tea. Soon the lower hall was filled, and: 'In the long run the unarranged thing turned out to be far better than was originally designed.' Following tea, a service was held in the Chapel, which, with guests and members, fairly well filled the church. There was singing, lanternslides and a gospel address.

This programme was repeated on the following evening; Saturday was the night for the Chapel's main effort 'to gain the ear of the soldiers who are in the city.' That evening, every stranger present had been brought in from the street by a personal invitation from a Chapel member. This outreach continued every Saturday at 6.30 p.m., with tea, a lantern display and a gospel message – further details are given in the next chapter.

## Communion before the sermon

Sunday 3 January 1915 was different as well. 'For long it has been felt we might occasionally give more prominence to the Supper of our Lord and it is fitting that such a change should take place at the New Year.' Instead of serving communion at the close of the morning service, which was the usual practice, it was served during the service and before the sermon. Members and others who wished to participate were asked in advance to occupy seats in the body of the church or in the gallery immediately above the clock. The elements were served in these areas only. About six hundred participated, and the format was so greatly appreciated that it was repeated on the first Sunday of subsequent quarters. Advance notice was given that 'members and friends who intend having fellowship with us' should sit in the areas mentioned. At the January 1917 service, seven hundred took part.

The elders were not sure when to uplift the collection in this format of service, so it was agreed on these occasions to abolish the offering at the Table and to take up a retiring collection on behalf of the Fellowship Fund instead. What was novel was to give the entire offering, on these Sundays, to the Fellowship Fund; since 1877, there had been boxes on the stairs at the end of the communion service, for a supplementary offering, as is done to this day – the only time when the elders, not the deacons, count the money.

## Wartime restrictions

By the spring of 1915, the war was affecting every aspect of Chapel life. Even the most popular summer social event, the Sunday School outing, had to be drastically curtailed. The railway company were reluctant to run a special train for a picnic party to Juniper Green on Saturday 5 June. They agreed to provide one, if the outing was not called a picnic and provided it was confined entirely to scholars and teachers. Mr and Mrs Kemp were allowed to go, but in view of the ruling about scholars only, their children could not be invited. This was the only outing held by any of the Chapel auxiliaries in 1915: 'There is little heart in any organisation for pleasure of any kind when so many of our brave fellows are pouring out their life's blood on the battle-field.' By the end of 1915, 96 of the Chapel's young men had volunteered for active service – there was no compulsory recruitment until 1916; three of them had been killed in action, and seven others had been wounded.

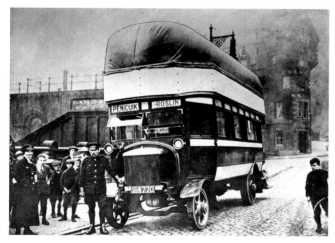

*Shortage of petrol led to some public buses being adapted to run on coal gas. Bags were attached to the roof, and they gradually shrank as the fuel was used up. As someone remarked at the end of the war: 'it seemed a good idea at the time.'*

## New York 'calls'

### Joseph Kemp's seventh visit to America

As mentioned in Chapter 20, Joseph Kemp spoke regularly at missions and conventions in other cities. Immediately after his thirteenth anniversary weekend in the Chapel, in February 1915, he went to Aberdeen for a ten-day mission, and then to Liverpool for a weekend, followed by meetings in one of the large Glasgow Baptist churches. However, his seventh trans-Atlantic visit, from mid-April to the end of May 1915, was for a different purpose. American evangelicals like Len Broughton and Wilbur Chapman, who had preached in the Chapel, were strongly urging him to settle there. Accordingly he went to preach for three consecutive Sundays in the vacant Calvary Baptist Church in New York.

His return was delayed because of the consternation in the shipping world, following the sinking of the unarmed British passenger liner *Lusitania*. He was about to sail on another British ship, but decided to wait for ten days and transfer to a (neutral) American liner. The Chapel were relieved to receive a telegram from Liverpool on Sunday 30 May: 'Safe in port. Meet at the Prayer Meeting to-morrow night.'

*Joseph Kemp's return from New York was delayed after the Lusitania, an unarmed British passenger ship, was torpedoed without warning off the Irish coast by a German submarine on 7 May 1915, with the loss of 1,195 passengers and crew.*

He received a formal 'call' to New York in the last week of June, and told the half-yearly members' meeting, on Monday 28 June, that he was giving it prayerful consideration. Within ten days, aged 43, he had decided to go. He wrote in the *Record*:

*For nigh fourteen years, we have sought, as far as in us lies, to give of our best to the church we now leave. Only those who pass through such years, and do the work, know the tremendous strain upon the body and mind. The taut string snaps sooner or later. To slacken off is safety. A prolonged temporary break in the present ministry did not seem possible and the only alternative was the acceptance of what we are assured is, at this stage, a truly divine call to another sphere.*

1 *Record*, 1915, p. 130.

## Why Calvary Baptist Church?

One of the office-bearers of Calvary Baptist Church heard Joseph Kemp preach in London in the summer of 1912, when Kemp was supplying for a friend. The pastor of the Calvary Church had just resigned after 43 years. The minister of the London church warmly commended Joseph Kemp to the visitor who, later in the same summer, came to Edinburgh and heard Kemp preach in Charlotte Chapel. He not only observed him in Edinburgh, but also entertained him in Glasgow. The facts that (1) both Mr and Mrs Kemp travelled to Glasgow to meet someone on the vacancy committee of the New York church, and (2) that they responded with alacrity when Kemp was invited to supply the vacant church in April 1913, show that the interest was not just one way, two years before any formal offer was made. On the other hand, Joseph Kemp's statement to the congregation in August 1914, set out at the end of the last chapter, shows that he had not yet decided to move to New York. It was the April-May 1915 visit that led to a meeting of minds.

## Farewell to the Chapel – Sunday 5 September 1915

The farewell services took place on Sunday and Monday, 5 and 6 September 1915. On the Sunday morning, a special communion service was held, presided over by the pastor; nearly seven hundred were present and 15 new members were received. After communion, Mr Kemp gave a farewell message to the church, based on Jude 24, 25, under the headings: (1) The Preservation of the Saints, (2) The Presentation of Believers, (3) The Praise of the Saviour. In the afternoon, he spoke to the School of Bible Study, again from the words of Jude. The largest gathering of the weekend was, predictably, the Sunday evening service. For many years it had often been impossible to get seats on Sunday evening, so by five o'clock, people were queuing at the church doors. Long before 6:30 p.m., the building was packed, every nook and corner, including the pulpit, choir seats, choir-room, vestry, bookroom (the room outside the vestry), and stairways. Many had to be turned away.

Mr Kemp conducted the entire service. He preached from 1 Corinthians 2.2. There were few personal allusions in the sermon, but he made clear that throughout his time in Edinburgh, he had deliberately avoided topics from the academic or political world, and that he had devoted his energies to preaching the Cross, as the only power to save the lost.

At the close of the service, Andrew Urquhart conducted an hour-long testimony meeting, with the church and the aisles still packed. Soul-stirring testimonies were given of what the gospel had done in individual lives. In drawing the day to a close, the pastor called for decisions for Christ, and nearly a dozen responded, coming forward to be counselled in the vestry. Although the combined services lasted for nearly four hours, there were no signs of weariness; all were full of praise for the Lord's blessing on this closing Sunday of the pastor's ministry.

## Farewell to Edinburgh – Monday 6 September

Tea was served in the lower hall at 7 p.m., but some went straight to the church in order to secure their seats. At 8 p.m., Andrew Urquhart presided over an audience occupying every inch of room in the Chapel. After reviewing the years from a spiritual perspective, he gave some statistics. Nine hundred and fifty had joined the church through profession of faith followed by baptism; 257 had transferred from other churches; 130 had joined by confession of faith after baptism elsewhere – a total of 1,337. Membership stood at 850, a true figure as Mr Kemp had insisted on keeping a purged roll. Of them, 94 were serving in the forces.

After Urquhart's farewell speech, seven visiting ministers paid tribute to Joseph Kemp's time in Edinburgh, summed up in four points made by his brother-in-law, Edward Last – his personality; his persistency in purpose; his prayer power; and his passion for souls. The wider Christian community was represented by, among others, Sir Alexander Simpson, the nephew of the discoverer of the anaesthetic properties of chloroform, who said: 'Whenever Mr. Kemp preaches he gives men room to think. When he takes you by the hand he gives you a good grip, which makes you feel his heart is big enough to take in Presbyterians as well as Baptists. I have been greatly struck by Mr. Kemp's great personality. He impresses you as meaning business. Our prayers will follow him to New York.'

As part of his tribute, the church treasurer, John Dovey, remarked on the splendid personal example that Joseph Kemp had set, by insisting that the collection bag was always sent up to the pulpit so that he could contribute to it. (This practice lasted until the 1970s, but now, sadly, has died out.) Mr Dovey then presented an Illuminated Address to Mr Kemp, together with parting gifts to Mrs Kemp and the children, John and Mary. In responding, Joseph Kemp mentioned that only 31 of the original congregation, which had called him to the pastorate, survived. He looked on the others as a father looks upon his children, for most of them had been born into the family of God through his instrumentality. 'You are my joy and crown. God bless you, one and all.'

Joseph Kemp honoured three prior engagements, to preach in Glasgow on Sunday 12 September, to induct the new pastor of the Leith Baptist Church on 13 September, and to address a Sunday School conference during the following week. On 22 September, he and Mrs Kemp and their son and daughter, together with Mrs Mary Ann Binnie (Mrs Kemp's widowed mother), and their domestic helper, Annie Wighton, sailed from Liverpool to New York. They arrived on 1 October, after the stormiest crossing he had ever experienced.

## Calvary Baptist Church

Calvary Baptist Church in New York was crowded for Joseph Kemp's induction and welcome services on 8 October 1915. He took, as his model for Calvary, the pattern of church life he had hammered out patiently and experimentally at Charlotte Chapel. He proposed 'to alter the order of service during the week and to adopt Monday for prayer meeting and Thursday for Bible Study as at C.C.' He invited the Chapel deaconess, Miss Elizabeth Boyle, to help him in the work of the Bible Correspondence Course. A year later, *The British Weekly* reported: 'The new pastor of Calvary Baptist Church … has dropped 1331 members out of the 2300 whose names are on the Church roll because they were not sufficiently active and did not attend regularly.' He cared little for statistics and hoped never to be brought under their tyranny.

Joseph Kemp's style of leadership aroused opposition, which took a heavy toll of his strength; he resigned in 1917 and became the pastor of another Baptist church in New York. However, the strain was too much and in 1919 he had a breakdown in health; he and the family returned to Edinburgh for a period of rest. Six months later, Graham Scroggie, his successor at the Chapel, was asked to recommend a minister for the Auckland Baptist Tabernacle; Joseph Kemp was delighted at the opportunity and had a very happy pastorate there from August 1920 until his death in 1933.

158

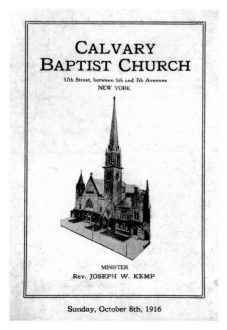

*Induction to the Calvary Baptist Church, New York.*

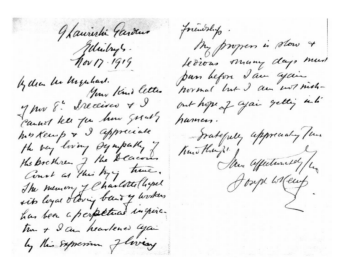

*Joseph Kemp returned to Edinburgh in October 1919, for a period of rest, to recover from a breakdown in health in New York. This letter expresses his thanks for the support he received from the Chapel office-bearers at this time. On medical advice, he did not preach in the Chapel before he left for New Zealand in May 1920, in response to a 'call' to the Auckland Baptist Tabernacle.*

159

## Review of 1902–1915

### Why were Kemp's years so successful?

A colleague, who knew Joseph Kemp well, suggested three reasons why his 14 years in Edinburgh were so successful; two of the reasons involved the laity, whom he inspired to work with him in the cause of the gospel. It was a partnership between pastor and people:

*First, by the preaching of the word. The Pastor presents the truth of God in all its simplicity, preaches the Gospel from the depths of his heart, faces his audience with a true soul-winning passion, and pleads with them, in Christ's name, to be reconciled to God. No new-fashioned themes are touched upon, but the old words of the Bible – sin, faith, repentance, forgiveness, justification, eternal life, heaven, hell – are forcibly expounded.*

*Second, by the prayers of God's people. Prayer meetings are held almost every day in the week, and at these intercession is made for the salvation of the people. Sometimes the names of unsaved ones are mentioned in prayer, and we have known cases where the person prayed for in the early prayer meeting was brought to the Lord at the evening service.*

*Third, by the band of Scouts who are ever on the lookout for opportunities of speaking to souls. These Scouts scatter themselves throughout the audience and watch for anxious ones, and take them into the vestry for conversation. Not in the services alone do these Scouts do their work, but at the open-air meeting, in the Infirmary at the bedside of the sufferer, and in the homes of the people.*

---

2 *Record*, 1912, p. 55.

### Dispensational preaching

As he left Edinburgh, Joseph Kemp made a remark that some modern readers may find puzzling. He himself had written the editorial of the *Record* since its inception in 1907, and he had personally supervised its contents month by month. He was anxious to leave it in safe hands. One of the Chapel elders, who had assisted Kemp with the magazine, agreed to take over as editor until a new pastor arrived. In announcing this, Kemp said: 'those who know our brother are aware that the present attitude of the *Record* to things spiritual, moral, biblical and dispensational will be maintained.'

Why 'dispensational'? Because Joseph Kemp interpreted Scripture within a framework that had become known as dispensationalism, that God had dealt differently with people during seven different eras of biblical history – innocence (before the fall), conscience (from the fall to Noah), human government (from Noah to Abraham), promise (from Abraham to Moses), law (from Moses to Christ), grace (the church age) and the kingdom (the millennium). Scripture (he believed) had to be understood in the context of the dispensation in which it took place. Although he had no say in the Chapel's choice of successor, he was delighted when Graham Scroggie, the next pastor, continued to expound these views. Scroggie asked the elder in question to write the editorials, and gave him freedom to put the *Record* together as he thought best.

### Kempites

At a senior citizens' party in the Chapel in January 1955, special provision was made for Kempites – the word appears in the official report of the event. Kempites were those who had been converted under the ministry of Joseph Kemp, and who took every opportunity of meeting and reminiscing. As there were more than 40 on the Chapel roll, who had been in membership continuously since 1907, two large, central tables were reserved for them. However, so many of them turned up that a third table had to be set. These get-togethers continued for as long as there were sit-down social functions in the lower hall. When Joseph Kemp's daughter visited Edinburgh in 1967, 50 members who had known her father were invited to a reception, and 40 attended. The last person to be described in print as a Kempite was Rev. Campbell Dovey, in his obituary in the *Record* in January 1983; after that, there were clues in obituaries, such as: 'She loved the Chapel and had long connections with it, having been baptized by Mr. Kemp in 1902'.

### For his grandfather's sake

The Chapel's continuing affection for Joseph Kemp was demonstrated in two other ways. Many members named their sons after him, and one father, a drunkard converted through Kemp's ministry, named his daughter Josephine when no sons were born to him. Secondly, when Joseph Kemp's grandson, Ian, visited Edinburgh in 1948:

*Someone in CBC must have thought that the mantle of Joseph Kemp had automatically fallen on this raw young 21 year old from 'down under' [New Zealand] and invited me to preach. So high was their regard for my grandfather's ministry even 33 years after he had left CBC that they indicated the warmth of their welcome to me by a loud rumbling of their feet on the floor as I was introduced.*

3 E-mail from Ian Kemp to the writer.

Ian did not feel that 'what in my youthful ignorance could not possibly have passed for a sermon' did him any credit, but the fact that he was invited to preach, and was so warmly welcomed, is testimony itself to the Chapel's memories of his grandfather.

### The testimony of the *Record*

When the *Record* reached its jubilee in 1957, Gerald Griffiths, the pastor at the time, commented on Joseph Kemp's statement of purpose when he started the monthly magazine in 1907. It included providing 'Notes of the Lord's doings at Home and Abroad.' Reflecting on that phrase, Mr Griffiths wrote:

*How wide were his interests! He writes about all the Lord's work, whatever the label the workers may bear. The Church of England, the Salvation Army, the Methodists, the Presbyterians (of all varieties!), the Congregationalists, the Brethren, as well as his own denomination – wherever Christ was preached he rejoiced. He was first and foremost a man of one passion – evangelism, as his book, 'Soul Winning' indicates.*

4 *Record*, 1957, p. 7.

### Mrs Kemp's memories of her Chapel years

When the Chapel celebrated its Ter-jubilee in 1958, Mrs Kemp, living in New Zealand, was invited to send greetings by tape. Her memories of 1902–15, 43 years later, included:

*I can go back in thought to the days spent in the old building and the wonders God worked there. How many of you remember the wonderful open-air meetings at the corner of Princes Street with Mr Robert Aitken in the lead, or the occasional marches along Princes Street with Mr Andrew Urquhart and Mr Dovey well to the fore? These were the days when miracles were being wrought in the salvation of many souls…. This present building in which you are now is the*

*result of faith, prayers and sacrificial giving of God's people. Here He continued His work and richly blessed my husband's ministry…. Good-bye and God bless you all.*

5 *Record*, 1958, p. 73.

Additional information on the following topics, mentioned in this chapter, is available on the CD.

Annie Wighton
Campbell Dovey
Chapman-Alexander mission
Church officers from 1912
Deaconess (for Elizabeth Boyle)
Fellowship Fund
Joseph Kemp – Andrew Urquhart's farewell
Joseph Kemp after Charlotte Chapel
Joseph Kemp's appreciation by the editor of the *Record*
Joseph Kemp's funeral
Joseph Kemp's Illuminated Address on leaving the Chapel
Joseph Kemp's obituary in the *Scottish Baptist Yearbook*
Joseph Kemp's publications
Mary Ann Binnie

# Chapter 22
## Vacancy (1915–1916)

### Wartime pastoral concerns

#### A testing twelve months

The pastorate was vacant for 13 months (September 1915-October 1916) after Joseph Kemp's departure. It was a testing time for the church, which had experienced 12 years of revival blessing. Had the revival been of God, or was it due to the man who had been their leader during those exciting years? Was it the work of the Holy Spirit, or nothing more than an emotional upsurge? The church remained a hive of spiritual activity and blessing during the vacancy, showing that the revival had indeed been of God. Before looking at the 'call' to Graham Scroggie, the next minister, it is appropriate to ask how the Chapel was responding to the Great War.

#### The men who volunteered

As mentioned, many pages of the monthly *Record* were devoted to news about individual Chapel members who had volunteered for military service. (The *Record* invariably referred to them as 'army and navy', although two were pilots in the Royal Flying Corps.) The Monday and the Thursday evening prayer meetings regularly and faithfully remembered both the physical safety and the spiritual welfare of the Chapel's young men in the Forces. Two letters on consecutive pages of the *Record* illustrate what they were facing. Lieut. W. MacDuff Urquhart (he no longer used his first name, William), son of Andrew Urquhart, volunteered for the Dandy Ninth, the only kilted battalion in the Royal Scots regiment. The journey from Edinburgh to Belgium was grim enough, and that was before they went into the trenches. He wrote in March 1915:

*We had an exceedingly strenuous journey. Leaving the Caledonian Station we were eighteen hours in the train, embarked on board ship, lay out in the roads for twenty-four hours, disembarked the next morning, marched in a blazing sun to a rest camp. Rose at 5, entrained in cattle trucks, and for twenty-two hours crawled across Europe until we arrived at –. We then marched ten or twelve miles; over the border and here we are. We are within six miles of the firing line and hear the roar of artillery intermittently all day and night…. The country is one sea of mud, and it is most difficult to keep clean.*

1 *Record*, 1915, p. 51.

Young men from Christian homes faced challenges on the moral front as well, illustrated by another Chapel member who wrote at the same time:

*Obscenity, gambling, and drinking is prevalent in many camps. The filthy language of many instructors, non-commissioned officers and others entrusted with a little brief authority in our Army and Navy, have given unnecessary annoyance and pain to the men from our Churches who are at present in training and who are powerless to protest against the insults offered in terms which are sometimes blasphemous and repulsive in the extreme.*

2 *Record*, 1915, p. 52.

An impressive feature of the Chapel's pastoral concern was regular mention of young men who had attended the Chapel on Sunday, but who were neither members nor the sons of members. John Ingram, the writer's maternal grandfather, was a loyal and active member of the United Free Church in Newhaven and the superintendent of its Sunday School. On Sunday evening, he brought his wife and three children to the Chapel, so that they could 'hear the gospel properly'. That was the only link which his son, Alexander, had with the Chapel. Nevertheless, when Sandy volunteered as a private for the Scots Guards, again when he was posted to the Front, and again when he was wounded there and hospitalised in England, there were seven or eight lines about him in the *Record* every time.

#### Soldiers' comforts

As a practical expression of their concern, the women of the Chapel, led by Mrs Kemp, made and despatched 269 pairs of socks, 38 mufflers, 65 shirts, 38 helmets, 54 pairs of gloves and mittens, 141 body belts and 7 jerseys to the army and navy volunteers in the first five months of the war. Letters of appreciation were printed in the *Record*. Having successfully appealed for money to buy more material, the same women sent another 66 pairs of socks, 14 mufflers, 9 helmets, 14 pairs of mittens and 8 body belts in the first three months of 1915. Mrs Scroggie took over in September 1916 and continued the work throughout the war. Everyone connected with the Chapel received a Christmas parcel, with chocolate and soap as well as hand-made items. One hundred and fifty men's parcels were sent for Christmas 1917, one hundred of them abroad, and six different parcels to nurses.

## Outreach in Edinburgh

The Chapel had held a Saturday Night Gospel Campaign during the winter months for some years before the outbreak of the Kaiser's War. The huge number of servicemen flooding into Edinburgh from 1914 onward led to a change of emphasis. Scouts went to Princes Street and invited anyone in uniform to tea in the lower hall from 6.30-8 p.m on Saturday evening, followed by a gospel address. This was so much appreciated by the men that some wanted the indoor services to continue when the Chapel switched in June to open-air activities for the summer months. One night, 20 servicemen signed decision cards. The meetings resumed on 13 November 1915, and throughout that winter, the scouts brought in a good number of men in uniform; there was no Saturday night without some clear decisions.

The indoor services continued between November and June in 1916, 1917 and 1918, with between 150 and 200 men on most Saturday nights; no doubt they were initially interested in the offer of a free tea, which the Chapel women supplied throughout the war for an outlay of £2 per week, but, one night, 23 men accepted Christ. As the war intensified, the Chapel workers noted the huge turn-over in those attending – men, who obviously appreciated the fellowship, came for a few weeks and were then posted away, often to the Front.

The hundreds of thousands who had been mobilized could not all be discharged at once when the war ended in November 1918, so the Saturday night meetings continued for as long as servicemen were wandering along Princes Street. The last Soldiers and Sailors Meeting was held in March 1919, when it was calculated that over ten thousand men had heard the gospel in this way; hundreds of New Testaments and thousands of gospel booklets had been given and accepted. In presenting his annual report for 1918, the church secretary said: 'C.C. never did a better bit of work in its history, and we praise God for His goodness to us.'

## The Home Front

The City of Edinburgh's Order for obscuration of lighted windows (what we now call black-out) in February 1916 required the Chapel to put blinds on all its windows. This was because Zeppelins were bombing areas of England, causing death and damage. It was not practicable to turn off the gas lamps in the streets quickly, in the event of a raid, so they were not lit; this made attendance at evening services difficult for older folk. The city fathers debated whether or not to install sirens, to warn the public about an imminent attack. They decided against it for two reasons: in other places, crowds had rushed out into the streets, to watch the Zeppelins, whenever the sirens sounded, and so made themselves more likely casualties. Secondly, one Zeppelin was passing over a blacked-out town in England, unaware of its existence until the crew heard air-raid sirens going off below; they turned and released their bombs on the invisible town.

On the night of Sunday 2 April 1916, two Zeppelins flew slowly over Edinburgh, dropping high explosive and incendiary bombs. Eleven people were killed and 24 properties damaged. The nearest one to the Chapel is still commemorated by a plaque above the path between King's Stables Road and Johnston Terrace, which reads: 'On this spot a bomb fell during the German air raid – 2nd April 1916.' The obscuration of lighted windows and the absence of gas lighting in the streets lasted until the armistice in November 1918.

*This is not a photograph of the Zeppelin raid on Edinburgh in April 1916, which was carried out in darkness, but it was taken during a courtesy visit after the war.*

## 'Call' to Graham Scroggie

### Invitation to preach

For the first six months after Joseph Kemp left Edinburgh, the Chapel office-bearers received no clear guidance about the vacancy. The deacons met every fortnight, for prayer and discussion, but the church secretary had to report to the members on 24 February 1916:

*After exhaustive enquiries and anxious consideration, the Deacons specially invited several brethren to preach in the hope that one of these might be thought suitable for the pastorate of the Church. But, although all were men of marked spirituality and ministerial gifts, none of them was able to command unanimity among the Office-bearers.*

3 *Record*, 1916, p. 53.

Graham Scroggie had spoken in the Chapel in 1907 – his sermon was printed in the *Record* – and he was a well-known Keswick speaker by 1915, but the deacons did not consider his name until a fortuitous return visit to Edinburgh of Wilkinson Riddle. As mentioned in Chapter 20, Riddle had supplied the pulpit for the month of May 1913, while the Kemps visited America. His ministry was greatly appreciated, and he was among those considered for the pastorate. (There is no embarrassment in saying that, because he published it in his memoirs.) During a visit to Edinburgh in December 1915, Wilkinson Riddle suggested that Graham Scroggie might be invited to fill the vacancy.

CHARLOTTE CHAPEL, WEST ROSE STREET
ANNUAL MEETING
OF
WEST END BROTHERHOOD
In the Church, on Friday Evening, 17th December
AT 8 O'CLOCK
Chairman, Sir ALEXANDER SIMPSON, M.D., D.Sc., LL.D.
Address by Rev. T. WILKINSON RIDDLE, London
THE CHURCH CHOIR WILL SING
ALL ARE HEARTILY INVITED
Collection on behalf of Funds for Soldiers' Comforts and Saturday Evening Meetings
Rev. Mr RIDDLE will also address Brotherhood Meeting on Sunday, 12th December, at 3 o'clock. Subject—"The Human Chariot."

*While in Edinburgh for the annual meeting of the West End Brotherhood on Friday 17 December 1915, Wilkinson Riddle suggested to the church secretary that Graham Scroggie would be a suitable successor to Joseph Kemp.*

On Riddle's recommendation, Graham Scroggie was invited to preach on Sunday 7 May 1916. In the meantime, two deacons went to Sunderland at the end of March, to observe him in his own pulpit. What happened next needs to be recorded, because it has been claimed that they took Scroggie's text – 'Art thou He that should come, or look we for another?' (Matthew 11:3) – as guidance to recommend his name to the church. In fact, they brought back a negative report, and the deacons approached someone else. However, Scroggie was already booked for May; after he had conducted three services on the Sunday, given a lecture on Monday 8

May and conducted the Bible School on Thursday 11 (which had to be moved from the hall to the church because of the number attending), the deacons unanimously decided on Friday 12 May that Graham Scroggie was the man for Charlotte Chapel.

## The 'call' sent

It was an excellent decision. Joseph Kemp was primarily an evangelist, and there were now hundreds of new believers in the Chapel, who required to be built up in the faith. Graham Scroggie's systematic Bible teaching was exactly what was needed. In 1916, he was in his fortieth year, with 17 years experience in the ministry. His life, since completing his training at Spurgeon's College in 1899, had been a mixture of sweetness and bitterness. He had to resign from his first charge in London (1899-1902), because of theological liberalism in the church, and also from his second charge in Halifax (1902-5), because of worldliness in the congregation. He was out of the pastorate for two years, but by 1916 he had completed nine happy years at Bethesda Church, Sunderland.

The deacons called a church meeting for Thursday 25 May, and then set about persuading Graham Scroggie that they might bring his name to it. He raised formidable questions, to test whether the invitation really was the 'call' of God. The office-bearers were able to answer all his queries, and the church unanimously supported the recommendation. Graham Scroggie accepted the 'call' on 1 July 1916.

He came on the basis that power in the pulpit required prayer in the pew:

*You, no doubt, are looking to me for spiritual instruction. I am looking to you for spiritual inspiration. You are looking to me for counsel. I am looking to you for confidence. We are a Body, and the health and usefulness of the whole depends on every separate part fulfilling its function.... Let it never be forgotten that a minister is a man of like passions with his people, and, under God, is greatly dependent upon their sympathy and co-operation.*

4 *Record*, 1916, p. 132.

The manse throughout Graham Scroggie's time in Edinburgh was 37 Cluny Gardens. After his father became paralysed in

1922, both his parents spent their remaining years in peace and comfort there; his father died in 1927 at the age of 84, and his mother in 1932, at the age of 86.

*Graham Scroggie chose 37 Cluny Gardens, Morningside, as his manse (2005 photograph).*

## Death of Andrew Urquhart

Graham Scroggie was due to commence his ministry on 1 October 1916. Just a month before he arrived, Andrew Urquhart, whose earnestness had persuaded both Joseph Kemp and Graham Scroggie to come to the Chapel, died on the morning of Sunday 3 September. He had been church secretary for 31 years. Graham Scroggie led the prayers at a service in the Chapel and then at the committal in Warriston Cemetery, on the following Thursday. The many oral tributes included a reminder that, as church secretary, he had ushered Joseph Kemp into the Chapel pulpit more than thirteen hundred times, and that he had never failed to bow with the pastor in prayer before doing so, commending the preacher to God.

## Four essentials

In an open letter to the church in September 1916, just before he took up the pastorate, Graham Scroggie wrote that the essentials of his ministry were: (1) Exposition of the Word on Sunday morning, (2) Proclamation of the gospel on Sunday evening – with this order sometimes reversed, 'for sinners needing to be saved come in the morning, and saints needing to be edified come at night', (3) a School of Bible Study, lasting for six or seven months every year, one lecture a week, probably on Thursday evening, and (4) a week-night prayer

meeting. The next chapter looks at the first two of these, that is the Sunday services, and Chapter 24 describes the other two.

Joseph Kemp's 13 years in Charlotte Chapel were described chronologically in Chapters 13-21. Graham Scroggie's 17-year ministry will be looked at thematically, taking a topic and following it throughout his pastorate. Kemp came to an almost lost cause, with only four services a week, and rapidly expanded the Chapel's activities. Scroggie came to a church humming with activity and, as an older man with years of experience in the ministry, he quickly established the areas that he wished to develop.

*Rev. W. Graham Scroggie and his first wife, Florence. They were married in 1900, when he was aged 23 (above photograph). His fourth anniversary at the Chapel, in October 1920, coincided with his twenty-first year in the ministry (left photograph).*

Graham Scroggie joked in October 1920, on the twenty-first anniversary of his entering the ministry, that 'although often regarded about 55 or 60 years of age, he had been in the ministry half of his life, so they would know how old he was.'

## Lasting impressions

Asked about their recollections of Graham Scroggie's pulpit ministry in Edinburgh, older members have commented to the writer on: (1) his prayers, which lasted for 10 or 15 minutes – 'they were so worshipful that one could have gone home after the prayer, without waiting for the sermon', (2) the length of the sermon, up to one hour morning and evening, (3) the dignity of the service, with the big pulpit Bible reverently opened and read from, and (4) his immaculate morning coat and, always, a ministerial collar.

Graham Scroggie started a practice that has endured to this day; he asked the elders to meet with him in the vestry, before both of the Sunday services, for prayer. As mentioned, Andrew Urquhart had never failed to pray with and for Joseph Kemp, before every service, but apparently on his own. When the writer became an elder in 1965, he found a dozen or more elders gathered in the vestry, half an hour before both of the Sunday services, literally kneeling in prayer for 15 minutes for the Lord's blessing on the preaching of the Word. They stopped a quarter of an hour before the service, partly to go to their own duties and partly to give the preacher a little time on his own; visiting preachers often remarked how helpful this pattern was to them. Scroggie expected the elders to join him in the vestry on Monday also, before the prayer meeting, and on Thursday, before the Bible School.

Additional information on the following topics, mentioned in this chapter, is available on the CD.

Graham Scroggie before Charlotte Chapel
Graham Scroggie's 'call' to Charlotte Chapel
Graham Scroggie's family
Graham Scroggie's first address in Charlotte Chapel
Wilkinson Riddle
Worldliness

# Chapter 23
## Sunday with Graham Scroggie (1916–1933)

## Sunday morning

### Full surrender

Graham Scroggie commenced his ministry in Charlotte Chapel on Sunday 1 October 1916. On Sunday morning he usually spoke to believers on Christian doctrine and Christian living and Christian character. From the beginning it was evident that God was going to do a great work through him. Scroggie's physical appearance was solemn, almost austere; he was tall and slim and gaunt. He scarcely moved while preaching, making little use of his hands, but his personality was deeply impressive. He had an analytical mind and was a master of English. He made sparing use of illustrations, but taught the Word in expository preaching. He reigned like a prince in the pulpit; he was an iceberg on fire. When he left the vestry to mount the pulpit steps, a deep hush fell on the congregation, who knew that the preacher was coming to them with the words of the living God in his heart and on his lips.

At the morning service on Sunday 26 November 1916, that is just eight weeks after he came to the Chapel, Graham Scroggie preached on Ephesians 5:18 and entitled his sermon: 'Be filled in the Spirit – What it is and what it is not.' He then appealed for any who wished to make a full surrender of their lives to Christ to stand.

*Amidst intense stillness and the quiet hush which betokens the presence of the spirit of God, friends quickly and quietly arose all over the building. To many, we are sure, it has meant the entrance into a new experience, and will mark an epoch in the spiritual life of not a few.*

_____
1 *Record*, 1917, p. 3.

What Graham Scroggie meant by being filled in the Spirit will be explored in the section on the Keswick Convention in Chapter 29.

As in the opening months of every succeeding pastorate in the twentieth century, the stewards could not find seats for everyone who wanted to attend. The aisles were filled with campstools, people were packed into the vestry, onto the communion platform, on the pulpit steps and even into the pulpit, leaving the preacher just room to stand. Until 1931, there was no technology for relaying messages to an overflow meeting in the lower hall, so the stewards were drilled with

military precision to fit thirteen people into every pew in the centre of the church and seven into every side pew – an art that was lost when closed-circuit television became available. If extra large numbers were anticipated, a separate preacher had to be engaged to speak in the lower hall.

As with the other ministries mentioned, numbers gradually found their own level. After a few months, the one thousand seats were normally well filled but not usually the aisles. Throughout Graham Scroggie's years in the Chapel, the *Record* reported large congregations, or that the church was nearly filled, on Sunday morning. Those who today have difficulty in squeezing past earlier arrivals, to get into a pew, may be interested that in August 1921 the elders discussed 'the difficulty experienced in people placing themselves in the corner of the pews and manifesting unwillingness to either move up, or come out, to let others in.' No solution was arrived at, then or now. Some people queued before the doors were opened, in order to get their own seat, and they were not going to move from it.

In one of his lectures on preaching, Graham Scroggie defined a sermon as 'an oral address, to the popular mind, on religious truth, as contained in the Christian Scriptures and elaborately treated, with a view to persuasion'. During the Revival period under Joseph Kemp, there was sometimes spontaneous comment from the congregation, like 'Hallelujah!', 'Amen!', 'Glory!', 'Praise the Lord!' Mr Scroggie found this disturbing and unhelpful to his style of preaching. A former soldier, Edmund Trickett, had the voice of a regimental sergeant major. When he shouted 'Praise the Lord' or 'Hallelujah', everybody heard him. One Sunday morning, Mr Trickett had been particularly vociferous. Graham Scroggie stopped preaching, looked down and said: 'My dear brother, if you are going to speak, I'll be silent, but when I'm speaking, you'll be silent'. The rebuke was graciously given and just as graciously received, and from then on, the 'Hallelujah' chorus was muted.

### One visitor's impression, in 1928

*As we entered the door [Sunday morning, 23 September 1928] there was the consciousness that we were in God's house. Many people hurried in for the few remaining seats about us in the large gallery, but they were quiet and reverent and worshipful.*

167

*Each seemed intent on meeting the Lord. Each sought Him.… the organ prelude drew our hearts further away from other things.*

*The songs selected and sung were of the deeply spiritual kind that reach to the heart.… The Scripture passage was a long one and exceedingly well read. Practically all of the people followed the reading with open Bibles as the minister pronounced the words.…*

*The highest point reached was the powerful message delivered by the scholarly pastor, Dr W. Graham Scroggie. He is one of our greatest preachers. He is dignified, calm, and forceful in his delivery, combining all the powers of the orator with an intense earnestness and a firm conviction that he had come to deliver God's message to that congregation.… . His heart seemed to be fired with a passion for the lost.… It was God's call to our hearts.*

*After the benediction every person sat quietly in the seat for a moment before going out into the busy street. As we left our seats the choir sang those familiar words that seemed to be echoing in our hearts: 'We have heard the joyful sound, Jesus saves! Jesus saves!'*

2 *Record*, 1928, p. 184.

### Another visitor's impression, in 1929
After visiting the Chapel on Sunday morning, 3 November 1929, a Presbyterian minister from Glasgow wrote in the *Glasgow Citizen*:

*Immediately on entering I experienced my first glad surprise. I was surrounded by office-bearers. One shook hands, another gave me hymn books, a third led me to a little table in the vestibule, and before I knew what was happening I was signing my name in a memorandum book. I was not, I may explain, in 'clericals'. A lesson on how to receive visitors, which many churches might study with profit.… by 11 o'clock the church was almost uncomfortably filled. The large number of men was remarkable.…*

*There was no invocatory prayer; nor any word of prayer until well on in the service.… there was something tense in this man in the pulpit all the time, even in his unemphatic intimations. The first real escape of personality came, with*

*the children's address on Jeremiah's rescue from the well. The story was told and lessons drawn quietly but arrestingly.*

*The sermon was the climax. The subject was 'Faith Without Works', a hackneyed theme. The treatment was an extraordinary blend of the Bible expositor, the cold logician, the man who knows the world he lives in, and the irresistible evangelist. He disposed of apparent contradiction between Paul and James (as I knew he would), but in his own way, and in the Bible way – taking the passage as it stood and illuminating it with many revealing remarks.… Through all, the intensity grew until at last in the preacher's plea for practical Christianity, we were caught up in the sweep of a spiritual passion which was more than any mere eloquence. It was great preaching – the only worth-while preaching – Bible truth, careful thinking, and illuminating expounding linked to the needs of the hour in a passionate final appeal.*

3 *Record*, 1929, p. 185.

That visitor was fortunate to hear Graham Scroggie talk to the children. Scroggie thought that he was not much good with children, and used to say: 'Children's addresses are not in my line', so he seldom gave them at this stage of his ministry. When he went to the Tabernacle in London in 1938, he was told that 150 children from the orphanage came every Sunday morning and that they expected a regular talk. He found, to his surprise, that when he applied his mind to it, both he and they greatly enjoyed this part of the service.

### A third visitor's impression, in 1930
A representative of *The Baptist Times* attended on Sunday morning, 15 June 1930:

*The service is as plain as the building. The amazing thing is the presence of hundreds of young people of the student type.… Five or ten minutes before the commencement of the service the spacious building was comfortably filled, and when Dr Scroggie ascended the pulpit there did not seem to be an empty seat.*

*It would be difficult to fit Dr Scroggie into either of the categories of preachers. He is emphatically himself; the only one of his kind. Gaunt and thin as he stands with the bent shoulders indicating the student, the slow speech of the Scot – an accent unmistakably belonging to the Land of the Thistle; hair turning from grey to white; an ascetic face and eyes slowly*

*taking fire, till their slumbering light seems to burn and blaze;*
*a personality with a message as individual as himself.*

4 *Record*, 1930, p. 125.

## Youth Sunday

There was no junior church in Graham Scroggie's day, as there is now. Children of all ages sat with their parents through the service; they were remarkably well behaved, considering there was usually nothing specifically for them in the morning service. As many of them stayed on for Sunday School at 1.30 p.m., Graham Scroggie was asked, at his first elders' meeting in 1916, to make every effort to close the 11 a.m. service by 12.30 p.m.

However, from June 1917 onward, one Sunday morning a quarter was devoted wholly to young people; from October 1918, the entire Sunday School joined this quarterly morning service, and there was no school that afternoon. When Scouts and Guides were started (Chapter 24), they sat together, in uniform, in the centre seats of the gallery on these Sundays. From 1919, one Sunday in June or July was Sunday School Prize Day, when the children filled the area of the church and prizes and certificates were presented.

## Young Worshippers League

In June 1928, the Sunday School teachers embarked on a new project, with the twin objectives of encouraging children to come regularly to the Sunday adult services, and of maintaining personal contact with them during the summer holidays. Teachers stood on the stairs and stamped a card (retained by the children) as the youngsters arrived. Annually in June, from 1929, a morning service was designated for the Young Worshippers, who sat together in the area of the church. 'For 51 Sundays in the year these boys and girls are scattered throughout the congregation, but the 52nd Sunday is their day, when we older folk take a back seat and look on.' Prizes were presented at the end of the service, for perfect attendance, once absent, or regular attendance.

Eighty signed up right away, of whom 45 received prizes at the end of the first year. By 1931, the number of the roll was 102, and during that year 3,497 attendances were marked, an average of 67 children per Sunday. In June 1931, four had three years' perfect attendance – 52 Sundays a year in some church; ministers in holiday resorts were permitted to mark

the cards – while 15 others had two complete years and 11 more had one complete year. At the end of the fifth year, in the summer of 1933, three boys had five years' perfect attendance.

A visitor in June 1930, who came expecting a normal morning service, was pleasantly surprised and wrote:

*The occasion was a special service; the minister presented*
*prizes to the Young Worshippers League.... The sermon was*
*addressed to boys and girls. It concerned the familiar passage*
*in the Epistle to the Hebrews, describing the Christian race.*
*Dr Scroggie is analytical in his method. He presents a triangle*
*of thought, firstly, secondly, and thirdly every time, and yet*
*without monotony he talked of the road, the runners and the*
*reward; the start, the track, and the goal. The little people*
*listened with evident relish.... The service was quite unusual, it*
*could easily have been spoiled by the introduction of a prize*
*distribution, but it was all of a piece, harmoniously thought*
*out and carried through.*

5 *Record*, 1930, p. 125.

Like all Chapel organisations at the time, the League had its own social life. Annually on a Saturday evening in the spring, there was a lively party in the lower hall, with a feast of sandwiches and cakes, followed by games interspersed with recitations, solos and piano pieces, ending with family worship. The only negative comment on the League was the deliberate absence of any provision for genuine illness; children with infectious diseases were brought to the vestry, after the minister vacated it, to preserve their perfect attendance record. Apart from that, it was an excellent scheme, and encouraged children to attend regularly at Sunday services.

## Hymnbooks

The morning hymnbook, when Graham Scroggie arrived, was still *Psalms and Hymns*, produced in 1858 and introduced to the Chapel in 1877. The choirmaster proposed the *Baptist Church Hymnal*, but Scroggie flatly refused: 'It lacked in his judgment warmth and life, and moreover the expense incurred would be a millstone round the neck of the church.' However, a year later the deacons overcame Scroggie's misgivings, and on Christmas Day 1922 the

Chapel started using it for the morning service; 'the praise has been much improved by the adoption of [it]'.

From 1911 to 1921, *Redemption Songs* was the hymnbook for Sunday evening and Thursday evening, then *Sankey's Sacred Songs and Solos*, which had been used from 1875 to 1911, came back into favour. Members were exhorted to 'buy your own copy so that there will be plenty available for visitors'.

## Sunday evening

### Directly evangelistic

'The Evening Services are rightly regarded as a great opportunity for evangelism and the services are entirely conducted with that in view.' After preaching the gospel, Graham Scroggie called for decisions, and there were conversions to Christ nearly every Sunday evening.

*At our evening service, January 29th [1922], the Lord was present in mighty wonder-working power. Our Pastor took for his theme, 'What shall it profit a man if he shall gain the whole world and lose his own soul?' He spoke with great power and … made an appeal which resulted in forty decisions for Christ, and twelve others stood up indicating their willingness to accept Christ as Lord. The fifty-two who signed cards were spoken to at the close of the meeting.*

6 *Record*, 1922, p. 18.

*February 19th [1922] the Lord again visited us in all His fullness at an after meeting; when Mr. Scroggie gave the appeal fourteen young men and women accepted Christ as their own personal Saviour. And the following Monday evening others came to the Vestry to see our Pastor on spiritual matters, and we rejoice to know that several that night also came to Jesus for the first time.*

7 *Record*, 1922, p. 18.

As with the morning service, the *Record* reported a crowded church on Sunday evening throughout Graham Scroggie's years in the Chapel. The gallery filled up first, and many queued before the doors opened at 6 p.m. in order to get a gallery seat. When it was discovered that some, who should have been in the queue, were letting themselves into the church by the unlocked side door, the internal door from it into the sanctuary had to be locked until the front doors were opened at 6 p.m. Older members remember with affection the congregational hymn singing, led by the choirmaster while the congregation was gathering, partly to keep the interest of those who had been in their seats since six o'clock, and partly to discourage idle chatter.

On special occasions, every seat in the church was taken by 6.10 p.m., for the 6.30 service, and people had to be turned away. A visitor in October 1923 expressed astonishment at the ingenuity of the stewards – 'the camp chairs were out in full strength, and even the organ loft held its quota of listeners', as they packed latecomers in behind the tenors and the basses in the choir.

### Focus on young people

On Sunday evening, the larger part of the audience were young men and women, and 'One of the most gratifying features of those services is the presence of so many young people.' This was the happy consequence of Graham Scroggie deliberately focusing his addresses on topics of interest to younger people during the evening service.

*A common standard of a Pastor's success is his ability to retain a hold of the youth of his congregation. By this standard Mr. Scroggie is an eminent success. His ability in this direction is seen in the large percentage of youth in our Sunday evening services, and then on Monday night. Why! It might have been a young people's rally. What a picture! A Pastor imbued with a passion to win the youth for Christ. A congregation of young folk all devoted to their Pastor.*

8 *Record*, 1922, p. 83.

This remained the position throughout Graham Scroggie's time in Edinburgh. At his farewell service in 1933, the church secretary ranged over the 17 years and particularly singled out:

*At any Sunday evening service, young people, young men and young women, have predominated. Now that, I understand, is rather unusual, and we immediately ask why. The answer, to my mind, lies in the fact that in Dr Scroggie's ministry and his preaching, and particular his Sunday evening preaching, he has insisted on the young people facing up to a question, and that question is one which has rung down through the ages, and will go on till the end of time, and which every soul has to answer: 'What will ye do with Jesus?'*

9 *Record*, 1933, p.170

### Relay of services to the lower hall

A London company, Acousticon for the Deaf, had been pressing the Chapel since early 1930 to accept a free trial of its equipment, which could broadcast the service to the lower hall and also provide individual earphones for hard-of-hearing members in the sanctuary. The Baptist Union of Scotland tried it out in Dundee in October 1930, and, duly impressed, asked the Chapel to install a temporary acousticon to the lower hall for the 1931 Assembly in Edinburgh. It was so successful that the deacons asked the company to make the link permanent, and also to provide twelve earphones in the northwest corner of the church. When the deacons proposed to remove the latter in 1945, one of the deacons pled for at least one to be retained, for his wife.

**SCOTTISH BAPTIST UNION ASSEMBLY.**

**DELEGATES WILL HEAR EVERY WORD**
of the Addresses at
WARD ROAD AND RATTRAY ST. CHURCHES
By means of the ACOUSTICON.
Installed in over 5000 Churches.   Upkeep only 5/- Per Year.

# DEAFNESS

**IS A TERRIBLE HANDICAP.**
And every Church should provide the Acousticon for their
Deaf Members.   It is so simple—fool proof and gives perfect
results.   No matter how Deaf or where Seated, every word
**CAN BE HEARD.**

*The Baptist Union of Scotland had an acousticon at its Assembly at Dundee in 1930, and asked the Chapel to install it, temporarily, for the 1931 Assembly in Edinburgh. The deacons, in turn, were so impressed that within a month, they set up a permanent link.*

After one particularly crowded series of meetings, the editor of the *Record* wrote: 'Indeed, many late-comers had to have a firm belief in the Apostle's words that "faith cometh by *hearing*", as they found their steps directed downstairs to the overflow'. The earphones in the sanctuary were operated for the hard of hearing, whether or not there was an overflow into the lower hall, although from time to time, police radio messages competed with the sermon.

Electrical loudspeakers were first installed in the sanctuary itself about 1936, to amplify the voice of the preacher; the acousticon continued to transmit the message to the lower

hall and to assist the hard of hearing with earphones. Technology had come a long way in 60 years, since 'the Secretary was authorised [in 1877] to arrange for the removal of the ear trumpet from the pulpit'.

## WIRELESS AID TO WORSHIP

### Edinburgh Innovation

A wireless innovation was tried in connection with last night's service at the Charlotte Baptist Chapel in Edinburgh, of which the minister is the Rev. Dr W. G. Scroggie. The church has been só crowded on Sunday evenings that numbers of persons have had to be turned away, and to meet the situation there have been installed in the hall under the church two loud speakers, through which the service can be broadcast. The experiment was inaugurated with success last night, a crowded congregation in the church, which holds 1100, and some 200 persons in the hall below worshipping together. The innovation includes a number of appliances for deaf persons.

*On Monday 22 November 1931, the* Edinburgh Evening News *rightly described the Chapel's link to the lower hall as wireless (the popular name for what is now called radio), because it was broadcast, not transmitted over a physical wire.*

### Sunday prayer meetings

As many as possible were encouraged to meet in the ladies' room in the Chapel for half an hour at 10.15 a.m. on Sunday morning and 5.30 p.m. on Sunday evening, specifically to pray for the service to follow. When Graham Scroggie came to Edinburgh, between 50 and 100 attended; a year later, the meetings were 'maintained by a score or thirty faithful souls'. The next year, support was even less and the church secretary was greatly concerned. One factor may have been that Graham Scroggie's health did not permit him to attend these meetings, and an elder was in charge. Both meetings opened with a hymn and a reading from Scripture, after which all were free to pray – and most did.

In 1921, the elder in charge noted sorrowfully: 'While grateful to those who so faithfully support them, it still seems that no meetings are so unpopular as prayer meetings'. Every time these two meetings are mentioned in the *Record* throughout the 1920s, it is with a plea for more to attend. In 1931, average attendance was 10, and the leader said, 12 months later: 'I appealed last year for your support, but I

171 must confess with little result, as our numbers are still very small, taking into account the size of our congregation.'

### Travel to Charlotte Chapel

People came to Rose Street from all over the city. In 1916 (when Graham Scroggie arrived) and in 1933 (when he left), not one elder or deacon lived in the postal district EH2, where the Chapel is located. The first column (below) gives the address of the 8 elders and 12 deacons in 1916; the second column translates these addresses into postcodes; the third column locates the 16 elders and 18 deacons by postal district in 1933.

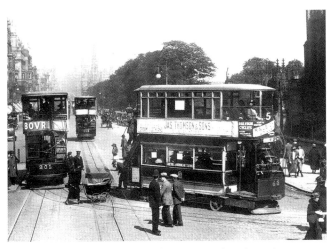

*This 1919 photograph of the West End of Princes Street shows the continuous open slot between the tramlines, through which the driver wound down a gripper, under the tram, to clamp onto the moving cable underground; this provided the propulsion for the tram.*

| Where elders and deacons lived: | 1916 | 1933 |
|---|---|---|
| Gayfield Square and the High Street | EH 1 | 0 |
| (no one in 1916, nor in 1933) | EH 2 | 0 |
| Clarence Street, Henderson Row, | | |
| Inverleith Avenue, Inverleith Row, | | |
| St. Peter's Place and Summerbank | EH 3 | 3 |
| Belford Road | EH 4 | 6 |
| Laverockbank Avenue | EH 5 | 1 |
| (no one in 1916) | EH 6 | 2 |
| Elm Row | EH 7 | 1 |
| Kenmure Avenue | EH 8 | 1 |
| Spottiswoode Street | EH 9 | 4 |
| Greenhill Terrace and Hartington Place | EH10 | 5 |
| Polwarth Crescent | EH11 | 4 |
| Saughtonhall Drive and Stanhope Place | EH12 | 6 |
| (no one in 1916) | EH14 | 1 |

Chapel members who used public transport on Sunday (some would not; Chapter 20) found travel much easier after Edinburgh Corporation took over the tramway and the bus networks in 1919 and extended their routes into the suburbs.

Even when public transport was available, people were more ready to walk long distances than they are now. The Young Peoples Meeting arranged a picnic in Davidson's Mains Park in May 1919; they met at the church, and then, instead of taking the train from the Caledonian Station to Davidson's Mains station (the site of the present supermarket), they walked the three-and-a-bit miles to the park. At first, Graham Scroggie used public transport, but after a year he obtained approval from the deacons to take such taxicabs as he found necessary for his visitation of the sick.

## Eight special Sundays

### Backs to the wall – Sunday 24 March 1918

Most of the references to the impact of the First World War on the Chapel have been held over until Chapter 28, but three services are included in this selection of eight notable Sundays during Graham Scroggie's ministry.

In March 1918, the German army launched an offensive against the British army in Flanders. The British commander-in-chief coined the phrase: 'We've got our backs to the wall' to describe the crisis. Thousands of British soldiers, including four Chapel boys, died in repulsing the German advance.

*Few who were present at the morning service on March 24 [1918] will forget the peculiar circumstances in which we met. The situation at the front was extremely critical, and grave concern was felt by many. Our Pastor, led we believe of God, after the usual opening hymn and prayer read a portion of the Prophecy of Habukkuk, and after some remarks, full of intensity and passion, bearing on the condition of things amongst us in the Church and the State, turned the service into one of intercession. The Spirit of God was present in power, moving many to audible prayer, in which we believe every heart was moved to join.*

10 *Record*, 1918, p. 66.

## Memorial service –
### Sunday evening, 8 December 1918

Thirty of the Chapel's young men died in the Great War. Their sacrifice was commemorated at a solemn memorial service in a packed Chapel on Sunday evening 8 December, shortly after the armistice was signed. At the conclusion of the service, which greatly moved both Graham Scroggie and the congregation, he read the names of those who had made the supreme sacrifice. He then appealed to the youth of the congregation to be 'baptized for the dead', calling on 'those who would take the places of the thirty men who had fallen, who would step into these gaps by consecrating themselves then and there to Christ, to come forward.' There was an instant response. Young men rose in every part of the Chapel and to Graham Scroggie's astonishment: 'when I counted those who had taken the great step just thirty had come forward'.

## Welcome home – March 1919

During the war, 173 Chapel men and 7 women served with the Colours; three were decorated. The survivors were welcomed home during a Sunday service in March 1919. Contrary emotions struggled to find expression as they rose in turn, reported their regiment and rank, and the fields in which they had served. The joy of reunion was tempered by the consciousness of 30 empty places and silent voices.

## Settlement of an industrial dispute –
### Sunday evening, 12 October 1919

During Sunday 12 October 1919, news came through that the national railway strike had been settled. Graham Scroggie announced this at the beginning of the evening service. It is difficult to imagine a Chapel congregation, now, responding as they did, but the congregation rose and sang with great heartiness the hymn, 'Praise God from whom all blessings flow' and the first verse of the national anthem. Seven years later, Graham Scroggie wrote passionately in the *Record* against the general strike of 1926 – 'those who promoted it have suffered a most humiliating defeat, as they deserved to do'.

Not all evangelical leaders shared his view; another member of the Council of the Keswick Convention, soon to be its chairman, was equally outspoken in asserting the 'righteous demands of the miners' during the strike. 'The Church', he claimed in a sermon, 'has assisted the privileged classes to keep Labour in chains.'

## Visit of the ex-prime minister –
### Sunday morning, 27 May 1923

On Sunday 27 May 1923, David Lloyd George, who had been prime minister of Great Britain from 1916 to 1922, was staying in Edinburgh and came, unexpectedly, to the morning service in the Chapel, with his wife. Graham Scroggie preached an eloquent sermon on John Mark, and then invited the ex-premier to say a few words. The congregation stood while he made his way to the pulpit. He spoke appreciatively about his visit and after the communion service, he and Mrs Lloyd George shook hands with many of the worshippers at the door as they left.

*David Lloyd George signed the visitors' book in the vestry on Sunday 27 May 1923. This book has the names of guest preachers from 1916 to 1960, together with their church or society and the subject on which they preached. Graham Scroggie added the third line in this entry.*

## Remembrance Day –
### Sunday morning, 11 November 1923

The remembrance of armistice (11 November 1918) fell on a Sunday for the first time in 1923. In order to observe the two minutes' silence, the Chapel, along with most churches throughout the country, commenced the morning service at 10.45 instead of 11 a.m. After two hymns, a Scripture reading and prayer:

*On the gun signal being heard the audience stood amidst a silence, that was indeed intense, and when the further gun signal was given announcing the termination of the period, the Pastor called the roll of the lads of our number who had made the supreme sacrifice….*

173

*The service, which was marked by a spirit of deep reverence, was concluded by the singing of another of Watt's Hymns, 'When I survey the Wondrous Cross', followed by the benediction and the singing of the National Anthem.*

11 *Record*, 1923, pp. 91-2

From then on, Remembrance Day was observed on the Sunday nearest to 11 November, not on armistice day itself. The congregation stood reverently while the pastor read the roll of those who had been killed; many could still put faces to the names of family and friends who had gone and not come back.

## Harvest Thanksgiving

Harvest Thanksgiving, which now features in the autumn calendar for the church, was initiated by the primary department of the Sunday School on 31 October 1926, as part of their Sunday afternoon meeting in the top hall. Fruit and vegetables overflowed the platform and windowsills and tables, as the children brought their gifts. Simultaneously, a similar occasion took place in the High Street mission primary Sunday School, where the teachers supplied the gifts. Anticipating that the High Street children might be expecting a 'dookin', because it was Hallowe'en, every child there was given an apple. The teachers then distributed the fruit and vegetables to members ill at home and in hospital and to about 35 parents of High Street children.

## Family service – Sunday morning, 13 May 1928

'The congregation was rather surprised when our Children's Choir occupied the usual choir seats,' at the first family service. The children sang three pieces, which were greatly enjoyed, but there is no indication that the congregation applauded them, as happens now. The Sunday School children attended and Graham Scroggie gave a talk, which was much appreciated by both young and old.

Additional information on the following topics, mentioned in this chapter, is available on the CD.

Graham Scroggie and the general strike, 1926
Lloyd George's visit to the Chapel
William Whyte
Young Worshippers League

# Chapter 24
## From birth to baptism (1916–1933)

## Sunday School

### 'From the Cradle to the Crown'

To supplement the four essentials described at the end of Chapter 22, that is two Sunday services, the Monday prayer meeting and the Thursday School of Bible Study, Graham Scroggie encouraged a wide variety of other activities 'to organize our corporate life on all sides, from the Cradle to the Crown'. This and the following two chapters look at aspects of the Chapel's corporate life for its members and adherents; Chapters 27 and 28 look at the gospel outreach.

### Cradle roll

The primary department of the Sunday School maintained a cradle roll, entering the names of babies on a large scroll as soon as possible after birth. Children were asked every Sunday to report any new arrivals in their family. From 30 names when it started in 1923, the roll grew rapidly to over one hundred names by 1932. Twice a year (May and Christmas) the mothers were invited to bring their infants to the top hall on a Sunday afternoon, to introduce them to the Sunday School. The cradle roll was called and every baby received a bouquet of flowers with a text-card attached, coloured by the Sunday School children. The scene on Sunday 31 May 1925 was typical:

*Early on Sunday afternoon, May 31st, there was an unusual scene outside the backdoor of the church. Mothers with babies in their arms were arriving for Sunday School. Why? Because this was Baby Sunday in the Primary – perhaps the most important Sunday of the year. That afternoon the teachers gathered early and the room was made gay with flowers. Bunches were made up for all the babies with an appropriate text-card attached to each.*

*No sooner was all ready than our important visitors – the babies – came and took their seats. The day had really come to which we had looked forward for so many weeks. The children sang a hymn-prayer asking God's blessing on our Sunday School, and an opening hymn. Then after prayer we sang a welcome hymn to the babies [text follows]. A word of welcome was then spoken to the mothers and babies, and some of the babies helped us to sing 'Jesus Loves Me' – some venturing as far as the front of the hall. Those who were courageous enough marched round and gave their pennies for their brothers and sisters in other lands who do not know Jesus.*

*For a short time the children went to classes. Into these a few of the older babies stole and sat with their big brothers or sisters, quite happy listening to the story. Since then two of the babies have come every Sunday. After the lesson the babies were presented with their bouquet of flowers, our Cradle Roll hymn was sung, and the happy service was closed with prayer.*

1 *Record*, 1925, p. 119.

Mothers were exhorted to bring their children every Sunday from the age of two and a half, with the promise that they would soon settle in. In 1960, it was noted that many of the parents who attended that year with their children had memories of coming themselves, as youngsters, many years before.

### Infant dedication

Charlotte Chapel, as a Baptist church, does not practise infant baptism, but offers a service of thanksgiving and dedication on the gift of a child. In April 1917, Graham Scroggie told the elders that he preferred public dedications, as part of a church service, but the elders insisted he should continue to conduct them in the home, as was the Chapel's tradition. Shortly before he left Edinburgh in 1933, Graham Scroggie obtained the elders' approval for one couple to bring their child into the closing part of a Sunday morning service, where he welcomed them and conducted the dedication publicly. This was well received by the congregation, and people asked why it had not been done before, but the next minister, Sidlow Baxter, reverted to private family occasions, as discussed in Chapter 32.

There is no record of when the practice of dedicating infants (which includes the dedication of their parents to their upbringing) began in the Chapel. In 1834, during the ministry of Christopher Anderson, there were discussions among the Scotch Baptist churches about the propriety of 'infant dedication services'. The Edinburgh church advised against them on two grounds, first that some people might see them as infant baptism by another name and, secondly, that there was not unanimity of view among the churches and so the issue might be divisive. Whether this was the position in Charlotte Chapel at that time, is not known.

## Lambs and sheep

Unless parents brought their children to the Sunday morning service, the youngsters' first involvement in Chapel life was to attend the Sunday School. Graham Scroggie gave it the highest priority and he personally chaired the committee. He said: 'Farmers who look after their lambs usually get good sheep.' The Chapel school, which numbered 180 with 26 teachers when he came to Edinburgh in 1916, had three aims; first, to train children in habits of worship and reverence, and to teach them the Word of God; second, to win them in their tender years to allegiance to Jesus as Saviour and Redeemer; third, to hold them for Christ's service in the church. The first and second aspects were accomplished by dedicated teaching and by holding annual Decision Days, as described below.

The third aspect greatly concerned Graham Scroggie. Many adolescents, not only in the Chapel but also in other churches, stopped attending Sunday School about the age of 15. Scroggie had a number of strategies to stem the leakage. In November 1919, he reorganized the senior department, so that the classes for young men and women of 16 were no longer designated as Sunday School. For them, he created two Junior Bible Classes, one for lads and another for girls; each was attended by about 18 and each had its own syllabus and proceeded at its own pace. When girls reached 15, they were encouraged either to attend this class or to become teachers in the primary department – the lads became teachers in due course in the junior school, which required more maturity. The prospect of teaching was, for many, motivation for attending the Bible Classes, especially since there was continuing training, every Friday, after they were recognized as teachers.

## Sunday School reform

Graham Scroggie inherited an ongoing debate about the best time for Sunday School. Should it continue at 1.30 p.m., which meant teachers and scholars who attended the morning service either bringing a packed lunch or having nothing to eat until after 2.30 p.m., or should it move to 3 p.m., which would mean going home for a hurried lunch, returning for the teachers' prayer meeting at 2.45 p.m., teaching until 4 p.m., and then going home again for tea before the evening service? Graham Scroggie asked the teachers if they would support a change of time; nearly all said that they would, so the parents were consulted. By 1918, he had secured unanimous agreement to try 3 p.m.

The experiment was an instant success. For the first time in nine years, attendance increased; the primary department almost doubled, and more came to the senior school, particularly boys. In the following year, there were 25 new scholars, bringing the total on the roll to 228, with 28 teachers; average attendance was 134. Both the school and the Bible Classes increased in number during the remainder of Scroggie's pastorate, totalling 376 scholars and 65 teachers when he left. The time stayed at 3 p.m. until 1985, except for the early years of the Second World War (Chapter 34).

Graham Scroggie's reforms went beyond the time of day – he put in place a seamless progression through the various departments. The smooth transition of several hundred youngsters from department to department, as they grew up, called for considerable ingenuity, but by the autumn of 1919, he had his system in place. From three o'clock to four o'clock on a typical Sunday afternoon, the primary department of the Sunday School occupied all the rooms on the top floor, the junior department the sanctuary and the intermediates the lower hall. The two Junior Bible Classes met in committee rooms, the lads studying the book of Joshua and the girls following Israel through its forty-year wilderness journey. The Men's Bible Class met in the vestry and the Women's Bible Class in the ladies' room facing the back door (now much reduced in size because of the enlarged kitchen, and known as the committee room).

## Primary department

The primary department was officially for children from four to eight years, but the indefatigable Agnes McPhail encouraged toddlers from the age of two and a half. They met in the top hall, with a membership of 70 and a staff of 15; classes averaged five or six in number, according to age. After some singing and opening devotions, the four-year-olds went to a room by themselves and were taught Bible stories, illustrated on sand trays; the others were provided with crayons, and after the teacher had told the lesson for the day, the children wrote out the text and drew pictures according to their own understanding of the story. By the time they went downstairs at the age of eight, they were well grounded in the faith.

## Junior and intermediate departments

The junior department, for 8 to 11 years, met in the church, with a membership of 75 and 13 teachers. The intermediates, for 12 years to 15 years, had a membership of 70 and 15 teachers; they started together in the lower hall, and then purpose-built wooden partitions were pulled out from the walls, giving separate and private areas for individual small classes – maximum size of six.

## Bible Classes

The Lads Bible Class and the Girls Bible Class catered for 15 to 18 year-olds, almost entirely former Sunday School scholars. Initially, attendance at each was about 18; over the remaining years of Scroggie's ministry, numbers fluctuated between 20 and 8 on each roll, with average attendance about two-thirds of membership. Since equipping youngsters for service in the church was one of the aims of these classes, low numbers were not a discouragement, because they usually meant that members had moved on to become Sunday School teachers; in 1930, 60 per cent of the 60 teachers had come up through these classes.

In the autumn of 1929, most of the intermediate department reached the age of 15 at about the same time; the pragmatic solution was to rearrange the age bands, and to have four Bible Classes (two for 14 to 15 year-olds, lads and girls, and two for those over 15). All four met together for opening devotions and then divided into classes. This proved so successful that it continued until the whole system was revised in 1985. All were eligible to enter the honours shields competition (below), and did so with conspicuous success.

## Decision Days

'The old question why do so many leave the School at 15, has the answer, because they are not converted at 14. Hence the importance of aiming at definite decisions for Christ at an early age.' Decision Days (Chapter 17) became annual events in 1919, when Graham Scroggie made a direct appeal to children aged 12 and over, for conversion and dedication; the usual classes were then held, so that the teachers might follow up the pastor's talk. Cards were available for scholars who wanted to record a decision there and then. At the first Decision Day, on Sunday 4 May 1919, 58 cards were handed in, 36 for decisions that day, 22 as recommitment of a previous decision. On the corresponding day in 1925, 65 accepted Jesus for the first time and another 22 made a rededication of their lives; 30 scholars handed in cards in 1927, and 48 in 1928.

## Sunday School socials

The primary and junior sections initially had a combined Christmas party in the lower hall, on a Saturday before Christmas, with tea, games, recitations and a visit from Father Christmas, who had a present for every child. As numbers grew, they held separate parties. The primary, which included the cradle roll and their mothers, met from 3 p.m. to 6 p.m., with over 100 boys and girls and about 80 babies, supervised by 30 teachers. The juniors met on another Saturday, with about 130 boys and girls, from 5.30 p.m. to 9.30 p.m. Early in January, the intermediates had their own social (without Father Christmas), jointly with the two Bible Classes, about 80 in all. In between, there was a combined meeting for the whole Sunday School on a Saturday afternoon in the church, called the Annual Christmas Entertainment. Graham Scroggie chaired; this was not for games, but for choir pieces, recitations, and lantern displays, etc., and latterly Graham Scroggie's own cine films of his American and African travels. This was when the Sunday School's book prizes for attendance were presented; the Annual Entertainment lasted for three hours.

## Summer picnics

Summer excursions (picnics) usually started with a special train from the nearby Caledonian Station, to Spylaw Park, Colinton, or to Balerno or Gogar or Ratho or Dalmahoy or Newhailes. Nearly five hundred children and adults were at a typical Sunday School picnic, which was usually voted the best of all the Chapel summer outings. The June 1923 picnic was at the Inch, Liberton; instead of chartering a train, the superintendent told scholars and parents to take the electric car to Lady Road. Liberton Park became a favourite for Sunday School picnics during the Second World War, because it was easier to hire tramcars than to charter special trains. After the picnic, the school met together for a closing Sunday, and then went into recess for the summer, reopening on the last Sunday in September.

*One Saturday afternoon in June, not (fortunately) the day of the Sunday School picnic, the driver left his tram at the terminus at Liberton without securing the hand brake. It moved off on its own, with the driver and conductor running after it, jumped the rails at the first bend in the road, and ended up in the garden of a house. Two elderly passengers, both over 70, took the next tram into town as if nothing had happened.*

## Sunday School honours shields

For many years, the Baptist Union of Scotland, of which the Chapel was a member, held Scripture examinations on a Friday evening in the spring, open to all Sunday School scholars, with questions based on the lesson scheme for recent months. Typical questions for the senior division, aged 12-16, were: 'What lessons concerning faith are taught by the healing of the Nobleman's son?' and 'Compare in detail the several accounts of the feeding of the five thousand'. Typical questions for the junior division, aged under 12, were: 'When the Nobleman came to Jesus at Cana, what did they say to each other?' and 'Tell the story of the feeding of the five thousand'. Up to four thousand entered, from over one hundred churches. Certificates and prizes were awarded on an individual basis, and these were presented in the Chapel on the final Sunday of the session, at the end of June.

From 1908 onward, the Union also offered two shields, one for churches with more than one hundred scholars and the other for churches with less. The shields were awarded to the Sunday School with the highest average mark. To avoid a monopoly situation, the winning school had five per cent deducted from its marks in the following year and ten per cent if it held the shield for two years in succession. The Chapel won the shield for larger churches for the first time in 1916, but its finest hour came in 1921, when it won the shield for a third consecutive year, despite the ten per cent penalty.

It was top again in 1925, when the guest preacher at the presentation was Eric Liddell, just before he left for China. For months before the exam, 'both teachers and scholars have untiringly and enthusiastically bent their energies', going over and over the passages of Scripture on which the exam was based. There were even special weeknights for cramming classes; the Chapel won again in 1926 and 1930.

## Systematic visitation

In 1927, systematic visitation of houses within three-quarters of a mile of the Chapel yielded an excellent return. The area was divided into districts, to each of which a group of teachers was allotted. They visited homes and personally invited children to come to the Sunday School. A card was left with details, and this resulted in an increase in the roll of 44; primary department membership went up to 102 and its cradle roll to 85.

To the delight of the teachers, newcomers brought their own chums and playmates. Visitations at the beginning of the 1928, 1929 and 1930 sessions attracted another 17, 40 and 58 new scholars respectively, bringing the roll to a record 338 (122 in the primary, 146 in the junior section and 70 in the Bible Classes), a net increase of exactly 100 in three years, nearly 30 per cent. Loyalties varied from year to year and from group to group, but the average attendance in the years 1932 and 1933 was 66 per cent and 70 per cent in the primary department, 80 and 85 per cent in the junior department and 90 and 77 per cent in the Bible Classes.

# Youth organizations

## Boy Scouts

At a Sunday School executive committee in September 1919, Graham Scroggie suggested forming a Boy Scout Troop and a Girl Guide Section. The link between the Sunday School and the Scouts and Guides was quite deliberate – it was another way of keeping young people interested in the Christian faith as they reached adolescence. Membership of the Sunday School was a condition of joining the new uniformed organisations.

The Scout Troop was outstandingly successful. W. Edgar Evans (affectionately known by the boys as Pa Evans) was its first leader. Joseph Kemp had resisted all suggestions of having Scouts and Guides in the Chapel, but Graham Scroggie had a different attitude and approved of a Warrant being granted to the 6th Waverley, Charlotte Baptist Chapel Troop in January 1921. Covering the age range from 11 or 12 to 19, the Troop began with 16 Scouts; in its first six years, it attracted and held 74 boys through the crucial years of their development. Over these six years, the Troop numbered between 20 and 28 at any one time, rising to 36 in Graham Scroggie's last year in Edinburgh.

## Scout meetings

They met on Friday evening for games and training, and always closed the meeting with prayer. Initially this was in the top hall in the Chapel, but Pa Evans, who was a bachelor and who devoted all his spare time to the Troop, rented premises for them in Rose Street Lane in 1924. When that proved inadequate for the growing numbers, he bought a larger clubroom in the same lane in 1928. From the beginning, there were frequent outings to the countryside on Saturday afternoon.

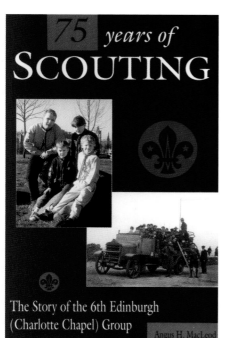

*In 1921, a Warrant was granted to the 6th Waverley, Charlotte Baptist Chapel Troop; 'Waverley' was later changed to 'Edinburgh', and this book in 1996 commemorated 75 years of Scouting in the Chapel.*

By far the most profitable activity, spiritually, was the Scouts Own, for singing hymns and choruses, Scripture reading, prayer and a Bible talk. For the first five years, this was held in the top hall in the Chapel at 10 a.m., before the morning service, which many of the Scouts then attended. The Scoutmaster and the boys took turns to lead these meetings, which had an average attendance of 12. In 1926, the time was changed to 6.30 p.m., and they met in their own clubroom. Attendance doubled. Although this meant the boys missing the Chapel's evening service, the leadership felt that these peer meetings were more valuable. From 1927, they met on alternate Sunday evenings in the club and went to the Chapel service on the others.

Second only to the Scouts Own, for training boys in the Christian way, were the devotional sessions at Scout camps. Through Evans' foresight and generosity, a permanent campsite was secured at Canty Bay, near North Berwick. It took its name from the time when sailors moored their boats at the high-water mark there, so the boats would 'cant' over onto their sides as the tide went out, enabling scraping and painting of the hull to take place. It proved of incalculable value to the boys, not only physically but spiritually; many of them were converted at camp. Edgar Evans died in 1963; his contribution to the welfare of the Chapel's young men was marked by one of the first Scouts designing and donating the wrought-iron memorial gates that still guard the entrance to the site (picture in Chapter 50).

Along with the Cubs, Brownies and Guides, the Scouts attended a monthly (later, from 1923, quarterly) parade to one of the Chapel's morning services. They sat together, in their uniforms, in the central gallery of the church, above the clock, and Graham Scroggie directed his message to them. The history of the Chapel Scout movement was published for its seventy-fifth anniversary in 1996. The book demonstrates how the emphasis was, and still is, on the spiritual welfare of the Scouts. Evans wrote: 'May I remind those who will be in charge hereafter that their first objective must ever be the winning of young lives under their care to the service of the Lord Jesus Christ in all sincerity. Fail in this fundamental necessity, and all other efforts to help and influence the boys, however sincerely undertaken, can be but to "plough the sand", to build without a "sure foundation". This first objective has been wonderfully achieved in the dedication of many of the boys to the service of the Lord Jesus. Many became faithful members of the Chapel, some serving as office-bearers and in other capacities, and ten have become ministers or missionaries.

### Rovers

A Rover Scout Troop was started in 1924 for older boys, from 17 upward, but the Chapel could not recruit a suitable leader and boys of that age had competing interests. The Rovers disbanded in 1929.

### Wolf Cubs

Much more encouraging is the story of the Wolf Cubs (usually abbreviated to Cubs) for boys in the age range of 8 to 11. The Chapel Cub Pack was founded simultaneously with the Scout Troop. Starting with 6, numbers grew rapidly to 26. The Cubs were no pale imitation of the Scouts, but had their own identity and their own activities, although it was expected that, at the age of 12, they would become Scouts. They met in the top hall from 6.15 to 7.30 on Friday evening and from the beginning they had access to Canty Bay. Nearly half of the Pack were also members of the Young Worshippers League and attended the Chapel regularly on Sunday. More than one-third of the 1929 Chapel Scout Troop had come up through the Cubs.

### First Girl Guide Company

It was hoped to start a company of Girl Guides at the same time as the Scouts and Cubs, but initially no one could be found who met the exacting requirements for a Guide leader. It was June 1921 before the Girl Guides (84th Division) were presented with their flag during a morning service in the Chapel. They gave demonstrations at socials, camped in the summer at Biggar and came second in the Girl Guides' Annual Athletic Sports in the King's Park. By 1924 they had 30 enthusiastic members.

What went wrong? At the deacons' meeting on 6 May 1925, Graham Scroggie reported that disbanding the Guide Company was being considered, and a few weeks later this took place; the Brownies (below) kept going until 1926.

### Second Girl Guide Company

The 186th Girl Guide Company was formed at the beginning of 1931, with a roll of 36 and an average attendance of 30; they met weekly in the top hall, for two hours on Tuesday evening. Every meeting ended with the singing of choruses, a

Scripture lesson and prayer. In the summer, there were country rambles on Saturday afternoon and often during the week as well. The Guides attended the church parades mentioned above, now back to monthly (from quarterly). Their outreach was to distribute tracts in three areas of the city. Pa Evans openly favoured the Scouts, to the disadvantage of the Guides, but they were given access to the site at Canty Bay for a weekend camp in the summer of 1932.

### Brownies

The first Brownie Pack was formed principally for the Chapel's Sunday School scholars, but in 1924 they admitted one or two others, who were particular friends of the Brownies; the gratifying result was that the newcomers soon joined the Sunday School and signed cards on Decision Day. Average attendance at the Tuesday meeting (Wednesday from 1926) was 20, for one hour, and there were summer excursions to Canty Bay. The maximum permitted for a Brownie Pack was 24, and for most of the time they were just under that figure. At the age 11 or 12, they were encouraged to 'fly up' to the Guides. There is a curious comment about Christmas Day 1924: 'the Brownies entertained their mothers and a few friends to tea, after which they gave a short demonstration of how the time is spent at the weekly meetings'. Presumably their fathers were either working, as was common on Christmas Day in Scotland at that time, or did not wish to spend the holiday with their family – or perhaps they weren't invited?

### Young Peoples Meeting (YPM)

After he had been in Edinburgh for two years, Graham Scroggie asked the young men and women of the congregation to devise some structured way of meeting with their peers. One of the catalysts was the need to welcome back the young men who had been away for the war, and to integrate them into church life again. Scroggie was also concerned about lonely young people in the city, who were homesick and who had nowhere to go. He suggested a meeting on Wednesday evening, from 7.30 to 9 p.m., to be called the Charlotte Chapel Young People's Movement. The young folk discussed the proposal among themselves for a week, and then called at the manse to express their support, but with the suggestion that it should be called the Young People's Forward Movement. They agreed to form its first committee, and to have a public meeting in the lower hall on Wednesday 13 November 1918, to launch the concept. This was two days after the armistice had been signed, so everyone was in patriotic mood, and decorated the tables with the flags of the allies.

Seventy attended, and Graham Scroggie came well prepared. He suggested a syllabus, consisting of several Bible studies, two missionary evenings, two musical evenings, two prayer meetings, two social evenings, one question evening and practical guidance on reading material, the use of money, etc. He also suggested a motto, which continues to this day: 'The utmost for the highest'.

Four Missionary Study Circles, with a total of 45 members, were already meeting every second Wednesday, so Scroggie recommended that the new syllabus should cover only alternate Wednesdays; he believed (as happened) that the new committee would soon absorb the small groups into one organisation. He proposed that it should be called simply the Young Peoples Meeting (no apostrophe), in place of their rather ponderous suggestion. The subjects dealt with 'would be taken by the young people themselves and should bear on the application of truth rather than the interpretation of it'.

### SYLLABUS :: :

| Date | Subject |
| --- | --- |
| 1919 Oct. 1 | Opening Meeting - - - |
| ,, 15 | The Church and the Young People |
| ,, 29 | Prayer Meeting - - - |
| Nov. 12 | Missionary Lantern Lecture—Africa |
| ,, 26 | Our Spare Time - - - |
| Dec. 10 | Citizens in Training - - |
| ,, 25 | Social - - - - |
| 1920 Jan. 7 | Our Personal Work - - |
| ,, 22 | Church Mission - - |
| Feb. 4 | Prayer Meeting - - - |
| ,, 18 | Missionary Meeting—China - |
| Mar. 3 | Question Evening - - |
| ,, 17 | Lantern Lecture—"How we got our Bible" |
| ,, 31 | Experience Meeting - - - |
| April 14 | Missionary Meeting—South America - |
| ,, 28 | Closing Meeting - - - |

*For its first two years, the YPM met on alternate Wednesdays, so as not to compete with existing missionary study groups; the two committees then merged, and the YPM met weekly until the new structures of September 2006 (Chapter 58).*

The meeting enthusiastically adopted all the pastor's suggestions, and soon there was an average fortnightly attendance of about one hundred. In 1920, the secretary pleaded for more older young people to come – a concern which has been echoed time and again over the years. The age bracket was 15 to 30, but at times the YPM has been very young. The secretary's other plea was for more young men to support the meetings. Graham Scroggie was a regular speaker and a regular attender at their social activities, which was an encouragement to them. Over the next decade, numbers fluctuated between one hundred and two hundred on the roll, and attendances between 70 and 150, averaging about one hundred at the Wednesday meeting.

### YPM activities

Like most of the Chapel auxiliaries, the YPM closed its indoor sessions from the beginning of June to the beginning of October every year. However, in addition to rambles and regular tennis matches on a court hired for the season at Murrayfield, near the site of the present rugby stadium, they were responsible monthly for the Sunday night open-air meeting in South Charlotte Street. *En masse*, they supported the Chapel's Monday evening prayer meeting once a month. Throughout the year they had outings to places which may be fondly remembered by older readers – the Easter Road Glass Works, the General Post Office, Granton Gas Works, Haymarket Engine Sheds, Inveresk Paper Mill, Lauriston Place Fire Station, Newtongrange Colliery, the North British Rubber Mill, *The Scotsman* Office, the Telephone Exchange, the Tramway Depot and other places where manufacturing processes of interest could be seen. Many of these were still favourites for youth groups after the Second World War.

The YPM committee was, and continues to be, a training ground for Christian leadership and for service within the church. To encourage diversity, no member of committee could hold the same position for more than one year (later two). The YPM was soon an outstanding contributor to Chapel life; its emphases have always been on prayer and Bible study, with evangelistic projects such as the distribution of tracts and open-air preaching. The challenge of full-time Christian service was kept to the fore; a number of YPM members have gone overseas with the gospel or entered the ministry. The camaraderie is evident from the numbers attending reunions, the first in 1934 and the next on their twenty-first birthday in 1939.

In February 1927, the YPM formed an Evangelistic Party, from which groups of 10 to 15 went to sing and speak the gospel at missions and other meetings; sometimes they contributed to the programme and sometimes they took full charge. It was 1928 before the Representation of the People Act gave women over 21 the right to vote in parliamentary elections on the same basis as men; the YPM had recognized their potential and effectiveness ever since it was formed ten years before.

## Baptism

Graham Scroggie encouraged those who had been converted in the Chapel to be baptized as soon as possible. Two months after his arrival, he conducted his first baptismal service, on a Monday evening, his preferred day. The candidates were one married couple, four single men and two single women. The next was on Monday 12 March 1917, when seven were baptized, some of them the firstfruits of Scroggie's ministry. Sometimes he led the whole service, consisting of singing, prayer and Scripture reading, and sometimes one of the elders led that part, but Graham Scroggie always preached on baptism and, assisted by one of the elders, carried out the immersions.

There was no oral testimony from the candidates, as happens now, so a large number could be baptized in one evening. Even so, it was sometimes necessary to hold two consecutive Monday services – for example, 16, including the Scroggie's son, Marcus, were baptized one Monday in December 1919, and another 14 a week later. March was a popular month, as the winter's work drew to a close. On Thursday 15 March 1928, 21 (14 women and 7 men) were baptized, and two weeks later another 20 (17 women and 3 men). This was not due to any delay in interviews, because 23 had been baptized just three weeks previously (14 women and 9 men), and there were still another 8 for a further service on 19 April – 72 baptized in eight weeks.

Graham Scroggie interviewed candidates in the vestry on Monday evening, from 6 p.m. until the congregational prayer meeting at 8 p.m., and he continued after it, if necessary – once, in February 1922, he was still seeing new people at 9.45 p.m. What particularly delighted him was that most of the applicants were young, and most of them took the initiative in seeking out their pastor to request baptism. This continued throughout Scroggie's years in Edinburgh. Usually the church was full, sometimes packed, although all baptisms took place on a Monday or a Thursday evening. Sometimes both Monday and Thursday were needed, as in

the third week of February 1933, when 17 (11 women and 6 men) were baptized on the Monday and another 12 (10 women and 2 men) on the Thursday of the same week. In total Graham Scroggie baptized 650 while he was in Edinburgh.

All who had been baptized were encouraged to join the Chapel. On Thursday 27 March 1923, 37 were baptized in one evening and 33 of them came into membership at the communion service on the following Sunday. However, Graham Scroggie provided the facility of baptism for 'members of other churches, not holding believers' baptism, but convinced of its Scriptural order.' As in earlier years, baptism was excused when applicants for membership suffered from some physical infirmity. At his second elders' meeting after he arrived in Edinburgh, Graham Scroggie brought forward 28 applications for membership, of whom two were accepted without actual baptism for medical reasons.

Additional information on the following topics, mentioned in this chapter, is available on the CD.

Agnes McPhail
Charlotte Chapel Scout Troop
Girl Guides
Sunday School statistics
Sunday School
Tract Society
Young Peoples Meeting Constitution, 1925

# Chapter 25
# From baptism to maturity (1916–1933)

## Membership

### Three ways to join the Chapel

Membership, as under previous Chapel ministers, was available: (1) following baptism in the Chapel, (2) by transfer from another Baptist church, or (3) on profession of faith, for applicants who had been baptized as believers elsewhere and who had no current Baptist church membership. At the first communion service of 1917, 26 new members were received, 7 by baptism (1 married couple, 4 single men, and 1 woman), 13 on confession of faith (5 married couples, 1 man and 2 women) and 6 by transfer from other churches (2 married couples and 2 women). Graham Scroggie alone made the decision, after interview, whether to baptize; membership, however, required the approval of the elders and then of the church. It was a commendably swift process. The elders met for an hour on Monday evening, prior to the church prayer meeting at eight o'clock; the names which they recommended, sometimes as many as 29 in one evening, were submitted to 'the Church Meeting at the close of the Prayer Meeting the same evening in accordance with our usual procedure.' If there were questions, the application was deferred for another meeting with the applicant. The doctrinal statement, which Graham Scroggie asked applicants to affirm, is set out in Chapter 47.

The first fortnight of May 1924 is worth mentioning. Graham Scroggie was about to visit the United States until the end of September, so a large number applied for membership. The elders met on Monday 5 May and recommended, to a church meeting that same evening, 13 for membership. However, they had another 14 names, of people who had not yet been baptized. The elders brought their names also to the church meeting, on the basis that they would be received as members after baptism. On Monday 12 May, Scroggie baptized them; the June communion was brought forward to Sunday 18 May, and all 27 were received into membership.

Toward the end of Graham Scroggie's ministry, it was common, because of his lengthy absences, for 25 or 30 to be welcomed at a communion service – everyone waited until he was back and the elders did not, as happens now, receive new members in the pastor's absence; on 5 March 1933, there were 34. In total, he received 950 into membership of the Chapel.

## Transfers from Edinburgh churches

Applications for transfer of membership to the Chapel from other Edinburgh Baptist churches were not a problem for Graham Scroggie until November 1923. He then received several applications from members of the Gorgie church, three more from Abbeyhill and three from Dublin Street. There was no problem with the Abbeyhill people, but there had been trouble in the Gorgie church and Graham Scroggie was also concerned about the reasons for the applications from the Dublin Street members. He met with the applicants and spoke with their minister and their church secretary; after careful deliberation, the elders decided that they could not see their way to admit the Gorgie dissidents. The applications from the Dublin Street members were to lie over for a time. By 1928, the Chapel elders had a firm policy that applications from members of other Edinburgh Baptist churches would automatically lie on the table for six months, before any action was taken, to test the genuineness of the move and also to discourage people from moving quickly while in a huff.

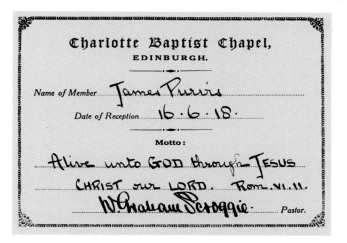

*Everyone joining the Chapel received (and still receives) a membership certificate with a text chosen by the interviewing elders. James Purves joined on 16 June 1918, along with his wife; they celebrated their diamond wedding anniversary with a party in the Chapel in December 1976.*

The church secretary had to remind members, from time to time, that absence from the Lord's Table for more than six months, without satisfactory reason, rendered them liable to be removed from the church roll. 'We do not wish as a Church to have a roll of members many of whom are merely on paper.' The elders were conscientious about purging the roll, but made every effort to restore those who were not attending. When people moved away, without notifying the Chapel of a new address, the elders went to extraordinary lengths to try to make contact. They enquired at the last address, they asked church meetings for information, and they even posted a list of missing persons in the lobby of the church before names were removed. No one was taken off the roll for any reason, not even at their own request, until the elders had considered it, recommended it to a church meeting, and received its approval.

### Adherents

Then, as now, a substantial number attended the Chapel regularly, and regarded it as their church, without ever applying for membership. This posed a dilemma for the leadership, when they were planning the memorial for the men who had fallen in the war – 'whether members of the Church only or of the Congregation as well should be placed on a Tablet.' There were 12 of the former and 16 of the latter, indicative of the number of young men who had not got round to joining, even when volunteering for combat. The office-bearers realized that it would be indelicate not to include them all, so the 28 names appeared in alphabetical order, not distinguishing 'members of the church' from 'members of the congregation', that is adherents.

Three sisters attended the Chapel continuously from 1916 to 1958, but never joined. On the death of two of them, in 1958, the Chapel expressed sympathy to the survivor, describing her as 'a very faithful adherent'. A married woman attended with her husband between 1948 and 1964; on her death, her obituary said: 'though she never came into full membership with us, she was known and loved among us.' There was no official roll of adherents, but the deaconess kept an informal list for the purpose of visitation.

### Associate membership

With Edinburgh's large student population, the Chapel has always had a mobile segment among its membership. With them in mind, Graham Scroggie inaugurated associate membership in 1931, for students and others of any denomination who were resident for a limited period, 'without disturbing their Church connections in any other place'. The first 35 associate members represented 12 different denominations and 20 different places, from Aberdeen to Dover, from Ipswich to Canada. They had all the

privileges and responsibilities of membership, except the right to vote at church meetings.

> ## CHARLOTTE CHAPEL
> EDINBURGH
>
> ### ASSOCIATE MEMBERSHIP.
>
> In view of the special circumstances of many with whom we have fellowship, and to meet oft expressed wishes, we have now instituted in connection with our Church an Associate Membership.
>
> Those who are eligible for this are :—
> (a) Any of the Lord's people who are in residence in Edinburgh for a limited period of time, and who desire to have fellowship with us as a Church meanwhile, without disturbing their Church connections in any other place, at home or abroad.
>
> (b) Students who are at the University, or any College, whose homes are not in Edinburgh, but who, for the period of their studies here, wish to identify themselves with us as a Church.
>
> Two things we wish to make quite clear, namely, first, that this fellowship is extended to all Christians, of whatever denomination ; and second, that this facility does not apply to anyone who is a member of any Church in Edinburgh.
>
> If you desire to identify yourself with us in the way suggested, will you please fill in the following Form, and send it to :—
>
> Dr. W. GRAHAM SCROGGIE,
> 37 Cluny Gardens,
> Edinburgh.

*Preamble to the application for associate membership.*

The associate members' roll served a second purpose, not stated on the preamble to the application form. Members who had moved away from Edinburgh, and who could not find a Baptist church to join, were liable to be removed from membership because they had not attended communion in the Chapel for six months. If they wished to retain their link with the Chapel, they were permitted to apply for associate membership. Two points jump out of the elders' minutes – first, that the elders themselves decided on these applications, and did not (as with all other membership matters) refer the names to a members' meeting, and secondly, that Graham Scroggie was answering a felt need, because several from this category applied within the first month of application forms being available.

## Communion

### Integration

Graham Scroggie constantly sought ways to make the weekly celebration of the Lord's Supper more meaningful. At his first elders' meeting, he said: 'owing to the length of the [morning] service, the communion service which followed did not receive the recognition it ought to have.' On the first Sunday of every quarter, he made communion an integral part of the morning service, instead of holding it at the end. 'This will give the ordnance a more prominent place. All who love our Lord are invited to gather in the body and front gallery of the Church.' The new arrangement was instantly popular, 'pervaded with the deep sense of reverence, and there was nothing to divert the mind from the simplicity of true worship.'

Some, however, could never be present on a Sunday morning – many were in domestic service – and for their sakes Graham Scroggie conducted communion in the evening. He experimented, first with the last Sunday of every alternate month; on these days, the ordinary evening service was curtailed and there was no forenoon Lord's Supper. However, after only two such services, in June and August 1918, he moved it to the evening on the first Sunday of every quarter. This became known as the United Quarterly Communion, and it was well supported. At the close of the normal evening service, there was an interval of ten minutes, for those who wished to participate to occupy the area of the church and, if necessary, the front of the gallery. On one occasion, this service lasted until 9.15 p.m. On all other Sundays, the Lord's Supper was celebrated weekly at the conclusion of the morning service.

## Communion cups

When Graham Scroggie came to Edinburgh, there was a growing movement throughout Scotland for Baptist churches to use individual cups for communion, instead of the traditional communal cup (actually nine communal cups in the Chapel, because of the large number of communicants). A Scottish Baptist Individual-Cup Communion Association had been formed in 1907, not just to encourage others to adopt it but also to demonstrate the practice by holding a united communion service, using individual cups, on the last Monday of every month.

Graham Scroggie suggested it for the Chapel, when he came, but it was not taken up until 1922; at the close of the Monday evening prayer meeting on 26 June, a church business meeting was held to consider individual cups. The idea was unanimously approved, with the proviso that the deacons should avoid, if possible, boring holes in the book boards to

hold empty glasses. This was achieved by the members drinking the wine as they received the glass and returning it to the tray; in most Baptist churches, communicants put empty glasses into a space in the pew or chair in front, and they are collected after the service. (The Chapel's practice greatly extends the time needed for the trays to be passed around.) Individual cups were first used in November 1922. The initial order was for 12 trays of 24 cups, that is 288, not a lot for a congregation of nearly one thousand. When the frequency of communion was changed from weekly to monthly, as described in the next paragraph, the deacons had hurriedly to purchase another 3 trays and 72 more glasses.

**Danger at the Communion Table**
Doctors and Public Health Officers pronounce the use of the **Common Cup** as liable to convey Infectious Diseases. Has your Church adopted the Individual Communion Cup, so avoiding this danger? If not, write for Free Illustrated List and Literature to—
**TOWNSHENDS, LTD., Ernest Street, Birmingham.**

SAFETY AT THE COMMUNION TABLE

Doctors and Public Health Officers pronounce the use of the Common Cup as liable to convey Infectious Diseases

IF YOUR CHURCH HAS NOT ADOPTED THE INDIVIDUAL COMMUNION SERVICE

WRITE FOR FREE ILLUSTRATED LISTS
(Dept. 12)

TOWNSHENDS, LTD.
ERNEST STREET, BIRMINGHAM

*The above advertisement appeared monthly in the Scottish Baptist Magazine from 1929 to 1935, urging the adoption of individual communion cups. In 1935, the supplier modified his advertisement to the rather more positive wording in the left-hand notice.*

## Frequency of communion

Another and graver problem troubled Graham Scroggie. The numbers attending the weekly communion service were falling – one morning, only 60 stayed out of a congregation of nearly a thousand. Even allowing for the fact that only believers were invited to stay, the underlying problem was serious. In his annual report for 1923, the church secretary expressed concern at the poor numbers, and at the absence of many younger members.

The elders analyzed the reasons, such as the inability of Sunday School teachers to be there and to teach on the same day, a sense of hurry because of the restricted time, and a feeling that the frequency diminished appreciation of the privilege. In June 1924, a fundamental change took place, establishing a pattern that has remained, almost unchanged, to this day. Communion was now observed monthly (not weekly), eight times on Sunday morning and four times (the first Sunday of the quarter) in the evening. The experimental and popular United Quarterly Communion was therefore made permanent, with a particular appeal to the younger members to remember their privilege and obligation. The first part of the morning service now finished at 12 noon on communion Sundays, not the usual 12.30 p.m. New members, who had been welcomed at any communion service, were now received on the first Sunday of the month. There was, however, flexibility about the first Sunday, and it was not infrequently moved to another Sunday to accommodate Graham Scroggie's itinerary or some special event in the Chapel.

Another emotive question, whether the wine used at the Lord's Supper had to be unfermented, will be looked at under the temperance movement in Chapter 26.

## Weeknights

### Monday evening prayer meeting

In contrast to the handful who now attended the Sunday prayer meetings, the Monday evening was 'always good and those of our members who do not come, or cannot come, lose much.' Graham Scroggie led it whenever possible; he introduced the time of prayer by a talk, for 15 or 20 minutes, usually as part of a series on some aspect of Christian life and service. The meeting was held in the lower hall from 8 to 9 p.m. In the autumn of 1917, when numbers varied from 60 to 150, Mr Scroggie changed the order and followed, not preceded, the time of prayer with a short address on some topical issue. In November and December 1918, he gave six talks on the Holy Spirit – His Personality, Deity, Dispensations, Titles, Communion and Ministry. Although these were at the close of the Monday night prayer meeting, they were an integral part of it and led to the lower hall and its gallery being crowded, meaning that several hundred were present.

Enthusiasm continued to grow, and the 1921 *Record* noted: 'Our Monday Evening Prayer Meetings have been wonderfully well attended these past weeks and there has been a keen spirit of intercession present.' Graham Scroggie continued to give a 15-minute talk, whenever possible, right through to the end of his time in Edinburgh. Usually the prayer part of the meeting lasted for exactly one hour, but occasionally: 'Such was the spirit of prayer and thanksgiving prevailing, that the meeting lasted much longer than the normal closing time, and one felt it was a pity to stop.' When Graham Scroggie put out a box for requests for prayer, which were read at the meeting, and prayed for, the meeting was lengthened by 15 minutes to 9.15 p.m., to allow for this.

The first Monday of the month was a missionary prayer meeting, usually with a talk from a missionary on furlough or 'systematic instruction on the Missionary Enterprise' by invited speakers. From 1929, imaginative use of lanternslides focussed prayer on Chapel missionaries by projecting three or four slides about their work onto a screen during the time of prayer; this led to fuller attendance. From 1930, an enlarged and framed photograph of every Chapel missionary was displayed on these Monday evenings.

The offering was usually for the Baptist Missionary Society, no matter which body the speaker represented, but Graham Scroggie occasionally persuaded the deacons to give the offering to the society that provided the speaker. That was exceptional, and in 1930 the deacons confirmed that the normal practice was still to support the BMS with the missionary prayer meeting offering. It was 1954 before the deacons gave those responsible any discretion to vary this rule on occasion.

### Thursday School of Bible Study

Graham Scroggie started a Thursday School of Bible Study soon after his induction as pastor – he had held similar schools in Sunderland. The meetings were at 8 p.m., opening with a hymn, prayer, offering and Scripture reading. He then gave an hour's Bible study without any frills. From the beginning, the lectures were held in the sanctuary of the Chapel, as numbers were too large for the lower hall. The first 24 lectures were a rapid survey of the Bible, book by book, under the title 'The Unity of the Bible'. To him, it was the Word of the Living God and the passion of his heart was to preach that Word, so that the people of God might be built up in their faith. The church secretary commented: 'This is going to be a bigger thing than Charlotte Chapel, for this ministry is touching many who are not members here, and is affording a splendid illustration of the value and fascination of systematic Bible study.' 'The Bible is like a new book', one attender reported, 'and we are learning the mind of God from the Word of God and are discovering that this book is the best thing in the world.' Numbers grew quickly until the Chapel was nearly full; non-members, from every Protestant denomination in the city, formed the larger part of the congregation, so the name was changed to The Edinburgh School of Bible Study.

The second series, from October 1917 to April 1918, was on the New Testament. More than 450 syllabi were sold and the church was soon well filled, week after week. Especially encouraging was the large number of young people attending. One of them said: 'Mr. Scroggie is putting his best into these lectures and the hour each week is far too short', and again: 'The lectures are bringing us into a deeper knowledge of Christ and to know Him is to love Him and trust Him.' By popular request, the third series, from November 1918 to May 1919, 30 lectures in all, was on the Book of Revelation. From the beginning, the Chapel was nearly filled and one wrote: 'We have been led to fresh discoveries in the Word of God and have been finding its treasures an inexhaustibly rich mine. It is the old Bible, but some of us have seen it with new eyes.' Graham Scroggie's clear, systematic, scientific analysis of the sacred page was bearing the fruit he sought.

The syllabus from October 1919 to May 1920 was more complex, covering biographical, biblical, doctrinal, evangelical and practical subjects. For the closing meeting, Graham Scroggie invited questions, in advance, on Scriptural problems. He received 150, but by going on until 10 p.m., he covered them to the apparent satisfaction of the questioners in particular and the audience generally. The 1920-21 series was different again, as the first Thursday of every month was used to explain the message and the meaning of the Keswick Movement. The other Thursdays, from December to the end of May, were taken up with a study of the English Bible, 21 lectures in all, with six hundred present weekly throughout the series.

The sixth session, October 1921 to May 1922, on the Book of Daniel, was exceptionally popular and closed with between eight and nine hundred attending every evening. In 1922-3,

the Letter to Philemon was studied over 18 lectures, and the eighth session, in 1923-4, was a survey from Nebuchadnezzar to Nehemiah. The start of the 1924-5 session had to be delayed until February 1925, because of Graham Scroggie's operation for appendicitis in the autumn of 1924, showing how personal these studies were. The planned series on the Apostles' Creed was postponed for a year, and instead he spoke on one of his favourite subjects, the Lord's Return. 'The Church is well filled, and people come from all denominations to hear the exposition of this great truth.'

There does not seem to have been the same interest in the 1926-7 lectures, 'How to Know and Enjoy the Bible', because only the body of the Church was used and 'the Church can accommodate many more'. The 1929-30 series had the lower part of the Chapel quite full, but, aided by publicity from the pulpit, the 1931-2 series attracted about five hundred. The subject in 1930, before Scroggie had to go to Madeira for his health in January 1931, was the Psalter; these lectures were the foundation of his major book on the Psalms. Graham Scroggie's last series in Edinburgh, over the winter of 1932-3, was on the Apostle Paul. The Bible School continued during the vacancy of 1933-4, with a guest preacher.

## Student involvement

University students had attended the Chapel since the days of Christopher Anderson, but Graham Scroggie's ministry attracted more than ever. Among those from New College, whom Chapel members got to know and who spoke at meetings in the Chapel after they were ordained, were James S. Stewart and Donald Caskie, later nicknamed 'The Tartan Pimpernel'.

Men returning to university life from the 1914–18 war found that the Student Christian Movement had become theologically liberal, and that the conservative evangelical position, upheld by Graham Scroggie and the officer-bearers of Charlotte Chapel, was now to be found in the newer Christian Unions. This will come up again in 1952 (Chapter 39), when the Chapel was deeply involved in ecumenical issues, but an incident in 1919 is worth recording; it illustrates the Chapel's position, although the Chapel was not involved in this particular exchange.

The president and secretary of the evangelical Cambridge

Inter-Collegiate Christian Union met, at the request of the secretary of the liberal Student Christian Movement, to discuss the reunification of the two movements, which had separated in 1910. The CICCU president reported that after an hour's talk: 'I asked Rollo [the SCM secretary] point blank, "Does the SCM put the atoning blood of Jesus Christ central?" He hesitated, and then said, "Well, we acknowledge it, but not necessarily central." Dan Dick [CICCU secretary] and I then said that this settled the matter for us in the CICCU. We could never join something that did not maintain the atoning blood of Jesus Christ at its centre; and we parted company.'

### Thursdays out of term

When Graham Scroggie came to Edinburgh, 36 auxiliary organizations reported verbally at the annual general meeting of the church. Recognising that this was information overload, the office-bearers utilized some of the Thursdays, when there was no Bible School, to hear a detailed report from one auxiliary at a time. This attracted reasonable numbers, meeting in the lower hall for a leisurely evening, with opportunity for questions.

## Pastoral care

### Deaconesses

Regular pastoral visitation was carried out, although not by Graham Scroggie himself. One of his priorities, while he was waiting to come to Edinburgh, was to find a new deaconess, as Elizabeth Boyle had followed Joseph Kemp to New York. Sister Lilian (Miss E. Tipper) was headhunted on his recommendation from the Cardiff City Mission and started before the end of October 1916. She took over the key elements of deaconess work in the Chapel, that is visiting the housebound and the sick, contacting outsiders evangelistically and running the women's meetings in Rose Street. She was well received, and started a Women's Bible Class on Sunday afternoon in the Chapel. After four busy years, she found the duties too demanding physically, and tendered her resignation in November 1920.

Elizabeth Boyle was back in Scotland, as her father and mother required her help. The Chapel 'called' her as soon as Sister Lilian resigned, and she restarted in April 1921. In a

typical year, about 270 Chapel members were classified as aged, housebound or temporarily unwell, and her visits to them, several times, totalled over one thousand home visits a year. In addition, another couple of hundred in the congregation were 'under the cloud of bereavement, and other kinds of affliction', and required pastoral attention; she also had a special interest in women and girls, not in membership, who lived in Rose Street. Fortunately, she herself was never ill throughout these years. In addition to the meetings mentioned above under Sister Lilian, Lizzie (as everyone called her) started a Girls Own on Sunday afternoons, for fellowship and for outreach.

*Miss Elizabeth Boyle, or Lizzie as everyone called her, was Chapel deaconess for 36 years, from 1907-16 and again from 1921-48.*

### *Charlotte Chapel Record*

Popular though the monthly magazine was, particularly among folk living away from Edinburgh, it struggled financially throughout Graham Scroggie's years. In 1923 it was reduced in size to eight pages per month and reduced in price to twopence (much under cost) in the hope of boosting circulation. Typical contents were a meditation by the pastor, Chapel news, a précis from the School of Bible Study and letters from missionaries. Persistence paid off, and from 1925 onward the size was doubled to 16 pages a month. It is a meticulous record (hence the name) of what took place week by week, and the editor was not bashful at printing letters of appreciation, particularly from the missionary family, to whom it was posted free of charge.

### Social meetings

Although Graham Scroggie had made clear that the Chapel could have either his head or his feet (expository preaching or pastoral visitation) but not both, he was far from being unsociable. He attended most of the social gatherings and picnics of the Chapel organisations. A year after his arrival, he divided the membership of eight hundred into four and invited two hundred at a time to a series of social meetings over the four Tuesdays of November 1917. Tea was served in the lower hall and, as the guests sat in small groups, Mr and Mrs Scroggie went round, speaking to everyone. For many, it was their first opportunity of shaking hands with their pastor personally, because he was too exhausted, after preaching on Sunday, to go to the door of the church. The response was gratifying, and justified the effort. The gatherings were delightfully informal. There were similar meetings, on a regular basis, with the leaders of the Chapel auxiliaries. Socials were held in the lower hall to mark Graham Scroggie's semi-jubilee in the ministry (1922), and again to mark his tenth anniversary in Edinburgh (1926), 'when an opportunity was given for all who cared to have a word and shake hands with our beloved Pastor.'

*The Scroggies regularly attended summer picnics arranged by Chapel auxiliaries, such as the choir, the male voice choir, the Sunday School teachers, the Chapel Sunday School, the High Street Sunday School, the YPM and the Girls Own.*

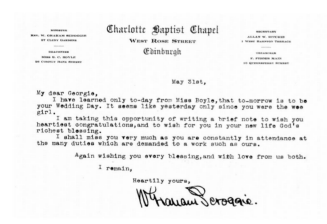

MINISTER
REV. W. GRAHAM SCROGGIE
97 CLANY GARDENS

DEACONESS
MISS E. C. BOYLE
90 COMELY BANK STREET

Charlotte Baptist Chapel
WEST ROSE STREET
Edinburgh

SECRETARY
ALLAN W. RITCHIE
1 WEST BARNTON TERRACE

TREASURER
F. FIDDES MAIN
40 QUEENSBERRY STREET

May 31st,

My dear Georgie,
I have learned only to-day from Miss Boyle, that to-morrow is to be your Wedding Day. It seems like yesterday only since you were the wee girl.
I am taking this opportunity of writing a brief note to wish you heartiest congratulations, and to wish for you in your new life God's richest blessing.
I shall miss you very much as you are constantly in attendance at the many duties which are demanded to a work such as ours.

Again wishing you every blessing, and with love from us both.

I remain,

Heartily yours,

W Graham Scroggie.

*Graham Scroggie had baptized the resident caretaker's daughter, Georgie, in March 1923, but he was not involved in her wedding. Later, when Georgie was expecting her first child, she came to stay with her mother and Freda was the last baby to be born on the Chapel premises. She grew up to become Mrs Topping, who, although not a member of the Chapel, helped regularly in the Mustard Seed café in the lounge until it closed in December 2005.*

## Marriage

Until 1925, Graham Scroggie, in common with most Baptist ministers at the time, performed marriages at the manse. The first reference to a wedding on the Chapel premises is on 7 January 1925, and it was held in the vestry rather than the sanctuary. This had the advantage for poorer members, that no gratuity was payable to the caretaker if the wedding was in the vestry. The first mention of what many would now regard as the norm, that is a public service in the Chapel followed by a reception at a hotel, is a large wedding in the church on Thursday 14 June 1928, followed by a reception in the nearby Roxburghe Hotel. Darling's Regent Hotel was used similarly, three weeks later, following a marriage in the Chapel, but more often than not, from 1929 onward, everything took place in the hotel. The Palace Hotel, the Caledonian Station Hotel, Darling's Regent Hotel, the Bruntsfield Links Hotel and 82 Great King Street were favourites.

Scotland's marriage laws were different from England's, in that the licence was for the person, not for the building, so Graham Scroggie could marry the couple wherever they chose. In his last year in Edinburgh, there were nine weddings, three in the church and six at the manse. Some Chapel brides preferred other Edinburgh churches – Morningside Baptist Church, Dublin Street Baptist Church, Morningside Parish Church and others. The steep staircase up to the sanctuary, the size of the building and the many licensed premises near the Chapel, deterred some families from coming to Rose Street for their big day.

## Sunshine Band

Routine visitation of the elderly and the shut-in was, until

1926, the responsibility of the deaconess and the elders. The pastor called in extreme cases, and he declined the offer of an assistant in 1918, because he 'did not wish to be a mere preaching machine'; he wanted to keep in touch with his people. The creation of the Sunshine Band in January 1926 met a need that the YPM nobly filled until the Second World War. 'A number of the members [of YPM] have undertaken to visit any people of the Church or YPM who are in the sick room or hospital and to cheer them by smile and song.' They went in twos and threes, and wherever possible held a devotional service in the home. Every year the Sunshine Band made up to 240 visits to the sick, the aged and the infirm, carrying fruit and flowers and 'sunshine'. One of the Chapel members, Andrew Ewing, who owned a chain of retail dairy shops, donated every egg laid on a Sunday to the Chapel, and the YPM were given five dozen freshly laid eggs every Monday for free distribution to the sick and needy.

In addition to visiting senior citizens throughout the year, and taking them for outings to the country in the Hallelujah Bus (Chapter 27), the Sunshine Band held an annual winter party for them. By arranging for members who had cars to transport elderly folk to the Chapel, the Band was able to bring a large number of infirm people together in the lower hall for this social occasion around Christmas or New Year. In 1929, at the height of the industrial depression, Father Christmas gave all the guests a present from a huge hamper.

*The tea tables were a sight to behold, decorated as they were and lit by candles, and literally laden with a rich variety of good things. During the afternoon a long programme consisting of games, solos, pianoforte solo, choruses, etc., was thoroughly enjoyed, and the items contributed by the old folk themselves were much appreciated by all. A couple of charades, one giving an impression of the 'Loch Ness Monster', by members of the Band, created much merriment. Family worship was conducted … and the Doxology ended the happy event on a note of praise. Finally the guests were presented with bags of Edinburgh Rock as they dispersed. The Sunshine Band are to be congratulated on the able and enthusiastic way in which they bring brightness into the lives of the suffering, sad and weary ones.*

---

1 *Record*, 1934, p. 24.

## 'We love you and we tell you so'

The people of Charlotte Chapel exuberantly expressed their affection for their pastor by twice (at least) hanging a banner from the gallery, opposite the pulpit, with the words: 'We love you and we tell you so'. Recorded instances are the Monday of his third anniversary, in October 1919, and his return from the United States in the following October. When Joseph Kemp visited Edinburgh in 1926, on holiday from New Zealand, a streamer with the same words (? the same banner) was displayed from the gallery; the phrase was used also during Sidlow Baxter's ministry (Chapter 37).

## Funerals

*Home Call. – Miss Young, 21 Tarvit Street, has passed away at the age of 91. Though not a member, Charlotte Chapel had been her spiritual home for many years. Dr Scroggie conducted the funeral service in the house, and Rev. A. C. Dovey, M.A., Dunfermline, officiated at the grave service.*

---

2 *Record*, 1928, pp. 167, 183.

That note from the 1928 *Record* is quoted for three reasons. First, it is not just a twenty-first century habit for some Christians to regard the Chapel as their spiritual home without ever joining; secondly, the norm was to have a service in the home followed by a committal at the cemetery. In Graham Scroggie's time, indeed until the 1960s, only male mourners went to the graveside. Female mourners either remained at the family home (or went there if the service had been in the church), to await the return of the men, or they went to the cemetery and stayed in the official cars while the men went to the open grave. The growing popularity of cremation in the 1930s led to women attending committal services there, but not at the graveside until the 1960s.

Thirdly, it was prudent for Graham Scroggie not to go to the perishing cold of a graveside service during Edinburgh winters, as he suffered badly from bronchitis. Miss Young died just before he had to call off preaching on Sunday 4 November 1928, through illness, having, perhaps unwisely, struggled to the Bible School on the previous Thursday with a bad cold. Graham Scroggie was diligent in pastoral concern, especially for the sick and the bereaved, but there was no point in inviting bronchial attacks. He did, however, sometimes conduct both parts of the service, that is at the house and at the grave.

When (unusually) a memorial service was held in the Chapel, it was not dissimilar to services today, but there were two differences. First, it was called the 'Funeral Service of the late …' and not, as is usual now, 'Thanksgiving for the life of …'. Secondly, the coffin was brought down the aisle at the beginning of the service, with the congregation standing, and laid on the platform; now it is usually placed there before the mourners arrive.

*Although Mr Fraser, a member of the Chapel, advertised monthly in the* Record *from January 1940, that his firm offered facilities for cremation as well as burial, there is no note of any Chapel member being cremated until 1952.*

*John Edward Dovey died on Friday 15 February 1918, as he was entering the vestry for a meeting of the elders. A member of the Chapel for 50 years, and treasurer for 38 of those, he had spoken a few Sundays before with great vigour at the open-air meeting at the corner of South Charlotte Street and had given thanks for the bread at the communion service on the Sunday before his death.*

Cremation was first available in modern Britain in 1874, and in Edinburgh in 1929, when Warriston crematorium was built. Many evangelical Christians disapproved of cremation until the 1960s, saying that non-believers cremated their dead in order to destroy the body and so undermine the New Testament pattern of burial with the sure and certain hope of resurrection.

At the same time as Charlotte Chapel was installing its first pipe organ (described below), the owners of Warriston were looking for a pipe organ for the crematorium services. The Christian Brethren meeting in Bellevue Chapel, which they had bought from the German church at the end of the First World War, sold their organ to Warriston, as they were not using it. The Bellevue organ has twice been reconditioned, and it is still in daily use.

## The Chapel building

### First repainting of the new building

Some will recollect the minor disruption to the Sunday services, when the inside of the Chapel was redecorated in 1989. It was not necessary to hire alternative accommodation, and the services proceeded as normal, although some could see the pulpit only by peeking through tubular scaffolding. Redecoration in 1920 (and again in 1970) was a major task, and the Synod Hall was hired for the months of July and August 1920. The congregation did not have happy memories of their enforced use of the Synod Hall in 1911-12, not least because a spiritual atmosphere among the half-empty 1,900 seats 'has to be created, and we have to do it'. To make it worse, Graham Scroggie was away for the whole two months, but there was nowhere else more suitable. In the event, attendances were encouraging, particularly the number of men in the evening; the guest preachers continued Graham Scroggie's pattern of speaking primarily to 'saints' on Sunday morning and 'sinners' on Sunday evening (the *Record*'s description). When the members returned, they were delighted with the newly painted Chapel.

### Pipe organ

In November 1921, the congregation voted to replace the inadequate 1879 organ with a proper pipe organ, but there was no possibility of the church finding the estimated £1,250 at that stage; they made do by hiring a piano, to play along with the organ. By 1924, the problem had again become acute, and the time had come for action. Graham Scroggie called a special church meeting in February 1925, and 85 percent voted to install a pipe organ. They agreed to place the order as soon as half of the estimated cost was in hand.

However, not many of those who had voted in favour were prepared to contribute toward the £850 needed – the price had come down from £1,250 – and some continued to grumble that a pipe organ was too expensive. Scroggie wrote caustically in the *Record*: 'I cannot understand the point of view of people who are quite agreeable to the use of an organ in a church, *so long as it is not a good one!*' Three years later, the organ fund had crept up to £400. On the eve of his departure for three months in the United States and Canada in June 1928, Graham Scroggie called a further church meeting. It is the first time that the number attending such a meeting is recorded – approximately 400 out of a membership of 963.

There was much debate as to whether the console should be part of the organ, as in this picture, or whether it should be detached and sited at the back. The communion table was a plain table at that time – the present carved table was not given until 1936.

It was preceded by a huge public relations exercise by the office-bearers. Tea was served from 7 to 8 p.m. in the lower hall, during which Mr and Mrs Scroggie circulated among the members. The church secretary then presented the case for implementing the previous decision, 'to install an organ such as will be adequate for the worthy maintenance of the Praise at Charlotte Chapel.' While no one opposed the principle, the church treasurer and another veteran of the struggle to fund the new building in 1912 moved an amendment, that the order should not be placed until the whole money (a further £450) was in hand. However, the overwhelming majority voted to begin installation right away, and to raise the money while the organ was being assembled. The significance of the pastor's lead in such schemes is underlined by the decision

not to launch the appeal until his return at the end of September.

There was still a shortfall of £350 on the required £850 when the organ was dedicated in May 1929, but the opening weekend, which included Graham Scroggie sitting in the vestry all Monday afternoon as he did for Thankofferings, brought in £260. The other £90 was carried forward as a debit in the Chapel accounts for many years, while those who openly praised the new organ did nothing to square the books.

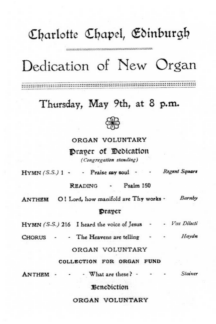

### Charlotte Chapel, Edinburgh

## Dedication of New Organ

#### Thursday, May 9th, at 8 p.m.

ORGAN VOLUNTARY

**Prayer of Dedication**
*(Congregation standing)*

| | | | |
|---|---|---|---|
| HYMN (S.S.) 1 | Praise my soul | *Regent Square* |
| READING | Psalm 150 | |
| ANTHEM | O! Lord, how manifold are Thy works | *Barnby* |

**Prayer**

| | | | |
|---|---|---|---|
| HYMN (S.S.) 216 | I heard the voice of Jesus | *Vox Dilecti* |
| CHORUS | The Heavens are telling | *Haydn* |

ORGAN VOLUNTARY
COLLECTION FOR ORGAN FUND

| | | | |
|---|---|---|---|
| ANTHEM | What are these? | *Stainer* |

**Benediction**

ORGAN VOLUNTARY

*The dedication of the organ was on Thursday evening, 9 May 1929, but the choir also gave recitals and voluntaries on the Friday, Saturday and Monday evenings.*

Additional information on the following topics, mentioned in this chapter, is available on the CD.

Andrew Ewing
Associate membership
Church officers from 1912
Deaconess

# Chapter 26
## Specialist groups (1916–1933)

## Sunday

### Twin expectations

When someone was converted under Graham Scroggie's ministry, he expected that two things would follow. One was that the person would engage in some Chapel activity, in addition to the four essentials mentioned at the end of Chapter 22, in order to grow in the Christian faith. The other was that the person would support one or more of the Chapel's evangelistic outreaches. The opportunities for the former, that is growing in faith, are set out in this chapter, going chronologically through a typical week and a typical year; the opportunities for the latter, that is evangelism, will be explored in the next chapter.

### Sunday morning, 10 a.m. –
### Young Men's Bible Class/Fellowship

When Graham Scroggie came to Edinburgh, this group was meeting every Sunday morning at ten o'clock, to cultivate the spiritual and devotional life of young men through the study of the Bible and prayer. Average attendance was 20. They worked through an international course of Bible readings, which gave them opportunities of learning to speak and to pray in public. When Scroggie reorganized the Sunday School in 1919, its functions were taken over by a new Sunday afternoon class, and the Sunday morning meeting was discontinued.

Within a year, the young men of the Chapel asked for it to be restarted. With the pastor's blessing – he attended the first meeting and often spoke at it – the Young Men's Fellowship came into being. Studies included the miracles of Jesus, the Apostles' Creed and *Pilgrim's Progress*; 15 minutes were devoted to prayer. Some came from long distances, and until 1923 they all came on foot; whether this was on principle, or whether it was too early for public transport, is not stated. In 1929, the fellowship was given a wider remit – the study of doctrine, the preparation of addresses, and counselling. The entire group, now averaging 12-15, supported open-air meetings as an essential part of their Christian service. Once a month, they led the 8 p.m. Sunday open-air. In the vacancy after Graham Scroggie left in 1933, there was a dearth of leadership; the members took up other activities, such as the Infirmary ward services, and the fellowship dissolved.

### Sunday afternoon, 3 p.m. –
### Young Women's Bible Class (Sisterhood)

When Sister Lilian was appointed deaconess in 1916, she took over the Bible Class for young women, held from 3-4 p.m. on Sunday afternoon, and renamed it the Sisterhood. It flourished under her leadership, with a membership of 98, even although many who attended the Chapel's morning service found it difficult to get home for lunch and back by three o'clock. The class had a strong missionary interest, and sent substantial monies every year for the support of Chapel and other missionaries. Like most auxiliaries, it had a social life of its own, including a summer outing and picnic – no men were invited. Like most auxiliaries, it broke up in June and resumed in October. Sister Lilian's motto was: 'Work hard and don't talk about it.' Many in the class were in domestic service, so they appreciated her reminder that the good Lord watched, helped and led even the silent and the humble. As with the Young Men's Bible Class mentioned above, the 1919 reorganisation meant that the Girls Bible Class, under the auspices of the Sunday School, replaced the Sisterhood.

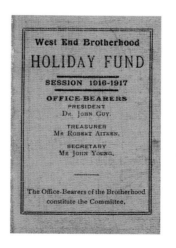

*An invitation to the West End Brotherhood. Its holiday fund encouraged men to deposit one shilling per week with the treasurer, in order to have something available for Christmas and their summer holiday.*

## Sunday afternoon, 3 p.m. – West End Brotherhood

The Brotherhood, described in Chapter 16, met in the Chapel from 3-4 p.m. between October and June. Until the armistice in 1918, many of its members were away on military service. The remainder focused on bringing soldiers and sailors into the afternoon meeting, offering tea in the lower hall, having a time of singing and testimony and encouraging their guests to stay on for the Chapel's evening service. Between 70 and 100 were brought in every Sunday by the scouts. When the elders considered changing the time of the Sunday School from 1.30 p.m. to 3 p.m., 'it was felt advisable to consult the Brotherhood Committee.' There was no longer room for the Brotherhood in the Chapel premises, and it seems to have disbanded in 1919.

## Sunday afternoon, 5 p.m. – Girls Own

This was first held in the top hall on Sunday afternoon 9 October 1921, starting with tea at 4.30 p.m. and followed by two hours of informal fellowship activities. The girls participated in the singing, prayer, Scripture reading and talk, hence the name Girls Own. Graham Scroggie was anxious that lonely people, away from home, could find friendship in the Chapel, so this meeting (unlike most auxiliaries) continued through the summer. Many were maids in domestic service, whose off-duty was Sunday afternoon and evening, and they had nowhere else to go. The girls, aged 18 and upward (later 17), brought their fellow servants, many of whom became Christians through the contact.

They were encouraged, but not required, to stay for the Chapel's evening service at 6.30 p.m. On a typical afternoon, about 30 places throughout Scotland were represented among the 45 or so attending, out of a membership of 60. They supported other Chapel activities, regularly assisting with the Infirmary ward services, tract distribution, open-airs, giving testimony and singing. The leader, Elizabeth Boyle, was greatly encouraged to count 16 of her girls at one of the open-air meetings. As with every other Chapel auxiliary, Graham Scroggie took a personal interest in the class, and attended and spoke from time to time.

Because most of the girls had come to Edinburgh for work, there was a high turnover in membership, as they moved on or got married. Successive deaconesses acted as counsellor to many of the girls in social as well as spiritual problems, finding them employment, lodgings, etc. Ministers in other places were grateful to have a name, to whom they could pass details of young girls coming to Edinburgh, in the confidence that the deaconess would look after them. The *Record* carried many letters of appreciation from former members, who looked back gratefully to the friendly times they enjoyed in the class. As well as the Sunday afternoon gathering, there was a picnic in the summer and at least one social during the winter, with tea, games, music and recitations, lasting from 6.30-10 p.m.

During and after the Second World War (1939-45), some of the Girls Own went out to Princes Street, inviting strangers to Edinburgh to join them. Although the meeting was open to all women, the average age went up, as the original members grew older. There was no upper age limit, and the deaconess pondered whether to change the name to reflect the reality. However, Girls Own remained the official title until 1969, when it was changed to Sunday Afternoon Fellowship, as described in Chapter 44.

# Weeknights

## Tuesday, 7.30 p.m. – Christian Service Class

The need for 'the training of young men and women for the service of Christ at home and abroad, training which is spiritual, intellectual, and practical', led Graham Scroggie to form a Christian Service Class. From 1921 to 1926, it met on Tuesday from 7.30-9.15 p.m. between October and May. Initially 90 enrolled, and membership soon rose to 130, nearly all attending every week. On the first night of the third session, 114 were present, 70 women and 44 men.

The class provided early training for those who were considering full-time Christian work, as well as for others who wished to be better equipped for evangelism in their free time. It was primarily for Chapel members, but it was open to all Christians; people came from nearly all the evangelical Protestant denominations in Edinburgh. The home mission committee of the Baptist Union of Scotland enrolled its students as members. Many became missionaries and ministers, some carefully preserving their notes for the rest of their lives.

Graham Scroggie invited a distinguished and varied body of lecturers; it was as strenuous, and had as rigid a discipline, as a university class. Applications for enrolment had to be in writing to the president, Graham Scroggie, stating the applicant's reason for wishing to join the class, the particular service in which he or she was interested and the degree of experience already gained. A note of apology for absence had to be sent to the class secretary. Membership for each session was half a guinea (52.5 new pence), on payment of which the accepted candidate was given a detailed syllabus. The course included Bible knowledge, psychology, elocution, missionary enterprise and preparation and delivery of addresses, besides practical and experimental work and a social gathering. Homework was set:

*This session I would like you to read Augustine's* Confessions, *once; Law's* Serious Call, *once; Myers'* St. Paul, *three times; Thompson's* Hound of Heaven, *twelve times; and the New Testament, once; one chapter each week-day, and two on Sunday.... Let all your reading begin and end with prayer.*

---

1 Christian Service Class syllabus, 1922-23, p. 11.

All members were encouraged to take part and thereby stir up the gift that was in them. The art and habit of note-taking was inculcated and a spirit of fellowship was fostered. Care was taken to encourage the devotional life of the class, so censoriousness and unfriendly criticism was strictly forbidden, in the hope that members would learn that strong conviction was not incompatible with Christian charity.

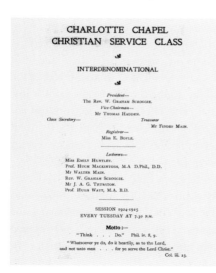

CHARLOTTE CHAPEL
CHRISTIAN SERVICE CLASS

INTERDENOMINATIONAL

*President—*
The Rev. W. Graham Scroggie.
*Vice-Chairman—*
Mr Thomas Hauden.
*Class Secretary—*        *Treasurer—*
                      Mr Fiddes Main.
*Registrar—*
Miss E. Boyle.

*Lecturers—*
Miss Emily Huntley.
Prof. Hugh Mackintosh, M.A D.Phil, D.D.
Mr Walter Main.
Rev. W. Graham Scroggie.
Mr J. A. G. Thurston.
Prof. Hugh Watt, M.A. B.D.

SESSION 1924-1925
EVERY TUESDAY AT 7.30 P.M.

*Motto :—*
"Think . . . . Do." Phil. iv. 8, 9.
"Whatsoever ye do, do it heartily, as to the Lord,
and not unto men . . . . for ye serve the Lord Christ."
Col. iii. 23.

*For five years, the Christian Service Class provided the Chapel with raw material for evangelistic teams. It met on Tuesday evening between October and May. Having achieved its purpose, it closed at the end of the fifth session in 1926.*

## Tuesday and Wednesday evening – area prayer circles

In July 1926, Graham Scroggie suggested that the scattered membership should meet in homes around the city for prayer. He had in mind those who could not manage to the Chapel for the Monday evening prayer meeting, and suggested they should meet 'on days and at hours suitable to those who are able and willing to open their homes for such a purpose.' Five groups started right away, and Scroggie hoped that there would soon be 'a belt of prayer meetings encircling and upholding the work' of the Chapel. Only two of the five endured. One met from 8-9.15 p.m. every Tuesday evening throughout the year in 2 George Place in Pilrig. An elder and a deacon sent invitations to members of the Chapel living in Leith and Pilrig, initially with little response. Ironically, for what was meant to be an area meeting, most support came from members and adherents who lived at a distance.

Attendance averaged 12, occasionally reaching 16. After singing and reading Scripture, they spent 45 minutes on their knees. Everyone present took part audibly, and they covered all aspects of the church's work. Two points are worth noting. When Alan Redpath introduced zone meetings in 1964, as a novelty imported from America, the daughter of the Pilrig elder remarked to the writer that there was nothing new about such groups, as she and her father had run one for nearly 40 years. Secondly, when they said that they spent 45 minutes on their knees, they meant just that. Alan Redpath's home groups sat in a circle to pray, as fellowship groups do now, but until about 1964, evangelical Christians, engaged in intercession, usually knelt at their chairs rather than sitting on them.

The other enduring group met on Wednesday evening at 7:30 p.m. at 46 Elm Row. It followed much the same pattern as the one in George Place, except they had a time of Bible study after the Scripture reading, and they had rather more singing and sharing of information; but they had more time, because they did not finish until everyone present had taken part. When the George Place group heard about this, they adopted the same pattern, and many who had never before prayed in public were ready to do so among friends. Both area prayer circles found that once friendships were formed, no one wished to discontinue them, and both meetings continued for many years. Graham Scroggie encouraged them, and in February 1933 another one was started on Wednesday evening at 7 Roseneath Terrace. At the same time, the Elm Row one moved to 12 Marchmont Street.

## Wednesday, 3 p.m. – Women's prayer meeting

About 20 women of the congregation (up to 50 during World War One) met in the ladies' room in the Chapel for an hour every Wednesday afternoon, from 3-4 p.m., 'to pray for the members of our families and for the work of the Church generally'. Two themes run through the reports of this meeting, from the first record of it in 1908 until Mrs Scroggie left Edinburgh in 1933. The first is the blessing felt by the women who attended it – the faithful band, as they called themselves; the second is their regret that not more came – 'One wonders why, in our large church, so few women avail themselves of this privilege, and share with us in the blessing,' especially since 'the day and the hour were chosen as the most convenient for those for whom the meeting was intended'.

Mrs Scroggie personally led the meeting during her time in Edinburgh; it went on all the year round. After a hymn, some verses of Scripture and a few words of encouragement based on the passage, the remainder of the hour was given to topics for prayer and individual prayer for them. Every week, the pastor, office-bearers, and all the church organisations were prayed for; those who were unwell were named by the deaconess and remembered, along with the missionary family. Time was left for wider interests; if any one had a personal problem, it was sympathetically supported in prayer.

Neither the pattern of the meeting nor the loyalty of the women altered when the Scroggies left Edinburgh in 1933 and Mrs Baxter, the wife of the next pastor, took over leadership in 1935. At the height of the Second World War, in 1943, one of the regulars wrote:

*The meeting begins with a hymn of praise. Prayer follows, then another hymn. Thereafter Miss Boyle reads the sick list, giving enough details of each case to enable us to pray intelligently and sympathetically. The remainder of the hour is devoted to intercession. The various Church activities, our missionaries, the lads and girls of the Forces, those whose homes have been desolated through bereavement, all are faithfully remembered.*

2 *Record*, 1943, p. 125.

The meeting still continues, now at 2.30 p.m., although the numbers in recent years have seldom reached double figures. For that reason, it has become necessary to close for the summer months, but a special effort is made whenever a missionary on furlough is able to attend.

## Friday, 7 p.m. – Children's meeting

The weekly Friday evening meeting for boys and girls, which had been suspended during the war, resumed in October 1920 at 7 p.m. in the lower hall. Numbers soon build up to one hundred, about two-thirds of whom also attended the Sunday School. It also attracted quite a number from Rose Street itself. It was for one hour, and included gospel chorus singing, lanternslides and blackboard illustrations, which greatly interested the children. Attendance dropped off as the nights became lighter, and this meeting, like many others, had a break from the late spring until the first week of October.

## Friday evening – Lads gymnasium class

Started in the autumn of 1918, this was held weekly during the winter months and 25 attended. It lasted for an hour and a half and was closed with a reading and a prayer; in summer, there were outings and picnics.

## Friday, 8 p.m. – Choir practice

The choir, which under Joseph Kemp 'not only helpfully led the congregational praise, but has on many occasions carried the Gospel message of salvation in song to many weary and heavy-laden hearts', numbered 47 when Graham Scroggie arrived. Spirituality was maintained by opening devotions at the Friday evening practice (average attendance 30) and a time of prayer at 6 p.m., before the Sunday evening service. From 1914, many of the men were away on military service – the organist, Edmund Craig, was killed in action – and the choir was glad to have the support of all believers, not just members of the church. The choir's new constitution, in 1917, confirmed the 1886 decision (Chapter 12) that: 'Members of the Chapel and other Christians who are regular worshippers or workers in the Chapel' were eligible.

With the cessation of hostilities in 1918, membership rose to 56 and average attendance to 35. The choir continued to be both an aid to worship and a call to salvation. They enjoyed a fine spirit of fellowship among themselves, with their own winter socials and summer picnics. Their outing to Canty Bay on 27 May 1933, attended by 50, is the first mention of anyone other than Scouts, Cubs and Guides being granted access to Pa Evans' seaside site. The earliest cine film in the Chapel archives shows their 1948 summer outing to the Trossachs.

## Occasional events

### Chapel cricket club

There is one tantalising vague reference to Graham Scroggie having encouraged competitive cricket matches in the Chapel's name. Cricket had been part of Sunday School picnics since at least 1875, but Scroggie wanted something more. He himself was an able batsman and bowler – at the age of 35 he took 4 wickets and scored 19 runs for the Sunderland clergy against the Sunderland Corporation. What was he referring to when he wrote in the *Record* in 1923?

*we do not deny a place to the worthy things that claim a subordinate place, and so we have our Guides and Scouts, and Brownies, and Cricket Club, etc.*

3  *Record*, 1923, p. 65.

The Chapel has never lacked for cricket enthusiasts, although there was more enthusiasm than skill when they played the Granton Baptist Church in July 1945 – the Chapel team was bowled out for 44 runs, which the Granton team passed for the loss of one wicket. Douglas Lawrence, who died in July 2000, opened the fast bowling for Scotland from 1956 to 1958, and went on to become one of Scotland's selectors and president of the Scottish Cricket Union in 1990.

### Temperance

With Graham Scroggie's encouragement, Chapel members actively supported the temperance movement. Licensing was a live issue for a church in Rose Street, because although the street was sparsely populated by the end of the Great War, it still had 17 public houses and the disorder after closing time was disgraceful. When the Temperance (Scotland) 1920 Act made provision for local veto polls, the Chapel was in the forefront of the campaign for Edinburgh to go dry. Chapel members canvassed from door to door with literature about 'the curse of the drink traffic, and the havoc it was working in

our midst', seeking to get at least 35 per cent on the municipal register to vote in favour of having no licensed premises in the city.

The pastor, office-bearers and many members joined a no-licence march in the Meadows on Saturday 16 October 1920. The Chapel also arranged a rally in the Usher Hall, on the night before the poll was taken, attracting about fifteen hundred. When the result was declared the next day, allowing the sale of liquor to continue, the Chapel members were disappointed, but pledged themselves to continue educating the public about the awful bondage of drink. Success in these local polls was rare, but Kirkintilloch and Wick voted for prohibition.

The Chapel Young Women's Temperance Association, formed in May 1926 with 55 members, was particularly active in promoting the temperance agenda. They met monthly in the lower hall and distributed temperance tracts along Rose Street. They also ran a Band of Hope in the Cowgate every Friday. Graham Scroggie presided and spoke at the opening of their winter session; he encouraged the young women to persevere, telling them: 'what a wonderful thing it was for America to vote for Prohibition'.

On Sunday 1 April 1928, the Chapel's evening service was given over to a temperance rally, with supporters from many outside organisations. Graham Scroggie led the service and preached on the evils of the drink trade. It took courage for businessmen to associate with such rallies, because the trade were pressing just as strongly for increased sales as their opponents were pressing for prohibition. On the morning after the eve-of-poll rally mentioned above, a licensed grocer called at his local branch of the Union Bank, where the writer's maternal grandfather was the manager, and closed his account because the manager, Jack Ingram, had been on the platform in the Usher Hall.

The churches' unequivocal stance against the drink trade – the Baptist churches in Scotland were proud to say in 1923 that there was not one single licence-holder in membership – drove a wedge between them and non-churchgoers, but they preached the gospel to liberate men, women and children from, among other things, their slavery to alcohol.

## Unfermented wine

The Baptist Union of Scotland encouraged churches to use unfermented wine at the Lord's Supper; its *Yearbook* listed those who did, and by 1923 every Scottish Baptist church was on the list. The *Yearbook* also published the names of Abstaining Baptist Ministers in Scotland, that is ministers who had signed the pledge; Joseph Kemp's name was on this list from the beginning, and, again by 1923, it included every Scottish Baptist minister and student.

The Chapel may have used unfermented wine at the Lord's Table continuously since 1882, when the elders had a discussion about the desirability of changing to it. A month later it was reported that a suitable unfermented wine was available, so the elders decided to experiment for a month. A member offered to give the wine, which suggests that he may have been the one pressing for the change. The experiment was to be reviewed in June 1882, but the records do not say what happened; it cannot be assumed that the experiment continued, because there were those who argued strongly that wine, to be wine, had to be fermented. At this time, some Baptist churches in Scotland offered a choice at the communion table, but then, as mentioned, all were using only unfermented wine by 1923.

## Watchnight and New Year's Day

Graham Scroggie's first Hogmanay (31 December) in Edinburgh was a Sunday; he preached at the usual two services, then led a large Watchnight service at 10.30 p.m., followed by the traditional hour of open-air evangelism at the corner of South Charlotte Street. On New Year's Day (Monday), he held a morning service, devoted largely to prayer; in the afternoon he gave an address on prophecy, which brought out the crowds and the lower hall was over-crowded. An evening of praise and testimony, again in a packed lower hall, flowed for two hours; Scroggie counselled some who wished to 'surrender all' (the words of the closing hymn). The *Record* commented that these must have been the busiest two days of Mr Scroggie's ministerial life.

In subsequent years, when New Year's Day was not a Sunday, Graham Scroggie continued the pattern of the previous decade, except for the morning service. He devoted the afternoon to some aspect of the Second Coming, followed by a praise and testimony meeting at 7 p.m. After the armistice, the pre-war practice of serving tea on 1 January, for those who had come from a distance (many Christians, not Chapel members, thought it was a marvellous way of spending New Year's Day), was resumed, together with the question time that occupied visitors between the two meetings. This pattern continued until Scroggie left Edinburgh in 1933.

## Anniversaries, Thankofferings and socials

From 1875 to 1889, the Chapel commemorated the founding of the church, on 24 January 1808, by holding anniversary services on the nearest Sunday to that date. In 1889, this was moved to become the anniversary of the current ministry commencing. Two years later, an evening social on the Monday was added. As described in Chapter 16, Joseph Kemp, whose anniversary was in February, sat in the vestry from 12 noon until 8 p.m. on the Monday, for members to place Thankoffering gifts (amount unknown to any but the giver) in a box.

Graham Scroggie initially retained the Thanksgiving Monday in mid-February, including a social in the evening, but moved the anniversary services to the date of his own induction, which was the first weekend of October; he also held a Monday social then. It was like passing the offering bag round twice, and Scroggie realized it was illogical to separate the two events; from 1918, the Thankoffering was on 'the date of my settlement among you'.

Scroggie, like Joseph Kemp, preferred not to have a guest preacher for the anniversary Sunday services, but to occupy the pulpit himself. The Monday began with a public prayer meeting in the church, from 12 noon to 1 p.m. (until 1927, when it was discontinued). The pastor then went to the vestry for the whole of the afternoon, to receive the Thankoffering. Twelve years after he came to Edinburgh, Graham Scroggie enthused:

*The Annual Thankoffering Day is a God-honouring and a Church-enriching occasion. Saving yourselves the labour and risks of bazaar or sale of work, and the humiliation of whist drive or mystery supper, you bring on this occasion what you feel you can and ought to give to the Lord … since the end of the Great War, the Memorial Fund has been steadily fed by your generous offerings on Thanksgiving Day, part of it being devoted to assisting our young people who are in training for Christian ministry at home or abroad; and part of it being used for our evangelistic extension work at home.*

---

4 *Record*, 1928, p. 132.

The anniversary social started with tea in the lower hall at 6.30 p.m., followed by a public meeting in the church. There were usually several invited guest speakers. The Thankoffering was counted during the social and the total (so far) was announced at the end of the evening. From 1924 onward, enough was given to support the two funds mentioned by Graham Scroggie (above) and also to send a Christmas gift of £10 to every married missionary and £8 to the single ones.

TENTH ANNIVERSARY
of the Settlement of

The Rev. W. GRAHAM SCROGGIE,

SABBATH, 3rd October.

11 o'clock and 6.30 o'clock : Preacher—The Minister.

THANKSGIVING DAY,

MONDAY, October 4th.

The Rev. and Mrs W. Graham Scroggie will be in the Church Vestry from 1 o'clock, to receive the Freewill Offerings for the **Memorial Fund,** for Evangelization at Home and Abroad.

PUBLIC MEETING

At 7.45. Tea will be served in the Lecture Hall from 7 p.m.

*From 1918, the anniversary Sunday in October was followed by a Thanksgiving Day on Monday. This commemorated the settlement of the present minister, not the anniversary of the founding of the church. In this 1926 leaflet, Sunday is still called Sabbath.*

### An observant visitor

A visitor from Sunderland recorded his impressions of the Chapel in October 1921:

*The band of open-air workers, forgetting their Saturday tiredness, were preparing to go out into the streets. Their prayer time over, they emerged with lamp and organ, buttoning coats and humming a cheery hymn tune, looking as keen and happy as men on holiday. Up in the gallery the choir was at work, preparing for the next day's singing. They were putting their hearts into it, singing with a will, although it was Saturday night. Down below lay strewn clusters of flowers, awaiting the deft fingers of the gentlemen who were arranging them round the pulpit....*

*Sunday brought a medley of impressions. The prayer meetings before the services were remarkable for their 'aliveness'. The services themselves were marked by a great stillness, and an*

*intentness on the part of the worshippers, in spite of the discomforts of crammed pews and crowded aisles. One was reminded again of the strange 'aura' that clings to Keswick. And the quiet, penetrating voice from the pulpit probed the hearts already hushed, bringing them into a new realisation of the 'unsearchable riches of Christ'....*

*This was seen again on Tuesday night, when the Christian Service Class met. One felt the inspiration of the sight of so many young people, with life's possibilities before them, offering themselves, their time, and their talents to be trained for the service of their King.... A hundred young lives in a single Church aflame for God!*

---

5 *Record*, 1921, p. 92.

### Guest missioners

Graham Scroggie regarded himself as a sower of the seed, and regularly invited evangelists to come to Edinburgh to reap the harvest; as they did, he was happy to sit in the congregation and to support their work. Typical of his guests was Paul Rader, the minister of the Moody church, whom Scroggie had met in Chicago in 1920. Learning that Rader was to visit Great Britain in the autumn of that year, Scroggie arranged a fortnight of special meetings in Edinburgh. The weeknight services practically filled the Chapel; the Assembly Hall, which seated 1,250, was crowded on the first Sunday morning and hundreds were turned away that evening. For the second Sunday, Graham Scroggie booked the Usher Hall, which seated nearly three thousand; again, hundreds had to be turned away. Rader was a gifted evangelist, and many were converted at every meeting.

Additional information on the following topics, mentioned in this chapter, is available on the CD.

Choir
Temperance

# Chapter 27
## No parochial view (1916–1933)

### Evangelism indoors

#### Sunday – Infirmary services

Until religious pluralism became politically correct in the late twentieth century, the management of Edinburgh Royal Infirmary encouraged churches to hold a Christian service in every ward, every Sunday morning and afternoon. From 1890 (Chapter 11) until the early 1990s, the Chapel provided teams of four or five for a half-hour Christian service at 9.30 a.m. every Sunday morning, and another on Sunday afternoon. This involved someone to play the ward piano, another to lead the singing of hymns, another to read the Scriptures and that person (or another) to give a short message.

Older members conducted the afternoon service in ward 20, and once the Young Peoples Meeting was constituted in 1918, it provided the morning team. Later, from 1969 until at least 1978, the YPM went also to wards 9 and 34 at the Infirmary every Sunday afternoon, as well as holding a Sunday School in the Royal Hospital for Sick Children and the children's unit in the Astley Ainslie Hospital. One of the Chapel's peer-groups, Group 45, was still holding a monthly service in ward 34 of the Infirmary in December 1993, from 4.15-4.45.

CHARLOTTE CHAPEL
**FELLOWSHIP OF SERVICE.**

After prayerful consideration, as a member of the Church, I would like to serve the Lord Jesus in the way indicated below (put a cross, thus **X**).

Name,....................................................
Address,..................................................
Date,......................................................

**SPHERES OF SERVICE.**

| | |
|---|---|
| Sunday School Teaching, ... | Sunday Afternoon at 3. |
| The Choir, ... ... ... | Practice—Friday Night at 7.30. |
| Open-Air Work, ... ... | During the season—To Scout, Sing, or Stand. |
| Missionary Study Circle, ... | Wednesday Night (alternate). |
| Missionary Preparation for the Foreign Field, ... | Under the direction of the Pastor. |
| Tract Distribution and Visitation, ... ... ... | |
| Young People's Fellowship Meeting, ... ... ... | Wednesday Night (alternate). |
| Scouting for Souls, ... | |
| Young Women's Missionary Auxiliary, ... ... | Tuesday Night Working Party. |
| Girls' Missionary Auxiliary, | Saturday Afternoon Working Party. |
| Home Mission Work, ... | Cottage Meetings, Singing Bands, etc. |
| Prayer Circle, ... ... | Formation of groups to keep the fires always burning. |
| "Helps," ... ... ... | Knitting, Needlework, etc., at home, for Home and Foreign need. |

N.B.—When filled in, return this page to
**Rev. W. Graham Scroggie, Charlotte Chapel.**

*Graham Scroggie issued a pamphlet to members and adherents, urging them to consider which aspects of the Chapel's activities they could support.*

#### Sunday – Rock Mission.

Dr Maxwell Williamson, an elder in the Chapel and Medical Officer of Health for Edinburgh, had long been concerned about the condition of people living in the lodging houses and derelict slums of the city. He was a director of the Free Breakfast Mission, which he supported by his presence on Sunday morning in the Grassmarket. Not content with that, he later obtained the use of a large room in the Livingstone Dispensary of the Edinburgh Medical Missionary Society at 39 Cowgate, and provided a free tea to men living in the area who were willing to listen to a gospel message afterward. He called it the Rock Mission and led it until his death in 1923. (In 1930, another Chapel elder, Dr John Gray, was appointed as Edinburgh's Medical Officer of Health – he too kept the Chapel keenly aware of the social implications of the gospel.)

The Chapel's evangelistic committee took over the Rock Mission and appointed one of the elders as superintendent. The work was difficult and largely unrewarding, but there were many willing helpers, both men and women, of whom one wrote in 1926:

*To us these men are not broken earthenware neither down-and-outs. We resent to hear them referred to as such.*
*We see in them souls for whom Christ died and we have learnt to love them for His sake. The men appreciate the effort and with such a Saviour of Whom to tell them,*
*we go on rejoicing in that we are counted worthy to have been called into this service.*

1 *Record*, 1926, p. 72.

Throughout the year, between 75 and 100 men gathered in the Livingstone hall at 4.30 p.m. on Sunday afternoon, for tea and sandwiches followed by a bright evangelistic service. Clothing was provided, and money for a bed in a lodging house. Numbers were steady throughout the year, even in the summer. The hour's meeting (5-6 p.m.) was followed by heart-to-heart talks with some of the men – casual labourers, alcoholics and gaolbirds; a few professed acceptance of Jesus as Saviour. That was when the real challenge started – no work, no food, no decent clothing and no bed was a test to try the faith of established Christians, far less of men old in sin, but young in the faith.

Up to 140 came to the New Year social, for which a larger hall was hired; a special tea was laid on, followed by community singing, recitations, a guest singing group and a closing message. The men listened attentively; visitors remarked on both their good behaviour and their obvious attention to the service. One well meaning but inexperienced guest speaker went to the platform, and could not find his chosen passage in the lectern Bible. In perplexity, he whispered to the chairman: 'The parable of the prodigal son is in Luke 15, isn't it?' The chairman whispered back: 'It is, but the men removed that page from the lectern Bible many years ago.' When the Edinburgh Medical Missionary Society sold its Cowgate Livingstone Dispensary (where the Rock Mission met) to the University of Edinburgh in 1952, the work was transferred to the nearby Grassmarket Mission, as described in Chapter 38, and continued until 1987.

## Wednesday – District Women's Meeting

Sister Lilian took over the kitchen meetings that Lizzie Boyle had started, in sympathetic homes in Rose Street, for mothers with young children and others unable to attend church services. She moved them to the Chapel, on Tuesday evening. When Miss Boyle returned, she preferred Wednesday evening, but kept the meeting in the ladies' room in the Chapel; numbers grew steadily over the next decade, from 30 to 50 or more. She had a team of Chapel women to assist her, providing soloists, pianists and speakers. She visited the women and their families in their homes, sometimes with parcels of clothing or gifts of money to relieve desperate situations.

The women appreciated this oasis in the desert of Rose Street. The spiritual response was difficult to gauge, but the gospel message was faithfully sown and annual reports mentioned conversions. Women who had moved away from Rose Street continued regularly to come for the fellowship, although the outreach was specifically toward Rose Street. When Graham Scroggie left Edinburgh, the Rose Street Meeting, as it was sometimes called, was in good heart, meeting every Wednesday from October to April, with three social gatherings a year in the lower hall, and outings in the summer.

A typical social was:

*The meetings for the session closed with a Social on April 25th [1923]. It was a bright and happy company. Tea was first served, and then during the evening solos were beautifully*
*rendered by [names].... Mr. Butler, our Church Officer, struck up the refrain of a Scotch hymn, and a most enjoyable and inspiring meeting was brought to a close by the company singing the refrain, 'That's what I'll dae wi' Jesus, I'll jist tak' Him hame wi' me.'*

2 *Record*, 1923, p. 42.

and a typical summer outing:

*Miss Boyle's District Meeting Members held their outing on June 7 [1933]. They travelled by char-a-banc to Garvald, and then back to Harvieston for lunch and tea. During the afternoon games and races were heartily gone into, and Mr William Inglis having his concertina we had plenty of music, and opportunities for the women singing many of their favourite choruses which they learned at the women's meeting.*

3 *Record*, 1933, p. 105.

The District Meeting continued under the supervision of successive deaconesses until 1971, by which time most of those who had grown up with it had either moved too far away or were too frail to travel back to Rose Street regularly. Like the Girls Own on Sunday afternoon, it was very much appreciated by its loyal members, but it did not attract the next generation. In 1971, it merged with the flourishing Women's Thursday Morning Fellowship.

*Thomas Butler, church officer from 1918 to 1939. He and his wife lived in a flat on the top floor of the Chapel (now a kitchen and a classroom).*

There was no phone or 'intercom' at the back door of the Chapel until 1962, so if anyone rang the doorbell, Mr or Mrs Butler had to go all the way downstairs from their flat on the top floor to see who it was and what was wanted.

## Deputation and male voice choir

The Christian Service Class (Chapter 26) provided not only personnel for the Chapel's Evangelistic Association (below), but also supplied lay preachers for churches of all denominations, lodging houses, hospitals and prisons. From his roll of 71 in 1924, the deputation secretary sent 40 or 50 speakers a month to outside meetings.

A male voice choir was formed in 1920, to assist in deputation work. Its members either took whole services in churches and mission halls, or contributed the choral element. In 1924-5, it was wholly responsible for 98 services and sang gospel pieces at 40 others; in the following year, invitations fell to only 21 full services and 19 part-services, but one open-air meeting in a park was attended by over a thousand people. Like many Chapel auxiliaries, it took a break for the three summer months; letters printed in the *Record* showed how much it was appreciated.

The evening of Sunday 14 December 1924 deserves mention, because one cannot imagine the chairman's conduct being acceptable today. The male voice choir was singing in the McEwan Hall in Edinburgh, at the invitation of the Grassmarket Mission. As always, they put across the gospel message in their songs, to which the audience listened appreciatively. However, when the speaker 'rose towards the end of the service, several people tried to leave the building, unwilling to listen to the Word of God, but the doors were not opened for their exit, at the order of the Chairman, and they had perforce to stay where they were.'

## Edinburgh Evangelistic Union

Graham Scroggie was, from its beginning, the vice-chairman of this interdenominational union, the successor of the Edinburgh Evangelistic Association (Chapter 20). It was launched in November 1924 by two hundred Edinburgh ministers and Christian workers. Many of its activities directly involved the Chapel, such as a return visit of Gipsy Smith in April and May 1925. Lunchtime and evening meetings in St Cuthbert's Church on weekdays were attended by over two thousand, and Sunday services in the Usher Hall, at 3 p.m. and 8 p.m., attracted three thousand a time, plus an overflow. Graham Scroggie reported enthusiastically on the mission, and again the Chapel was involved in following-up enquirers and converts.

In January 1926, the Union invited Graham Scroggie to conduct a fortnight of evangelistic meetings in the United Free Church at Haymarket, Edinburgh, a mile to the west of the Chapel. A reporter from the *Edinburgh Evening News* was greatly impressed:

*The services, which commenced last Sunday evening, and were largely attended, may well develop into one of the most genuine and satisfying Revival movements ever held in Edinburgh. Many people associate evangelism with emotionalism, excitement, and other objectionable features. In the present mission these things are conspicuous by their absence. The addresses of the evangelist remind me very much of the summing up of a judge. He puts his hearers into the position of jurors. With consummate skill and a closely reasoned appeal to the intellect, he sums up the evidence in favour of Christ and His Kingdom, and then calls upon 'the jury' to give their verdict.*

4 *Record*, 1926, pp. 23, 27.

## United Services

Graham Scroggie participated enthusiastically in a series of meetings in the first week of February 1927, arranged by the eight churches in the west end of Edinburgh. Known as the United Services, they were held in St George's Parish Church in Charlotte Square, now the New Register House, at 8 p.m. every evening. Their purpose was the deepening of Christian life, not evangelism, and up to one thousand attended nightly for the week.

## Religious broadcasting

On the first Wednesday of January 1922, Graham Scroggie's son gave the YPM a demonstration of wireless radio transmission in the hall in the Chapel. Wireless was a mystery to most, but Marcus had made a study of it. He rigged up the necessary apparatus to pick up signals from Stonehaven and Stavanger in Norway, to the delight and astonishment of his peers. There was a marked increase in the attendance that Wednesday evening.

In April of the following year, the BBC began religious broadcasting in Scotland, to the few people who had wireless receivers. In 1927, it was the Chapel's turn to conduct a service. This had to be from a studio, so Graham Scroggie and the Chapel choir attended and broadcast live at 8.15 p.m. on

Sunday 15 February. Most members did not have a wireless receiver of their own, so they gathered in the Chapel to listen. Graham Scroggie was a gifted communicator, and it is instructive to read, today, how he began his sermon – he could assume a fair bit of background Bible knowledge. He started:

*Sooner or later we must all leave home, but it makes a lot of difference how we go. The PRODIGAL went voluntarily, in order to have, what he imagined to be a good time. JOSEPH went involuntarily, sold into Egypt by his brethren, yet in the favour and care of God. JACOB went as a fugitive, in order to escape his brother's wrath. Most of us go of necessity, in order to pursue one calling or another, and to establish for ourselves a home. No doubt a gracious providence over-ruled Jacob's out-going, and absence, but it was his SIN that drove him out. He had many lessons to learn, and only in a severe school could he learn them. This experience on the Bethel upland is the beginning of his discipline. Let us then endeavour to understand what Bethel meant to Jacob: and what it did for him.*

5 *Record*, 1927, p. 33.

## Marconi wireless message spans Atlantic

*The young Marconi soon after his arrival in England from Italy.*

*Until December 1901, it was thought that radio signals went in straight lines, and so disappeared into space as the earth curved. Guglielmo Marconi believed that they followed the curvature of the earth, and positioned himself in a hut on the cliffs of Newfoundland. He picked up a faint radio signal from Cornwall, 1,700 miles away, and so paved the way for global radio communication.*

Four years later, the evening service on Sunday 28 June 1931 was broadcast live from the Chapel itself; this was directly evangelistic, ending in an appeal.

## Evangelism outdoors

### Saturday, Sunday and Wednesday

Open-air preaching was still a feature of Chapel life, although not quite so intensive as during Joseph Kemp's years. The Chapel had three open-air meetings a week during Graham Scroggie's time, Sunday evening (all year round) and Wednesday and Saturday evening (May–October). In addition, a group went along Rose Street at 6 p.m. on Sunday evening, singing and giving invitations to the evening service; occasionally there was a march along Princes Street as well.

The corner of South Charlotte Street and Princes Street was still the preferred spot for open-airs, as it was near the Chapel and the harmonium and the platform had to be carried to the venue. Organizing an open-air meant not just getting soloists and speakers, but also enough supporters to form a crowd and draw in others. They met in the Chapel at 7.30 p.m., sometimes to sing a hymn, always to read a portion of Scripture and to have prayer. At eight o'clock they went to the street corner and started the meeting; they sang gospel hymns, prayed, preached, and offered booklets to all who listened. At 9.30 p.m. they took the furniture back to the Chapel. If it rained, the workers held a Bible study and prayer meeting in the Chapel instead.

*Open-air services were still held at the corner of Princes Street and South Charlotte Street, but, as this 1925 postcard shows, motorcars, taxis and electric trams were making Princes Street noisier and even congested at times.*

As the postcard shows, horse-drawn transport was on its way out in 1925, being replaced by motorcars, taxis and electric trams. The picture shows Edinburgh's first drinking fountain for people, horses and dogs. Shortly after this picture was taken, it was removed, as a traffic hazard, and it was never re-sited.

The Wednesday and Saturday evening outreaches in the summer and autumn were different from the Sunday evening in two ways. First, workers had to turn out specially – they were there, anyway, on Sunday, for the evening service in the Chapel – so numbers were always fewer. Secondly, the public houses of Rose Street (not open on Sunday) attracted a rough crowd during the week, so young men were needed to make an outer ring to protect the women; sometimes, sympathetic police were required as well. The 1919 season was hard, 'owing to the sparsity of workers – an average of six – and the indifference of the people'. The 1921 season had more support and a better response. The 1928 season was even more encouraging, growing in numbers and in enthusiasm; nine conversions were reported and one backslider was restored.

There was an amusing exchange of views just after Graham Scroggie left Edinburgh. Some of the young men asked the deacons for permission to form an official Charlotte Chapel football team, to compete in a local league. The deacons were not persuaded this was a good idea, and pointed out there was an urgent need for support at the open-air meetings. None of the young men 'could see their way to stand in', and nothing more was heard about a football team until 1994 (Chapter 50).

### Tract distribution

The Chapel started delivering gospel literature to homes in Rose Street in 1886, as mentioned in Chapter 12, and revived this outreach in 1903. Graham Scroggie wholeheartedly supported their noble work. When he came, 36 members were delivering 1,250 copies of 'The Evangel' every month, covering Rose Street and both of its lanes, Thistle Street, Hill Street, Melville Street, Upper Bow, Bread Street, Spittal Street, William Street, Grindlay Street, India Place, India Street, Lower Broughton, part of Jamaica Street and the married quarters at the Castle.

The cost was covered by voluntary subscription, one penny a week, not only from the distributors but also from anyone willing to contribute. Increasing subscriptions in 1917 enabled the team to buy 1,800 tracts monthly and to add every home in Cumberland Street and St Stephen's Street to their districts. There were now 47 distributors, all women (at least during the war), and they tried, wherever possible, to make personal contact with the residents as they handed the literature into the homes. If anyone expressed an interest, they were initially offered a copy of John's Gospel, and personal discussion if they wanted to know more.

By the end of 1918, distribution had risen to 2,300 a month, through 54 workers, with Greenside, Saunders Street, Johnstone Terrace and part of the Lawnmarket now included. Only a year later, it was 2,750, with 61 distributors, and Bedford Street, Cheyne Street and Dean Street were added. By 1923, 4.000 copies a month of 'The Evangel' were taken round by 70 women, rising in 1925 to 4,500 copies and 78 helpers, which enabled Drumdryan Street, Tarvit Street, Horne Terrace, Thistle Place, McNeill Street and Dorset Place to be visited as well.

Numbers increased steadily throughout Graham Scroggie's time; when he left Edinburgh, 60,000 tracts were being distributed every year – 5,000 a month – through 84 distributors. The work continued throughout the year, with no break. Home Street, Leven Street, Lochrin Place, Lochrin Terrace and Crichton Street were the last to be added. Tract distribution continued until December 1964, by which time the number of distributors had greatly reduced and appeals for new workers were unsuccessful (Chapter 43).

### Evangelistic Association – village outreach

Graham Scroggie had a vision to take the gospel into the villages and towns outside the boundaries of the city. To achieve this, he channeled the enthusiasm and dynamism of the Christian Service Class (Chapter 26) into forming a Charlotte Chapel Evangelistic Association in 1920. Under his presidency, young men and women ran it, but they employed an experienced evangelist for the main preaching. William Whyte was the first, for the six summer months of 1920, and then William Park.

In June 1920, the Association purchased a large tent for £200 and pitched it by the sands at Portobello. In cooperation with Portobello Baptist Church, they invited visiting preachers to assist William Whyte in the conduct of a two month campaign. The Chapel repeated this enterprise every summer until 1926, and then handed it over to the local church.

*The Chapel's Evangelistic Association pitched a large tent at Portobello every summer from 1920 to 1926, and employed an experienced evangelist to lead the meetings. They called it the canvas cathedral.*

In 1922, the Association purchased a second tent, smaller than the Portobello one, but still capable of accommodating 240 people. This (more portable) tent was moved from place to place, fulfilling Scroggie's wish to take the gospel to the communities surrounding Edinburgh. Mr and Mrs William Park travelled with this tent. Finding suitable accommodation for them was difficult, so the Association purchased a motor-caravan, which doubled up as a home for them and as a mobile platform for speakers at open-air meetings; Mrs Park sang the gospel effectively, accompanied by a small harmonium on the platform.

*This motor-caravan provided residential accommodation for the evangelists, as they moved around the Lothians, and also served as a platform for speakers at the meetings.*

In 1924, the Association employed one of the Chapel's own young men, Walter Main, as a second evangelist. A Chapel member, Andrew Ewing, presented the Association with a minibus, to convey people quickly to wherever the evangelists were working at the time – it became known as the Hallelujah Bus. The Christian Service Class supported the full-time evangelists by (many of them) giving up their summer holidays to take part in the outreaches, as instrumentalists, choristers, stewards, supporting speakers and counselors. 'No one appreciates such help more than the evangelist, who regards it as an inspiration to see a bus load of helpers with their smiling faces arriving to assist him in the work that at times he finds so difficult.'

From 1928 until it was wrecked in a storm in 1935, the smaller tent was pitched for the summer at the Old Canal Basin, at the corner of Morrison Street and Lothian Road. While it did not attract great holiday crowds as at Portobello, the Lothian Road work reached city dwellers, and more Chapel members were able to take part.

Curiously, Graham Scroggie's attempt to start a Workers' Training Class did not attract enough interest for even one meeting. He offered to teach elocution, grammar, deportment, address and sermon preparation, Bible knowledge and the cultivation of devout life, which the deacons endorsed as much needed. A flyer was put in the *Record* in 1921, but nothing came of it.

## Three mission halls

### The High Street mission in 1921

When Graham Scroggie came to Edinburgh, some members of the Chapel had been running an afternoon Sunday School in the High Street of Edinburgh for three years; its early stages were described in Chapter 20. Unlike the school in the Chapel, where a high percentage of the scholars came from Chapel families, the parents of the children attending the High Street School had no church connection. Graham Scroggie encouraged and promoted it, both for its own sake and as an avenue of service for Chapel members. When its founding member entered the ministry in 1921, he asked the Chapel to take it over, which it gladly did. There were then about 150 scholars and 15 teachers.

By 1926, there were 26 teachers (all Chapel members) and 220 scholars on the roll, 45 seniors in Bible Classes, 105 in the junior Sunday School and 70 in the primary department. Attendance averaged 150, unless the weather was good; on warm Sundays, many families went to the seaside at Granton or Portobello. The teachers did not mind unduly – encouraging family life, in an area of great social deprivation, was part of the Christian message.

Between 25 and 40, out of a roll of 60, came to a boys' club every Saturday evening, to play games, read or have discussions. The Chapel gave the club an electric lantern, and also supplied a library, both of which the boys greatly appreciated. In the summer, they had open-air games and went on rambles. The annual picnic in June, usually to Riccarton, attracted up to three hundred children and their mothers; no fathers came – 'Church and Mission were associated but distinct; one gave charity and the other received it. Women and children attended the Mission Hall and self-respecting working men were absent.'

The Christmas social – tea, singing, games and a visit from Father Christmas, with a present for all – was held in the Chapel, partly to provide a large enough hall (250 children attended) and partly to cement the link with the parent church; Father Christmas' parcel on these evenings was probably the only Christmas present the High Street children received. The aim of the mission was directly evangelistic, to win the children for Christ and, through them, the parents.

Despite every effort to retain their interest, boys generally disappeared from the Bible Class and the club as they grew into adolescence. Attempts to have a Sunday evening meeting for the parents of the children got nowhere – 'Not that they go elsewhere, which would solve our problem, but because they go nowhere.' Yet the mission was appreciated, and when they held a social evening in the High Street premises, to meet the parents, they had to close the door when the hall, built for 90, had 130 mothers inside.

### The High Street mission in 1928
In 1928, the Monday evening girls' club began to cater for a wider age range, 14-25, meeting at 7.15 p.m. for sewing, talking and playing games. There were 20 on the roll, with an average attendance of 13, starting and finishing with family worship. A junior girls' club, meeting for the hour before

7.15 p.m., was meant to be for the age range 9-13, but any girl aged 3 upwards, who wanted to come, was made welcome. A weekly women's meeting on Thursday evening, started in 1928, was an instant success, even although it was directly evangelistic, and decisions were recorded. Numbers averaged from 30 to 40, but despite extensive canvassing, not one single man turned up for the equivalent men's meeting.

Finding sufficient accommodation was a problem until 1930; by 1925, the mission was renting four separate halls every Sunday afternoon. Things changed when the 1929 reunion scheme in the Church of Scotland made the West St Giles church hall, on the first floor above street level at 128 High Street, surplus to requirement. The Chapel purchased it in 1930, and after repair and cleaning, it was ready for the Sunday School opening in October. Permanent accommodation enabled the mission to extend the girls' clubs on Monday evening, to add a girls' study class on Tuesday evening, to expand the Thursday women's meeting, to start a Friday evening Bible study and a Sunday evening gospel service. An open-air meeting was held in Hunter Square from 7.30-8 p.m., which never attracted large crowds, but a few came in to the meetings in the new hall because of it. When Graham Scroggie left Edinburgh in 1933, 11 different auxiliaries were using it.

*In 1930, the mission purchased a hall on the first floor of 128 High Street. The stairway to number 128 (through the arch behind the pedestrian with the red jacket in this 2006 picture) is no longer used, as the hall has been incorporated into the Wee Windaes restaurant, entering by number 144.*

The High Street mission, alone among the Chapel's outreaches, had to contend with active opposition from the local Roman Catholic priests. This took two forms; they ordered Catholic parents not to attend, nor to allow their children to attend; more subtly, they purchased a large building opposite the mission and fitted it out lavishly, so that the boys attending the Chapel club were seduced by better facilities across the road. Graham Scroggie's inter-denominational sympathies were strictly toward fellow Protestants, and he deplored such activities by those loyal to Rome.

The mission wanted to have an occasional communion service, but Graham Scroggie absolutely forbad it, reminding them that the mission was an auxiliary of the church, not a detached body. However, they showed their semi-independence by holding jumble sales every May between 1927 and 1935, 'although the [Chapel] office-bearers would … prefer if we could find some other means of raising funds'. That was quite a concession by the Chapel, not to overrule the mission, because the deacons replied frostily to the Scottish Temperance Alliance, whose work they supported: 'We regret that we cannot see our way to take any part in a Grand Bazaar to be held in the Music Hall'.

The High Street mission had splendid semi-jubilee services in October 1938, but it was badly affected by the restrictions imposed during the Second World War, and had to close in June 1943, as described in Chapter 34.

### The Jamaica Street mission

When the tract distributors expanded their area to include Jamaica Street in 1915, they were concerned about the unlovely situation of the folk living there, just downhill from the lovely Heriot Row; it was drab and depressing, with little sunlight coming over the high tenements. The need for evangelistic work in the area led the deaconess, Elizabeth Boyle, to start a kitchen meeting, along the lines as the one in Rose Street. Sister Lilian took it a stage further, securing the let of an empty shop and turning it into a meeting hall in October 1916. It could (and often did) accommodate one hundred children, provided the platform was used as well as the seating area.

The mission flourished there for 25 years, with Sunday and midweek services, socials and outings. The first (pleasant) surprise was when twenty young men, over school age, came to a lads' class every Sunday afternoon, and said: 'the Mission Hall is a sort of home.… they would not miss their class.' They suggested having open-air meetings in Inverleith Park

on Sunday afternoon, from June to September, between 3-4 p.m.; they themselves collected money to purchase a portable organ, and this outreach continued summer after summer until 1931.

*The Chapel rented an empty shop in Jamaica Street (the service road for Heriot Row) and turned it into a meeting hall in 1916.*

The younger women formed a girls' class, which met on Wednesday, with 72 names on the roll and an average attendance of 50; in the spring of 1917, there were 30 professions of conversion among them. They formed a choir, specifically for 16-18 year old Jamaica Street girls; it took courage to sing at gospel meetings in their own district, but they were radiant. Throughout the years of the mission, one of its most encouraging features was the commitment of young people – especially in the Junior Christian Endeavour on Thursday, and the Band of Hope on Friday. One of the Jamaica Street boys went into the ministry and another became a missionary.

The people of Jamaica Street themselves asked for a Sunday evening adult service. It was well attended from its inception in 1917, especially by younger adults. An open-air meeting in the summer months preceded it, and scarcely a week went by without someone accepting Christ as Saviour during the prayer meeting that followed the evening service. The Tuesday evening Women's Meeting filled a large place in the otherwise empty lives of the women in the district; attendance averaged between 40 and 50, sometimes up to 80. Like most Chapel auxiliaries, it closed for the summer, from the middle of May to the beginning of October, but the Chapel workers made a point of keeping in touch any who were unwell or in difficulty.

The Second World War (1939-45) made life in Jamaica Street even more difficult for the residents. The Chapel workers carried on until 1952, when the owner of the shop, which they rented for the mission, sold it. The population was shifting and the old houses were scheduled for demolition. It was reluctantly decided in May 1952 to discontinue the work and to concentrate on the new housing area of Longstone (Chapter 39). However, members still visited and encouraged children to come to the Chapel Sunday School; they held open-air services on Sunday afternoon in Jamaica Street until the area was cleared of houses in the late 1960s.

### Stenhouse Baptist Church

In the late 1920s, the Chapel started a church plant in the new corporation housing area of Stenhouse; house-to-house visitation was carried on systematically. A Chapel business meeting voted in March 1932 to purchase ground at Stenhouse Cross, to build a hall and to meet the cost of ministry until the new venture was self-supporting. Things moved quickly; the foundation stone was laid in July 1932 and seven months later, the opening service was conducted by Rev. Andrew MacBeath, who acted as pastor for two months before sailing for Africa with the Baptist Missionary Society.

There was no lack of willing workers for such evangelistic outreach. The people loved their Lord and they wanted to serve him and others in every possible way. This was the thrust of the pulpit ministry, and there were numerous opportunities for everyone to develop their particular gifts. Graham Scroggie used to say: 'this place is not a museum, it is a workshop.'

The theological issues of the day were pinpointed when the Chapel interviewed a potential pastor for the new work in February 1933. Rev. James McAvoy was already an accredited minister with the Baptist Union of Scotland, but the deacons decided that they had to ask him point-blank:

(1) Did he believe in the full and proper deity of Christ?
(2) Did he believe in the sacrifice of Calvary as atoning?

His answers were satisfactory and he was inducted to his new charge in June 1933, at a salary of £250 a year. On 9 July 1933, 61 members sat down at the first communion service, 12 of them Chapel members who had transferred to help the new cause. The Chapel watched with interest and affection as, under Mr McAvoy's leadership, its first daughter church adopted a constitution, formed its own deacons' court, and later purchased a manse for £900 and rapidly paid off the mortgage over it of £700. James McAvoy was 'called' to Jarrow in 1938.

CHARLOTTE BAPTIST CHAPEL
WEST ROSE STREET, EDINBURGH

Minister—Rev. W. GRAHAM SCROGGIE, D.D.

▾ ▾ ▾

## FOUNDATION STONE LAYING

OF

STENHOUSE BAPTIST CHURCH HALL

AT

STENHOUSE PLACE EAST, EDINBURGH

ON

**SATURDAY, 30th JULY, 1932, 3 p.m.**

▾ ▾ ▾

Chairman, - - F. FIDDES MAIN, Esq.

*Laying the foundation stone for the Stenhouse Baptist Church on Saturday 30 July 1932. From left to right: Rev. A.D. Sloan, Rev. John M'Neill, W. MacDuff Urquhart (the Chapel secretary), Professor Henry Curr, Rev. Peter Fleming, (father of Tom Fleming of broadcasting fame), and James Scott (a former assistant at the Chapel and then secretary of the Baptist Union of Scotland).*

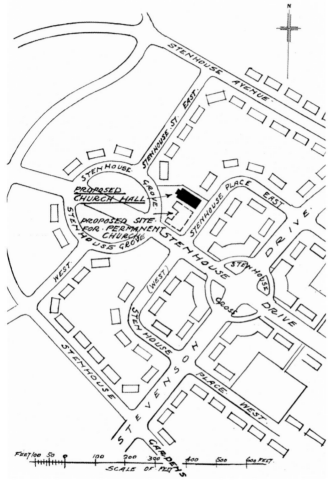

*This map shows the strategic site chosen by the Chapel in 1932, in the new housing area of Stenhouse. A hall seating three hundred was quickly built at a cost of £1,200, but the intended church building beside it (see map) never materialized; that ground may soon (2007) be sold for development.*

Additional information on the following topics, mentioned in this chapter, is available on the CD.

Christian Endeavour Society
Church officers from 1912
Graham Scroggie's first broadcast
High Street mission
Jamaica Street mission
Kitchen meetings
Marcus Scroggie's obituary
Stenhouse Baptist Church
Walter Main
William Whyte

## Frank W. Boreham

Those (mostly of the older generation) who find Frank Boreham's books compulsive reading – the writer has 40 of them – will be interested to know that he spoke in the Chapel on Tuesday 12 June 1928. He had emigrated from London to New Zealand, but came back in 1928 for a tour of Britain. He was invited to address the General Assembly of the Church of Scotland, where the moderator introduced him as: 'the man whose name is on all our lips, whose books are on all our shelves, and whose illustrations are in all our sermons'. Graham Scroggie took the opportunity of his being in Edinburgh to get him to tell the Chapel, at a special weeknight meeting, about his experiences.

# Chapter 28
# Missionaries (1916–1933)

## Thanksgiving and Memorial Fund

### A missionary heart

Through the Christian Service Class and through his pulpit ministry and in pastoral counselling, Graham Scroggie stimulated considerable interest in overseas ('foreign', as it was then called) missionary service. He constantly advocated the need to take the gospel to the whole world; sending out witnesses was one of his dominant passions. During his ministry in Edinburgh, 32 young men entered the ministry at home and 51 missionaries, men and women, were valedicted from the Chapel. As late as 1958, over half of the Chapel's serving missionaries had first gone abroad under Graham Scroggie. Older members have told the writer about some of the quiet talks they had with him, when he pressed on them the claims of the unevangelised and changed the course of their lives.

### Memorial service

Of the 173 young men from the Chapel who served in the 1914-18 war, 30 were killed, 29 in the army and 1 in the Royal Flying Corps (which later became the Royal Air Force). Their sacrifice was commemorated in three ways. First, Graham Scroggie conducted a solemn memorial service in a packed Chapel on Sunday evening, 8 December 1918, 'for our own young men who have fallen in the Great War.' In his own words:

*Just before the sermon, the congregation standing, the Roll was called. Well do I remember how difficult it was to get through, difficult for us all. The sermon was an appeal to the rising youth of the Church to be 'baptized for the dead'. That finished, the two front benches in the area were cleared, and we rose to sing the hymn, 'Take my life and let it be consecrated Lord to Thee.' I asked that, while we were singing it, those who would take the places of the thirty men who had 'fallen', who would step into these gaps by consecrating themselves then and there to Christ, would come forward and stand in these empty seats. At once they began to come, from area and gallery, and, the hymn finished, I asked the people to remain standing while I counted those who had taken the great step. Just thirty had come forward: the two front benches were full.*

1 *Record*, 1926, p. 147.

**Charlotte Chapel**
**Edinburgh**

**Memorial Service**

FOR OUR OWN MEN WHO HAVE
FALLEN IN THE GREAT WAR

**1914-1918**

*Sabbath Evening, 8th December, at 6.30*

*"Blessed are the dead who die in the Lord"*

*Everyone who attended the memorial service received a leaflet, with the order of service and the names of the men killed.*

Secondly, the names were inscribed on a memorial plaque in the vestibule of the Chapel, dedicated during the morning service on Sunday 9 January 1921. The plaque had to be moved to the stairway to the lower hall when the present lounge was constructed in 1983. In the 1990s, one of the Chapel deacons painstakingly traced all available information about them, and it is now available in pamphlet form and on tape.

*The Scottish National War Memorial in Edinburgh Castle has been described as a nation's grief etched in stone. It remains as solemn and impressive as when it was opened in 1927. The Chapel decided to remember those killed in the war, not in stone, but by setting up a fund to train people to carry the gospel all over the world.*

## Memorial Training Fund

Thirdly, Graham Scroggie established a fund, to express the church's gratitude for the members who had fallen in the war. He suggested:

*that instead of a costly material memorial, we should establish a Fund, by means of which many might express their gratitude to God, for having had spared and restored to them their men who had been in the ranks, and by means of which others, indeed all of us, might keep in loving remembrance those who had laid down their lives; and so, the institution is called the Thanksgiving and Memorial Fund.*

2 *Record*, 1933, p. 131.

After meeting the cost of the memorial plaque just mentioned, the remainder of the money (the bulk of it) was used to establish a fund 'to assist such of our young people who might go into training for the work of God at home and abroad and also to help such to reach their respective fields'. Although Scroggie initially called it the Thanksgiving and Memorial Fund, it soon became known as the Memorial Training Fund. It was replenished through the annual Thankoffering and lasted until 1995; the fund was then running low, so it was merged with the Dr Scroggie Memorial Fund, which had been set up on his death in 1958, and the joint fund continues to provide grants for members in training.

The Memorial Training Fund, established in 1919, is still available (now merged with the Dr Scroggie Memorial Fund) to assist Chapel members preparing for Christian service.

Mr Scroggie also had a deep concern for the young men who had returned from the war and did everything possible to re-establish them in the life of the church.

## Thankofferings

As Graham Scroggie left Edinburgh in 1933, he was proud to report that:

*Throughout these years my wife and I, with some of the Office-bearers, have received, on the first Monday in each October, your freewill offerings, and the results, in actual giving, have been truly wonderful. The figures [rounded to the nearest £] are as follows:*

| | |
|---|---|
| *1919 – £430* | *1926 – £470* |
| *1920 – £470* | *1927 – £503* |
| *1921 – £467* | *1928 – £505* |
| *1922 – £389* | *1929 – £498* |
| *1923 – £610* | *1930 – £512* |
| *1924 – £516* | *1931 – £515* |
| *1925 – £529* | *1932 – £406* |

*During a part of this period the whole world has been passing through a period of unprecedented economic distress, and still the average of giving to this Fund has been maintained.... no single gift has exceeded £35, and ... in no year have there been half-a-dozen gifts of more than £25 each; the balance has been made up of pound and half-pound notes, and cash, down to the pennies of the little children.*

3 *Record*, 1933, pp. 131-2.

The economic depression, mentioned by Graham Scroggie in that quotation, reached its depth toward the end of his time in Edinburgh. Twenty-seven per cent of Scots men, practically all of whom were the main breadwinners in the family, were out of work. Graham Scroggie had to balance: (1) his pastoral concern for a congregation struggling with unemployment, and (2) his pastoral concern for those who depended on the Memorial Fund for their training. £500 was needed from the Thankoffering every October, to replenish the fund, so Scroggie wrote to the congregation in September 1931:

*Only too well do I know how difficult many of you are finding it.... the Apostle Paul writing to the Corinthians of the*

*Macedonian Churches, says that 'in a great trial of affliction the abundance of their joy and their deep poverty abounded unto the riches of their liberality'. Giving is never so precious to God as when it is sacrificial....It is on this ground that I appeal to you again for our Memorial offering.*

4 *Record*, 1931, p. 131.

As the figures above show, the response was almost as generous as any other had been.

## Raising missionary awareness

### Valedictions and ordinations

Missionaries who were valedicted during a Sunday morning service were expected to take a leading part in the evening service. Graham Scroggie used them to drive home both his regular Sunday morning call for dedicated Christian living, and his regular Sunday evening call for conversion. On Sunday 13 July 1919, Douglas Robertson and Nurse Rebecca Cowie were about to sail to different missions in China. Scroggie had them in the pulpit in the morning, after which he issued a powerful challenge to full-time Christian service; Douglas gave his testimony in the evening, and Scroggie used it as the basis for an equally powerful sermon on conversion. He did not ask Nurse Cowie to speak, but that was not because she was a woman – one Sunday morning in the previous month, a woman missionary on furlough delivered the whole sermon. Departing missionaries often added their own pleas for overseas needs, of which Grace Chalmers' valedictory address was typical:

*The China Inland Mission are appealing for 200 volunteers in two years to finish up the work God has given them in China. My own society is needing men and women for several different parts of the field where Christ has never been named. They are waiting for their first missionary, and to-night God is waiting for volunteers. Won't some of you young people make glad the heart of God by saying, 'Lord Jesus, here I am, take me now and use me in Thine own place of choosing'. God needs you, won't you give him the chance to use you; won't you make His heart glad to-night by saying, 'Here am I, send me?'*

5 *Record*, 1929, p. 172.

Graham Scroggie reintroduced ordination services (that is, ordination for ministry) to the Chapel. Between 1881, when James Balfour was ordained, and 1916, when Scroggie came to Edinburgh, the Chapel held 'recognition services', but they did not include ordination. Andrew MacBeath was ordained on Sunday morning, 6 April 1924, and preached at the evening service. Graham Scroggie used both ordinations and valedictions to press the need for more to volunteer for full-time Christian service.

### Christmas parcels for missionaries

Mrs Scroggie shared her husband's missionary zeal, and she began a Missionary Christmas Parcels Scheme in 1919 (as she had done at Bethesda in Sunderland, both of which continued long after the Scroggies moved on). Building on the Christmas parcels for service men and women during the war, mentioned in Chapter 22, Mrs Scroggie appealed to every member of the church to contribute at least one item toward a parcel for the Chapel's missionary family. If they could make something themselves, so much the better; if not, they could buy it and hand it to one of the 30 women whom she enlisted to carry on the scheme. Every year from 1920, they met monthly in homes around the city on Friday afternoon, or in the ladies' room on Wednesday evening, to make up materials purchased or handed in. This was complementary to the work of the three auxiliaries mentioned next, whose goods went only to the Baptist Missionary Society.

At the beginning of October, there was an exhibition of goods, prior to their dispatch. With the high profile that Mrs Scroggie was able to give it, this was a splendid social evening, with tea and a talk and an appeal for funds for next year.

*On Wednesday, October 19 [1921], our sober Church took on an unusual aspect. Willing workers had decked pulpit and stairs, platform and tables with the many beautiful gifts which had come in. Festoons of bright jerseys and caps wonderfully fashioned from old stockings and socks, so useful for our missionaries' work, radiated from the pulpit, and from 6.30 until 7.30, when the meeting commenced, a steady stream of friends passed along admiring the work and commenting upon the many hours of loving sacrificial labour that must have been put in; one or two expressed a wish to purchase some article, and had to be reminded that 'this was not a Bazaar'.*

---

6 *Record*, 1921, p. 88.

As soon as the exhibition was over, the women made up the parcels and got them away, so they would arrive in China, India, Africa and Palestine in time for Christmas. Starting with 15 parcels in 1920 and 24 in the following year, the number rose steadily to 61 in 1929. That did not mean 61 recipients, because until 1930, the maximum weight on overseas parcels was 11 pounds, so most missionaries received 2 or 3. When the limit for parcel post went up to 22 pounds, the Chapel took advantage of it, partly because packing was easier and partly because the recipients had less import duty to pay on one large parcel then on several smaller ones. It was, however, a daunting task to fill 30 boxes, all weighing 22 pounds, and to finance their postage; Mrs Scroggie remarked, as she closed the last parcel in 1931, 'these take some filling'. A missionary on furlough, who had come to watch, remarked in astonishment that the women filled these huge parcels 'as if they were peeling tatties'.

Those on furlough received exactly the same gifts, and all were effusive in their letters of thanks. From 1924, a money gift of £10 for a married couple or £8 for a single missionary was sent at the same time, from the October Thankoffering. This often enabled the recipients to get the goods out of custom, because over the years, some gifts to missionaries had to remain uncollected because they could not afford to pay the duties on the parcels.

As soon as the parcels for one year were away, Mrs Scroggie began planning for the next. She canvassed for gifts of material and money, cannily using the sales pitch that money given before the end of the year would enable her to buy material cheaply in the January sales. The scheme continued after the Scroggies left Edinburgh, and Mrs Baxter, the wife of the next pastor, was just as enthusiastic a leader. In a happy touch, the Scroggies were added to the list of recipients from Christmas 1933 onward.

The parcels had to be suspended for the duration of the Second World War, and a larger gift of money was substituted. The last parcel sent to a mission station in China in 1939 was delivered nine years later, by which time the original addressee had retired, but she told the station to treat it as their own; this delighted them, as scissors and other items were unobtainable locally at that time. For a few years after the war ended in 1945, it was difficult to get material – the rationing authorities refused to issue any coupons for the project, and people desperately needed their own – but by 1950 parcels were posted regularly to Congo, Damascus, Gold Coast (now Ghana), Nigeria and Pakistan.

## Missionary auxiliaries

### Sunday School missionary committee

The Sunday School had its own missionary committee, which originally had three functions – to arrange missionary meetings in the Sunday School context, to look after the missionary library in the church, and to propose the disbursement of missionary collections. When the School was not meeting, in July and August, this group took the initiative in arranging open-air meetings at Saughton and Granton, which were well supported over many years. Quarterly from 1928, the departments of the Sunday School came together for their hour from 3-4 p.m. and invited parents and friends to join them for a missionary rally. Graham Scroggie took the chair, and the scholars gave demonstrations and recitations and generally raised the awareness of the mission field (as it was known at that time).

CHARLOTTE CHAPEL SUNDAY SCHOOL

INAUGURATION OF MISSIONARY MUSEUM

**EVENING TOUR**
**"ROUND THE WORLD IN 90 MINUTES"**

To visit our Missionaries, their Work and Fields

ILLUSTRATED BY

**NATIVE CURIO, LANTERN, and SONG**

In Lecture Hall, Charlotte Chapel
Saturday, 26th March, 1932

Exhibition of Curios from 6.30 p.m.      Lantern Service at 7 p.m.

COLLECTION

*The Sunday School asked Chapel missionaries to send some native curios, for a missionary museum. They also put together exhibitions, focussing on an area of the world and the Chapel missionaries in it, to stimulate the children's interest.*

## Women's Missionary Auxiliary

Three groups met regularly, from the beginning of October to the end of April, to sew and knit garments for Baptist Missionary Society hospitals and schools. The goods were exhibited at separate social occasions in April or May, before being sent off via the Society. Graham Scroggie and his wife greatly encouraged all three by attending and speaking at their opening and closing sessions, whenever possible; the pastor's personal involvement was a significant factor in their growth.

The largest of the groups was the Women's Missionary Auxiliary, which had started in Mrs Urquhart's home in 1905 as the Girls Auxiliary, and divided 11 years later into a Women's Missionary Auxiliary and a Girls Auxiliary, meeting separately. The Women's group met in the Chapel from 7-9 p.m. on Tuesday evening; average attendance expanded throughout the 1920s from 27 to 38. The purpose, from the beginning, was to make garments to send to BMS missionaries, especially those working in hospitals.

While knitting and sewing, they had a missionary speaker or listened to letters from missionaries being read. Most were married women, who valued the fellowship, and every evening closed with family worship. They made goods to order, when Andrew MacBeath sketched out a pattern for boys' suits and was delighted when they fitted perfectly. They made peculiarly shaped garments for Moslem girls and Mohammedan pyjama trousers, when these were requested for women's hospitals in India. Although the three auxiliaries existed to support the work of the BMS (only), this group bent the rules when one of their own members, Bessie Hamilton, went to Morocco in 1926. Like the other two, they also collected generously and sent gifts of money as well as goods. They supported a teacher at one of the CIM schools at a cost of £10 a year and also a Bible woman, who travelled around villages in India.

## Girls Auxiliaries

The Girls Auxiliary (later renamed the Young Women's Missionary Auxiliary) met at the same time on Tuesday evening, with much the same agenda but with a concentration on children's garments. They sewed and knitted for hospitals in China, Congo and India and for a boarding school in India, where they also financially supported one teacher and one pupil. When Graham Scroggie arrived, 22 were attending, but this soon rose to a membership of 49 and attendance of nearly 30. They studied a country or listened to a talk while they worked in the ladies' room in the Chapel.

The Girls (Junior) Missionary Auxiliary, started in November 1916 at the initiative of Graham Scroggie, was initially for girls aged between 10 and 17; it was soon restricted to those aged over 12. It met on alternate Saturday afternoons from 3 -4.30 p.m., with 40 on the roll and average attendance of 32. They too met in the ladies' room and they too made garments for girls at a boarding school in India; they also met the cost of the upkeep of an orphan girl at the school. They varied the destination of their gifts from year to year, according to need. Numbers remained steady over the years, to the pleasant surprise of the leaders, who had initially doubted the wisdom of arranging a missionary meeting on a Saturday afternoon. Like the other groups, their year closed with an exhibition of their goods in April or May.

In 1933, the Girls Auxiliary, as the youngest group was often called, moved its meeting to alternate Tuesdays in the Chapel from 7.30-9 p.m.; numbers had dropped and they hoped to attract more than were now coming on Saturday afternoon. It was a good move – 10 new girls joined right away, bringing the membership up to 26 and the average attendance up to 16. As a branch of the National Girls Auxiliary of the Baptist Missionary Society, they also had meetings with similar groups in other churches.

## Missionary Study Circles

Missionary Study Circles met on alternate Wednesday evenings, to look into books on mission and to hear talks on mission. Thirty-five attended; they divided into four circles, each under the leadership of a senior member. A chapter of a book was set for every evening, and discussion of it followed. When Graham Scroggie started a fortnightly Young Peoples Meeting in 1918, on alternate Wednesdays (Chapter 24), he suggested that the two should merge, and this soon took place.

# Who is a missionary?

## Our own missionaries

The Chapel used the word 'missionary' in several different ways during Graham Scroggie's time. He kept reminding the congregation that:

*You cannot all go abroad as missionaries, but you can all be missionaries here. If it may not be Persia, then, let it be Princes Street; if it may not be China, then, let it be Charlotte Street. Say a word, sing a song, stand around, carry the organ, or lamp, or platform, or hymn-books, and pray for all the rest, and when the Accounts are made up, you will be surprised at your Dividend.*

7 *Record*, 1929, p. 91.

However, the Chapel divided members in full-time Christian service into four categories, of which only the first were 'missionaries'. They were listed as such in the *Record* every autumn, to encourage people to send Christmas letters. To be included in this category, one had to be: (1) in membership at the Chapel, (2) working in Africa, China, India, Palestine or the West Indies, and (3) supported through a missionary society, not a secular organization. Wives of Chapel missionaries were not included on the list, unless they themselves were in membership.

### Secular employment in missionary countries

The second category was for members who worked with secular organizations in the countries listed above. They were encouraged to send reports, they were prayed for, and some received Christmas parcels, but they were not 'our missionaries'. For example, nursing sister Kathie Brown worked for three years in a hospital in Ceylon and another five in Nigeria, placed through the BMS, but she was not a 'missionary' because she was employed by the government. Missionaries had 'furloughs'; others had 'vacations'. The distinction was pointedly made at Kathie Brown's wedding in the Chapel in 1934, when Graham Scroggie said: 'We take this opportunity of saying how much Miss Brown's work was appreciated at Onitsha, Southern Nigeria, though not a missionary working under a society.'

This was also the situation if a member went abroad with a missionary society and then moved to a government post, even if doing identical work. Dr Ian Dovey, son of the Chapel treasurer, was on the missionary list while working with the London Missionary Society at the Shantung Hospital in Shanghai. He was taken off the list when he moved to a colonial appointment in Hong Kong, even though he was working in a hospital, as in Shanghai, and supervising an orphanage run by the Church Missionary Society.

### Pastoral ministry

A third list was kept, and printed in the *Record* from time to time, of 'men who have entered the Christian Ministry from Charlotte Chapel'. There was, unfortunately, some antipathy at that time toward the Baptist Theological College of Scotland, which trained men for pastoral ministry. Andrew MacBeath's suggestion that one Sunday offering a year should go to the College was turned down, with the explanation that Graham Scroggie had told Mr MacBeath about unsatisfactory features of the College's teaching. When another of the Chapel's old boys, William Cassie, asked for an annual grant from the Memorial Training Fund to be given to the College, he was told that the church could not on principle support the College, but would give aid to individual students.

### Other full-time Christian service

The fourth list was of Chapel men and women, including former members, who were carrying out full-time evangelistic or teaching work in non-missionary countries, such as Australia or Canada or Great Britain. (The latter are listed under 'Home mission' on the CD.) They were regularly mentioned in the *Record*, but not in the missionary section. Examples included James Forbes, who went to Australia in 1922 as an itinerant evangelist, and Margaret Govan, who worked with a caravan mission in Norfolk and Essex.

There was some flexibility with the Christmas missionary parcels; Annie Wighton, whose membership was elsewhere until 1935, received them as regularly as the supported missionaries, and one went in 1930 to Mr Watson, Sianfu, Shensai, China, although he is not mentioned anywhere else and he was never one of the Chapel's missionary team.

## Missionary support

### District collections

Graham Scroggie was determined to increase the Chapel's financial support for its missionaries, and also for the work of the Baptist Missionary Society. Shortly after he arrived, he formed the Charlotte Chapel Foreign Missionary Society, representing all aspects of Chapel missionary interest, with himself as chairman and his wife as secretary. He divided the city into 20 districts, and asked members of the congregation to encourage everyone in their district to give regularly to missionary causes, by means of boxes or envelopes. All unallocated gifts went to the BMS.

## Fully supported missionaries

In 1929, the cost of fully supporting a BMS missionary was £125 a year for a single man, double that for a married man, plus an allowance for children. At a special church meeting in February, it was agreed to undertake the support of Mr and Mrs Andrew MacBeath, as the Chapel's missionaries in the Congo. This was an appropriate gesture, as Andrew had grown up in the Chapel, had already served abroad, and had been married just a fortnight before. The large number of guests at their wedding were among those who set about raising £250 a year, every year.

It was quite a challenge; the Chapel's missionary giving for the calendar year 1929 was £409, of which £126 was divided among the other 18 missionaries and £107 was sent to 24 societies in which the Chapel had an interest. That left £176, so far, toward the MacBeaths' £250. The BMS financial year ended on 31 March; this was the deadline to bring the MacBeath fund up to the promised amount. It was achieved, and the momentum built up was so great that on 31 March 1931, the required amount (now £265) was in hand plus £34 over, to start the next financial year.

## Missionary travel

Douglas Robertson showed both initiative and good stewardship when, in 1929, he and his family returned to China overland, via Siberia, instead of the usual steamship route through the Suez Canal. Another Chapel missionary sailed from Liverpool on 12 October and arrived in Hong Kong on 14 December, which was 9 weeks; the Robertsons took 18 days. From 1936, Imperial Airways offered flights from London to Hong Kong, but no Chapel missionaries took advantage of them, for two reasons. Ships were much more reasonably priced – the airfare was £175 one-way, at a time when the average worker's wage was £4 a week, and a small car cost £100. Secondly, the time on the boat gave missionaries a much-needed rest; flying was no holiday, as Imperial Airways made 16 stops in 13 countries, using a number of different aircraft.

## Missionary map

From June 1932, until the construction of the lounge in 1982, a map of the world dominated the wall behind the platform in the lower hall, with markers for the location of the Chapel missionaries. A member, who proposed the idea and then painted it himself, kept it up to date. The original map (photograph below) was replaced by a more modern one in 1971, of which there is a photograph in Chapter 45. The map disappeared with the reconstruction of the lower hall in 1982.

*This map of the world, showing the location of Chapel missionaries, dominated the lower hall from 1932 to 1971.*

## Photographs of missionaries

As mentioned under the heading 'Monday evening prayer meeting' in Chapter 25, the Chapel made good use of photography to keep missionary interest before the congregation. From 1930, photographs of all the missionaries were framed and displayed in the lower hall on the first Monday of the month, when the prayer meeting had a missionary focus. Copies of 33 photographs from that album are on the CD under 'Missionaries, 1936'.

Additional information on the following topics, mentioned in this chapter, is available on the CD.

Andrew MacBeath
Home mission
James Balfour
Walter Main
Missionaries, 1936

# Chapter 29
# Graham Scroggie's wider ministry (1916–1933)

## Conference ministry

### Great Britain

When the Chapel 'called' Graham Scroggie in 1916, he was already well known as a speaker at the Keswick and other conventions for the consecration of life and Christian service. His response included the query: 'Is Charlotte Chapel prepared to give me the same facilities [six or seven conventions a year] that the Church at Bethesda allows?' Andrew Urquhart replied: 'Mr Kemp … was allowed the fullest liberty. We never said "No" to a single request of this kind he ever made.' Accordingly, Scroggie continued to accept invitations to preach at conventions throughout Great Britain and Northern Ireland, and (for example) his conference diary in 1919 included:

| | | |
|---|---|---|
| April 2-8 | Wed.-Tues. | Liverpool convention |
| May 19-22 | Mon.-Thurs. | Swansea convention. |
| May 23 | Fri. | Cheltenham Bible Society. |
| May 25 | Sun. | Metropolitan Tabernacle, London. |
| May 26-29 | Mon.-Thurs. | Leicester convention. |
| June 13 | Fri. | London. Annual Meeting of Heart of Africa Mission. |
| June 15-19 | Sun.-Thurs. | Brighton convention |
| June 20 | Fri. | London. Bayswater convention. |
| June 23-27 | Mon.-Fri. | Ireland. Port Stewart convention. |
| August | | Holiday |
| Sept. 14-19 | Sun.-Fri. | Aberdeen Conference for the Quickening of Spiritual Life |
| Sept. 27-30 | Mon.-Thurs. | Manchester and Birmingham Keswick conventions |
| Oct. 6-10 | Mon.-Fri. | Birkenhead convention |
| Oct. 20-23 | Mon.-Thurs. | Baptist Union of Scotland Jubilee |

In 1924, he was in London in January, Oxford in February, Belfast in March, then in the United States and Canada from 19 May to 4 October. All that was in addition to one or two pulpit exchanges in a typical month. There was a very practical reason for Graham Scroggie accepting so many invitations to minister away from Charlotte Chapel, and he told the Chapel frankly what it was: 'it lessens the strain necessary when continuous preparation for pulpit ministry is involved.' He could (and did) give the same address on

numerous occasions in different places, which saved having to prepare new material every week for the Chapel.

Before the days of tape-recording, it was possible, indeed expected, for well-known speakers to deliver the same address many times in different locations. Scroggie made a careful entry, in the top right-hand corner of his notes, of where and when he had preached a sermon, and the list is often a long one. In 1917, he gave a series of talks around the country on The Book of Joshua entitled, *The Land and Life of Rest*. That was the subject for his Bible Readings at the Keswick Convention in 1950. A study of his 1917 notes, compared with the book in 1950, shows that he had hardly altered his material; the fruit of his early studies nourished generation after generation.

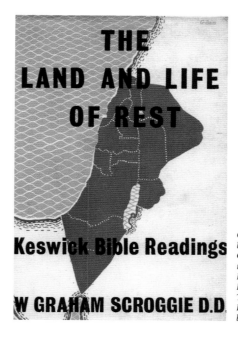

*On 12 occasions, between 1914 and 1954, Graham Scroggie gave the Bible Readings at the Keswick convention. His 1950 talks, entitled The Land and Life of Rest, were published in book form.*

### North America

As mentioned in Chapter 26, Graham Scroggie visited the United States of America in 1920, from early June to the beginning of October. He travelled even more extensively in North America in 1924 (above), covering twenty thousand miles. He returned in 1928, sailing on 27 June, preaching in Philadelphia, New York, Chicago and Toronto, and returning to the Chapel on 23 September. On these overseas travels, Graham Scroggie met many gifted preachers, whom (like Paul Radar in 1920) he persuaded to visit the Chapel.

## Impact of conference ministry

Graham Scroggie never gave an address or Bible exposition at any convention or conference that he had not first given to his own people – a feature of his ministry that they greatly appreciated. His Thursday Bible School in 1925-6, on the Apostles' Creed, was the basis of his talks at the Keswick Convention in 1929. His theme was that, given the conflicts in the 1920s over theological modernism (with fundamentalists calling for evangelicals to leave their denominations), it was preferable for everyone to accept the Apostles' Creed than for small groups to construct their own basis and then to split from Christians who had a different one. When a critic protested that Scroggie was undermining the interdenominational nature of Keswick, he replied that the Apostles' Creed 'was no more the peculiar property of the Anglican Church than the doctrine of the Second Advent was the possession of the Plymouth Brethren.'

Ian Randall has admirably assessed the impact of Graham Scroggie's conference ministry at this time, but what was the impact of the Keswick movement on Charlotte Chapel during his ministry? Scroggie printed the full text of convention addresses in the Chapel *Record*, together with articles on 'The Aim and Appeal of Keswick'. He encouraged members to attend the annual week in the Lake District, and he held open meetings in the Chapel, after it, for people to give testimony to the blessings they had received at it. He wanted his people in Edinburgh to understand what lay on his heart as he took the platform in Keswick, where he gave the morning Bible Readings 12 times.

## Keswick's new emphasis

In 1922, Graham Scroggie deliberately and emphatically steered the Keswick Convention away from the dangerous precipice (as he regarded it) of an emotional revivalism, which bypassed the intelligence. Furthermore, in the 1921 and 1923 Bible Readings, he deeply influenced Keswick's understanding of consecration and the reception of the Holy Spirit. He particularly opposed 'speaking in tongues' as a sign of Spirit-baptism. He moved Keswick from an emphasis on the Spirit to an emphasis on the Lordship of Christ. His message could be summed up in the exhortation: 'You have accepted Christ as your Saviour; now make him also your Lord.'

In another deliberate move in the 1920s, Graham Scroggie and other Keswick leaders prefixed the word 'evangelical' by the word 'conservative', to distinguish Keswick (by far the largest pan-denominational event in evangelicalism) from the 'liberal evangelicals' of the inter-war period; they dropped it when the latter disappeared from the scene, as a party, in the 1960s, and 'evangelical' again meant all evangelicals. Liberal evangelicals reappeared in the late 1980s, as described in Chapter 51, although they preferred, then, to call themselves 'open evangelicals'.

Graham Scroggie's stature at Keswick was acknowledged when the BBC first broadcast from the convention, in 1933; the Council invited him to give the address.

## Keswick in Edinburgh

When Graham Scroggie came to Edinburgh in 1916, he immediately proposed holding a local convention, along Keswick lines, during the last week of July 1917. Facing down local scepticism, he arranged for a tent, seating over one thousand, to be pitched in the grounds of St Luke's Church of Scotland in Comely Bank. It was nearly full for the opening Monday night, after which, following the Keswick pattern, there was a 7 a.m. prayer meeting, then morning, afternoon and evening gatherings from Tuesday to Saturday.

The nine speakers included Wilkinson Riddle from London (who had suggested Scroggie's name to the Chapel), and Scroggie himself took a major part. He led the consecration meeting on Friday evening, 'when many yielded themselves wholly to God, marking the entry into a new experience of our Lord's ability to cleanse and deliver, and to give victory over self, sin and the world.' The convention closed on the Saturday, with a morning praise meeting and a missionary gathering for five hours in the afternoon. Unlike the parent convention, the tent was also utilized for two evangelistic meetings on the Sunday, when there were definite conversions.

This pattern was followed, at the same location, until 1925, and then the Edinburgh Evangelistic Union took over the arrangements (although Scroggie was still deeply involved) and moved the tent to Meggetland in Colinton Road, for a week in June. The gathering was popularly known as the Keswick Week, although the official title was the Edinburgh Convention. These meetings continued after Graham Scroggie left Edinburgh, latterly in a church building; they still continue, now called the Annual Bible Convention (Chapter 52). There was no need to have them from 1956 to 1968, because the Monday-Thursday evening meetings from the large tent in Keswick were relayed to the Chapel by telephone link, but they resumed after the landline was discontinued (Chapter 39).

## Missionary appeals

Graham Scroggie's conference ministry included a strong appeal for overseas missionary service. On the closing day of the 1922 Keswick Convention, he summed up the week in this way:

*We have seen the glory of God; we have felt the power of God; we have heard the voice of God, and Divine revelation is intended to lead to holy experience that shall find its last expression in sacrificial service, This Convention cannot and will not leave any one of us where it found us. We are facing the most tremendous issues of our life. What are you going to do?*

---

1 *Record*, 1922, p. 67.

He then invited fathers and mothers, who were willing for their sons and daughters to go into the foreign mission field, if God should 'call' them, to stand, first inviting his own wife to stand with him. Over two hundred men and women followed their example. In very solemn accents, Scroggie then appealed to the young people present to listen to the cry from far-off lands; more than 350 young men and women rose in their places. In response to a further appeal, the whole audience rose as a sign that they were willing to give to the utmost limit of their power for foreign missions. Graham Scroggie then closed the meeting by asking the congregation to change the verb in the last line of a familiar hymn, from 'Demands' to 'Shall have'; they sang, with intense feeling:

*Were the whole realm of nature mine,*
*That were an offering far too small,*
*Love so amazing, so divine,*
*Shall have my life, my soul, my all.*

---

2 *Record*, 1922, p. 67.

## Edinburgh Baptist Association

In April 1929, Graham Scroggie, who had been active in the Edinburgh Baptist Association throughout his time in Edinburgh, consented to be its president, for the ensuing year. It was no light commitment, because the monthly meeting was held on Tuesday evening, his only day off in the week. Support for the Association had never been strong – less than 150 attended normal meetings, out of 3,300 Baptists in Edinburgh – but Scroggie set about increasing its usefulness. He made a point of exchanging pulpits, during his year in office, with every one of the other 11 churches in the Association. He concluded his year with the first-ever united communion service, which packed both the Chapel and its lower hall, with twelve hundred present on 12 March 1930. It was the last time that a separate speaker had to be appointed for the overflow meeting, because the acousticon, mentioned in Chapter 23, was installed shortly afterward.

## Meticulous filing

Graham Scroggie hoarded every piece of paper that came his way. He had a series of notebooks, which he kept in the pockets of his waistcoat. He filed everything – counterfoils of tickets, a note of restaurants where he had eaten, the cost of the meal and even the tip given to the waiter. He chronicled the details of every photograph that he took, the exact time, the aperture and the shutter speed. There are two examples in the Chapel archives. In his Scripture Union notes (below) for November 1928, he asked readers to say whether they were appreciated. Letters poured in from all over the English-speaking world; he carefully sorted and bundled them and kept them. When his house was cleared, following the death of his second wife in 1989, they were sold in bulk to philatelists for the value of the foreign stamps; the one who bought the Australian letters passed dozens of unwanted envelopes, still with the letters inside, to the Chapel. The other example (photograph below) is even more surprising. The writer's parents were friendly with Graham Scroggie, so it is not surprising that they notified him about the arrival, but it is astounding that he bothered to file it away in one of his notebooks.

*Ian Leslie Shaw*

*Mrs Frank Balfour*

cordially thanks you

for your kind enquiries and congratulations.

18 Denham Green Terrace,
Edinburgh.                            16th June, 1932.

*Graham Scroggie filed away every scrap of paper that came his way, but, even so, the writer was astounded when a mutual friend, going through Scroggie's papers after his death, found this card and passed it on.*

## Writing ministry

### Scripture Union notes

Graham Scroggie wrote the daily notes for the Scripture Union over a number of years, starting in 1923; this meant composing about 350 words a day, explaining and applying the Bible passage for that day. He had to give it up while he recuperated from appendicitis in the winter of 1924-5, but he took it up again in July 1927. There were soon a quarter of a million readers worldwide. He encouraged the Scripture Union method more than any other reading scheme, because it covered the whole Bible in the course of five years, and did not just select portions here and there. Scroggie remarked that after five years: 'you will have a Devotional Commentary on all the Scriptures', and, for the price of one shilling and sixpence, 'that was a bargain not to be missed'.

### *Sunday School Times*

An even wider opportunity came during Scroggie's summer tour of America in 1924; he was asked to write the weekly lesson for the *Sunday School Times*, an international publication for Sunday School teachers, students of the Bible and Christian workers generally. He reproduced the first one in the Chapel *Record*, but the *Times* then exercised its copyright exclusive; anyone who wanted the material from then on had to send two dollars to Philadelphia for a year's subscription.

### Four Years' Bible Correspondence Course

In addition to all his other work, Graham Scroggie conducted a monthly Bible correspondence course, involving four years of systematic Bible study; he had started it in 1904, and during his years in Edinburgh, over three thousand enrolled. He continued it after he left the Chapel, and by 1940 (when his wife, who did the clerical work, died) more than five thousand people, in all parts of the world, had participated.

### *A Treasury of W. Graham Scroggie*

An excellent introduction to Graham Scroggie's writings is contained in a 220-page book (Ralph G. Turnbull, *A Treasury of W. Graham Scroggie* [Baker Book House, Grand Rapids, 1974, Pickering and Inglis, London, 1975]) compiled by one of the Chapel's young men who, converted in the Chapman-Alexander mission in 1914, attended Scroggie's Christian Service Class and went into the Baptist ministry. The material is taken from the Chapel *Record*, arranged under sections such as Sermons, Thoughts, Bible Notes, Monthly Meditations and Lecture Notes; there is also an introduction to Scroggie's life. As there is no published biography of Graham Scroggie, and unlikely ever to be one now, books like this are a valuable resource for looking at his ministry.

### The *Record*

Graham Scroggie was not a hands-on editor of the *Record* in the way that Joseph Kemp had been, but the assistant editor (a Chapel elder, who was responsible for production) included much of Scroggie's material. Rises in the cost of printing led to a serious proposal in 1920 to discontinue it. This provoked such a reaction that the church treasurer gave in and continued the annual subsidy, although he reduced the size and kept trying to increase the circulation. This rose gradually from eleven hundred copies a month in 1925 to fourteen hundred in 1929. Casual sales varied, and if there were 60 copies left unsold at the end of the month, it made the magazine financially precarious. The number posted all over the world rose steadily, from four hundred in 1927 to six hundred in 1930. The story of the *Record* will be continued when the next minister, Sidlow Baxter, remodelled it in 1935 (Chapter 33).

### Doctor of Divinity

Graham Scroggie's growing influence led to an honorary degree of Doctor of Divinity, conferred by the University of

Edinburgh on 1 July 1927. He had earlier received an honorary DD from an American university, but he never used it and few members of the Chapel knew about it. It was different when Edinburgh University honoured him – the church were delighted. At a meeting in the Chapel on Thursday 23 June, they presented him with his doctorate robes, after which the choir rendered the anthem 'The Lord bless thee and keep thee' and later the 'Te Deum Laudamus'.

In responding, Graham Scroggie's sense of humour, deliberately repressed while he was preaching, came bubbling out in a series of stories about robes, the focus of the evening. They may not seem hilarious to present readers but they went down well that evening, such as: 'There were two ministers at the front [during the war], one an Episcopal and the other a Baptist. The Episcopal, asking the Baptist if he would speak first, said: "Will you have a surplice?" "No," replied the other, "I am a Baptist minister, and we generally have a deficit."'

*Students from New College, who had attended Graham Scroggie's early Thursday Bible Schools, and who by 1927 were influential figures in the Church of Scotland, proposed his name to the University of Edinburgh for an honorary degree of Doctor of Divinity.*

The graduation ceremony took place in the McEwan Hall; the Dean of the Faculty of Divinity introduced Scroggie with the citation:

*The Reverend Graham Scroggie, minister of Charlotte Baptist Chapel, Edinburgh. His first charges were in London, Halifax, and Sunderland, and since his call to Edinburgh in 1916 he*

*has exercised unusual influence in the City and neighbourhood as a preacher and missioner. He is also known as a prominent representative of the Keswick Movement, which has done much to deepen the life and refine the ideals of Evangelicalism. The work to which Mr. Scroggie has specially devoted himself, he has stated, is the study and teaching of the English Bible in its twofold character of a Divine Revelation and a great Literature. In the capacity of teacher he has conducted Correspondence Classes for 3000 pupils through a four-years Course of Systematic Bible Study. The fruits of his devotional study of the Scriptures have been given forth in a long series of expository volumes and articles, which are distinguished by lucidity and grace of expression, as well as, by spiritual fervour.*

---

4 *Record*, 1927, pp.120-1.

It was a great occasion and the church, together with Dr Scroggie's many friends in all denominations, rejoiced with him in the well-deserved honour.

## Some distinctive emphases

### The Lordship of Christ
Asked what was the distinctive message of Keswick, Graham Scroggie replied that it could be summarized in four words: 'The Lordship of Christ'. That phrase encapsulates also his distinctive message in the Chapel pulpit. He defined spirituality as obedience to the Lordship of Christ in everyday life:

*At the heart of the spiritual life, for Scroggie, was a conscious decision to make Christ Lord of one's life. Scroggie argued that although Keswick spoke of the 'Spirit-filled' life, this idea was derived from that of Christ's Lordship, which in his view was Keswick's distinctive message.*

---

5 **Timothy Larsen (ed.),** *Biographical Dictionary of Evangelicals* **(Inter-Varsity Press, Leicester, England, 2003), p. 594.**

### Revival
Graham Scroggie regularly took part in revival conferences. The month of January 1922 was typical – 1922 is selected because that was the year in which he intervened to dampen down excessive revivalist fervour at Keswick, as mentioned above. On Saturday 14 January, he spoke at a conference on

revival in North Berwick; on Sundays 8 and 15 January, he led revival rallies in the Assembly Hall in Edinburgh, at which 60 young men and women were converted amid much emotion. His editorials in the *Record* set out his rationale for revival.

*Scroggie considered that errors over the baptism of the Spirit were especially due to the desire to associate the blessing of the Spirit with the gift of tongues. The careful Scot also believed that in many Pentecostal meetings there was a 'surrender of common sense'…. Despite his caution, Scroggie did not deny the possibility of contemporary speaking in tongues.*

6 Larsen (ed), *Biographical Dictionary*, pp.593-4.

### The Second Coming of Christ

While Graham Scroggie faithfully and carefully expounded the three differing views on the Lord's return, he left his hearers in no doubt that his own ardent belief was in Christ's pre-millennial return for the saints – 'this energising hope', as he described it. In the first six months of 1918, when the Great War made many think of eternity, 24 of the 96 pages of the *Record* were on aspects of the Second Coming. In the autumn of that year, Scroggie's preaching supplemented his printed teaching; he lectured at the Thursday Bible School on 'The Bible and Christ's Return', and he gave a series on Sunday evening on 'The Last Things' – 'if you wish a seat you must come early'. Scroggie also published seven addresses under the title 'Studies Short and Simple on the Lord's Return'.

Graham Scroggie was both reflecting, and at the same time promoting, the advent teaching that had become intertwined with the Keswick message. 'Every day', remarked an incredulous Methodist, 'they are waiting for the saints to be caught up – the captain from his ship, the engine-driver from his locomotive, the mother from her family, etc'. Belief in the rapture of the church (at the Second Coming) was promoted by the hugely popular Scofield Bible, published in 1909, with footnotes expounding dispensationalism; presentation of a well-bound copy of it, to students and missionaries and others leaving Edinburgh, or as a thank-you for long service in one of the Chapel auxiliaries was, as mentioned in Chapter 18, common from 1913 to 1950.

The pre-millennial view of the Second Coming received huge publicity when the former suffragette, Christabel Pankhurst,

embraced it; she published *The Lord Cometh* in 1923, and championed its teaching around the country. Dispensationalists taught that no events were to intervene before the sudden and unexpected return of Christ to earth, first to collect true believers and then to set right all the wrongs of earth in a display of kingly power.

Sermons were illustrated with references to the housewife who said, as she pulled the curtains every evening: 'Perhaps tonight' and, when she opened them again in the morning: 'Perhaps today'. Another was about the visitor to a well-kept country estate, who remarked to the gardener that his master must be very proud of his work. The gardener replied that the owner was an absentee landlord, who had not visited in the last 20 years. Noting the immaculate condition of the garden, the visitor commented that it was maintained as if the owner might return tomorrow. 'Perhaps today' was the gardener's reply.

Brought up in this ethos, the writer assumed, until the death of his father in 1974, that his understanding of the Second Coming was a product of his maturer years. However, on reading his father's diary posthumously, he learned just how powerfully such teaching could impact on children brought up in evangelical Christian homes. An entry under Sunday 19 May 1940, a month short of the writer's eighth birthday, reads: 'Ian asked me today, "if a Christian was being buried, when Jesus came, and caught him up, would the men burying him notice suddenly there was no one in the coffin?" A very proper question…'. He did not record his answer to it, and the writer's embarrassment, in reading the diary now, is the assumption that none of the gravediggers would be going as well.

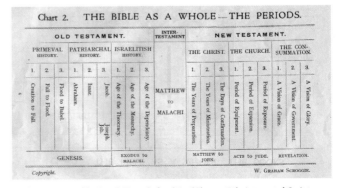

*Graham Scroggie, like Joseph Kemp before him (Chapter 21), interpreted Scripture within a framework known as 'Dispensationalism', that God had dealt differently with people during different eras of biblical history. These were his guidelines for his Christian Service Class.*

James Monihan, the Chapel's organist and choir master from 1958 to 1965, and who still helps out at weddings and funerals, loves to tell how, as a boy, he accepted the Lord Jesus as his Saviour after hearing his parents discussing a lecture by Graham Scroggie on 'The Second Coming of our Lord', given at the Thursday Bible School, and realising that he was not ready. Mabel McLean, a Chapel missionary in Nepal from 1952 to 1981 and then the matron of the Chapel's Beulah Home for five years, 'was not particularly interested in spiritual things until one night in bed I woke up and because everything was so quiet I thought the Lord had come, the family had gone to Heaven, and I was left behind. … It was the crossroads for me but there was a sense of peace when I did take the important step'. Many others, brought up in evangelical homes in the inter-war period, had similar conversion experiences.

## 'Telegrams – "Theophany"'

Older readers will remember when businesses, and some private houses, had a telegraphic address as well as a telephone number. Telegrams were charged by the number of words used, so brevity was essential; enterprising people registered a single (unique) word with the Post Office. For example, any telegram, sent from anywhere in the world to Balfroned (the key letters of Balfour & Manson, followed by 'Ed' for Edinburgh) would be delivered to 58 Frederick Street here. Telegraphic addresses were printed on stationery, along with telephone numbers.

Graham Scroggie's wry sense of humour shines through the Chapel's choice, because after 7198 Central (many telephone numbers until after the Second World War had an exchange name and four digits), were the words 'Telegrams – "Theophany"'. That is the word for the appearance of God to the patriarchs in the Old Testament in the form of an angel or in human form, or, in New Testament theology, the incarnation and Second Coming of Christ. One wonders how many opportunities Graham Scroggie had to speak about his sure and certain hope of the return of Christ, to those who enquired why he had chosen that particular telegraphic shorthand.

*Graham Scroggie's wry sense of humour shines through his choice of telegraphic address for the Chapel – 'Theophany' means the appearance of God in human form.*

## Roman Catholicism and Anglo-Catholicism

Graham Scroggie had wide Christian sympathies, as he stressed in his response to the invitation to come to Edinburgh: 'This is a day of catholic sympathies and widespread interfellowship among Christians of all the Protestant Churches, and it has been my privilege for many years to have a not inconsiderable share in this'. However, his catholic sympathies were confined to fellow Protestants. He gave an address, which occupied six pages of the *Record* and which was later printed in pamphlet form and reprinted in the *Expository Times*, entitled: 'Why are we Protestants?' It detailed the errors of Roman Catholicism, as Scroggie saw them in the 1920s, and was particularly critical of Anglo-Catholicism. Apart from that, the Chapel *Record*, which he edited, commented adversely on the activities and doctrines of the Roman Catholic church only three times, in contrast to the sustained attack which his successor, Sidlow Baxter, maintained through the pages of the *Record* (Chapter 33).

Additional information on the following topics, mentioned in this chapter, is available on the CD.

# Chapter 30
# Graham Scroggie's resignations (1925, 1933)

## Head or feet

### Social pastoral visitation

Graham Scroggie accepted the invitation to Charlotte Chapel on two conditions, which the church agreed. First, as mentioned in the last chapter, the office-bearers promised to give him the same facilities as he enjoyed at Bethesda, to speak at conventions. The other was that he would not be expected to do social pastoral visitation. When at Sunderland, he had told the office-bearers that they could have 'either my head or my feet, but you can't have both'. He did not claim to be either an evangelist or a pastor but a Bible teacher. He used to say that if he was to look after the souls of others, he needed time to look after his own soul.

There was another and very practical reason for allocating his time in this way. He was not strong physically, and one member, who lived at the top of an Edinburgh tenement, recalled how the pastor was exhausted by the time he got to the flat for an urgent pastoral visit. He confined pastoral work to the sick and the sorrowing, following the example of the Chapel's founder and first pastor, Christopher Anderson, who resolutely declined to undertake 'so-called pastoral visitation'. The church accepted that. It was not Graham Scroggie's attitude to pastoral calls that gave rise to the unhappiness described in the first part of this chapter, but the amount of time he was away from Edinburgh, and so not available to make any pastoral calls at all.

### Consequences of conference ministry

In the autumn of 1925, some of the members, including some of the office-bearers, tried to re-visit the issue of the convention facilities promised to Graham Scroggie when he came. There were four very human responses in Charlotte Chapel to Graham Scroggie's frequent absences at conferences. First, there was a noticeable drop in attendance at the Sunday services when he was away. In 1920, the church secretary pleaded with the members to be loyal to the church, 'no matter who may be the preacher, when our Pastor is absent. Remember that the task of filling our pulpit is not an easy one.'

Secondly, the pastor personally interviewed all applicants for baptism and membership, so huge backlogs built up during his absence. His four months in the United States, from June

to the beginning of October in 1920, resulted in a drop of 33 in membership over that year – dozens of new applicants were not able to get the necessary interview. When Graham Scroggie baptized 23 new Christians on 27 June 1921, their names could not be brought to the church, for membership, until after his return from his summer vacation. The Chapel today delegates this function to the elders, but in the 1920s there was a clear distinction between what a minister should do and what lay people could do. The elders suggested appointing an assistant minister, which Scroggie refused to consider, but the elders did not offer to do 'ministerial' work, even when the minister was away for months.

### MINISTERIAL
### SEMI-JUBILEE
1897——1922

"HITHERTO"  ::  "HENCEFORTH"

### Rev. W. GRAHAM SCROGGIE
EDINBURGH

*Graham Scroggie at the age of 45, photographed for his semi-jubilee in the ministry, in 1922. He carried a very heavy workload, but resolutely declined all offers of an assistant minister.*

Thirdly, the spiritual health of the Chapel at that time depended largely on the presence of the pastor. When Graham Scroggie was recuperating from appendicitis in the winter of 1924-5, the elders commented on the decreased attendance and diminished interest at prayer meetings, 'the lack of the old spirit of abounding life, the lack of emphasis on prayer, the difficult situation caused by the illness and absence of the Pastor.'

Fourthly, those Chapel members who had been rightly apprehensive at Joseph Kemp's visits to the vacant Calvary

Baptist Church in New York, between 1913 and 1915, were again alarmed at reports that Graham Scroggie had been invited to remain in America during his 1920 visit. On his return, he said publicly that he had seriously considered an invitation to Minneapolis, but he then said: 'I shall write back and tell him I won't be coming to America, as I can't leave home'. This lifted a load from the minds of office-bearers and members alike, as they had heard of the 'call' through religious periodicals. Graham Scroggie qualified that assurance a short while later, by writing in the *Record* that he would not consider moving for at least 15 months. It was all rather unsettling, and lengthy absences at other churches' conferences were part of the problem.

## Unhappiness

To complete Graham Scroggie's recuperation from the appendicitis operation, mentioned above, his medical advisers asked the deacons to give him an extended vacation from preaching and pastoral duties from 1 June 1925 to the middle of September. He spent June in France, came back to Edinburgh for the communion service on Sunday 5 July and the valedictory of Andrew MacBeath on Thursday 9 July, and then gave the Bible Readings at the Keswick Convention. After that, he retired to the north of Scotland for a complete rest, returning to the Chapel for 20 September. His speaking for a full week at Keswick, while not taking more than a couple of services in the Chapel, led to unrest, and he came back to Edinburgh in September 1925 to a very unhappy church. There is no breach of confidence in writing about it here, because it was reported in the press at the time (both *The Scotsman* and the *Edinburgh Evening News*) and Graham Scroggie himself published a full explanation in the *Record*.

The first weekend in October 1925 followed the familiar pattern for anniversary services, including a social gathering for tea in the lower hall before the public meeting on the Monday evening. Graham Scroggie was upset, although he did not say anything at the time, by the church secretary's opening remarks at the main meeting. Scroggie thought that they implied a connection between his absence at conventions elsewhere and a lack of pastoral care for the Chapel congregation. At the regular monthly meeting of deacons two days later, Scroggie proposed: 'that this Court should meet for the special purpose of considering the future of the Ministry of Charlotte Chapel.' At it, a week later, he read a statement about his concerns, following which several

deacons expressed their feelings. Graham Scroggie responded, and the meeting was adjourned for a fortnight, for reflection.

At the adjourned meeting, the deacons carefully reviewed the terms of the 'call' in 1916 and Graham Scroggie's response to it at the time. Had the position changed? They assured their pastor of their continued loyalty and appreciation of his ministry, but also said that more consideration must be given to the needs of the 'sick and sorrowing members, whose numbers had increased over the intervening years' – 'the problem remains with us and for the surmounting of which we as a Court are responsible to the Church.' They did not ask him to do more pastoral visitation while he was in Edinburgh, but asked him to be in Edinburgh for more of the year, to be available to the sick and sorrowing.

## Resignation

Graham Scroggie's response was to resign. The deacons would not accept his resignation and asked to meet with him, which led to a useful discussion. Scroggie's position was that the deaconess, Miss Boyle, did all necessary visitation and did it so efficiently that cutting back on his conference engagements would not make any difference – he would still not do social visitation. That was not, however, the point of the deacons' concern; they wanted him to be more available to give pastoral support to those whom he did ordinarily meet, when he was here. Scroggie responded that he was balancing his time as had been agreed when he accepted the 'call'; the church should either affirm this or tell him to go. He insisted that his offer to resign be put to the members, so a congregational meeting was called for Thursday 3 December.

At it, the correspondence was read and a vote taken by secret ballot. While individual voting was private, the result was made public in the *Edinburgh Evening News*:

*Out of a membership of approximately 850, about 400 were present at the meeting, and they voted as follows: Declining to accept the resignation, 246; prepared to accept, 144, while 14 who were present refrained from voting. The Church, we understand, now awaits with interest and anxiety Mr Scroggie's final decision, as it is felt that the comparatively small majority may not be sufficient to alter his original intention.*

---

1 *Edinburgh Evening News*, 5 January 1926.

225

Four members (in favour of resignation) called for a plebiscite, saying that the members not present (more than half) should be given an opportunity of voting on the issue. The deacons steered a middle course on a plebiscite, telling Graham Scroggie (who was not present) the result of the vote and asking whether he would withdraw his resignation. If he would not (that is, if he resigned), there would be no need for a plebiscite; if he remained, and if there were still calls for one, they would deal with the request then.

Discussion and correspondence went on for more than two months, in the hope that Scroggie would withdraw his resignation and that the four would withdraw their request for a plebiscite. The sticking point was how to define a pastoral visit. The passing of many weeks, without a resolution, led to much anxiety throughout the congregation. The YPM committee debated whether to send a letter to the pastor, expressing the confidence and loyalty of the committee, but decided they should not get involved. Others were less restrained; on 16 February, six very disgruntled members wrote to the deacons, saying that the uncertainty was intolerable and that unless Graham Scroggie made his position clear immediately, he ought to go. This jolted the deacons into action. They worked hard at some long-term understanding, in consequence of which Graham Scroggie withdrew his resignation on 24 February 1926 and no more was heard of the plebiscite. Scroggie made a statement at both services in the Chapel on Sunday 28 February, which included:

*It is, of course, a matter of common knowledge that four months ago I tendered my resignation from the Pastorate of this Church; and that a month later, at a meeting specially convened, a majority of the Church declined to accept it. Since then I have been in doubt as to what I should do in view of certain aspects of the situation which perplexed me, but ten days ago, action was taken by the Office-Bearers of the Church, which enables me to say, in reply to the Church's request, that I now withdraw my resignation.*

2 *Record*, 1926, p. 41.

The first practical step, to solve the visitation question, came when the deacons recommended the appointment of three additional elders and one additional deacon; Graham Scroggie was to continue his conference ministry, both in this country and abroad. For a while, the monthly *Record* tactfully gave less prominence than previously to his outside engagements, but by 1928 it was back to giving full details of his conference ministry – Cambridge in January, Belfast in February and March, London and Paisley in May, Canada and the United States for all of July, August and September, London in November and Glasgow in December, all in 1928.

## Graham Scroggie's humour

After the narrative of those four grim months, this may be the place to expand on one lighter aspect of Graham Scroggie's personality, which has been briefly mentioned several times, his rich store of pawky humour. Only occasionally did it flash out in his preaching and even then it was usually in asides, so it rarely appears in printed versions of his addresses and sermons. One of his friends, Alexander Frazer of Aberdeen (later of Tain), was celebrated for his humour and used it freely while preaching, usually with great spiritual effect. On one occasion when the two were together, and having an uproarious time, Fraser said to Scroggie: 'Why don't you take your humour into the pulpit?' Scroggie answered: 'I wouldn't come down to it'. Fraser remarked on this publicly at Scroggie's tenth anniversary in the Chapel, saying: 'he would not be satisfied until our Pastor brought some humour into the pulpit. He was sure his reputation would not suffer; his own had not'. He then proceeded to tell a hilarious story, but Graham Scroggie's humour was always under strict control when preaching.

However, he used it freely on other occasions, such as while recuperating from his appendicitis operation:

*It is now three weeks (as I write) since, with little ceremony (not being given time even to make my will!) I was hurried away to the 'theatre' – the only time I have been in a theatre for twenty-five years! Out of that I came minus my appendix. It's a good thing it was not my preface that they removed.*

3 *Record*, 1924, p. 89.

One of his best-known quips came on his last appearance on the platform at the Keswick Convention in 1954. He was very frail and special arrangements had been made so that he could sit at the rostrum to give his address. He introduced himself by saying: 'I am here in consequence of prayers and pillows, penicillin and pills. I thank you for your prayers, my wife for the pillows, and my doctor for the penicillin and the pills. It is a grand privilege to be here once more.'

The writer met Graham Scroggie only once, socially, in addition to being in the congregation when he spoke at public meetings. Just after the Second World War, when petrol was still scarce and motorbikes were relatively expensive, a group of us had gathered for an open-air meeting at the entrance to Inverleith Park. Graham Scroggie passed by, during one of his visits to Edinburgh. He readily engaged the young men in conversation, spanning the generation gap without difficulty. Turning to those who were on pedal cycles and the few who had come on motorbikes, he asked: 'what is the difference between these [indicating the bicycles] and these [pointing to the motor bikes]'? Noting with amusement the puzzled silence, he said: 'these [indicating the powered machines] are spirit filled'. Of such small incidents are lasting impressions made.

## Graham Scroggie's health

### Administration

When Sister Lilian resigned in November 1920, Graham Scroggie took the opportunity of saying to the elders: 'He had found it quite impossible in view of the many committees etc calling for his presence and interest to give his best attention and the time necessary to the work of pulpit preparation.' The elders accepted that: 'If Charlotte Chapel is to come to the front as a force in this City, as regards its pulpit ministry … our pastor will have to be relieved of much of the committee work and business meetings', and they arranged accordingly.

### Doctor's orders

Graham Scroggie's health had never been robust. He suffered repeated attacks of bronchitis and was troubled by catarrhal inflammation of his lungs. As mentioned earlier, he took, on medical advice, an extended vacation from preaching and pastoral duties from 1 June 1925 to the middle of September. As the winter of 1930-31 approached, one of the elders, who was Edinburgh's Medical Officer for Health, called an urgent meeting of the deacons and expressed concern that any repetition of last year's bronchial attacks could be serious; he suggested, and the deacons agreed, that Graham Scroggie should take a complete rest in a better climate for the first

three months of 1931. Asked how he wished this communicated to the church, Scroggie wrote a personal statement for the *Record*:

*the Office-Bearers unanimously recommended, and the Church as unanimously and heartily agreed that I be given three months leave of absence, from January to March, in the hope that in a sunnier clime this trouble may disappear, or, at any rate, so far improve as to enable me to 'carry on' in the work which is so dear to my heart.*

4 *Record*, 1931, p. 4.

He spent the three months in Madeira, but on his return he developed another attack of bronchitis.

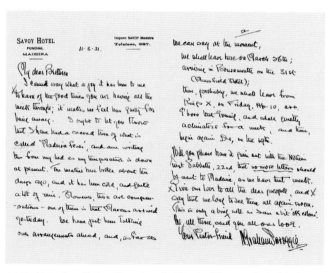

*A typical letter from Graham Scroggie to the Chapel, while on medical advice he spent the first three months of 1931 in Madeira, away from the rigours of an Edinburgh winter.*

## Six months in South Africa

In December 1931, the office-bearers proposed that Graham Scroggie should be given six months leave of absence, with salary, from the spring to the autumn of 1932. This was not sick leave, they emphasized, but what is now called sabbatical leave, in recognition of 15 years of ministry in the Chapel. (Such leave is now usual every seven years.) Scroggie expressed both his surprise and his pleasure, and he sailed for Cape Town on 4 March; he was back for the first Sunday in September.

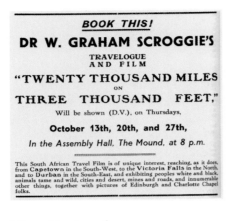

*Graham Scroggie visited 32 places during his tour of South Africa in 1932; he recorded them on cine film, which he showed over three consecutive Thursday evenings on his return.*

## New Zealand

### Invitation from Auckland

On 8 May 1933, Graham Scroggie received an invitation from Joseph Kemp's church in Auckland, New Zealand, to come as pulpit supply from October 1933 to the following March. Kemp was seriously ill. Graham Scroggie laid the letter before the deacons, without expressing his own views. They debated it carefully and courteously at two special meetings. Was it wise for an outstanding preacher to go to any church while the pastor was absent from his pulpit through illness? What about pastoral care for the older members in Edinburgh, and guidance for the younger members, over a period of eight months (allowing for travel)? On the other hand, it was Scroggie who had recommended Kemp to the Tabernacle in Auckland, and so he had a pastoral concern for them.

The deacons arranged to meet Graham Scroggie on Tuesday 6 June, to talk through the whole matter. However, and perhaps significantly, Scroggie was taken suddenly ill just before the services on Sunday 4 June, necessitating (as so often before) a replacement preacher at very short notice. He was unable to take part in the opening social for the Chapel's daughter church at Stenhouse on the following day, Monday 5 June, through serious illness. He could not meet the deacons on the Tuesday. Bearing in mind that he had had to leave Edinburgh for the winter of 1931, would it not be sensible to send him to the southern hemisphere for the winter of 1933? On the other hand, October to April was the busiest and most fruitful time in the Chapel calendar, and, as someone put it: 'the Spiritual tide in the Church was on the flow again, and that this could best be taken advantage of, if the Pastor were here.' It was a real dilemma.

The deacons, very commendably, considered only whether they should regard this invitation to be in the will of God. Selflessly, they proposed to the congregation: 'that Dr. Scroggie accept the Call to the Auckland Tabernacle (involving an absence of approximately eight months) his salary to continue during the period, subject to Dr Scroggie providing pulpit supply and a satisfactory arrangement as to pastoral work.'

### Response to the invitation

A special meeting of members on Monday 19 June unanimously accepted the first part of the deacons' recommendation, to give the pastor leave of absence for eight months. However, an amendment was moved from the floor, that instead of paying his salary and making him responsible for finding guest preachers, the church should make its own pulpit and pastoral arrangements, and that Scroggie should not receive his salary while he was away. The amendment attracted 91 votes, but was defeated by 111 voting for the motion. Some of the deacons supported the amendment – not, apparently, feeling bound by the rule that members of a committee must support the committee's recommendation unless they have reserved the right, when the decision was made, to speak and vote against it at its next stage (no one had).

Graham Scroggie was deeply upset by the strength of support for the amendment, which he regarded as an attack on his integrity and a breach of the fundamental relationship between a pastor and his people. He felt that the only course open to him was to tender his resignation. The deacons made every effort to retrieve the situation, sending a deputation to meet Scroggie, and this persuaded him to take time to reconsider his decision. The deacons called another meeting of the congregation, hoping that the membership would urge their pastor to withdraw his resignation, and to continue with them on his return from New Zealand.

The congregational meeting was, however, a non-event, because Scroggie wrote an open letter to the members, printed in the *Record* a few days before the meeting, to say that although 'those who were responsible for the amendment at that Church meeting intend to withdraw from it, and to identify themselves with what then was the motion', he had 'come to the definite conclusion that in the interests of us both the time has come from me to lay down my task here'. The church secretary reported that he had had a long talk with Graham Scroggie, and that it was clear he would not change his mind. He was, however, persuaded to remain until the second week of October, and to conduct the anniversary services.

## The best years of my life

Graham Scroggie's resignation was received with deep regret, not only by the church but also by non-members who attended the Thursday Bible School. He gave three reasons for his decision:

*First, that I have been with you a long time, seventeen years; second, that my health has been very uncertain during the past three or four years; and third, that I think I hear the call to a wider ministry, a ministry to the Church of God in this and other lands.... I shall always look upon my time with you as having been the crown of my pastoral career and the memory of these years will be eternally fragrant.*

5 *Record*, 1933, p. 117.

He said twice during the farewell services, and repeated it again 20 years later, that his years in Charlotte Chapel were 'the best years of my life.'

**CLOSING SERVICES**
OF
**Dr SCROGGIE'S MINISTRY.**

**THE ANNIVERSARY AND THANKOFFERING.**
SUNDAY and MONDAY, October 1st and 2nd.
October 1st, 11 and 6.30—Preacher, Dr W. GRAHAM SCROGGIE.
October 2nd—The Pastor and Mrs Scroggie, and some of the Office-Bearers, will be in the Vestry from 1.30 p.m. until 7.45 p.m. to receive your offerings to the Memorial Fund. This will be the last time that Dr Scroggie will accept your gifts, and we sincerely trust that they will be specially liberal.
7—7.45—TEA will be served in the Lecture Hall.
7.45—PUBLIC MEETING in the Church.
Chairman—MR W. MACDUFF URQUHART, M.A., LL.B., S.S.C.
As this will be Dr Scroggie's last anniversary service in Charlotte Chapel, the speakers will be all members of the Church, instead of visitors as in other years. The Choir will again give us their valuable assistance.
The freewill offering taken at this meeting will be for the Memorial Fund.
**This will be the Church's Farewell to Dr and Mrs Scroggie.**
A full attendance is requested.

**MISSIONARY PARCELS EXHIBITION,**
THURSDAY, October 5th, at 7 p.m.
Public Meeting at 8 p.m.
Chairman—DR W. GRAHAM SCROGGIE.
It is expected that Miss Vonda Sturrock, Mr Alex. Clark, and others will speak. This will be Dr Scroggie's last service in Charlotte Chapel.

**THE FINAL SERVICES**
will be held in the ASSEMBLY HALL, The Mound,
On SABBATH, October 8, at 11 and 6.30.
Preacher—DR W. GRAHAM SCROGGIE.
Soloist—Mr JACQUES HOPKINS, L.R.A.M., M.R.S.T.
Doors open at 10.30 and 6. Souvenir Programmes will be provided.

MONDAY, October 9th, at 7.30 (Doors open at 7).
**PUBLIC FAREWELL SERVICE.**
Chairman—W. MACDUFF URQUHART, Esq., M.A., LL.B., S.S.C.
Speakers—Rev. DONALD DAVIDSON, B.D., B.Litt., Ph.D.
Rev. JAMES SCOTT, M.A., Ph.D.
Rev. GORDON EWING, M.A.
Rev. PETER FLEMING.
Dr C. H. MILNE.
Dr W. GRAHAM SCROGGIE.
Soloist—Mr JACQUES HOPKINS, L.R.A.M., M.R.S.T.
This service will conclude Dr W. Graham Scroggie's seventeen years of ministry in Edinburgh. On October 10th, or 11th, he and Mrs Scroggie will leave the City for London en route to Auckland, New Zealand. There will be reports of all these services in the November *Record*. Those who are not subscribers are advised to order copies early to avoid disappointment. *Record Secretary*—Mr Blair, Charlotte Chapel.

*The Chapel's domestic farewell to Graham Scroggie was held over the first weekend in October 1933, followed by a public farewell over the following weekend.*

## Farewell

The farewell services were held over two weekends. The first, Sunday 1 and Monday 2 October 1933, also marked Graham Scroggie's seventeenth anniversary at the Chapel. On the Sunday, the church was packed to capacity at both services. Scroggie preached in the morning on Hebrews 6:1: 'Let us go on unto perfection … and this will we do', and in the evening on 1 Kings 20:28: 'The Lord is the God of the hills and He is the God of the valleys as well'.

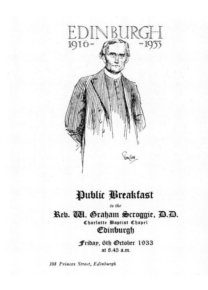

EDINBURGH
1916- ~1933

**Public Breakfast**
*to the*
**Rev. W. Graham Scroggie, D.D.**
Charlotte Baptist Chapel
**Edinburgh**
**Friday, 6th October 1933**
at 9.45 a.m.
*108 Princes Street, Edinburgh*

*The programme for the Public Breakfast on Friday 6 October 1933, attended by ministers and lay people from many denominations in Edinburgh.*

A family get-together was held in the Chapel on the Monday evening. Eight leaders of Chapel organisations expressed their appreciation of Dr Scroggie's ministry, and their love for both him and Mrs Scroggie. In his reply, Graham Scroggie said, among many other things:

*All the speakers have overlooked a very important matter. I would remind the secretary of the Church and my brother elders and deacons that I have resigned as pastor of the Church but I have not sent in my resignation as a member.... this is our home Church. You have had many valedictory services here, and in my view this is not a farewell but a valedictory service.... I am going from here to the world.... It is not goodbye but only good-night for a while. Maybe in a year or a little more when we return from the other side, one of the first places we shall want to see again will be this place and you folk. The Lord bless you, and we thank you.*

6 *Record*, 1933, pp. 168-9.

229

A Public Breakfast was held on Friday 6 October, attended by ministers and lay people from many denominations in Edinburgh. Two of the speakers are of particular interest to the writer. One was Peter Manson, the 'Manson' of the legal partnership of Balfour & Manson, founded by the writer's grandfather and Mr Manson in 1888; the other was Charles D. Nightingale, vice-chairman of the Methodist Conference, and the founding partner of Nightingale & Bell, a two-partner legal practice established in Edinburgh about the same time. Little could Peter Manson and Charles Nightingale have imagined, as they both spoke on that memorable occasion in 1933, that their successors would come together in one merged firm in 1990, still opening every partners' meeting with prayer.

### The final weekend

Over the next weekend, services were held in the Assembly Hall on the Mound. Large numbers gathered on the Sunday, and many were turned away in the evening. Graham Scroggie preached memorable sermons, in the morning on Nehemiah 8:10: 'The joy of the Lord is your strength', and in the evening on Galatians 6:14: 'God forbid that I should glory save in the cross of our Lord Jesus Christ'.

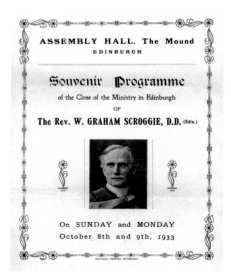

*Assembly Hall brochure*

The final service was on Monday evening, 9 October; the Assembly Hall was again packed to capacity. The church secretary spoke about the amazing attraction that Dr Scroggie's ministry had for young men and women, and that during the 17 years of his pastorate, 650 believers had been

baptized and 950 received into membership. After five others had paid tribute, Dr Scroggie picked up on some of the comments:

*It has been said that my ministry has not been a denominational or sectarian ministry. I hope that is true, but I want also to say, side by side with that, that I have never toyed with my convictions as a Baptist. We should all come to think in terms of the Kingdom of God, in terms of a campaign rather than a battle, in terms of the Holy Catholic Church instead of a denomination, and we can do so without being disloyal to our denomination and our convictions. It was in the infinite goodness and providence of God that I was brought into touch with the great Keswick Movement in 1900, and have had the opportunity and privilege all these years of meeting brethren of most denominations, meeting them in the happiest fellowship.*

7 *Record*, 1933, pp. 171-2.

On the following morning, a large crowd gathered at the Waverley Station, to sing 'God be with you till we meet again' as the train drew out for London.

Curiously, there was no mention, during the farewell services, of Mrs Scroggie's ministry to students in Edinburgh, but one of the tributes, following her death in London in February 1940, was that:

*One of her special activities during the seventeen years of Dr. Scroggie's ministry in Edinburgh, was to have 'open house' to students of all Faculties in the University, every Sunday afternoon. She could never be certain how many would come, but she would busily prepare for her guests, and then dispense the happiest possible hospitality to the many of all nationalities who greatly appreciated finding a 'home away from home', and always a motherly welcome. On one occasion twelve Chinese students arrived together! Mrs. Scroggie was indeed in her element when entertaining, and nothing seemed a trouble to her.*

8 Mary R. Hooker, 'Mrs W. Graham Scroggie', *The Sword and the Trowel*, 76 (1940) 57.

Graham Scroggie served the church in Auckland for six months, as he had promised, and then became 'minister at large' (his phrase) from 1933 to 1937, under the auspices of the Movement for World Evangelisation. He visited Australia, South Africa, Canada, the United States of America and Great Britain, conducting interdenominational Life and Service Campaigns. In 1938, he offered his services for a few months to Spurgeon's Metropolitan Tabernacle in London, and was there for seven years. He was then briefly the first principal of London Bible College (now the London School of Theology), and then professor of Biblical Exegesis at Spurgeon's College.

Graham Scroggie came back to the Chapel as guest preacher from time to time. His longest return visit was in March 1938, when he spoke at a week of special meetings and showed more travel films in the Assembly Hall. He occupied the pulpit for three consecutive Sundays in May 1950, while his successor, Sidlow Baxter, was on a world tour; the building was packed, with overflows to the lower hall. His last visit was for Sundays 19 and 26 July 1953, during a vacancy. He had not been strong enough to preach anywhere for a year, and so he confined his ministry in Edinburgh to the two Sunday services.

Until 1957, he was much in demand for pulpit supply and convention ministry; after that, he was too frail to continue. He died at home on 28 December 1958 and was buried in the Grange cemetery, Edinburgh (Chapter 40).

### VISIT OF DR. SCROGGIE.

Following up our earlier intimations, we are glad to announce that the former Pastor of Charlotte Chapel, the Rev. W. Graham Scroggie, D.D., will be with us for Five Days of Special Ministry this month. Please make the Meetings widely known.

SUNDAY, 13th MARCH, 11 a.m. and 6.30 p.m.

MONDAY, 14th, to THURSDAY, 17th, each evening at 8 p.m.

N.B.—On Friday evening, 11th March, Dr. Scroggie will give his Travel-Film on North America, in the Assembly Hall, The Mound, at 7.30 p.m. Tickets, 6d.

Pray for much Blessing on all the Meetings.

*Graham Scroggie's visited the Chapel in March 1938, for a week of special meetings.*

## Basis of his ministry
Graham Scroggie spoke with authority and deep conviction, because he believed with all his heart and mind that the Bible was the inspired revelation of the Living God. What was the secret of such a ministry? One of the speakers at his farewell meeting in Edinburgh analysed it as: (1) intensely, emphatically, and exclusively a Bible ministry. 'Not that our friend', said the speaker, 'is a man of one book – I have seen his library, and it is the envy of many – but all books are laid under contribution to the Book of Books,' (2) a Christ-exalting ministry, (3) a spiritual ministry, and (4) an ethical ministry. He was one of the outstanding Bible expositors of his generation, reigning like a prince in the pulpit, both in preaching the Word and in teaching it.

However, no minister can give of his best unless he has the warm-hearted support of his office-bearers, and Graham Scroggie had that in full measure. He was always ready to acknowledge the debt he owed to the loyal support he received from the elders and deacons who served with him.

Additional information on the following topics, mentioned in this chapter, is available on the CD.

Graham Scroggie after Charlotte Chapel
Graham Scroggie: evaluation by Ralph Turnbull
Graham Scroggie: tribute from the church secretary
Graham Scroggie's 1925 resignation (head or feet)

# Chapter 31
## Vacancy (1933–1935)

### First year of vacancy

#### A positive attitude

The vacancy in the pastorate, caused by the resignation of Graham Scroggie, faced the Chapel with a serious problem; it would not be easy to find someone to follow such an outstanding ministry. Nevertheless, the church secretary encouraged the membership to take a positive, not a negative, view of the position. At the annual church business meeting in May 1934, he said:

*As you know, the release of Dr Scroggie from the pastorate here has enabled him to enter a very wide field of service in the Master's cause, and we confidently believe that his usefulness has been thereby extended. He is presently engaged in a world-wide campaign, and although this corner of the vineyard may have suffered, we can look abroad to the wider fields which will benefit from his ministry.*

---

1 *Record*, 1934, p. 100.

The Chapel responded to this positive approach. The building was often packed for both Sunday services, particularly if a well-known guest preacher was due. The elders received many new members, 23 on one Sunday and 25 on another. Baptisms continued regularly on Thursdays, sometimes with 16 at a time. There was a particularly happy occasion when Sheila Dovey, the fourth generation of her family to be baptized in the Chapel, and also Ronald and Elspeth Urquhart, the third generation of theirs (grandfather Andrew and father MacDuff) were among nine young people baptized. The Thursday Bible School flourished from October 1933 to the end of April 1934 under one guest lecturer, the rector of St Thomas' Episcopal Church, which was then a near neighbour of the Chapel.

#### Auxiliary growth

After a year of vacancy, the church secretary observed: 'this leaderless period has been beneficial to us. We have become more knit together as a congregation and have learned to rely more upon ourselves where the human element of leadership was necessary.' The tract distributors increased their deliveries to five thousand broadsheets a month; the Sunday School had 65 teachers, the highest number ever, with 311 scholars and another 65 in the Bible Class; the Scouts and the Guides were in good heart. The District

Women's Meeting packed 80, the most ever, into the ladies' room in the Chapel; the Girls Own had 120 on Sunday afternoon; the Jamaica Street mission started additional meetings, and 130 men came to the Rock Mission's Christmas social. In short: 'The work in Charlotte Chapel has continued with unabated zeal during the year that has elapsed, and the Church today has not only a larger membership then it had a year ago, but all the agencies [auxiliaries – there were 33 of them] are in a flourishing condition.'

#### Vacancy committee

The church appointed the whole diaconate (34 men) to be the vacancy committee. They made a list, quite a long one, of those whom they would like to see in the pulpit at the Chapel before considering any one name. Although some visiting preachers made an instant impression on the congregation, the committee stuck to their policy, and did not apply themselves seriously to the question of a recommendation until the middle of June 1934.

**HAVE YOU FIXED YOUR HOLIDAY ?**

**NETHERHALL, LARGS, AYRSHIRE.**

A Christian Holiday centre on the Scottish West Coast. 12 Acres of Grounds; Hard Tennis Courts, etc.; Bedrooms with Hot and Cold Water; Spacious Public Rooms; Library and Recreation Hall; Good Catering.
Apply Mr W. E. Taylor, Netherhall, Largs, Ayrshire; or 'Phone 2204.

*One of the advertisements in the Chapel Record. A member who was on holiday there in 1934 sent his vote from Netherhall in favour of Sidlow Baxter. Many today remember holidays and conferences there, until it was sold for housing development in the 1990s.*

The committee had a particular interest in Graham Scroggie's successor at the Bethesda Free Church in Sunderland. He had been invited to write the monthly meditation (the first two pages of the *Record*) for February 1934, and also to take the services on the last Sunday of that month. Following his visit, the vacancy committee sent a small deputation to hear Sidlow Baxter in his own church. Unlike the corresponding group in 1916, which brought back a negative report, the three delegates were enthusiastic, and Sidlow Baxter was invited to preach again on 17 June. Three days later, the committee decided that he should be invited to the pastorate. Individual notices were sent to all members, calling a meeting for Thursday 5 July, and advising that Mr Baxter was the unanimous choice of the vacancy committee. Those on holiday were invited to express their views by letter, and 'It was also agreed that an opportunity be given to those unable to attend the meeting to endorse the Call by signing a suitable document in the Vestibule of the Church on the two following Sundays.' A large majority, with only ten dissenting, carried the motion and a 'call' was sent to Sidlow Baxter.

### The first 'call' declined

Sidlow Baxter came to Edinburgh to discuss the position at length with the church secretary and then wrote, on 31 July, declining the invitation. He gave two reasons. First, he had been at Bethesda for only two and a half years and the church was enjoying great blessing. Secondly, he had no conviction that this was the right move for him, and he was not prepared to leave Sunderland until he was at peace with himself. However, he ended the letter by saying that he would like to be invited as pulpit supply from time to time in the future; the significance of that comment became apparent nine months later, as set out below.

## Second year of vacancy

### Another reluctant candidate

It was November 1934 before the committee seriously considered another name. Following a visit to the Chapel by a guest preacher, two office-bearers attended his church in London. This time, the vacancy committee decided to approach the candidate before they called a members' meeting. Two senior elders went to London, and asked him whether he would give serious consideration to a 'call' if the members invited him. He responded that while he had no thought of leaving his present church, he was always ready to go where the Lord led him. The committee therefore called a members' meeting for 10 December, seeking endorsement for an invitation to be sent. A large majority carried this, with only 12 voting against. However, on considering the whole position, the man in London advised that he was not ready for a move.

### A challenging year

The second year of vacancy proved to be more difficult for the Chapel than the first had been. At the annual members' meeting in May 1935, MacDuff Urquhart said: 'I cannot but think that we as a congregation are being tested in preparation for some great work yet to be done in this place. I am sure the right man for Charlotte Chapel will be sent among us.' The area that suffered most during the vacancy was the Chapel's missionary interest, with comments like 'so few present' at the Monday missionary prayer meeting, and poor support for the BMS annual deputation. The Carey centenary rally (to commemorate his death) attracted an 'audience unworthy of the occasion'. On the other hand, when three missionaries were valedicted on Sunday 2 September 1934, the church was packed morning and evening, largely with young people in the evening; the effective policy was again employed, of following up the formal dedication in the morning by asking the missionaries to take a significant part of the evening service. Clearly the potential was there, but the absence of an under-shepherd was also evident.

### Second invitation to Sidlow Baxter

The vacancy committee discussed several names, following the disappointment of December 1934, but there was no unanimity and there did not seem any immediate prospect of a settlement. Then word reached Edinburgh in March 1935, that other churches were making approaches to Sidlow Baxter. If anything were to be done in regard to him, it would need to be done without further delay. One of the elders went to Sunderland, had an informal discussion with Baxter, and gained the impression that if a unanimous 'call' to the Chapel was sent, it would be accepted. Sidlow Baxter gave the elder three reasons for this. First, he had not thought himself capable of succeeding Dr Scroggie so quickly, but now that nearly two years had elapsed, it would be much easier for any successor. As he put it in an interview 60 years later: 'I was waiting for the ghost of Graham Scroggie to get out'. Secondly, schemes that he had introduced at Bethesda were now up and running and could be carried on by others. Thirdly, he had received several calls, which made him think that the time had come to move from Sunderland.

On Thursday 21 March 1935, the vacancy committee broke the first rule that all such committees should observe – they discussed two names together. Sidlow Baxter was already

233

booked as pulpit supply for 19 May, but the committee asked two of their members to visit someone else, again in London, in early April, and to find out whether he was 'movable'. They reported favourably; it seems incomprehensible today, but the committee invited this other man to preach on the Sunday after Sidlow Baxter. There are few secrets in evangelical circles, and when they got the reply that he was not free for 26 May, nor any Sunday in the near future, they took the hint and concentrated, as they should have been doing all along, on one name only.

On 6 June, MacDuff Urquhart proposed to a church meeting that a further invitation should be sent to Sidlow Baxter, on the basis that the first reason for his former refusal (a short time at Bethesda) no longer applied. The motion was carried by a large majority and after the 'kindly pressure of a renewed invitation', Sidlow Baxter yielded; on 16 June 1935, he accepted the 'call' to come to Edinburgh.

## Rev. J. Sidlow Baxter

### Background

Sidlow Baxter was born in 1903 in Sydney, Australia, to which his parents had emigrated a few years previously. When he was nearly two, his father deserted the family and disappeared; his mother returned to England, and settled in Lancashire. Sidlow had a natural musical talent and a family friend recollects the young boy coming to their house to play the piano and sing.

He intended to become a chartered accountant, but when he was converted in November 1919, during evangelistic meetings held in Lancashire by the Wood Brothers, in connection with the National Young Life Campaign, they encouraged him to think of full-time Christian service. After some months of itinerant evangelism as their pianist, he started at Spurgeon's College, London, in the autumn of 1924; he was one of the youngest students in the college. After graduation, he had pastorates in Northampton (four and a half years) and Sunderland (from January 1932), before he came to the Chapel on 20 October 1935.

In 1927, he married Ethel Smith, and their daughter Miriam, born in 1929, was with them throughout their years in Edinburgh. Ethel was a true helper to him, sharing fully in his ministry. She came to the Chapel with a quiet dignity, tact and a good sense of humour. She was an excellent housewife and homemaker, and also an efficient secretary and typist. She was willing to be in the background, supporting her husband by her prayers and her presence. However, she was a member of the augmented choir during the Usher Hall services and also assisted in the enquiry room after these services.

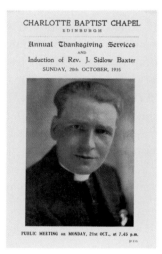 

*Sidlow Baxter and wife, Ethel, when they came to Edinburgh in October 1935. The induction service was combined with the church anniversary.*

### Induction

The vacancy had lasted for two full years. Rev. John MacBeath, a former Chapel boy and president of the Baptist Union of Scotland for that year, conducted the induction during the morning service on Sunday 20 October 1935. The building could not accommodate all who wished to attend, and about one hundred had to be content with the lower hall. Mrs Kemp, the widow of Joseph Kemp, was present as she was on holiday from New Zealand. It was even more crowded in the evening:

*Not for many days have the Deacons and Stewards had such a job to find seats for the flow of people, all anxious to see and hear Mr Baxter. The queue commenced to form at the door about 5 o'clock and by 6 o'clock the flood had to be diverted to the Lecture Hall, which was filled to capacity by a slightly disappointed gathering; but if they could not see they certainly could hear.*

2 *Record*, 1935, p. 128.

The evening service, conducted by Mr Baxter, received the seal of the Lord's approval in the conversion of six souls.

## Manse

The minister was still responsible for finding a manse, and for financing it out of his stipend. As Sidlow Baxter did not have a car, he looked for one reasonably near to the Chapel, but he also wanted three public rooms and three bedrooms. A house nearing completion at 14 Ravelston Dykes was ideal, but it was not available for rental and the builder was asking for £1,600 to sell. The deacons were not interested in purchasing a manse, partly because they did not have £1,600 and did not want to borrow, and partly because any bought house might not (they said) suit the next minister. The idea of selling that house and purchasing another, for the next minister, never entered their discussions. Various schemes were discussed, and eventually the stipend was fixed at £600 per annum, out of which Mr Baxter was to make his own arrangement for a mortgage of £1,000. That was £100 more than the figure originally offered, which was £400 of stipend and £100 to rent a manse, but it was what Dr Scroggie had been receiving when he left.

Incidentally, the word 'stipend' was, and still should be, used to describe the emoluments paid to the pastor of a Baptist church; 'salary' implies a different legal relationship, set out in the section 'Legal status of ministers' on the CD.

*Sidlow Baxter bought 14 Ravelston Dykes in 1935 and used it as his manse until 1949. This photograph was taken in 2004.*

Throughout his time in Edinburgh, Sidlow Baxter never owned a motorcar. It was not that he could not afford one, but walking and cycling gave him much pleasure. On weekdays, he cycled to the Chapel. When one of the Chapel elders, William Tregunna, was on police points duty at the West End (which was then an open junction), and when he saw his pastor cycling toward him up Queensferry Street, he stopped all traffic from Shandwick Place, Princes Street and Lothian Road, and waved Sidlow Baxter through, with the salutation: 'Good morning, pastor.' Baxter replied: 'Good morning, Mr Tregunna', and then the constable allowed the buses, trams, cars and lorries to move again.

## A 'gathered' congregation

As noted in Chapter 8, the membership in 1851 was drawn from many parts of the city; Chapter 23 recorded how the office-bearers in 1916 and 1933 lived in almost every postal district except the Chapel's own. The membership that greeted Sidlow Baxter was too large to analyse here, but the locations of the homes of the elders and deacons are worth another look. A few office-bearers had cars but most travelled long distances by public transport, to take up their duties in the Chapel. They lived in:

| | |
|---|---|
| EH2 | East Register Street |
| EH3 | Glengyle Terrace, St. Peter's Buildings, Torphichen Street |
| EH4 | Barnton, Clarendon Crescent Comely Bank Avenue, Dean |
| EH5 | Laverockbank Terrace |
| EH6 | Agnew Terrace |
| EH8 | Piersfield Terrace |
| EH9 | Lauder Road, Marchmont Crescent Marchmont Street, West Savile Terrace |
| EH10 | Falcon Avenue, Greenbank Road Montpelier, Riselaw Road, Viewforth Square |
| EH11 | Balgreen Road, Briarbank Terrace, Ogilvie Terrace Robertson Avenue |
| EH12 | Anwoth Villas, Belmont Gardens (2) Clermiston Road (2), Saughton Crescent Saughtonhall Avenue, Saughtonhall Drive |
| EH14 | Craiglockhart Quadrant |
| EH16 | Esslemont Road |

On the other hand, Mrs Margaret Armstrong, whose home was at 161 Rose Street (the Chapel's number is 204) joined the Chapel in 1902, before the revival under Joseph Kemp, and lived there and attended regularly until her death in 1958.

## More about the new pastor

Sidlow Baxter's life between his birth in 1903 in Sydney and his induction to the pastorate of Charlotte Chapel in 1935 has been described by his authorised biographer, Ernest A. Johnston, in *J. Sidlow Baxter, A Heart Awake* (Baker Books, Grand Rapids, Michigan, 2005). It is no part of this book to duplicate that, but there is one significant aspect of Sidlow's early life, not included in Johnston's biography, that may be lost to posterity if it is not recorded here. Mrs Marjorie Baldock, the granddaughter of the Mr and Mrs George Taylor mentioned below, told the writer about it in 2002.

Sidlow's mother, Alice, returned to England in 1905, with her three children. Arriving by ship at Southampton, they took the train to Waterloo Station, London, where Alice's money ran out. She had no idea what to do or where to go. She was sitting on a bench in Waterloo Station, with the children, considering whether to approach the Salvation Army, when she 'opened her eyes' (Marjorie did not know whether she had been praying or whether she simply looked up) and saw three people standing in front of her. They were complete strangers, who introduced themselves as Mr and Mrs George Taylor and an unmarried school headmaster called Ford. They were evangelical Christians, returning from a holiday together on the Isle of Wight; the Taylors had felt 'led' to speak to the little family sitting forlornly on the station bench.

When Alice told the Taylors about her plight, they took all four Baxters to their own home in Ashton-under-Lyne in Lancashire, and looked after them until Alice found accommodation nearby. She became the deaconess at the Scarhall Mission in Ashton, and also worked as a Police Court missionary there, while forming a new home for her children.

How different Sidlow Baxter's life – and his (Lancastrian) accent – would have been if the family had not by chance (or was it divine guidance?) met the Taylors in Waterloo Station. Sidlow's older sister, Margaret, married a Congregational minister in Ashton-under-Lyne.

One other aspect of the Baxters' friendship with the Taylors is worth recording. Young Sidlow was passionately fond of music, particularly the piano. One of George Taylor's friends was a widower, James Arthur Yoxhall, who played the organ at the United Methodist Church in Stamford Street in Ashton; he was also the official pianist for the Keswick Convention. James Yoxhall encouraged Sidlow's musical gifts, and he thought about taking up music as a career. When Sidlow decided to go instead to Spurgeon's College, Yoxhall financed him through his student years.

Additional information on the following topics, mentioned in this chapter, is available on the CD.

Graham Scroggie's 'call' to Charlotte Chapel
Legal status of ministers
Sidlow Baxter before Charlotte Chapel
Sidlow Baxter's biography to 1936

# Chapter 32
## Sidlow Baxter settles in (1935–1936)

## Sunday

### Overview

Sidlow Baxter came to a lively, expectant church, with well-attended Sunday services, 33 active auxiliaries and many overseas missionary links. His 18 years in Edinburgh divide into: (1) the four years from his induction in October 1935 to the outbreak of the Second World War in September 1939 (Chapters 32 and 33), (2) the six war years (Chapters 34 and 35) and (3) his eight years of post-war ministry (Chapters 36 and 37).

During the first period, life in Charlotte Chapel continued much as it had during the pastorate of Graham Scroggie. The auxiliaries grew in strength and in effectiveness, the Sunday services filled the building to overflowing, membership rose to its highest ever at 1,123, missionary support increased and the Thursday Bible School flourished. This chapter focuses on developments during Sidlow Baxter's first four years; if activities are not mentioned, it is because they were continuing along the lines described in the last few chapters.

### Pulpit ministry

As a preacher, Sidlow Baxter was expository and warmly evangelistic, with a popular appeal. At his first anniversary, he publicly thanked God that there had not been one Sunday in the previous 12 months without some conversions at or after the services. Published sermons rarely do justice to the preacher, but the following transcript from a tape may, if one imagines his slow diction and his broad Lancastrian accent, give the flavour of a typical Scripture reading at the beginning of a Sunday service. The words in brackets are Baxter's comments on the Biblical passage as he read it.

*The Epistle of Paul the apostle to the Ephesians, chapter 1 and verse 4. I think I'll wait until you find it – there's heavenly music to my ears in the rustle of those Bible pages.*

*Well now, here it is. Ephesians, chapter 1 and verse 4. 'According as He (that is God) hath chosen (or elected) us (that is Christian believers) in Him (that is in Christ) from before the foundation of the world (with this tremendous objective in view) that we should be holy and without blame before Him (not just before men; that is where, long ago, the originally well-meaning but latterly hypocritical Pharisees*

*went tragically wrong; they wanted a demonstrative sanctity, merely before men) that we should be holy and without blame before Him (before God), in love.'*

*Now, don't you agree, is not that an expressively tremendous statement of truth, and before I dare to make my first reverent comment upon it, let me slowly read it once again?*

---
1 Tape in the Chapel archives.

The adjective most often applied to Graham Scroggie's pulpit ministry was 'dignified'; the corresponding description of Sidlow Baxter was 'charming'. It took the congregation a little time to adjust to the more relaxed and genial style of their new pastor; as mentioned earlier, Graham Scroggie had a great sense of humour, but would not use it in the pulpit. Sidlow Baxter introduced one Sunday sermon with the words: 'My dear friends, this morning I am going to preach about three seconds' – pause for reaction, which was incredulity and curiosity, as expected – 'the Second Birth, the Second Blessing and the Second Coming.' Although he invariably preached in a three-quarter-length frock coat and clerical collar, his natural charm came through; he had a fresh and warm popular appeal, and the Chapel was usually crowded at both services on Sunday. When all the pews were filled, the boys in the congregation were asked to give up their seats and to squat on the pulpit steps or even in the pulpit itself. Many men, now long past retiring age, still speak fondly of those evenings when they perched precariously at the preacher's feet.

However, the practice was reviewed after an incident in the summer of 1939. A group of boys, unconnected with any church, had arrived in good time; they were embarrassed at the request to move out of their seats and to sit in full gaze of the congregation on the pulpit steps. One of them walked out and was never seen again. The deacons ruled that in future:

*no one in a seat should be dis-lodged to provide a seat for a late-comer, nor should anyone be seated on the steps. It was decided that the practice of seating the Platform with extra chairs should also cease, and that when the Church was full, cards should be hung on the ropes at the foot of the stairway, intimating that the Church was full and that the service would be relayed to the Hall downstairs.*

---
2 Deacons' Minute, 7 June 1939.

When the Chapel leadership were approached in 1937, in the same way as they had been in 1900, to sell the property to a commercial concern, they did not turn down the £20,000 offer immediately; they explored the possibility of putting up a bigger building in the same general area. The idea was dropped only when they could not find a suitable alternative site in the city centre.

## Communion table

The beautifully carved oak communion table, on which a Bible is placed and illuminated throughout Chapel services to this day (except at communion services), is the Chapel's memorial to Joseph Kemp. It was dedicated during the morning service on Sunday 3 May 1936, and unveiled by Mrs Kemp. Sidlow Baxter explained:

*a Communion Table is primarily, and indeed supremely, 'the Lord's table'– looking back to Calvary's never-to-be-forgotten altar of Sacrifice, and looking on to the Lord's Second Coming in glory. Yet while we are quick to recognise that this table is peculiarly and supremely 'the Lord's table', we are not conscious of the slightest incongruity in unveiling it as a monument, also, to memorialize the beloved former pastor of Charlotte Chapel, the Rev. Joseph W. Kemp, and his great ministry in this place.*

3 *Record*, 1936, p. 98.

The inscription on the communion table reads: 'To the glory of God, and in memory of Joseph W. Kemp, pastor of this church, 1902-1915.' The book board on it was in memory of Graham Scroggie. The open Bible, illuminated during all church services except communion, was the gift of David Wallace.

Six elders joined Sidlow Baxter on the platform, to serve communion. All who remember those days speak of their immaculate dress for this solemn occasion – some in morning coats and the others in striped trousers and a black jacket. The latter were still *de rigueur* when the writer became

an elder in 1965, but shortly after Derek Prime took up the pastorate in 1969, they were made optional; an elder in formal dress, now, would look distinctly out of place. Lounge suits were usual until the early 2000s, but there was no adverse comment when, in June 2006, an elder gave thanks for the bread in an open-neck, short-sleeve cream shirt, and another elder gave thanks for the wine in a green t-shirt, neither with jacket. Until the 1950s, the caretaker was expected to wear striped trousers and a black jacket on Sunday, every Sunday, not just on communion days. By 1935, the word 'Sunday' had almost completely replaced the older word 'Sabbath', although 'the Lord's Day' was still frequently used.

## Sunday School anniversaries

Until 1937, the Sunday School anniversary was held on a Sunday afternoon in June, for the children only. Sidlow Baxter reintroduced the practice (last noted in the Chapel in the 1870s) of using the two normal Sunday services, once a year, to focus on the work of the Sunday School; this was common in Free Churches in England, but unknown in Scotland. The choir stalls and surrounding pews were taken over by excited youngsters; Sidlow Baxter always turned round, after the benediction, and told them how well they had sung, for which they adored him.

*The Sunday School Flower and Fruit Services, held on 13th June [1937], introduced features which were new and interesting. An augmented junior Choir occupied the choir seats, and was supported on either side of the gallery by the other scholars of the Sunday School and Bible Classes, while the very small people of the Primary made an attractive group in the front seats of the area. Mr Baxter received the children's gifts as they entered, adding them to those sent in earlier. These were beautifully arranged before the pulpit, and all were distributed later in the day.*

*The Evening Service was the occasion of the presentation of prizes to members of the Young Worshippers' League. Instituted in 1928, the League has a membership of eighty, and an average attendance each Sunday of fifty. Of these, eighteen recorded perfect attendance for the year, four for two years, four for three years, one for four years, one for six years, and one had nine years' perfect attendance to his credit.*

4 *Record*, 1937, p. 110.

## Dedication of infants

The dedication of infants (more correctly, the dedication of the parents and the church to the upbringing of children) was encouraged in the Chapel, although most ceremonies still took place in the home of the parents (Chapter 24). The elders did not share the enthusiasm of some members, after Graham Scroggie incorporated a dedication into a Sunday morning service in 1933; all dedications during the vacancy took place in homes, and Sidlow Baxter maintained this practice until May 1936. The first public dedication during his ministry may bring a fond smile to some readers:

*Dedicated to the Lord. – At the close of the morning service on Sunday, May 31st [1936], two of our younger members, Mr and Mrs David Murray, brought their little son, Derek Boyd Murray, and in the presence of the members dedicated him to the Lord. God richly bless their little son!*

5 *Record*, 1936, p. 121.

That wish was abundantly answered. Derek had three fine pastorates, in Paisley, Kirkcaldy and Dublin Street, Edinburgh, lectured for five years at the Scottish Baptist College (as it is now called), was chaplain to St Columba's Hospice, Edinburgh, and on retiring, spent time teaching in India. David Murray remained active in mind, although latterly frail in body, until his death in June 2005.

Public dedications were a Murray initiative, and there was not another one in the Chapel until Derek's half-sister, Irene, was born 14 years later, in March 1950. Sidlow Baxter was on a world tour and would not be back until November; Graham Scroggie was providing pulpit supply in May. David Murray asked Dr Scroggie to conduct a service in the vestry, but he responded: 'a Dedication Service should either take place in the Church or in the home.' Mr Murray preferred the former, 'but he was aware that it had not lately been Mr. Baxter's practice and desired the ruling of the [elders'] Court.' The elders had no objection, provided it was not seen as a precedent to bind Sidlow Baxter on his return. In consequence:

*Dedication – After the morning service on the 14th May [1950], a touching little service was held in the Chapel when Mr and Mrs David Murray brought their infant daughter, Irene Donald, to be dedicated. The service opened*

*with the singing of 'Jesus is our Shepherd', after which Dr Scroggie took the baby into his arms and prayed that she might have true blessing as she grew up, and that her parents would find Divine guidance in all their prayers and desires for her. A large and sympathetic audience remained behind for the very happy little ceremony.*

6 *Record*, 1950, p. 90.

Many members liked it, and several other dedications followed this pattern while Sidlow Baxter was still away. He took heed of the trend, and twice in April 1951 he dedicated children 'at the close of the Sunday morning service … in the presence of the Lord's own people.' From then on, parental choice determined the location; Sidlow Baxter would go to a home, or bring the family into the church at the close of the morning service or receive them in the vestry, as they wished. The practice in the vacancy, after Sidlow Baxter left in February 1953, is examined in Chapter 41. Typically, the minister said to the parents:

*In presenting this child to the Lord, do you promise, in dependence on divine grace and in partnership with the Church, to teach him the truths and duties of the Christian faith; and by prayer, precept, and example, to bring him up in the discipline and instruction of the Lord?, to which they replied: 'We do'.*

The minister then said to the congregation:

*Do you, as members of the Church, acknowledge and accept the responsibility, together with the parents, of teaching and training this child that, being brought up in the discipline and instruction of the Lord, he may be led in due time to trust Christ as Saviour, and confessing him as Lord in baptism, be made a member of his Church? If so, will you signify your acceptance of this responsibility by standing? Let us now look at the four things you and the Church members dedicate yourselves to do, by making these promises [an exposition of these followed].*

7 Stephen F. Winward, *The Dedication Service* (The Baptist Union of Great Britain and Ireland, London, 1960), p. 5.

## Music and choir

Sidlow Baxter's musical talent found outlets in various ways.

He frequently played the piano at the Monday prayer meeting, the Thursday Bible School and other weeknight meetings. He took these opportunities to teach the members new hymns (many written by himself) or new tunes for familiar words. When he came, the choir was 50-strong, and for three decades it had been an outstanding feature of the Church's worship and evangelistic work. Sidlow Baxter built on this, and asked that after the benediction on Sunday evening, the choir should always sing an evangelistic piece, so that the congregation dispersed with the gospel ringing in their ears. A suggestion in 1939, that the Chapel should change to the new *Revised Baptist Hymnal* for the morning service was not agreed, although it was approved a year later. The hymns composed by Sidlow Baxter himself were collected and published; this hymnbook was used at Chapel mid-week meetings, but did not sell sufficiently well outside the Chapel to merit a second edition.

## Weekdays

### Prayer meetings

When Sidlow Baxter came to the Chapel, he noted that the Monday prayer meeting and the Wednesday open-air was not as well supported as other activities, so he set about reviving interest in them. He led by example, attending and giving an introductory message at the main church prayer meeting, as well as playing the piano; after only two months in Edinburgh, he wrote: 'Nothing has been more heartening than the revived interest in the Prayer Meeting on the Monday night each week. This augurs well; but we here appeal for a still bigger response. Nothing can compare, for gripping interest and worthwhileness, with a Spirit-filled prayer meeting.'

Mrs Baxter encouraged attendance and participation at the women's prayer meeting on Wednesday afternoon at 2.45 p.m. in the ladies' room – 'an oasis in the desert to all who attend. Each week sees fresh faces, and the increase in numbers testifies to the influence of our beloved leader, Mrs Baxter'. The deaconess supplied prayer-requests from the sick and lonely, and the Chapel missionaries, elders and deacons, open-air workers and auxiliary leaders were regularly remembered in prayer. The closing meeting of 1935 was 'of a Christmassy nature', with the pastor leading the singing and

bringing a message; 130 attended, so they had to move from the ladies' room to the lower hall.

### Open-air meetings

The Chapel still had three regular open-air meetings at the corner of Princes Street and South Charlotte Street. They were held after the Sunday evening service, all the year round, and at 8 p.m. on Wednesday and Saturday through the summer. The Wednesday outreach was poorly supported, despite Sidlow Baxter's regular appeals for more to attend, even if only to carry the platform and the harmonium from the Chapel and to be part of the crowd.

The faithful few persevered, and there were regular conversions. The majority of the population had, by today's standards, a considerable knowledge of the elements of the Christian faith and morals. This came from a substantial biblical content in religious education in schools, and attendance of large numbers at Sunday schools. Christian morality was generally accepted as the norm, even when it was not practised; as a result, most people had some sense of being sinners. Open-air preaching could therefore be blunt, calling for repentance from sin.

*The favoured spot for open-air evangelistic meetings was still the corner of Princes Street and South Charlotte Street, although by 1936 the noise of traffic, which forced the abandonment of the location after the Second World War, was a problem from time to time.*

Sidlow Baxter also encouraged the annual two-month summer open-air campaign. The Chapel employed evangelists to head up this outreach, but many Chapel members provided supporting roles for all of July and August. Prior to Mr Baxter's coming to Edinburgh, the campaign was carried on at two sites, one near the beach at

Portobello and the other at the canal basin at Lothian Road. The Portobello Sand Services continued until the Second World War, but, as mentioned in Chapter 23, the 'canvas cathedral' at Lothian Road was wrecked in a storm in 1935. Instead of replacing it, the Chapel workers drove the motor caravan (also mentioned in Chapter 23) to the Mound (not Lothian Road) and used it as a platform. Meetings were held there on Tuesday, Wednesday, Thursday and Saturday evening; at the conclusion of the Wednesday and Saturday meetings, the assembled crowd marched along Princes Street to join the open-air at the corner of South Charlotte Street.

## Thursday Bible School

Sidlow Baxter maintained the high profile that Graham Scroggie had given to Bible study, leading by example at his Thursday Bible lectures from October to June. The lower part of the Chapel was well filled, although the gallery was never required, as he went through First John (1936), an overview of the New Testament (1937), and then, in 1938, he began his monumental series 'Through the Bible Book by Book', which became the basis for his four-volume commentary, *Explore the Book.*

When he came to Exodus in 1939, he spent some time on the details of the tabernacle; not much had been said about it in the Chapel since Joseph Kemp's studies in 1909. He also invited a guest speaker to give a series on the tabernacle in 1942, nightly from Sunday through to Thursday, illustrated by large charts hung across the full width of the Chapel. Baxter himself went on to lecture on the significance of the high priest's garments – 'a subject of rich interest'.

## Reverence for Scripture

The reverence for Scripture as the Word of God, which has characterized Charlotte Chapel throughout its history, was fully maintained. 'We approach the Bible', Mr Baxter wrote, 'as being in its totality the Word of God in our studying of it. Therefore we are seeking to learn under the illumination of the Holy Spirit, the mind and the truth and the will of God.' He shared Graham Scroggie's insistence that the Bible must not be displaced by any commentary on it, saying: 'it is no use reading the following studies instead of the Bible.... What we are after is that the Bible itself shall be read, part by part, several times over, and the present scheme of studies used alongside with this.' 'The Course', he wrote elsewhere, 'was meant to give a practical grip on the Bible as a whole.'

He described this method of study as 'interpretive', and his aim was 'to get hold of the controlling thought, the outstanding meaning and message of each book and then see it in relation to the other books of the Scriptures.' Furthermore, 'in our study of the Bible we need ever to guard against becoming so engrossed in the fascination of the subject that we lose sight of the object. Our Lord Jesus Christ Himself has taught us that He is the focal theme of all the Scriptures and everywhere, therefore, we want to see beyond the written Word to Him, who is the Living Word.'

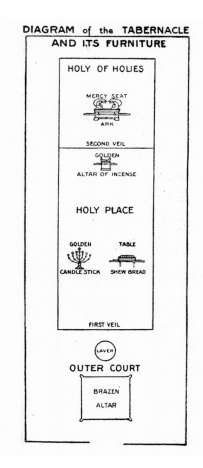

*When Sidlow Baxter came to Exodus in his Thursday evening Bible lectures, he spent some time on the furniture in the tabernacle in the wilderness, illustrated by this reconstruction.*

## Dispensational teaching

Sidlow Baxter, like Joseph Kemp and Graham Scroggie before him, expounded the Bible within the framework known as dispensational teaching – that God dealt differently with people during seven different eras (dispensations) of biblical history (Chapter 21). Even those listeners who did not accept that particular approach – with its sharp antithesis between

240

law and grace, justification and sanctification, etc. – found his Thursday Bible School outstandingly helpful. Gerald Griffiths, the next minister, preferred the Reformed framework, but for the first half of the twentieth century, the Chapel thrived on a steady diet of the dispensational method of biblical interpretation.

### The Second Coming of Christ
All dispensationalists are necessarily pre-millenialists, although the reverse is not the case. Sidlow Baxter, like Graham Scroggie before him, therefore regularly taught that Christ's Second Coming might take place at any time, and that the believer should not only look for it but be prepared for it.

*Who is to say which day He will not come?… We are given clear signs: yet the day itself is left in suspense. His coming is certain some time. It is possible any time. It is imminent all the time. It is likely very soon. He is coming without delay. 'Behold I come quickly!'*

8 *Record*, 1947, p. 164.

Until the 1940s, the pre-millennial view was normative, although not universal, among evangelical Christians. From then on, Evangelicals still believed in the personal and visible and bodily return of the Lord, but other timetables for the end-times (a-millennial, post-millennial) gained in popularity and today it is mostly the older generation who are pre-millennial; the Scofield Bible, which promoted it, is rarely used in this country now.

### Encouragement of auxiliaries
While the minister of a church, particularly a large church like the Chapel, has a significant leadership role both in and out of the pulpit, many of the auxiliaries continue from pastorate to pastorate under dedicated lay members. Nevertheless, Sidlow Baxter visited them assiduously, as Graham Scroggie had done before him. He rarely missed their three key dates, the re-opening for the winter's work in September or October, the Christmas social and the closing meeting in May or June. 'While the offering was being received, Mr. Baxter taught us a new chorus, composed by himself, specially for the High Street.' He was usually asked to speak when he visited an auxiliary, and his wife Ethel, who made her own contribution, often accompanied him. Two

examples will suffice – they thoroughly enjoyed the Sunday School annual prize giving on Friday 5 February 1937, which lasted for nearly two hours, and Sidlow presided at the YPM's Sunshine Band party for the older members of the church, on Saturday afternoon 22 January 1938:

As mentioned, most of the Chapel auxiliaries had their own picnic in the early summer, to close off their session; usually this involved taking the train to a park on the outskirts of Edinburgh. However, in 1937 both the Women's Missionary Auxiliary and the District Women's Meeting hired charabancs and went for a drive. The former drove to Stirling, Callander (lunch), the Falls of Leny and St. Fillans, and came back by Loch Earn and Crieff (tea and shopping), while the latter toured Stirling, Balloch (lunch), Helensburgh (tea) and then sailed on the Gareloch. To see such places, which people today can easily go to by car, was novel in 1937, and increasingly popular until the Second World War put a stop to travel for pleasure.

### Baptism and church membership
Baptisms continued to be held on Monday or Thursday evening, or on both days in the same week if required – in April 1936, 50 were waiting for a date to be baptized. Typically:

*On Monday evening, 1st March [1937], an impressive Baptismal Service was held, the Pastor officiating. A pleasing number were present, including – we have cause to think – some who were not the Lord's, and who, we pray, may have been influenced for Him. The Pastor, in a brief message, spoke of love to Christ, and its expression in obedience to the Lord's commands. Then followed a season of prayer, after which eleven friends [named] gave glad witness to their Lord Jesus in His Own appointed way.*

9 *Record*, 1937, p. 58.

There was no opportunity in those days for candidates to speak, other than to respond 'Yes' to questions, immediately before their baptism, about their repentance and faith, so it was possible for 20 or more to be baptized in one evening.

Membership rose and rose, with over one hundred new members in Sidlow Baxter's first year. The numerical totals (987 in 1936, 1,078 in 1937, 1,117 in 1938 and 1,123 in

1939) are, however, misleading, because not one single name was purged from the roll over these years, even if members had stopped attending or had disappeared. The church secretary promised that one of the first duties of the elders, after the 1938 election, would be to revise the roll. The elders duly brought their lists of missing persons to the court, but the court had no power to remove names; only a church meeting could do that, and no one got round to calling one until 1940. Even then, revision reduced the roll by only 16, because the elders were reluctant to recommend removal. When they eventually grasped the nettle in 1944, they admitted that some of the missing members had not been seen for over a decade, without action being taken, and the church removed 80 names from the roll.

Five unrelated comments are worth making about membership. When a man was 'called' to pastoral ministry elsewhere, his name (and his wife's name) was kept on the Chapel roll, whether or not they formally joined the churches where they were serving. Secondly, there were still junior members, as described in Chapter 20, who had been baptized when under the age of 17 and who were not yet entitled to attend church meetings. One of the 13 admitted to junior membership on Sunday 7 June 1936, was Donald Fleming, who was active with the China Inland Mission (later the Overseas Missionary Fellowship) from 1952 until he retired in 2005. Thirdly, associate membership, which was popular when it was first introduced, was hardly used in Sidlow Baxter's time – two applicants in 1937 are the only mention in his first four years. Fourthly, there were people, then as now, who were regarded for all practical purposes as members of the Chapel, although they would not join; typically: 'Mrs Shaw, of 9 Warrender Park Terrace, has passed to her reward; although not actually a member, she attended the Chapel for many years.' There is further discussion, in Chapter 35, about those who attended the Chapel but were reluctant to join.

The fifth comment concerns one of the questions on the membership application form. Joseph Kemp had introduced: 'Do you see the necessity, as a Christian, of separating yourself from the pleasures of the world? (2 Cor. 6:14-18, Rev. 18:4, Jas 4:4, 1 John 2:15-17).' When the deacons asked Sidlow Baxter what this meant, he amended it to read: 'As a Christian do you see the necessity of dissociating yourself from all such practices and pleasures as

might be considered questionable or of a "worldly" nature? (2 Cor. 6:14-18, 1 John 2:15-17)'. One senior deacon, who had joined the Chapel in 1904, before Joseph Kemp amended the application form, asked: 'What are worldly pleasures, and will an applicant be refused membership if he or she answers in the negative?' The elders talked around the issue in 1936, without coming to any conclusion, and Sidlow Baxter's question remained on the application form for another 39 years; it was rephrased in 1975 (Chapter 47).

## Weddings and funerals

The majority of weddings continued to be in the home of the bride or in the vestry, not in the body of the church. Funerals on Sunday afternoon were increasingly popular in the late 1930s, including one of the largest funerals of Sidlow Baxter's time in Edinburgh, when hundreds went to the graveside to pay respects to a Chapel stalwart, Donald Cormack, grandfather of the present member of that name. Sometimes there was a service in the house first, but on other occasions, particularly on a weekday, the minister officiated only at the grave.

## Missionary recognition

Sidlow Baxter gave missionaries the same high profile as his predecessors had done. Within a month of coming to the Chapel, he valedicted four members, one to Bolivia, for the first time, and three who were returning to China or India. He did this during a regular Sunday service, and, as Graham Scroggie had done, he preached on a missionary theme after the missionary had given his or her testimony. The Baxters joined those who went to the railway station to bid them farewell. For example:

*About thirty members and friends, including Mr and Mrs Baxter and Miriam, gathered at the Caledonian Station, West End, on Tuesday morning, 29th August, to see Miss Wighton away. At her request the company gathered sang, 'He lives', and later, as the train drew out of the platform, they struck up 'No, never alone'.*

---

10 *Record*, 1946, p. 141, but typical of 1936.

That may have been an unusually low number, because when Mrs MacKenzie (Eleanor Dovey) spoke at a rally in the Chapel in 1952, 39 years after first sailing for China, 12 of those present had been at her send-off at the station in 1913.

243

On that occasion, as on many others, the final hymn was 'No, never alone'.

A Chapel missionary, Mary Harrison, was evacuated by plane from Belgian Congo in 1936, after being taken seriously ill at her mission station there. That is the first account of a Chapel member in a civilian flight; two members were military pilots in the 1914-18 War.

*There is no photograph of Mary Harrison being evacuated by plane from Belgian Congo, so the writer's family holiday to Westray, Orkney, in 1938, will have to suffice. School uniform, including cap, was the norm for travel, even on vacation. Left to right: Bill Balfour, Mrs. Frank Balfour (Isabel), Miss Frances Berwick (nannie), the writer.*

## BMS Birthday Scheme
The Baptist Missionary Society encouraged churches to adopt what was then called their Birthday Greetings Scheme. They supplied cards and envelopes to volunteers in local churches, who then found out the birthdays of members and sent a card, together with a return envelope, shortly before every anniversary. The Chapel adopted the scheme in 1937, particularly for the MacBeaths, who had gone to the Belgian Congo with the BMS in 1929 (Chapter 28). It was enthusiastically supported, and at the date of writing (2007)

there are still over 80 subscribers in the Chapel, and over £1,100 is sent annually to the Society; this is for general missionary support, as no Chapel members are overseas with the BMS at present.

Additional information on the following topics, mentioned in this chapter, is available on the CD.

Authority of Scripture
David Wallace
Donald Fleming
Mary Mein Harrison
Membership statistics
Preaching styles
Preaching – audio-tapes (Sidlow Baxter)
Scofield Bible
Second Coming of Christ
Worldliness

# Chapter 33
## Expansion in all directions (1936–1939)

### Evangelism

#### Usher Hall services

Shortly after Sidlow Baxter came to Edinburgh, the Chapel was due for repainting. The Synod Hall, which the Chapel had used during the 1911-12 rebuilding, was no longer available, so the Assembly Hall, where the farewell services for Graham Scroggie had been held, was hired for February and March 1936. The first Sunday attracted 1,500 and numbers increased over the seven weeks. Meeting in a neutral venue, especially one where there was no need to close the doors through overcrowding, sowed the thought in Sidlow Baxter's mind for evangelistic services in the Usher Hall, which seated nearly three thousand, the largest auditorium in Edinburgh.

When he suggested holding Sunday evening services there at 6.30 p.m. for the months of November and December 1938 and January 1939, the deacons were supportive, but only on condition that he would be personally responsible for any financial shortfall. Sidlow Baxter was no mean negotiator, and accepted the challenge on condition that if there was a surplus, he personally should decide where it went. He obtained a reduced rental from the City Council, the owners of the Usher Hall, paying only £150 for all eleven Sundays, including the use of the organ and the amplifiers. The deacons' hesitation disappeared when congregations exceeded two thousand every Sunday evening, easily covering the costs. The services were warmly evangelistic with bright, hearty singing; Mr Baxter preached with great fervour, and never failed to win some for Christ.

*The Usher Hall, when the Chapel first made use of it in 1938. It then had 2,902 seats (1,192 in the area, 428 in the grand tier, 813 in the upper tier, 349 behind the platform and 120 on the platform).*

He planned a similar series for the winter of 1939-40, but had to cancel it on the outbreak of war in September 1939; the Chapel's next Usher Hall outreach was in October 1946.

*Sidlow Baxter encouraged small groups for Bible study and prayer. In this 1938 photograph, the teenager on the left is Bertha Gillon, who became the pastor's secretary in 1963, the first such appointment. Women wore hats throughout such occasions.*

#### Calvinist or Arminian?

How did Sidlow Baxter justify, theologically, this style of evangelism? At an early stage of his ministry in Edinburgh, he dealt with the issue, which had perplexed Christopher Anderson and contemporary Scottish Baptists, in a typically Baxter way. Again, imagine the Lancastrian accent:

*During the eighteenth and nineteenth centuries, there was much controversy in England, between the two rival theological systems, Calvinism and Arminianism. It is wonderful how with changing times, the tides of human thought ebb and flow. The controversy between Calvinism and Arminianism has so far receded now, that comparatively few people even know the meaning of the two names.... Somebody who heard C.H. Spurgeon preach with a decidedly Calvinistic flavour, to Christian believers, one Sunday morning, and then heard him, the same Sunday evening pleadingly urging the 'whosoever will' invitation of the Gospel, to the unconverted, charged him with contradicting himself. Mr Spurgeon replied that since his commission was to 'declare all the counsel of God', he was a Calvinist to the saints, and an Arminian to the unsaved!*

---

1 *Record*, 1936, p. 81.

The doctrinal statement, which Sidlow Baxter asked applicants for membership of the Chapel to affirm, is set out in Chapter 47.

*From January 1939, the Chapel printed its own monthly tract, with details of the services and one of Sidlow Baxter's sermons. Over one hundred members distributed 7,500 copies every month, until wartime paper restrictions reduced the number to four thousand.*

## Jamaica Street mission

This chapter does not attempt to list all that took place in the Chapel during Sidlow Baxter's first four years, but one auxiliary deserves an update; it follows naturally from mention of the Tract Band. The Jamaica Street mission had been started in 1915, because the tract distributors were concerned about the miserable housing there (Chapter 13). The Chapel turned an empty shop into a meeting hall in October 1916 and its progress up to 1933 was described in Chapter 27. In 1936, a Sunday afternoon meeting was started

for young men, a girls class was formed to knit and sew for those in need and to study the Scriptures, and a weekly boys club, for ages 8 to 12, averaged 16 for games and an epilogue. In the following year, they held their own Watchnight service, which was described as excellent; they began a tea meeting for 'keeping old and young out of mischief on Saturday evenings'. With socials and outings and pastoral visitation, the mission had a life of its own. Two young men, whose homes were in Jamaica Street, obtained university degrees and went into the Baptist ministry. The mission was an example of the rewards that can come from years of faithful Christian service; it continued until 1952.

*March 1939 – the first extant photograph of a Chapel congregation; people have been asked to move into the aisles, but even so, the camera could not include many in the gallery and the sides of the church.*

## Ministry

### Sidlow Baxter's conference ministry

Sidlow Baxter was in great demand as a speaker at conventions and rallies in every part of the United Kingdom. He did not accept nearly as many engagements as Graham Scroggie had done, but wherever he went, his Bible teaching, fresh, penetrating and richly illustrative, was deeply appreciated. Only one aspect is commented on here. He spoke many times at local 'Keswick' conventions, but never appeared on the platform of the parent convention in Keswick. He declined their invitations, because he would not accept the requirement to follow a certain pattern of ministry from Monday through to Thursday; he said that if he spoke, he would do so as he was led at the time, and this was not acceptable. Alan Redpath, pastor at the Chapel from 1962 to 1966, used to tell a story against himself; he had preached at Keswick with great power, but was chastened when the chairman said to him afterwards: 'Thank you, Alan, but do remember that this is Tuesday, not Wednesday.'

In October 1937, Sidlow Baxter received a 'call' to the Metropolitan Tabernacle Baptist Church in London, but the elders in the Chapel persuaded him to stay in Edinburgh. Within a year, the Tabernacle called Graham Scroggie instead. Early in 1938, Mr Baxter received an invitation to visit North America from early July to September. Although the older office-bearers could not help remembering what had followed when his two predecessors had accepted similar invitations, they graciously agreed that he should have leave of absence.

## Another view of the Chapel
Eric Lomax was born in Joppa, a suburb of Edinburgh, in 1919. On his own admission, in his autobiography in 1995, he was a loner. During his teenage years, his passion was train spotting; being a choirboy in an Episcopal church at the age of 11 was his only Christian experience before the age of 17.

In 1936, he was working for the Post Office by day, and watching trains, in the glorious age of steam, in the evenings and at weekends. A favourite haunt, at which the writer spent many happy hours when he was similarly smitten in the late 1940s, was the Dalry Road station (now demolished), where several lines converged. One summer Sunday evening in 1936, Eric Lomax was approached by an older man (Jack Ewart, a member of Charlotte Chapel), who struck up a conversation about trains and about recent sightings at this station. 'He really did seem to know a great deal about locomotives. Then, once he had hooked me, the talk turned to religion.' Ewart introduced the lonely young man to the Chapel:

*It was a powerful magnet for a young man looking for a centre to his life. Looking back, I can recall little except an extraordinary arrogance – the members of the Chapel were better than everybody else, they were saved, they were exempt from normal rules and they were certainly above compassion. I didn't know it, but I was now living in a matchbox with*

*people who thought they could rule the world. This was, after all, a church with but one chapel which financed its own missionaries to Africa and Asia.*

*The Chapel was famous for the extremity and ferocity of its preaching. The minister, J. Sidlow Baxter, who was a real fire and brimstone orator, reminds me of those tent gospellers who now make fortunes on television channels in the USA. An accountant before he found the Lord, he relished the tabulation of human weakness. He would rant, cajole, pray, threaten and demand; his sermons were the high point of our services, which were otherwise pretty routine affairs with announcements, readings and hymns....*

*I went to Chapel several times a week: to two Sunday services, and once or twice during the week. There were also sedate social occasions, tea and fundraising efforts. And of course like any sect it had 'policies' about things you could do and a great many more about things you could not, like going to the cinema, to dances, pubs or watching the new medium of television. They would have banned the radio too, but it was too well-established by now and they all listened to it anyway.*

*The older members were immensely bitter and obsessed with status. If newcomers or visitors occupied a pew which an older member felt that he or she had a claim to, the interlopers were the object of furious resentment.... But for all that they made me feel welcome. Ewart, my proselytizer, was still my closest contact in the group. I discovered that he made a speciality of recruiting young men and that he was genuinely interested in trains: a fairly unique form of evangelism.*

2 Eric Lomax, *The Railwayman* (Cape, London, 1995), pp. 33-6, 208.

In 1939, Eric Lomax was called up for military service, and he was posted to Malaya in 1941, at the age of 21. While waiting for embarkation, he became engaged to a Chapel girl, aged 19. His courtship had consisted of: 'walking out together, avoiding the temptations of the city or the world. Dances and films and similar occasions of sin were out of the question for us; we visited each other's houses, took long walks in the country and busied ourselves with Chapel affairs.' Contemporaries remember him as active among the young folk of his day, presenting and reading papers in the Bible Class.

After three and a half years as a Japanese prisoner of war, Eric Lomax returned to Edinburgh, and was married in the Chapel. 'J. Sidlow Baxter was still in command, still denouncing sin and evil with his evangelical bookkeeper's fervour, and he was glad to enter me again on the credit side of his flock.' However, the years in South-East Asia had left Lomax shattered psychically and physically, and he did not settle. He went to the Gold Coast of Africa in 1949, where he drifted away from the Chapel and all that it stood for. His recollections, quoted above, were written 40 years later, but they record one young man's impression of the Chapel between 1936 and 1949. He is, of course, quite correct in his observation that the Chapel was a fairly close community, and, evangelism apart, there was no need to look outside it for friends, social life, and seven-day-a-week activity.

## World events

### The *Record*
One of Sidlow Baxter's main ways of communicating with the scattered Chapel membership was through the monthly *Record*. He stamped his own personality on it: 'Why is the *Record* like an anaemic person? Because it needs a better "circulation"'. He remodelled it, starting with an evangelistic page, followed by a devotional study, then church and missionary news, sermon and lecture outlines, and something for the children. He commented more freely than his predecessors had done on public issues; to four of them, mentioned below, he returned again and again.

### Sunday trading
Sidlow Baxter urged readers of the *Record* to find out the views of candidates in political elections, both municipal and parliamentary, on Sunday trading, and to vote for those who opposed shops, theatres and cinemas opening on Sunday. He attributed Westminster's passing of the Sunday Trading Restriction Bill in 1936, by 191 votes to 8, to Christian lobbying of candidates.

He carried on a relentless campaign against 'the beaming, bland-faced, Sabbath-commercialising Sunday-amusement agitator, pretending to want his gayer Sunday for the benefit of the public, [who] is nothing but the mouthpiece of this world and its downright anti-Christian godlessness, under the guise of humanitarian magnanimity'. As the Second World War increasingly encroached on the traditional British Sunday, he wrote and spoke tirelessly against government and local authorities caving in, as he saw it, to shopkeepers, cinema-owners and brewers, whose self-interest was increased profit under the guise of freedom of choice.

### Christianity or Churchianity
Through the late 1930s, Sidlow Baxter's articles in the *Record* repeatedly challenged nominal religious belief and practice, which Evangelicals described as Churchianity instead of Christianity:

*The truth of the matter is that our churches to-day are mostly filled with unconverted clergymen. In so far as the organised churches are concerned, there are as many atheists in the pulpits as in the pews. We accept the Book as binding in all matters of faith and practice. They accept it only when convenient.… As for the Report on Doctrine in the Church of England, it gives a tragic modern instance of the blind leading the blind.*

3 *Record*, 1937, p. 101; 1938, p. 18.

The Chapel did not, and largely still does not, observe Trinity Sunday, Whit Sunday and other dates in the ecclesiastical calendar. Sidlow Baxter's mother encouraged the women of the Chapel to observe the 'days which come round in "the church year", which never fail to speak a wonderful message to us if our hearts are ready to listen', but most of the church year passed (and still passes) without mention. This included an Easter Sunday in the 1960s, when the guest preacher, from the Free Church of Scotland, had no Easter hymns and did not mention the resurrection in the entire morning service.

### Roman Catholicism
Sidlow Baxter protested strongly and repeatedly against Roman Catholic influence in national and international life. He stressed that his invective (his word) was against the Romanist system, not the individuals within it. One of his concerns is still topical today – the extent to which denominational schools should receive public finance: 'If Roman Catholic authorities insist on keeping their children separate from others, and demanding for them a purely Romanist education, then it is only fair that they themselves should pay for it.'

Baxter was particularly vocal about papal foreign policy. He was convinced that the pope said nothing against 'Italy's butchery campaign in Abyssinia' in 1936 because the pope wanted Protestant missionaries to be killed and replaced by Roman missionaries – 'We hear that four hundred Roman Catholic missionaries are even now ready for being sent into Abyssinia'. He said the Vatican purposely condoned the Japanese invasion of China in 1938 so that 'special facilities would be accorded to the Roman Church in the spheres of Japanese influence'. When neutral Eire covertly assisted the enemy in the Second World War, Sidlow Baxter explained why: 'The promises of any Romanist nation to Britain are not to be trusted. They have never proved so throughout our history, and they will never be better.'

Sidlow Baxter realized, but made no apology, that he was going on and on about Rome:

*We have uttered ourselves again and again recently concerning the accentuated menace of Papal Rome in our day.... No country can have flirtations with that harlot of the seven hills without ruing the day. No Samson can toy with the Delilah of the Vatican without having his eyes put out in the end, and grinding the millstones for the Philistines. With the history of the Popes and the Vatican before us, we pray: God save Britain from Rome!*

4 *Record*, 1944, p. 4.

Fear that Roman Catholicism was working to dominate the church, worldwide, was widespread in Sidlow Baxter's day; it was not until Vatican II, in the 1960s, that evangelical Christians began to see Rome in a more sympathetic way.

### The League of Nations
Like many of his generation, Sidlow Baxter had high hopes that the League of Nations, set up after the First World War, would mediate in international disputes and so avoid another armed conflict. However, by the time he came to Edinburgh, he despaired of it as little more than a talking shop: 'The League, like all other human methods, tries to work from the outside, and fails. God's method is to begin with the heart of man himself. When that is right, all is right. Not international co-ordination, but individual regeneration, is the solution.' Baxter became increasingly critical of the British government's European policy.

## Domestic matters

### Advertising in the *Record*
The circulation of the monthly *Record* nearly doubled during 1938, from seven hundred copies per issue to thirteen hundred. Even so, it needed to be subsidized, as it still is, from the general funds of the church. Advertising revenue had been important for many years, but Sidlow Baxter allocated three full pages per issue for advertisements, and encouraged contributions:

*We wish to put on record our gratefulness to those who advertise in our magazine, some of whom, without a break, have advertised for many years, and whose financial help to our magazine in this way has meant a great deal to us.... the least we can do is to express our thanks and to make the following appeal, namely: – Will our readers kindly examine the advertisements, and where possible patronise the advertisers?*

5 *Record*, 1940, p. 185.

*Robert Aitken, the founder of Aitken & Niven, was the senior elder in the Chapel at the time of his death in 1937. The* Record *relied on advertising revenue from businesses like his, and many others with a Chapel connection, to make publication viable.*

Chapel members were generous in taking space – it was a way of contributing financially to the church while also promoting their businesses. Aitken & Niven, then in Queensferry Street, afterwards in George Street and now in the suburbs, took a full page every month and varied the advertisements according to the season. Advertising continued (although restricted by wartime conditions) until Alan Redpath revamped the magazine in 1964; he dispensed with all advertising by substantially increasing the price.

### Cine films in the Chapel

As mentioned in Chapters 12 and 16, cinematograph films were popular at socials and other occasions in the Chapel from the early 1900s. In February 1938, the Sunday School showed a film, which the elders described as unfortunate; it depicted puppets which came to life when their creator breathed on them. Sidlow Baxter suggested that in future only religious films should be shown, and only after he or two elders had previewed them. The deacons reacted even more strongly and by a large majority imposed an immediate ban on all cinematograph films on the church premises.

Six months later, one of the Chapel missionaries wished to show a film of his work in Nigeria. Sidlow Baxter came back to his original suggestion, and the deacons relented to the extent of allowing 'religious films to be shown – that is those setting forth some aspect of Christian truth, or bearing directly upon the life and activities of our own Church', provided the film had been approved by the pastor or two elders. Films were, however, to be shown only in the top hall or the lower hall, never in the sanctuary, and never, anywhere, on a Sunday. This was the position until 1959, when the rule was grudgingly relaxed, as set out in Chapter 41; there was, however, one exceptional situation in 1951, when the numbers wishing to see Sidlow Baxter's film of his world tour (Chapter 37) necessitated using the sanctuary – on a weeknight.

### Christmas morning

Although Christmas Day was not generally a holiday from work in Scotland at this time (unless it fell on a Sunday), Sidlow Baxter led a service in the Chapel on Christmas morning, 1939. It was well attended, with many from all over the town. In addition to regular Chapel worshippers; from then on, a Christmas service was held until a year into the vacancy after Baxter left in 1952 – there was a brief but profitable service at 11 a.m. on Friday 25 December 1953. It was then discontinued until 1963, and, in a different form, is still a popular and well-supported event in the Chapel calendar.

### The wider Baptist scene

Over the inter-war years of 1919-39, Charlotte Chapel exhibited many similarities, but also a few striking differences, compared with other Baptist churches in the central belt of Scotland. All (of the dozen surveyed) had teaching for Christians on Sunday morning and preached the gospel on Sunday evening. All (except the Chapel, which had *Psalms and Hymns*) used the *Baptist Hymnal* in the morning and either *Redemption Songs* or *Sankey's Sacred Hymns and Solos* at night. Nearly all started the morning service with a psalm or paraphrase, and half of them repeated the Lord's Prayer together. All had a choir, although some choirs sang only in the evening. In only one (not the Chapel), children left partway through the morning service; all had Sunday School and Bible Classes on Sunday afternoon, for children aged between 3 and 15. All used the Authorised Version of the Bible, although some had readings from Moffat's translation as well. Sermons were generally shorter than those in the Chapel, averaging 30 minutes in both morning and evening (although some churches regularly expected 40 minutes). All the churches had open-air evangelistic work and tract distribution, although not many were as active as the Chapel.

Charlotte Chapel was, however, different from the others in several ways. They held communion weekly – the Chapel was monthly – and most did not allow unbaptised believers to take part. The Chapel was one of the first (1922) to stop using a common cup. All but one of the others had a talk to the children as part of the Sunday morning service, whereas neither Graham Scroggie nor Sidlow Baxter would do this regularly. Both did so occasionally – Sidlow Baxter had a series on the Lord's Prayer, which he addressed directly to the children.

The other churches expected between 25 and 50 per cent of the Sunday congregation to attend a mid-week prayer meeting, but only the Chapel had a prayer meeting on one night and a Bible School on another; it was a good evening if 20 per cent of the Chapel's Sunday congregation were at the Monday prayer meeting. In only half of the other churches did women pray in mixed company, whereas it was expected in the Chapel. Two-thirds of the others held sales of work, which were still anathema in Charlotte Chapel.

In answer to the question: 'Were there any taboos which we now [1960 questionnaire] accept?', the other churches listed: dancing, make-up, nail varnish, lipstick, whist drives and going to the cinema. That was the Chapel's position also, but in a quarter of the other 12 churches, a few of the members drank, some of the males smoked and some of them watched football matches. That was quite worldly by Chapel standards.

The participating churches were two from Edinburgh, Morningside and Marshall Street; one from Fife, Leslie; three on the west coast, Ayr, New Prestwick and Clydebank; and six in the Glasgow area, Cambuslang, George Street in Paisley, Harper Memorial, Partick, Queen's Park and Rutherglen.

### Sidlow Baxter's review of 1935-39
Sidlow Baxter summarized his first four years in the Chapel in this way:

*The Chapel continued to be crowded out. Many were seeking membership. Letters and telephone calls told more and more frequently of blessing received through the ministry. Members were increasingly trusting me with their confidences. Real friendships were forming between many of them and ourselves. And practically every Sunday souls were being converted to Christ. All these things were clear seals of the Holy Spirit on the ministry, and I felt encouraged. Besides this, I began to see more clearly the type of ministry which would be most appreciated. I planned a systematic course of Bible teaching. About 600 people were coming every Thursday for the Bible lectures. Then, for three months we took Edinburgh's largest auditorium, the Usher Hall, for Sunday evenings, and despite the worst winter weather for years we saw that place filled week after week. Also, our prayer meetings at the Chapel were noticeably growing. Our income was continually increasing. The time was ripe for a 'big push'. Revival seemed almost upon us. Alas, just at that point, with desolating blow, the war came.*

While there was general support among Scottish Baptists for the British government opposing Hitler, there was not the same universal approval for war as there had been in 1914. At the 1940 Assembly, 13 delegates dissented from a resolution in favour of the country's 'heroic stand against Nazism', and there were moves to form a Baptist Pacifist Fellowship within the Scottish churches. There is, however, no hint of pacifism in the Chapel's monthly *Record*; Sidlow Baxter, while deploring the evils of war, was fully behind the need to resist militant Germany, by force if necessary.

Additional information on the following topics, mentioned in this chapter, is available on the CD.

Calvinist or Arminian?
Christmas morning
Ministry
Jamaica Street mission

---

6 *Record*, 1945, p. 165.`

# Chapter 34
## The war years from 1939 to 1942

### War is declared

#### Our cause is righteous

As people all over Scotland came out of morning services on Sunday 3 September 1939, they were told by those who had not been in church about Prime Minister Neville Chamberlain's radio broadcast at 11.15 a.m. German troops had invaded Poland on 1 September; the British government presented Germany with an ultimatum, that unless they undertook, by 11 a.m. on 3 September, to withdraw from Polish territory, a state of war would exist between Britain and Germany. No assurance was received, so Chamberlain told the nation that Britain was once again at war. Sidlow Baxter commented:

*We ourselves deplore war, even as the extreme resort, but we are at one with all our fellow-Britishers in believing that our cause is righteous. The war was thrust upon us.... ample facts have accumulated before us to expose Hitler's hypocrisy and his blame for the newly broken out conflict. The fact remains, therefore, that in this war we are without doubt championing right and truth against a brutal system of oppression which threatens our very civilisation.*

---

1 *Record*, 1939, pp. 177, 193.

Three members of the Chapel were conscientious objectors, and successfully applied to the Board of Trade for exemption from military duties, on condition that they went down coalmines instead. Throughout Great Britain, there were 16,500 'conscies', but only 73 Baptists; most accepted the government's war policy.

#### Air-raid precautions

The Chapel office-bearers reacted immediately to the declaration of war. Looking back, it might be said they over-reacted, but they were not alone – within days, Edinburgh Corporation evacuated twenty-six thousand schoolchildren and their teachers, many to camps at West Linton and Middleton near Gorebridge; they had been planning it for months. War was declared on Sunday, and Sidlow Baxter called an emergency meeting of the deacons for Wednesday. It was widely expected that within days the Luftwaffe would rain bombs on British cities during the hours of darkness, so strict blackout was imposed. The deacons considered that older people should not venture out after dark, so all

meetings commencing after 3 p.m. were cancelled with immediate effect. This included the Monday evening prayer meeting, the Thursday Bible School and the Sunday evening service. A meeting was arranged for Saturday afternoon at 3 p.m., to combine the Monday prayer meeting and the Thursday Bible lecture. Recognising the need for both special prayer and outreach, the Saturday afternoon meeting was preceded by a prayer meeting at 2.30 p.m. and followed by an open-air at 4 p.m.

*Poison gas in the Kaiser's War of 1914-18 prompted fears that it might be dropped from enemy aeroplanes at any time, so gas masks had to be carried by everyone at all times. Masks for babies were operated by adults, suitably masked themselves. Fortunately, they were never needed for real.*

To replace the cancelled Sunday evening service, a meeting was scheduled for 3 p.m. to last for not more than one hour. This meant moving the Sunday School from 3 p.m. to 1.45 p.m., but with mass evacuation, there were only 26 Primary children, 75 in the Junior Bible Class and 68 in the Senior Bible Class, a total of 169, half the usual number and by far the lowest figure since 1902. When the Sunday afternoon service stopped with the lighter evenings at the end of February 1940, the Sunday School was restored to its usual time. Before the winter of 1940, with its resumption of the three o'clock adult service, the Sunday School had completely rearranged its classes and was able to keep its usual time.

There were only two exceptions to the not-after-3 p.m.-start ruling; they were the deaconess' Young Women's Meeting at 4.15 p.m. on Sunday and the Young Peoples Meeting, which had been on Wednesday evening; it now met on Sunday afternoon at 4.30 p.m., after the public service. The windows at street level, which gave light to the lower hall (present readers will have to imagine the building without the lounge) were bricked up and sandbagged, in case bombs were dropped during a service. It was October 1943 before the caretaker, acting on his own initiative and without authority, removed some of the bricks covering the windows of the ladies' room, which had been unventilated for over four years. The other brickwork remained in place until the deacons decided, in March 1945, that the danger of air raids was now minimal.

**A.R.P.:** In the event of an "alert" during a Service, please note that there is accommodation for **500 persons in the Hall downstairs.**

If the congregation is asked to take shelter when the church is full, persons under **30** are requested to use the nearby public shelters outside.

Occupants of this pew please leave in orderly manner by door numbered

All reasonable precautions for your safety have been taken.

*A buzzer was installed in the pulpit, to alert the preacher if evacuation was required. The public shelters mentioned in that notice (which was displayed in every pew) were under Charlotte Square gardens.*

The first air raid of the Second World War took place during the afternoon of 16 October 1939, when 14 German bombers attacked shipping anchored near the Forth Bridge. A fortnight later, the first Luftwaffe aircraft to be brought down on British soil was chased by Spitfires over the Pentlands and Dalkeith and crash-landed near Humbie in East Lothian. There was then a lull and the Chapel realized, at the end of November, that the expected blitzkrieg was not imminent. The Monday evening prayer meeting was resumed, and any auxiliary that wished to meet at its usual time in the evening was free to do so. The Sunday services remained at 11 a.m. and 3 p.m. until the middle of December, when the pastor called a special meeting of the deacons; they agreed that a third service should be held, at 6 p.m. This meant keeping every window absolutely lightproof, because Edinburgh's seven thousand volunteer air raid wardens patrolled the streets and rigidly enforced the blackout regulations. The practicality of getting home for tea after Sunday School and then back to Rose Street for 6 p.m. soon put the evening service back at its usual time of 6.30 p.m., from the first Sunday of February 1940.

Realising that the Chapel might be damaged in an air raid, the deacons had it surveyed in December 1940, so that they could state its true value in any insurance claim. From its pre-war value of £20,300, it had risen to £25,400 in less than two years.

*In 1940, the word EDINBURGH was (as seen in this picture) carefully obscured on the façade of the head office of the EDINBURGH SAVINGS BANK at the corner of Rose Street (a short distance east of the Chapel) and Hanover Street.*

Road signs, names on railway stations, shop names, even addresses on butchers' and bakers' vans, were removed so that German invaders would not know where they had landed.

## A sermon on evacuation

As mentioned, twenty-six thousand Edinburgh schoolchildren were evacuated to camps in the Lothians, but other schools went further afield; the writer's class and teachers were sent to Grantown-on-Spey. Some families preferred to make their own arrangements; Angus Ferguson recollects how his parents, not wishing him to go with his school contingent, arranged for his mother, his sister and himself to stay at a remote farm under Schiehallion mountain in Perthshire; the writer's wife, then aged four, went with her family to Strathyre, also in Perthshire. Looking back, it all seems unreal, but it was taken very seriously then, at least initially. The writer and the Fergusons were back in Edinburgh by the end of October. This was not untypical – the writer's father travelled by train from Oban to Glasgow on Saturday 16 September, a fortnight after the declaration of

253

war, and noted: 'Swarms of evacuated parents and kids returning to Glasgow; had enough of a country life.' By the beginning of 1940, when the expected German blitz had not taken place, nearly half of the evacuees, nationwide, had returned to their homes.

Ever topical in his preaching, Sidlow Baxter's afternoon sermon on Sunday 1 October 1939 began by drawing a parallel between the events of the past four weeks and the Evacuation/Exodus of Israel from Egypt:

*When the 'evacuation' was in progress, I could not help thinking of another and even greater evacuation which took place over three thousand years ago – that greatest evacuation in all history, namely, the exodus of Israel from Egypt. Most people have little idea what a stupendous transportation the Israelite 'Exodus' really was. Think of it – an entire race of people suddenly and forever flinging away the shackles of a generations-long servitude, and emigrating to a new country and a new corporate life.... Our 1939 'evacuation scheme' becomes small in comparison with it!*

---

2 *Record*, 1939, pp. 205, 214.

He went on, continuing the Exodus theme, to speak of the sacrifice of Christ as our Passover (1 Corinthians, 5:7).

*The farthest evacuation from the Chapel was when Angus MacLeod, aged 14 and a patrol leader in the Scout troop, went to New Zealand under the Children's Overseas Reception Scheme; this photograph was taken at his farewell party in 1940. From left to right: Donald Fleming, Graham Rae, Arnold Walker, Jack Cochrane, Jackie Cairns, Tom Scott, Eric Brown, Robert Aitken, Walter Lang, Angus MacLeod, Francis Miller.*

After six years in New Zealand, Angus came back to Scotland for tertiary education. He was ordained, married a girl from the Granton Baptist Church in Edinburgh, was student-pastor of the Peebles Baptist Church and had a pastorate in Whitley Bay for three years from 1954; in 1957 he accepted a 'call' back to New Zealand. In 1994, he spent three months in Edinburgh, researching and writing *75 years of Scouting: The Story of the 6th Edinburgh (Charlotte Chapel) Group*.

## Wartime activities

### Knitting for the Forces
Immediately after the declaration of war, Mrs Baxter mobilized the women of the Chapel to send parcels of knitted goods on a regular basis to everyone called up for military service. 'As wool price will increase, it is urgent to buy large quantities early.' Within three months, 20 were on the mailing list. Bars of chocolate and tablets of soap were slipped into the knitted articles. Letters of appreciation were printed regularly in the *Record*. In the first 18 months of the war, 631 items (socks, scarves, mitts, gloves, pullovers, chocolates, soap, toothpaste) were sent in 173 parcels.

*These Articles*

are sent with all kindly thoughts and with prayerful remembrance, from—

**Charlotte Baptist Chapel, Edinburgh.**

May God shield and bless the receiver of them during these days of war. The texts given below are full of cheer and comfort from the word of God, the Bible. May God bless you!

---

*Isaiah, chapter 41 verse 10 ; Hebrews, chapter 13 verse 6 ; John, chapter 3 verse 16 ; and chapter 5 verse 24.*

*This card was enclosed with every parcel sent from the Chapel to soldiers, sailors and airmen, whether in membership or not, who had any connection with the Chapel or who were relatives of members.*

The Missionary Christmas Parcel Scheme (Chapter 28) was discontinued; the goods that had already been assembled for the 1939 parcels were sold and the proceeds distributed as monetary gifts. The decision to stop sending these parcels seems, with hindsight, to have been premature – the Chapel's Women's Missionary Auxiliary continued to knit for Baptist Missionary Society stations and in 1942 sent three parcels to Nigeria and two to China, all of which arrived safely. The Chapel sent generous financial gifts to the missionaries in lieu of Christmas parcels.

## Meetings return to near-normality

During what has since been described as the 'phoney war', that is the lull between September 1939 and the German invasion of France and the Low Countries in May 1940, the Chapel gradually resumed normal activities. There was a Watchnight service on 31 December 1939, and the New Year conference on 1 January 1940 included an evening meeting. The Thursday Bible School resumed at 7.45 p.m.; with the lighter nights of spring, attendances picked up. The YPM moved back to Wednesday evening, but the deaconess' District Women's Meeting stayed with its blackout time on Thursday afternoon. The only casualty of the war was the 9.45 a.m. Young Men's Fellowship on Sunday, which had to be discontinued in November 1940 because most of those attending had been called up for military service.

From late May 1940 onward, until the imminent threat of cross-Channel invasion receded, the Chapel was open every day from 12.30-2 p.m., 'for prayer for our nation in its hour of crisis'. There was an open invitation to all Christians to attend, even if only for part of the time; Sidlow Baxter was encouraged by the number who came. The successful evacuation at Dunkirk was widely regarded as a miracle, in answer to prayer.

## Anniversaries and Thankofferings

The practice of holding a weekend of special meetings (Sunday and Monday), on the anniversary of the settlement of the current pastor, was continued throughout the war. Mr and Mrs Baxter and some of the elders were in the vestry on the Monday afternoon to receive gifts, and they continued to announce the total received at the end of the Monday rally. When the sirens sounded for an air raid during the Monday

meeting in October 1940, which proved to be genuine as several bombs were dropped on Edinburgh, Mrs Baxter remarked, as the congregation filed down to the security of the lower hall, 'we shall always be able to say that our fifth anniversary "went off with a bang!"' The 1940 Thankoffering was, despite wartime austerity, £100 more than the 1939 figure. As before, the anniversary weekend at the beginning of October marked the reopening of activities after the summer break and the launch of the winter work.

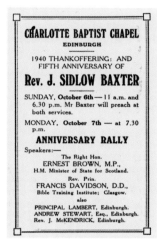 

*The 1940 anniversary leaflet. One of the guest speakers was the Member of Parliament for Leith, a fine Christian who spoke regularly in the Chapel.*

Just how much went on, despite the blackout and the shortage of leaders through conscription and ARP (air raid precautions) duties, is illustrated by a paragraph from Sidlow Baxter's anniversary letter in September 1940:

*Week by week, under consecrated leaders, the work goes on in our Sunday Schools, at the High Street and Jamaica Street missions, and at the Rock mission; in the hospitals, in the open air, in the monthly distribution of tracts, in the various missionary auxiliaries, in the Scouts and Guides, in the Young Peoples Meeting, and among the men of the forces, besides those other regular meetings and services connected with the work and witness of our Chapel. Obviously, such many-sided activity entails much expense; and, as costs have risen all round, we make confident appeal for a corresponding generosity in our Thankoffering this year.*

3 *Record*, 1940, p. 129.

## Closure of the High Street mission

Of all the auxiliaries mentioned by Sidlow Baxter in that anniversary letter, the one that struggled most with wartime restrictions was the High Street mission; adult meetings ceased and the work was fraught with many perplexities and difficulties. When an offer was received from a business in December 1941, the Chapel negotiated a sale of the premises, on the basis that the workers could continue as tenants until August 1943. The Chapel hoped to channel the funds and the personnel to a new mission in Sighthill, although the High Street remnant were not enthusiastic about that. The final meeting in the High Street premises, on 24 June 1943, concluded more than thirty years of dedicated outreach in a particularly needy community. By contrast, the Jamaica Street mission continued to be both vibrant and expanding throughout (and despite) the war. In October 1945, it rented two further rooms because the work was still growing.

## War-time conditions

Services in the Chapel may have given the appearance of near-normality, but life in Edinburgh was far from normal. On Sunday 3 November 1940, the writer's father attended the early morning prayer meeting, the morning worship service, the young people's class in the afternoon and the gospel service at night in Bellevue Chapel. When the sirens went off at 3 a.m. on the Monday morning, he got up and wrote in his diary:

*We carry identity cards; gas masks; tin hats.*

*Our houses are blacked-out; lights are masked; sand and water stand about for incendiary bombs, and stirrup pumps are handy. Windows are plastered with gauze or criss-crossed with strapping.*

*All sign-posts, directions and place-names are gone.*

*In the streets, there are sand-bags, anti-tank traps; in the country, barbed wire entanglements, trenches, posts & pillars to obstruct enemy aircraft; playing fields and parks are littered with rollers, seats, anything to make them useless as landing-grounds; everywhere are shelters for air-raids – basements, cellars, surface ones; every pleasant garden and many parks have been tunnelled into.*

*We cannot go where we would; the Western Highlands, Orkney & Shetland are debarred; much of the coast is closed off. Trains are uncertain. Motoring is almost excluded for want of petrol.*

*Separation is universal. Children are sent away from parents, wives from husbands. Irritation comes from unwilling guests thrust upon resentful hosts.*

*We are not free to speak as we want; letters are censored; it is hardly safe to use a camera. Even the weather forecasts are stopped.*

*The moon is unwelcome; it lights the way for the bomber. The darkness is equally hostile; people fall over obstacles, and lose the way; torches may only be used when considerably dimmed. Cars with their darkened lights can scarcely find their way, even with white lines on the streets.*

*Shortage prevails in many commodities. A pinch of sugar only in tea; a scrape of butter; strictly rationed tea, etc. Scarcity of paper; limited supplies of razor-blades; and many others.*

*Enormous taxation. Income tax 8/6 per £. Postage on a letter is 2½d. On a card 2d. Greatly diminished business for many.*

*Wailing sirens, warning us of the bomber; the explosions when the bombs drop; the fires started by incendiary bombs; demolished houses; fine old buildings, statues, works of art, reduced to dust; and the constant loss of life; mutilation; disease contracted through exposure; unsanitary conditions in shelters, which are packed all night to suffocation.*

*And yet with it all, we have much to give praise for; we really lack nothing essential; we are kept in perfect peace. God is over all. And we should be ever so much worse on the Continent.*

*This has been written during a heavy raid over Edinburgh, with German planes droning overhead, bombs bursting, and machine guns rattling, while the skies are brilliant with searchlights.*

4 Francis E. Balfour, unpublished diary.

*Air raid sirens sounded as Chapel members were going home from the annual general meeting on Monday 7 April 1941; many had to spend an uncomfortable night in the public shelters before the 'raiders gone' signal was given in the morning. This picture shows people (not Chapel members) leaving the shelters in Princes Street Gardens.*

### Sunrise on Arthur's Seat

As many activities were suspended for the duration of the war, it is encouraging to record one which started in 1940 and which has continued ever since. Chapel members responded to an invitation by the minister of the Canongate Church to attend Christian worship on the summit of Arthur's Seat at daybreak on 1 May 1940 (May Day). Appropriately, he included readings from the Sermon on the Mount. People also indulged in the ancient (pagan) practice of washing their faces in dew as the sun rose – although, strictly speaking, this was a ritual for females only, to make themselves more beautiful.

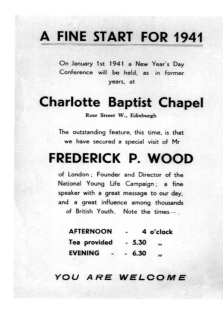

**A FINE START FOR 1941**

On January 1st 1941 a New Year's Day Conference will be held, as in former years, at

**Charlotte Baptist Chapel**
Rose Street W., Edinburgh

The outstanding feature, this time, is that we have secured a special visit of Mr

**FREDERICK P. WOOD**

of London; Founder and Director of the National Young Life Campaign; a fine speaker with a great message to our day, and a great influence among thousands of British Youth. Note the times—.

| AFTERNOON | - | 4 o'clock |
| Tea provided | - | 5.30 „ |
| EVENING | - | 6.30 „ |

**YOU ARE WELCOME**

*Sidlow Baxter tried to maintain Chapel life as near to normality as possible, arranging events as in former years. The New Year's Day conference included an evening meeting, even under blackout conditions.*

## Evangelism in wartime

### Sunday services

The morning service was held at 11 a.m. throughout the war, and was often described as well attended. As mentioned, another service was started at 3 p.m., for older people and others who were advised not to venture out during the blackout; it was held from the beginning of October to the end of February in 1939-40, 1940-41 and again in 1941-42. It was for Christians and it too was well attended; Sidlow Baxter preached on contemporary topics, which were not appropriate for the main worship service on Sunday morning. In January 1940, the evening service was resumed,

in addition to keeping the afternoon one. All three were relayed to the lower hall, not from necessity but because some were nervous about sudden air raids.

As during the First World War (Chapter 22), Chapel scouts invited service men and women, who were wandering along Princes Street, to come into the lower hall for tea and to stay for the evening service. It had always been evangelistic, with a particular appeal to the younger generation, but Sidlow Baxter now spoke directly and plainly to service people and other visitors to Edinburgh, who might never again be under the sound of the gospel. Bright singing with a piano and a straight gospel talk not only filled the building, but also had people coming back and back again. There were many Canadians from the beginning, and after the United States of America came into the war in 1941, Americans too responded well to the invitation, perhaps because they were more accustomed to church-going than young Britishers. The parallel outreach on Saturday evening is described in the next chapter.

Because of the nature of the wartime evening service, there was no evening communion for 18 months. Then some, who could never get to a morning service because of their employment, persuaded the elders to alternate the celebration of the Lord's Supper between morning and evening of the first Sunday of the month – and it also gave the opportunity of receiving new members on these evenings.

## Sunday Night at Seven!

This is to welcome you to the bright Sunday night "rendezvous" for young men and women of the Forces, and all others who can join in, at

### Charlotte Baptist Chapel
ROSE STREET (just off Charlotte Square)
"Community Singing"; cheering fellowship; and vital "Talks-to-the-Point"

## Every Sunday Night at Seven
BE SURE TO COME!

*During March 1942, 156 service men and women and 49 civilians accepted invitations from scouts on Princes Street, for tea in the lower hall prior to Sunday Night at Seven! (as described on the card).*

257

Scouting continued until the start of the service and the Chapel was usually full. As the nights grew lighter, people were reluctant to come indoors from the warm sunshine, so in April 1942, Sidlow Baxter moved the evening service back to 6.30 p.m., followed by a special Forces Meeting at 8 p.m.. This pattern continued for the rest of the war – in the summer months, the Chapel held a special Forces' outreach on Sunday at 8 p.m., after the evening service, preceded by tea, and for the rest of the year, the scouts invited service men and women walking along Princes Street to tea, and to stay for the ordinary evening service.

To cater for service personnel who wanted more, the caretaker and his wife held open house from November 1939, with up to 30 lonely lads and girls (as they described them) in their home for a cup of tea and family worship. This grew into the Upper Room Fellowship, held in the top hall during the winter months of 1941-42 and 1942-43, following the evening service in the Chapel; attendance varied from 15 to 48. In summer, another couple opened their home to any visiting service people who wanted Christian fellowship.

### Open-air outreach

Open-air preaching was held during the three summer months, as before the war, on Tuesday and Thursday at the Mound and on Wednesday, Saturday and Sunday at the corner of Princes Street, all at eight o'clock in the evening. Wartime visitors to Edinburgh, including troops, were more ready than the citizens of Edinburgh to stop and listen. The speaker had to use a portable pulpit, carried nightly from the Chapel to the location, because the authorities would not issue petrol coupons for the gospel caravan, which had been used as a platform. A rechargeable car battery powered the portable electric organ.

### Granton Baptist Church

Fortunately, the war did not dull the Chapel's appetite for evangelistic expansion in the Edinburgh area. Plans to build a mission hall in the new housing development at Sighthill, where the Chapel Sunday School had been carrying on summer open-air services for young people for some time, had to be discontinued when the city architect would not allocate a suitable site. However, as soon as the Chapel paid off the final cost for establishing the Stenhouse Baptist Church, in January 1940, the deacons responded to an appeal from the Edinburgh Baptist Association, for help with a new outreach in the Granton-Pilton area. The Association had reserved a site in Crewe Road North in 1938, and there were now twenty-four thousand people living in the area, mostly from slum clearances in older parts of the city. Money and building materials were in short supply, so a Chapel member, Andrew Ewing, owner of the Buttercup Dairies, provided a large wooden hut – his business included building huts for hens, to produce eggs for his shops. This allowed the new outreach to start on 9 July 1940, and it soon became the Granton Baptist Church. The initial membership was 19, and the first pastor was inducted on Saturday 14 December 1940. The Chapel contributed annually until a permanent building (the present one) was opened in 1952.

Andrew Ewing's death, in 1956, deprived the Chapel of a benefactor who for 50 years had quietly honoured the Sabbath day by (as mentioned in Chapter 25) giving all the eggs that his hens laid on Sunday to the Chapel deaconess or to the YPM, for distribution to shut-in and impoverished members. Many a guest preacher, at the Chapel or at one of its missions, found a pound of butter or a packet of bacon in his overcoat pocket, along with the pulpit fee.

*While the pastor was the editor, the* Record *depended on lay volunteers for its production and distribution. Robert Gillon (top left) and Lizzie Boyle (top right) were the assistant editors throughout the war; David Blair (bottom left) was* Record *secretary for 20 years, and was succeeded by John Coutts (bottom right).*

The Chapel's monthly magazine, the *Record*, which Sidlow Baxter had expanded to 20 pages and which was enjoying its highest ever circulation at the outbreak of war, had to be cut back through wartime economy to 12 pages (of which 2 were full-page advertisements to subsidize the cost).

## Public issues

### Broadcasting standards
Prompted by the congregation, Sidlow Baxter wrote to the chairman of the British Broadcasting Corporation on 28 June 1940:

*Our appeal to you is against the permission of indecent language in broadcasts. The other day, the postscript to the news began: 'We must work like hell'. Other terms, like 'damn' and 'devil' and 'God' and 'bloody' have been coming through, used in their profanest sense. We suspect, sir, that the strange idea exists in the minds of some at Broadcasting House, that these expressions give added emphasis – or what is commonly called 'pep' or 'kick' – to utterances; but the truth is that to all but a vulgar section of Britishers they are most revolting.*

5 *Record*, 1940, p. 125.

The reply would do credit to a twenty-first century spinner:

*I can assure you that the B.B.C. does indeed take upon itself the responsibility of ensuring that only suitable material is included in the broadcast programmes, and any questionable item is excluded whenever it can be detected in time.*

6 *Record*, 1940, p. 135.

### Actors speaking as Christ
Sidlow Baxter had another running battle with the wartime BBC. He and many others petitioned vigorously when the BBC persisted, despite many protests, in allowing actors to speak in religious broadcasts as if Christ was speaking. They distinguished reading Scripture on the wireless, of which they fully approved, from plays and dialogues where actors were given biblical characters to read, one of whom spoke his lines as if Christ was speaking – 'degrading our Lord's words to slangy paraphrases or distasteful jargon' such as 'You have been playing ducks and drakes with the estate'. When he got

no satisfaction from the BBC, Sidlow Baxter wrote an open letter to the king.

Present readers may not appreciate why Christians were so upset, especially as the author of the offending plays was Dorothy Sayers, but the writer recollects his father's distress when, in the late 1940s, a Christian film was released in which the Saviour was depicted as a glow of light among real actors (unobjectionable) and an actor spoke the words of Jesus as if from the light (objectionable, even although it was straight text from the Gospels, because no human should speak as if he were Christ).

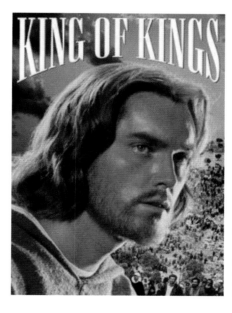

*There was even more concern when* King of Kings *was released in 1961, with the person of Jesus played on screen by an actor. Such films are now accepted without comment.*

### Commended standards
Mention of BBC standards may remind some older readers of the popular radio programme, *Two-Way Family Favourites*. As soon as the war was over in 1945, the BBC in London linked up with presenters attached to the British Army of Occupation of the Rhine. At Sunday lunchtime, while parents (including the writer's) were preparing lunch after attending the kirk, the family listened to Jean Metcalfe playing records requested by soldiers in Germany for their families at home, and vice versa. 'Aunty' had strict guidelines about who could participate and what could be played. Only married couples could take part – no requests were accepted from engaged couples and certainly not from girlfriends. No jazz (it was Sunday); acceptable music was 'Sheep May Safely

Graze' or Kathleen Ferrier singing 'What is Life Without You?', interspersed with Gilbert and Sullivan and ending with the 23rd Psalm or the 'Hallelujah Chorus'. No pop; no Mantovani.

## Government policy on intoxicating liquor

Sidlow Baxter had other wartime campaigns, in addition to those aimed at the BBC. He was outraged at government policy on intoxicating liquor. The Chapel had always campaigned for temperance (ideally for total abstinence), and regularly petitioned the government to reduce, not to increase, licensing hours and the availability of strong drink.

*The Brewers, by their intensive campaign, are filling our land with beer-drinkers again, are increasing our road-accidents, and are bringing moral ruin to numberless homesteads. Again and again young married people come to us Christian ministers, and tell us, through their streaming tears, of matrimonial unfaithfulness, of blighted hopes and blasted lives, of havoc and agony. My own experience is that in almost every case the beginning of the tragedy is traceable to the influence of drink, or the picture house, or both.*

---

7 Sidlow Baxter, *Britain's Greatest Need* (Warwick, Edinburgh, n.d.).

Sidlow Baxter had a point, when he reminded the authorities: 'Barley, grain, rice, and sugar, are being used in huge quantities to manufacture beer, while farmers, poultry-keepers, are very severely rationed.'

Additional information on the following topics, mentioned in this chapter, is available on the CD.

Andrew Ewing
High Street mission

*One page of the writer's ration book in January 1940. Bacon, butter and sugar were the first foodstuffs to require coupons, then meat, jam, biscuits, breakfast cereals, dairy products and canned fruit were added. Clothing was rationed from June 1941.*

# Chapter 35
# The war years from 1943 to 1945

## Pastoral work

### A war of attrition

As the war continued, most of the Chapel's young men and women were called up for the armed forces or other government service. It was not easy to replace them in the various organisations, especially since many of the older men volunteered for the Home Guard or became air-raid wardens, and were on duty on Sunday. From May 1941, women were required under government direction to be bus conductresses ('clippies') for the first time, initially on single-deck buses and then on all bus and tram services.

For a downtown church like Charlotte Chapel, the blackout created real problems; many members, especially the elderly, could not travel safely through darkened streets to get to evening meetings. Nevertheless, the church secretary counted 1,541 meetings on the Chapel premises during 1943. This included committee meetings – not even the war could eliminate them – but MacDuff Urquhart was delighted to find that 723 of the 1,541 were prayer meetings, which averaged two a day for every day of the year. In addition, there were 67 meetings arranged by outside organisations, such as missionary societies and the Baptist Union of Scotland, which involved the Chapel in caretaking, stewarding, catering and cleaning.

Sidlow Baxter quickly realized that people under stressful wartime conditions required a different message from the pulpit of pre-war days:

*Again and again, during those years, when I looked round the congregation from this pulpit I could see that you were in no disposition for elaborate sermonic analyses or closely reasoned treatises which might have been suitable enough in pre-war days. The need was for messages conveying sympathetic encouragement of a brotherly but discerning kind.*

1 *Record*, 1945, p.166.

### Membership statistics

When war broke out in 1939, membership stood at its highest-ever total of 1,129; however, the church treasurer kept questioning the accuracy of the roll. He pointed out that throughout the late 1930s, no names had been brought to

the congregation for removal, even of people who had moved away or who had stopped attending. Only those who had died, or who had asked for a certificate of transfer, or who were known to be attending another church, had been deleted. He wanted exact figures, because every Baptist church in Scotland was expected to pay an annual fee to the Baptist Union of Scotland, based on the membership figure returned to the Union. He persuaded the elders to look over the roll in 1940, but only 16 of the missing names were removed (Chapter 32). When the elders eventually took themselves in hand in June 1944 (below), they acknowledged that many of the names deleted then could not have been traced even before Sidlow Baxter came in 1935.

Chapel men, who had been 'called' to pastoral ministry elsewhere, but whose names were kept on as members of the Chapel (Chapter 32) were not the only anomalies. When Sister Sadie McLaren married a director of the well-known Kilmarnock publishing firm, John Ritchie & Co., she remained for the rest of her days on the Chapel roll, although living permanently in Ayr. When Chapel missionary Thomas Draper left India and took up medical practice in Leicester in 1946, his membership remained with the Chapel; contact was obviously minimal, because when someone spotted him at the morning service on Sunday 8 April 1951, the elders were astonished to learn that he was on his way back to India and that he had come to Edinburgh only to see his sons who lived here. The rule, which the elders enforced from time to time, that absence from the Lord's Table for six consecutive months was deemed to be resignation from membership, applied only to people who lived in the area and who could attend, and not to those who lived far away.

Another complicating factor, which worked the other way, was the large number who regarded the Chapel as their church, who attended faithfully and who brought their families, but who never joined. The obituaries in the *Record* regularly included phrases like: 'who was for years one of our most regular worshippers' and: 'though not a member with us, he was a very familiar figure as he often worshipped at our Sunday morning service'. Another entry on the same page of the *Record* read: 'The bride is a member with us … and the bridegroom, though not a member, is a regular worshipper at Charlotte Chapel'.

**Chapter 35**
The war years from 1943 to 1945

In the early 1940s, a new phrase appeared in the church secretary's annual report, the removal of those who had joined the Church of Scotland following marriage – 14 in 1941, 16 in 1942 and 7 in 1943. However, the treasurer kept pressing for a proper review, and when this was done in June 1944, 80 names were removed at a special congregational meeting. The church secretary explained:

*The Pastor and the Elders have for some time past been concerned about the state of the Church Roll of Members as there were so many names on the Roll, which undoubtedly ought to come off, as many of these former members had left the city without any notification, many of them had married and gone with their husbands to other Churches and a number could not be traced at all....*

*The actual figures are as follows:*

| | | | |
|---|---|---|---|
| *Last Year's Membership [1943]* | | | *1108* |
| | | | |
| *Additions:* | *By Baptism* | *11* | |
| | *By Transfer* | *5* | |
| | *Total additions:* | | *16* |
| | | | |
| *Removals:* | *By Death* | *17* | |
| | *By Transfer* | *14* | |
| | *By Revision* | *80* | |
| | *Total removals:* | | *111* |
| | | | *95* |
| | | | |
| *Present Membership [1944]* | | | *1013* |

2 *Record*, 1945, p. 77.

### Family occasions during the war

Funerals were still usually on Sunday, conducted by the pastor. The normal pattern was a service in the home, followed by a committal at the grave. For very well-known members, there was a service in the Chapel itself, prior to going to the cemetery, but one had to be exceptionally well known for this to happen – for most, the family met in the home and other mourners gathered at the grave.

Dedication of children was mostly in the home, some on Sunday, and others on every day of the week. There was,however one in the vestry at the end of the Sunday afternoon service, so the choice was there. This continued to be the pattern after the war – one weekend in November 1947, a family invited Mr Baxter to their house on Saturday afternoon, while another family brought the baby to the vestry after the Sunday morning service. There were weddings galore, under wartime conditions, some in a hotel, but the majority in the Chapel.

Elizabeth Boyle, the deaconess, continued to make over one thousand home visits every year – 1,460 in the year 1944, when there was a lot of illness and an exceptional number of bereavements. Members dropped a note into a box in the vestibule, with particulars of anyone needing a pastoral visit. Sidlow Baxter called personally in serious cases. Mrs Beatrice Ferguson, Angus' mother, related, with a twinkle in her eye, how she had been in the Edinburgh Royal Infirmary for a minor operation. Unknown to her, another Chapel member was further down the ward, seriously ill. Sidlow Baxter came into the ward, looking for the latter. As he passed, he spotted Mrs Ferguson and came over to her bed. 'Mercy, pastor', she said in genuine alarm, 'I knew I was ill, but am I ill enough to have a visit from you?'

### Lack of news from the Forces

In contrast to the monthly list in the *Record*, of Chapel members serving in the Forces during the Kaiser's War, followed by lengthy excerpts from their letters, there was almost no mention in the magazine of members, men or women, called up for active service during World War Two. Acknowledgements of parcels gave only the recipient's initials; there is no obvious explanation for this difference in editorial policy. It cannot have been security, because the vice-president of the YPM wrote a full page every month, mentioning by name those of YPM age who were away, and where they were stationed.

The first Chapel fatality of the war was when HMS *Calypso* was torpedoed in the Eastern Mediterranean, south of Crete, in June 1940. In December 1941, more than 70 Christmas letters were sent from the Chapel, 20 of them to men and women serving overseas. For the following Christmas, 1942, the pastor sent a letter and a monetary gift of five shillings to 150 members or regular attenders, who had been conscripted. From January 1943, their names were read from the pulpit on the second Sunday of every month, but there was still no list in the *Record*. For Christmas 1943, Sidlow Baxter wrote to two hundred young men and women who were either members or attenders.

These were anxious days for parents, wives and children. The *Record* sympathized with the widowed mother of young Robert Smith, of Arden Street, who heard nothing for nearly two years after the Japanese over-ran his camp in the Far East; eventually, a card arrived to say that he was a prisoner of war. Another member, whose son had been reported missing when the Japanese captured Singapore in 1942, also waited anxiously for two years before word came that he too was a prisoner (and not killed). The Japanese would not accept letters from this country with more than 25 words, so pastor and friends devised a telegraph style and collated their messages.

## Mini conferences

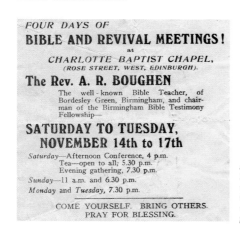

*A feature of wartime life in the Chapel was mini-conferences, that is, days of consecutive meetings with a guest preacher.*

Following Mr Boughen (above) in November 1942:

*From Saturday to the following Thursday, March 6th to 11th [1943], we had the Rev. W. Myrddin Lewis, of Birmingham, at the Chapel for special meetings for the deepening of the spiritual life. We look back on them with gratitude. They brought uplift and challenge to all who came, and the growing attendances testified to the enjoyment of the gatherings.*

3 *Record*, 1943, p. 39.

One of the three guest speakers at the October 1944 conference was Alan Redpath, later minister of the Chapel from 1962 to 1966.

## Deeds of covenant

The Chapel was slow to use deeds of covenant, through which charities could reclaim income tax – 'the chancellor gives you the choice of paying your tax to the government or to the Chapel'. It was not the church treasurer but the deacons' court secretary who pressed for action in 1944. Mr Baxter was enthusiastic and the elders resolved that the scheme should be commenced without delay. However, some members had reservations about whether Christians should use it; when the deacons learned that a respected senior and influential member had very strong views against the adoption of the scheme, they did not take it to the membership. The article that Sidlow Baxter had written for the January 1945 *Record* did not appear until March 1952.

Even then, the scheme attracted only three covenanters. With the top rate of income tax at 50 per cent, the (now enthusiastic) treasurer pointed out that over the next seven years, he would recover £2,000 from the Inland Revenue through these three alone. Since, however, deeds of covenant were binding for seven years, although never in practice enforced if the donor's circumstances worsened, few were prepared to commit themselves. Eighteen years later (1970), the number of covenanters had risen to 50, contributing (including tax recovered) £6,034 of the Chapel's annual income of £9,657. Regular publicity over the next 34 years, and the introduction of one-off Gift Aid in place of seven-year (later four-year) deeds of covenant, meant that in the year 2004, 430 members and regular attenders used the Gift Aid scheme; the Chapel received £851,560 (including tax refund) from them and £160,596 from everybody else, although half of the Gift Aid figure came from one-off donations for a new building at Niddrie (Chapter 56).

## Sunday School in wartime

### A typical twelve months

The Chapel gave high priority to its Sunday School during (perhaps because of) the disruption of normal life during the war. Going chronologically through a typical year:

*Annual prize giving*

The Sunday School ran with the calendar year, so in late December or early January, all the departments met together on one Sunday, for the presentation of book prizes for good attendance. This was not a social occasion, but various choirs participated and Sidlow Baxter spoke.

### Sunday School Scripture Examination

Organized by the Baptist Union of Scotland, this was held in the spring, and was fiercely competitive, both against other churches and internally. As mentioned earlier, it was intensively coached and prepared for. Prizes were presented on the closing day of the Sunday School in June; the Union donated prizes for only the top five places, but in order to encourage all Chapel children, the Sunday School committee presented a prize to everyone who achieved 90 per cent or more. A dozen or more regularly did so, and in 1942, two Chapel scholars in the lower senior category achieved one hundred per cent, the only ones in the United Kingdom to do so. Both of them, Sheila Meiklejohn (Finlayson) and Angus Ferguson, were still in active membership until Sheila died on 21 January 2007.

### Young Worshippers League

Every Sunday, markers were positioned on the stairs to stamp the card of every Sunday School pupil who had joined the league; prizes were given out during a morning service in June. Evacuation disrupted the league for a while, but soon many were again achieving perfect attendance, 52 weeks in the year at either the morning or the evening service, or holiday equivalent.

### Picnic

This was held on a Saturday in June; Liberton Park or Spylaw Park, Colinton, which were accessible by trams, chartered for the outing, were popular venues during the war. Parents were invited, and there were games and refreshments. The Sunday School closed for the summer on the following day, until the autumn. It was 1949 before special trains could again be chartered, and the first post-war all-day picnic went back to Ratho. The Sunday School claimed that their chartered train to Kirknewton in June 1951 took them farther afield than ever before. Many local railway stations operated around the Lothians until the Beeching axe in 1955; the Chapel's Longstone Sunday School chartered a personal train from Kingsknowe to Davidson's Mains for their outing in 1950, and to Midcalder in 1955.

### Camps

The Scouts and Guides were part of the Sunday School, so their summer camps, the boys at Heriot and the girls at Carlops in 1942 and at Heriot again and Balerno in 1943, were an integral part of Chapel life.

### Saughton Park

While the Sunday School was in summerrecess, the teachers encouraged pupils to support an open-air Sunday School at 3 p.m. on Sunday afternoon, at the bandstand beside the paddling pool in Saughton Park. The teachers visited the area in the morning, encouraging local children to attend, and many useful contacts were made. Up to two hundred gathered every Sunday for the ten weeks of the summer vacation. Conversions were reported and good seed was sown. The outreach continued after the war, but the teachers found it increasingly hard to gather children – in 1946 they saw themselves as 'Pied Pipers', combing the park for an audience while others led singing and speaking for those already at the bandstand.

The driving force behind the summer Sunday School in Saughton Park was Miss Agnes McPhail. Professionally, she taught for 22 years in the primary day school in Balgreen, from its opening until her retirement; her love for her pupils motivated her not only to run a Scripture Union group in the school but also to reach out to others in the local Saughton Park.

*Miss Agnes McPhail, the driving force behind the summer Sunday School in Saughton Park, was superintendent of the primary department of the Chapel's Sunday School for 40 years. This photograph was taken in 1950 in the garden of her home in Lanark Road.*

### Sunday morning in Princes Street Gardens

When Edinburgh Corporation arranged 'Holidays at Home' activities for children who could not get away for a summer vacation, the Chapel Sunday School seized the opportunity of contributing, even although it meant missing the Chapel's morning service for those involved. Chapel members led the convention (as it was called on the publicity leaflet, below) in July 1943, 1944 and 1945, while the Sunday School choir led the singing and rendered special pieces as well.

**CHILDREN and YOUNG PEOPLE OF EDINBURGH**

During the Summer Vacation Period at

**THE BANDSTAND AND ENCLOSURE**
PRINCES STREET GARDENS

under Edinburgh Corporation Holidays at Home Programme

**A SERIES OF**
**SUNDAY FORENOON OPEN-AIR CONVENTIONS**

will be held, weather permitting, each Sunday,
commencing on

**SUNDAY 4th JULY, at 11.15 a.m.**

Bright Community Singing     Interesting Addresses for Young People

**ALL SEATS FREE**

*In addition to presenting their own adult service in the bandstand on Sunday afternoon (below), the Chapel provided leaders for the Corporation's children's programme on Sunday morning in July from 1943 to the end of the war.*

### Church parades

From time to time, the whole Sunday School attended the Sunday morning service and sat together in the centre area of the church; either Sidlow Baxter or a visiting speaker addressed them and their parents. In addition, there was an annual (or oftener) parade of the uniformed organisations, that is Scouts, Cubs, Rangers, Guides and Brownies. They sat together in the gallery, in full array; since participation in these groups was (then) conditional on membership of the Sunday School, it was another way of introducing young people to the Chapel's adult services.

### Anniversary

Apart from the heightened profile that the Sunday School anniversary service gave to its regular work, all the offerings on that Sunday went for the work of the School. A junior choir occupied the choir stall at both services, and contributed a couple of pieces as well as leading the congregational singing.

### Christmas parties

The Primary, Junior and Senior departments had their separate socials during December, much as before the war.

## Evangelism in wartime

### Saturday evening meetings

As described in the previous chapter, Sunday evening services were resumed in January 1940; Sidlow Baxter soon adapted them to appeal directly to the soldiers, sailors and air force personnel who had been brought in from Princes Street by the scouts. Equally effective were the Chapel's Saturday evening gospel meetings, held weekly at 7.30 p.m. from December 1939 to June 1945. As on Sunday afternoon, Chapel scouts invited anyone in uniform wandering along Princes Street to come into the Chapel for tea, followed by singing and a clear gospel message. From the beginning, there were usually more than 50 servicemen present.

Only men were invited at first, and the meeting was officially called the 'Homely Hour for the Men of the Forces'. The scouts were delighted at how many of their guests made professions of conversion after the meeting. In 1942, the leader recommended that they should invite everyone in uniform, and he soon reported: 'since our meetings were opened to the young women as well as to the young men, many conversions have taken place among the uniformed young women.' The earliest extant visitors' book for the Forces Fellowship Meeting, from April 1943, has many women signatories – 50 per cent on some pages.

While many accepted invitations to Saturday evening meetings during the autumn, winter and spring, few would come indoors between July and September; accordingly, the Saturday outreach to the Forces, like most Chapel auxiliaries, broke for the summer months. A Christian soldier, who turned up early on Easter Saturday 1944, recorded his impressions:

*As I waited patiently in the Lecture Room [lower hall], in came scout after scout, some bringing four, others six members of the Forces. Meanwhile tea was being served by the other workers, and still the lads and girls came in; and strange to narrate, there was an unusual number of A.T.S. girls. After tea the leader introduced a deputation led by Mrs Baxter (wife of the pastor) … The large audience listened with rapt attention, and throughout it was a happy and impressive gathering.*

4 *Record*, 1944, p. 70.

Neither the Saturday nor the Sunday Forces' meetings were restarted after the summer break in 1945, partly because the war was over (although many service people were still coming to Edinburgh on holiday and in uniform) and partly because the workers were exhausted.

### Ross Bandstand services

The Town Council gave the Chapel permission to use the auditorium known as the Ross Bandstand in West Princes Street Gardens for evangelistic services on five consecutive Sunday afternoons in May and June 1943. The Hammond organ and amplifiers were included in the let, so the gospel message could be heard throughout the large seated area (still there) and all over the gardens. It was the first time that a single congregation had been allowed to have evangelistic services in this location. Sidlow Baxter led and preached in his own inimitable way, supported by solos, duets, community singing and testimonies.

About three thousand people in total came into the seated enclosure over the five weeks, but others listened in the gardens or leaning on the Princes Street railings. Similar permission was given for three consecutive Sundays in May and June 1944, when the crowds were even larger, with over two thousand on the last Sunday, in addition to hundreds more listening along the length of the gardens. From 1945 to 1947, the Chapel was allotted the last two Sundays in May and the first two in June (all of June in 1947); except when the weather was poor, there was a wonderful crowd. In 1948, a United Churches group asked for these dates, so the Chapel could no longer hold its own service.

*The sitting area of the Ross Bandstand in West Princes Street Gardens. There are no extant photographs of a Chapel service – these people are at a children's concert, in which the Chapel took part, as set out above.*

### Missionary activity during the war

When war was declared in 1939, there were 25 Chapel missionaries. Five were in China, one in Hong Kong, three in India, three in Congo, three in Nigeria, two in Bolivia, one in Colombia and seven were on furlough in Edinburgh. Travel permits were hard to come by, and those who got permission for sea voyages were exposed to submarine attack. The five in China were worst affected – May Weightman, who married in China in 1940 (now Mrs Kennedy), received no mail from the Chapel between 1939 and 1944; neither George Bolster nor his sister Maida (now Mrs Contento) was able to leave China throughout the war; Douglas Robertson and Alison Ballantyne came home on furlough from China in October 1939 and December 1941 respectively, and both were still waiting in 1945 for government permission to return. John Fisher was interned in Hong Kong in May 1942. Christian McTaggart, home from Ludhiana in India in October 1941, was still here at the end of 1944. The two families in South America were trapped there – the McNaughtons in Colombia until 1944, nine years without furlough, and the Clarks in Bolivia until 1946.

No new missionaries were commissioned from the Chapel during the war, but when Sidlow Baxter arranged a meeting in the Chapel at Christmas 1943, for missionaries on furlough to meet prospective new missionaries, seven members in training outnumbered the six then on furlough.

## Chapel guests

### Baptist Missionary Society

Every year in March, the Chapel invited the Baptist Missionary Society to provide speakers for the Sunday morning service, the Sunday School and the Monday evening prayer meeting, in what was called their 'annual deputation'. The elders were slightly defensive when the missionary nominated for the 11 a.m. service was a woman, so Sidlow Baxter did everything except give the sermon; to their credit, the elders were fulsome in praise for the messages given. On Sunday 25 July 1948, they invited a French woman, the pastor of the Tabernacle Church in Paris, to preach the sermon at the morning service, and they reported favourably on her impassioned appeal for evangelistic work.

## Baptist Union of Scotland

The most robust meeting ever held in Charlotte Chapel came to its climax on Thursday 25 October 1944. What has become known as the modernist debate started with widespread concern that 35 Baptist ministers had resigned in the previous 30 years, many moving to other denominations. The Baptist Union of Scotland set up a commission of inquiry in 1941, to find out what was wrong. Its report, largely blaming the financial strain endured by ministers in smaller congregations, was discussed at the 1943 Assembly and remitted to the churches for comment; decisions were to be taken at the 1944 Assembly. During the discussion year, John Shearer, president of the Union in 1936, wrote a booklet denouncing the conclusions of the inquiry as sheer evasion of facts. He claimed that the real cause of denominational malaise was that modernism was being taught to students at the Baptist Theological College of Scotland. Sidlow Baxter reproduced the entire booklet in the *Record*, and gave his personal endorsement of it. The Chapel's position at the 1944 Assembly was basically that of Shearer, although more temperately expressed.

The press were excluded from the debate in the Chapel on that Thursday morning in October 1944 – just as well. The formal minute is bland – that some wanted the Union to dissociate itself from its allegedly wayward College, and that others wanted the Union to take over direct control of it. However, when George Hossack, mentioned in Chapter 1 as the leader of the Baptist Heritage Trail, died in 1997, his family offered his books to the College. He had been away on military service in 1944, but tucked inside the papers from the 1944 Assembly was a full transcript of the debate, which his wife, May, had taken down in shorthand and sent to him that very night. It describes the passion and personalities involved in the debate, argument and counter-argument, which the formal minute does not even hint at.

Not only was the teaching policy of the College bitterly attacked, but also the orthodoxy of individual staff members by name. Shearer

*shouted that it [the material produced] was full of Modernistic teaching – it denied the Miracles of Christ.... There were jeers and cat-calls, and calls of support too, from all over the meeting ... the row and hubbub was terrific. It was proposed that the Union should take over the College, because of what Shearer*

*called 'the cancerous growth of Modernism.' 'The College,' he said, 'denies that this Book is the Word of God.... It is robbing us of our evangelical faith.... The College is an evil thing and unclean.... I have proof that ... two of the present tutors are Unitarians.*

---

5 K.B.E. Roxburgh, 'The Fundamentalist Controversy Concerning the Baptist Theological College of Scotland', *Baptist History and Heritage*, Winter/Spring 2000, 36.1/36.2, pp. 252-3.

The principal of the College challenged Shearer to name the two leaders of the College who were Unitarians. Shearer stood up and yelled at Holms Coats: 'The two are yourself and Dr Miller'. May Hossack commented that 'the meeting went quite wild at this point.'

## The Evangelical Baptist Fellowship

The Assembly debate did not solve anything, so John Shearer and others formed a rival Evangelical Baptist Fellowship, which sponsored its own Bible College (the contrast in name was not accidental). The leadership of the Chapel was deeply involved in it, although when the delegates from the 1944 Assembly reported to the next deacons' court, there was no discussion and the subject was officially closed. There is, however, no doubt where Sidlow Baxter's sympathies lay: 'Despite wintry weather, an eager and expectant company gathered in Charlotte Chapel on Saturday 17th February [1951], to witness the induction of Dr Henry S. Curr [an old Chapel boy] as Principal of the new Evangelical Baptist College.' Mr Baxter chaired the meeting, conducted the induction and said: 'Dr Curr has caught our own vision as to the college.' The *Record* carried a verbatim report of his defence of the project 'which we now sponsor'. It lasted for a few years, but then as passions cooled, both its former secretary and its former treasurer were elected presidents of the Union, in 1959 and 1965 respectively.

There was, nevertheless, a legacy for the next 60 years. Union-College relationships were on the agendas of both bodies from time to time; the writer, as law agent to the Baptist Union of Scotland from 1966 and also honorary secretary of the Baptist Theological College of Scotland (later the Scottish Baptist College), not infrequently had to soothe the antagonistic memories of those who, or whose parents, had been hurt by the personal nature of the exchanges in 1944. It was October 2002 before the two bodies entered into a formal and mutually acceptable relationship, and unhappy memories passed into history.

## Pocket Testament League

Helen Cadbury, one of the family of English chocolate-makers, believed from her schooldays: 'If only we can get people to read the book for themselves, it will surely lead them to Christ.' She began the Pocket Testament League in 1893, and after she married the evangelist Charles Alexander (of the Chapman-Alexander mission team) in 1904, it became a worldwide movement. It has now given away more than ninety-five million copies of its distinctive copy of the New Testament, Psalms, pictures, hymns and membership card.

*Elizabeth Rudland was converted in Charlotte Chapel at the age of ten. She was baptized by Sidlow Baxter on 22 February 1943 and joined the church on the following Sunday. At her funeral in 1998, her family asked the Chapel to accept her Pocket Testament as a memento of her life.*

## VE Day and VJ Day

### Anticipation

In the spring of 1945, the Chapel made plans to hold a public thanksgiving service as soon as hostilities in Europe ended. The public knew nothing about the development of an atomic bomb, and assumed that the war against Japan still had a long way to go. Advertisements in *The Scotsman* and *Edinburgh Evening News*, from the first week in April onward, announced that an evening service would be held on the day that armistice was announced – Chapel auxiliaries were alerted to cancel whatever they had planned for that evening and to join the larger gathering:

Sidlow Baxter was not able to contribute to the preparations for this. He had not taken a proper holiday throughout the war, but had given himself unstintingly to the preaching and pastoral needs of the Chapel. His 'stupid, long-continued overstrain of the nervous system' (his words) led to a breakdown in health in January 1945. The doctors ordered complete rest until the beginning of May. He was back just in time to conduct the 'Victory in Europe' thanksgiving service on Tuesday 8 May. In the meantime, a retired minister, in Chapel membership, led the Thursday Bible School and conducted weddings and funerals, while visiting preachers supplied the pulpit.

'Now that the war is over, there will be no more black-out'; the deaconess moved her Women's District Meeting, an outreach to tired women and mothers in the Chapel neighbourhood, from Thursday afternoon back to its pre-war time on Wednesday evening. Attendance increased right away – including some who had not been able to attend since the outbreak of war.

### Demobilisation

Almost immediately, two Chapel members who had been prisoners of war in Germany, one since Dunkirk in 1940, were welcomed back, together with key figures from the pre-war Chapel Sunday School, such as Donald Cormack (father of the present member), who had been called up in September 1939 and who had been in France and India ever since.

Sidlow Baxter was recuperating on holiday when Japan surrendered on Wednesday 15 August 1945, after the detonation of an atomic bomb over Nagasaki. The elders led a service of thanksgiving that same evening, after which the caretaker plugged in his radio receiver and the congregation listened to a broadcast to the nation by King George VI.

There was particular relief when three members, who had been prisoners of war of the Japanese, and another who had been interned by them, came home safely in November 1945. Eric Lomax, mentioned in chapter 33, was welcomed back to the Chapel on Sunday 7 November and married there on Tuesday 20 November. That fortnight was not untypical of the calls on Sidlow Baxter to conduct weddings for those who had waited so long to be together – he officiated on Saturday 10, Monday 12, Tuesday 20 and Wednesday 28 November 1945.

Slowly, other servicemen and women were demobilized. The first welcome home meeting was held in the lower hall on 19 December 1945, when 25 were given a handshake and presented with a book by Mr Baxter. The next one was on 22 May 1946, when 19 men and 6 women were the guests at a social and tea in the lower hall.

## War memorial

Sadly, nine men did not come back. Their names were added to the plaque on the wall of the vestibule, commemorating those who died in the 1914-18 war. It was dedicated at an impressive service on Sunday morning, 29 April 1951. The uniformed organisations paraded at the front of the church and, with the congregations standing, one young man and one young woman, who had served in the war, carried wreaths from the communion table and hung them on the tablet.

## Vestry hour

With the ending of blackout regulations, Sidlow Baxter was able to resume the practice, which Christopher Anderson had started in 1806 and which all the pastors of the twentieth century had continued, of being available in the Chapel vestry, without prior appointment, between 7 and 8 p.m. on Monday evening. This was to interview any who wished to discuss baptism or membership, or who had pastoral problems on which they sought advice. It was a natural time to be there, because Sidlow Baxter usually led (and also played the piano at) the church prayer meeting in the lower hall at 8 p.m. His repeated statement, that he could not sustain his ministry unless the members gathered on Monday evening for prayer, led some of the older folk to protest when the day was changed to Tuesday in 1996. The objection was not just to change, but also to a conviction that Monday evening was the time to pray home the messages of the previous day.

## The effects of war

Shortly before the end of the war, Sidlow Baxter expressed a concern, shared by many Christians, about the long-term moral cost of the conflict.

*So far as the outward and visible contest of armed forces is concerned, we are definitely winning; yet in another sense which is even more vital, we are losing the war badly.... we are throwing away those very same Christian heritages for which we are ostensibly fighting.... Never has the secularization of the Lord's Day gone to such lengths in Britain as during this war. Never within memory has there been such drunkenness, obscenity and unchastity. Never has there been more abandon to vulgar amusement or a more contemptuous disregard of divine things.... the war which is being won in the outward and visible sense is bleeding away the nation's truest life.*

---

6 *Record*, 1945, p. 4.

Additional information on the following topics, mentioned in this chapter, is available on the CD.

Agnes McPhail
Annual report
Deaconess
Deeds of covenant
Maida Contento
Mary Weightman (Kennedy)
Ministry
Missionaries
Thomas Draper
Young Worshippers League

# Chapter 36
# Post-war reconstruction (1945–1948)

## Renewed missionary interest

### Around the world in four days

With the end of the war in sight, Sidlow Baxter planned a long weekend missionary conference, from Friday 25 to Monday 28 May 1945. The children's programme on the Friday extended over two and a half hours, consisting of 15-minute talks on Africa, China, India and Palestine, interspersed with the exhibition of curios and refreshments. There was a further six hours of meetings for adults over the weekend. It was hailed as a great success, and a similar four-day event took place in September 1946.

> **WORLD-WIDE-MISSIONS' EXHIBITION**
> at
> **Charlotte Baptist Chapel**
> ——————
> Curios from Africa, China, India, New Hebrides,
> Palestine, Syria, and South America
> Interesting Missionary Items, Lantern Slides,
> Native Music, etc.
> FRIDAY, (for Children) 6.30 to 9 p.m.
> SATURDAY (for Adults) 3 to 9 p.m.   TEA, 5 p.m.
> **Tea Tickets, 1/-**
> *All Offerings to be for World-Wide Missions*
> SUNDAY, 27th MAY, 11 a.m., 3 and 6.30 p.m.
> **Special Missionary Services**
> MONDAY, 28th MAY, 7.30 p.m.
> **Final Missionary Rally**

*The May 1945 missionary conference attracted so much interest that another was held in September 1946.*

Missionaries, whose travel had been severely restricted during the war, were now free to move again. When Marjory Sommerville eventually got a berth on a ship for China in 1946, she discovered 69 other missionaries on board, 13 of them with her own Society, the China Inland Mission. When she changed ships in Hong Kong, for the final section to Shanghai, she met not only another Chapel member, John Fisher, whose ship had 45 missionaries bound for China, but another ship where 400 of the 1,500 on board were newly-arrived American missionaries.

### Thirty-two Chapel missionaries

In October 1945, 32 Chapel members were on overseas missionary service, the highest number in the Chapel's history so far. Of these, 17 had been valedicted by Graham Scroggie, 8 had been commissioned by other churches but had later transferred their membership to the Chapel, while the other 7 had answered the missionary 'call' during Baxter's ministry. In addition: 'about twenty of our younger men and women are at this very moment just completing training, or in the midst of training, or about to enter training, for full-time ministry at home or abroad.' These commitments grew out of a lively interest in the missionary cause from a young age, illustrated by the formation of a monthly Missionary Band.

### Missionary Band

Because of the interest shown by the children and young people of the Chapel in the May 1945 conference and exhibition, a Missionary Band was started in October. It met monthly, at 4.30 p.m. on the third Sunday of the month, until 1982. Tea was provided in the lower hall at the conclusion of the Sunday School at 4 p.m. – the children brought their own eatables – after which a missionary on furlough (not necessarily from the Chapel) spoke and missionary magazines were available. A decade later, when it restarted after the summer in 1955 – because, like most Chapel auxiliaries, it broke for the summer – 64 youngsters were present, an equal numbers of boys and girls. Most of them stayed on for the evening service.

In common with other Chapel auxiliaries, the Missionary Band had its own summer outing. When the writer became missionary secretary in 1963, it was a pleasure to attend the Missionary Band, and to see the enthusiasm of the youngsters for news from 'Foreign Fields', as they were known at the time. This was before the days of package holidays to far-away places, so a speaker from France could be as novel as one from China. In 1970, up to 80 stayed after Sunday School, for it was essentially an extension of the 3 p.m. Sunday School, and ages ranged from 8 to 16.

The format was so popular that when Gerald Griffiths suggested, in 1957, having a similar hour for adults on the last Sunday of every month, at 4.30 p.m., 60 turned up for the first meeting of the Missionary Circle. A different region of the world was studied every month, with the object of stimulating prayer interest for new areas and new missions. 'Come prepared to think as well as pray!'

## Steady growth

### Sidlow Baxter's tenth anniversary

Two months after the Japanese surrender in August 1945, Sidlow Baxter celebrated his tenth anniversary in the Chapel. The weekend followed the traditional pattern, except that no blackout was necessary for the evening meeting. It is difficult, now, to appreciate the psychological boost of having windows and streets illuminated for the first time since 1939. There were packed congregations on Sunday morning and evening, with 19 new members received during the Lord's Supper after the morning service. 'Packed' in those days meant that there was not a single vacant seat – the stewards shoehorned 13 people into the central section of the pews downstairs and 7 into each of the side pews.

On the Monday, Mr and Mrs Baxter and some of the elders were in the vestry from one o'clock to seven o'clock, to receive gifts for the Thankoffering and to exchange friendly greetings. There was the usual public rally in the evening, with two guest speakers. The total of the Thankoffering was announced at the end of the meeting, and mention of just over £800 prompted the heartfelt singing of the doxology.

Sidlow Baxter took the opportunity of reviewing the ten years – four of them years of peace, and six of them years of war.

*during these ten years it has been our privilege to welcome nearly 600 new members. And remember that in an evangelical Baptist Church like this, such a number means more than in certain other churches and denominations where a clear-cut confession of conversion and baptism by immersion are not made a prerequisite of membership. Each applicant here is required to fill in a questionnaire, including a declaration of belief, then come for interview with two of the Elders and the Pastor, and to obey the Lord's command in baptism. unless either already baptised or excusable on physical grounds.*

*Second, we gratefully record that besides these 600 new members there have been close on 400 baptisms. And again remember that there are no persons baptised here without satisfactory evidence to us that there has been a real experience of saving grace in the heart.*

1 *Record*, 1945, pp. 166, 173.

## Unusual baptisms and membership

Baptisms continued to be held on Monday or Thursday evening, and new members were received at the communion service on the first Sunday of the month. The autumn of 1945 saw three departures from established practice. At the Lord's Supper on Sunday 5 August, 20 new members were received, 6 men and 14 women. There was nothing unusual in that. On Monday 6 August, 17 were baptized, 4 men and 13 women. There was nothing unusual in that either. But 3 of the men received on the Sunday, and 10 of the women, were not baptized until the Monday. Membership (at that time) was restricted to baptized believers, or those excused on medical grounds, so the sequence over that first weekend in August was back to front.

There was another novelty at the baptismal service on Monday 17 December 1946.

*Just after the benediction had been pronounced a fine-looking Canadian soldier made request for immediate baptism – having been much impressed by the service. He was able to give a good confession of his faith in the Saviour, and was well-known to one or two of our members who were able to confirm his testimony, so he quickly prepared and was baptised, with many of those who had been at the meeting staying behind to witness it.*

2 *Record*, 1946, p.10.

The third unusual occurrence was at the October communion. Three new members were received in absence, along with 16 others who were present – the first time this phrase was used. It seems they were absent on military duties, while their spouses were to be received personally, so they were accepted at the same time, instead of waiting until they had leave. The next record of a welcome in absence was in 1994, when a Chapel member who had been studying in America was delayed on his way back. The final one was in 1996, when a recently converted schoolteacher volunteered to give the first year of her retirement to work in a school for missionaries' children in Malaysia; she was on her way there when she was received in absence. In 2006, an applicant for membership who was shortly to go overseas was received during the morning service – not a communion Sunday – in the middle of August; unusual, perhaps unique, but a more imaginative way around a tight timetable than being received *in absentia*.

271

*Most travel within the city boundary was by tram, which was cheap and efficient, but if one broke down, there was no way of others passing it – hence this spectacular tram-jam in Princes Street in 1950.*

## 'Sunday Night at 7' in the Usher Hall

Every year from 1946 to 1952, the Chapel hired the Usher Hall on Sunday evening for several consecutive months, and held the evening service there, as in 1938. From the first Sunday, 13 October 1946, the meetings attracted wide attention and the area and the grand tier were filled. The aim was to get the upper tier filled as well, and this was achieved from time to time. Chapel members went scouting in Lothian Road, inviting passers-by to come in. Sidlow Baxter relied on the congregation to take the initiative in speaking to strangers:

*the persons who came into the experience of Salvation would not have come forward at all had it not been that some member had spoken a personal word at the end of the service…. that 'follow-up word' of discreet individual 'button-holing' is required to clinch the matter. In this way most of us can be partners with the preacher in Sunday evening evangelism.*

3 *Record*, 1947, p. 139.

The *Edinburgh Evening News* commented on the 1949 Usher Hall venture of 20 February to 8 May:

*Charlotte Baptist Chapel under the leadership of its efficient minister, the Rev. J. Sidlow Baxter, has again justified its annual campaign of evening services in the Usher Hall. The twelfth and closing service was held last Sunday when the spacious auditorium was full…. One of the most encouraging features of the work was the response made every night, without exception, by hearers of the message, who were led to a reconsecration of their lives. The embarkation on such a scheme for three months is, of course, a great financial responsibility, but it is gratifying to know that Charlotte Chapel emerged from it without loss.*

4 *Record*, 1949, p. 94.

That last point in that report is worth emphasising. Not only were the expenses of hiring the hall and advertising the services paid for, but after the ordinary Sunday evening offerings were deducted (to cover the cost of running the Chapel), the treasurer had a credit balance of £21. Sidlow Baxter reached the peak of his preaching career in the Usher Hall services, and deservedly earned the title, which he loved to apply to himself, of the 'preaching elder'.

## 13 South Charlotte Street

The Chapel's office, which is now the centre of its complex administrative activity, is located on the second floor of a tenement block, overlooking the Chapel but entering from the main road, South Charlotte Street. This was acquired in 1946, when the first, second and third flats came on the market and the Chapel purchased them for £3,750. The property was chosen in the hope (never realized) that some day it might be physically linked to the church building, to give the Chapel a frontage onto Charlotte Street.

There was no church office then, so the Sunday School, the Scouts and Guides, the Young Peoples Meeting, the missionary auxiliaries and miscellaneous smaller meetings all submitted bids to use the new accommodation. The top flat had tenants, protected from removal by wartime legislation, so it was not available. The rooms in the second flat were made into one large hall, by knocking down internal walls; imagine entering the present church office – all the rooms on the right were linked, plus the room facing the door, to give a large L-shaped hall. The internal walls had to be restored when this flat became the caretaker's home in 1959 (below).

In a move that present auxiliaries (always short of space) may regret, the deacons decided in 1952 to sell the first and third floors. The first one, which the Baxter family had used as a manse from 1950 to 1952, attracted quite a bit of interest and went for £3,000 to a businessman wishing to create a city-centre office, which it still is. The five-room third (top) flat was still subject to wartime tenant's rights, meaning that the owners could not get possession until the tenant or his widow chose to leave. That depreciated its value, and the Chapel were pleased to get £900 for it. The second floor was retained, to become the caretaker's house between 1959 and 1992 and then, from 1992, the church office. The top flat came back on the market in June 1982, but the Chapel had no interest in it. It was on the market again, for months, in the spring of 2006, but again there was no thought of repurchasing it.

## Sidlow Baxter's travels

### Home and away

Sidlow Baxter, like Joseph Kemp and Graham Scroggie before him, believed that the pastor of Charlotte Chapel should be set free by his home church for a wider ministry, both for special occasions in other churches and for Bible teaching conventions.

*The past year [May 1945–May 1946], of course, has been rather exceptional because of our Pastor's presidency of the Edinburgh Baptist Association. He has, among other things, visited every one of the Baptist churches in the Edinburgh area, in most cases for a Sunday morning and a Monday and a Tuesday evening.*

5 *Record*, 1946, pp. 87, 153-4.

The presidency over, Sidlow Baxter travelled widely during the summer of 1946. In May, he gave the Bible Readings and addresses at the Leicester Keswick, took the anniversary services at two Baptist churches in London (one of them being Alan Redpath's sixth anniversary in Richmond), and addressed a Sunday School teachers' conference and a ministers' conference. In June he lectured for five days at Cliff College in Derbyshire, and gave the Bible Readings at the Portstewart Convention in Northern Ireland. In July he took part in the jubilee of Woolwich Tabernacle in London and spoke at the four-day Rothesay Convention; he also preached

at the Hillhead Baptist Church in Glasgow, had a short break and then went to Bristol for meetings. He took the services at Westminster Chapel, London, on the first two Sundays of September, and spoke at rallies in Northampton and Leicester. From the middle of September, he concentrated on the Sunday services and the Thursday Bible School in the Chapel, and on the plans for the Usher Hall outreach.

*Sidlow Baxter and his wife Ethel at a Christian conference at Hildenborough Hall in 1946. As well as speaking throughout a full week, he was challenged by the young guests to various sports. After his 1949 visit, he said: 'I came down here very tired, but I am going back completely exhausted.'*

### America beckons

In January 1946, Sidlow Baxter advised the deacons that he was thinking of touring South Africa and Australia in 1947, but before he could progress these plans, Dr Donald Gray Barnhouse invited him to America for the first three months of 1947. The deacons could hardly demur when he said, at the same time, that he had already arranged pulpit supply and that (his words): 'C.C. would not lose a penny'. It may seem cavalier, but the concept of sabbatical leave – three or six months study leave every seven years – did not come to Scottish Baptist churches until the 1970s; until then, a minister's normal break from congregational duties was one day a week and four weeks a year.

Knowing that Sidlow Baxter would be away for over three months, 34 new members hastened to join the Chapel at the December communion service. Mr Baxter sailed (his wife did not accompany him on this occasion) on 19 December, and obtained permission to hold a service on board on Christmas Day – the best-attended service ever seen on that liner. For three months, he preached every Sunday in Philadelphia, lectured at noon on Monday to students in that city, gave Bible Readings in New York on Monday evening, repeated them back in Philadelphia on Thursday, addressed a business men's lunch on Wednesday, and spoke every morning at one of the Philadelphia theological colleges.

He enjoyed his visit so much that when he was invited to say a little about it on the Thursday after his return, he spoke for 90 minutes and the church, packed to capacity, listened throughout with eager interest. Baxter, this time accompanied by his wife, was back in America for August and September of both 1948 and 1949, to speak at the Canadian Keswick and other rallies. From the reports in the *Record*, it is clear that America was 'calling'.

## Features of Chapel life

### The office-bearers' passion

People did not speak in those days about 'having a passion', in the sense of a driving ambition, but it aptly describes the dedication of the Chapel's leadership to evangelism. In October 1946, they declined to send representatives to a proposed Edinburgh Baptist Men's Fellowship, where all ages would meet weekly around the city, to discuss topics 'religious, political, evangelistic, scientific etc.'

*What would be the purpose of these meetings? (1) Could be to win the outsider, or (2) to cater for the Christian. If the first – to win them to what? The only answer could be surely to win them for Christ and therefore the meetings should certainly be religious and evangelistic; and if for the second – to cater for Christians – we feel that this type of meeting is not required. We believe that the truest fellowship is ever in outright service for Christ. It was suggested therefore that for the time-being we have no contact with the movement.*

6 Deacons' Minute, 2 October 1946.

That is not to say that the deacons were insular. In 1949, they acted on a suggestion from the Edinburgh Baptist Association, to have a combined communion service on Good Friday – the first ever. Sidlow Baxter led it, assisted at the communion table by eight ministers from other churches.

Nor did the deacons lack vision for indirect evangelism. For a week in April 1948, they mounted an Exhibition of Ancient Bibles and Manuscripts in the lower hall, attended by 2,500 pupils from Edinburgh schools and their teachers, for one-hour sessions during school hours. The evening lectures for adults were not well supported, but to arrange nine consecutive evenings on ancient manuscripts, and to expect them all to be well attended was, perhaps, optimistic.

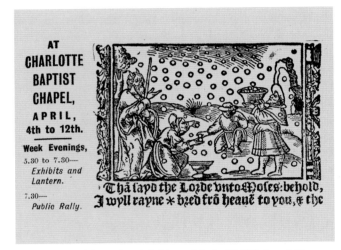

*The April 1948 exhibition showed the history of the English Bible through 55 exhibits, including Hebrew scrolls, Greek manuscripts and early printed editions. This carving illustrates the manna given to the children of Israel in the desert.*

## Golden weddings

With life expectancy a great deal less than it is today, golden (fiftieth) wedding anniversaries were comparatively rare, and merited a telegram from the king and queen (as with diamond (sixtieth) weddings and hundredth birthdays now). When the senior elder and his wife reached fifty years of marriage in August 1948, the elders and their wives arranged a party in the Charlotte Rooms. It was 1957 before a diamond wedding was celebrated, another decade before the next one, and another decade again before the third.

Three points are worth noting about the 1948 party. First, the couple were referred to throughout as Mr and Mrs David Ronald; in the social convention of the time, the wife's Christian name was never mentioned. Secondly, the programme included a solo and a recitation – both *de rigueur* for such an evening. Thirdly, Mr Ronald's reminiscences included memories of five ministers under whom he had served as deacon or elder – Reverends Way, Bardwell, Kemp, Scroggie and Baxter; he was the only surviving male member of the congregation that 'called' Joseph Kemp in 1902.

*The clock in the lower hall, until it was divided horizontally to create the present lounge in 1983, was from the original building of 1797. The door above the clock and to its right, allowed worshippers to come from the vestibule and hang their coats in the gallery.*

He told the party that the two silver chalices, which stood on the communion table month by month – individual cups were distributed, but common cups were on the table, filled with wine, partly symbolic and partly in case the individual cups were all used – were the original ones, from Richmond Court in 1808. The offertory box in the vestibule had, he recollected, been there when he joined in 1891; the clock in the lower hall (removed when the present lounge was created in 1983) was the clock from the original sanctuary, demolished in 1911.

Better health care gradually raised life expectancy, and by the later 1950s, ninetieth birthdays became common among the women – no men as yet; in 1958, one member died in her ninety-seventh year. It was 1983 before any Chapel member reached one hundred (Chapter 41).

### Change of deaconess

Lizzie Boyle, as everyone called the deaconess, retired at the end of 1948. She was the first Chapel deaconess, starting in 1907, in her early twenties, during Joseph Kemp's ministry. When he went to New York in 1915, he persuaded her to help him there, as she had done in Charlotte Chapel, but for family reasons she returned to Scotland within 18 months, When her successor in the office of deaconess left to go elsewhere in 1921, she was invited to pick up the threads where she had left off.

At annual meetings over the next 28 years, members were increasingly amazed as the number of her home and hospital visits rose to about fifteen hundred a year, together with leading the Young Women's Meeting on Sunday afternoon and the Wednesday night District Meeting. She also brought the sick list to the women's prayer meeting on Wednesday afternoon, maintained the church register, worked the addressograph machine, helped with Chapel correspondence and prepared the copy for the *Record*. The grateful Chapel awarded her superannuation of £2 per week for the rest of her life and that, together with a leaving gift of £160, met all her needs. She did not live long to enjoy retirement, and died in November 1954.

Miss Boyle's successor, appointed after four excellent applicants had been interviewed, was Miss Margaret (Peggy) Gillon, the daughter of Chapel members. She had been through Sunday School, as scholar, teacher and then leader, had studied at the Bible Training Institute in Glasgow, had served with the Liverpool City Mission, and was, in 1948, on the staff of the YWCA of Scotland in Aberdeen. She was welcomed and set apart for her duties in the Chapel during the morning service on Easter Sunday 1949. Mr Baxter preached appropriately on Romans 16:1-2: 'I commend unto you Phoebe our sister, a servant of the Church…'. Peggy Gillon soon endeared herself to all, especially to the women and the aged. She made 1,760 visits in her first year and 1,900 in her second, but lamented that there were still a hundred Chapel homes that she had not been able to visit. For the next 18 years, she ministered graciously and sympathetically to the sick and the sorrowing.

*Miss Elizabeth (Lizzie) Boyle, who retired in 1948 after 37 years as deaconess, and her successor, Miss Margaret (Peggy) Gillon.*

Peggy's father, Robert Gillon, typified the lifetime of Christian service that many of his generation gave to the Chapel. He became a member in 1924, a deacon in 1927, and was the assistant editor (in other words, he did all the work) of the *Record* during the ministries of Graham Scroggie and Sidlow Baxter. He then convened the house committee, caring for the fabric of the building.

*Mr and Mrs Robert Gillon celebrated their golden wedding in August 1955; their daughter Peggy (right of picture) became the Chapel deaconess in 1949 and their other daughter Bertha (left of picture) was the first full-time secretary to the pastor, from 1963 to 1972.*

## Church flowers

The first reference to fresh flowers around the Chapel pulpit is in 1921, when men were responsible (Chapter 26). Flowers are not mentioned again until February 1949, when a member, who had made it her service for some years, had to give it up. Sidlow Baxter thought about the contemporary American practice, as he had observed it, of inviting named donors and publicizing the reason for the gift, such as a birthday or an anniversary. He intimated from the pulpit, that people might wish to provide flowers on family occasions, perhaps in memory of a loved one. When members asked whether they were to supply flowers or to send money, the deacons realized the implications of what the pastor had said. Concerned (human nature being what it is, even sanctified human nature) that families might try to out-do each other – 'care will have to be taken that no display of flowers will become so pretentious as to cause critical comment' – the deacons decided that donors should not arrange their own flowers, but that the whole congregation should be encouraged to make donations to a flower fund.

A rota of six women purchased flowers and arranged them. Anyone wishing to provide flowers for a special occasion, as Sidlow Baxter had suggested, subscribed to the fund (no amount specified) and received a personal (not a public) acknowledgment. This satisfied everyone, and soon a couple of dozen women took turns at doing the actual work; many of them bought the flowers for their day from their own money, but they could recover the cost from the flower fund if they wished. In 1954, the caretaker and his wife took over responsibility for the floral decoration of the communion table, and they also put up two external window boxes, which became a source of beauty and fragrance in Rose Street, summer and winter.

*One can see when there has been a wedding in the church on a Saturday, by the character of the floral display left over for the Sunday.*

When the caretaker resigned on medical advice in October 1956, the rota system was restarted. It ran short of volunteers in 1959, so Kitty Griffiths (the pastor's wife) asked Lorna Hunt to take over. Once a month, the church secretary announced from the pulpit that Mrs Hunt would be in the vestibule after the service, to receive donations for the flower fund. From the monies given, she personally purchased (or picked) suitable flowers on Friday and spent the morning arranging a display for the front of the pulpit and sometimes for the pedestals as well. Except for weddings, when professionals were brought in, she did this for 24 years.

When she passed on responsibility for flower arranging in 1983, a team of 18 women did it in turn – about three times a year each. Generally, the volunteers provided the flowers themselves, but they could draw on the flower fund, no longer collected in the vestibule on Sunday but given through the offering bags, suitably marked. From 1983, there have been displays in both the sanctuary and the lounge.

Every Sunday, after the evening service, volunteers remove the flowers, divide them into suitably sized bunches and take them to people in hospital or unwell at home. In 2006, the distribution team was given the name 'Flower Power', and became a recognized auxiliary.

## On the footplate

Flash floods in the Borders swamped the east coast railway line in August 1948. One of the Chapel elders, Jim Paterson, was a top-link driver on the Edinburgh-London service; for bringing his train safely through the havoc – the last one before the floods closed the track – he was presented with a watch: 'In recognition of his special services to British Railways during the Border flooding.' He was in the news again in 1954, when his train broke the Waverley-King's Cross speed record, and he twice drove the royal train. The *Daily Record* (headline below) reported how he spent Sunday 4 September 1955, a fortnight before he retired, after 47 years with the railway.

*Yesterday he drove the 10 a.m. King's Cross-Edinburgh train....*
*Mr. Paterson stepped down from his engine at 6.20 p.m.*
*He was met as usual by his wife and after a bath and change*
*into his Sunday best he hurried to the evening service at*
*Charlotte Baptist Chapel, where he is an elder. Then on*
*to the foot of the castle [Castle Street], where he set up*
*a harmonium and preached in his vigorous style.*

7 *Daily Record*, 5 September 1955.

In those days, drivers were given a particular engine; only Jim and one other drove *The Union of South Africa* on a shift system for nine years. 'Every day of my railway life was happy but the nine years I had of her, and she was my very own, were the happiest years of my railway career.'

Additional information on the following topics, mentioned in this chapter, is available on the CD.

Deaconess
Preaching – audio-tapes (Sidlow Baxter)
Sidlow Baxter's review of 1935-45

# CRACK ENGINE DRIVER IS A LAY PREACHER IN HIS SPARE TIME...

"Record" Reporter

WHEN a large, jolly, immaculately-dressed lay preacher conducted a service at the junction of Princes Street and Castle Street, Edinburgh, last night, most of the strollers who noticed him didn't know that only a few hours earlier the preacher—Mr. James Paterson, of 60 Gorgie Road—had been at the controls of the London-Edinburgh express.

They didn't know either that he holds the world record for the longest, non-stop train speed.

Mr. Paterson broke the record on the "Elizabethan" run from Edinburgh to London last year. He did his last "Elizabethan" run on Saturday to King's Cross.

## He holds speed record

He said last night: "I am very sorry to have to give it up. It will be hard giving up my engine. I've driven the same one for nine years."

*Jim Paterson, a Chapel elder, was both a top-link driver and an articulate lay preacher, especially at open-air meetings.*

# Chapter 37
## A mid-century globetrot (1949–1953)

### Wider yet, and wider

#### 'Look for my successor'

At Sidlow Baxter's tenth anniversary in October 1945, the church secretary said: 'Mr Baxter has finished his first ten years with us, and now he starts the second ten.' It was not to be a full ten; four years later, he began to loosen his ties with the Chapel, and four years after that he resigned his charge, for a wider ministry of itinerant Bible teaching.

Sidlow Baxter's widespread ministry at conventions and anniversaries and other special occasions (Chapter 36 for 1946) continued, and in 1949 he spoke at the annual meeting of the Advent Testimony Movement in London on 19 April, the Liverpool Keswick Convention from Monday 25 to Wednesday 27 April, the Bible Testimony Fellowship in London on 14 May and the Baptist Union of Ireland from Monday 23 to Thursday 26 May. The elders were, as ever, generous in sharing their pastor with others, regarding it as part of the ministry of a large and self-sufficient church, but Sidlow Baxter proposed a new dimension at a specially convened members' meeting on Monday, 30 May 1949. It was the best-attended members' meeting ever held in the Chapel – between six and seven hundred. Baxter said:

*As you know, I am now in my fourteenth year at the Chapel, and I myself am now well into my forties. Through all those fourteen years you have been consistently kind to me;… for some time now I have felt that a point has been reached where both you and I should seek some special guidance respecting the future. For one thing, I feel the time has come when I ought to accept some, at least, of the pressing invitations which come from places abroad; and again I have felt a pressure on my spirit to visit various missionary fields.*

---

1 *Record*, 1949, p. 100.

Sidlow Baxter then submitted three proposals: First, that he should make a tour, including visits to as many of the Chapel's missionaries as possible, from December 1949 to October 1950. Secondly, that while he was away, the pulpit should not just be supplied, but that potential successors in the pastorate should be invited. Thirdly, that he would return for the anniversary weekend in October 1950, and that he would see the Chapel through as much as necessary of that winter's work, depending on the office-bearers' progress in finding a new pastor. In other words, he did not want a long vacancy.

Mr Baxter then withdrew and MacDuff Urquhart took the chair. A full and frank discussion took place, and a number of members expressed themselves. The chairman showed the sagacity for which he was renowned, and called on two of the Chapel missionaries on furlough to speak. After both had expressed the incalculable benefit which a visit from the minister of the church to the missionaries labouring in lonely foreign fields would mean, all amendments were withdrawn and the meeting unanimously approved the first proposal. They also agreed, although sadly, to begin looking for a successor. Mr Urquhart, who had refused to allow any discussion on the financial aspects until the principle had been established, then brought a recommendation from the deacons' court – that the pastor should receive his full salary and that the church should meet the cost of pulpit supply during his absence.

Sidlow Baxter responded:

*It is with affection and appreciation unfeigned that I write this note of thanks for what you did last Monday. It has placed a shining crown upon your royal record of kindness through fourteen years.… We wish to donate £500 [from the stipend] to our Charlotte Chapel Beulah Home project.*

---

2 *Record*, 1949, p. 103.

At a farewell social on Monday 21 November 1949, a streamer stretching around the gallery bore the same words as had greeted Joseph Kemp and Graham Scroggie (Chapter 25): 'We love you and we tell you so.' As mentioned in the last chapter, a large number had hastened to join the Chapel at the communion service before Sidlow Baxter left for three months in America in 1947. There was a similar rush before he left for his world tour. On Thursday 17 November, 19 were baptized, the largest number that anyone could recall at one time – Mr Baxter baptized the candidates himself, without assistance; friends and well-wishers overflowed into the gallery after the area of the church was filled. On the following Sunday, 31 joined the church, 14 men and 17 women, of whom a dozen were married couples, many of them having been baptized on the Thursday. This was also the pattern when Sidlow Baxter announced his resignation in November 1952 (below); 30 were baptized (14 men and 16 women) and 44 joined the Chapel in December and January.

## World tour

Sidlow Baxter left Edinburgh on 24 November 1949, with a large crowd singing 'God be with you till we meet again' on the station platform; Mrs Baxter stayed in Edinburgh until mid-January, when their daughter Miriam's school resumed, then flew to Los Angeles and joined Sidlow for the remainder of the tour. By this time he had fulfilled preaching engagements right across the USA; they then visited Canada, Honolulu, Fiji, New Zealand and Australia. Unexpectedly, it took two months to find a sea passage from Australia directly to South Africa, so the Chapel's October 1950 anniversary services were put back to the end of November, while the Baxters completed their tour through South Africa, Nigeria, the Belgian Congo, Egypt, Syria, Pakistan, India and Israel.

Sidlow Baxter's sense of humour did not desert him, even after nearly twelve months of gruelling travel. Their luggage was lost in Cairo airport, so he demanded to see the president of Egypt personally; when an anxious official asked why, Sidlow replied that he was going to 'Su-ez Canal'. They just made it back for the (delayed) fifteenth anniversary services on 26 November; the sanctuary was crowded, with overflows into the lower hall.

**"A MID-CENTURY GLOBE-TROT"**

In response to many requests,
the Rev. & Mrs J. Sidlow Baxter re-show their

**ALL-COLOUR ROUND-THE-WORLD FILM,**

Depicting their 1950 global Lecture and Missionary
tour, on the two evenings, March 31st and April 2nd,
at 7.30 in

**THE CENTRAL HALL, TOLLCROSS.**

Part 1.  Fijis to Congo.      Mon., March 31st
Part 2.  Egypt, India, etc.   Wed., April 2nd

*No admission charge; but silver collection for overseas missions.*

*The Baxters covered seventy thousand miles and took four thousand feet of coloured cine film; Sidlow showed films in the Chapel and in the Central Hall, Tollcross, under the title 'A Mid-Century Globe-Trot'.*

## An ambassador for Edinburgh

Many who had heard or met Sidlow Baxter on his world tour made a point of seeking out Charlotte Chapel when visiting Edinburgh on holiday or on business. The visitors' book for July and August 1950, while he was still on the later stages of the tour, included people from eight cities he had visited. This continued over subsequent years: 'this year [1952] there have been visitors from such varied and distant lands as Canada, U.S.A., Australia, New Zealand, Africa and India … the desire to make first-hand acquaintance had in many cases been gained during our Pastor's recent world tour.'

Another consequence of the tour was 950 new subscribers to the Chapel's monthly magazine, the *Record*. Until then, it had required an annual subsidy of about £130, but the increased circulation, plus a 50 per cent increase in its price, from 4d a copy to 6d (2.5 new pence), opened a new era in its life. However, many of the overseas readers did not renew their subscriptions, and the new era was quickly over; the remainder of the decade required an annual subsidy, from general funds, of about £150.

The world tour led to further invitations. Sidlow Baxter was back in Canada (Toronto) and America (Philadelphia and New Jersey) for July, August and the early part of September 1951, but the Chapel were not prepared to take seriously his request to look for another pastor. They kept hoping that things would go on and on, as they had done for 17 years; by doing nothing, they enjoyed another 27 months of their beloved preaching elder.

## Missionaries and mission

### Mr H. C. Teng

As Sidlow Baxter arrived back in Edinburgh in November 1950, a young Chinese Christian was leaving. Three years previously, one of the Chapel missionaries in China, Maida Contento, had asked the Chapel to sponsor an exceptionally talented student to come to Edinburgh for further study. There were all sorts of complications, financial and diplomatic, but he completed his BD degree in New College and endeared himself to the congregation by his evangelistic zeal. He did not seek to remain in Britain, as some have done after gaining a professional qualification here, but returned to teach his countrymen in Hong Kong.

*Maida and Paul Contento, who asked the Chapel to sponsor H. C. Teng. Maida was a Chapel missionary in China, then in Singapore and finally in Saigon, from 1928 to 1982.*

The Contentos were due furlough in 1958. Rather than sailing home, they spent their boat fare (provided by the mission) on a second-hand Land Rover and drove it all the way from Singapore to Edinburgh. They wanted to meet local Christians and to see indigenous churches and missionary work on the way. They covered twelve thousand miles in 87 days, including preaching 10 times in 7 days in Calcutta, and following in the footsteps of the apostle Paul through Turkey and Greece.

### New ways to communicate

On the first Monday of every month, the Church prayer meeting was given over to missionary matters. In January 1951, an experiment was tried, which has lasted and been developed ever since. In the absence of a speaker, the convenor read excerpts from letters received from the 'Field', and the meeting took up the topics in prayer. It was so much appreciated that excerpts were read at future meetings, even if there was a speaker, and missionaries began to time their airmail letters to arrive for the meeting.

*When Mary Harrison (centre of picture) first went as a missionary to the Belgian Congo in 1923, it took her three months to get there. When air travel became available in the 1950s, it took her a day and a half. Her husband (left in picture) died in 1946, but she continued on her own until 1965.*

In June and in August 1951, two first-time Chapel missionaries went by plane to their stations, instead of by ship. Ted Emmett was in Kano, Nigeria, only 14 hours after leaving London, and Nurse Jean McLelland flew to Israel to work at the EMMS hospital in Nazareth. These are the first recorded departures by air. The opportunity for crowds to gather at the Waverley or the Caledonian station, to sing hymns on the platform as the train left, continued for another decade, as some (especially those with heavy luggage) still went by sea until 1967, but by 1953 many missionaries were routinely using the speediest form of transport. Mary Harrison remarked in 1958, that when she first went to Belgian Congo in 1923, she had taken three months on the journey which now took only a day and a half.

### New missionaries

No new missionaries could be commissioned from the Chapel during the 1939-45 war, but in the seven years between VJ Day (Victory over Japan) in August 1945 and Sidlow Baxter's resignation in 1952, 11 young men and 13 young women left for full-time service in Palestine (both Israel and Arab), Africa (Belgian Congo, Cape Province, Dahomey, Gold Coast, Nyasaland), India and Pakistan, South America (Paraguay) and Malaya (China being closed to missionaries). Most of them were doctors or nurses; the others were teachers or evangelists. In addition, another 25 or so were in training for work abroad or at home. One of the features of Sidlow Baxter's ministry was the thrusting out of Christians for active service.

## While the pastor was away

### Typical Sundays

Although the Chapel missed Sidlow Baxter's genial leadership while he was on his world tour, it is worth running through a typical Sunday to see how much went on, pastor or no pastor. The Young Peoples Meeting conducted a thirty-minute service in one of the wards in the Edinburgh Royal Infirmary at 9.30 a.m. every Sunday; the Young Men's Fellowship met at 10 a.m. in the Chapel; at the same time, choir members had a final practice, while others supported the 10.00 a.m. prayer meeting. The stewards had to be in their places for the doors to open at 10.30 a.m., and the queue (yes, a queue began to form from ten o'clock) poured into their favourite seats. The markers for the Young Worshippers League were in position on the stairs, to stamp the cards of the 40 or more children competing for prizes for regular attendance.

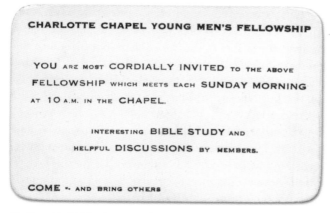

*The Young Men's Fellowship, at ten o'clock on Sunday morning, was suspended during the war – the young men were called up – but resumed in January 1947, to promote a deeper knowledge of the Scriptures and to give training in leadership and evangelism.*

Following the morning service, families with children went quickly home for lunch, in order to be back for the Sunday School and Bible Classes at 3 p.m. (teachers' prayer meeting at 2.30 p.m.); 53 teachers and 314 children met in the Chapel, with another 230 children at Longstone. A group of older members led an afternoon ward service in the Infirmary, while others prepared the tea and the talk for the average of 80 single homeless men at the Rock Mission in the Grassmarket. Women packed out the top hall for the Girls Own at 4.45 p.m., with tea and a speaker; it retained its name, even although the members grew older with the passing of the years.

There was another prayer meeting at 5.30 p.m.; entry was by the side door, as the main doors were kept firmly closed until the stewards and choir were ready for the invasion at 6 p.m. The evening service was usually the best attended of the week; to occupy the rapidly gathering congregation, the organist led congregational singing up to the start of the service at 6.30 p.m. There was an open-air after the service, at 8 p.m. at the corner of Princes Street and Castle Street.

The elders invited the pastor of the Baptist church in Eday, one of the Orkney Islands, to come with his wife, and conduct the annual service for the Baptist Union of Scotland Home Mission. Their combined travel costs were £18, and the preaching fee was £2 2s. A retiring collection for the Mission (in addition to the general offering taken up during the service) was £42, at a time when the average Sunday offering was £28 in the morning and £24 in the evening.

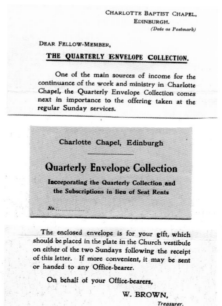

*Quarterly gifts through envelopes were a significant part of the Chapel's income from 1881 to 1964 (when the scheme was stopped). William Brown was church treasurer from 1933 to 1951.*

## Charlotte Baptist Chapel

### Order of Services

| Date |
|---|

| Morning | Evening |
| 11 a.m. | 6.30 p.m. |
|---|---|
| Prayer | Prayer |
| Hymn | Hymn |
| Reading | Reading |
| Hymn | Choir |
| Intimations | Intimations |
| Offertory | Offertory |
| Prayer | Prayer |
| Hymn | Hymn |
| Sermon | Sermon |
| Hymn | Hymn |
| Benediction | Benediction |
| Communion | After-Meeting |
| Hymn | Hymn |

*Guest preachers while Sidlow Baxter was away got no choice in the order of the Sunday services. They were sent this sheet to complete and return. It made for continuity, as ministers from a wide variety of backgrounds conducted the services.*

## Typical weekdays

The congregational prayer meeting was on Monday at 8 p.m., and no other activity was permitted to compete with it – the Chapel would not advertise any outside services scheduled anywhere in Edinburgh for Monday evening. A good number who were not in membership supported it, but they had to leave at nine o'clock if there was members' business after the time of prayer. The first Monday of the month continued to be devoted to missionary topics, sometimes with a speaker on furlough.

On Tuesday, the Women's Missionary Auxiliary met at 7 p.m., for two hours of knitting, sewing and exchanging missionary news. They had previously met in one of the committee rooms, but while Sidlow Baxter was away, numbers grew to an average of 27, and they had to move into the lower hall to get room to work. At the same time, the Girls Missionary Auxiliary grew so rapidly in the top hall that they had to form a junior branch for girls under 12.

Some of the Chapel young people preferred the Christian Endeavour on Tuesday evening in Carrubbers Close Mission (now the Carrubbers Christian Centre) to the Chapel's YPM on Wednesday. From 1946 to 1954, it provided complementary yet different training for Christian service. When 80 of them held a jubilee reunion in 1996, they were thrilled to discover that most of the original members were still going on with the Lord.

Wednesday was a busy day, with between 40 and 50 at the women's prayer meeting at three o'clock in the afternoon. The District Women's (gospel) Meeting in the evening had to move from the ladies' room (which could accommodate about 60 if they were not making garments) into the lower hall, as numbers rose to over 90. More than a quarter came from Rose Street itself, and this was the Chapel's main evangelistic outreach to its immediate community. At the same time, the Young Peoples Meeting (average attendance 70) met in the top hall for two hours from 8 p.m. There was an open-air outreach at the Mound every Wednesday, all the year round. The tract distributors worked their way through their districts at their own pace and time, once a month, every month of the year.

Thursday was Bible School night in the Chapel. Typically the area was well filled, often using 'our own special hymnbook', compiled by Sidlow Baxter, even when he was away.

On Friday evenings, the uniformed organisations met, Cubs and Brownies at 6 p.m., Scouts and Guides at 8 p.m., the boys in the lower hall and the girls in the top hall. The choir practised in the choir stalls from 7.45 p.m.; in addition to rehearsing their pieces for Sunday and going over the congregational hymns, they prepared a Sankey hymn, to be

sung as the Sunday evening congregation dispersed. This vesper, as it was known, became so significant that many people were unwilling to leave their seats until it ended; the elders had to reassure those who were anxious to get away that the service closed with the benediction, and that they were free to go during the final choir piece.

On Saturday, there was often a conference of some type, and always an open-air meeting at 8 p.m. at the junction of Princes Street with South Charlotte Street (Castle Street when traffic noise made the former impractical). Once a month the YPM held an outreach Saturday Night Fellowship, which saw over 20 young people won for Christ in one year.

*As traffic increased in the early 1950s, the Chapel moved its open-air meeting, especially during the summer, from the junction of Princes Street with South Charlotte Street to its junction with Castle Street.*

## Summer evangelism

In May/June, many of the auxiliaries broke up until October, and energies were redirected to the three-month summer open-air gospel campaign. When this was last mentioned, in chapter 32, Chapel members were supporting evangelistic outdoor meetings at two venues, led by guest evangelists. After the war, a new pattern was established; meetings were held at the Mound every Tuesday, Wednesday and Thursday, from the beginning of June to the end of August, in addition to the regular open-airs, all the year round, on Saturday and Sunday at the junction of Princes Street with Castle Street (South Charlotte Street in the winter).

The summer meetings started at 8 p.m. and lasted for not less than two hours. A rota of Chapel elders led them; occasional guest speakers were involved but no professional evangelist was engaged, as had happened before the war. Gospel tracts were handed out freely to all who would accept them. Over one hundred titles were available from the Victory Tract Club in Croydon, mostly for general distribution but some themed for children, teenagers, old people, Christmas, Easter, etc.

### Hallowe'en

Some Chapel members became concerned, toward the close of the twentieth century, at children attending Hallowe'en parties on 31 October, because of Halloween's association with witchcraft. There were no such reservations in the 1940s and the 1950s – Hallowe'en parties were all the vogue, and the Chapel auxiliaries vied to put on the best one. Turnip lanterns, 'dooking' for apples, nuts, treacly scones, splashes, gurgles and shouts for help, were followed by other party games, and a Bible quiz. The Girls Own (Sunday afternoon) used Hallowe'en in 1952 for an outreach meeting, which packed the lower hall. The first recorded protest is a letter to the elders in October 1967, objecting to the YPM having a Hallowe'en party; the elders agreed to take no action. Both the YPM and the Cub Scouts had parties in 1968.

## Three new ventures

### Church family holiday

A family weekend away is now an annual event in the Chapel calendar, but it was 1952 before anyone (Sidlow Baxter and the church treasurer) put forward such an idea. Netherhall Christian guesthouse in Largs had long been popular with individuals, but the Chapel booked all 130 beds for a church holiday during the Edinburgh trades fortnight (the first two weeks in July) in 1952. Sidlow Baxter gave morning Bible Readings and spoke at an after-supper rally; the time between was free for excursions, shopping and games in the grounds, or simply relaxing together.

*Netherhall Christian guesthouse in Largs. The dining and games areas were on ground floor of the grey building in the background, with bedrooms above. This wing was demolished when Netherhall closed as a conference centre in 1994, but the main house is still there.*

### Harvest Thanksgiving

The Sunday School flower and fruit service, held in June from 1937 onward (Chapter 32), had been discontinued for some years. In 1952, the teachers suggested bringing the whole School to a Sunday morning service, not in June but as a harvest thanksgiving in October. This soon became a popular annual event; the next minister, Gerald Griffiths, expanded the idea and asked adults to contribute as well. They were encouraged to deliver their gifts on Saturday afternoon, so that the flowers, fruit and vegetables could be artistically arranged on the platform at leisure. The children's gifts were slotted in as they filed past the platform, just before the service started.

*'It is a particularly pleasing part of the service when the children file into the Church and give their gifts to the teachers.' (They formed up in the lower hall and filed in as the service started.) No photograph is available to illustrate that comment in October 1953, but this one shows the 2003 practice of children coming forward with their gifts during the service.*

On the Sunday afternoon, teams took the produce to over one hundred members in hospital or confined to their homes. Any surplus fruit, vegetables or flowers were offered to Dr Barnardo's Homes and similar institutions.

### Beulah Home

Another project started during Sidlow Baxter's ministry was the Chapel's Beulah Home. In 1931, Miss Boyle, the deaconess, drew attention to the need for accommodation for elderly members; many were in tied accommodation, where the house went with the job and had to be vacated on retiral, to make way for the successor. Some members, who had come to Edinburgh for work many years before, had nowhere to go. It was 16 years before anyone took up the challenge; one of the deacons, John McGuinness, described what happened:

283

*I became very concerned about the old people of our church. It seemed that we did not hear about some of them until it was almost too late, sometimes they were dead, and I felt a great tugging at my heart to do something about it. It was not until 1947 that I answered the call and one night at a Deacons' Court meeting I tabled a motion to empower us to start a fund.... the Church Secretary, in his manner, which is dear and familiar to all of us, said: 'Mr. McGuinness, this is your pigeon – you must be the convener'.*

---

3 'Beulah Home' on the CD.

*Notice of Motion 5.3.47.*

*I will move at the next monthly meeting of the Deacon's Court, that a committee of Elders and Deacons be appointed to consider some scheme, in the interest of aged Christians.* John McGuinness

John McGuinness' notice of motion to the deacons' court in 1947. To humour him, the deacons told him to get on with it himself, which he did, leading to the purchase of Beulah Home in 1955.

**Christmas Song and Praise**
CHARLOTTE CHAPEL CHOIR
under the leadership of our organist
Mrs ROSE PENWELL, L.R.A.M., A.R.C.O.,
will give a
CHRISTMAS CHORAL AND CAROL SERVICE
in the Chapel on
SATURDAY, 17th DECEMBER, at 7.30 p.m.

*The Offering will be on behalf of the Beulah Homes Fund*

DO NOT MISS THIS CHRISTMAS TREAT BY OUR OWN CHAPEL CHOIR

BEULAH HOMES ANNUAL THANKSGIVING SOCIAL
ON THURSDAY, 11th MAY 1950
*Chairman :*—REV. JAMES DUFF.
*Speakers :*—
    Mr J. T. LOCKHART,
        President of the Baptist Union of Scotland.
    REV. A. H. DUFF STEVENSON, Glasgow.
        *(Subject:—"Scotland Through Irish Eyes")*
    REV. JAMES D. KIRK, Carluke.
*Duettists :*—Mrs J. D. KIRK and Miss M. GILLON.
    TEA commences at 6.45 p.m.

*Offering on behalf of the Beulah Homes Fund.*

Rallies were held in the Chapel from 1948 to 1955, to raise the £7,000 needed for an eventide home.

The cost of setting up an eventide home for a dozen residents and three living-in staff was estimated at £5,000. John McGuinness arranged tea parties and Saturday rallies in the Chapel during the winter, usually with a visiting choir and a guest speaker; there was no television in Scotland at that time, and people were glad of somewhere to go on Saturday evening. These rallies generated offerings of about £50 a time; Sidlow Baxter gave £500, as mentioned above, and Miss Boyle left £262 in her Will. Every year from June 1951, the Sunday services, followed by a public meeting on the Monday, were designated the Beulah Weekend, with all the offerings going to the project. By the spring of 1952, the target of £5,000 was in sight, but inflation over the intervening five years had pushed up the cost of acquiring and equipping a home to £7,000. It was autumn 1955 before a suitable property, at an affordable price, became available; Beulah Home was opened in June 1956, as described in chapter 39.

## Sidlow Baxter's last two years

### Usher Hall services

In 1951, the Usher Hall services (eight Sunday evenings in February and March) started at eight o'clock instead of the usual seven, with an organ recital from 7.30 p.m. and community hymn singing from 7.45 p.m. This allowed people to support the evening service in their own church, from 6.30-7.30 p.m., and then get a tram to Lothian Road in time to draw spiritual inspiration from the gatherings in the Usher Hall. Eighty thousand handbills were delivered to homes or handed out in the street; the Lord Provost of the City of Edinburgh was invited to attend the opening meeting, although not to speak.

Sidlow Baxter's final Usher Hall meetings were from March to May 1952. He himself played the Steinway piano for the solo gospel songs. The main auditorium and the first gallery, seating together over two thousand, were filled throughout, and the upper gallery was required for Easter Sunday. As before, there were many conversions.

### Death of King George VI

King George the Sixth died on 6 February 1952, greatly admired and loved. Sidlow Baxter's sermon on the following Sunday morning made a deep impression on the church. He was conducting a series, but interrupted it to speak from Isaiah 6, a powerful address that kept the congregation spellbound.

*His Majesty was a true Christian man. Deeds and words bear elegant witness. Four things above all others give cause for profound thankfulness – his deep regard for God's BOOK, the Bible; for God's DAY, the Sabbath; for God's HOUSE, the Church; and for God's TRUTH, the Gospel.... A nation's true strength is not in its military forces or material resources, but in its Christian citizens. Throughout the reign of his Majesty, King George the Sixth, we have had on our throne a truly Christian king, leader, exemplar. God be thanked for his noble reign!*

4 Record, 1952, p. 33.

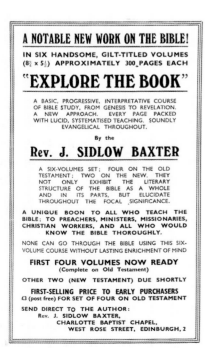

A NOTABLE NEW WORK ON THE BIBLE!

IN SIX HANDSOME, GILT-TITLED VOLUMES
(8¾ x 5½) APPROXIMATELY 300 PAGES EACH

"EXPLORE THE BOOK"

A BASIC, PROGRESSIVE, INTERPRETATIVE COURSE OF BIBLE STUDY, FROM GENESIS TO REVELATION. A NEW APPROACH. EVERY PAGE PACKED WITH LUCID, SYSTEMATISED TEACHING. SOUNDLY EVANGELICAL THROUGHOUT.

By the

Rev. J. SIDLOW BAXTER

A SIX-VOLUMES SET: FOUR ON THE OLD TESTAMENT: TWO ON THE NEW. THEY NOT ONLY EXHIBIT THE LITERARY STRUCTURE OF THE BIBLE AS A WHOLE AND IN ITS PARTS, BUT ELUCIDATE THROUGHOUT THE FOCAL SIGNIFICANCE.

A UNIQUE BOON TO ALL WHO TEACH THE BIBLE; TO PREACHERS, MINISTERS, MISSIONARIES, CHRISTIAN WORKERS, AND ALL WHO WOULD KNOW THE BIBLE THOROUGHLY.

NONE CAN GO THROUGH THE BIBLE USING THIS SIX-VOLUME COURSE WITHOUT LASTING ENRICHMENT OF MIND

FIRST FOUR VOLUMES NOW READY
(Complete on Old Testament)

OTHER TWO (NEW TESTAMENT) DUE SHORTLY

FIRST-SELLING PRICE TO EARLY PURCHASERS
£3 (post free) FOR SET OF FOUR ON OLD TESTAMENT

SEND DIRECT TO THE AUTHOR:
Rev. J. SIDLOW BAXTER,
CHARLOTTE BAPTIST CHAPEL,
WEST ROSE STREET, EDINBURGH, 2

*Explore the Book was an expansion of Sidlow Baxter's Thursday evening Bible School lectures in the Chapel.*

### Sidlow Baxter in print

Sidlow Baxter's Sunday evening sermons in Charlotte Chapel were published in 1939 under the title *Enter ye in*; some of his Sunday morning sermons appeared in 1947 as *Mark those Men*. The material for his Thursday Bible School was published in 1960 under the title *Explore the Book*, originally in six volumes; since 1966, it has been available in one large volume.

### 'Everything in the garden is not lovely'

These words, spoken publicly at the annual church meeting in April 1951 by the man who had been church treasurer for 17 years, expressed the slightly unreal nature of Mr Baxter's relationship with the leadership at this time. He was giving mixed messages about his future. He had asked that while he was away from November 1949 to October 1950, the pulpit supply should be used to find a successor. He had said that he would see the Chapel through part or all of the winter of 1950-1, depending on the office-bearers' progress in finding a successor. The membership took this seriously; after one weekend, a member wrote to the deacons: 'If the preacher yesterday is one of the prospective candidates when/if there is a vacancy, well, let him stay at home, we got nothing yesterday, there being no depth in his messages.'

The office-bearers were going through the motions of seeking a successor, but they did not take any active steps – they kept hoping that if they did nothing, their pastor would stay. Sidlow Baxter formally tendered his resignation in March 1951, but withdrew it a few weeks later. He did not wish the church to purchase a proper manse for him – on his return from his 1949-50 world tour he lived in the Chapel's flat at 13 South Charlotte Street – yet he accepted the chair of the Edinburgh Evangelistic Union in October 1951, hardly the action of one who was thinking of leaving the city. On the other hand, he spoke at week-long conventions in Torquay and Preston in February 1952 and addressed various other meetings in March. He was away from Edinburgh for long spells in the summer of 1952. The deacons were uncertain whether they should arrange any further Usher Hall services or plan a church family holiday for the summer of 1953.

### Resignation

Sidlow Baxter took the initiative to regularize the situation. In October 1952, he wrote a letter of resignation from the pastorate, concluding: 'on no consideration are we prepared to reconsider our decision.' His letter was read to the deacons after the morning service on Sunday 26 October; they met on the following Wednesday and agreed: (1) to announce the resignation at the morning service on 2 November, and (2) to hold a members' meeting on 10 November. Mr Baxter was due to celebrate his semi-jubilee in the ministry on Sunday 1 February 1953, so the office-bearers persuaded him to stay until then – the day of his ordination 25 years before. As Mr and Mrs Baxter were not leaving the city, but making it their base for a wider ministry, they were asked to remain in membership with the Chapel.

CHARLOTTE CHAPEL ANNUAL THANKOFFERING ; AND SEVENTEENTH PASTORAL ANNIVERSARY

AT CHARLOTTE CHAPEL

OF THE

Rev. J. SIDLOW BAXTER

SUNDAY and MONDAY, OCTOBER 19th and 20th

Sunday, 11 a.m. and 6.30 p.m.

Rev. CHARLES T. COOK, D.D.,
of London

Monday (from noon onwards). Mr and Mrs Baxter and Elders will be in the vestry to receive the thankofferings of members and friends.

MONDAY EVENING AT 7.30

Chairman
Rev. J. Sidlow Baxter

Speakers
Rev. CHARLES T. COOK, D.D.
Rev. G. W. BROMILEY, Ph.D., D.Litt.
W. M. URQUHART, Esq., M.A., LL.B., S.S.C.

The Choir will render special Music
Everybody will be made Welcome

*October 1952 was Sidlow Baxter's seventeenth and last anniversary weekend in the Chapel.*

Some suggested that the farewell services should be held in the Usher Hall, but Mr Baxter would not hear of it: 'I am saying farewell to the Chapel, not to the city', he said. So the 'greeting meetings' (as they were popularly called in Edinburgh at the time, 'greeting' meaning 'weeping') were held in the Chapel over the first weekend of February 1953, three weeks before his fiftieth birthday. Both services on the Sunday, and also the Monday meeting, overflowed into the lower hall. Mr Baxter thanked the Chapel for their gifts and continued:

*The mid-war and early post-war years were a grim testing time. But our beloved Chapel not only survived, it has*

*flourished; and it wonderfully prospers today, spiritually, numerically, departmentally and financially.... It is seventeen years and four months since we settled in Edinburgh. That is a big slice of any man's public usefulness. I was thirty-two when I came. I am now forty-nine.... around 850 new members (averaging 50 per year) [have been received]; and over 584 baptisms (some 35 per year). And to crown it all, nearly 50 sent out into full-time service all over the world.... I have conducted some 340 funerals among you.*

5 *Record*, 1953, pp. 47-8.

Inset: Mr J. Begg. Standing at Back: Messrs J. Cochrane, J. Balmer, D. L. Macnair, J. Cossar, J. Oliphant. Inset: Mr J. McGuiness.

Second Row (Standing): Messrs J. Whitlie, D. M. Jenkins, J. Ritchie, D.S. Cormack, D. Blair, J. Hudson, J. E. Coutts, D. Steele, G. H. Rae.

First Row (Standing): Messrs D. Petrie, J. B. Purves, T. S. Currie, W. A. D. Somerville, W. Tullis, J. M. Tullis, G. Davidson, R. M. Hadden, D. M. Murray, G. Rae.

Sitting: Messrs J. Bethune, P. Armstrong, R. D. Clark, W. M. Urquhart, Rev. J. Sidlow Baxter. Messrs R. Aitken, R. J. Gillon, P. B. Murray, J. Paterson.

*Sidlow Baxter with the office-bearers (elders and deacons) of Charlotte Chapel in Charlotte Square Gardens in 1952.*

## A twinge of conscience

Sidlow Baxter's survey of his years in Edinburgh, and his gracious parting remarks, made some of the deacons wonder whether they had appreciated their pastor as much as they should – now that he was going. They asked themselves four questions at their next meeting: (1) had they been paying an adequate stipend and proper expenses in lieu of providing a manse, (2) should they have offered more clerical assistance, (3) had they been sufficiently supportive of his wider ministry, away from Edinburgh, and (4) why had they not provided a motor car for his pastoral visits to the scattered membership? They took retrospective action on the second point only. Betty Waugh, remembered by some to this day for her work at the Humbie Village and the Pathhead Café (Chapter 44), had voluntarily helped the pastor with his voluminous correspondence, calling at South Charlotte Street for shorthand dictation; the deacons recognized this by sending her a gift of £25.

## Sidlow Baxter's ministry in Edinburgh

Preaching was Sidlow Baxter's dearest and best role. It is said that preachers are not made but are born, and he certainly was born to it. In the pulpit, he was a dignified figure with his tail-coat, striped trousers and magnificent head of hair. His command of language put him in a field of his own; his published sermons and his books demonstrate to this day his individualistic style, with his unusual choice of words and phrases. He had no modern aids – no car at any time while in Edinburgh, no secretary (apart from Betty Waugh's help over his last few years, his wife did most of his typing), no pastoral assistant except the deaconess, and yet he conducted two services on Sunday (three during the war), plus the Ross Bandstand in the afternoon during the summer, the Monday prayer meeting, the Thursday Bible School and he visited the auxiliaries regularly. Everything was done with dignity, but the communion service was the highlight of the month, with the elders in tail-coats (morning suits) or black jackets and striped trousers; everything was carried through with great reverence.

Sidlow Baxter never avoided hard questions. He preached on, and subsequently published, helpful guidance on problem texts in the Bible, such as the suicide of Judas, the unpardonable sin and the sons of God in Genesis 6:1-4; he addressed poignant pastoral issues like: 'Are those who die as children lost?'

Before setting off on his world tour in November 1949, Sidlow Baxter sold his house at 14 Ravelston Dykes. On his return, he occupied the first flat of the Chapel's property at 13 South Charlotte Street, as the manse, until the spring of 1952. He then bought a house in Hillpark Avenue and made it his base until December 1954. The deacons were so appreciative of the improvements he had made to the flat that they paid for laying out the garden for the new house.

The church secretary explained the strength of the Chapel in general, and Sidlow Baxter's ministry in particular, in this way:

*First there has always been the insistence on the necessity for 'conversion', an old fashioned word with a modern significance acknowledged by all psychologists – a change of life, of heart and mind, brought about by a surrender of the will to God, with a handing-over to Him the controls of thought and action. Second, there has always been the recognition that this change of heart must be publicly professed (and how difficult that was for many of us!). Third, there has ever been our insistence on the Deity of Christ, as absolute and final, with no whittling away of its meaning and significance. Fourth, there has ever been our stand on and for the inspiration of the Bible – our regard for it as the Holy Book, the word of God and our realisation of the consequent need to study it carefully and hide its words in our hearts.*

6 *Record*, 1952, pp. 72, 170.

*35 Hillpark Avenue, Davidson's Mains, as it is now; it was the Baxters' home from 1952 to 1954.*

*Sidlow and Ethel Baxter at the end of his ministry in Charlotte Chapel.*

Mr and Mrs Baxter stayed in Edinburgh until 8 December 1954, and then set off on their wider ministry, with engagements for the next four years, chiefly in America. Fifty-

**Chapter 37**
A mid-century globetrot (1949–1953)

five Chapel members bade them farewell on the platform of the Caledonian Station (now demolished – only the Caledonian hotel remains). They sang 'Blest be the tie that binds our hearts in Christian love', and 'God be with you till we meet again' as the Baxters said good-bye to Edinburgh.

### Sidlow Baxter's remaining years

The Baxters came back in December 1966, when many who remembered them travelled considerable distances to be in the Chapel for the Sunday services. Sidlow's next – and last – Sunday in the Chapel was in late May 1968, after which he spoke on 'Deeper Spiritual Life' from Monday to Thursday evening. He was at the Women's Morning Fellowship and the Bible School in May 1970, but he was not free for the Sunday.

The Baxters made their home in Santa Barbara, California. Ethel died there on Christmas Day 1977. Sidlow continued his itinerant ministry, and there is a video recording in the Chapel archives of him preaching in a Baptist church in Memphis, Tennessee, in 1991, aged 88, but still fresh and powerful.

On 29 April 1979, he married Isabella (Isa), a widow originally from Ross-shire in the North of Scotland. For the next 20 years, they hospitably entertained Chapel members visiting Santa Barbara. Sidlow died there on 28 December 1999. He had told Isa that he wanted his remains to go back to 'Bonnie Scotland', so she arranged a thanksgiving service in Invergordon (near her original home) on 18 July 2000. She kindly invited the writer to attend, and after a service in the parish church, Sidlow's ashes were scattered there. Isa died at home in Santa Barbara on 1 July 2004.

Additional information on the following topics, mentioned in this chapter, is available on the CD.

Beulah Home
Christian Endeavour
Maida Contento
Mary Mein Harrison
Missionaries
Sidlow Baxter after Charlotte Chapel
Sidlow Baxter's obituary
Sidlow Baxter's publications

# Chapter 38
# Gerald Griffiths' first year (1954–1955)

## Events during the vacancy

### The vacancy committee

When Sidlow Baxter resigned in November 1952, the deacons appointed themselves (all 34 of them) as the vacancy committee. They also formed a sub-committee for pulpit supply, with the remit to let the congregation hear as many potential pastors as possible. In April 1953, one of the members wrote to the deacons, suggesting that a certain approach should be made. The response is revealing: 'After careful consideration, the Court agreed that the time was hardly ripe for such a move as there were a few excellent brethren still to be heard.' It was a full year after Mr Baxter's farewell before the vacancy committee held their next meeting. The agenda was: 'to discover if they were sufficiently drawn to any one preacher to warrant recommending him to the members.'

One name immediately went to the top of the list and stayed there; before the meeting concluded, the deacons recommended that a 'call' be sent to Rev. Gerald B. Griffiths, BA, BD, minister of the Metropolitan Tabernacle Baptist Church in London (Spurgeon's Tabernacle). As a young man of 29, in his second pastorate in Wales, he had been one of the 17 visiting preachers while Sidlow Baxter was on his world tour in 1949-50. He made such an impression when he occupied the pulpit for two Sundays in August 1950, and led the mid-week services, that he was invited back for a conference in January 1951.

Every guest preacher during Sidlow Baxter's world tour was (deliberately) a potential successor, but normally candidates are asked to preach 'with a view' before the congregation considers a name. Gerald Griffiths had not been in the Chapel for over three years, but such had been the impact of his ministry in August 1950, and at the conference a short while later, that a members' meeting on 15 February 1954 – about five hundred packed the area of the church – sent him an immediate 'call'. Those who had not heard him preach were content to go along with the enthusiastic recommendation of those who had. Before considering his response, four events during the vacancy should be recorded.

### The Rock moves

Every Sunday afternoon since 1923, Chapel members had served tea and sandwiches to men who lived rough in the Grassmarket area. This was followed by a short service, and attracted about 80 men weekly; the annual social in January brought in up to two hundred. Just as Sidlow Baxter was leaving Edinburgh, the Edinburgh Medical Missionary Society sold their Cowgate dispensary (where the Rock met) to the University of Edinburgh for development. A quiet word on the old-boy network secured the use of the nearby Grassmarket Mission; the Rock Mission continued there until 1966, when it moved for 12 years to the Church of Scotland's People's Palace in the Grassmarket. It then returned to the Grassmarket Mission, until the Rock closed in 1987 (Chapter 51).

### Graham Scroggie's last Sunday in the Chapel

One of the highlights of the vacancy was a return visit – the final visit – of Graham Scroggie, on Sundays 19 and 26 July 1953:

*As a prelude to his sermon on the morning of the 19th July, Dr Scroggie said, 'The best years of my life were spent here. This is the one place on earth about which I cannot think without emotion'.... both morning and evening the main building was packed to capacity, while disappointed ones – who could by no means be described as late-comers – were ushered into the Lecture Hall where the service was relayed to them. The sight of young men and lads 'adorning' the pulpit steps brought back vividly to mind the great audiences of Dr Scroggie's pastorate at the Chapel.*

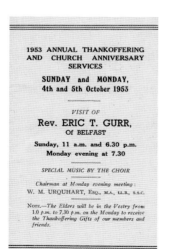

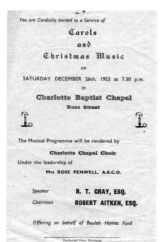

*In the absence of a pastor, the Chapel elders chaired the anniversary services and the carol concert and other public events; there was no interim moderator.*

1 *Record*, 1953, pp. 109, 126.

### Thursday Bible School

The activity that suffered most during the vacancy was the Thursday Bible School. 'Time was when the area of the Chapel was filled to capacity. What has caused this definite decline?' The editor of the *Record* answered his own question, writing: 'Christianity is just one of a number of interests today.... Christ is one of a number of hobbies run by Christian people! That is why we get nowhere!'

That rebuke calls for comment. In 1988, the writer invited one of the honorary elders, Robert Hadden, to speak at the fellowship group meeting in his home about the old days in the Chapel (inter-war, wartime and post-war). Mr Hadden had run a successful ornamental ironmongery business, but he was at or around the Chapel every weekday evening and all weekend, not just listening or praying but also actively evangelising; his wife – they had no children – played the portable organ at the open-airs. The group in 1988 listened with incredulity to the commitment of the Haddens and others of their generation, who would not miss a Thursday Bible School or other regular church activity.

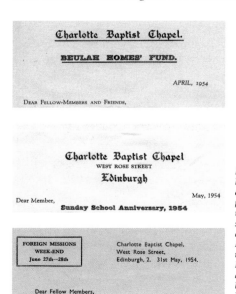

*Nine times a year, a letter with an offering envelope enclosed, was posted to every member, urging donations for specific projects, as described below. In April, May and June 1954, it was the turn of Beulah Home, the Sunday School and Foreign Missions. All had their own style of letter.*

Equally demanding were the calls on Chapel members for financial support. Nine times a year, a letter enclosing an offering envelope was posted to every member, urging donations to Beulah Home (April, £652 in 1953), the Sunday School (May, £81), foreign missions (June and December, £325), the anniversary (October, £645) and the quarterly offering in lieu of seat rents (March, June, September and December, £369). Although only half of the members responded to the quarterly letter, the treasurer persevered; the Sunday morning and evening offerings in 1953 were £1,530 and £1,345, so another £369 was not insignificant.

### Billy Graham's Greater London Crusade

The Chapel followed, with interest and delight, the Greater London Crusade in the Harringay arena from March to May 1954. On Thursday 13 May, the rally was relayed by landline to the Chapel. The doors had to be closed after 1,600 people packed into the sanctuary and both halls – the largest number to assemble on the premises so far – and a hundred more were turned away. (There were more in the building during the 1986 Commonwealth Games, Chapter 50.) Seats were not reserved, so people queued from 4.30 p.m. for the doors opening at 6 p.m.; the building was full by 6.30 p.m., for a 7.30 p.m. start; 15 responded to the appeal.

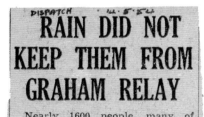

**RAIN DID NOT KEEP THEM FROM GRAHAM RELAY**

Nearly 1600 people, many of whom had travelled by bus from the Borders, Fife, and the West of Scotland, crowded into Charlotte Baptist Chapel, West Rose Street, Edinburgh, last night, to hear a broadcast relay of the address given by the American evangelist, Mr Billy Graham, at the Harringay Arena, London.

The queue of admission began to form up in the rain shortly before five o'clock, and the main hall was packed an hour before the relay started. The others were admitted to the lecture hall in the basement and to a hall on the top floor.

Half an hour before the relay began, all the seating had been taken up, and over 100 who had been waiting outside in the drenching rain had to be turned away. All but six left disappointed that their wait had been in vain.

**LISTENED OUTSIDE**

The six — four of them young women—were determined to hear something of what Dr Graham had to tell them from Harringay, and although they were soaked by the rain, they went round the side of the Chapel, where they could faintly hear the voice as it came through the loud-speakers to the 1600 enthusiasts inside.

*Edinburgh newspapers were impressed that people queued for over an hour in drenching rain to hear the voice of an American evangelist in London. A press photograph of the six people standing in the rain and listening through open windows is not clear enough to reproduce.*

## Acceptance of the 'call'

The day after the members issued their 'call' to Gerald Griffiths in February 1954, three office bearers travelled to London to present the invitation in person. The timing was providential. The Tabernacle had been badly damaged during a German air raid in 1941; in the early 1950s, the six hundred members were thinking of restoring the building and re-establishing the Tabernacle as a preaching centre, with seating for 1,700. Gerald Griffiths' priority was evangelism in the immediate neighbourhood, but as he was still in his twenties when he went to the Tabernacle, he did not wish to disagree too vocally with the leadership's new idea. He had declined invitations to preach in the Chapel after Sidlow Baxter left, not wishing to alarm his own church by preaching in a vacancy situation, but as 1953 drew to a close, he had less and less peace about the rebuilding proposal. The Tabernacle leadership did not agree with his alternative vision (direct evangelization of the district); they genuinely wanted him to stay, but they wanted him to stay and promote their building plans. The invitation to Edinburgh solved the impasse. On Sunday 7 March 1954, the church secretary informed a delighted congregation that the end of the vacancy was in sight.

*In 1954, the Chapel bought 550 Queensferry Road, Barnton, as a manse for the Griffiths family.*

In anticipation of their new pastor's arrival, the deacons purchased a manse, the first time the Chapel had done so; previously, they had left it to the minister to rent one or, in Sidlow Baxter's case, to buy his own. Mr and Mrs Griffiths (in

London) were not consulted – houses were hard to come by in Edinburgh in 1954, and the manse committee (five men) snapped up a house in Barnton. It turned out to be an unsuitable location for a Chapel manse, and a better one was found in 1958 (Chapter 40). Queensferry Road is nearly four miles long, but the Chapel always gave the Griffiths' postal address as simply: 'Craigatin, Queensferry Road'; it was a tribute to the postman's local knowledge that such letters reached number 550.

## Gerald Griffiths' ministry

### The Griffiths family

Gerald Bader Griffiths was born in Wales in 1921 and grew up there. At the age of 14, he had a profound spiritual experience and prepared whole-heartedly for Baptist ministry. He studied arts and divinity (graduating BA and BD) at the University of Wales in Cardiff. Through the university Christian Union, he met a fellow-student, Kitty Anna Coe, who had been brought up in a Christian Brethren home in a village in Suffolk. During his studies, he was asked to be student pastor at the Archer Road Baptist Church in Ely, Cardiff (1944-47); the pastorate included a manse, so they were able to get married on 29 December 1943, earlier than would otherwise have been possible. On completion of his studies, he was 'called' to the Tredegarville Baptist Church, also in Cardiff (1947-51), then the largest Baptist church in the area, with a membership of five hundred. From 1951 to 1954, he was pastor of Spurgeon's Metropolitan Tabernacle in London. The Griffiths came to Edinburgh with three children, Ian, Myfanwy and baby Jonathan.

### Induction

The induction was on Sunday 13 June 1954. The pattern at that time was for a senior minister to lead both services, and to give a public 'charge to the minister' in the morning and a 'charge to the congregation' in the evening. Many members had not seen their new minister until that morning, and they were deeply impressed:

*As our new Pastor stood before us we could not but be conscious that here was a man 'full of the Holy Ghost and wisdom'.... Our hearts warmed towards him as he declared his belief in the Word of God as being fully inspired by the Holy Ghost....*

291

*All his preaching would be based on 'What saith the Scriptures?' There were three things which as a minister he regarded as fundamental. (1) The Word of God, (2) Evangelism, and (3) Prayer.*

2 *Record*, 1954, p. 99.

*Gerald and Kitty Griffiths at the induction in June 1954.*

## Believers' baptism

Gerald Griffiths told his first Sunday congregation that he and two of the elders would be in the vestry on the following Thursday, to receive enquirers for baptism; over the next few days, he interviewed 23 of them. It was the start of a remarkable six months. At services in June, September and December, 48 women and 20 men were baptized; others came forward, on all three occasions, in response to Mr Griffiths' appeal, some for conversion and some to be baptized at a future date. A further 41 were baptized over the next six months – 109 in the pastor's first year. Sixty per cent of them joined the Chapel, but Gerald Griffiths did not discourage Christians from other denominations, who wished to be baptized while still retaining their membership in their own churches.

## Overcrowding on Sunday evening

Gerald Griffiths regarded the Sunday evening service as supremely an evangelistic service, so that the Chapel might be the scene of constant and numerous conversions. Accommodating everyone who wanted to come on Sunday evening, and to bring unconverted friends with them, soon became an acute problem. When the 1954 summer holidays were over, sections of the Chapel membership were grouped according to the first letter of their surname and requested to go to the lower hall, in order to leave space in the sanctuary.

Gerald Griffiths did not apologise for this 'voluntary occupation of the Lecture Hall by our own members'; he urged them to be satisfied with nothing less than a full Church *and* a full Lecture Hall. When both were full, the last resort was to ask the elders to sit on the platform, facing the congregation, so the stewards could put latecomers into their seats. The alphabetical system of diverting certain sections of the membership to the lower hall remained in operation over the winter of 1954-5.

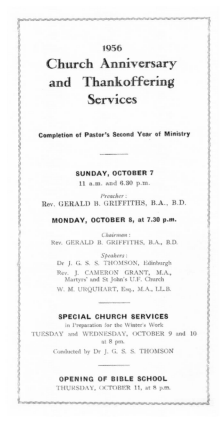

1956
**Church Anniversary and Thankoffering Services**

Completion of Pastor's Second Year of Ministry

**SUNDAY, OCTOBER 7**
11 a.m. and 6.30 p.m.
*Preacher :*
Rev. GERALD B. GRIFFITHS, B.A., B.D.

**MONDAY, OCTOBER 8, at 7.30 p.m.**
*Chairman :*
Rev. GERALD B. GRIFFITHS, B.A., B.D.
*Speakers :*
Dr J. G. S. S. THOMSON, Edinburgh
Rev. J. CAMERON GRANT, M.A.,
Martyrs' and St John's U.F. Church
W. M. URQUHART, Esq., M.A., LL.B.

**SPECIAL CHURCH SERVICES**
in Preparation for the Winter's Work
TUESDAY and WEDNESDAY, OCTOBER 9 and 10
at 8 pm.
Conducted by Dr J. G. S. S. THOMSON

**OPENING OF BIBLE SCHOOL**
THURSDAY, OCTOBER 11, at 8 p.m.

*The church anniversary, over the first weekend in October, no longer commemorated the founding of the church (in January), nor the start of the present ministry (in June), but was used to launch the winter's work.*

Anniversary services on Sunday were followed by a Thankoffering rally on Monday and special services on Tuesday and Wednesday, in preparation for the winter's work; the Bible School started on Thursday.

## Monday night

Ministers, coming to a new church, look for areas that need to be developed. Gerald Griffiths encouraged greater priority for the Monday evening prayer meeting at eight o'clock, and soon the lower hall was almost filled – over two hundred people. He continued the practice of giving news about Chapel missionaries, and leading in prayer for them, on the first Monday of the month.

When some auxiliaries asked for a higher profile in the life of the church, the novel suggestion was made (it happens so regularly now that it seems obvious) of occasionally starting the Monday meeting at 7.30 p.m., to allow a presentation by an auxiliary without reducing the hour for prayer; there was the added benefit that the intercession was based on the information just given. In January 1956, in response to popular request, every meeting started at 7.30 p.m. instead of 8 p.m., and closed at 8.30 p.m., but the business community found this was too much of a rush, and after six months, the regular meeting returned to 8 p.m.

### Thursday night

Attendance at the Thursday Bible School improved substantially, as Gerald Griffiths provided 'meat' from the Scriptures. The area of the Chapel was packed for the first study in 1 Corinthians in October 1954, and the gallery was needed on subsequent Thursdays. Numbers were even greater for his two-session studies in the Gospel of John, from October 1955 to April 1957; many non-members came regularly. Small Bible study groups met on Thursday as well; as an experiment, the Bible School started at 7.30 p.m., for an hour, and the groups followed, but the School soon reverted to an 8 p.m. start, and the groups met at 7 p.m.

The application of spiritual truth to personal experience and conduct was a marked feature of Gerald Griffiths' ministry of the Word. His knowledge of Hebrew and Greek kept him from straying into bypaths of interpretation, and Scottish minds responded readily to his deep interest in Reformed theology, especially Puritan theology. His acquaintance with the broad structure of systematic theology, as distinct from biblical theology, gave his teaching a balance and proportion that maintained the true Reformed tradition.

### Sunday golf

In March 1955, the deacons learned that Edinburgh Corporation, the owner of Carrickknowe golf course, was planning to allow play on Sunday. They were not the only ones to express concern, and their letter of protest, along with others, persuaded the Corporation not to open the course. How different it was less than thirty years later, when the

Royal Highland Show started on a Sunday, without protest from anyone. However, a letter in the *Scottish Baptist Magazine* in 1983 provoked a number of reactions:

*Dear Sir, Glasgow Marathon, [Sunday] September 11 [1983]. Would any Scottish Baptists hoping to run in the Glasgow Marathon please correspond with … so that we can co-ordinate sponsorship, BMS Dedridge / local church projects. Perhaps a special dispensation can be arranged for ministers and members of church house staff wishing to absent themselves from pulpit to take part in the event.*

---

3 *SBM*, May 1983, p. 2.

Although the second part was humorous, the first part was serious; the editorial and contributed articles, responding to the letter, were generally supportive – what Baptists did and did not do on Sunday was changing.

### Tape recording of services

Tape-recording was in its infancy in the early 1950s. Gramophone records of the Chapel choir were on sale in 1953, because one of the members possessed a tape-recorder, and he also recorded, with appropriate background railway noises, the testimony of the Chapel elder, James Paterson, who was a driver on the Edinburgh–London route (Chapter 36).

In June 1955, a member gifted £85 to purchase a tape-recorder, so that shut-in people could hear the Chapel services. A team was formed to carry the heavy equipment to their homes and to play the tapes to them. By March 1956, 30 such visits had been made; housebound Chapel members, always looking for ways to testify to their faith, invited curious neighbours to the novelty of hearing a recorded church service. It was so novel that the *Record* published the names and addresses of those who had been visited. The technology was so unfamiliar that the deacon in charge patiently explained to the readers of the *Record* in 1960 that a microphone in the pulpit 'picks up every word spoken or sung and sends them electrically by means of a short length of cable to the recorder in the Book Room at the back where they are magnetically recorded on a special tape. At the end of the service the tape is removed from the recorder, stored in a small box and placed in an attaché case.'

Chapel missionaries in isolated places particularly appreciated tapes of the services being sent to them, although one pointed out that unless the Chapel was prepared to gift a tape player as well, there was not much point in sending recordings. No one dreamed that only 42 years later, anyone, almost anywhere in the world, would be able to listen to the sermon on the Internet shortly after it was preached, and to view the PowerPoint illustrations that went with it. By 2005, Chapel sermons were being downloaded at the rate of four hundred a week, and the demand for tapes almost disappeared.

### Charlotte Recordings Limited

The tape ministry remained one-to-one (someone visiting the shut-in person with a machine and a tape) until 1963. Then an Edinburgh chartered accountant, a member of St Matthew's parish church in Morningside but a great admirer of the Chapel, catered for the growing number who had their own tape players at home, by building up a lending library of all the Sunday services and the Thursday Bible School. He did this as Charlotte Recordings Limited, a non-profit-making company recognized by the Revenue as charitable. Tapes were sent free of charge; there was no time limit for borrowing, but a second tape was not sent until the first had been returned. Requests came from 70 different countries, 178 requests in 1965 and 200 in the first five months of 1966.

## Billy Graham, All Scotland Crusade

### Welcome

The Chapel enthusiastically supported the first visit to Scotland of the American evangelist, Dr Billy Graham. Gerald Griffiths had been active in the earlier campaign at the Harringay arena in London, and led the Chapel's involvement in the meetings in the Kelvin Hall in Glasgow and elsewhere for six weeks, commencing on 21 March 1955. Books have been written about this, but a few aspects of the Chapel's contribution to the crusade deserve mention here.

### Prayer meetings

The Chapel office-bearers responded warmly to a request from the organisers of the crusade to form special prayer groups, including several all-night prayer meetings in the Chapel. The first was on Friday 18 March 1955, not just for Chapel members, and seven hundred were present for the start at 10 p.m. There were four sessions of two hours, with a break for light refreshments at 2 a.m. 'The tide of prayer flowed spontaneous and free. It was an inspiration to be present. Our oneness in Christ, though all denominations were represented, was abundantly manifest.' Five hundred were still present and participating when the meeting concluded at 6 a.m. Two similar nights were held in the Chapel on Fridays 1 and 22 April. They reminded veterans of the Kemp years of the not infrequent whole nights of prayer during the Revival. There was also a daily meeting for prayer in the Chapel at lunchtime throughout the month of April.

### Special transport

Admission to the Kelvin Hall in Glasgow, where the main rallies were held, was by (free) ticket only, although others could usually find a place in the televised overflow. The Chapel laid on buses from Charlotte Square every Tuesday and, when these were fully booked, arranged special trains to the nearest station in Glasgow. An encouraging number of Chapel members took non-Christian friends.

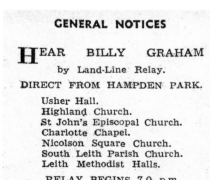

**GENERAL NOTICES**

HEAR BILLY GRAHAM
by Land-Line Relay.
DIRECT FROM HAMPDEN PARK.

Usher Hall.
Highland Church.
St John's Episcopal Church.
Charlotte Chapel.
Nicolson Square Church.
South Leith Parish Church.
Leith Methodist Halls.

RELAY BEGINS 7.0 p.m.

Be Seated at 6.45 p.m.

TO-NIGHT.

*For those who could not get to Glasgow, the Chapel (and others) arranged for the Hampden Park rally to be transmitted by landline; this was sound only, although the relays to the arena adjoining the Kelvin Hall had picture as well.*

### Meetings in Edinburgh

For the last ten days of the crusade, there were audio relays from the Kelvin Hall to the Chapel and to 40 other centres throughout Scotland. In addition, Tynecastle Park, the home of the Heart of Midlothian Football Club, was hired for a rally on Wednesday 20 April at 2 p.m. Twenty thousand (including the writer) were present and after a service lasting for 90 minutes, 922 came forward and recorded their decisions for Christ. Two days later, Billy Graham spoke to students in the McEwan Hall. For all of these, counsellors were trained, so that when an enquirer went forward, someone of the same sex and of approximately the same age went with them, and then talked with them; 80 Chapel members were involved in this.

*Billy Graham and his wife, with the Edinburgh leaders of the crusade, coming onto the pitch at Tynecastle Park on Wednesday 20 April 1955. Twenty thousand were present and 922 came forward in response to the appeal.*

*The singing, led by an augmented choir in the Kelvin Hall, conducted by Cliff Barrows, was an inspiration to many and introduced Scotland to new hymns and tunes.*

## Referrals

From the Kelvin Hall and the relay mission, 60 people were referred to the Chapel for shepherding and growth in the faith. Gerald Griffiths answered criticism in *The Scotsman* about the crusade's appeal to children. He pointed out: 'Children need to be converted, children can be converted, children have been converted and the earlier children are converted the better.' This echoed Joseph Kemp's defence of calling for decisions from an early age, and anticipated Derek Prime's explanation of his position 30 years later, as set out in Chapter 46.

## Pastoral matters

### Sunday morning

In May 1955, the elders considered the length and the style of the 11 a.m. Sunday service. Gerald Griffiths believed that it should close not later than 12.30. He was unwilling to curtail the sermon, nor to omit the children's address, since he wanted to recognize the presence of many children, including those in the Young Worshippers League – in those days, children of all ages sat with their parents throughout the service. He asked the choir to shorten the anthem. The Chapel used the *Revised Baptist Hymnal* in the morning, with the metrical psalms and the paraphrases incorporated. The evening hymnbook was still *Sankey's Sacred Songs and Solos*.

To encourage children to read their Bibles, Gerald Griffiths based his talks to them on Sunday morning on the Scripture Union portion for that day, and invited them to draw a picture to illustrate it – giving prizes for the best entries.

### Young Worshippers League

The Young Worshippers League deserves further mention, because of its influence on family life in the Chapel. Started in 1928, for boys and girls up to the age of 16, Sunday attendance averaged between 70 and 80 out of a membership of over one hundred. Most of them received a prize after a Sunday morning service at the end of May. In 1956, medals were presented to three girls, two of whom had been absent only twice in seven years and five years respectively, while the third had perfect attendance over three years.

## CHARLOTTE BAPTIST CHAPEL

### YOUNG WORSHIPPERS' LEAGUE

As the Annual Prize-giving takes place on Sunday morning, 24th May, you are requested to be present in the Lecture Hall below the Church at 10.30 a.m.

*Presiding.*

*There were 47 prizewinners in May 1959, including one perfect attendance for six years, once absent in five years, perfect attendance for four years and perfect attendance for three years.*

## Chairs in the aisles

Chairs were regularly placed down the aisles of the church in Graham Scroggie's time (Chapter 23). Although some deacons were concerned in the mid 1950s about fire risks, the practice continued:

*The Services on Sunday, the 7th [October 1956], were memorable for the power which rested upon the Pastor as he preached to a completely packed church. Extra seats had to be placed in the aisles on Sunday morning in order to accommodate all who wished to worship with us.*

4 *Record*, 1956, p.168.

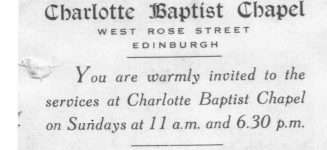

## Charlotte Baptist Chapel
### WEST ROSE STREET
### EDINBURGH

*You are warmly invited to the services at Charlotte Baptist Chapel on Sundays at 11 a.m. and 6.30 p.m.*

Minister - Rev. GERALD B. GRIFFITHS, B.A., B.D.

(OVER)

*Cards, inviting attendance at the Sunday services, were widely distributed, and the Chapel was regularly filled to overflowing.*

Stewards had to put chairs in the aisles for the Thursday of the Ter-jubilee services 1958 (Chapter 40). In September 1960, the superintendent of stewards obtained a ruling from the deacons: 'That no chairs in future are to be set in the aisles when the pews are overcrowded', but he had problems enforcing it; a year later, the deacons hung cards on the stairs, prohibiting chairs at the doors and in the passages of the church during services.

## Usher Hall

When an American choir, coming to London for the Baptist World Alliance Jubilee, asked if they could sing in the Chapel on Sunday evening, 24 July 1955, there was clearly going to be a monumental accommodation problem. In faith, the office-bearers hired the Usher Hall for 7 p.m.; 2,500 attended, the choir sang the gospel, Gerald Griffiths preached and several people, invited by Chapel members, were converted.

## Great Usher Hall Meeting

### SUNDAY EVENING RALLY

arranged by
CHARLOTTE BAPTIST CHAPEL,
EDINBURGH
On SUNDAY, 24th JULY 1955, at 7 p.m.

THE ATLANTA BAPTIST ASSOCIATION CHOIR (U.S.A.)
Direct from the Royal Albert Hall, London

PREACHER:
Rev. GERALD B. GRIFFITHS, B.A., B.D.

ALL FRIENDS ARE VERY WELCOME.    OFFERING TO DEFRAY EXPENSES

*For the first time since Sidlow Baxter left Edinburgh, the Chapel hired the Usher Hall in July 1955. Two thousand five hundred attended, and several were converted.*

## Non-attendance at communion

Absence from the monthly communion service for six consecutive months was meant to alert the elders to a potential spiritual malaise and, unless a satisfactory explanation was given, could lead to removal from membership. The practical difficulty, in a crowded church, was to identify those who were not there. In May 1955, Gerald Griffiths suggested: 'some record of attendances at these services should be kept so that members failing to attend could be interviewed and reasons ascertained'. He proposed: (1) some form of attendance tokens (communion cards), (2) a visiting committee, to include a number of women, to follow up the absentees and (3) a roll secretary, who would check the cards against the membership roll. The elders agreed in principle, but some had reservations about the details, so the proposal was shelved. Mr Griffiths' successor tried it for two years in 1972-3, and then abandoned it; no satisfactory method of recording attendance at communion in the Chapel has ever been devised (Chapter 45).

## National Service

From 1948 to 1962, every able-bodied young man in Great Britain was required to spend two years in the armed forces or in the merchant navy, starting either at the age of 18 or on completion of full-time study. Over two million were conscripted and the Chapel felt a pastoral responsibility for its own youngsters. If they had been brought up in Chapel families, and if their friendships had been in Sunday School and the Young Peoples Meeting, the crudity of barrack life was bound to be a shock, as their fathers, who had come through the Great War, knew well. During basic training, the period which no National Serviceman will ever forget, the barrack-room was the nation in microcosm, where boys from every type of background, social and educational, found that they had to sink or swim. 'Let us not fail them, praying especially for those overseas, facing new temptations and difficulties, that they may keep themselves "unspotted from the world", and that any who are still strangers to grace and to God, may find Him in a foreign land.'

The Chapel sent a parcel to every one of them at Christmas, with a personal letter, assuring them of the Chapel's prayerful remembrance. In December 1953, seven were with the army overseas, six with the army and three with the Royal Air Force in this country; two were in the Royal Navy and two in the Merchant Navy. The parcels continued until the end of National Service in 1962.

## Veterans

### Thomas Draper

Dr Thomas Draper, who retired in 1955 after nearly 50 years in India, was both exceptional in some respects, and yet typical in others, of the Chapel's missionary family. As a young pharmaceutical chemist in London, he knelt down at his bedside on 23 October 1905 in a room behind the chemist's shop in Belgrave Square; as he meditated on John's Gospel, he received, by the Spirit of God, the assurance of salvation. Two years later, he went to India, to work as a pharmacist in the Salvation Army hospital at Travencore, a post he filled for eight years. Dissatisfied with his own preparation for the mission field, and appalled at the tremendous need and unnecessary suffering in India, he came to the Edinburgh Medical Missionary Society and to Charlotte Chapel in 1915. He graduated as a doctor in 1920 and immediately went back to India, for medical missionary work. In 1931 he returned to Edinburgh for post-graduate training, and in 1932 he was elected a Fellow of the Royal College of Physicians of Edinburgh.

*Dr and Mrs Thomas Draper spent 48 years as missionaries in India. This photograph was taken in 1936.*

Returning to India, he took up missionary hospital work, but he was compelled for economic reasons to undertake private practice until 1944, when he became Professor of Pharmacology at the Christian Medical College in Vellore.

Even when he returned to England in 1952, and entered general medical practice in Leicester, he kept his membership with the Chapel – two of his five sons lived in Edinburgh. It is typical of the link, forged when people study in Edinburgh and join the Chapel, that the relationship endures for the rest of their lives. In 1954, at the age of 70, the call of India took him back to the tribe where he had started in 1920. Only failing health in 1955 compelled him to return to the United Kingdom.

## Veterans' party

The annual Christmas party, arranged by the Sunshine Band of the YPM for older members of the church, did not survive the war (Chapter 25). Gerald Griffiths noticed the gap and arranged a Saturday afternoon tea in January 1955 in the lower hall. It was followed by an evening of singing, a film of the Holy Land, an interval for chatting, more singing, a violin solo, another interval, another film (Chapel personalities, missionaries, the Baxters, etc.), family worship and a closing hymn. It was a great success, and the presence of the three young Griffiths (Ian, Myfanwy and Jonathan in his baby chair) brought as much delight to the 90 veterans as anything else.

This became an annual event, from 4-7 p.m., hosted by the office-bearers and their wives; the title 'Senior Members Party' replaced the description of 'Veterans'. Among the hundred guests on these Saturdays was one who had joined when George Way was pastor in the 1890s, and two who had been baptized at Joseph Kemp's first baptismal service. They loved singing the old hymns, but they were intrigued by new ideas as well; when one of the deacons produced a camera that took flashlight photographs, they thought it was fascinating.

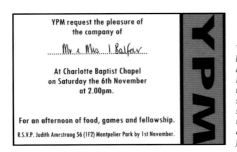

*When the YPM took back responsibility for the annual Senior Members Party in 1962, the writer was aged 29; they were still running it with the same enthusiasm when the writer and his wife qualified, 36 years later, for an invitation.*

In the next vacancy, the YPM took it over again, and made it the best party of the year – as they still do. From 1977, they also arranged a mystery bus tour (two coaches) in the month of June. A typical outing was to Crieff, with the opportunity of looking around the town, followed by tea in the Baptist church hall there.

Additional information on the following topics, mentioned in this chapter, is available on the CD.

Charlotte Recordings Ltd
Elders and Deacons – history 1877–1995
Gerald and Kitty Griffiths before Charlotte Chapel
Manses
Rock Mission
Thomas Draper
Young Worshippers League

# Chapter 39
## Branches over the wall (1956–1957)

## Ongoing activities

### Overview

The title for this chapter – Branches over the wall – comes from Gerald Griffiths' anniversary letter in October 1956. He picked up three phrases from Genesis 49:22, which reads: 'Joseph is a fruitful bough, even a fruitful bough by a well, whose branches run over the wall'; he commented on them: (1) the Chapel was experiencing much fruitfulness, with crowded Sunday services, baptisms, Usher Hall meetings and a sense of unity; (2) fruitfulness included supporting the Monday prayer meeting; (3) neighbours, over the wall, should be told about, and share in, the good things going on in the Chapel.

It would be repetitive to refer to events, even significant ones, which took place year after year; on the other hand, there would be gaps in the Chapel's history if they were not mentioned occasionally. This chapter opens with news about seven regular activities, going chronologically through 1956.

### Sunday Night at Seven

Holding the Chapel's Sunday evening service in the Usher Hall for two months in the spring, which had been so successful during Sidlow Baxter's ministry, was resumed from 29 January to 25 March 1956. Intensive preparation by prayer and by distributing thirty thousand handbills and by displaying four hundred window-bills brought about fifteen hundred to the opening meeting. An augmented choir of 140 sat behind the platform, and Gerald Griffiths preached a serious gospel address for half an hour. Decisions were made at the close of every meeting, eight on the first night alone. By mid-February, about two thousand came nightly and the top gallery was needed. The *Edinburgh Evening News* commented on two aspects: (1) 'one of the most impressive features of the services is the community hymn-singing', and (2) 'a large section of the audiences are people who have no church connections'.

A second series, again for nine weeks, was held from 3 February to 31 March 1957. Fifty thousand handbills were distributed – climbing Edinburgh tenement stairs was excellent exercise – and five hundred posters were displayed in shops, offices and factories. The Monday evening prayer meeting was extended by an hour, to concentrate on

intercession for the Usher Hall services. They were well attended throughout the nine weeks, with never less than sixteen hundred present and, on the last night, two thousand three hundred.

*The Usher Hall is the white-domed building on the right of this picture; the Chapel's white west wall can be seen on the left. The Caledonian station and railway lines dominate the area between. The Western Approach Road now runs along the lines of the track and the Sheraton Hotel stands opposite the Usher Hall in Lothian Road.*

In 1958, Gerald Griffiths and the elders arranged eight consecutive Sunday evenings during February and March – the best time of year for such services – and the Usher Hall was well filled. This time, he did not hold an after-meeting for enquirers, as it presented logistical difficulties, but he asked seekers to come to the front during the closing hymn. Encouraged by the response, the Chapel arranged a ten-week series in 1959.

Not so visible, but crucial to the success of these meetings, were Chapel members who did not sit in the auditorium, but who met in the hall behind the platform to pray throughout the service. Gerald Griffiths felt so strengthened by this that he arranged for similar contemporaneous prayer during the Chapel's regular Sunday evening service.

### Annual missionary conference

The annual Foreign Missions Sunday was expanded in June 1955, to include both Saturday and Monday evening. Films and a speaker on Saturday, a guest preacher for both services on Sunday and an information meeting on Monday, set a pattern that lasted for a decade. In 1957, the conference moved from June to November, to attract better numbers; the lower hall was full on Saturday, with nearly three hundred

299

people, but 'Monday night did not see the great crowd which we had hoped, but a thoughtful and concerned group of two or three hundred with the mission field on their consciences.'

CHARLOTTE BAPTIST CHAPEL,
WEST ROSE STREET.
FOREIGN MISSIONS WEEK-END.
TO-NIGHT, in Lecture Hall, at 7.30 p.m.
Mr JAMES BALLANTYNE
will show his 2 new Colour Films of
INDIA and ARABIA.
All will be made welcome.
N.B.—Owing to indisposition, the Rev.
John Savage, of E.U.S.A., has had to cancel
his week-end engagement at Charlotte Chapel.
SUNDAY, 26th, 11 a.m. and 6.30 p.m.
Preacher:
Rev. GEORGE E. J. BIRD,
of Ipswich.
MONDAY, 27th, at 7.30 p.m.
Speaker: Dr A. M. KERR of E.M.M.S.
All offerings during week-end on behalf
of Missionary Work Overseas.

*The annual Foreign Missions Sunday became, in 1955, the Foreign Missions Week-end and then, in 1956, the Overseas Missions Week-end.*

## Secular missionaries

Until Gerald Griffiths came to Edinburgh, the Chapel's definition of a missionary was someone working overseas with a missionary society. Members in government posts, or who moved from a faith mission to secular employment, came off the list of 'Our Own Missionaries'. Mr Griffiths realized that the role of mission was changing in the post-war world, especially in countries where indigenous churches could take over the work of evangelism. He persuaded the Chapel to hold a valedictory service for members who, out of concern for the salvation and welfare of others, took secular employment in a 'missionary country'. The first three to be valedicted in this way went to: (1) a rural government school in Sarawak, (2) the Girl Guide movement in Kenya and (3) the education department of the Nyasaland government. Gerald Griffiths changed the title of the missionary news pages in the monthly *Record* to 'The Field is the World', and included letters from the three just mentioned.

Alan Davis had gone as a Chapel missionary to the Gold Coast in 1950, with the Worldwide Evangelisation Crusade, to work among lepers. When the nation became independent in 1956, he felt it right to transfer to the Ghana State Medical Service; under the new arrangement, that made no difference to his missionary status in the Chapel. By 1958, seven of the thirty missionaries on the Chapel's prayer list were in secular employment for missionary ends. Nevertheless, there were still opportunities for direct missionary evangelism, particularly among the expatriate Chinese in Asia, the villages of India and the tribes of tropical Africa and South America.

## Keswick Convention

Annually from 1956 until 1968, the Monday-Thursday evening meetings from the large tent in Keswick were relayed to the Chapel by telephone link. The reception was uniformly faultless and the messages came over with the ring of reality to the five hundred or so who gathered nightly in the Chapel. Throughout Great Britain, 112 centres shared Keswick teaching in this way; the annual Convention lasted for only one week at this time (now it is three). When the link was discontinued in 1969, the Convention made tapes available at the end of the week, but the Chapel felt this was too remote and did not take up the offer. Instead, it supported the resumed 'Keswick in Edinburgh' week in June, which Graham Scroggie had started in 1917 (Chapter 29). This Monday-Friday convention, with a guest speaker, moved around the Edinburgh churches and was held regularly in the Chapel until 1994 (Chapter 52).

KESWICK
CONVENTION

RELAYS
Charlotte
Baptist Chapel,
Rose Street, Edinburgh 2.
July 18th to 21st, 1960
at 7.30 p.m.

*Gerald Griffiths was one of the speakers at the Keswick Convention in July 1956 and again in July 1958; a Chapel member took this snap of the Griffiths with Rev. and Mrs Herbert Cragg. When he was not in Keswick, Gerald Griffiths chaired the services relayed to the Chapel.*

## Youth organisations

The annual remembrance service, on the Sunday nearest to 11 November, was an opportunity for the uniformed organisations (Brownies, Guides, Cubs and Scouts) to parade together. It was also an opportunity for the Longstone Sunday School (described below) to attend the Chapel. About this time of year, but on a Saturday, the Sunday School held an evening for parents and friends, conducted by the scholars themselves, culminating with the presentation of prizes for good attendance.

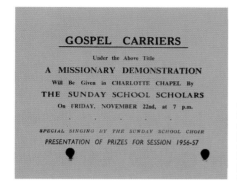

**GOSPEL CARRIERS**

Under the Above Title

A MISSIONARY DEMONSTRATION

Will Be Given in CHARLOTTE CHAPEL By

THE SUNDAY SCHOOL SCHOLARS

On FRIDAY, NOVEMBER 22nd, at 7 p.m.

SPECIAL SINGING BY THE SUNDAY SCHOOL CHOIR

PRESENTATION OF PRIZES FOR SESSION 1956-57

*A Saturday evening meeting in November, at which prizes were presented for good attendance at the Sunday School, was popular with parents and friends in 1956.*

## Sunday baptisms in the Chapel

Gerald Griffiths, like his predecessors, conducted believers' baptism on either a Monday or a Thursday evening, and the Chapel was usually well filled. However, on 9 December 1956, he included baptisms in a Sunday evening service – as several of his predecessors had done in the nineteenth century (Chapter 11). The building was crowded to capacity, with an overflow into the lower hall. In an atmosphere of reverence sustained by the large congregation during the service, ten were baptized, thirteen more signified their desire for future baptism, and ten others accepted Christ as Saviour. The Sunday pattern became established, with similar services, and similar responses, in January, March and June 1957.

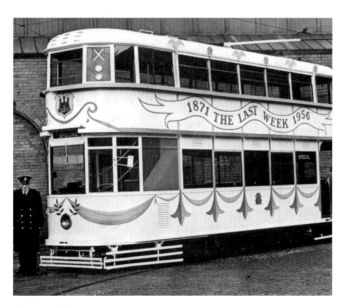

*November 1956 was a nostalgic month for many in Edinburgh, as buses replaced the last trams. There was no longer any hesitation about using public transport on Sunday (Chapter 20).*

## Christmas and New Year

The turn of the year was always a busy time in the Chapel. In 1956, there was a carol concert on Thursday 20 December, Christmas services on Sunday 23 December, and a Monday evening prayer meeting on Christmas Eve. There was no longer a Christmas Day service in the Chapel, but there were full services on Sunday 30 December, and a Watchnight service on Hogmanay. Shortly after midnight, many of the congregation went to the corner of Princes Street and South Charlotte Street (or South Castle Street, if traffic was heavy), for an open-air meeting and to rededicate the work for the new year. The faithful were back for the afternoon and evening conference on Tuesday 1 January 1957.

**CHARLOTTE BAPTIST CHAPEL**
WEST ROSE STREET, EDINBURGH

**ANNUAL**
**NEW YEAR'S DAY CONFERENCE**

on

1st JANUARY 1960
CONFERENCE SESSIONS at 3.30 and 7 p.m.

Guest Speaker:

**Rev. GEOFFREY R. KING**
West Croydon Tabernacle

Soloists:
Mr Gordon Borthwick     Mr Thomas S. Currie

Chairman:
**Rev. GERALD B. GRIFFITHS, B.A., B.D.**

Tea served in Hall at 5.15 p.m.

**ALL FRIENDS FROM TOWN AND COUNTRY ARE WARMLY INVITED TO ATTEND.**

Printed by Warwick & Sons Ltd., Edinburgh and Portobello

*At the New Year's Day conference, a guest preacher gave an address in the afternoon and then, following tea in the lower hall, at an evening session as well.*

The Watchnight usually saw the Chapel filled to capacity by 11.15 p.m. Two strangers, who attended on Saturday 31 December 1955 because their own congregation did not have a service, were so impressed that they wrote to the *Edinburgh Evening News*:

*Some hundreds of people were present, but what delighted and astonished us most was the fact that more than half of the gathering was composed of young men and women. The youth of to-day has no time for the religious formalism which is so prevalent, but this service demonstrated that the*

301

*living Christ, when He is presented, still saves and captivates the young with the abundant life into which He leads them.*

1 *Edinburgh Evening News*, 3 January 1956.

The New Year conference, held on 1 January unless it was a Sunday, brought in Christians who had nothing comparable in their own churches. Numbers ranged from three hundred to the Chapel being well filled.

## Beulah Home

### The vision

As described in Chapter 37, one of the Chapel deacons, John McGuinness, began campaigning in 1947 for funds to provide a home for elderly members, who had been in tied accommodation and who had nowhere to stay when they retired. Eventide homes were almost unheard of in those days; the only Baptist one in Scotland was in Dundee, set up by the Rattray Street Church there in 1947. By the spring of 1955, enough was in hand to purchase and renovate a home for fourteen residents, with a staff of three living in.

> **SPECIAL BEULAH HOMES WEEK-END**
> **at CHARLOTTE CHAPEL**
> on Sunday and Monday, 12th and 13th July
> MONDAY EVENING RALLY AT 7.30
> *Speaker :* REV. W. G. CHANNON, OF PURLEY, SURREY.
> *Monday (from 1 p.m. onwards). Office-bearers will be in the vestry to receive the gifts of our members and friends.*
> **Everybody will be made welcome**

*The Beulah Homes project (the name was plural until one home in Newhaven Road was chosen in 1955) was publicized every summer from 1951.*

A house at 134 Newhaven Road came on the market in the spring of 1955. It was ideally situated, with a well-kept garden and overlooking Victoria Park; it had three public rooms, a large kitchen, and could accommodate fourteen people, plus staff. The seller, an Edinburgh bailie, was so delighted at the proposed use of his home that he reduced the price and planted the front garden with antirrhinums and asters. The £8,000, collected painstakingly over eight years since the appeal was launched, covered the purchase and the adaptation of the building (fire escapes etc.); the home opened free of debt. At that point, the deacons changed the name of the house from Beaufort to Beulah.

*The house purchased by the Chapel at 134 Newhaven Road; John McGuinness, who promoted the scheme; Miss Margaret Innes, a hospital sister and a member of the Chapel, who offered to be matron.*

### Opening

Beulah Home was opened on Saturday 30 June 1956, when over three hundred filled the carriageway and the street outside. They sung the 23rd Psalm, Gerald Griffiths dedicated the home in prayer, and then John McGuinness presented Mrs Griffiths with a key (see photograph on next page); she gave a gracious speech and opened the front door. The crowd sang the doxology and moved through to a marquee in the garden, where a service of thanksgiving took place.

*The opening of Beulah Home on Saturday 30 June 1956, and John McGuinness handing over a key to Mrs Griffiths, who formally opened the door.*

The home quickly built up to full occupancy. The first Christmas was celebrated by the Griffiths family and the McGuinness family leading a short service, followed by Father Christmas, a turkey dinner for the residents, the Queen's broadcast on the radio and a quiet evening. A garden party was held on Saturday afternoon every May, with a marquee on the lawn.

## Closure

Family worship twice a day, regular visits from Chapel auxiliaries and then, from 1969, listening to Chapel services as well, made Beulah special for fifty years; updates are given

in Chapters 40, 44 and 49. By 2006, those for whom Beulah had been established were, as a matter of social policy, being looked after at home, either by family or by social services, until only a nursing home could provide for them. Beulah could not be adapted for nursing care, and as there were no applications from Chapel members, it was decided, after full consultation, not to continue beyond the summer of 2010.

## The Baptist Union of Scotland

### A tangled maze

In his seven years at the Chapel, Gerald Griffiths proved himself to be not only a great preacher and Bible expositor, but to possess the qualities that make a Christian statesman. He inherited a confused and uncertain situation about the relationship of the Chapel to the Baptist Union of Scotland, with particular reference to the World Council of Churches. He led the church carefully through the tangled maze of doctrinal issues, which were at times mixed with expediency. Ever patiently listening, he brought the church to a position of almost complete unanimity under circumstances where one false move or injudicious meeting could have split the church and possibly the Union as well. He stressed: 'our action was not motivated by antipathy on the part of any members of the Court against the Baptist Union, but simply with a desire to maintain our clear Evangelical position.' What was it all about?

### 1948

The World Council of Churches was founded in Amsterdam in 1948; the Baptist Union of Scotland's representative recommended that the Union should affiliate to it. At the 1948 Assembly in Aberdeen, the leadership pressed for this, and it was approved by a majority of one (81 votes to 80). Chapel elder Robert Aitken wrote in his memoirs: 'it was with very considerable concern that the Chapel observed the Baptist Union Assembly, in 1948, join the World Council of Churches'. He and another elder, James Cossar, attempted to have the decision overturned; they were unhappy about the doctrinal basis of the WCC and the narrowness of the decision. Having failed to persuade the Union to withdraw from the WCC, they raised the issue with the Chapel elders: 'A number of the smaller churches are looking to Charlotte Chapel to give a lead.'

**Chapter 39**
Branches over the wall (1956-1957)

*William MacDuff Urquhart, the church secretary, and Robert Aitken, the church treasurer, during the ecumenical debates of the 1950s.*

## 1952

The elders invited the American vice-president of the International Council of Christian Churches to address them in the summer of 1952. He told them unpleasant facts about the World Council of Churches, so that: 'it was obvious that we as a Court, would have to review the whole position, especially as Charlotte Chapel was linked to the World Council of Churches through the Baptist Union of Scotland.' Literature in support of his position was distributed, and by the autumn of 1952, two different attitudes emerged: should the Chapel withdraw immediately from the Union, in protest at its affiliation, or should the Chapel try to persuade the Union to disaffiliate from the WCC?

Incidentally, Chapel members who were students at the Universities of Edinburgh and St Andrews in 1952, and who supported the evangelical Inter-Varsity Fellowship Christian Unions there, found themselves involved in much the same issue at student level. The more liberal Student Christian Movement, whose interests were in discussing the relevance of Christianity to politics and social and university problems, made ecumenical overtures to the evangelical Unions, whose priority was evangelism and teaching within a clear doctrinal basis. In Edinburgh, the Chapel students were united in opposing the approach; in St Andrews, the SCM had the grace not to press for divisive joint activities.

## 1953

At a meeting of Chapel members in July 1953, during the leaderless period of the vacancy, the elders told them about the doctrinal basis of the new body. Although it read: 'The World Council of Churches is a fellowship of churches which accept our Lord Jesus Christ as God and Saviour', it was followed by a declaration that: 'The WCC does not concern itself with the manner in which the churches will interpret the foundation.' This, the elders said, 'rendered the doctrinal statement void of meaning as a basis on which to unite'. The lowest common denominator approach was so vague as to be unacceptable; the WCC (they said) did not uphold the fundamental truths of Scripture.

The members agreed that the doctrinal basis was not scripturally adequate, and called on the Union to disaffiliate. When notice of this motion was given to the Union, prior to the Assembly in Dundee in October 1953, the Union office-bearers persuaded the Chapel that it was not desirable to have another public debate on this emotive issue, so shortly after the debates at previous Assemblies. A meeting of Chapel members, called early in October, agreed that instead of the Chapel's motion, a Committee of Enquiry should be appointed, consisting of the five Union office-bearers and eight ministers and eight laymen, of whom two (the two elders who felt so strongly on the matter) should be the Chapel representatives.

## 1954

While the committee was formulating its report, Gerald Griffiths took up the pastorate of Charlotte Chapel. He supported the Chapel's stance, saying that the doctrinal basis of the WCC could be interpreted in any number of ways; he compared it with the Chapel's evangelical basis of faith, and agreed that the Chapel had been right to protest at the affiliation of the Union with the WCC.

## 1955

The committee's report was circulated with the papers for the Assembly in October 1955. Nineteen recommended the status quo, that the Union should remain in the WCC pending a revision of the latter's basis of faith in 1961. Only two members of the committee dissented, and they were the two Chapel elders. They circulated their views to every Scottish Baptist church, calling for immediate withdrawal. Prior to the Assembly, the Chapel agreed, almost unanimously on a paper ballot: 'to withdraw now from membership of the Baptist Union of Scotland in view of its affiliation with the World Council of Churches'. The exact wording of that decision became very significant, as set out below.

The Chapel was therefore committed to withdrawing from the Union, if the Union remained in affiliation with the WCC. The question in October 1955 was one of timing – whether to withdraw before the Assembly, and so have no right to speak there, or whether to go to the Assembly, have a vigorous debate, and risk not only defeat and subsequent withdrawal, but also the withdrawal from the Union of a number of like-minded churches. Both approaches had serious and far-reaching consequences.

With Christian love and grace, which was misunderstood by some, Gerald Griffiths recommended immediate withdrawal. He summarized the Chapel's fundamental objection to the WCC: it will not commit itself to bow to the final authority of the Scriptures. With many of the objectives of the Council, and particularly its Refugee Relief Programme, the Chapel was in entire sympathy, but its basis of faith was too ambiguous and inadequate for any united evangelical Christian witness. The Chapel's resignation was submitted to the Union, and a lengthy printed statement of its position was circulated to all the churches in the Union.

As the Chapel had resigned before the report was debated, it could not take part in the Assembly discussion. Nevertheless, the Assembly decided, in deference to the strongly expressed view of the largest Baptist church in Scotland, to reject the majority report and to accept the minority recommendation. The Assembly disaffiliated from the WCC for seven years, that is until the review of 1961; it would then look at the situation afresh. The debate was not really about the World Council of Churches, but about the unity of the Baptist Union of Scotland.

## 1956

The Union having, as it thought, met the Chapel's demand, invited the Chapel to withdraw its resignation and resume normal relations. This was the first of five formal approaches to the Chapel for reconciliation, the others coming in 1967, 1987, 1992 and 1996, as described below. After full discussion among the Chapel office-bearers and the Union, a special meeting of Chapel members was held in December 1956. The chairman said:

*At first glance the obvious thing seemed to be that we should go back into the Union now that they had withdrawn from the World Council of Churches; but it was not so simple as that. For one thing the Baptist Union Assembly had acknowledged the scriptural inadequacy of the basis of the World Council of Churches, and yet was apparently content to continue in affiliation with the British Council of Churches and with the Scottish Ecumenical Movement whose doctrinal basis was precisely the same.*

2 Members' Minute, 17 December 1956.

The meeting decided that the Chapel should remain out of the Union because of the British Council of Churches anomaly. This moving of the goal posts by the Chapel (as the Union saw it, but see below for the Chapel's position) was widely misunderstood and caused embarrassment to those in the Chapel who had close personal links with the Union. The Chapel was the only church to withdraw at that time.

The writer shared that embarrassment until Robert Aitken's widow gave him, after her husband's death in 1970, notes that Mr Aitken had made at the time. They may not excuse the Chapel's attitude, but at least they explain it. Mr Aitken's own words, about the events that followed the Assembly decision in October 1955, are:

*We had stated our case and won our brethren but our lack of foresight in 1953 still left us isolated. The Union had disaffiliated from the World Council but not from the British Council of Churches, nor from the Scottish Ecumenical Conference, which have the same basis to which we had already stated our objection. We had not mentioned this problem earlier. Very humbly, as a Church, we now asked the Union to address itself to this situation and undertook should the issue be satisfactory, to give our full support to the Baptist Union. This was not done. Our resignation was allowed to lie on the table for two full years until the Assembly of 1957, by a majority vote, agreed to accept it.*

3 Robert Aitken's notes.

As that note states, the Union thought carefully about this further call, but decided in October 1957 that enough was enough. Despite the Chapel's resignation, there have always been good relationships at personal level. Rev. William

304

305

Whyte, the president of the Union in 1960-61, retired from active ministry during his presidential year, rejoined his home church (the Chapel) and became an elder in 1961. When the Union arranged a holiday summer school in Holland in 1961, it was led by two of the Chapel's boys, Donald McCallum and Peter Barber, and there was an open invitation to the Chapel's youth to join in. The writer was the Union's law agent from 1966 to 1997 and president of the Union in 1976-7. The Chapel was the home church of two consecutive general secretaries, Andrew MacRae (1966-80) and Peter Barber (1980-94). Alastair Hay was the Union's financial and pension adviser for many years, succeeded by another Chapel office-bearer, David Whitlie.

*Although the Chapel withdrew from the Baptist Union of Scotland in 1955, the post of general secretary of the Union was subsequently held by two of the Chapel's boys, Andrew MacRae (upper) from 1966 to 1980 and Peter Barber (lower) from 1980 to 1994.*

### 1962–1964
In 1961, the World Council of Churches looked afresh at its doctrinal basis, as promised. The Union re-examined its relationship, in light of that, but the 1963 Assembly concluded that nothing significant had changed. The issue was raised again at the 1964 Assembly, which reaffirmed the position. The Union remained outside the WCC, and the Chapel stayed outside the Union.

### 1967
Withdrawal from the Union meant (it was thought at the time) that the Chapel was no longer eligible to be a member of the Edinburgh and Lothians Baptist Association (Chapter 12). Nevertheless, many individuals in the Chapel worked with Elba, as individuals, particularly when Elba hosted the Union's annual Assembly. In February 1967, someone asked how this squared with the Chapel's relationship with the Union. The deacons decided to meet with the office-bearers of the Union, to ask what the Union stood for and what it was doing, and secondly what its attitude was to the Ecumenical Movement.

A full and positive meeting took place in the Chapel in the following month, after which the deacons met again to reflect on the position. The writer proposed: 'while this Court cannot support certain policies and aims of the WCC, BCC and SCC, it is desirous of expressing fellowship with our Baptist friends throughout Scotland and resolves to make application to the Council of the Baptist Union for readmission to that body.' This was approved by 23 votes to 11; it was agreed to hold a special meeting of members, early in May 1967, for the proposition to be put as a majority recommendation from the Court.

At the members' meeting, there was what the *Record* called a full and lively discussion, following which 107 voted for the recommendation, 134 against and there were 10 abstentions. Over the next few months, some in the congregation tried to keep the discussion going; eventually, the deacons gave every Chapel member a leaflet and an explanatory letter, supplied by the Union to set out its position, and then, in January 1968, declared the matter closed.

### 1987
In March 1987, the Union wrote to the four Baptist churches in Scotland that had, at various times and for various reasons, withdrawn from membership, suggesting exploratory meetings. As Derek Prime, the Chapel's pastor, was due to leave in October, the elders decided that any discussions

should be in consultation with the next pastor, when appointed. Furthermore, they were aware that some members had strong feelings about the Union, and they resolved that if exploratory meetings seemed likely to threaten the unity of the congregation, they should be discontinued – the unity of the Chapel was as important, if not more important, than relationships outside.

The Union regularly reviewed its relationship with the ecumenical movement in Scotland, and never approved of Baptists being other than observers at multilateral conversations aiming for unification of the Scottish churches. The last major debate was at the Assembly in October 1989. The Scottish Churches Council, the local expression of the World Council of Churches, was to be re-formed under the name ACTS (Action of Churches Together in Scotland). The options were full membership, associate membership, observer status or no participation. The Union leadership, recognising the reservations of some churches, proposed associate membership. Those fully committed to the ecumenical movement moved for full membership, which provoked a backlash and the decision, after a full debate, was not to associate with ACTS in any way.

Many thought that the 1989 decision cleared the way for the Chapel to rejoin the Union, because the issue on which they had left in 1955 had finally become Union policy. However, when informal soundings were taken, it was apparent that some members of the Chapel still had a deep-rooted antipathy to the Union.

## 1990

The 1989 decision did, however, cause some to ask why the Chapel could not take a full and official part in the Edinburgh and Lothians Baptist Association. In April 1990, the Chapel asked to rejoin Elba, with Dr (now Professor) Donald Meek as its representative; Elba responded gladly to the Chapel's approach, and Donald was the Elba president in 1992-3.

## 1992

After preaching in the Chapel as pulpit supply in January 1992, Peter Barber, a Chapel old boy who was now general secretary of the Baptist Union of Scotland, wrote to say that both he, and some who had spoken to him, hoped that the relationship might now be reconsidered:

*When Baptists outwith Scotland ask me why Charlotte Chapel is not part of the Union I find that a very difficult question to answer. They know the issue cannot be ecumenical; they wonder if there is some sense in which the Union is not evangelical enough. When I assure them this is not the case, I am left – as is my questioner – wondering what is the problem?*

4 'Baptist Union of Scotland – Peter Barber's letter', on the CD.

The elders thought about his letter for several months; some were in favour, some were against. They recognized that it would be folly to bring a recommendation to the members unless they themselves were united about it, which they were not. In May, they replied: 'the letter has been discussed, but there is no desire for the matter to be taken further at this stage'.

## 1996

The fifth and final approach by the Union to the Chapel was in November 1996. The Union's annual Assembly had met in Edinburgh in October, and the minister of the Chapel, Peter Grainger, had been invited to preach at one of the meetings. He did so, and when the Union's general secretary wrote a letter of thanks, on 6 November, he went on to 'wonder whether there is any way in which we might strengthen the links between Charlotte Baptist Chapel and the Union'. Peter Grainger read the letter to the next meeting of the Chapel elders.

It so happened that the elders had had a lengthy discussion on that very question at their October meeting. The Chapel's fellowship groups were encouraged to advise their elder about any item that the group wanted to air, and several had asked about the Chapel's relationship with the Union. In consequence, a background paper was prepared over the summer of 1996, and the elders spent time discussing it on 2 October. They concluded: 'if membership was important enough we should pursue it but otherwise it was best left alone, being potentially divisive. It was clear that there remained division in the Court regarding the matter and there being no sense of unanimity to proceed, we should take no action.'

Accordingly, when the Union's letter of 6 November was read, some said: 'we made a decision about that just a month ago, so there is no point in discussing it again'. It was clear that to press the invitation would have been divisive, so Peter Grainger replied courteously but without offering any encouragement. The writer, who had been present at the elders' meeting as church secretary, was also at the receiving end of that letter, because, as the Union's law agent, he was on its executive committee. The general secretary read the reply, and there was genuine and heartfelt disappointment around the table. The writer still remembers Bill Slack's wistful comment, as he filed the letter: 'Ah, well, perhaps some other time.'

## New youth work

### YPM September weekend

For the last 50 years, a major event in the YPM's calendar has been going away together for the Edinburgh September holiday weekend. Mr and Mrs Griffiths began the idea with an invitation (below) in 1957. It was so successful that they went annually to the youth hostel in Kinross until 1964, when increasing numbers forced them to relocate to Wiston Lodge, Biggar. From September 1968 to 1985, the YPM rented the Gean House in Alloa or St Ninian's in Crieff or the Abernethy Outdoor Centre at Nethy Bridge, and then went back to Wiston Lodge for 1986 – finding somewhere large enough, at a competitive price, was more difficult than finding a speaker on their wavelength. New venues have now become available, Lendrick Muir (2001-2002, 2006), Gartmore House (2003, 2005) and Blaithwaite House in Cumbria (2004).

*YOUNG PEOPLE'S WEEK-END*
(15-30 years)
**AN INVITATION**
*Rev. and Mrs Gerald B. Griffiths request the pleasure of your company at a Young People's Week-end Conference from 13th to 16th September, at "Broomleigh," West Linton.*
*R.S.V.P. to Craigatin, Queensferry Road, Barnton.*

*YPM September weekends began with this invitation in 1957 from the pastor and his wife. As mentioned in Chapter 38, it is a tribute to the postman that letters to the manse were delivered without a street number in the four-mile Queensferry Road.*

### Longstone Sunday School

The Chapel Sunday School held summer open-air services for young people in the Sighthill district of western Edinburgh in the years before the Second World War (Chapter 34). The Chapel also tried to purchase ground in the area, for a permanent outreach mission, but the city architect would not make anything available. When open-air services were resumed after the war, the Council was building further to the west, in Longstone; the Chapel obtained permission to hold a Sunday School in the day school building there.

Fifteen teachers visited houses in the area on Saturday 9 October 1948, door to door, inviting children to the school on the following day. More than 80 turned up, and 57 enrolled in the Longstone Baptist Sunday School. On the following Sunday, 100 came, between the ages of 3 and 14, and soon there were 130 on the roll; about 100 attended on most Sundays, which demonstrated the enthusiasm of both the children and the teachers. As numbers increased, the school was divided into a primary department of 100, and a junior school, with 140.

So many parents wanted to come to the first summer picnic, in 1949, that two double-deck buses were required; there were seven hundred at the picnic in the following year. This challenged the leaders to do something for the grown-ups as well as for the children, because there was no church in the new estate at that time. Nothing was possible for adults until 1955 (below), but by 1950 the Sunday School was using every room in the day school building, organized into beginners, primary and junior departments. Soon a Guide Company and a Brownie Pack was added, and the classes overflowed into the passages and cloakrooms of the school. In April 1954, the Chapel rented the Slateford-Longstone village hall on Sunday afternoon and started a Bible Class for older scholars. From an initial roll of 16, it increased rapidly to 29. Most were aged 14 or over and had previously attended the Sunday School; they came back because of the creation of a separate Bible Class.

When a new Longstone day school was built in 1957, magnificently equipped, the Sunday School expanded to include two Guide Companies, three Brownie Packs, one Scout Troop and one Cub Pack, with 43 Chapel members involved as leaders and teachers. From the beginning, the Chapel insisted that there was only one Sunday School, meeting in two places (Rose Street and Longstone), both fully supported by personnel and prayer backing from the Chapel.

The Longstone school gave the same prominence to overseas mission as the one in Rose Street. On the first Sunday of the month, all the offerings at Longstone went to purchase Bibles in the African Hausa language. The leader of the Junior Sunday School, who was also Brown Owl, went to Kenya on a two-year assignment, giving the scholars a personal focus on Africa. As the Chapel met all current expenses for both schools, they were able to send all the children's offerings to evangelistic home and missionary enterprises – teaching the children early the importance of supporting such work. Up to £200 annually was sent overseas in this way, usually by direct gifts to individual Chapel missionaries.

**Missionary Demonstration—Longstone Bible Class—Parents' Night**

*The Longstone Sunday School gave the same prominence to overseas mission as the parent school in Rose Street. These scholars presented tableaux in national costumes on parents' night in 1957.*

## Longstone adult services

A Sunday evening gospel service was started in the Slateford-Longstone public hall in October 1955. The district was circulated with handbills, and the response was encouraging. It was also an excellent way for the Chapel's YPM to gain experience in public singing and speaking. Eighty Chapel members provided a nucleus for the congregation. This encouraged the Chapel to renew its search for land for building its own premises, but none was available. What happened over the next 18 years, and how this led to the establishment of the Wester Hailes Baptist Church in 1973, is taken up in Chapter 46.

## Two new auxiliaries

Between 1955 and 1958, two new activities started in the Chapel itself – a Deaf and Dumb Christian Fellowship and a Women's Morning Fellowship. Both deserve more space than is available in this chapter, so their story will be taken up in Chapter 40.

Additional information on the following topics, mentioned in this chapter, is available on the CD.

Baptist Union of Scotland
Baptist Union of Scotland – Peter Barber's letter
Baptist Union of Scotland – 1996 Chapel document
Beulah Home
Edinburgh University Christian Union
Longstone
Robert Aitken

# Chapter 40
## The Chapel's Ter-jubilee (1958)

### Domestic celebrations

#### Home and away

The office-bearers had twin plans for the Chapel's Ter-jubilee. One was to commemorate events in Rose Street, for which a souvenir brochure was prepared. The other was to raise the profile of the Chapel's foreign mission work, for which another brochure was prepared and a large missionary conference arranged. The first part of this chapter looks at the domestic programme, and the second part at overseas mission.

#### 24 January 1958

Although Christopher Anderson had constituted the church on Sunday 24 January 1808, the Chapel did not start its Ter-jubilee celebrations until April; this was to avoid snow and icy streets during the first three months of the year. On 24 January 1958, one of the Chapel missionaries, Mabel McLean, left Edinburgh for her second term of service in India; since Christopher Anderson had promoted mission in India for fifty years (Chapter 5), it was an apposite coincidence (neither planned nor mentioned at the time). A large group of friends gathered at the Caledonian station (now demolished) to wish Mabel God-speed. It was one of the last instances of such a gathering; modern trains do not permit passengers to lean out of the window as the train moves off, waving good-bye, while people on the platform sing a farewell hymn.

*Mabel McLean left Edinburgh for India on 24 January 1958, 150 years to the day since Christopher Anderson inaugurated the church that became Charlotte Chapel.*

#### A week in April

A week of Ter-jubilee meetings in April started with a Great Open Air Rally in South Charlotte Street at 8 o'clock on Saturday:

*A good company filled the wide pavement on the South Charlotte Street side of MacVittie's on Saturday evening, 12th April, for the opening meeting of our Celebrations. Mr James Paterson acted as leader, some half a dozen brethren spoke and the Hebron Choir, under the conductorship of Mr James Monihan, rendered choral items. This, with the fervent congregational hymn-singing, must have made an impression on the hundreds who passed by as well as those who stood to listen.*

1 *Record*, 1958, p. 76.

**Charlotte Baptist Chapel**
WEST ROSE STREET.
**TER-JUBILEE SERVICES.**
TO-NIGHT (SATURDAY), 12th April.
**GREAT OPEN AIR RALLY**
at SO. CHARLOTTE STREET, 8 p.m.
SUNDAY, 13th April.
11 a.m. in CHARLOTTE CHAPEL.
7 p.m. in USHER HALL.
Preacher:
Dr D. MARTYN LLOYD-JONES
(Westminster Chapel, London).
MONDAY, 14th April,
in the USHER HALL, 7.30 p.m.
Speaker:
Dr D. MARTYN LLOYD-JONES.
Tues. and Wed., 15th and 16th in Charlotte Chapel, at 7.30 p.m. Speaker: Rev. W. LESLIE LAND, M.A., B.Litt. (Melbourne Hall, Leicester).
All are welcome to these services.

*Both* The Scotsman *and the* Edinburgh Evening News *carried this advertisement for the April Ter-jubilee celebrations.*

The guest preacher for the weekend was Dr D. Martyn Lloyd-Jones, minister of Westminster Chapel, London. The morning service was in the Chapel and the evening service in the Usher Hall. For many, the highlight of the weekend was the Monday evening, when Lloyd-Jones preached for an hour:

*It was the thrill of a life-time to look from the platform of the Usher Hall out on to the great sea of faces extending right up to the top of the building. The vast hall was virtually filled to capacity and the platform too.... This was no great inter-church rally; it was just one local church congregation gathered with its friends to celebrate the goodness of God and worship Him.... An outstanding feature of the meeting was the presence of many hundreds of young people. They filled the top gallery and spilled over into every part of the great hall.*

2 *Record*, 1958, pp. 68-9.

Thursday was Reunion night. A queue formed well before the 5.30 p.m. tea in the lower hall, which was a time of nostalgia for past and present members. Then, by putting chairs down the aisles (Chapter 38), the stewards got everyone into the sanctuary for the final event of the week, at 7 p.m. For 20 minutes, recorded greetings were played from Mrs Kemp in New Zealand, Graham Scroggie in London and Sidlow Baxter in the United States. What memories those loved voices kindled as they spoke their warm-hearted greetings to the old church. Scroggie finished by saying: 'I do not suppose I shall ever stand in that dear old pulpit again.' That was true; he died before the end of 1958, and tributes to him are noted at the end of this chapter.

## A weekend in October

The church secretary explained why the Chapel described its services over the first weekend of October 1958 as the 150th Church Anniversary:

*Charlotte Chapel refuses to be bound by mere dates and it is true to say that the actual date on the Calendar when the Church was founded was not the 6th October, nor did Mr Griffiths come to us on that date, but the Anniversary Services have for very many years been celebrated in the beginning of October and they have always been an inspiration and a send-off to the winter's work here.*

3 *Record*, 1958, p. 168.

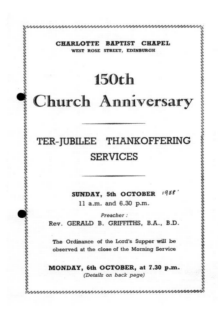

*The final evening of the April Ter-jubilee celebrations included tape-recorded greetings from Mrs Kemp in New Zealand, Graham Scroggie in London and Sidlow Baxter in America.*

*Charlotte Chapel celebrated its Ter-jubilee in April, October and November 1958, although the actual date was 24 January.*

*Most auxiliaries closed from the end of June until after the Edinburgh autumn holiday, the third weekend in September. This press notice publicizes the re-openings in 1957.*

## Renovation of 13 South Charlotte Street

The Ter-jubilee activities included substantial renovation of the premises; there was even talk about extending the building. Because of pressure on accommodation, the remaining flat at 13 South Charlotte Street (the first and third floors had been sold) was turned into a house for the caretaker and his family. This released several rooms on the top floor of the Chapel, which were used for the Guides and Scouts, a committee room and a study for the pastor.

## Niddrie Mission

In view of the Chapel's involvement in Niddrie, on the east side of Edinburgh, since 1996 (Chapter 55), it is worth noting that Gerald Griffiths performed the dedication of the Edinburgh City Mission's new hall at Hay Drive on 18 September 1958. It was an ideal site for a mission, at the junction of three large housing schemes, but it was a tough area; the workers had to remove boys who were playing noisily on the roof during the dedication service. This building was obsolete by 2000, and was replaced (by the Chapel) at a cost of £650,000 in 2005; it is now the Niddrie Community Church.

## Ter-jubilee gifts

Among the Ter-jubilee gifts from members were two new praise boards, which were in weekly use for the next 40 years, displaying the numbers of the hymns to be sung. They were removed when PowerPoint replaced hymnbooks in 2001; one of them forms the background to a photograph in Chapter 55.

The last gift was in December 1958, when two plates of polished oak were given to the church 'for the purpose of receiving the offerings at each of the Sunday services.' Initially they were placed on the communion table and the deacons laid the offertory bags on them; later, the deacons placed the bags on them at the back and brought the plates forward for a dedicatory prayer; they are now used only to take the bags to the counting room.

## Missionary Events

### Missionary exhibition and conference

The Ter-jubilee missionary conference, from Saturday 15 to Sunday 23 November 1958, involved 35 missionary societies as guests. Those with a regional base were grouped together in the lower hall, under the title 'The Seven Regions of the World'; societies whose work was not confined geographically to one area (RBMU, WEC, BMS, etc.) exhibited in the top hall under the title 'Seven Intercontinental Missions'. In addition to being open to the public, daily and free, from 3-10 p.m., the exhibition was open all Wednesday morning as well.

Every evening except Sunday, tea and light refreshments were served, for people coming straight from work, and films were shown from 6.30-7.20 p.m., prior to the main meeting at 8 p.m.; every region of the world's mission fields was represented on a different evening. It was an ambitious programme but:

*By picture and word, by native costume and model, by tract and book, we have seen the world for which Christ died holding out beseeching hands to us to come over and help them. We have seen so much that none of us ought to be the same again.*

4 *Record*, 1958, p. 179.

Insert left: George Davidson, Donald Cormack. Insert right: Norman Hunt, John McGuiness

Back row: David Murray, Tom Sim, Jack Oliphant, John Coutts, John Balmer, Robert Hadden, David Petrie, Peter Armstrong, Jim Hudson, George Rae, William Tullis.

Second row: William Somerville, David Wallace, Robin White, Oscar Barry, Robert Findlater, William Tregunna, Douglas Macnair, Jim Cossar, Jack Cochrane, Charles Steele, John McGregor, Tom Currie.

Front row: Jim Purves, Jim Paterson, Peter Murray, Robert Clark, MacDuff Urquhart, Gerald Griffiths, Robert Aitken, David Blair, George Rae, David Jenkins, John Whitlie.

*The Chapel elders and deacons in the Ter-jubilee year.*

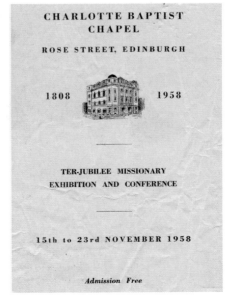

**CHARLOTTE BAPTIST CHAPEL**

ROSE STREET, EDINBURGH

1808　1958

TER-JUBILEE MISSIONARY EXHIBITION AND CONFERENCE

15th to 23rd NOVEMBER 1958

Admission Free

*The Ter-jubilee missionary exhibition in November 1958 was the largest ever mounted in the Chapel.*

## Ongoing missionary challenges

The Sunday School had its own missionary weekend, with boys and girls giving a biography of all the current Chapel missionaries, in costumes peculiar to the area in which the missionaries were working. They regularly sent money for the support of an orphan boy on Andrew McCabe's station in India. The congregation was constantly exhorted from the pulpit to pray daily for its missionary members.

One quarter of the Chapel's monthly magazine, the *Record* – three pages out of twelve – contained news from members in overseas missionary service. Letters from them were read on the first Monday evening of every month, prior to prayer for them. Chapel missionaries were invited to speak at that meeting on their return from the field and prior to their departure.

## Three tiers of Christian 'calling'

The ethos in the Chapel throughout the 1950s (and at other times as well) was that the highest Christian 'calling' was to lifelong overseas missionary service, especially if it was with a faith mission; for a church or an individual to be described as missionary-minded was the highest possible accolade.

Failing overseas mission, full-time Christian ministry was next best. There was, however, a third 'calling'; those who did not take up full-time service, either abroad or in a church at home, were expected to be active as lay people in local church life. This three-tier view of Christian service was not peculiar to the Chapel; it was widely advocated at this time by, for example, the Inter-Varsity Fellowship (now the UCCF). A report from the Chapel YPM illustrates the emphasis:

*Dr Gih [see the press advertisement two pages back] delivered a stirring message on life in China to-day. His talk rather surprised us, as we had expected a challenging address on our daily lives in relation to YPM. What we expect and what the Lord has for us, are often two different things.... I see the Lord laying a positive missionary outlook before our minds.*

5 *Record*, 1957, pp. 171.

This was mirrored in other auxiliaries. The meetings run by the deaconess, the Girls Class on Sunday afternoon and the District Women's Meeting on Wednesday evening, combined to take the lower hall for tea and to hear missionary speakers.

## Chapel missionaries

Over the 150 years, 102 members (58 women and 44 men) had been valedicted for missionary work; by 1958, they had given more than 1,500 years of service. They played many parts – teaching, doctoring, nursing, building, evangelising (door to door, open-air and hospital ward services), edifying the local church in Bible classes and training indigenous pastors. They endured hardship and separation – Tom Allan was away from his wife and family for 15 years for the sake of the gospel in Nigeria.

No one society monopolized the Chapel's missionary interest. Members went wherever there was an evangelical witness, and wherever they recognized the personal leading of the Lord. The 102 missionaries up to 1958 were associated with 43 missionary societies. The BMS headed the list with 13 Chapel members, followed by the CIM (now the OMF) with 11 and the RBMU with 9. Six served with the Church of Scotland, retaining, without any inconsistency, membership with the Chapel; they demonstrated not only fellowship in the gospel but also spiritual unity in Christ Jesus.

The Chapel had a special relationship with the Edinburgh Medical Missionary Society, which, among other things, provided accommodation for medical students in George Square. In 1958, 18 of the 102 had trained through the 'Mish'; 6 of these 18 joined the Chapel during their student days. Medical missionary work was carried on largely through mission hospitals, in which 34, that is exactly one-third of the 102, served. Seventeen others spent the major part of their working lives teaching overseas, from elementary schooling to universities.

## Mission fields represented

Until 1971, a coloured map of the world, showing the location of Chapel missionaries (photograph in Chapter 28), formed the background to the platform in the lower hall. One-third of the Chapel's missionaries (33) worked in Africa, 25 were in India and 14 in China, until it closed its borders to foreign missionary work in 1953; 11 were in the Near East, especially Palestine and Syria. South America was a neglected field of missionary enterprise in 1958, not only for the Chapel, and only six Chapel members had gone there. As part of the Ter-jubilee celebrations, two long wooden plaques were erected on either side of the rostrum in the lower hall, bearing the names of all the Chapel missionaries, past and present. Two of these plaques can be seen in the photograph of the 1971 map, in Chapter 45.

### Financial support

In 1958, it cost, on average, £500 a year to support a missionary on the field, and the Chapel had 18 missionaries. Although four shillings (20 new pence) a week from every member would have covered this, a good shorthand typist was fortunate to earn £4 a week in 1958, and there were other calls on members' generosity. The Chapel contributed about one-fifth of the support needs of its members overseas. How the foreign missionary committee tackled the shortfall is taken up in the next chapter.

## Two new auxiliaries

### Deaf and Dumb Christian Fellowship

As mentioned at the close of the last chapter, the mid-1950s saw the start of two new activities in Charlotte Chapel, and it is now time to catch up with them. The first was a ministry to the deaf and dumb. In May 1955, a widowed deaf woman, a member of the Chapel, felt a burden for others in her silent world; she invited a number of them to a meeting in her kitchen and gradually others joined them. Soon they were meeting in larger premises every second Friday, and looking for somewhere to worship together on Sunday. In October 1956, she asked Gerald Griffiths whether the Chapel could provide facilities. He put together a team for simultaneous interpretation, by sign language, of the whole evening service. A room off the lower hall was equipped with a loudspeaker for the interpreters, and also with an epidiascope, which projected the words of hymns and the Scripture reading onto a screen. When the *Edinburgh Evening News* featured the fellowship in an article, two married couples came along and were converted; within three months, one of the husbands was baptized.

*Nobody present at the Baptismal Service on Sunday evening 1st June [1958] could have been unmoved. It was a season of great rejoicing for our Deaf and Dumb Fellowship: five of their number bore their witness to a saving knowledge of our Lord Jesus in baptism.... We could not but admire their courage and praise God for the radiance of their new-found faith.*

6 *Record*, 1958, pp. 56, 105.

About a dozen came regularly to the Chapel on Sunday evening, as well as meeting in a home, now every Friday, alternating Bible study and prayer with a social gathering. Forty attended their first weekend residential conference in October 1959. A family moved to Edinburgh from the south of England, so that their deaf daughter might enjoy the fellowship available here.

There was never a corresponding involvement with the blind, although the Chapel provided Braille hymnbooks and Scriptures at the Sunday services. From 1992, the Chapel's tape librarian read the whole of the monthly *Record* onto audiotape, for the benefit of the blind and partially sighted.

### Women's Morning Fellowship

One December morning in 1956, as Kitty Griffiths was washing dishes in the manse in Barnton and keeping an eye on her children, she thought about other Chapel women who were doing the same thing at about the same time – very few wives were in employment in those days. 'We feel cut off, and yet in bringing up our family to love and serve the Lord Jesus Christ we are doing the greatest job possible.... We long for spiritual strength and fellowship.' The thought came to her of starting a midweek morning meeting, with a crèche. Afternoons were difficult, because of children coming home from school, and evenings were out of the question. However, a morning meeting, finishing promptly by 11.30 a.m., seemed viable.

The first was on Wednesday 16 January 1957, with coffee and tea from ten o'clock and an informal meeting in the lower hall, chaired by herself, at 10.30 a.m. It was an instant success, with over 150 at the weekly meeting, and about 40 children, under school age, looked after by 'aunties' in the top hall – games and choruses for those able to participate. Although there were readings, recitations and solos, and a distinguished speaker to close the hour, it was Mrs Griffiths' chat and banter that delighted young and old. All ages were welcome, but it was primarily to provide Christian fellowship for younger women. 'The little children ask their mothers daily: "Is this the day for me to play with toys at church?"' Members of other churches in the city heard about it, and were made equally welcome. Like most auxiliaries, the fellowship went into vacation for the school summer holidays, from early July to early September.

CHARLOTTE BAPTIST CHAPEL.
WEST ROSE STREET.
THIS SUNDAY 11 a.m. and 6.30 p.m.
Preacher:
Rev. GERALD B. GRIFFITHS. B.A., B.D.
All are Welcome.
WEDNESDAY, 30th October, 10.30 a.m.
Women's Morning Fellowship. Special
visit of Mrs JEAN REES, of Hildenborough
Coffee, Tea, 10 a.m.
THURSDAY, 31st October, 8 p.m.
BIBLE SCHOOL.
Lecturer: Rev. GERALD B. GRIFFITHS.

*When Jean Rees was the guest speaker, six hundred attended the Women's Morning Fellowship.*

When Jean Rees was the guest speaker at the Women's Morning Fellowship in October 1957, four hundred came for coffee and six hundred to the meeting. When Marjorie Saint, widow of the martyred Ecuadorian missionary, Nate Saint, spoke, the building was packed to its one thousand capacity.

Occasionally, a Husbands' Evening was held on a Saturday, featuring a Brains Trust. Jean Rees' husband, Tom, was on the panel at one of these Saturday meetings in March 1958. The use of 'make-up' had been a contentious issue among Chapel members, and others, for about three years. During Billy Graham's All Scotland Crusade in 1955, evangelical Christians noted with incredulity that his wife, Ruth, used it. In Charlotte Chapel at that time, worldliness, which any keen Christian was expected to avoid, was defined as drink, tobacco, the cinema, the theatre, make-up and dancing. Billy Graham was from a conservative background, and for many he was a model of modern evangelicalism. That his wife 'made up' her face concerned some of the more conservative in Edinburgh, although it helped others to see that such things were not really important. Tom Rees was asked what he thought about women 'making-up' their faces. Ever the one to bring common sense into emotive issues, he replied: 'If men shave off from their faces what nature intended to be there, what is wrong with women putting onto their faces what nature did not intend to be there?'

## Hyacinth day

On the Wednesday before Christmas, helpers brought about one hundred pots of pink hyacinths, with ferns, to the lower hall, where they were wrapped in Christmas paper, with a greeting card for everyone connected with the fellowship (much wider than Chapel members only). The Griffiths family personally delivered them; in 1960, the Hyacinth Marathon involved delivering 162 pots of hyacinths, three in a bowl, plus ferns. The Women's Morning Fellowship continued Hyacinth Day after the Griffiths left Edinburgh,

and it was as popular as ever until the mid-1990s. The pastoral team then took over, and they preferred to wrap parcels and to deliver them over a more extended period.

The fellowship had another focus at Christmas. One hundred members offered hospitality to boys from Dr Guthrie's Approved School in Gilmerton (boys under Local Authority supervision), and welcomed them into their homes over the festive period.

## Prayer support

When the 1958 series of Sunday evening evangelistic rallies in the Usher Hall was being planned, the Women's Morning Fellowship wanted to do their bit, but what could they contribute on a Sunday evening, with family commitments? 'We have decided to meet at the Chapel for prayer every Sunday morning during the Usher Hall Campaign at 7 a.m.' They did, and it was so powerful that they continued to meet even after the special services were over. This early morning prayer meeting continued for the rest of the Griffiths' time in Edinburgh, and at their farewell Gerald mentioned: 'Every Sunday morning, even when the snow was thick and the roads were treacherous, our car has left in the biting darkness for the 7 a.m. prayer meeting.' It never achieved the same publicity or the same numbers as the Wednesday morning meeting, but it was a powerful influence in the life of the Church.

*In June 1958, the Chapel purchased 23 Cluny Gardens as a new manse for the Griffiths family, at their request. Barnton was more than four miles from the Chapel, and even further from the main hospitals, which the pastor and his wife regularly visited.*

Not to be outdone, the men met for prayer at a time convenient for them, Saturday evening, from 9-10 p.m. in the Chapel, to pray especially for the Sunday services. That brought the regular meetings for prayer to six in the week – the women on Sunday morning at 7 a.m., the meetings preparatory to the morning and evening services at 10 a.m., and 5.30 p.m, the congregational meeting on Monday evening, the women's prayer meeting on Wednesday afternoon (40-50 crowded the ladies' room, some of whom had attended for over 50 years) and the men's meeting, just mentioned, on Saturday evening.

*Chapel members were loyal in paying for advertising space, month after month, to subsidize the* Record. *Many of those who advertised in the 1930s (Chapter 33) were still taking space in the 1950s (above).*

## Subsidising the *Record*

Chapel members were generous in financially supporting both the general funds of the church and missionary enterprise. There was a surplus on the church accounts, even after making grants to numerous Christian organisations, covering the cost of the Usher Hall services, increasing the stipend of the minister and the deaconess, sending half-yearly and Christmas gifts to the missionaries and supporting younger members in training for full-time Christian service. However, not even the Ter-jubilee celebrations could prevent the need for a substantial annual 'sub' to produce the *Record*. Despite every plea to members, to buy more copies or to make donations, it incurred deficits of £124 in 1957 and £140 in 1958. In consequence, four of the sixteen pages still had to be given over to advertisements, leaving nine for general items and three for missionary letters.

## Rev. William Graham Scroggie, DD

### Memorial services

On Friday 2 January 1959, the mortal remains of Graham Scroggie were brought to the Chapel for a memorial service at 12 noon. He had died at his home in London on Sunday evening, 28 December, after long months of patient suffering. Men converted and commissioned to Christian service during his years in Charlotte Chapel (1916-33), together with Edinburgh ministers and the Principal-emeritus of Spurgeon's College, paid warm tributes to his memory.

*The last portrait of Graham Scroggie. He was buried in the Grange cemetery, Edinburgh. At the interment, three of his favourite hymns were sung: 'In heavenly love abiding', 'When I survey the wondrous cross' and 'The Lord's my shepherd'.*

A memorial service was held in Westminster Chapel in London on Wednesday 4 February. No biography has ever been published, but *The Life of Faith* (the unofficial organ of the Keswick Convention) devoted much of its issue on 8 January 1959 to tributes, and the February Chapel *Record* did the same.

### 'It is given to few to reach the Eighties'

Graham Scroggie died at the age of 81. As noted under golden weddings in Chapter 36, life expectancy was much less than people look for now. Golden wedding anniversaries were comparatively rare in 1959; after commenting on one, the editor of the Record went on: 'It is given to few to reach the Eighties, but several ladies in C.C.'s history have got into the Nineties!' – one of them had reached her ninety-seventh birthday in December 1958. A man – probably the first male in the Chapel to do so – reached 90 in 1961, and David Blair, who had been active in the Chapel since he joined in 1911, died in 1980 in his ninety-ninth year.

It was 1983 before any Chapel member became a centenarian; Derek Prime presented Miss Euphemia Bowden with a hundredth birthday cake during a Sunday after-church fellowship in June 1983. On 24 July 1990, Miss Sarah Hudson not only celebrated her hundredth birthday in Beulah Home but also hand-wrote a letter of appreciation to the Chapel for the congratulations sent to her. In the following three years, 1991, 1992 and 1993, three other residents of Beulah reached the same landmark. On 6 August 1996, one of them, Mrs Catherine Reid, celebrated her one hundred and fourth birthday, the highest so far in the Chapel's history; she died, still in Beulah, a few weeks later.

### The final Ter-jubilee event

1958 ended, as every year since 1906 had ended, with 'the Lord's people meeting in the Lord's house' at 11.15 p.m. on 31 December for a Watchnight service. Although much of the Chapel's open-air outreach was now located at the corner of Castle Street and Princes Street, because of the volume of traffic turning into South Charlotte Street, it was to the traditional site at MacVittie's corner that the members went a few minutes after midnight, for a brief service. A new year had begun.

Additional information on the following topics, mentioned in this chapter, is available on the CD.

Andrew McCabe
Church officers from 1912
Committee structure 1808-1958
Graham Scroggie after Charlotte Chapel
Graham Scroggie: tribute from Spurgeon's College
Graham Scroggie: tributes in *The Life of Faith*
Graham Scroggie's 1958 message to the Chapel
Mabel McLean
Niddrie Mission
Overseas mission
Women's Morning Fellowship
Worldliness

# Chapter 41
# Common grace (1959–1961)

## Reactions to the Ter-jubilee

### Spiritual exhaustion?

Were there any signs of spiritual exhaustion in the Chapel at the beginning of 1959, after the intense activity of 1958? The key Chapel figures, most of whom had leadership responsibilities in their daytime jobs, had worked tirelessly throughout the year. But they worked tirelessly every year; it takes dedication to run open-air meetings on Princes Street in the depth of an Edinburgh winter. Gerald Griffiths was more concerned about spiritual exhaustion in the pew.

*He felt that there was considerable slackness creeping in among the members in general and that a greater emphasis should be laid on the Congregational Prayer Meetings, attendances at which were less than should be expected. He urged the members of the Court as Elders of the Church to support him in his efforts to remedy this state of affairs and to raise the spiritual temperature of the Church which in his view was below the normal for Charlotte Chapel.*

---

1 Elders' Minute, 3 December 1958.

Others shared this concern, and the elders thanked the pastor for not sounding only the note of thanksgiving, and for not allowing the congregation to feel complacent among such tangible evidences of prosperity in the church. Gerald Griffiths continued to press onward and upward. At the first office-bearers' meeting of 1959, he reminded the elders and deacons that they should be at both services on Sunday, at least one of the week-night meetings and especially at the office-bearers' prayer meeting in the vestry on Monday at 7 p.m., for an hour before the public prayer meeting.

### Baptism and membership

Not as many came forward for baptism and membership in 1959 as in the early days of Gerald Griffiths' ministry; only 33 joined the Chapel in 1959, and there were only 27 candidates for baptism, at 3 baptismal services. There was, however, a reason for no baptisms between June and December 1959. Older readers may remember the remarkable summer, the driest in two hundred years, which emptied the city's reservoirs; water rationing was enforced and it would have been a criminal offence to fill the baptistry.

### Outreach

For five Sundays in February-March 1959, and four more in April-May, the evening service was held in the Usher Hall. The response was sufficiently encouraging for the Chapel to resume its spring offensive for ten Sundays in 1960, attended by about two thousand every evening. Young people were more inclined to come to a neutral venue than to a traditional church, so six Sunday evenings were tried in the autumn of 1960 as well. They were even better attended than the spring ones, so the Usher Hall was hired for five Sundays in September and October 1961.

**Summer Open Air Campaign**
6th JUNE to 7th SEPTEMBER
TUESDAYS, WEDNESDAYS, THURSDAYS
8 p.m.
**THE MOUND, PRINCES STREET**
THESE WILL AUGMENT OUR NORMAL WEEK-END MEETINGS
PREPARE BY PRAYER

*As auxiliaries closed for the summer months, evangelistic focus switched to the mid-week open-air campaign at the Mound.*

As the notice (above) states, the annual open-air campaign at the Mound lasted from the beginning of June to early September, with meetings every Tuesday, Wednesday and Thursday. This augmented the Saturday and Sunday evening open-airs, which were held all year round in South Charlotte Street or South Castle Street. The 1959 summer campaign was both encouraging and effective:

*The speaking has often been with marked power and the listening at times most intent. The hands of our stalwart open-air workers have been strengthened by the appearance of new workers. The Young People's Meeting conducted some effective meetings as they have done in previous years. For the first time the ladies of the Women's Morning Fellowship, under Mrs Griffiths' leadership, took a Saturday evening meeting.*

---

2 *Record*, 1959, p. 126.

### Giving

If generosity is a barometer of spirituality, the Chapel was in good heart in 1959; the Sunday and Thursday offerings went up steadily during Gerald Griffiths' ministry, and in 1959, exceeded £5,000 for the first time. The collections at the three meetings totalled £3,749 in 1954, £4,463 (1955), £4,626 (1956), £4,692 (1957), £4,875 (1958) and £5,053 (1959). Furthermore, a revolution was taking place in missionary support during 1959; this deserves a closer look.

## Missionary financial policy

### Full support?

Only once did the Chapel attempt to support two of its missionaries fully; in 1929, the church aimed to cover the whole cost of Andrew and Emmie MacBeath's work in Belgian Congo, every year (Chapter 28). The promised money was always sent to the Baptist Missionary Society, but often a subsidy from the general funds of the church was needed to meet it. This made the foreign missionary committee cautious about putting forward any other projects that they might not be able to finance.

As mentioned in the previous chapter, the Chapel contributed only one-fifth of the cost of its members working overseas in 1958. There were three reasons for this low figure. Many members banded together, in small groups, and directly supported individual Chapel missionaries, whose work they admired; that did not go through the church books. Secondly, the foreign missionary committee's method of collecting was outdated. They sent a letter to all Chapel members twice a year, with a return envelope, inviting gifts on two specific Sundays in March and two in November; in other words, the committee relied on giving from capital rather than from income. Thirdly, the half-yearly offering did not necessarily benefit Chapel missionaries, as the envelope (sample below) gave donors other options.

*Half-yearly envelopes for the Chapel's missionary fund were replaced in December 1959 by a weekly envelope, distributed annually in advance, with every Sunday shown; missionary giving almost doubled under the new scheme.*

### A new approach

The missionary convener was Norman Hunt, Professor of Economics at the University of Edinburgh. In 1958 and again in 1960, he was invited by the Indian government to spend the month of February in India, as their guest, to advise them on how to move from a medieval peasantry to a modern industrial state. A Christian economist with international connections could hardly be sanguine about either the level of the Chapel's missionary support or the method of collecting it. The missionary secretary was Oscar Barry, who had spent seven years as a missionary doctor in Palestine and Ethiopia, They persuaded the deacons to call a special meeting of members in October 1959. With Gerald Griffiths in the chair, they stressed that the issue was primarily a spiritual challenge.

The meeting responded positively, and agreed that there should be continuous education about the privilege of supporting fellow-members overseas. Packets of 52 envelopes, date-stamped for every Sunday in the year 1960, were issued free to every member and adherent. One envelope was to be returned every Sunday, to a box in the vestibule; if a week was missed through holiday or other absence, the unused envelope was a reminder (and an opportunity) to catch up. The envelopes were not identified, and no allocation of money was permitted through the scheme; everything that came in was divided equally among the missionary family. Numbered envelopes were available for those who wished to covenant their gifts.

### Weekly envelope scheme

The result was spectacular. Soon, about 450 envelopes were returned every Sunday, bringing in about £250 a month, that is £3,000 a year. The Chapel was able to send quarterly remittances of £35 to every missionary, £5 as a personal gift and £30 to their society for their support. That was in addition to the £10 Christmas gift from the October Thankoffering. The project flourished because the missionary committee kept plugging away at it; when the second year brought in £323 less than the first, the convener wrote in the *Record*:

*Missing – over Three Hundred Pounds. The loss of £300 would be a serious matter to most people; in this particular case the loss is especially tragic and could be critical, for the losers are the missionary societies which are responsible under God for the maintenance of our own Charlotte Chapel missionaries on the field.*

3 *Record*, 1962, p. 45.

The message slowly got through; by the autumn of 1962, weekly giving was over £75, bringing in nearly £4,000 a year. The average cost of keeping a missionary on the

318

field, including allowances, travel and headquarters' administration, was now £550. Since there were 18 Chapel missionaries (disregarding those in paid employment), £10,000 a year was needed. Even the Chapel's increased giving left other Christians to subsidise Chapel missionaries, but not to the extent of £6,000 because many members still sent personal gifts directly to missionaries whom they knew – they did not approve of the equalization of everything that passed through the Chapel books.

The Chapel's weekly envelope scheme was more successful and lasted longer than another good idea introduced in December 1959. To prevent buses and cars from skidding when the Mound was covered with ice and snow, the Corporation installed an electric blanket for the five hundred yards between the Lawnmarket and Princes Street. It was switched on for the first time in December 1959, and prevented ice forming or snow lying. It was a good idea, but the combination of frequent breakdowns and high running costs led to the blanket being discontinued a few years later.

*In December 1959, an electric blanket was laid underneath the Mound, to prevent buses and cars from skidding when ice formed or snow lay on the surface.*

## Pastoral matters

### Visitation

In May 1959, Gerald Griffiths suggested that every member should automatically and regularly receive a home visit from an elder. For many years, the deaconess had looked after women who were unwell, bereaved or otherwise needing pastoral care, and Mr and Mrs Griffiths were assiduous in

hospital situations and other serious problems. However, the 1877 ideal of the systematic visitations of members of the church, by dividing the congregation into districts and allocating families in them to an elder, had long since fallen into disuse.

Instead of dividing the membership equally among the available elders, the 1959 scheme created five districts (only) and three elders were allotted to a district, so every triumvirate shared responsibility for about 120 Chapel families. At the next election, in 1960, four additional elders were appointed, and an additional district was created, with consequent boundary changes. This paved the way for the much more ambitious scheme which the next pastor introduced, of elders not only visiting members in their homes but arranging for them to meet regularly together in groups in suitably large houses.

### Quinquennial elections

Every five years, all elders and deacons stand down, together with those appointed by them (the church secretary, treasurer, convener of stewards, etc.) and all the committees demit office. This has advantages – it focuses the minds of older office-bearers as to whether they should stand for re-election, and encourages the congregation to look around for younger people. The quinquennial election, as it is known, was due in May 1960. The absurdity of the elders' reluctance to review the roll regularly was demonstrated when the ballot papers had to be printed with some candidates described as 'address unknown'. They had not been in the Chapel for years, but until they were removed from membership by a congregational meeting, they remained eligible for election. Understandably, they did not receive a single vote.

### Roll revision

This led to a review of the roll, including the first instance of church discipline for over 40 years. An Edinburgh member had not attended for a long time; when the elders called on him at home, as they did several times, he heaped unkind and critical remarks on the minister, the officers and the church in general. Eventually, the elders instructed the church secretary to call a special members' meeting, after the prayer meeting on Monday 9 January 1961, with a view to removing his name because of the hostile attitude which he had adopted, as well as his refusal to attend communion. MacDuff Urquhart, having reflected on this instruction, did not call the meeting and explained to the elders that he felt it would give undue prominence to the man concerned; he suggested, and the elders agreed, that when the next list of missing members was brought to a church meeting, this name should be among them. It was good advice, and the deletion took place as part of a roll review at the annual meeting in May 1962, when 36 names were removed.

## Infant dedication

During the 1953-4 vacancy, all dedications were in the vestry, not in public at the close of a morning service. The elders insisted that Graham Scroggie (whose preference for the latter was noted in Chapter 24) conform to this, when he was supplying during the vacancy. For his first six years at the Chapel, Gerald Griffiths followed this pattern. However, in March 1961 a father and a mother, both from long-standing Chapel families, urged the pastor to arrange a public dedication.

The elders pointed out that when this had been done some years previously, a few members had voiced objections and so, in order to avoid offending anyone, recent dedication services had been held privately. Mr Griffiths persuaded the elders in 1961 that a dedication in front of the congregation would be a good example to all young parents; anyone who was unhappy could leave the church after the main service, and before the dedication, because the pastor had to come down from the pulpit and go into the vestry to collect the family. The dedication took place at the close of a Sunday morning service, in the presence of a large congregation.

## Films on Sunday

Three items on the deacons' agenda in the early 1960s may seem, to present readers, to indicate a censorious attitude in an otherwise progressive church, but they were live issues and passionately safeguarded at the time.

One was showing films in the Chapel. Since 1938, the policy had been that no films could be shown anywhere on Chapel premises on Sunday under any circumstances (Chapter 33). At the request of the Missionary Band, where youngsters met on the third Sunday of the month, it was reluctantly agreed that missionary slides (not moving pictures) might occasionally be permitted, but their use was to be kept to the minimum. On weekdays, films could be shown in the two halls, but not in the sanctuary, provided the film had the

prior approval of the pastor or two elders. There was a more stringent test if a film was to be shown in the sanctuary on a weekday; application had to be made well in advance for a decision by the full elders' court.

In 1963, one of the more innovative elders proposed that films might be shown on a Sunday, provided prior approval had been obtained; after much discussion, this was agreed. The elders did not always give permission – a request from the Young Peoples Meeting in April 1967, to show *Friends of Israel* after an evening service, was turned down. One elder was outraged when Alan Redpath (the next pastor) asked the church secretary on a Friday in February 1968 whether he could show a film of his travels in the Far East and Australia after the evening service on the Sunday. The secretary, believing that the majority would approve, gave permission; the elders, at their next meeting, made plain that they expected to be consulted and that in future prior sanction from the whole court should be observed strictly, with no right to waive it under any circumstances. The same elder was still objecting when the elders agreed in 1970 that the Bible Class could show a film strip (a series of still pictures, mounted on film instead of individual slides) at a guest service in the church on a Sunday afternoon.

## Selling on Sunday

Secondly, the elders were dismayed to learn that the Chapel magazine, the *Record*, was being sold in the vestibule after Sunday morning services. They had no objection to the *Record* being given out at the end of the service, but there was a long-standing prohibition against money changing hands on the Chapel premises on a Sunday. They were in something of a dilemma about visitors who wanted a copy of the magazine:

*it was agreed that it was very undesirable that in the vestibule there should be an obvious buying and selling and giving of change as that would undoubtedly have the effect of dissipating any atmosphere of worship which the church Service had produced and was open to grave criticism particularly by visitors.... if a visitor desired a copy of the* Record *that could be handed to him and a plate or box made available so that if desired visitors could make a contribution.*

---

4 Elders' Minute, 23 July 1958.

Tickets for the Sunday School outing, which all members were encouraged to attend, were available after every weeknight activity, but never sold on a Sunday at this time.

## Suitable literature

Thirdly, a missionary society, holding a meeting in the Chapel early in 1959, displayed some books 'which proved theologically unacceptable to us as a Church'. Many outside organisations had meetings in the Chapel, so the elders reacted by absolutely forbidding the sale of any books. When the Baptist Union of Scotland asked for the use of the Chapel for a week in October 1959, to hold their annual Assembly, this was granted 'provided that a new ruling, applicable to all outside organisations, be adhered to, namely that there should be no bookstall.' When the Union asked for a waiver for the Assembly, the deacons reluctantly agreed, provided it was 'confined to books pertaining to Baptist propaganda, the choice of which would be made in consultation with the pastor.' This was a better formula than an outright ban, and organisations could, from then on, sell their own literature (but nobody else's), under supervision.

## Common grace

The sermon which the writer has found the most helpful and lucid and challenging of his life so far was Gerald Griffiths' Sunday morning exposition of Luke 6:32-6, where the Lord spoke about unbelievers who put believers to shame by their good deeds. How, he asked, can unbelievers 'be good' and 'do good'? He explained the Christian doctrine of common grace (given by a good God to all of his creation, because they are his creation), and contrasted it with saving grace (which alone leads to salvation through Christ). The text of the sermon is available on the CD with this book.

Sadly, there was not much common grace in the attitude of some in the Chapel in the spring and summer of 1961. Gerald Griffiths announced from the pulpit on Sunday morning 2 July 1961 that he was leaving Edinburgh. The writer and his wife were so taken aback by the intimation that Mr Griffiths' sermon that morning is etched on their memory. He developed the theme, which has often been used but never better expressed, that prayer should consist of four elements, Adoration, Confession, Thanksgiving and Supplication (Acts). These, he said were the Christian's weapon to defeat the wiles of the devil.

The writer asked one of the elders, 'Why has the pastor resigned?' The answer was, 'the less said, the better'. That was good advice; the remainder of this chapter will say only what is necessary to explain the premature end of an outstanding pastorate.

## South Africa calls

### Find a preacher

Every minister of Charlotte Chapel receives many invitations to preach at special events in other churches. Gerald Griffiths declined most of them, but in February 1960 he sought guidance from the elders about a third and pressing request to conduct ten days of special meetings in May 1961 at Rosebank Union, a white, English-speaking church in Johannesburg. The invitation came after a businessman, who was secretary of the Rosebank church and who was touring Great Britain on behalf his employers, visited the Chapel on 27 September 1959. He had been commissioned by his church to find a British preacher who would conduct an inner mission, that is, a series of meetings for renewal of the membership.

Rosebank was a fashionable suburb of Johannesburg, and the church recognized that its own people did not have the necessary spiritual vitality to mount an inner mission; they needed an outsider. The visitor came to the vestry after the service and urged Gerald Griffiths to lead this mission. Initially he declined, but the Johannesburg church kept pressing, so eventually he brought the invitation to the elders. They encouraged him to go, considering it an honour for the Chapel; it turned out to be a very happy and successful time.

### Two unexpected events

Between the invitation and the event, two unexpected things happened. The first was a 'storm in a teacup', which developed into a tempest. In October 1960, the elders issued an invitation to a well-known preacher to come as pulpit supply. His letter of acceptance indicated that he was aware the invitation was on its way. This prompted the church secretary to remind the elders that all discussions in the court were confidential, and that no business should be mentioned elsewhere. The principle was readily accepted and that seemed to be an end of the matter. However, although no names had been mentioned, one elder felt that others were assuming that he was the culprit. He said that he had had no contact with the guest preacher, and his assurance was accepted.

Sadly, that did not close the issue, as it should have done. Other grievances were aired or, worse still, festered; four elders resigned from the court. Some members (not office-bearers) raised imagined discontents at a church meeting. The irony was that while some were determined to make their pastor's life a misery, it was a time of great spiritual blessing. At the conclusion of the evening service on Sunday 30 April 1961, after 11 had been baptized, 22 others responded to the appeal to come to the front of the church. All were young people, 16 of whom came forward for baptism, 3 for salvation and 3 more to apply for church membership.

The second unexpected event was the resignation of the minister of the Rosebank church, just before Gerald Griffiths fulfilled his ten-day engagement there. He flew from London to Johannesburg in a Comet 4, similar to the one now at the Museum of Flight at East Fortune. While the technology that produced Comets was spectacular, telegraphic services in 1961 were less so. He wanted to tell his wife that he had arrived safely, but there was a 24-hour queue for sending cables. His host managed to get a telex to his London office, which phoned the message to Cluny Gardens.

## Providence, again

The Johannesburg congregation was very taken with Gerald Griffiths' ministry and urged him to consider their vacancy. There was, however, unfinished business in Edinburgh; on 7 June 1961 he had a lengthy meeting with three of the four disgruntled ex-elders. They refused to modify their hostile attitude to him; the church secretary and the senior elder, who had accompanied their pastor to the meeting, advised that nothing would be achieved by further discussion. Mr Griffiths, like his predecessor, Christopher Anderson, a century before (Chapter 7), remained calm and dignified, although he might have echoed Anderson's wish: 'Oh, to be delivered from unreasonable men!'

In the same way as the Chapel's approach to Gerald Griffiths in 1954 had been providential, solving his dilemma about the rebuilding programme at the Metropolitan Tabernacle, so the equally unexpected approach from the Rosebank church in May 1961 solved the seemingly intractable problem of

deep-seated hostility from a vocal minority of Chapel members. On 28 June, aged 40, he told the office-bearers that he had received, and was going to accept, a unanimous invitation to the pastorate of the Rosebank church. Many tried to persuade him to change his mind, but he was convinced that it was the 'call' of God to a wider and much-needed ministry in a South Africa divided by Apartheid.

Since Gerald and Kitty Griffiths had contributed so much to the missionary cause, by encouraging missionaries and missionary candidates, and by promoting the missionary offering scheme, it was appropriate that the next stage in their ministry was to 'come over to South Africa and help us'. The farewell services were held over the weekend of Sunday 25-Monday 26 September 1961.

## A journalist's impression

As an antidote to the depressing narrative in the previous few paragraphs, it is worth repeating the observations of a journalist in the first week of June 1961, when relationships were at an impasse. He was visiting various Edinburgh churches, incognito, and he slipped into the Thursday Bible School. 'The chapel was well filled', he wrote in *The Scotsman*; 'the atmosphere was alive and expectant. The organist was playing a devotional chorus that I had learned as a boy nearly 40 years ago'. He was impressed with both the congregational singing and the Bible teaching that followed:

*'Sacred Songs and Solos' may not be everyone's choice in devotional hymnology but it has a very respectable evangelical ancestry. As sung in Charlotte Chapel these hymns have a robust vigour and an enlivening vitality which are exhilarating in their thrust and power. For wholehearted, joyous exuberance the congregational singing can hardly be excelled in Edinburgh....*

*The preacher's task was the exposition of the Word and to this he addressed himself with penetration and insight – as well he might. This was an audience, intimate with Scripture, educated in things of the Spirit and urgent for thoughtful teaching. They would not put up with pious platitudes or glib moralisings. But they responded with rapt attention to one who mined deeply in his text and rightly divided the word of truth.*

5 *The Scotsman*, 3 June 1961.

**Chapter 41**
Common grace (1959-1961)

## Historical perspective

Gerald Griffiths had been, for seven years, an expository preacher, a beloved pastor, a keen evangelist, an able biblical scholar, a leader, guide and friend – not one or two of these but all of them and more, a combination which is rare indeed. His preaching was entirely biblical, thoroughly conservative and evangelistic, demanding a verdict. The *Record* described the farewell services as 'a sad milestone in the history of Charlotte Chapel … he will be sadly missed'.

Gerald Griffiths told the writer, when they discussed these events 30 years later, that his only problem in the Chapel was the misunderstanding just mentioned; he had been supportive of the Chapel's position in the ecumenical debate, even although he had inherited it, rather than initiated it. He knew that there was as much support for him in the Chapel when he received the 'call' to Johannesburg as there had been when he came to Edinburgh. Most were unwilling to accept his resignation, but he insisted that he had to move on.

## Return visits

The Griffiths were welcomed back to the pulpit on a number of occasions, the first on Sunday 5 December 1965, following their return from South Africa. For two years, they assisted the vacant Gorgie Baptist Church in Edinburgh, and then accepted a 'call' to Calvary Church, Toronto. Mr Griffiths ministered there for 23 years, retiring in November 1990, although he continued to take preaching and conference engagements. Mrs Griffiths began her fifteen-minute radio Bible stories, 'A Visit with Mrs G', which, by 1974, were (and still are) broadcast round the world, round the clock.

Gerald Griffiths, as the chairman of the Africa Inland Mission International Council, regularly passed through Great Britain on his way to and from Africa; on ten Sundays between 1969 and 1995, he came to Edinburgh and preached in the Chapel. Particularly memorable was 10 May 1987, Beulah Home's thirty-first anniversary, when Kitty spoke to the children as 'Mrs G'. During their last visit, in April 1995, she spoke to the Women's Morning Fellowship, which she had started 38 years previously.

## Vacancy events (1961-1962)

Rev. William Whyte and his first wife rejoined the Chapel in 1961, when he retired from the pastorate. He provided invaluable assistance during the vacancy between Gerald Griffiths leaving and Alan Redpath arriving.

*Rev. William Whyte and his wife. Striped trousers and a black jacket were expected for communion, but many elders wore them every Sunday.*

The first casualty of the vacancy was the summer open-air campaign at the Mound. The Tuesday meeting had to be discontinued, through lack of support, and the deaconess applauded 'the faithful few who carry on this noble work on Wednesdays and Thursdays'. This was unfortunate, because there was usually a good crowd to listen and to accept gospel tracts. The evangelistic committee chivvied, pleaded and cajoled, not just to get speakers and singers but for supporting workers to transport the portable lectern, organ, hymnbooks and evangelistic literature, all of which had to be brought to the Mound from the Chapel and returned after the meeting.

*A well-supported Chapel open-air meeting at the Mound in 1958; support fell away during the vacancy of 1961-1962.*

The YPM threw their weight behind the Sunday evening open-air meeting, which was advanced from the usual 8 p.m. to 5.45 p.m., partly to secure better attendance from older Chapel members and partly to encourage passers-by to come in to the evening service.

A fortnight after Gerald Griffiths made clear that he would not reconsider his resignation, the church secretary approached a minister with a passion for evangelism; open-air meetings were high on his agenda. Within a few months, Alan Redpath had accepted a 'call' to the Chapel; how this came about is described in the next chapter.

Additional information on the following topics, mentioned in this chapter, are available on the CD.

Common Grace
Church discipline
Gerald Griffiths after Charlotte Chapel
Norman Hunt
Preaching styles
Visitors – 'Raven' in *The Scotsman*, 3 June 1961

# Chapter 42
## Attacking on all fronts (1962–1963)

### 'Call' to Alan Redpath

**Clear guidance**

There are few secrets in evangelical circles. It was known that Alan Redpath, who had spoken at conferences in the Chapel in the 1940s, and who had gone from Richmond Baptist Church in Surrey to the Moody Memorial Church in Chicago in 1953, wanted to return to Britain. As soon as it was clear that Gerald Griffiths could not be persuaded to stay in Edinburgh, and without waiting for a vacancy committee to be formed, MacDuff Urquhart, the church secretary, wrote to Alan Redpath 'exploring the possibility of him being able to help us with a series of meetings during the vacancy'.

Alan Redpath read into this coded message exactly what the Chapel intended, and he came to Edinburgh for eight days (Sunday to Sunday) at the beginning of December 1961 – preaching 'with a view'. The congregation was deeply impressed with his ministry, not only on the two Sundays but also at the prayer meeting, the Bible School, the YPM and other meetings. The vacancy committee unanimously recommended to a church meeting on 22 January 1962, that a 'call' should be sent. Alan Redpath telegraphed his acceptance at the end of February; the news was given to the Monday prayer meeting, which turned into a praise meeting. Owing to commitments in Chicago, he could not start until the first Sunday in November 1962.

## 'RADIO PASTOR' FROM CHICAGO TO TAKE OVER

THE congregation of Charlotte Baptist Chapel, Edinburgh —one of the biggest and liveliest Baptist churches in the country—think so highly of the man who will be their next minister that they are prepared to wait until he is free to come from America in November.

*In 1962, the settlement of a new minister was still sufficiently newsworthy for the secular press to publish a photograph and an article.*

### Rev. Alan Redpath, FCA

Born in Gosforth, Newcastle-upon-Tyne, in 1907 and schooled there and in Durham, Alan Redpath was nearly 20 and training in Newcastle to be a chartered accountant, when he was converted through the witness of an office colleague in the Christian Brethren. For the next few years, the appeal of his former life – especially rugby: he played for Northumberland – was so strong that he did not grow as a Christian. He qualified in 1928, and joined the staff of Imperial Chemical Industries in London. He did well in business, but the same colleague who had brought him to faith said to him over lunch one day: 'You know, it is possible to have a saved soul but a wasted life.'

That convicted him. He had married in 1934, so both he and his wife, Marjorie, linked up with the Wood brothers, who ran the National Young Life Campaign; Sidlow Baxter had done the same when he felt the 'call' to full-time Christian service in 1923. They encouraged the young couple to attend a school of evangelism in London, and both of them became increasingly involved in Christian work. Thirteen months later, typically for an accountant, Alan drew a line on a piece of paper and listed on one side: 'Arguments in favour of staying in business', which included opportunities for witnessing to colleagues and obligations to his parents, who had given him a business training; on the other side he listed: 'Arguments in favour of going into the ministry', which included more opportunities for preaching and for study. The latter outweighed the former, so he joined the staff of NYLC in 1936, as an itinerant evangelist.

Nowadays, a young man having such a 'call' would probably be encouraged by his church to attend a Bible college or theological seminary. Alan Redpath had no such opportunity, as there were no grants available, and he had a family to maintain. He asked Graham Scroggie to recommend 50 books to a young man with business training but no theological background, who had a great burden in his heart to preach the gospel and enter the ministry. Over the next four years, he worked his way through them, while evangelising up and down the country with the Wood brothers' teams.

In May 1940, the Duke Street Baptist Church in Richmond, Surrey, impressed by a tent campaign that Alan had conducted for them in 1937, invited him to become pastor of the church 'temporarily, until we can get a proper one'. Alan knew what they meant – a man theologically trained and accredited – but he believed the Lord was in it, so he accepted and stayed for 13 years.

*Alan Redpath in
1950, while the
pastor of the
Duke Street
Baptist Church in
Richmond, Surrey.*

During these 13 fruitful years, membership rose from 60 to 360; from 1946, Sunday evening services were held in the Richmond theatre, because the church could not accommodate the congregation. In 1953, he accepted a 'call' to the Moody Memorial Church in Chicago. In 1961, a New York Christian college awarded him an honorary DD degree.

*Alan Redpath and his wife, Marjorie, were accompanied to Edinburgh by their
younger daughter, Caroline, who was still at school. Their elder daughter, Meryl,
who was married and expecting her first child, stayed in America.*

## CCTV

During the vacancy of 1961-2, an enterprising company offered the Chapel a free demonstration of the comparatively new concept of closed-circuit television. On 27 May 1962, black-and-white pictures were transmitted from the sanctuary to the lower hall. They were impressive (for their day), and Alan Redpath agreed that CCTV could be used for

the expected overflow at his induction in November. Those who were too late to get into the sanctuary appreciated seeing, however dimly, what was taking place in the pulpit. Should the church install it permanently? Technology was improving all the time, and also becoming cheaper, so the deacons kept putting off a decision; it was 1980 before they placed an order (Chapter 48).

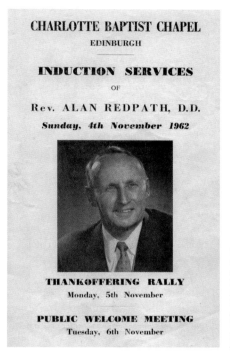

*The induction services
were combined with
a (delayed)
Thankoffering in
November 1962.
The public welcome
on the Tuesday was
in the Assembly Hall,
with Rev. George
Duncan as speaker.*

## A new manse

The manse in Cluny Gardens was kept on a care and maintenance basis until the Redpaths indicated, in April 1962, that it was too large for them. The deacons put it on the market, and almost immediately received an offer of £6,600. To give the new minister time to look around, after his arrival, the deacons leased a furnished flat at 11a Queensferry Terrace, for £36 a month. In due course, the Redpaths were attracted to a stone-built villa-type house at 11 Midmar Gardens, on the market at £6,000; the owner agreed to sell for £5,500, and from the profit on the transactions, the deacons installed central heating. The Redpaths 'flitted' (the traditional Scots word for moving from one house to another) in June 1963, and invited the office bearers and their wives to a service of dedication in their new home at the end of the month.

327

*The Redpaths chose a new manse at 11 Midmar Gardens, a stone-built villa-type house with two public rooms, four bedrooms, maid's room, kitchen, scullery and bathroom. It was the Chapel manse until December 2006, and then sold in June 2007 (Chapter 58).*

## A dozen new ideas

### Novel in 1963

Alan Redpath came to the Chapel with wide experience, boundless enthusiasm, a passion for evangelism, especially among younger people, and a commitment to full Christian living as taught at the Keswick Convention. At the age of 55 he was older, when starting his pastorate, than his three predecessors had been when they left. He was in Edinburgh for only a short time, but from among the whirlwind of new ideas that he introduced, the following dozen may give some flavour of his first year. Many of them, like home meetings, weekly bulletins, a church office, discipleship classes and oral testimony at baptisms, are so familiar now that people may ask if they are worth mentioning? They are mentioned because of the impact they had on the Chapel in 1963 – they were unheard of, then; 1963 was an adventurous and exciting year, and the way that the Chapel 'did church' changed dramatically and forever.

### Discipleship classes

Within a month of his arrival, Alan Redpath saw a gap in the Chapel's programme. In order to disciple the large number of young people who were responding to his appeals for commitment to Christ, he set up a 13-week course, repeated as soon as the first one had finished, in the vestry at 5 p.m. on Sunday afternoon. 'It is the distinction between making a convert and making a disciple.' Of the 18 who attended the first one, 15 were subsequently baptized. When 30 applied for the third course, he decided it was too taxing to hold it just before the evening service, so he moved it to Monday evening, before the church prayer meeting. It was for all new Christians and all applicants for membership of the Chapel. Subjects included the need of salvation, repentance, forgiveness, the work of the Holy Spirit, discipleship, Bible study, prayer, stewardship, baptism and church membership. These classes continued until the 1990s, and are further described in Chapter 46.

### Zone meetings

At his first meeting with the elders, Alan Redpath told them about American-style cottage prayer meetings. He wanted every elder's group to meet at least once every six weeks, in a house large enough to accommodate 30 or so. One elder and one deacon were to be in charge of the group, but not necessarily to host the meetings. He intended to call them 'district home prayer meetings', but when his newly appointed secretary (see below) divided the city into zones and the members resident in each zone had been tabulated, the groups were popularly known as 'zone meetings'. Alan Redpath saw them as an essential step in the binding together of the congregation in a closer fellowship. Typically, he announced that he would attend the first meeting of all 18 groups – they were held on different nights, at the elder's discretion.

People are now so accustomed, nationwide, to the concept of house groups that it is difficult to imagine how revolutionary the concept was, not only in the Chapel but also in Scotland as a whole. Prior to 1963, the elders had visited members in their homes, but the members never met together in groups. The editor of the Church of Scotland magazine, *Life and Work*, asked Alan Redpath to explain the warmth and friendliness that he (the editor) found among the Chapel members:

*Dr Redpath explained to me his rather unique scheme whereby the congregation (which has about 1000 members – all baptised by a total immersion) is divided into twenty zones, with an elder or deacon in charge of each. [Two of the original 18 had sub-divided by this time.] By arrangement they meet regularly in different houses in each zone for Conversational Bible Study and for prayer. It is a sort of halfway house to the church. 'This,' he explains, 'makes it finally into a real church. This prevents it from being only yet another preaching centre.'*

---

1 *The Scots Magazine*, July 1965, p. 328.

In addition to meeting for Bible study and prayer, the groups were responsible for the pastoral care of everyone in their zone. This was carried out effectively, by going over the list of members at the beginning of every meeting, and asking someone to visit those who had not been seen in the Chapel recently. In addition, one or two of the Chapel missionaries were allocated to every group, which corresponded with them and entertained them when they came on furlough.

Alan Redpath had great hopes that: (1) the zones would evangelise their neighbours, by holding 'squashes' in homes, and (2) that when 15 attended regularly, the group would divide. How the zone meetings fared over the next few years will be taken up in the next chapter. In addition to Alan attending the first meeting of every zone, he and Marjorie subsequently entertained them all, in turn, at their temporary manse in Queensferry Terrace; when they had worked their way though all 18, they had had 450 people in their home (average attendance of 25).

**CHARLOTTE BAPTIST CHAPEL**
WEST ROSE STREET
**EDINBURGH, 2**

Telephone No. CALedonian 4812

Dear Friend/s,

ZONE PRAYER MEETING No. _____

*You are invited to attend the above meeting in the home of..................................................................................
on...............................................at..............p.m.*

*It is very much hoped that you will be able to be present and share in the blessing of an evening like this.*

*Yours very sincerely,*

*The 18 zone meetings arranged their own timetables, so the elder sent out postcards, as a reminder. The title emphasized the prayer aspect of the meeting.*

## Crèche

Noting how pre-school children were looked after admirably during his wife's Thursday Morning Fellowship (below), Alan Redpath persuaded the Sunday School to organize a crèche for the care of younger children, from ages two to four, during the Sunday morning service, 'so that parents of young

children would be able to remain throughout the Service without distraction and the children will be looked after in the Upper Hall by volunteer Nannies.' Until then, a nursery for babies had operated, but children of two and over were expected to stay with their parents for the whole service.

## Prayer meetings

Five months after his arrival, Alan Redpath suggested holding a prayer meeting in the Chapel on Friday morning from 7.30 to 8.30, for the spiritual quickening of the whole work of the church. He himself led it, and over 30 attended right away, rising in a few months to 70. He also continued, and encouraged, the existing prayer meetings on Monday evening (for everyone), on Wednesday afternoon (for women) and on Saturday at 9 p.m. (for men). For special occasions, such as the Usher Hall services and the annual missionary conference, he arranged a half-night of prayer from 10 p.m. to 2 a.m. on the Chapel premises, on the basis of 'come when you can and leave when you must'. The writer recollects MacDuff Urquhart, by now an elderly church secretary, saying apologetically at midnight: 'Sorry, but I must go – I have to conduct a case in court later this morning'.

*On Good Friday 1962, the choir honoured John Balmer's 50 years as a chorister. Suitable tribute was also paid to Mrs Balmer, for sitting alone every Friday for fifty years. The choir secretary, Jim Fenwick, presented Mr Balmer with (his choice) an electric fire.*

Mr Balmer's choice of an electric fire (caption for photograph) was timely. Smoke control zones were being introduced to Edinburgh, because the city, then nicknamed Auld Reekie (Old Smoky), still had coal fires heating individual rooms in some homes, offices and public buildings. Charlotte Square was designated a smoke control zone in 1962, so the deacons had to replace the coal fire in the sitting room of the caretaker's house with an electric fire.

## Testimony at baptisms

During the vacancy, it had been felt inappropriate to ask guest preachers to conduct baptisms as part of the Sunday service; Rev. William Whyte, who had joined the Chapel on retiring from the Baptist ministry, officiated on Thursday evenings (except for Easter Sunday 1962, when seven were baptized during the evening service). When Alan Redpath arrived, there was discussion as to whether Sunday was appropriate for baptisms, because of pressure on time and overcrowding of the building; however, as he settled into his ministry, it was not a question of 'either/or' but of 'both/and', that is Sunday, Monday and Thursday, to reduce the queue of those waiting to be baptized.

What was novel under Alan Redpath's ministry was the opportunity for candidates to give an oral testimony to the reality of their faith in the Lord Jesus and of their personal experience of his saving grace and keeping power, before going down into the baptistry. All seven did so at his first baptismal service on Sunday 10 March 1963, when the Chapel was filled to capacity and many had to be turned away long before 6.30 p.m. When an appeal was made at the close of the service, many indicated their desire for baptism in the near future, and others came to a knowledge of the Lord Jesus as Saviour and Lord. It was the same on two consecutive Sundays in April and another at the end of May.

Some (older) elders did not approve of candidates speaking before their baptism; they regarded going under the water (symbolising death to the old way of life) and coming up again (symbolizing rising with Christ to a new way of life), as testimony enough – but they were loyal enough never to criticize their pastor. The practice had come to stay, although not at that stage with the lengthy statements that became common when candidates were invited into the pulpit; in 1963, they spoke from the platform, just before they were baptized.

Derek Prime (pastor from 1969 to 1987) permitted testimonies, although he did not encourage them. He stressed the importance of the candidates' answers to the questions that he addressed to them in the water. It was 1993 before an extended statement from the pulpit was introduced, and Peter Grainger explained (Chapter 53) why he encouraged this.

## Infant dedication
The Chapel had long encouraged parents to dedicate their newly born children, usually in their home or in the vestry after a Sunday morning service (Chapters 24, 32 and 41). Two weeks before Alan Redpath arrived, William Whyte carried out a 'simple, sweet service of dedication' in the vestry. The new pastor had other ideas. When he was preaching 'with a view' in December 1961, he anticipated the pattern that he established when he became pastor; he conducted dedications on the platform (not in the pulpit) during the Sunday morning service. He gave shy parents the option of a private occasion, but he believed that public dedications should be the norm. He conducted them in his own inimitable way, an informal, friendly and cheerful approach, which brought smiles to the faces of the parents, the congregation, and sometimes the baby as well.

## The first pastor's secretary
Alan Redpath, after eight years' experience of American church life, suggested that he should have full-time secretarial assistance. The deacons agreed and from eight applicants, Bertha Gillon, the sister of the deaconess, started on 18 February 1963 at a salary of £400. An office was created on the top floor of the Chapel, equipped with a typewriter, a telephone and a duplicating machine. In deference to her being alone in the Chapel for much of the day, the deacons installed an answer phone, coupled to an electronically operated lock, at the side door of the building – something that generations of caretakers would dearly have loved. She did the job with enthusiasm and dedication for nine and a half years, retiring in May 1972.

## Weekly bulletins
Having got a secretary, Alan Redpath introduced a printed weekly bulletin, to reduce the lengthy intimations at Sunday services. In addition to reminding worshippers of Chapel events, it was customary for the church secretary to publicize the activities of other organisations, whose aims the Chapel supported; these were now set out on the back page of the bulletin.

Sunday services did not, in those days, include mention of a sick list or family news – that was given at the Monday prayer meeting. Alan Redpath began to mention names before the intercessory prayer on Sunday morning; the congregation generally welcomed this, but some felt it was intrusive, so the elders decided in January 1967 to discontinue it. There were immediate protests from the membership; the elders resisted these until the annual general meeting in April, when the members insisted on hearing, on Sunday, the names of any in special need of prayer. It was January 1993 before family news for prayer was included in the weekly bulletin, after which the pastor referred to it, and prayed for the people mentioned, without having to give the details first.

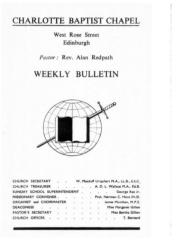

*Alan Redpath introduced weekly bulletins in September 1963. At first, they were placed in the pews, prior to the congregation arriving; later they were handed out as people came in. This one, for 26 January 1964, shows the winter programme in full flow.*

## Holy Week convention

For Easter 1963, Alan Redpath arranged meetings at 8 p.m. every evening from Monday to Friday of Holy Week (his phrase), to explore the significance and meaning of the cross. The convention (as he described it) culminated with a communion service on the Friday evening. He wrote in his diary:

*This has been a great week. We have had an Easter Convention with meetings every evening. While it has been tiring, it has nevertheless been a tremendous encouragement and inspiration to see so many people coming to the Chapel night by night. Each evening the ground floor of the Chapel has been well filled and to-night it was packed for the final meeting followed by a Communion Service. I am sure that this is something the Lord has laid upon our hearts and should be repeated another year.*

---

2 *Record*, 1963, p. 72.

He repeated it in 1964 but, recognising how much the first one had taken out of him, at a busy time of the year, he

invited a colleague from Ipswich to share the preaching with him. The Chapel did not continue the convention after Alan Redpath left, but held a communion service on the Thursday, instead of the Friday, because the Emmaus Choir, in which many Chapel members participated, presented a citywide chorale on Good Friday.

## Overseas Mission

Within a few weeks of his arrival, Alan Redpath arranged a closer link between the Chapel and the various missionary societies with whom members were serving. He asked them to allocate one full month during every missionary's furlough, for working with the Chapel team and getting to know new Chapel members; he also asked them to arrange for any Chapel member, applying to a society, to serve an internship with the church before the application was accepted.

*Iain Clayre, who worked on the construction of the Forth Road Bridge before going as a missionary to Borneo, attended the Chapel during his time in Edinburgh; this was his personalized Christmas card for 1963.*

Alan Redpath expanded the annual foreign missionary conference, held for eight days at the end of October. As well as arranging a half-night of prayer in preparation for it, he invited as many missionaries on furlough as he could find, to come for the week and to attend a Bible study at 11 a.m.; he spoke from the Scriptures to those who spent so much time 'giving out' that they seldom had the opportunity of 'taking in'. Thirty attended, and the week was greatly appreciated, both by the guests and by the Chapel families who gave hospitality to them. Alan Redpath put them to work every evening, arranging forums where the congregation asked them missionary questions. The format was so successful that it was repeated in 1964 and 1965.

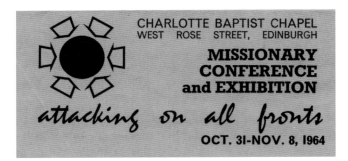

*The 1964 Missionary Conference resulted in 18 young people responding to the 'call' for overseas missionary service.*

### After-church fellowships

Starting in March 1963, Alan Redpath arranged occasional meetings after the evening service. For the first one, he anticipated an informal gathering in the lower hall, but about four hundred people stayed; after a cup of tea downstairs, they returned to the sanctuary, where the pastor outlined his plans for the immediate future.

These included more proactive ways of getting strangers into the Sunday evening evangelistic services. Beginning in April, an army of 'fishers' went out, half an hour before the service, to invite passers-by to come in. They did not, as in the past, simply hand out leaflets, but they invited people to come with them and to sit with them. If the building was already full, it was the duty of any members who did not have a guest, to vacate their seats and to listen to the service in the lower hall.

Some of these after-church fellowships were for the whole congregation, but others targeted peer groups within it. About one hundred young people stayed once a month, and at other times about 130 from Group 35 (that is, people between the ages 25-45) gathered. Alan Redpath found them stimulating and very worthwhile.

### Ready for anything

The last of the dozen innovations mentioned here, which are only a sample of Alan Redpath's modernization of Chapel life, was the creation of his RFA squad. Based on Phillips' translation of Philippians 4:13, 'ready for anything', he

gathered, and inspired, a band of people who would drop everything at a moment's notice to type, fill envelopes, stick on stamps, duplicate circulars or do anything else to help his secretary in a crisis situation. He publicly acknowledged, 18 months later, that Bertha Gillon could not have coped without them; true though that was, it was great fun for those involved and a time of real fellowship. The deacons had recently presented Alan Redpath with a battery-operated dictating machine, and curiosity overcame fatigue as the RFA squad transcribed his letters and sermon notes from this novel device. During the vacancy that followed his resignation in 1966, they were often called in to produce the weekly bulletin in time for the Sunday services.

## Charlotte Baptist Chapel

West Rose Street, Edinburgh

### *Thursdays at 10 a.m.*
### *Spring Programme 1963*

LEADER
MRS ALAN REDPATH

A Ladies' Meeting
that is Different

*Marjorie Redpath took over leadership of the Women's Morning Fellowship, which Kitty Griffiths had started. Since she was also responsible for the Wednesday afternoon women's prayer meeting, she transferred the fellowship from Wednesday to Thursday. The lower hall was usually crowded, and 'aunties' looked after about 26 pre-school children.*

As well as noting activities that were started and have continued, it is worth mentioning one that was significant then, but is history now. Until Alan Redpath came, the Thursday evening Bible School had studied a passage of Scripture. His first session was, characteristically, entitled 'Studies in Soul-Winning'; while firmly based on Scripture, it was subject-driven, interactive, question-and-answer, and was greatly appreciated by the three hundred or so who attended regularly. It was part of the syllabus for the students at the Faith Mission Training College (then in Ravelston Park), as it had been since Graham Scroggie's time. Their programme was rearranged in April 1968, and the students no longer occupied the front rows in their distinctive uniforms. Derek Prime continued the Thursday evening, but numbers dropped during the vacancy of 1987–92. Shortly after that, the night was taken over for a new style of group meetings in homes, modelled on the zone meetings mentioned above, which had fallen into disuse (Chapter 53).

## Moving up a gear

### Thankoffering

In addition to these dozen new ideas, Alan Redpath expanded many existing arrangements. For example, the pastor and some of the elders had traditionally been in the vestry on Monday afternoon for the October Thankoffering; he sat in the vestry all day for his first anniversary in October 1963, from 8.30 a.m. onward, 'being greedy'. As well as a public meeting on the Monday evening, he held a further gathering for members and adherents only on the following day, Tuesday, to speak to them privately and frankly about his vision for the next 12 months. For the following year, he made the Tuesday evening public and invited Dr Martyn Lloyd-Jones from Westminster Chapel, London, for what was described as the most outstanding part of the long weekend.

### New Year Conference

The Chapel had hosted a conference on New Year's Day since before the First World War, but Alan Redpath extended it to a second day and had two visiting speakers on both. He wrote in his diary for Thursday 2 January 1964: 'We have had two wonderful days at our New Year Conference. For the first time we extended this to a second day and the experiment was more than justified, the attendance on both days being excellent, and the ministry most powerful.' He used jocularly to misquote the Old Testament: 'See, here is a prophet, let us kill him [by giving him so many meetings].' Yet he was always available, leading by example. After preaching twice on Sunday, he loved to be invited to a home where groups of young people sat literally at his feet, as there were never enough chairs. He spoke about living the victorious Christian life until about 10.30 p.m., when he would say: 'Now for some horizontal quiet time' (his phrase for going to bed).

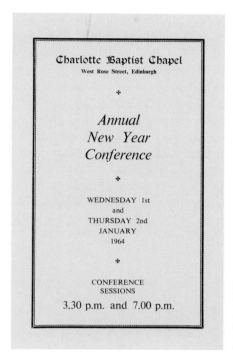

Charlotte Baptist Chapel
West Rose Street, Edinburgh

✦

*Annual
New Year
Conference*

✦

WEDNESDAY 1st
and
THURSDAY 2nd
JANUARY
1964

✦

CONFERENCE
SESSIONS
3.30 p.m. and 7.00 p.m.

*In 1964, Alan Redpath extended the New Year's Day conference to two days, with two visiting speakers on each day.*

### Ross Bandstand

When Alan Redpath learned that the Chapel had previously hired the Ross Bandstand in West Princes Street Gardens for evangelistic outreaches on Sunday afternoons, he suggested holding open-air services there for half an hour, starting at 9.30 p.m. on alternate Sundays, from the beginning of June to the middle of September 1963. Light refreshments on the Chapel premises (the YPM offered to wash-up, which demonstrated their enthusiasm to be involved) ensured that a good number stayed after the evening service in the Chapel, to support the singing, testimonies and preaching in the gardens. For 1964, Alan Redpath persuaded the Corporation to give him every Sunday evening in June, July and August for £1 per night. The official starting-time was 9.30 p.m. but he was often successful in hinting to the military bands or orchestras, engaged by the Corporation, that they might like to get away early, and that he would answer to the authorities if any questions were asked. He booked every Sunday evening for the same three months in 1965 and 1966, but had to get others to lead the services.

### Usher Hall services

Alan Redpath was determined to build on the success of earlier services in Edinburgh's largest auditorium. When he arrived, he was disappointed to find that the Usher Hall was free for only five consecutive Sunday evenings in the autumn of 1963, starting on 22 September, but he took them and made the best of them. He booked nine consecutive Sundays from March to May 1964 and six more from September to November. The BBC heard about them, and took the initiative in broadcasting one of them live. BBC guidelines precluded him from making an appeal on air for commitment to the Christian faith, but Alan Redpath managed to put the gospel across in his usual challenging way. Frustrated that so few days had been available in 1963, he tried to book the whole spring and summer of 1965, from the beginning of April to the middle of August, but others had already reserved two Sundays.

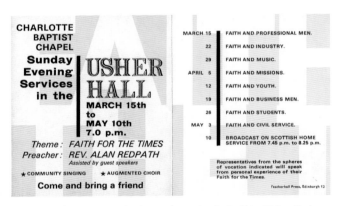

*Invitation to the spring 1964 Sunday evening services in the Usher Hall, with the titles of the talks.*

## Christmas morning communion service

Alan Redpath had one final new idea for 1963 and, like most of his ideas, it filled a felt need in Chapel life. The Griffiths family had started Christmas Day by visiting the Chapel's Beulah Home. The new pastor wrote in his diary: 'Wednesday, December 25th [1963]: A precious day as we remembered the birth and death of our Lord at a Christmas Morning Service. I understand this is the first which has been held in the Chapel, the ground floor of which was packed to capacity.' He asked the elders whether it should be repeated next year, including communion; they were enthusiastic, and although they cancelled other events when the pastor took ill in September 1964, as set out in the next chapter, they pressed his assistant to hold a Christmas morning service. It was so popular that by 1965 a full complement of eight elders (the number required on a Sunday) had to be on the platform to serve communion.

## Constitutional questions

Until 2007 (Chapter 58), the Chapel had no written constitution – it relied, as does Great Britain to this day, on precedent, decisions of meetings, accepted practice and consensus. There is a delightful pencilled comment on a set of 1963 minutes in the church archives. MacDuff Urquhart had made a ruling on some procedural point, although he admitted that he could not lay hands on the authority for it. Against the decision, one of the deacons jotted down, 'Does that mean that when Urquhart dies, the constitution goes with him!?'

Many a true word is spoken in jest. Urquhart's death two years later (Chapter 43) prompted the deacons to start drafting a constitution. In a series of lengthy meetings, they prepared one line by line 'with infinite care', and passed the draft to their successors after the quinquennial election in 1965. The new court doubled its length and complexity and added 'standing orders', by going through the last seven years of minutes and collating decisions on the sale of tickets, the use of films and slides, the closing hours of meetings, and much more. Both of them were still being discussed when a 'call' was sent to Derek Prime in 1969. Someone proposed that finalization of the documents should await the arrival of the new minister and his comments on them. No one was unduly concerned when neither the constitution nor the standing orders ever came back onto the agenda.

The spring, summer and autumn of 1964 brought rather more interesting developments, new excitements and some major disappointments, which are described in the next chapter.

Additional information on the following topics, mentioned in this chapter, is available on the CD.

Alan Redpath's family
Baptismal practice, 1962-1999
Christmas morning
Church office
Manses
Missionary furlough policy, 1980

# Chapter 43
# K.o.k.d. (1964–1965)

## Lay initiatives

### Explanation of the chapter title
When Alan Redpath said goodnight to an individual or a group, or finished a letter, his parting phrase was often K.o.k.d. (Keep on kicking the devil). When one of the Chapel elders visited him in hospital in 1989, as his end drew near, his farewell words were: 'brother, K.o.k.d.'

His second year in the Chapel brought new opportunities, deeper consecration and more active evangelism. Before looking at these, the first part of this chapter describes some initiatives taken by laypeople, to complement the pulpit ministry.

### Young Men's Fellowship
Some of the boys who had passed through the Sunday afternoon Bible Class took the initiative in asking for a meeting on Sunday at 10 a.m., prior to the Chapel's morning service. The elders responded enthusiastically, as they had been concerned for some time at the lack of consecutive Bible teaching for those between 16 and 24. This resumed, under new leadership, the class that had met at this time between 1920 and 1940.

### Summer camps
There is no space here to describe the activities of the uniformed organisations (Scouts, Cubs, Guides and Brownies), nor the developing Sunday School at Longstone. However, a glimpse at the summer before Alan Redpath's arrival illustrates how much went on quietly, month after month, among young people. The Chapel Scout Troop, 26 strong, camped for a week on the banks of Loch Tummel, while the Chapel Guides had their camp on a farm near Middleton, Midlothian. At the same time, the Longstone Scouts went to a farm in the Scottish Borders and the Longstone Guides camped at Trefoil, near Ratho. Another 39 of the Longstone Sunday School, not in uniform, took over the day school at Kirknewton for a week, getting to know the Chapel missionaries on furlough, who joined them for the week.

### Moredun
Several years before Alan Redpath came to the Chapel, the Edinburgh and Lothians Baptist Association (the new name, from 1952, for the Edinburgh Baptist Association) began an outreach in the Moredun housing estate, on the southeast of the city. In 1962, there was a Sunday School of 75, and numbers were growing, but they had no superintendent and they were short of teachers. Elba appealed for help from the Chapel, which was not involved because the Chapel had withdrawn from Elba in 1955 (Chapter 39). The Chapel did what it could, and also supplied speakers for the adult services. It was hoped to plant a church in Moredun, and when the Baptist Union of Scotland offered to support a full-time pastor, if the Association contributed £250 a year toward this, the Chapel promised £100. No such appointment was ever made, but the Moredun Baptist Fellowship worked conscientiously for another decade; in 1969, it averaged 25 at the Sunday morning service, 100 in the Sunday School and 28 at the Women's Auxiliary. However, none of the helpers were prepared to live in the community, and without resident members, the fellowship did not have long-term prospects. When the Christian Brethren established the Ferniehill Evangelical Church in another part of Moredun, the Chapel handed over its part of the work to them.

### Weekly envelope scheme
The success of the weekly missionary envelopes encouraged the deacons to introduce a corresponding scheme in January 1964, for the general funds of the church. It replaced the quarterly envelopes. Eight hundred sets of plain (unnumbered) envelopes were printed, one dated for every Sunday in the year, so that if regular worshippers missed a Sunday, they were reminded to use the envelope on a subsequent occasion.

A further three hundred numbered envelopes were printed, because anyone participating in the 'Government approved tax refunding covenant scheme' had to be identified. To the disappointment of the treasurer, only 30 of the latter were taken up – rising to 40 over the next two years. The new scheme dovetailed neatly with the existing missionary envelopes, as twin-packs were printed, with a perforation between the two parts. On average, 345 envelopes a week were returned over the first two months; the deacons, who had been apprehensive about the extra work involved, were delighted at the increase in giving – up by £54 in the first month.

### A new *Record*

Alan Redpath was embarrassed by the dated appearance of the *Record*. He introduced colour for the first time, and modernized the style and the quality of paper; he dispensed with all advertising by substantially increasing the price. Regular features were given new titles – 'The Message of the Month' (a transcript of one of Alan Redpath's sermons), 'News from all Fronts' (world-wide Christian events), 'From the Pastor's Desk' (editorial), 'Children's Page', 'For the Women' (by Marjorie Redpath), 'A Christian looks at the News' (three office-bearers took turns to comment on the secular scene), 'The Deaconess Reports', 'Flashes from the Fields' (missionary news) and 'Chapel Notes' (about people).

He had 1,250 copies a month printed; the new format was well received, but the circulation did not increase, as had been hoped, to meet the increased cost of production, so an annual subsidy from the general funds of the church was required. Nevertheless, the Chapel posted a free copy, with a letter of greeting from the church, to everyone who signed the visitors' book on Sunday; on average, 35 copies a week went all over the world.

```
DIRECTORY OF
CHURCH SERVICES

SUNDAY       10 a.m.  Young Men's Fellowship
             10 a.m.  Prayer Meeting.
             11 a.m.  Morning Worship.
             3 p.m.   Sunday School and Bible Classes.
             4.45 p.m. Young Women's Class.
             5.30 p.m. Prayer Meeting.
             6.30 p.m. Evening Service.
MONDAY       8 p.m.   Congregational Prayer Meeting.
TUESDAY      7 p.m.   Women's Missionary Auxiliary.
WEDNESDAY    3 p.m.   Women's Prayer Meeting.
             7.30 p.m. Women's Bright Hour.
             8 p.m.   Young People's Meeting.
             8.30 p.m. Open Air Meeting at the Mound.
THURSDAY     10.30 a.m. Women's Morning Fellowship.
                       Tea and Coffee served from 10 a.m.
             8 p.m.   The Bible School.
FRIDAY       7.30 a.m. Prayer for Revival.
             6 p.m. and 7.30 p.m. Youth Organisations.
             7.45 p.m. Choir Practice.

The Ordinance of the Lord's Supper is observed on the first Sunday
of each month after the Morning Service, except in January,
April, July and October, when after the Evening Service.

MISSIONARY MEETINGS
             The Congregational Prayer Meeting on
             the first Monday of the month is a
             Missionary one.
             The Missionary Band for all young people,
             8 years old to teenage, meets at 4.30 p.m.
             on the third Sunday of most months.
             The Missionary Circle meets at 4.30 p.m.
             on the fourth Sunday of every month.
```

*The calendar for the week in the new style of the monthly* Record.

## Initiatives in evangelism

### The swinging 60s

During the 1960s, Edinburgh (along with most of Britain) experienced a revolution in social attitudes, especially sexual attitudes. Many abandoned traditional Christian-based values, including those associated with family life; the role of women evolved quickly. The Chapel leadership, aware of the changes taking place around them, looked for relevant ways to evangelise this new world. If it meant 'breaking down the walls of partition between the sacred and the secular', so be it – although some members took a lot of convincing. How the leadership responded to the shifting moral standards in national life is taken up in the next chapter.

### Saturday evening

What could the Chapel do for the crowds of teenagers who wandered along Princes Street on Saturday evening? What would be on their wavelength, without compromising the gospel? The answer was one of the most remarkable and exciting ventures of Alan Redpath's many new ideas. The Young Peoples Meeting already had an outreach café in the lower hall once a month, attended by about one hundred, but they yearned to have their own premises and to hold coffee evenings every week. This was music to Alan Redpath's ears, and a year to the day after his induction, he told the elders that he had approached the owners of a nearby cinema and that:

*He had a vision of warm, well lighted premises, which would be under the control and supervision of the Chapel and where refreshments could be served in pleasant surroundings and opportunity given for discussion, games and social intercourse, but where at all times the claims of Jesus Christ on the lives of young people should be pressed.*

1 Elders' Minute, 6 November 1963.

*The Monseigneur News Café in Princes Street in 1963 (left). With its frontage on Princes Street, and its back entrance at the side door of the Chapel, it would have been ideal for youth outreach. From 1965 to 1973, it was the Jacey News Theatre (right); the site was then sold for redevelopment.*

He had his eye on the Monseigneur News Café, on Princes Street, whose back entrance was at the side door of the Chapel. It would have been ideal for youth outreach, but the selling price was beyond the Chapel's means. It was refurbished and opened in 1965 as the Jacey News Theatre. Over the next few years, more and more families could afford television at home, and 'news theatres' went out of business. The Jacey was sold for redevelopment in March 1973, before the Chapel heard it was on market, but having just funded the building of the Wester Hailes Baptist Church at a cost of £40,000 (Chapter 46), there was no way the Chapel could have considered another project at that time.

## Assistant to the pastor

Although that project was never financially viable for the Chapel, the dream of a youth centre would not go away. Any such outreach needed 'permanent leadership, youthful and enthusiastic'. Alan Redpath knew a young couple, Bryan and Joy Thomson, natives of Bristol. They had both trained for three years at the Moody Bible Institute in Chicago, and they were now back home, looking for an opportunity like this. A church meeting on 16 December 1963 approved their appointment, for an initial period of 12 months, to develop youth work in the city centre and also at Longstone. Bryan's background in commercial art was invaluable in the publicity for the various outreaches. He started at the beginning of March 1964, with overall responsibility for the Saturday evening café outreach.

## Contact Club

Encouraged by Alan Redpath, the YPM hired the Charlotte Rooms in MacVitties Guest restaurant in South Charlotte Street, for five consecutive Saturdays from 11 April 1964 – the only available dates before the restaurant's busy summer season. Thus Contact Club was born. Background gospel music was played from 8 p.m., while coffee and sandwiches were served, without charge, in an informal atmosphere; this encouraged guests to strike up conversations with Chapel youngsters, carefully allocated to all the tables. In almost no time, two hundred young people, aged between 16 and 30, filled the restaurant. Three-quarters of them had no Christian commitment – Chapel members were not allowed in unless they brought a guest. Some had previously arranged to meet friends, others went out to Princes Street, with invitation cards, and came back with complete strangers. Any Chapel members turning up without a non-Christian friend were politely directed to the street and asked to come back when they had found someone to bring in.

The Chapel-based musical group, the Heralds, played and sang; they were good – BBC Television heard about them, and invited them to take the epilogue for a week in August. There were a few games to break any remaining ice, and then, at 9.15 p.m., Alan Redpath introduced a film, which usually lasted no more than 45 minutes. Strangers were openly amazed at this new presentation of the Christian faith, and listened attentively to a clear gospel challenge from the pastor. Soft drinks were then served, while the hosts at the small restaurant tables encouraged discussion about what had just been said. Closing time was 10.45 p.m., but visitors made appointments to meet Alan Redpath during the following week, to hear more. The total cost to the Chapel was £30 a week – an excellent investment. Not only were strangers converted, but the Chapel's own young people were given a new vision of what the gospel could do. On the last evening, 225 people under the age of 30 were either seated or standing around the walls. As William Wordsworth put it in another context: 'Bliss it was to be alive, but to be young was very heaven.'

*The Heralds played and sang regularly at Contact Club. From left to right, Georgie Hume (vocalist), Graham Baker (banjo and clarinet), Donald Cormack (guitar), Campbell McKellar (guitar), David Brown (drums), Jim Whitlie (bass guitar), Fergie Milne (trombone), Ian Leitch (vocalist).*

## Charlotte Rooms and the Usher Hall

The five Saturdays in the Charlotte Rooms in April and May 1964 coincided with the Chapel's last five Sunday evenings in the Usher Hall. The two complemented each other; many, whose first contact with Christianity was at the club, felt unabashed at coming to a public auditorium on the following evening. At the end of the five weeks, over one hundred had either professed faith in Christ or wanted to know more. Groups of not more than six were invited to the homes of young married Chapel members, and soon ten such first-steps groups were covering a six-week syllabus with Billy Graham's follow-up material. After that, these new Christians were invited to the pastor's discipleship class.

this
is
your
invitation
to

# CONTACT CLUB

**MACKIES' RESTAURANT, 108 PRINCES ST.**

**SATURDAYS AT 8·0 P.M. MAY 23 TO JUNE 27**

refreshments

music

varied and intriguing programme

SPONSORED BY THE YOUNG PEOPLE OF CHARLOTTE BAPTIST CHAPEL

*As the Charlotte Rooms in MacVitties Guest were not available after Saturday 9 May 1964, Contact Club moved to the Buttery, the function room of Mackies' Restaurant, also on Princes Street.*

## International Club

Alan Redpath was now more determined than ever to find permanent premises, to fulfill the vision that he had shared with the elders (above). He looked at a basement in nearby Castle Street, but the cost of renovation was prohibitive. To keep the momentum going, he booked the Buttery, the function room of Mackies' Restaurant on Princes Street, for every Saturday evening from mid-May 1964 until the end of June. It could accommodate only 140, and the management did not permit the showing of films, but, as Bryan Thomson remarked: 'When "Contact Club" commenced no one dreamt that it would ever have become necessary to turn people away: yet this is the apology with which a number of folk have been greeted when arriving at the entrance of Mackies' restaurant.' The Chapel booked the Charlotte Rooms for every available Saturday evening through the autumn of 1964 and the spring of 1965, but it was not free from 20 March onward. The scene was set for Alan Redpath's biggest venture and, perhaps, his biggest disappointment.

A block of property at 127 Princes Street, formerly The Liberal and International Club, came to Alan Redpath's attention at the end of June 1964. It was just to the east of the Monseigneur News Café, and it too had a rear entrance a few yards from the Chapel's side door. Unlike the cinema, its frontage onto Princes Street was almost non-existent. Two years previously, the owners had turned the ground floor into shops, leaving only a small door onto Princes Street for the club, and this led to a narrow and steep stair to the upper floors. For this reason, although the property was in good condition, it had not attracted a buyer.

Alan Redpath showed it to the office bearers and their wives in July 1964, and arranged for it to be open on two Saturdays in August for all Chapel members to inspect. The young folk were wildly enthusiastic. The owners said they wanted £30,000 to sell, or £2,000 a year to let it to the Chapel; the writer and others believed they were bluffing, as no one else was interested, and recommended offering £15,000 to purchase or £300 to rent. To adapt the premises for Contact Club, and other Chapel organizations looking for accommodation, would cost £6,000, but it was hoped to attract a government grant of £10,000 for work among young people. The bottom line was therefore £11,000, a very large commitment for most Chapel members; average industrial wage in 1964 was £15 a week, £780 a year (in 2005, it was £480 a week, £24,960 a year), but, money apart, some of the elders and deacons thought this rambling property was 'a club too far'.

*When the Usher Hall was not available for Sunday evening services, queues began to form in Rose Street 15 minutes or more before the Chapel doors opened at 6 p.m. The editor of the Church of Scotland monthly* Life and Work *was so impressed that he wrote an article, accompanied by this photograph, in* The Scots Magazine.

## Alan Redpath's illness

### Cerebral haemorrhage

A week after the last open day for viewing the International Club (as everyone called it), on Saturday 5 September 1964, the Redpath family had lunch at the manse. Meryl was staying there with her husband and two children, while she completed her midwifery training in Edinburgh, prior to leaving for the Central African Republic with the Africa Inland Mission. Alan and Marjorie had just returned from being joint hosts at a conference at Hildenborough Hall in Kent. Alan was due to conduct a wedding later that afternoon, so he went to his study to arrange final details, and to complete his preparation for the Chapel pulpit on the following day.

Suddenly, as he was writing, his hand wandered all over the paper. A few moments later, he lost all speech, his right side was paralysed and he was unable to walk. The doctor diagnosed a slight stroke, and although his mind remained clear, and he did not suffer any pain, he was completely helpless for over a week. The services in the Usher Hall, from 27 September to 1 November, were cancelled. The plans to acquire the International Club were put on hold. Ever the optimist, Alan Redpath asked whether he could fulfil his planned visit to various Overseas Missionary Fellowship fields in Southeast Asia in November. He was told it depended on the outcome of a thorough examination in hospital, to discover the extent of the problem.

### Complications

The stroke had been mild and everyone was optimistic about a steady return to full health. If there had been no question of going to the Far East in November, there would have been no need for the gruelling hospital tests to allow the doctors to pronounce on that. During one of the tests, which revealed that the damage to the arteries was not severe, a main nerve in the back of his neck was damaged, with the result that his diaphragm ceased to function and his left arm was paralysed. For about eight weeks, he was in intense pain. As he gradually recovered, the specialist said that if he gave up all work, and took life gently, he would have normal life expectancy; if he resumed work, he would not live for more than five or ten years. He was aged 57.

There was, however, a factor that the medical specialist did not take into account. Billy Graham phoned from Nebraska, on the day after the stroke, to assure the family of much prayer. Alan's successor at Richmond Baptist Church, Stephen Olford, who was now in New York, heard the news just as he went into the evening service. He was so distressed that he called the whole congregation in Calvary Church to prayer and set his alarm clock for 3 a.m. on the Monday morning – 8 a.m. Edinburgh time. He telephoned at what was, for him, the middle of the night, saying that the love, thoughts and prayers of hundreds of Christians throughout the world were joined with those of the Chapel family for a speedy recovery. This prayer support, spearheaded by the Chapel, continued throughout the months of convalescence.

Given the choice (as he put it) of 'rusting out or burning out', Alan Redpath set out to confound the specialist. At his next examination, not one symptom of the illness was left, apart from slight damage to the right hand, which hampered his writing for the rest of his life. The doctors kept the brakes on him for as long as they could, but agreed that he could preach again on Easter Sunday, 18 April 1965. He received a fresh anointing of the Holy Spirit as he preached powerfully at the Keswick Convention in July, and he returned to the Chapel like a new man. 'Constant victory' remained both his message and his lifestyle.

**Alan Redpath**

**A TESTIMONY TO DIVINE HEALING**

*Alan Redpath wrote a leaflet about his illness and the lessons he had learned from it; he spoke frankly of the spiritual struggles he had had during times of physical weakness.*

**Chapter 43**
K.o.k.d. (1964-1965)

## Assistant to the pastor

Bryan Thomson had come to Edinburgh to spearhead evangelism, but Alan Redpath's illness rearranged his priorities. He conducted the wedding on the afternoon of the stroke, and a funeral two days later. He took over the Sunday morning services (William Whyte conducted the evening ones), welcomed new members, held infant dedications and a number of weddings, all despite the arrival of their second child in August – no one thought of paternity leave in 1964. Pulpit supply had already been arranged from late November until late February, because of Alan Redpath's planned visit to the Far East, but these two were invaluable for the remainder of the autumn and winter.

*For Your Diary . . .*

Services in the Ross Bandstand every Sunday at 9.15 p.m. until the end of August.

**Sunday, August 2nd:**
  *Guest Preacher*: Rev. John Caiger.
**Saturday, September 12th to Saturday, September 19th:**
  Filey Convention.
**Sunday, September 13th:**
  *Preacher*: Rev. Wm. Whyte, M.A.
**Sunday, September 20th:**
  *Preacher*: Rev. Bryan Thompson.
**Thursday, September 24th:**
  United Baptist Rally. *Speaker*: Rev. Peter Barber.
**Sunday, September 27th:**
  Harvest Thanksgiving.
**Sunday, September 27th to Sunday, November 1st:**
  Usher Hall Autumn Services.
**Monday, October 12th:**
  Stephen Olford Crusade Preparation Meeting.
  *Speaker*: Canon Herbert W. Cragg, M.A., of Beckenham.
**Sunday, October 18th to Tuesday, October 20th:**
  Church Anniversary Services.
  *Monday, October 19th*: Congregational Meeting.
  *Tuesday, October 20th*: Anniversary Meeting.
  *Guest Speaker*: Dr. Martyn Lloyd-Jones.
**Tuesday, October 27th to Thursday, October 29th:**
  Baptist Union Assembly in Edinburgh.
**Saturday, October 31st to Sunday, November 8th:**
  Annual Missionary Conference.

*The services in the Usher Hall had to be cancelled when Alan Redpath took ill, but all the other special events that had been planned for the autumn of 1964 were carried through in his absence.*

## Contact Club continued

### 127 Princes Street

During Alan Redpath's illness, the majority of the office-bearers saw the potential of the International Club, so they carried out surveys and kept the property on the agenda. However, a minority remained sceptical. Estimates for immediate repairs were pared down to £2,750, and the writer ascertained that the owners might now sell for £10,000, although they were still quoting £2,000 a year to lease it. As no one else was interested in the vacant building, things were allowed to drift until the pastor was fit to get involved again; when the YPM 'expressed deep concern over the delay in securing premises for the continuance of Contact Club', the deacons 'assured them that their zeal and enthusiasm was appreciated', but suggested that they use the Chapel's lower hall when the Charlotte Rooms were not available (which they did). There was never any doubt about the deacons' wholehearted support for the Contact Club style of outreach – they were thrilled by it – but never more then three-quarters of the deacons were in favour of acquiring the International Club premises, and some were vehemently and vocally against.

Convalescing in Bournemouth, Alan Redpath sent a tape-recorded message to the deacons in February, strongly advocating progress and believing that the whole church would respond to the opportunity. He came briefly to the March deacons' meeting, his first public appearance since September 1964, to press for a decision. They decided to wait until he was able to chair the necessary church meeting, and fixed this for 26 May 1965. He 'flew a kite' at the annual general meeting on 10 May; it soon became clear that while the membership supported the need for additional premises, they were doubtful as to whether this property was the right one. Alan Redpath continued trying to accentuate the positives in preparation for 26 May, pointing out that the International Club was on the doorstep of the Chapel, that there was ample accommodation, that planning permission had been granted, and that the premises were 'ours for the taking', because the restricted Princes Street access made it unattractive for commercial use.

The deacons had, however, picked up the negative vibes from the members' meeting, and two days later only 17 out of 32 were prepared to continue with the special meeting – 15 voted to abandon the project there and then. Alan Redpath had to open the members' meeting on 26 May by saying that the deacons had no recommendation to bring. He himself (and others) stressed the tremendous potential of this particular property, but others argued that it was too large, that the access was too restricted and that the cost was too great. A motion to proceed was defeated by a substantial majority, too decisive to require hands to be counted.

### Contact Club under new management

The next meeting of the deacons authorized Alan Redpath to continue looking for property, so that Contact Club could have its own premises for regular weekly meetings. A small group actively pursued every possibility in the vicinity of the Chapel. Nothing suitable came onto the market for purchase, but the New York Restaurant in Shandwick Place offered to rent its large Statten Suite every Saturday evening, for 5 shillings (25 new pence) per head. This was within the Chapel's budget, but the premises were licensed; there was no suggestion that Contact Club would serve alcoholic drink, but temperance (meaning total abstinence) was an important principle for most of those involved, and there were real hesitations about renting licensed rooms. While the committee debated, the young people threw their energies into the Edinburgh Christian Crusade (below). They got on so well with their peers in other churches all over the city, that they asked the Crusade Committee to assume responsibility for continuing youth outreach. Contact Club therefore reopened under new management in Romano's Restaurant in November 1965.

The small group, commissioned by the deacons to keep an eye out for suitable premises, brought various suggestions to the court. A church meeting was called to consider purchasing property in Coates Crescent, but by the time the required notice had been given, the property had been sold. That was the last serious enquiry; when Alan Redpath resigned from the pastorate in April 1966, as described in the next chapter, 'the question of the property did not [any longer] arise' and the search was discontinued. The International Club was still on the market in the summer of 1969; a Christian group, Edinburgh Youth Outreach, asked the Chapel whether they would rent some of the rooms for youth work, Sunday School and Bible Classes, if EYO purchased the whole property. By this time, the Chapel had a three-year lease of rooms at 127 Rose Street South Lane, and none of the auxiliaries were interested in 127 Princes Street.

### The Heralds at the ABC (and elsewhere)

The Saturday evening outreach continued for a while in Romano's, and then once a month in the YWCA in Randolph Place, under the name '3 C's'; on the other Saturdays, the young folk did what they could in the top hall of the Chapel. One special effort was on a Sunday evening in the ABC cinema in Lothian Road – now divided, but then one enormous single auditorium. Sunday 1 May 1966 was hot and sunny, and the manager of the picture-house was concerned that the Chapel's young folk had wasted their money in trying to get unchurched people into a religious

meeting on such a glorious day. He had not taken account of the prayer meetings, three times a week for the previous month, the one thousand posters in shop windows and the twenty thousand cards handed out in workplaces.

There was a queue when the doors opened, and soon 2,500 teens and twenties were listening to the Heralds' music, testimonies and preaching. When Ian Leitch invited those who wished to become Christians to stay behind, one hundred did so, and 40 of them came to a follow-up meeting in the next week. Eight years later the Heralds, supported by the Chapel, packed the Usher Hall on Sunday evening 28 May 1974, for singing, testimony and a gospel address. While the majority of those who came to the front in response to the appeal were young, some older folk in the 2,500 audience left their seats in order to learn more about the claims of Christ.

### Monthly tract distribution

1964 finished on a sad note for the systematic monthly distribution of the gospel leaflet, 'The Lightbringer'. The Chapel had restarted tract distribution in 1903, as mentioned in Chapter 13; by 1939, over one hundred members were calling at 7,500 homes every month. Wartime paper restrictions reduced the print-run to 4,000, but all through the war, over 60 volunteers kept calling. By 1964, only ten were still prepared to visit the districts around the Chapel and no new workers could be recruited. The Young Peoples Meeting were concentrating on the new housing estate of Longstone, where the Chapel had a thriving Sunday School, and they delivered suitable literature to nearly every home in that area once a month. It was therefore reluctantly decided to end 'tract society' business in the centre of Edinburgh at the end of 1964.

## Alan Redpath's return

### Monday prayer meeting

When Alan Redpath resumed active involvement after his illness, he was distressed to find that both the Monday evening and the Friday morning prayer meetings were poorly supported. The zone meetings may have been partly responsible, as many prayed aloud in these informal home groups, and so did not go to the larger meetings in the church as well. The Monday meeting was now 'small in number and weak in spirit'; the Friday meeting, specifically for revival, had dropped from 70 to only a handful. On Monday 14 June 1965, Alan Redpath led an opening session of praise and worship in the lower hall, and then divided the meeting into four groups, each led by an elder, one group for young people only. Some liked the new idea, others did not; when people were slow to participate in the groups, he arranged for a hymn-book to be passed around, and expected the person to whom it was handed to pray, however briefly. Positive reaction outweighed the negative, and group prayer on Monday continued for some time.

## Reverence

Another of Alan Redpath's ideas was for an elder to go into the pulpit, carrying the pulpit Bible, a few minutes before the start of the morning service. He was concerned that the hubbub of conversation, right up to the point where he himself stood there, was not a good preparation for worship; he felt it was positively off-putting for visitors who were accustomed to a sepulchral silence in church. The appearance of the elder invited people to settle down. Not everyone was happy at the idea, because lonely people enjoyed speaking with friends, and this involved moving about in order to greet one other; they were concerned that the Chapel should not lose its reputation as a friendly place. Subsequent ministers have tried various ways to achieve a reverent hush shortly before the service starts, but people do love to talk.

## Edinburgh Christian Crusade

Within three months of his arrival in Edinburgh, Alan Redpath proposed holding a citywide evangelistic crusade for three weeks in the autumn of 1965. He had a speaker and a committee already in his mind, but he was anxious that this should be an inter-church effort. This is not the place to reflect on what was indeed a citywide enterprise, held in the Usher Hall for 19 evenings in October 1965. Meetings were held nightly except Friday (when the Scottish National Orchestra had a prior booking), and well over two thousand attended every time, with closed-circuit television overflows to a nearby church at weekends. The public meetings attracted 46,000 people in total, of whom 1,200 were counselled, most of them young, and about half made a first-

time profession of faith. The Chapel was heavily involved in every aspect, planning, praying, publicity, choir practice, stewarding, counselling, etc. Alan Redpath was one of the two vice-presidents, Fergus Brown of the Chapel was treasurer and the writer was secretary. Enquirers were referred to a church of their choice for follow-up and 65 names were passed to the Chapel. A new sense of unity was forged among the evangelical churches in Edinburgh.

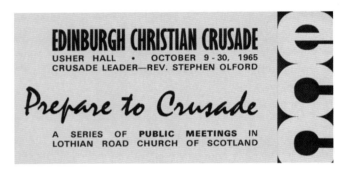

*Bryan Thomson, the Chapel's assistant minister, was in charge of the publicity for the Edinburgh Christian Crusade of October 1965.*

## Who will go?

Alan Redpath regularly challenged the congregation with the need for more overseas missionaries; six Chapel members were valedicted for the first time in 1964-5. Every one had a unique testimony, but there is not space to print more than one excerpt from the *Record*:

*In the course of the morning service on Sunday 7th February [1965], Sheila and Ian Finlayson were valedicted from the church to service in Nigeria. For them, it saw the fulfillment of a dream which started more than 10 years ago, when Sheila Meiklejohn (as she then was), and Ian Finlayson first wrote, independently, expressing the conviction: that God was calling them to service with the S.I.M. But time went by, and the way did not become clear. Ian has told something of the problems which he had to face [during National Service, Bible college, university and teaching training.]*

*Sheila, also a member of the Chapel, had (as she put it) 'always been accustomed to a strong missionary challenge', and she undertook nursing training with the mission field in view. Having qualified in that sphere, she then completed the course at B.T.I. – 'two very full and wonderful years'.*

*Ian had completed that course a few years earlier, and he and Sheila were married on 11th July, 1959. Although at that time Ian was still continuing his studies, they anticipated making formal application to the Mission in the not-too-distant future. [Health problems then kept them in this country for four years.] The Finlaysons sailed from Liverpool on 12th February, on M.V. Apapa bound for Lagos. They have been appointed to the staff on the Mission station at Egbe, where Ian will be teaching his own subject, mathematics, with some physics also, at Titcombe College. Sheila will be nursing in the Mission hospital there.*

2 *Record*, March 1965, pp. 20, 22.

*Ian and Sheila Finlayson and their family, Derek, Colin and Andrew, as they sailed for Nigeria for the first time in 1965.*

## 'Do you want me to stay?'

When Alan Redpath was invited to be the minister of Charlotte Chapel, he accepted for an initial period of three years. In October 1965, he reminded the deacons that the three years were nearly up, and that his recent illness made it impossible for him to carry full responsibility for pastoring the church and for taking the initiative in evangelistic outreach. Furthermore, he wished the opportunity to preach in the United States for six weeks at the beginning of 1966 and to visit some of the Chapel missionaries for another six weeks at the beginning of 1967. He regarded this as an extension of the ministry of the church. The deacons unanimously encouraged him to remain with the Chapel on this basis, indefinitely, until either party gave six months' notice. A special meeting of members endorsed this 'with heart-warming unanimity and ready approval'.

## Prayer before the evening service

At a day retreat to North Berwick in the autumn of 1965, the office-bearers agreed (among other things) that the elders should resume the practice from Sidlow Baxter's day, which had fallen into abeyance, of joining the pastor for prayer in the vestry at 6 p.m., before the Sunday evening service. This restarted what is, to this day, one of the most appreciated supports that the leadership gives to the pastor and to visiting preachers; a dozen or more kneel for 15 minutes of prayer with the preacher, morning and evening on Sunday.

## Review of the three years

What was accomplished in the first three years of Alan Redpath's ministry? The regular work of the church went on – new members were received almost every month, 50 in his first year and 33 until his illness in the second; 6 baptismal services were held in the first year, with 66 baptized, and 2 more, involving another 15, before September 1964; 9 couples brought infants for dedication in his first year and 7 more in the first part of 1964. Membership remained steady at about 1,050. The building was full on most Sundays and the congregation regularly overflowed into the lower hall. Alan Redpath held the evening service in the Usher Hall whenever it was available, attracting congregations of up to three thousand. A significant number of young people heard the call to overseas missionary service. As the church secretary put it:

*Dr Redpath is a man of dynamic energy and drive, prompted and guided by the Holy Spirit Himself and believe me, it takes some dynamism to move 1000 people – indeed, with some of us, dynamite would be needed. He is full of ideas and plans whereby we can be welded into a fighting unit, able and willing to fight evil, to proclaim the Gospel and to extend Christ's Kingdom. He has made it his business to get into close personal touch with all the agencies and departments of the work here, to inspire and to encourage and has always made time to visit the sick and the sorrowing to their joy and comfort.*

3 *Record*, 1963, p. 91.

---

### WILLIAM MACDUFF URQUHART, M.C., M.A., LL.B., S.S.C.

On Sunday 30th May 1965 at 4.30 p.m. Mr. W. MacDuff Urquhart was called into the presence of the Lord Whom he had loved and served so faithfully and so long.

He had been secretary of the Chapel for thirty-seven years, and it is impossible to express in words what this lifetime of service meant to all associated with the work of the Lord in this place. His keen mind, his helpful advice, and spiritual insight which enabled him to get to the real root of every matter have been God's gift to the church and will be sorely missed.

Only a fortnight before he passed on Mr. Urquhart wrote a letter to the Elders and Deacons reminding them of their sacred responsibility of office, and committed them to the grace of God. In the course of it he said, "Let us discuss without rancour and and argue without heat, remembering always that we are a body of men dedicated to the service of our Lord, and bound together by the golden cord of His love." This sums up the example he set during the many years he held prominent office in the Chapel, and which made him a man beloved by all who knew him.

A further tribute is paid on another page by one who knew him well over a long period, but I would take this opportunity of expressing the loving sympathy and prayers of the Chapel family to Mr. Urquhart's son and two daughters at this time of loss.

"I have fought a good fight, I have finished my course, I have kept the faith" (II Timothy 4. 7).

---

*MacDuff Urquhart, whose appreciation of his pastor is quoted just before this obituary, died as Alan Redpath returned to active service after his illness.*

### Zone meetings evaluated

As Alan Redpath's cottage meetings went into their second year, he was keen to make them welcoming points for new Christians, looking particularly to the Edinburgh Christian Crusade planned for October 1965 – it would be more natural for people, converted from a non-church background, to meet Christians first of all in a home rather than in a formal church setting.

Some groups gelled better than others. The writer and his wife were in the 'West End to Barnton zone' comprising 69 members, 25 men and 44 women, under the leadership of MacDuff Urquhart. His drawing room could accommodate the 40 or more who attended, but on his death in 1965, the zone was divided into two – those living south and those living north of Queensferry Road. Alex Cameron led the former and the writer, who was now an elder, the latter, which had 28 members. Initially, 17 (3 men and 14 women) attended regularly, but 11 never came. Outreach among neighbours and unchurched friends was attempted on several occasions through the group, but it never really fulfilled its objective. By the autumn of 1967, only 7 of the 20 zones were meeting, 3 regularly, 3 occasionally and 1 just once a year. Average attendance was about 15. In other words, just over 100 of the members were actively involved. The zone meetings became less and less significant in the life of the church after Alan Redpath left, but they were revived and renamed 'pastoral groups' under Derek Prime in 1970 (Chapter 45).

Other regular activities continued; it would be tedious to go through them, except to make one general comment. Alan Redpath had the gift of inspiring people, especially young people, to believe in themselves as evangelists, to join them together in imaginative outreach and to 'keep on kicking the devil'. The impact of this on the expanding work in Longstone will be mentioned in the next chapter.

Additional information on the following topics, mentioned in this chapter, is available on the CD.

Edinburgh Christian Crusade, 1965
Heralds Trust
William MacDuff Urquhart's obituary

# Chapter 44
## Onward, Christian soldiers (1966–1969)

### New life comes through

#### Open-air meetings

The summer open-air campaign, which had been held at the Mound on Wednesday and Thursday in 1964, was restructured from 1965 to 1971; it now focused on the Mound at 8.15 p.m. on Wednesday and the Ross Bandstand in Princes Street Gardens on Sunday at 9.15 p.m. Both ran weekly from the beginning of June to the end of August. The Young Peoples Meeting, which had been enthused for evangelism under Alan Redpath's leadership, actively supported both. They met in the Chapel for prayer with the regular Mound workers on Wednesday evening, before transporting a portable organ and a collapsible platform, music sheets (there was a lot of singing of hymns and choruses), and tracts and gospels in most of the European languages. Holidaymakers from all over the world stopped to listen, and some Christians among them responded to the invitation to come up and give their own testimony.

*The Chapel's open-air meeting at the Mound. This picture was painted by an art teacher at an Edinburgh school, who attended the meeting regularly, although he claimed to be an atheist; he presented his painting to the leaders of the meeting.*

Alan Redpath tried repeatedly, without success, to book the Ross Bandstand earlier than 9.15 p.m. on Sunday. It was quite a wait from the end of the Chapel evening service until then, but the suggestion of delaying the service until 7 p.m. presented more problems than it solved. The Chapel kept this outreach going through the pastor's illness, through the vacancy that followed and for many years more; in 1971, the Corporation gave the Chapel three-quarters of an hour, commencing at 5.45 p.m., and that (with variations) was the pattern until the facility was withdrawn in 1987 (Chapter 46).

SUMMER OPEN-AIR CAMPAIGN

**"Sunday Challenge"**

9.15 P.M. EVERY SUNDAY

ROSS BANDSTAND

PRINCES STREET GARDENS

———

OPEN-AIR MEETINGS AT THE MOUND

Every Wednesday at 8.15 p.m.

*The name 'Temple Twilight' for the half-hour in the Princes Street Gardens was changed in 1967 to 'Sunday Challenge' – and that was its focus.*

#### Longstone Christian Fellowship

The Chapel's outreach in the western suburb of Longstone was described in Chapter 39, from its commencement in 1948 to the first adult service in 1955. Through immense dedication by many Chapel members, everything grew and grew, except the Sunday evening adult service. By the spring of 1966, the Longstone Christian Fellowship (as it was now known) was active for five nights a week, with Scouts, Cubs, Guides, Brownies, Searchers (Tuesday, for children, attendance 70), Young Peoples Fellowship (Tuesday, attendance 18), Sunday School (140 in the afternoon) and a Sunday evening gospel service (45), all in the Longstone School. There were also occasional Saturday evening evangelistic squashes; apart from Sunday evening, the work was directed entirely toward young people.

The problem was reaching their parents. Encouraged by attendance at a fortnight's mission in November 1963, the fellowship restarted the Sunday evening evangelistic service for adults, which had been discontinued. It was well supported by Chapel members living in the area, with attendance of up to 50, but regrettably it made little impact on the community. Since parents came in large numbers to weeknight evenings, when their children were taking part, the fellowship arranged a mid-week Get-Together for adults. It attracted about 30 local people, all women; as they did not come on Sunday evening (as had been hoped), these meetings became evangelistic in themselves.

The parents of the Sunday School children applauded what the fellowship was doing, and when Chapel members visited them, many promised to consider coming to the Sunday evening adult service – but they never did. Sunday evening, intended as an outreach to adults, continued to attract between 35 and 45, mostly in their teens or early twenties. Several of them were baptized in the Chapel and two of them trained for full-time Christian service, one at London Bible College and the other at the Faith Mission.

In September 1964, the fellowship delivered a questionnaire to eight hundred homes in the area, along with gospel literature; 220 families responded, most saying that their allegiance was to the local Church of Scotland. Only 34 said they would like to receive the good news paper 'Challenge' every month. The parish minister made it plain that he saw no need for the Chapel to be involved in the area, and the workers began to wonder whether they should transfer their efforts to some other needy part of the city.

*Although Bryan Thomson came to Edinburgh for ministry and evangelism, the Chapel made extensive use of his artistic talents. These two syllabi are examples of the attractive work that he produced.*

Bryan Thomson had come to Edinburgh for 12 months from March 1964 (Chapter 43), to expand the work in Longstone. During Alan Redpath's illness, he took on many of the pastor's duties, for which the office-bearers were grateful, and they asked him to stay on. In April 1966, at the same time as Alan Redpath tendered his resignation (below), Bryan advised the deacons that he did not see a future for himself in Longstone and that he wanted to set up a business, Mission in Design, preparing Christian publicity material.

## Alex Hardie

When Bryan Thomson left in June 1966, the elders and the Longstone workers looked for a young man, fresh out of College, who would live in the district, explore sites for a building in adjoining areas, and give his undivided attention to the work. Bryan had found, in visiting homes, a genuine aversion to attending services in a school building – 'it doesn't take the place of the kirk'. No ground was available in Longstone, even if it had been desirable to build there when the allegiance of so many was to the parish church. Alex Hardie, a member of the Granton Baptist Church, who was completing his studies at the Baptist Theological College of Scotland, accepted the challenge for a period of not less than three years.

*Alex Hardie was the first to devote all his time to the Chapel's outreach in the western suburbs of Edinburgh. This led, six and a half years later, to the constitution of the Wester Hailes Baptist Church.*

He quickly proved that someone living in the area, and dedicated to the work, could expect a response. Within a month, 60 adults were attending the Sunday evening service, and this nearly doubled over the next month. The Youth Fellowship went up to 36 and Alex, setting an example by doing visitation himself, held training classes to prepare 36 others for evangelistic visitation. Every time there was a baptismal service in the Chapel in 1968 and 1969, a number of new Christians from the Longstone outreach (as many as eight at a time) were baptized by Alex Hardie on the same evening. The first communion service in Longstone was held in June 1968, with 55 present.

The Chapel was sufficiently encouraged to ask the Corporation for ground in the adjoining new housing area of Wester Hailes. Officials in the Housing Department laid out a plan of the Wester Hailes development, with the roads marked but with little else decided. They invited the Chapel team to select any three-quarters of an acre that they wished. The most appropriate site seemed to be at the intersection of several main arteries, just back from the main road. A Chapel members' meeting on 30 January 1969 unanimously accepted the challenge to erect a church building on this site within three years, to seat 300 in the sanctuary and 250 in a hall, at an estimated cost of £35,000. Robert Rankin, the architect for the Baptist Union of Scotland, cleverly designed it so that walls could be taken down and the building extended if expansion was required – which it soon was. The Corporation's Planning Department assumed – this was 1969 – that 18 car parking spaces would be sufficient for a congregation of 300.

Raising the money, acquiring a manse, and constituting the Wester Hailes Baptist Church in February 1973, all took place under the ministry of Derek Prime, and so will be described in Chapter 46.

## Evangelical Alliance

### '18 October 1966: I was there'

When the Evangelical Alliance opened its membership to congregations as well as to individuals, in 1965, six thousand churches (including the Chapel) affiliated almost immediately. Anglicans formed the largest group, with Baptists not far behind, followed by members of the Fellowship of Independent Evangelical Churches. The Chapel sent delegates to its National Assembly in London in 1965 and again in 1966.

The 1966 Assembly was eventful; one delegate entitled his report on it: '18 October 1966: I was there'. So was the writer, as one of the three Chapel delegates. Dr Martyn Lloyd-Jones, the minister of Westminster Congregational Chapel in London, had become increasingly concerned at 'the rising and revival amongst us of what is known as the ecumenical movement.' He was worried, as the Chapel had been in the previous decade, at the lowest common denominator approach; the stated aim of the British Council of Churches was to have organic church union in Great Britain by Easter 1980. The Alliance general secretary asked Lloyd-Jones to state publicly, at the 1966 Assembly, what he had been saying privately to their executive for some time. (He said afterward that this was 'probably one of my biggest mistakes'.)

The opening session was in Westminster Central Hall. A young London minister, Derek Prime, took the opening prayer; neither he nor the Chapel delegates had the slightest inkling that exactly three years later, he would be inducted to the vacant pastorate in Charlotte Chapel.

The chairman, John Stott, rector of All Souls Church, Langham Place, London, was a highly respected Anglican evangelical. He opened the session with extended chairman's remarks, giving his view on the ecumenical issue. Martyn Lloyd-Jones then made his case, as he had been invited to do. He asked passionately whether evangelicals were content to be 'nothing but an evangelical wing' in churches where the majority held liberal views of the Bible and theology. He questioned whether evangelicals should be in denominations affiliated to the World Council of Churches. He did not say, as some have thought they heard him say, that evangelicals should form a new denomination – his challenge was for evangelical churches to leave their denominational structure and, maintaining their individual identity, to form a confederation of evangelical ecumenicity.

*Martyn Lloyd-Jones (seated, left) and John Stott (right) in conversation, following their public disagreement at the Evangelical Alliance Assembly in Westminster Central Hall on 18 October 1966.*

John Stott was concerned that impressionable young evangelical Anglicans might immediately leave the Church of England, so he used the chairman's closing remarks, not to thank the speaker, but to repudiate the challenge laid down:

'I believe history is against what Dr Lloyd-Jones has said … Scripture is against him; the remnant was within the church, not outside it. I hope no one will act precipitately.'

Much has been written about that Assembly, but the writer has never seen comment on one aspect of it. Does a chairman have a right of reply to the invited speaker? This is what concerned the Chapel delegates – two of them being businessmen rather than theologians. Was a breach of normal business procedure the reason (humanly speaking) for the polarization of the evangelical scene in Britain for years to come?

## Vacancy

### Alan Redpath's resignation

Alan Redpath enjoyed his six-week tour of America at the beginning of 1966, and it guided his thinking about the years ahead:

*If, as it seems, I am bound to experience exhaustion while only carrying on a limited amount of work, then my great longing is to be exhausted in the thing that matters most: preaching the Word and offering Christ to others. I proved by my recent tour of Jamaica and the United States that I am able to carry a fairly full preaching responsibility, and experience great release in doing so, when free from all other commitments.*

1 *Record*, June 1966, p. 7.

He realized it was impractical, in his state of health, both to preach and to exercise pastoral care in a large church. In April 1966, he advised the deacons that he wished to resign from the pastorate in order to undertake itinerant ministry in the front line of battle, visiting missionaries, taking conferences and preaching throughout the world. A members' meeting on Monday 2 May accepted the resignation with reluctance and regret; in recognition of his short but outstanding time at the Chapel, it conferred on him the title of Pastor Emeritus; he was delighted by this, and regularly signed his letters 'Pastor-Em.'

### Sixty-four baptisms

As has been mentioned already, the announcement of a vacancy concentrates the minds of the undecided. Within weeks of Alan Redpath's notice of resignation, 64 young people applied for baptism, requiring five separate services in May, June, July, August and October 1966. Most of them, following his encouragement, gave a short oral testimony to their faith before being baptised. It was a particular pleasure to him that during his last communion service, in November, 14 young people joined the church; he had had a particularly effective ministry to the young. In addition to six new overseas missionaries, whom he valedicted in 1964-5, five more began training for missionary service during his pastorate and another three for home ministry.

### Pulpit supply

Alan Redpath stayed on as pastor until the end of 1966. As he was to embark on an arduous tour of mission fields in January 1967, the farewell services were held at the end of November. By invitation, the Redpaths used the manse as their base until a new minister was found in 1969, and Marjorie Redpath continued to lead the Women's Thursday Morning Fellowship. During 1967, Alan travelled widely under the auspices of the Keswick Convention, to Japan, South Africa, Brazil and America; in January 1968, he showed a film of his travels. When in Edinburgh, he supplied the Chapel pulpit during the vacancy – first on 13 August 1967; he preached twice on 29 June 1969, conducted a wedding on the Saturday, a dedication on the Sunday and spoke at the Morning Fellowship.

*Following his stroke, Alan Redpath resigned from the pastorate of the Chapel in 1966, in order to pursue a worldwide conference ministry.*

When the Chapel 'called' a new minister in 1969, Major Ian Thomas, a friend of the Redpaths, made a cottage available in the grounds of Capernwray Hall, near Carnforth in Lancashire, in exchange for Alan helping at the Capernwray Bible School and exercising an itinerant ministry for the Capernwray Missionary Fellowship. He was not back in the Chapel until the missionary conference in November 1974. He preached on Saturday evening, twice on Sunday, and then led an after-church rally. He brought powerful messages at evening rallies on the Monday and the Tuesday (from Ezekiel 47) and ministered to the missionary guests on the Monday and Tuesday mornings. He preached again on Sundays 17 December 1978, 1 April 1979 and 31 July 1983.

Alan Redpath was invited to the church anniversary weekend in October 1986. His health was failing, and he knew that this would be his last visit to the Chapel. His three messages summed up his three greatest passions. On Saturday evening, he challenged the church to greater evangelism. On Sunday morning, he preached on the principles of church growth. On Sunday evening, his last message to the Chapel was from Colossians 3 – 'self dethroned, Jesus enthroned'; this was one of his constant themes, that Christians are delivered from failure only by constant and renewed submission to the Lordship of Christ.

It reminded the writer of an earlier Sunday evening, when Alan Redpath still had full health and strength. His text was from Luke 7, the healing of the centurion's servant. What he said remains in the writer's mind to this day. The centurion said to Jesus (Authorized Version): 'I am a man set under authority, having under me soldiers.' For half-an-hour, Alan Redpath drew out the implications of this chain of command. The centurion had authority over his soldiers only because he had voluntarily subordinated himself to Caesar; the Christian could live victoriously in proportion to his or her voluntary surrender to our heavenly king. This distinctive message runs through Alan Redpath's many books, including *Victorious Christian Faith*, *Victorious Christian Living*, *Victorious Christian Service*, *Victorious Praying*, and *The Life of Victory*, daily readings compiled by Marjorie.

As with their predecessors, the Scroggies and the Baxters, who also went from the Chapel into itinerant ministry, the Redpaths retained their membership for the rest of their lives. Alan died peacefully at home in Edgbaston, Birmingham, on 16 March 1989, surrounded by his family. Marjorie stayed in Birmingham, and is still a member of the Chapel as this book goes to print.

348

## Memories of Alan Redpath's ministry

The writer asked Alan Redpath, after a weekend of challenging meetings and a large response to them, whether he was satisfied with the outcome; he replied: 'I will never be satisfied'. He led by example, and his four years were crowded with experiments. Setting up house groups for pastoral care was pioneering in Scotland at the time; tireless evangelism, especially in Princes Street Gardens, Contact Club and in the Usher Hall, showed Christians how a half-way house could reach the unchurched. Walking back from the Ross Bandstand one wet and cold Sunday evening, when only a few passers-by had listened to the half-hour 'Temple Twilight' in Princes Street Gardens, he remarked to the writer: 'You know, probably more unsaved folk heard the gospel this evening, even in the rain, than we got into the Chapel at 6.30 p.m. Hallelujah, anyway.'

*Rev. William Whyte, who joined the Chapel when he retired from the pastorate, guided the church through the vacancy of 1966 to 1969.*

## A different approach to vacancy

When he tendered his resignation to the deacons in April 1966, Alan Redpath expressed the hope that there might be a joint valediction and induction by the end of the year. This had happened when he left Duke Street in Richmond for Chicago in 1953; Stephen Olford was inducted as he left. The Chapel vacancy committee (again, the whole diaconate) made a prompt start, meeting for the first time on 8 June 1966, but they adopted a totally different method. When Gerald Griffiths resigned, they went straight for one name, Alan Redpath; in 1966, they were strongly guided by one of the elders, Rev. William Whyte, who had wide experience as a moderator in vacancies in both Scotland and England. He recommended that the deacons should draw up a list of all those who might be considered for the pastorate, and invite them one by one to preach for a Sunday as pulpit supply. He was strongly against a joint valediction and induction, so there was no urgency to fill the vacancy.

CHARLOTTE BAPTIST CHAPEL

YOUNG WORSHIPPERS' LEAGUE

As the Annual Prize-giving takes place on Sunday morning, 28th May, you are requested to be present in the Lecture Hall below the Church at 10.30 a.m.

Prize Winners.

SUNDAY, 28th May, 1967.
MORNING WORSHIP at 11 a.m.

Introit
Opening Prayer
Hymn No. 7
Scripture Reading - Joshua, chap. 9.
Children's Address
Children's Hymn No. 753
    Young children leave for Junior
    Nursery Department in Lower Hall.
Intimations and Offertory
Offertory Prayer
Message from the Choir
Prayer
Hymn No. 136
    MESSAGE: Rev. Derek J. Prime,
                M.A., S.Th., LONDON.
    Subject: "A Cause of many Mistakes
          in Life". (Joshua, 9:14).
Hymn No. 417 (verse 1 only)
*YOUNG WORSHIPPERS' LEAGUE PRIZE-GIVING*
Hymn No. 417 (verses 2 and 3)
Benediction.

*Derek Prime's first visit to the Chapel coincided with the Young Worshippers League's annual prize giving. He 'kindly presented the prizes, and pinned on the medals. He manifested a real interest in each child, and this added greatly to the success of the occasion.'*

Mr Whyte further recommended that if anyone coming as pulpit supply made an impression, a delegation should visit his church, and make enquiries about his background as a preacher and a teacher. If the deacons were then unanimous, or nearly so, the nominee would be asked to preach again 'with a view', which would be intimated to him and to the congregation. The deacons accepted this in theory, but in practice they worked their way through all the 16 names (below) before seriously considering any one name. They met every Monday evening at 7 p.m., for an hour of special prayer before the congregational prayer meeting.

Members of the congregation were invited to submit nominations, and they put forward 28 names. Other names came from the vacancy committee itself. From this long list, the committee decided to invite 16 ministers to come for a Sunday as pulpit supply. Among them was 'Rev. Derek J. Prime, West Norwood, London', who preached on 28 May 1967.

## Progress report

In November 1967, the vacancy committee reported to the church that all but one of the 16 men had preached, and that the last one would do so before the end of the year. The young people were pressing for action, as young people do, but the deacons reiterated that they were going to follow through the procedure that Mr Whyte had recommended. Despite the negative items mentioned in the next two sections of this chapter, many activities in the Chapel were in good heart, and some exciting new ones were started. They will be looked at in a moment, but a vacancy inevitably has its downside and that is looked at first.

## Changes during the vacancy

Alan Redpath's departure at the end of 1966 marked the beginning (although it was not the cause) of six months of rapid change in Chapel life. The deaconess reached retiring age, the Sunday School superintendent had to resign through ill health, the organist went elsewhere, the church officer moved on and the matron of Beulah Home resigned.

Other changes did relate to the absence of a pastor; attendance at both the Sunday services and the Monday prayer meeting dropped substantially. The Easter Conference, which Alan Redpath had found so challenging over five days, was reduced by the elders to communion on Good Friday in 1967. Missionary giving went down from £4,809 in 1966 to £4,087 in 1967, and down another £300 in 1968. The

Missionary Circles, meeting once a month for intensive study of areas of the world, were discontinued through lack of support. The eight-day annual missionary conferences, which included hospitality (for their benefit) for 30 or more missionaries, became a Saturday to Monday event from October 1967, with no ministry to missionary guests. The lower spiritual temperature meant that the circulation of the *Record* went down; two hundred of the five hundred printed weekly offering envelopes were uncollected by members. The church accounts, which had a surplus of £524 in 1967, showed a deficit of £520 in 1968. It was not all downhill, however, as £5,200 was given, during the vacancy, toward the building at Wester Hailes.

### Membership below 1,000

Membership, which had gone into four figures in 1930, remained there until 1967 although, as noted from time to time, roll review was infrequent and for many years the figure was artificially high. In the spring of 1967, the elders were concerned about 39 members who had not been seen for some time; they had no address for 13 of them. After full enquiry had been made, a members' meeting in December 1967 deleted 19 names. That brought the total membership, at the end of 1967, down to 996.

In the calendar year 1968, the vacancy took a further toll on the membership. 11 joined other Baptist churches, 11 more joined non-baptistic churches, 10 resigned, 14 died and 1 name was removed, 47 in all; only 12 joined (4 by baptism, 4 by confession, 4 by transfer), leaving the roll at 31 December 1968 at 961, a drop of 35. This was believed at the time to be accurate, but when a careful analysis was made, in preparation for the arrival of the new pastor in November 1969, it was found to be overstated by 85, 'due to a miscalculation at some unknown point in recent years'. In addition to the phantom 85, 20 more names were deleted in the year 1969, giving exact membership at 31 December 1969 of 856. It may have been exact on paper, but when Derek Prime asked for a list of those who had not been seen in the Chapel recently, 135 names had to be reviewed, as set out in the section 'Roll revision' in the next chapter.

### Secularisation

As mentioned in the last chapter, the Chapel leadership experimented with new ways to reach outsiders, in the rapidly changing world of the 1960s. They were aware, at the same time, of the revolution in moral standards in society, where Christian ethical teaching was widely repudiated. Parliament did not help; the Conservative government had introduced Premium Bonds (gambling under another name) in 1957, and a liberalized Betting and Gaming Act three years later. The 1966 parliament turned to more personal questions – abortion was legalized in 1967, and homosexual acts between consenting adults was decriminalized; in 1968, theatre censorship was abolished, and in 1969 divorce by consent was introduced. The Chapel rallied round Mary Whitehouse and her National Viewers' and Listeners' Association, set up in 1965, and supported her rallies in Edinburgh.

The Chapel saw issues like Sunday observance and licensing in black and white. When the government proposed legislation in 1967, to allow sport and commercial entertainment on Sunday, the Evangelical Alliance, of which the Chapel was a member, suggested working for an acceptable compromise. The Chapel officer-bearers rejected this and gave full support to the Lord's Day Observance Society, which opposed the Bill outright.

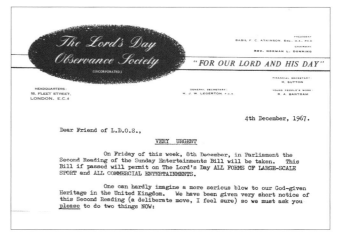

*The Chapel gave full support to the Lord's Day Observance Society, who refused any compromise on the Sunday Entertainments Bill of 1967.*

## Individual initiatives

### The Children's Village, Humbie

In 1964, two Chapel members, assisted by three others, started a Sunday School for children with learning difficulties. Although it was never an official Chapel activity, many Chapel members helped as leaders and drivers and musicians, and its work was regularly and enthusiastically reported in the *Record*. Initially, 30 children and parents were transported monthly from different parts of Midlothian to a schoolroom at Cockpen, where the Algrade Sunday School was held. Four years later, 150 handicapped children, accompanied by brothers, sisters, mothers, fathers and grandparents (330 in all) were collected monthly in 5 large buses, 25 cars and 4 dormobiles. They filled the largest primary school in the area. All abilities were catered for in an atmosphere of caring, of love and of hope. The monthly gatherings were so much appreciated by parents that a bungalow was obtained, in two acres of ground at Middleton, where parents could enjoy holidays with their handicapped child and family. Four hundred attended the open day in 1967 and over six hundred in 1968.

In 1968, the leaders rented the Children's Village at Humbie in East Lothian, to expand the holiday bungalow into a residential home for 'mentally handicapped children' (the contemporary phrase). A Chapel member gave up his job in journalism in order to acquire the necessary professional qualification to lead it. The village consisted of seven houses, a school and a hall seating two hundred, set in eleven acres of countryside, with every facility for children. Initially they were able to take a couple of dozen residents and as many again on a daily basis; by 1973 (when the Chapel's Christmas Day offering was for the village), they had 77 residents, some full-time and others for respite care. Many Chapel members helped at the village, and at the Algrade Sunday School, which now filled the Newbattle School building with four hundred children and parents every week.

## The Emmaus 4

In the same way as the Algrade Sunday School was run by Chapel members, without being an official Chapel activity, other initiatives were mentioned from time to time at the Chapel prayer meetings. One was the Emmaus 4 (Douglas, Alex, Jim and Bernard in the photograph below), a male voice quartet of Chapel members who sang and preached in towns and villages throughout southern Scotland, including Barlinnie prison.

*The Emmaus 4 were part of Jimmy Monihan's Male Voice Group. In this 1962 photograph, from left to right, back row: John Gibson, Douglas Lawrence, Alex McLean, Jim Fenwick; centre row: John Arnott, Ken Baker, Walter Johnston, George Balmer; front row: Bernard Howard, George Henderson, George Nash.*

## Chancelot Children's Hour

Another individual initiative was the Chancelot Children's Hour, held in the home of the Gillon sisters in Chancelot Terrace. Concerned that the children who played in the gardens and park around their home had no church connection, they approached nine homes in the Terrace. Immediately 18 youngsters, 8 boys and 10 girls up to the age of 12, came and continued to come to what was a Sunday School under another name.

## Landline to Beulah Home

Two members were able to connect the Chapel to Beulah Home by a permanent post office landline, in time for the Easter Sunday services in 1969; reception was very good. From then until the present day, the residents have been able to share in the Sunday services, the prayer meeting, the Thursday Fellowship and in any special occasions.

# Auxiliaries

## Young People

In 1966, the Young Peoples Meeting had 80 on its roll, with an average attendance on Wednesday evening of 70, including some converted through the Crusade and through Contact Club. They took back the management of the club, because running it through an inter-church committee was unwieldy, and renamed it 'The 3 C's'. This outreach was held one Saturday a month in the YWCA in Randolph Place. Light refreshments were on sale, with gospel rhythm groups, solos, duets, quizzes, sometimes a film and always an epilogue. Discussion about the message was encouraged, and the YPM valued the presence of a few older (but not too old) Chapel members to answer questions. As with Contact Club, the aim was either to bring non-Christian friends or to go out street fishing for young people: 'We have only one ultimate purpose, to win our generation for Christ.' The organisers were greatly encouraged by the response; even in the worst weather during the winter of 1967-8, over one hundred came in. On the other Saturdays, the club was held in the top hall in the Chapel, primarily to nurture those who had expressed an interest in the Christian faith at one of 'The 3 C's'.

Summer Schools with evangelism in view are common now, but the Chapel YPM was innovative in arranging one on the Chapel premises for a week in July 1969, encouraging school-agers to bring their friends and a packed lunch. In the morning there was singing and a talk, and then an outing for the afternoon.

*The 186th City of Edinburgh (Charlotte Baptist Chapel) Company of Girl Guides held a reunion in the lower hall on Tuesday 3 May 1966, to commemorate the formation of the company in 1931. For the map in the background and the boards on either side of it, see Chapters 28 and 45.*

The Young Peoples Meeting held a fiftieth anniversary reunion on Saturday 1 November 1969. It was originally hoped to invite all former members, but numbers were so large that invitations had to be restricted to members up to 1939. Sadly, it was noted that over 80 who had attended the YPM between 1918 and 1939 had died, but 160 sat down for a meal in the lower hall, which was their original venue.

## Junior YPM

The deaconess and the church officer started a Junior YPM in the spring of 1968, for boys and girls between the ages of 12 and 15, meeting fortnightly. About 35 attended for Bible study on the first Saturday of the month, in the home of the church officer at 13 South Charlotte Street, and for games and refreshments and singing, concluding with an epilogue, on the third Saturday; this was in the top hall, because the YPM were holding their outreach in Randolph Place. Further details of this remarkably successful enterprise are given in Chapter 47.

Twice a year, for Baby Sunday in May and for a Christmas party, mothers were invited to bring the children on the cradle roll to the top hall. On Baby Sunday, the roll was called, and every baby received a bouquet of flowers with a text-card attached, coloured by the Sunday School children. The invitations below are for May and December 1969. Sandy (misspelled in the invitation) was the first Chapel baby born after the Primes arrived in Edinburgh in October 1969, and the first to be visited by Betty Prime.

*The primary department of the Sunday School maintained the cradle roll, with the names of babies born to Chapel families.*

## Girls Own

Mention was made in Chapter 26 about a meeting in the top hall, started in 1921 for girls in service who had nowhere to go on Sunday afternoon. The original members grew older together, but they kept the name Girls Own for 36 years. Tea was served at 4.30, followed by informal fellowship, and most stayed on for the Chapel's evening service. Attendance in the early 1960s averaged 30, but 130 came to the Christmas social.

By 1968, numbers were down to single figures, and the elders thought the meeting had outlived its usefulness. When Miss Kate Young, who had been a key helper from the beginning, was advised that her meeting was to be discontinued, she thought otherwise. She renamed it the Sunday Afternoon Fellowship and had a recruitment drive, under the slogan:

353

'Ladies! Something for You!' Soon the weekly attendance was up to 20. She was its driving force until she retired in April 1970, after 52 years of arranging the teas, the speakers and generally organising the practical side of the meeting. The fellowship continued to meet for tea (only) in one of the committee rooms, as the members were no longer able to climb to the top hall. Instead of having their own activities, after tea, they joined the 5.30 p.m. prayer meeting, to the delight of the faithful few who attended it.

## Suffer the little children

During the 1960s, parents were encouraged to bring their children to church on Sunday morning, as part of family worship. In 1963, a crèche was started for babies in prams, in the committee room at the side door; provision was also made for toddlers up to the age of two and a half in the top hall from 10.45 a.m. In 1964, at the initiative of the writer's wife and Pearl Rendall, who both had lively offspring just turned three, a nursery class was started for children up to four (later five); they came into the first part of the service and then, after the children's talk, went to another part of the top hall.

In 1967, one of the Chapel missionaries, Marjory Sommerville, asked permission to take photographs of a Sunday service. The small groups in Malaysia, where she worked, could not visualize a thousand Christian people meeting together, and she wanted to show them pictures. It would have been unthinkable in 1967 to use a camera during a service, so the congregation was asked to remain after the benediction.

*Views from the pulpit and from the back of the gallery in 1967 – note the tripod in the first picture, from which the second one was taken. Eight elders normally sat on the platform only when the side benches were required for latecomers.*

## No hat?

As the 1967 photographs show, every woman and girl wore a hat to Chapel services. This was partly because of 1 Corinthians 11:10-13 and partly because it was good manners in Scotland in the 1960s. Hardly any hats are worn now. The change started on 16 June 1968. The guest preacher was Rev. Tom Houston, a Scotsman who had been minister of the Nairobi Baptist Church for eight years. Norman and Lorna Hunt had got to know him while Norman was seconded to Nairobi from the University of Edinburgh, and they offered hospitality when Tom was invited as pulpit supply in the Chapel during a furlough in this country. As they got ready for the Sunday morning service, Hazel Houston said that she had not brought a hat. 'In that case', said Lorna Hunt, 'I won't wear one either'. They got some strange looks, but gradually others came without a hat, initially on Sunday evening and eventually on Sunday morning as well. It was 1979 before the choir allowed younger women into the choir stalls without a hat, and most of the older women in the choir still came with their heads covered in the 1980s.

In February 1968, the deacons bought 250 stackable chairs for the lower hall. Members were invited to meet the cost of one or more, at 48 shillings (£2.40) each. The long wooden benches, which had been there since 1912, went to the Rock Mission in the Grassmarket; some said the lower hall would not be the same without them, but most appreciated the comfortable chairs.

*In February 1968, 250 stackable chairs in bright colours replaced the long wooden benches that had been in the lower hall since 1912.*

Primes were happy to occupy the manse at 11 Midmar Gardens, and the induction was fixed for early November. A new chapter in the history of the Chapel was about to begin.

Additional information on the following topics, mentioned in this chapter, is available on the CD.

Alan Redpath's family
Alan Redpath's obituary
Alan Redpath's publications
Alex Hardie
Charlotte Recordings Ltd
Girl Guides
Marjory Sommerville
Preaching – audio-tapes (Redpath)

## 'Call' to Rev. Derek J. Prime

Since Derek Prime had preached very acceptably in the Chapel in May 1967, why was it July 1969 before a 'call' was sent to him? The vacancy committee, having heard all 16 of the men on their list, had to decide on three basic principles before coming to a unanimous decision. (Perhaps they should have decided the principles before compiling the list.) The first was how much time the next minister would expect to be given for conference ministry elsewhere. The second was whether men actively involved in the Baptist Union of Scotland or the Baptist Union of Great Britain and Ireland should (because of the Chapel's strict view on ecumenical relationships) be considered. The third was whether it was fair to consider anyone who had recently settled into a new ministry.

To these questions, and many more, there were as many views as there were members of the vacancy committee. Suffice it to say that the only name ever to receive the unanimous recommendation of the committee was that of Derek Prime. A members' meeting on Wednesday 2 July 1969 endorsed the 'call'; he accepted it ten days later. The

# Chapter 45
# Pastoral care (1969–1975)

## Pastoral care by example

### The Prime minister

This chapter looks at pastoral care in the Chapel under Derek Prime's guidance during his first six years in Edinburgh; the next chapter looks at the teaching and learning opportunities of those years. First, however, who was the Prime minister (a joke that soon wore thin)?

Derek Prime was born in 1931 in South Lambeth, London, and attended Westminster City School. In 1944, at the age of 13, some school-friends persuaded him to go with them to a Bible class at Lansdowne Evangelical Free Church in West Norwood, near his home. There he heard the gospel and became a Christian. In June 1946, at the age of 15, he was baptized and received into membership. As many of the older men were away on military service, he had opportunities of speaking and preaching. One day his pastor asked him whether he had ever thought of the ministry. He had, but he was glad that his pastor, not he himself, had taken the initiative in mentioning it.

The conviction grew as opportunities for ministry arose both in the forces (National Service with the Royal Scots Greys in Germany) and in the Cambridge Inter-Collegiate Christian Union (he graduated MA in history and theology from Emmanuel College). The elders of his home church encouraged his 'call' to ministry, but suggested that he should get some wider experience first. Accordingly he taught history and religious knowledge for three and a half years, at Battersea Grammar School. During a pastoral vacancy in the church where he had been converted, and a year after he had become an elder there, the congregation asked him to become their pastor. He was ordained in 1957. In addition to pastoral ministry, he was given the opportunity of writing, and by the time that he came to the Chapel in 1969, he had published ten books, including *A Christian's Guide to Prayer*, *A Christian's Guide to Leadership*, *Questions on the Christian Faith*, *This Way to Life* and a series of six entitled *Tell me the Answer*, his children's talks over a period of two years.

Derek Prime was inducted to the pastorate of Charlotte Chapel during the morning service on Sunday 9 November 1969, in a weekend that combined Remembrance Sunday, induction, and the annual Thankoffering.

*The Prime family in 1969 – Derek, Esther, Timothy, Betty (back row), Jonathan and Priscilla (in front).*

### Need for pastoral care

After a vacancy of three years, during which two church meetings were divided 134/107 and 198/118 on the emotive topic of inter-church relations, and without the strong leadership of MacDuff Urquhart, who had guided the church through its previous two vacancies, an obvious priority was to improve pastoral care and fellowship among the 856 members. While enthusiasm for evangelistic and missionary work was not in question, as evidenced by the outreach in Wester Hailes, the open-air campaigns at the Mound, the Ross Bandstand and much else, the elders advised the new minister: 'the pastoral vacancy had not been helpful to the spiritual welfare of the membership; but … the faithful Bible ministry of our new pastor would be a major factor in remedying the situation.' Derek Prime, for his part, made clear that he did not wish to hear about the events of the previous decade in the Chapel. This was not avoiding the ecumenical issue, but giving a clear signal that the congregation must live for the future, not dwell on the past.

Church unity is first and above all a gift of the Holy Spirit, but it is not unspiritual to mention a dozen ways in which Derek Prime encouraged it during his pastorate in the Chapel.

## Call me pastor

How should one address a minister? Younger members in 1969 generally said 'Mister'; the fashion of calling everyone by first names was still a decade away. Older members, not wishing to be stiff, used Christian names. Those in between were not sure what to do – should they say 'Reverend'? Derek Prime insisted that everyone call him 'pastor'; the youngest child could use the word without undue familiarity; the oldest member could set a good example by using this neutral word; those in between had their problem solved.

For the same reason, the new pastor imposed two other disciplines on himself. Recognising that he could not entertain the great majority of the 856 members socially at the manse, he concentrated on those who could not be expected to reciprocate, like students, especially those from overseas, single folk and newcomers; groups, like the Young Peoples Meeting, were regularly invited for coffee and biscuits. Secondly, to avoid any impression of favourites among the elders, he deliberately refrained from closer friendship with any one office-bearer more than another. As the church secretary said regularly at annual meetings, the Chapel had a minister with a true pastoral heart.

*Derek Prime's induction to the pastorate of the Chapel, at the age of 38, was on Sunday 9 November 1969.*

## Pastoral groups

In place of zone meetings, which had met irregularly at the discretion of individual elders, Derek Prime reorganized the membership into 20 new groups, more or less equal in number, on a geographical basis. They met three times a year,

all on the same evening, a Thursday when the Bible School was in vacation. He called them pastoral groups, and gave them a new agenda; the concept is familiar now, but in 1971 it was all exciting and new. The groups were:

*(1) For people to get to know one another. (2) For prayer. (3) For visiting those who could not attend the group meetings. (4) For Bible study. (5) For listening to the concerns of members and assuring them that through the group, every member had a voice in the elders' and deacons' courts. (6) For discovering hidden talents among the group. (7) For joint activities with other groups. (8) For making evangelistic contacts in the area.*

---

1 Elders' Minute, 3 March 1971.

No other Chapel activity was permitted on pastoral group evenings. The first was on Thursday 11 March 1971, and then in September and January, just before the Bible School resumed. On every occasion, the elders sent a letter of invitation to every member of their group.

```
PASTORAL GROUP MEETINGS
THURSDAY, 20th Apr. 1972 at 8 p.m.
Details of Meeting-places.
Group No. 1 (Mr. Gordon): At Mr. & Mrs. Gordon's
home, 19 Bernard Terrace.
Group No. 2 (Mr. Armstrong): At Rev. & Mrs.
Sommerville's home, 69 Restalrig Road.
Group No. 3 (Rev. W. Whyte): At Miss Davis'
home, 16 Hillside Crescent.
Group No. 4 (Rev. Gerald Block): At Mr. & Mrs.
Norton's home, 67 Durham Terrace.
Group No. 5 (Mr. A. Wilson): At Mr. & Mrs.
Wilson's home, 406 Ferry Road.
Group No. 6 (Mr. D. Macnair): At Mr. & Mrs.
J. Ansdell's home, 12 Dean Park Crescent.
Group No. 7 (Mr. A. Cameron): At Mr. & Mrs.
Cameron's home, 24 Ravelston House Park.
Group No. 8 (Mr. I. Balfour): At Mr. & Mrs.
Balfour's home, 58 Murrayfield Road.
Group No. 9 (Mr. J. Cossar): At Mr. & Mrs.
Cossar's home, 10 Craig's Bank, Corstorphine.
Group No.10 (Mr. R. Hadden): At Mr. & Mrs.
Fraser's home, 4 Coltbridge Avenue.
Group No.11 (Prof. N. Hunt): At Mr. & Mrs.
Hudson's home, 34 Chessar Avenue.
Group No.12 (Mr. R. White): At Mr. & Mrs.
White's home, 38 Corstorphine Park Gds.
Group No.13 (Mr. K. Baker): At Mrs.
Vickerman's home, 3 Craiglockhart Bank.
Group No.14 (Mr. D. Wallace): At Mr. & Mrs.
Cook's home, 19 Frogston Terrace.
Group No.15 (Mr. D. Murray): At Mrs. Ritchie's
home, 36 Woodburn Terrace.
Group No.16 (Mr. J. McGregor): At Mr. & Mrs.
McFarlane's home, 59 Leamington Terrace.
Group No.17 (Mr. J. Beran): At Mr. & Mrs.
Ferguson's home, 4 Tay Street.
Group No.18 (Mr. J. Cochrane): At Miss
Denholm's home, 14 Roseneath Terrace.
Group No.19 (Mr. J. Simison): At Miss P.
Gray's home, 33/1 St. Patrick Square.
Group No.20 (Mr. G. Hutchison): At Mr. & Mrs.
Donaldson's home, 84 Liberton Brae.
```

*To give maximum publicity to the pastoral groups, the homes where they met were listed in the bulletin on the previous Sunday.*

Derek Prime visited all the pastoral groups in rotation, and from time to time he invited them to meet in the manse. Typical of his pastoral concern was his insistence that refreshments at the end of the evening should be confined to tea/coffee and biscuits – so there would be no competition or comparison among groups for the best spread. He encouraged the groups to move around, so that they did not become associated with any one house. How the groups fared, as they settled down, is discussed in chapter 48.

*Group 35 was a vehicle for Chapel members, aged between 25 and 45, to look out for and to integrate people in their peer-group into the life of the church.*

Group 35 was so named as the median between its lower (25) and upper (45) ages. It met once a month, for recreational, devotional or practical activities, including helping newcomers with their gardens or to move furniture or with painting and decorating.

## Membership

### Associate membership

Setting up pastoral groups, which were initially for Chapel members only, led Derek Prime to consider the position of adherents, a loosely defined list of those who attended the Chapel regularly but who had never joined. He recreated the concept of associate membership, which Graham Scroggie had instituted for students, but which was in abeyance. The new scheme gave students and nurses a pastoral link with the Chapel while they were in Edinburgh, without disturbing their membership of their home church, but Mr Prime's primary motivation was to create a permanent pastoral relationship with Edinburgh people who had never been baptized by immersion as believers and who, for various reasons, were not prepared to take this step.

If they had made a clear profession of faith and were living a consistent Christian life, and if they had no other church membership, Derek Prime wanted them to be under the Chapel's pastoral care. This would give them opportunities for service, open only to members or associate members

from October 1971, as set out below; also, it would make them subject to church discipline. Associate members applied in the same way as everyone else (except the application form did not require a statement about baptism) and they were welcomed at the monthly communion service in the same way as full members. They were entitled to attend and to speak at church business meetings, but not to vote. They were not eligible for election as elders or deacons, but otherwise they were encouraged to take an active part in all aspects of Chapel life.

### Implications of associate membership

There was a corollary to Derek Prime's proposal. He was concerned that some in leadership in the Chapel were not, and had no wish to be, members of the church. 'What do we do', he asked the elders, 'if a Sunday School teacher or a Scout leader is teaching contrary to Scripture, or is behaving in a way dishonouring to Christ? If that person is not a member, and so not subject to family discipline, he or she can legitimately say that we have no right to question them about it.' Accordingly, he proposed that after a year, during which non-members should consider their position, only full members or associate members would be eligible for leadership in the Chapel, defined as: teachers in the Sunday School, members of committees, the vice-president, secretary and treasurer of the Young Peoples Meeting, the committee of Group 35, leadership of the Scouts, Cubs, Guides and Brownies, and members of the choir.

Some elders were concerned that younger members of the choir and young Sunday School teachers might use this as an excuse to ease off their Christian commitment, on the ground that they were not yet ready for membership. However, the twelve months of grace were used to persuade them that if they were to be leaders, they must set an example of commitment. The only casualties were the brother and sister who ran the Young Worshippers League; they were not prepared to join, because they could not accept some aspects of the Chapel's teaching and discipline.

These discussions reopened the question of who should approve membership applications. For some time, the elders had taken the view that they had been appointed by the church to give spiritual leadership for periods of five years at a time, and that this included interviewing and accepting applicants for membership, without reference to the congregation. Some elders felt that all applications should be shared with the members, or at least notified to them, so that any objection could be lodged by the objector with his or her elder for submission to the elders' court. As always, it was good to review the procedure, but after discussion the elders continued to deal with membership themselves. They did, however, share with the congregation the names of those with whom the church had lost touch, before their names were deleted from the roll, as members often came up with an address or a point of contact.

## Absent members

Many ministers can recall, after a service, which of their regular worshippers were present. It is, however, a remarkable gift to look around a congregation of nearly one thousand people and to be able to recall, afterwards, which of the regular worshippers were not present. Derek Prime achieved this by using the membership list as a prayer diary, going over a page of ten names a day as part of his devotional time, and so he noticed instinctively those on the list whom he had not seen in recent weeks.

He recognized, however, that this should be put on a more formal footing. He therefore proposed the introduction of communion cards from January 1972. After the sermon, on the first Sunday of every month, the pastor or guest preacher explained that there would now be a service of communion, to which all who loved the Lord, irrespective of membership, were invited. To facilitate the distribution of the bread and the wine, those in the gallery who wished to participate were asked to come down to the area, and to take the place of those who were leaving. About half of the congregation, including many members, left, and only about four hundred remained, including visitors. Derek Prime reckoned that only one third of the 856 members regularly took communion.

## Communion cards

In December 1971 the elders distributed a booklet with 12 numbered cards to every member. Those attending the Lord's Table were expected to detach the card for the appropriate month and, on the way out, to drop it into the boxes on the stairs that were used for donations to the fellowship fund. These were then checked against the membership roll, and the elders were informed after four months of unaccountable absence. If the elders found that a

person was unwell or infirm, home visits, including communion, could be arranged; the absence of cards also identified those who had lost interest in regular attendance. 'Some of the sad situations we have faced in recent months would doubtless have been avoided and relieved if we had known earlier.'

*The writer was embarrassed, in looking through some old papers, to find his 1973 booklet intact – meaning he had not used any of the cards. Since, however, as an elder, he served communion every second month, he was not marked as absent for four months.*

It might be thought that pastoral groups made this unnecessary, but they met only every four months and, as Mr Prime himself said of the intervening weeks: 'With people sitting in different places in the Chapel (both upstairs and downstairs) – and rightly so – and using different exits, it is quite impossible by visual means to be sure that people are present.' The scheme was not, however, well received by the majority of the members, even after the senior elder made an impassioned plea at the 1973 annual meeting:

*The Elders are disappointed at the lack of response on the part of some members in the use of the Communion Cards.... We have in the Rev. Derek Prime a man with a Pastor's heart and he has a deep and sincere concern for each member of the fellowship, but it is impossible for him in a large congregation such as we have in the Chapel to check on absentees. Therefore, by using the Communion Cards regularly, we will be assisting the Pastor in his work and I am sure that must be the desire of every member.*

2 *Record*, June 1973, p. 5.

## A Verse for the Year

Owing to the lack of use by the majority of the congregation, communion cards were discontinued at the end of December 1973. The elder's visit to every home in his pastoral group to deliver the cards, in December 1971 and again in December 1972, had been so much appreciated that a Verse for the Year card was printed instead; elders were expected to deliver it to everyone in their group, along with a set of gift-envelopes, during the month of December. As Derek Prime preached on the verse on the first Sunday in January, woe betide the elder who had not been round by then. The verse for 1974 was: 'I will trust and not be afraid. (Isaiah 12.2)'; it was printed in two formats, a large card for the mantelpiece or wall, to attract comment and question, and a bookmark version. The card was so popular that it has been repeated every year since; however, as elders struggled during the 1980s to visit every home in December, cards and envelopes were made available in the lounge, and elders delivered them only to shut-in members of their group.

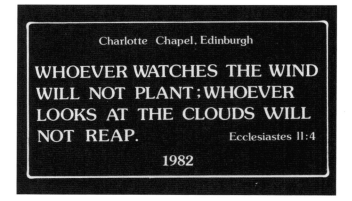

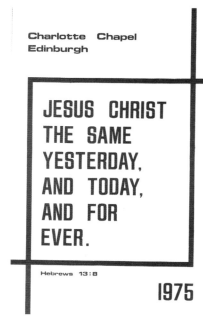

*Some Verse for the Year cards carried familiar texts, but others were chosen so that strangers would ask: 'What does that mean?' The verse in 1982 was a challenge to build a lounge at street level (Chapter 49).*

Delivery of gift-envelopes to members was crucial for missionary support. Sunday offerings went to general church funds, unless designated otherwise; making envelopes available was the best way of securing this. The Chapel partially supported 28 overseas missionaries in 1972, including some who were in this country after reaching retiring age. Following regular exhortations from the missionary treasurer, the missionary-designated part of the Sunday offerings went into five figures for the first time in 1973, £10,607.

## Roll revision

As has been mentioned several times, the elders took themselves in hand every decade or so, and went over the membership roll. Derek Prime encouraged this on a more regular and systematic basis. Of greater importance to him than not showing artificially high figures, was the false confidence it might give to those who had ceased to have any living link with the Chapel family, but who regarded their membership as some kind of spiritual security. Shortly after his arrival, he asked for a list of those who had not been seen in the Chapel recently and, as mentioned in the last chapter, this produced 135 names. 80 were in the Edinburgh area, 6 were in other parts of Scotland, 49 were 'furth of' (i.e. outside) Scotland and the Chapel had no current address for the other 18.

Personal contact was made, where possible, and letters were sent to those at a distance, inquiring whether they had joined another church and, if not, how they saw their membership of the Chapel. One letter was returned, with a note that the addressee in Thurso had been dead for 20 years. Those who had moved away were encouraged to join a local evangelical church; the Chapel was reluctant to delete a name from its roll without knowing that the person had established a new connection elsewhere.

*Sidlow Baxter and his wife, Ethel, when he last preached in the Chapel in May 1970, aged 67. He had lost none of his humour; when he came into the vestry, the church secretary greeted him: 'Mr Baxter, your hair has gone white'; he replied: 'Mr Cochrane, yours has gone altogether'. Ethel died on Christmas Day 1977.*

'Like painting the Forth Bridge' is a popular phrase in Edinburgh for a never-ending task. As soon as the painters worked their way to the far end of the railway bridge, it was time to start again at the beginning (until they replaced paint with a modern substitute in the early 1990s). Under Derek Prime's leadership, the membership roll was meticulously kept up to date, at least as far as people living in the Lothians were concerned. The roll call at the pastoral groups was an excellent way of alerting the elders to members who were not regularly worshipping at the Chapel. It was more difficult to keep in touch with those who lived at a distance. Four years after the review just mentioned, the elders went over the names of 86 other members, most of whom now lived too far away to attend the Chapel regularly. Again, they were exhorted to join their nearest evangelical church, which five did, and five more hoped to return to Edinburgh soon. Thirteen others, including Alan and Marjorie Redpath, who were engaged in itinerant ministry and who had no base elsewhere, were kept on the roll, but 63 names had to be removed in June 1974.

One name caused a great deal of debate, not about the individual but about the principle involved. He was the third generation of a well-known Chapel family, who had moved in middle life from Edinburgh to live in East Lothian. He attended the local parish church, and was its treasurer, but he had no wish to join it or anywhere else; he wanted to retain his membership in the Chapel, where he had been brought up and which he still regarded as his spiritual home. The problem was that if the elders took away membership from others on the roll, because they had not attended communion for six months without an acceptable reason, those affected could reasonably ask: 'Why me and not him?' Family discipline had to be seen to be fair, and when two elders called on the man concerned, he accepted the position.

## Prayer

### Opportunities for prayer

When Derek Prime came to the Chapel, there were four opportunities for collective prayer: half an hour before the Sunday morning and Sunday evening services, an hour on Monday evening and an hour for women on Wednesday afternoon. Monday was the main church prayer meeting; no competing activities were permitted in the Chapel, and events in other places on Monday evening, however worthy, were never intimated from the pulpit or put in the bulletin. Under the new pastor's leadership, numbers gradually increased and more people participated. Derek Prime made no secret of his hope that the meeting would increase in size to the point where it would have to move from the lower hall (capacity several hundred) into the main church. This did not happen, but in 1979 the Monday meeting was a source of encouragement for three reasons; it was well attended, a good cross-section of the church family was represented, and many different people took part.

### City-centre visitation

In October 1971, the Monday prayer meeting was linked with a personal visit to the sixteen hundred homes within a quarter mile of the church. Once a month, on the second Monday, as many as possible met in the Chapel at 7:30 p.m. for 20 minutes of prayer; those prepared to visit then went out in teams of two, with the intention of gaining entry to two homes during the evening. Between one third and one half of the meeting went out; if they could not make personal contact, they left literature and an invitation to the next guest service. The remainder of the congregation continued in prayer for them, and they quietly rejoined the meeting after they had completed their visits. There was then a time of sharing and encouragement. Derek Prime, who always went out as part of the visitation team, found:

*Now the prayer meeting on the City Centre Visitation evening seemed to me – in that period at least when I was back from visiting – to be quite different, and we were all encouraged by it. I think I can suggest some reasons for this which may be helpful.*

*First, many had made an effort to be there who cannot regularly be present.... Secondly, we are praying specifically – that is to say, we had definite visits and objectives in mind.... Thirdly, many short prayers were offered. It is probably better to pray several times briefly for different things than once at length for many things, so as to give others the opportunity of praying. Fourthly, prayer was being linked with action. We asked for God's help; we counted upon it in going forth to visit; and we returned to give thanks and to share in further prayer.*

3 *Record*, November 1971, pp. 2-3.

This continued for over a decade, with about one thousand visits every year, deliberately on the Monday before the monthly guest service, so that personal invitations to it could be given. In the winter of 1981-2, over 150 homes opened their doors and accepted invitations and portions of Scripture; those who expressed interest were revisited on a regular basis. A number said they would come to the guest services, although it was difficult to confirm whether they did. By 1984, the visitation was no longer monthly, but concentrated on specific events, such as Christmas, Easter and the Festival outreach.

### Prayer in the vestry

The elders had a long tradition of meeting with the pastor or visiting preacher in the vestry for 15 minutes of prayer before Sunday morning and evening services. Derek Prime not only encouraged this, but he also reverted to an earlier (discontinued) practice of inviting as many elders as possible to meet with him for prayer for the quarter-hour before the Monday prayer meeting and the Thursday Bible study. Guest preachers remarked on the fact that the elders always knelt for this time of prayer, as they do to this day.

## Inclusive thinking

### After-church fellowships

Derek Prime believed in sharing as much information as possible with as many people as possible: 'People want to know what is going on and they have the right to be informed so long as it is not confidential.' He encouraged everyone, of all ages, to stay behind after the evening service on the last Sunday of the month. 'The real advantage of these After Church Fellowships is that they bring us together as a church family, and such a benefit is worthy of encouragement.'

As well as sharing information, he asked what people would like him to cover in future teaching. The requests made at the October 1972 fellowship meeting illustrate the issues of the day: versions of the Bible; ecumenical involvement; the gifts of the Spirit; the use of contemporary language in prayer; entertainment evangelism; redefining worldliness; divine sovereignty and human responsibility; women and their ministry in the church; the Second Coming of Christ; and the wearing of hats or head-coverings to church. These Sunday after-church fellowships continued right through Derek Prime's time as pastor, and in 1984 he wrote:

*It's good to have the separate groups – according to age – meeting once a month after church, but at the same time we must seize every opportunity of coming together as a church family. The latter occasions are very important for sharing family news and the concerns we have as a church – and the After-Church Fellowships have an invaluable role here. I'm sometimes asked, 'Why don't you go into details beforehand and tell people what's going to happen on that particular Sunday night?' I generally don't because I honestly feel that he desire to have fellowship together as a church family is more important than trying to attract people simply because such and such a person is taking part or a particular subject is being dealt with.*

4 *Record*, October 1984, p. 3.

*After-church fellowships filled the lower hall and the gallery that looked down on it from street level, perhaps three hundred people in all. Crowded though it was, Derek Prime did not move the meeting to the sanctuary in case it lost its informality.*

### Church fellowship meetings

In addition to these Sunday evenings, which were open to everyone, Derek Prime also introduced church fellowship meetings. They had much the same purpose, but were confined to full and associate members, so that more confidential matters could be shared. The first was in September 1972, taking the place of the pastoral group meetings planned for that evening – which emphasized its significance. The format was to introduce a topic, to invite open discussion about it, and then to have a time of prayer about the issue; no decisions were made and no votes were taken, but the elders noted the views expressed. They were deliberately on an occasional basis, in order to maintain their informality, but by 1984 the pattern was to have three or four a year.

Mr Prime's pastoral concern for meetings to be as inclusive as possible is illustrated by an occasion when one of the Chapel missionaries on furlough suggested that people might arrange house-parties, inviting groups of their friends for a get-to-know-you-better occasion; the pastor pointed out the danger, namely of only meeting those who happen to be invited to such groups. He had a real fear of cliques.

## Harvest Thanksgiving

Harvest Thanksgiving had been a Sunday School occasion since its inception; Derek Prime broadened its appeal in two ways. He combined it with the Chapel's annual gift-day for Tearfund (The Evangelical Alliance Relief Fund, set up in 1968), as a reminder of countries where harvests were insufficient to provide for basic needs. Secondly, he encouraged everyone to contribute, adults delivering their gifts on Saturday afternoon and children bringing theirs with them on Sunday morning. The consequent increase in perishable goods was more than enough for all the Chapel shut-ins, so for the next year, Mr Prime recommended a mixture of 50 per cent of flowers, fruit and vegetables and 50 per cent of tinned and packaged goods, which could be stored on the Chapel premises and distributed by the deaconess over the next few months. Some contributors felt this was not the same, but the recipients appreciated the longer-term gifts.

*From 1974, everyone was encouraged to participate in the Harvest Thanksgiving, not just the Sunday School. It was combined with an offering for Tearfund, The Evangelical Alliance Relief Fund, whose commitment to third world development (as it was called in the 1970s) made social concern an integral part of the mission of the church.*

Once started, the practice of mingling tinned goods with fresh flowers and fruit continued for 25 years. The deaconess reported in 1998 that tins were no longer appreciated and

that she had to pass them on to the Bethany Christian Trust. When one door closes, another opens; in the autumn of 1998, Operation Christmas Child appealed for shoeboxes to be filled with packets of soup, coffee, biscuits, raisins, soap, gloves, etc., as Christmas presents for children in impoverished areas of Eastern Europe. The appeal has been renewed every autumn since, now with the addition of toys; the Chapel has contributed over one hundred crammed shoeboxes every year. Where it is culturally appropriate, the local distributors add a booklet with Bible stories in the children's own language. Also, a box in the lounge on the first Sunday of every month, for gifts of tinned food for the Edinburgh City Mission, has been there for as long as anyone can remember, and still continues.

## Deaconess

When Derek Prime came to the Chapel, Joan Wragg had been in post as deaconess for just over two years. In 1971, she was 'called' to missionary service in Nigeria with the Sudan United Mission, and left in July of that year. It happened that Dorothy Somerville, a Chapel member, a schoolteacher and a missionary (also) in Nigeria, required to come home to care for her elderly mother at this time, so she became the deaconess until 1972, when she returned to Africa.

### situations vacant

DEACONESS—Committed Christian lady required by Evangelical Baptist Church to assist in the pastoral care of the ladies of the congregation and in the visitation of the sick and elderly. Apply in writing to the Church Secretary, Charlotte Baptist Chapel, West Rose Street, Edinburgh, EH2 4AZ.

*This advertisement came to the notice of Shirley Tory, who had been working for seven years with the Faith Mission. She started in April 1972, and resigned on her marriage to Stewart McLeod in August 1975.*

## Anniversary weekends

Another example of Derek Prime's inclusive thinking was his approach to the anniversary weekend in October. Sensing that the traditional pattern of Sunday plus Monday evening was not family friendly, he experimented with Saturday evening and Sunday. This proved popular, although it meant the end of: 'the pastor and elders will be in the vestry on Monday afternoon to receive your Thankoffering'. Going on from there, he moved the Saturday meeting to the comparatively early time of 6 p.m. and (if the visiting speaker agreed) children of all ages were encouraged to attend. If the speaker was not happy with that, arrangements were made for the children to be looked after elsewhere in the building.

Transport was laid on for the elderly, with tea in the lower hall; Derek Prime's hope that the anniversary would become an occasion for the whole church family to gather was fulfilled.

His innovative approach to the annual spring-cleaning of the Chapel was another way of involving as many people as possible. Previously, professionals had been hired, but he suggested that it was a good opportunity for fellowship, as well as saving costs. The Saturday began with a short time of worship together, then the willing hands scattered all over the building to scrub, wash, dust, etc.

**CHARLOTTE BAPTIST CHAPEL**
WEST ROSE STREET, EDINBURGH, EH2 4AZ
TELEPHONE: 031-225 4812

| | | |
|---|---|---|
| Pastor | Rev. Derek J. Prime, M.A., S.Th., 11 Midmar Gardens, Edinburgh, EH10 6DY | Tel: 031-447 3419 |
| Church Secretary | John Cochrane, 25 Spottiswoode Road, Edinburgh, EH9 1BJ | Tel: 031-447 3678 |
| Church Treasurer | A. D. L. Wallace, M.A., M.Ed., 104 Biggar Road, Edinburgh, EH10 7DU | Tel: 031-445 2303 |

19 March 1974

Dear Fellow Labourer,

Chapel Spring Cleaning - Saturday, 30th. March, 1974.

As you are aware, the Spring Cleaning of the Chapel is to take place on SATURDAY, 30th. MARCH, 1974, between 9:00 a.m. and 12 Noon.

An inspection of the Chapel has revealed that a vast amount of work will require to be done within a very limited period of time.

You will recall that I was appointed by the most democratic of processes as Overseer of the work.

I am pleased to advise you that you have been nominated, appointed and enlisted to take a share in the work in the Spring Cleaning. I am sure that you will count this to be a privilege.

I shall be obliged if you will report to me for duty at the Chapel at 8:55 a.m. on 30th March, 1974, when the roll will be called.

Yours sincerely,

FERGUS J.M. BROWN
Overseer

*Fergus Brown requisitioned all able-bodied Chapel members in 1974. This was a popular way of spring-cleaning the building, and Fergus supervised it annually until 1978, when his work took him away from Edinburgh.*

### The Jesus Revolution

Derek Prime's policy of working with the whole church, wherever possible, made him cautious – and rightly so, as it turned out – when Arthur Blessitt visited Edinburgh for a week in April 1972. Blessitt had been promoting 'The Jesus Revolution' since 1969, walking through the streets of various cities and pulling a 12-foot cross. Mr Prime's concern was that the visit was organized and led by some enthusiastic students, without reference to any Edinburgh churches or church leaders. They distributed stickers, posters and banners, and organized a Jesus March; many in the Chapel were caught up in the activity and excitement. There were both conversions and renewed dedications when Arthur Blessitt addressed a packed Assembly Hall on the Tuesday evening; two young men, whom the writer counselled in the after-meeting, came to faith and went on to Christian maturity. However, some aspects of the follow-up showed the wisdom of involving sympathetic local churches in such outreaches, and being accountable to them.

*Arthur Blessitt in Edinburgh in April 1972, at the part of the Mound where the Chapel held open-air services. Sitting on the 12 foot cross, which he pulled through the streets to draw attention to its message, is his young son Joel.*

Arthur Blessitt was back in Edinburgh on Friday 6 May 1977; this time, the Chapel leadership were fully consulted. Blessitt spoke to students at lunchtime and to ministers in the afternoon, under other auspices, then the younger members of the Chapel, who had put in an immense amount of preparation in prayer and publicity, arranged the rest of his day. This included an evening rally in the Ross Bandstand, which the pastor hosted and led in prayer. At 9 p.m., everyone in Princes Street Gardens was invited to the lower hall in the Chapel for refreshments, and to talk with Arthur Blessitt; 25 made professions of faith.

## More pastoral concerns

### Unanimity in decisions

Derek Prime believed that decisions on spiritual issues should never be achieved by voting – the Holy Spirit would lead people to unanimity on what was right. During his 18 years in the Chapel, it was never necessary for the elders to vote at their monthly meeting; if there was initially any difference of opinion, the topic was carried forward for reflection and prayer.

*Whether we are in a church meeting, a committee meeting or in conversation informally with other Christians, we are to strive all the time to be in harmony.… it is important not only to do the right thing but to achieve it in the right manner.… What a difference it makes when every person concerned speaks and contributes solely with the motive of achieving unity. As a general rule, it is best to act only upon the things about which there is universal agreement and to leave matters which do not receive such agreement in abeyance.*

5 *Record*, September 1971, pp. 25-6.

This was not an excuse for inactivity, because Mr Prime and the elders reviewed some aspect of Chapel life at every monthly meeting, and made many improvements. Nine such reviews are analysed in Chapter 47.

### Missionary internship

Missionary members sent regular news, which was mentioned at the prayer meeting on the first Monday of the month, and printed in the *Record*; when they came on furlough, they met with the Chapel auxiliaries.

Derek Prime questioned whether this was sufficient exposure, in an increasingly mobile and fluctuating society. One particular example came up early in his pastorate

A nurse who had joined the Chapel in 1966, but who had been away from Edinburgh at Bible College, advised that she had been asked by a missionary society to go immediately to the Middle East, Derek Prime realized the pastoral implications. She was not known to most of the congregation, and he took seriously the New Testament principle of a local church 'sending' a missionary, which implied knowing the candidate and being supportive of her 'call'. He therefore proposed that she should spend six months working part-time with the pastoral team, and obtain secular employment to support herself during that time. This worked so well, in that she got to know the congregation and they got to know and to have confidence in her, that it was adopted as Chapel policy.

How that policy was communicated to the congregation illustrates the value of the church fellowship meetings, mentioned above. The missionary convener explained why the six months had been so successful, and why the deacons

recommended it as the norm for future candidates. Members asked whether someone who had been brought up in the Chapel would be expected to follow this pattern; the advantages and disadvantages were discussed. It was also recommended that missionaries on furlough should spend some time in the Chapel, free from deputation duties, in order to participate in Chapel life, and get to know those who had come into membership since their last furlough. This also produced a lively discussion, not least on the practicalities of accommodation. The deacons took note of all that was said, made the policy decision at their next meeting, and promulgated it through the *Record*.

*In 1971, Group 35 offered to update the map of the world that dominated the lower hall. In place of the 1932 rectangular map (Chapters 28 and 44), they painted a striking projection, which, although looking like a peeled orange, gave correct areas and dimensions for all countries.*

Two of the three tall boards that made up the missionary roll of honour, prepared for the Chapel's Ter-jubilee in 1958, are on the left of the map in the picture; as mentioned in Chapter 44, they listed the name, country and years of service of Chapel missionaries.

### The alternating principle

The Thursday Bible School was increasingly well attended, and Derek Prime was encouraged by the cross-section of the congregation and membership present. However, he had some advice to offer:

*There is great value in what we may describe as 'the alternating principle' which means quite simply that the parents take it in turns to attend at the Sunday evening services and the week-night activities. Besides strengthening the spiritual life of the parents, such an action is a godly example both to the children and the church. It is obviously not helpful to a child if it has to say, 'I never have any time with Daddy because he is always out at church.' The practice of the alternating principle will go some way to avoid this kind of situation.*

6 *Record*, March 1970, p. 4.

## Funerals

Funeral services (or 'thanksgiving services for the life of …', as Derek Prime called them) often brought neighbours and work colleagues of the deceased who had no Chapel connection. Mr Prime had a gift, unique in the writer's experience, of giving thanks for a life well lived, bringing comfort to the bereaved, expressing certainty in the resurrection, and encouraging faith in Christ, all in one service. What came across, perhaps more than anything else, was his assurance from the Scriptures of life after death. For example:

*God gives eternal life now to those who put their trust in Jesus Christ and at death, although the body sleeps, God ushers the spirit of those who believe in the Lord Jesus into God's presence, where there is fullness of joy.… Douglas [Lawrence] had found the Lord Jesus' greater love. Now he is filled with joy in the presence of God. His body awaits that glorious day of resurrection, when the body will be united with the spirit to enjoy forever God's everlasting kingdom. When John Bunyan in his* Pilgrim's Progress *caught a glimpse of believers entering into heaven, he said that if you could see what it was like in heaven, you wouldn't want to be here, you would want to be there. So for Douglas this morning, there must be no regrets for him. The regrets are for us, for we miss him.*

---

7 Thanksgiving service for Douglas Lawrence, 12 July 2000.

*Derek Prime invariably shook hands at the front door after the morning and evening services on Sunday, whatever the weather, and the duty elder took the other door.*

Under reference to James 5:14-16 members of evangelical churches facing serious illness sometimes ask the elders for prayer and for anointing with oil, usually on the palms and

forehead. There is deliberately no detail in this book about such personal requests, which were not infrequently made in the Chapel, except to say that the emphasis was always on the prayer, not on the application of the oil.

Additional information on the following topics, mentioned in this chapter, is available on the CD.

Associate membership
Communion cards
Derek Prime before Charlotte Chapel
Fellowship fund
Fellowship meetings

# Chapter 46
# Teaching and evangelism (1969–1975)

## Teaching

### Derek Prime's priorities

The last chapter described pastoral care in the Chapel in the early 1970s; this chapter looks first at Derek Prime's teaching over the same period, and then examines how evangelism and outreach developed under his leadership.

Shortly after he came to Edinburgh, Derek Prime publicly listed his priorities as pastor:

study of the Scriptures;
ministry of the Word;
prayer for the membership;
crisis visitation;
pastoral visiting of those in hospital;
visiting regularly those shut-in through age and illness;
interviews with those who sought them;
co-ordinating the activities of auxiliaries;
correspondence with overseas members;
care of the newly-converted;
follow-up of promising contacts;
regular systematic visitation of the membership.

In other words, ministry of the Word (preaching and teaching), flowing from the systematic study of Scripture, were his top priorities. Having been a schoolmaster before his 'call' to pastoral office, his teaching was professional in the best sense of the word.

### Children's talks

For the Sunday morning children's talk, Derek Prime divided *Pilgrim's Progress* into 40 episodes, and captivated the attention of both children and adults by coming to a crucial point in the narrative and asking: 'so what happened? – we'll find out next week'. By the end of Derek Prime's first year in Edinburgh, pilgrim had reached the celestial city; then came *Christiana's Progress* (pilgrim's wife, who followed him) and then John Bunyan's third classic, *The Holy War*. Every time that he repeated the series, a Chapel member prepared fresh flannelgraph illustrations for the pulpit blackboard; the artist was not averse to drawing figures that vaguely resembled people in the congregation.

At other times, Derek Prime described Biblical characters and asked: 'Guess who I am?': children raised their hands as soon as they identified the person. Another series was entitled: 'What the Lord Jesus means to me', beginning with 'a' for advocate and working through to 'z'; children were encouraged to make scrapbooks, and to hand them in at the end of the series. Yet another idea was to invite youngsters to give the pastor, a week in advance, any item that was mentioned in the Bible; he wove a story about it, explaining its significance, and said something useful about even the most obscure Old Testament objects.

### Sunday morning

Derek Prime systematically expounded the Bible to a crowded Chapel on Sunday morning, and he varied his way of making the message fresh and relevant:

*The variety of the Scriptures themselves should be reflected in our methods of presentation. Systematic expository preaching is not limited to preaching through the books of the Bible. We may equally well deal with Bible characters or Scripture's basic truths and themes.... When I have done an extended series on a New Testament letter like Romans, I have divided the exposition into periods of approximately ten weeks, and then paused for a few weeks to do something entirely different. Both speaker and hearers then come back to the main subject with freshness. A refreshing contrast from Romans, for example, would be the life of Abraham or Joseph, so that narrative provides relief from the closely connected thought and concentration required for Romans.*

_____

1 Derek J. Prime, *Pastors and teachers: the calling and work of Christ's ministers* (Highland Books, Crowborough, East Sussex, 1989), p. 108; revised edition with Alistair Begg, *On Being a Pastor: Understanding Our Calling and Work* (Moody Press, Chicago, 2004).

### Sunday evening

The Sunday morning service filled the sanctuary, often overflowing into the lower hall. The evening service was less well supported in the early 1970s. Community hymn singing from 6.10-6.30 p.m., which had been a feature of the evening service since the days when people came at six o'clock to secure a seat, became desultory. People no longer came early, or at least not in large numbers, because seats were available at 6.25 p.m.; some timed their arrival for then, because they did not like the hymn singing before the service. However, 'The real problem was the lifelessness in the Service and absence of unconverted people. This was a matter which concerned the whole fellowship.'

Television had been affecting evening church attendance from the early 1960s – Gerald Griffiths exhorted Chapel members in March 1960 to persevere with 'fishing' on the streets, to bring strangers into the Usher Hall services, because: 'For all the pull of television, there are still enough available pedestrians on our streets in the Usher Hall vicinity to bring in quite a few.' However, few had video recorders in those days, so when a popular television drama was screened on Sunday evening, services all over the country suffered – one either stayed at home or never saw it. When BBC1 showed *The Forsyte Saga* for 26 consecutive Sunday evenings in 1967, publicans and vicars complained that they might as well shut up shop, as 18 million people watched.

## Thursday Bible School

Until the renovation of the lower hall in 1982 required Bible studies to be held in homes, Derek Prime had a Bible School every Thursday evening during the academic term. Books or topics included: the life of Abraham (19 studies), Esther (9), Malachi (10) and Amos (13); the books of James (23 studies), Ephesians (16), Philippians (10) and Colossians (8). He believed in audience participation. When tackling a topic, as opposed to expounding a passage, he invited comment from all round the hall. He appeared to be noting the responses haphazardly with chalk on the blackboard but, as the theme developed, it became apparent that he was grouping the various comments into subject matter, so that the theme unfolded itself and he could then answer the questions logically and concisely from Scripture.

*Derek Prime with the YPM in the top hall on a Wednesday evening; his professional training as a schoolmaster made him an excellent Bible expositor.*

## The *Record*

In an early editorial, Derek Prime wrote that he wanted 'to give the magazine the "teaching" content which will make it of profit also', that is, in addition to family and other news. His articles on Christian life occupied a quarter of the 24 pages; Questions and Answers took up another six, so half of the monthly *Record* was now devoted to teaching.

This was popular, but circulation remained about six hundred copies a month. Mr Prime was unhappy that subsidies from church funds were needed to keep the price at one shilling (five new pence) a copy, but increasing the price usually diminished circulation. As printing costs went up, the subsidy had to be increased from £412 in 1967 and 1968 to £480 in 1969. That may not seem much today, but it was more than the deaconess' annual salary (£426 in 1970) and well over two-thirds of the salary of the pastor's secretary (£600 in 1970).

When printers' charges went up by another £13 a month in May 1970, Derek Prime suggested producing the magazine in-house, as had been done in his previous church. With volunteers typing stencils, which were run through the Chapel duplicator, the *Record* was produced in the church office from 1971 to 1988; the only outlay was for paper, and donation boxes in the vestibule helped with that, so the magazine could be given away free. Readers outside Edinburgh were asked to pay for postage. One unforeseen consequence of not charging for the *Record* was that some people took three or four copies, to pass on to friends; 650 were printed for the first free issue in January 1971, and 500 of them 'went' on the first Sunday. By 1974, 750 copies a month were handed out at the door and another 170 were posted, 40 of them abroad.

When the *Record* was professionally printed, before 1971, the type was justified, so that both margins were straight. Derek Prime was keen to keep this format for the in-house edition, and told the sceptical typists that it had been possible in his previous church. Justification is automatic on a word processor, but on a manual typewriter, every word had to be counted and spaced out before the line could be typed. The volunteers persevered for nine months, but for the October issue they just hit 'carriage return' when the bell rang for the end of the line, and the right-hand margin was ragged.

Revival in Rose Street:
Charlotte Baptist Chapel, Edinburgh, 1808-2008

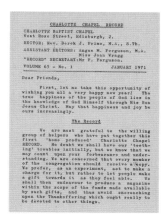

*By counting every word and spacing the lines accordingly, the volunteer typists justified the text of the in-house* Record *for its first nine months (left picture); from October 1971, they let the right-hand margin look after itself (right picture).*

## Flexibility

Because the *Record* was now put together on the premises, its size could be varied monthly between 16 and 32 pages, depending on the length and number of contributed articles, letters from missionaries and obituaries (long written appreciations have, unfortunately for the historian, gone out of fashion in the *Record*). Whatever its size, at least one-half was devoted to the pastor's teaching. The Christian doctrine of service (sample below) covered 138 pages in 1971 alone; this was consecutive teaching indeed.

A full outline of Derek Prime's Sunday morning sermons ('The life of Abraham', spread over 15 months in 1975-7), or even the full text of them ('The lion has roared: the message of Amos', spread over 15 months in 1977-8) took 10 out of 16 or even 15 out of 24 pages. Through this, those who had been present at the services could reflect at leisure on the verse-by-verse exposition and application of the Word, and readers away from Edinburgh could also benefit from the ministry.

*From 1971 to 1988, the* Record *was produced in-house, to save expense. Its cover progressed from a basic silhouette in 1971 to a line drawing by one of the members in 1976 and finally to a detailed sketch in 1984.*

## Christian service

As mentioned, 'The Christian doctrine of service' was the title of a series in the 1971 *Record*. The pastor's message was timely, for this was before the days of working mothers:

*On account of a false impression of Christian service, many a mother has been heard to exclaim, 'What with the children and the home, I'm not able to do anything now by way of Christian service.' The husband's duty is to see to it that his wife does not feel like this; and, in addition, that she has opportunities to enter into the fellowship and corporate service of the local church by means of him sharing some of the parental duties.*

2 *Record*, March 1971, p. 13.

Derek Prime was concerned that children could, and should, come to personal faith in Christ at an early age: 'If you are old enough to understand what is being said in the preaching of God's Word, you are old enough to be converted.'

## Recommended books

Through pulpit book reviews, through articles in the *Record*, and by setting up a Chapel bookstall, Derek Prime encouraged the congregation to read Christian literature. Initially open only during the Bible School on Thursday, the bookstall in the lower hall sold three hundred devotional books, mostly to younger people, within four months of opening in January 1970. The profits (because no one could sell books below the recommended retail price in those days, not even on church premises) were divided equally between giving books to Chapel members who were training for Christian service, and purchasing booklets for evangelistic work.

By popular demand, the bookstall was opened also on Monday evening from the end of 1972 but never, at that stage, on a Sunday; the sale of literature on Chapel premises on the Lord's Day, even Christian books, was still unacceptable. It was December 1991 before the bookstall (now in the lounge, following its construction in 1983) was open on Sunday, and then only on the basis that anyone who did not wish to buy goods on a Sunday could give an i.o.u. and settle up during the week.

Through the *Record*, Derek Prime encouraged readers to build up a basic library of Christian books; the problem, as he himself said, was knowing where to start and where to stop. In one article, carried over two issues, he advised Christians to gather 55 books, and he recommended, giving reasons, a selection of commentaries, dictionaries, concordances, books on doctrine, ethics, evangelism, church history, Christian service, missionary enterprise, biographies and heresies.

## A new hymnbook

Derek Prime saw the singing of hymns as a teaching opportunity. First, he said, hymns should encourage worship and praise; secondly, they should edify and teach believers; thirdly, they should reflect the call of the gospel. As numbers at the Sunday services increased under his ministry, the deacons were unable to purchase any further copies of the *Baptist Church Hymnal*, which was used in the morning, and they were concerned at the dilapidated state of many copies of *Sankey's Sacred Songs and Solos*, used in the evening. They therefore recommended getting one new hymnal, because: (1) using different books perpetuated the traditional distinction between Sunday morning (teaching) and Sunday evening (gospel), when every service should include both, and (2) maintaining one set of a thousand books in good order was half the work of maintaining two sets.

Three hymnbooks were studied in detail; many analyses were carried out over the next six months, with protagonists pointing out how many favourites were (or were not) in the three contenders, and how far modernising the wording had improved (or detracted from) the message. A special time of prayer together, following a unanimous recommendation from the music committee, persuaded the deacons to prefer *Hymns of Faith* (Scripture Union). Although some of its tunes were unusual, the words best matched the three criteria mentioned above. For a bulk order of one thousand, the publishers were prepared to include the Psalter and paraphrases for a small additional charge.

Changing a hymnbook can be divisive, but the careful and prayerful approach adopted by the pastor over six months brought everyone, no matter where they started, to a harmonious decision. Nostalgia prevailed for a while; when the leader of an Infirmary ward service asked for 50 copies of Sankey, the deacons declined as it was intended to use it from time to time in the Chapel. No such sentiment attached to the *Baptist Church Hymnal*, which was offered without charge to any small church looking for copies.

## Assistants to the pastor

If a young man, training for the ministry, had had little responsibility in his own church before he went to college, a time of apprenticeship was invaluable before he took up leadership of a congregation on his own. Mr Prime gave time to train six men in this way during his 18 years in the Chapel. They came with the title 'pastor's assistant'; when they had proved themselves, usually after about a year, they were ordained to the ministry and given the title 'assistant pastor'. After another year or so, working as an integral part of the pastoral team, they were expected to move on to a church of their own.

Mr Prime's pastoral heart was evident in the way that he contacted them. Realising that it could be intimidating, and could raise false expectations, if young men in college were invited to come to Edinburgh to meet the office-bearers, he contacted them informally in their own situations when he was in their area and had a chat with them. If he felt he could recommend them, he then invited them to visit Edinburgh, to take some part in the evening service, and to meet the elders; in all six cases, there was a mutual drawing from that point.

The first was Tom Lawson, a married pharmacist, with two boys, from Bethesda Chapel in Sunderland, who graduated from London Bible College in June 1972. He started in the Chapel in February 1973 and after two years, he accepted a 'call' to the New Prestwick Baptist Church. He was succeeded in the autumn of 1975 by a young Scotsman, Alistair Begg, recently married, who moved to the Hamilton Baptist Church in October 1977 and then to America. He became the best known of the Chapel's former assistants, and he has been invited to be the guest preacher at the Chapel's bicentenary weekend in October 2008. Kenneth Armstrong, an Edinburgh schoolteacher and a member of the Chapel, started working with the pastoral team on 1 January 1978; at the same time, he studied for the London Diploma of Theology through distance learning. He was ordained on the completion of his studies in the summer of 1981. A year later, he accepted a 'call' to the Wishaw Baptist Church.

## Yesterday's technology

One incident during Kenneth Armstrong's tenure of the Chapel's flat in Lauderdale Street is worth recording. The Post Office was not able to provide enough telephone lines to keep pace with the rapid housing development after the end of the Second World War. Accordingly, many subscribers (including the writer) had a party-line. This meant that one telephone cable served two homes; if one householder was speaking, and the neighbour picked up his or her handset, the conversation was audible without the original caller being aware of it. The Chapel's house convener discovered, in October 1978, that the assistant pastor's telephone was 'a shared or party line'. Concerned that confidential pastoral matters could be overheard, he persuaded the treasurer to upgrade the subscription and to have a direct line installed.

Kenneth Armstrong was followed by David Hunt, who had been President of the Cambridge Inter-Collegiate Christian Union, and who had worked for six years in industry before going to London Bible College. In the summer of 1981, he completed the Cambridge Diploma in Theology there; as his wife's sister was a member of the Chapel, he knew the Edinburgh situation. After meeting with the elders and taking part in the Sunday services in August 1981, he was invited for a period of two years, on the same basis as his predecessors. The other two, Jim Murdock and Peter Firth, will be mentioned in Chapters 49 and 50.

## Discipleship classes

For those wishing to become Christians, and also for those considering baptism or church membership, Derek Prime (or the assistant pastor) ran an almost continuous series of discipleship classes over a period of nine weeks. As soon as one group finished the course, new applicants were ready to begin another one. The class followed the same pattern as that established by Alan Redpath (Chapter 42), but the teaching material was now based on 1 Peter, which (as mentioned earlier) Mr Prime believed to be an excellent introduction to the basics of Christianity. The classes were held on Wednesday from 7 p.m. for an hour, to suit those coming to the Chapel for the Young Peoples Meeting at 8 p.m. Approximately 20 attended the weekly meeting, and in 1984 the classes were still running continuously throughout

the year, although by then, Monday evening was a better time – the hour before the congregational prayer meeting. Discipleship classes continued right through the vacancy of 1987-92, but were then held at 12.50 p.m. on Sunday, after the morning service.

For those wishing to go more deeply into the Christian faith, the Chapel began discipleship groups (as opposed to classes), based on the Navigators 2:7 series; this referred to Colossians 2.7, where Paul challenged Christians to be 'rooted and built up in him, strengthened in the faith'. There were six 12-week courses, so normally the group ran for two consecutive years. By 1990, it was necessary to start two new groups at the same time, such was the demand for them. By 1993, over 80 Chapel members had completed the course and 21 more were still working through it.

## Who to baptize and how?

The Chapel had always seen scriptural significance in going under the water in baptism (symbolising death to the old way of life) and coming up again (to new life). Membership was therefore open only to those who had been baptized as believers by immersion, unless the applicant accepted the principle but was excused on medical grounds from going into the water.

With many coming forward for baptism under Derek Prime's ministry (85 in his first two years, 22 men and 63 women), and with an encouraging percentage of them from non-Christian backgrounds, it was not long before exceptional cases had to be considered. Was there a minimum age for baptism? No, the elders decided, the maturity and understanding of every applicant should be assessed individually. Could someone who was about to give birth to a baby be excused baptism on medical grounds? No, she should wait and be baptized by immersion in due course – incapacity meant permanent incapacity. Should she then be received as a full member, now, on the basis that baptism would follow shortly? No, let events follow their usual sequence. What about a man who particularly wanted to be baptized by immersion but who suffered from hypertension? He was immersed in the presence of his family only, on a Saturday evening after the baptistry had been prepared for the following day. All these decisions were arrived at, unanimously, after a full discussion of the principles involved.

*Baptism took place on any Sunday during the year, but Easter Day was always a favourite, The pastoral studies class from the University Faculty of Divinity came every November, to observe and to learn, from discussion afterwards, about the Baptist understanding of the sacrament.*

## Baptism by effusion

It took six anxious discussions, over the decade from 1975 to 1985, before the Chapel elders came to a concluded view about applicants for full membership who had been baptized as believers but not by immersion. In the first discussion, an 18-year-old student had been converted at an Anglican church in London, from a non-Christian background; she had then been baptized by sprinkling. This was (she maintained) believer's baptism, in the presence of her parents and friends, in accordance with the practice of that church. On moving to Edinburgh 12 years later, she applied to join the Chapel as a full member. She accepted, now, that there was significance in immersion, and that if she had been converted now, she would have asked for it. However, she did not see her baptism at the age of 18 as invalid, and she did not see the need to be re-baptized. Some of the elders accepted that baptism with water, in the name of the Trinity, following confession of personal faith, was valid New Testament baptism, and that the Chapel should not ask for more; others felt that the significance of immersion should not be compromised; others, again, while accepting the importance of immersion, were concerned not to stumble a sincere believer.

As always, the elders took time to pray collectively and individually about it. A month later, they advised the applicant that while they did not question the validity of her earlier baptism, there was New Testament significance in immersion and they were convinced that immersion would supplement her earlier experience. She graciously agreed and went on to play an important part in Chapel life. Similarly,

when someone who had been baptized as a believer in Holyrood Abbey Church of Scotland, although not by immersion, applied for a position of leadership in the Chapel in 1976, she was willing to be baptized in the Chapel in its usual way.

The third discussion was even more delicate, because it involved an associate member, who would have made an excellent elder (if eligible). This man had been baptized as a believer in an evangelical church where the practice was effusion and not immersion; he had therefore joined the Chapel as an associate member. He now acknowledged and supported the Chapel's position on immersion, so the consensus of the elders was that he should be recognized as a full member, without further procedure, and he was duly elected to office.

## The key question

The fourth pastorally sensitive situation clarified the key issue, namely that it was the applicant's view of baptism now, not in the past, which was crucial. In 1983, a man applied for membership, who had been christened in a Presbyterian church as an infant. On coming to personal faith in Christ at the age of 37 in another Presbyterian church, he had sought believers' baptism by effusion, which was the practice of that church. The Chapel elders took the view that if he was now convinced there was symbolism in immersion, and if, on being asked about baptism now, he accepted that principle, they would accept him into full membership. However, this man still held a strong and scriptural conviction that effusion was the appropriate method of baptism, for those who came to faith in mature years. In that situation, associate membership was more appropriate for him

A fifth such application for membership cemented this view. A young woman applied for membership in 1984. She had been baptized by effusion, at the age of 15, on profession of faith in the Free Church of Scotland. She regarded this as believers' baptism, and the elders affirmed the principle, which they had followed on the two previous occasions, that if she was now of the view, following further consideration of the Scriptures and the practice of the Chapel, that there was significance in immersion, then full membership was appropriate. If, however, an applicant, who might be teaching others in the name of the Chapel, still recognized baptism by effusion as equally valid, associate membership should be offered instead.

In this fifth situation, the applicant confirmed that her understanding of baptism, now, was that of immersion although she still felt that her own baptism, by effusion, had been valid at the time; the elders invited her into full membership. They had come a long way in ten years; there was no requirement in 1984 (contrast 1974) for such a person to be baptized again. The sixth discussion, in June 1985, applied the same principle; a man, who said that if he was applying for baptism now, it would be by immersion, but that only effusion was on offer in the church where he was converted, was received as a full member.

### Oral testimonies

As mentioned in Chapter 42, Alan Redpath gave candidates the opportunity of speaking about 'the reality of their faith in the Lord Jesus and of their personal experience of His saving grace and keeping power … before going down into the baptistry'. When Derek Prime was asked about this, he made clear that it was optional and that if anything was said, it must be brief and to the point. Candidates observed the guidance given, and 13 were baptized during the Sunday evening service at Easter 1974, 16 at Easter 1976, 13 at Easter 1977, 9 at Easter 1978 and 13 at Easter 1979, without the services being unduly prolonged.

In December 1974, one of the seven baptized spoke at great length; 'the elders agreed that, subject to the pastor's approval, the opportunity to give testimony should not be denied to baptismal candidates; but that the insistence on brevity should be increased both in the discipleship classes and prior to participation in the ordinance'. Baptismal services were held about every 3 months, when between 7 and 14 were baptized; in the calendar years 1974-76, 44 men and 63 women were baptized at 11 different services.

## Evangelism

### Morning or evening?

From Christopher Anderson onward, successive pastors of Charlotte Chapel distinguished the purpose and content of the two Sunday services; the morning service was for teaching and the evening service was for preaching the gospel. When Derek Prime came to Edinburgh, the morning hymnbook was (as mentioned above) the *Baptist Church Hymnal* and the evening hymnbook was *Sankey's Sacred Songs and Solos*. He was not convinced that the distinction should be maintained, because social patterns were changing, and it was easier to get non-church going friends and colleagues to come to a religious service on a Sunday morning. Another tradition was to hold special gospel efforts from time to time, such as the three-week Edinburgh Christian Crusade in the Usher Hall in 1965. Again, and without detracting from the benefit of such special occasions, he was concerned that evangelism should be part of the regular ongoing weekly activity of the church. The remainder of this chapter looks at how he started where the Chapel was, and gradually moved its outlook to make evangelism more effective for the changing world of the 1970s.

### Monthly guest services

Building on the tradition just mentioned (an evangelistic service every Sunday evening, with a special effort from time to time), the new pastor designated 6.30 p.m. on the third Sunday of the month as a guest service. All who signed the visitors' book, on any Sunday, received a letter from the church office, welcoming their attendance and inviting them to come again; this was followed up by posting a guest service invitation over the next three months to those with an Edinburgh address. If local residents expressed any interest, when they were visited on a Monday evening (as described in the last chapter), they were encouraged to come to a guest service. It was designed to make strangers feel welcome, and to present the gospel in a clear and contemporary way. Derek Prime was, however, careful not to make guest services so different from regular services that those who came back were turned off by the difference.

The same reasoning applied to not taking the Usher Hall regularly for special evangelistic meetings, although there was a second reason; it was not good stewardship to pay for the Usher Hall until the Chapel was regularly overflowing on Sunday evening. Some were good at bringing non-Christian friends, but the number of 'oncers' (Sunday morning only) increased through the 1970s. Monthly guest services continued, although most members found it increasingly difficult to get non-church goers to come to an evening service. On the other hand, a testimony at the end of 1977, by someone who was invited to a guest service, came back and ultimately professed faith in Christ, was an encouragement to persevere. Two of Derek Prime's continuing concerns, throughout his time in the Chapel, were: the number of members who did not come on Sunday evening, and how few brought unconverted friends with them.

*Those who did not normally attend church were made particularly welcome on the evening of the third Sunday of the month.*

## Students and nurses

The Chapel has, since the days of Christopher Anderson, welcomed young men and women who have come to Edinburgh for study or nursing training. All students and nurses who ticked the appropriate box on a visitor's card during Derek Prime's ministry received a letter from him in the following week, followed by a personal visit by one or two from a team of 30, whose particular Christian service was to contact and encourage students and nurses. In a typical autumn term, about 90 such visits were made. The third Sunday in October was designated as a student welcoming service, and twice every term, tea was served at 4.30 p.m., prior to the evening service, with interviews, musical items and book reviews.

In addition, Chapel members visited everyone who filled in a visitor's card with an Edinburgh address. On a typical Sunday, 20 cards were handed to stewards, 14 from local people, but in the summer the number went up to 40; in the calendar year 1981, 1,029 cards were completed, and all visitors were sent a letter of acknowledgement and encouragement. The minister of a church in Essex wrote

back: 'In all my years of visiting churches around the U.K., I have not had this response before.'

**CHARLOTTE BAPTIST CHAPEL**
West Rose Street, Edinburgh

We warmly invite you to a

**WELCOMING SERVICE**

**for**

**STUDENTS AND NURSES**

to be held on

**SUNDAY, 16th October, 1983, at 6.30 pm.**

The service will be followed by an informal reception
at which refreshments will be served; all students and nurses will be most welcome.

We would also like to invite you to tea at 4.30 pm.
on Sunday, 9th Ocotber, in the Lower Hall.

**CHARLOTTE BAPTIST CHAPEL EDINBURGH**

**VISITORS**

We give a warm welcome to all visitors, and we shall be grateful if you will kindly fill in this card to help us get to know you.

Name ...................................
(MR/MRS/MISS)

Address ...................................

...................................
(BLOCK CAPITALS PLEASE)

Resident in Edinburgh ☐
Visitor to the City ☐
Nursing ☐
Attending University ☐
College ☐
School ☐

Please place a
√ in the
appropriate
box.

Please hand this card to a steward at the door or leave it on the table in the vestibule.

The Pastor, his assistant or any of the elders are always glad to meet visitors following our services.

*Everyone (not just students and nurses) who signed the visitors' book, or who filled in a visitor's card, received a letter from the church office during the following week,*

## Commonwealth Games outreach

Edinburgh was host to the Commonwealth Games for ten days in July 1970 (and again in 1986). About two hundred thousand visitors from all the Commonwealth countries came; the Meadowbank Stadium, the Commonwealth Pool and the Athletes' Village at Salisbury (afterwards the Pollock Halls of Residence, for students) were purpose-built. The

Chapel spearheaded a programme with two aims: (1) to offer fellowship to visiting Christians throughout the day, and (2) to hold evangelistic meetings in the open air and in the Usher Hall in the evening.

For the former, the Chapel premises were open from 10.30 a.m. to 5.30 p.m. every weekday, with light refreshments, a bookstall, a record stall, a film room, discussion groups and Bible talks at lunchtime. As an incentive for visitors who could not get tickets for the events, the televised programmes from Meadowbank were available in the lower hall.

*The Ninth Commonwealth Games, held in Edinburgh in 1970, became known as the 'Friendly Games'. The informality of the Scottish team entering the Meadowbank Stadium, during the opening ceremony, contrasts with the razz-ma-tazz and security at such Games now.*

For the outreach, Edinburgh Corporation provided the Chapel with kiosks along Princes Street, for the distribution of specially prepared gospel literature, and also made the Ross Bandstand in Princes Street Gardens available for half an hour every weekday evening. There was singing, testimony and a Bible message, followed by an open-air meeting at the Mound from 8-10 p.m. Two evangelistic cafés were held in the Chapel until 11 p.m., one in the top hall for teenagers and another in the lower hall for adults. People contacted at the Mound were invited back to the Chapel. On the two Sundays of the Games, the regular 45-minute service at the bandstand was followed by an evangelistic outreach in the Usher Hall at 7 p.m., with Christian athletes taking part. Many Chapel members gave up part of their holidays, in order to participate all week. They were rewarded by meeting believers from all over the world and by seeing a number of outsiders coming to faith in Christ.

## Festival outreach

Encouraged by the response to the Commonwealth Games outreach, the Chapel arranged something similar, although on a smaller scale, during the annual Edinburgh International Festival in August 1972. A Good News Café was open in the Chapel's lower hall from 8-11 p.m., Tuesday to Thursday, for all three weeks of the Festival. It provided a follow-up point for those contacted at the open-airs at the Mound, held from 8.15-9.30 p.m. The young people, who were responsible for the Wednesday evening, were delighted to find as many as one hundred strangers willing to come back with them from the Mound to the café.

The format was repeated in 1973 and 1974; in 1975, it was renamed 'At Home' and extended to Saturday; all refreshments were free. From 1977, the outreach started in the week before the Festival, and continued for the first two weeks of it, because the evenings were lighter and there were more visitors around. During the eighth annual programme in 1978, Derek Prime noted: 'Each open-air and cafe has been well supported by the Chapel family, and encouraging contacts have been made with people from all over the world.' With small variations, the Festival outreach continued in this form for the next decade.

## Ross Bandstand outreach

From the beginning of June to the beginning of September, services were held every Sunday afternoon in the Ross Bandstand in Princes Street Gardens. In Alan Redpath's time (Chapter 44), the Corporation offered the Chapel only from 9.15 or 9.30-10 p.m., but in 1971 they allocated three-quarters of an hour, commencing at 5.45 p.m. The Chapel's evening service was put back to 7 p.m., so that interested spectators could join Chapel people walking to Rose Street for the indoor service.

From 1974 to 1987, the bandstand service was for half-an-hour, starting at 5.30 p.m.; it was renamed 'Sunday Challenge', and the Chapel's evening service reverted to 6.30 p.m. While the number of Chapel members who supported the Gardens outreach by their presence was never large, those who did were enthusiastic. They held prayer meetings, with special emphasis on the Ross Bandstand, on two Saturday mornings in June 1979, from 7.30-8.15 a.m., with coffee and rolls afterwards. They also stayed for 20 minutes, after the

Monday evening prayer meeting, specifically to pray for the bandstand services.

### Ross Bandstand Programme
**Summer 1981 ● Sundays from 5.30pm–6pm**

| DATE | MUSIC | SPEAKER | TITLE |
|---|---|---|---|
| 21st June | James Monihan & Choir | Eric Smith | Who needs forgiveness? |
| 28th June | Graham Baker & Group | Ian Balfour | Can you believe the Bible? |
| 5th July | CCYPM Choir | Norman Wallace | Who Cares? |
| 12th July | Graham Baker & Group | Derek Prime | What is a Christian? |
| 19th July | Fountain of Life | Alex Cameron | Did Jesus have to die? |
| 26th July | James Monihan & Choir | Kenneth Armstrong | Life before Death? |
| 2nd Aug | Fountain of Life | Don Summers | What Good News? |
| 9th Aug | James Monihan & Choir | Dick Saunders | Jesus, The only Way? |
| No meetings on the 16th and 23rd August due to Festival activities | | | |
| 30th Aug | James Monihan & Choir | Eric Smith | Is there a God of love? |
| 6th Sept | Graham Baker & Group | Alex Cameron | Faith, fact or fiction? |

*Ross Bandstand, Princes Street Gardens, Edinburgh*

*The programme for the 1981 Sunday afternoon outreach in the Ross Bandstand in Princes Street Gardens, entitled 'Sunday Challenge'. The Chapel used the bandstand in this way during every summer from 1963 until the facility was withdrawn in 1987.*

### Crosstalk Café

Encouraged by the interest shown in Contact Club (Chapter 43), the young people arranged monthly outreaches on Saturday evening in the top hall in the Chapel, under the name 'Crosstalk Café'. It was not ideal to take strangers round to the back door of the Chapel, and then up three flights of stairs, so in 1975 they rented the Queensfare Restaurant in Queensferry Street, for seven consecutive Saturdays from 1 November to 13 December. The café was open (exclusively for them) from 8.15-10.15 p.m., during which they either brought friends with them or invited passers-by to come in; the gospel message was sung and spoken, but the main outreach was through personal conversations, informally around the tables. Ten young people came to know the Lord Jesus through the café, and many more were challenged with the gospel. Everyone who attended was invited to the Chapel's Sunday services. The pattern was repeated in the same restaurant for three Saturday evenings in December 1976, but widespread indifference to the gospel, which had been setting in through the mid-1970s, was increasingly evident; they knew of no conversions in 1976, although the seed was faithfully sown.

## Wester Hailes Baptist Church

### Preparation

Between the decision of the Chapel members in January 1969, to erect a church building in the new housing development of Wester Hailes, and the opening service in February 1973, an almost indescribable effort was put in by both the folk based in Rose Street and those in Longstone.

### Costing

Derek Prime inherited the Chapel's pledge to raise £35,000 for the new building, but during his first year: (1) the quantity surveyor predicted £11,000 more would be needed, (2) building costs escalated, and (3) donations slowed down. He therefore applied a principle, which he used again when the Chapel needed a new organ, and on several other occasions. He called a meeting of members in November 1970, and put the proposition: the budget would be the money received or pledged by 31 December of that year – not a penny more. The congregation responded magnificently and the Wester Hailes fund went up from £11,673 on 1 December to £45,493 on 31 December (including promises and anticipated covenanted tax refunds).

Keeping something back for furnishings, the deacons instructed the architect to put up the best building possible for £40,000. This was positively fixed as the total amount available for the new building, including all fees and expenses; it was up to the architect to decide how to use it. From time to time, he suggested that for a small additional amount, he could (for example) use hardwood instead of softwood for the floor, which would be a better investment in the long run; he was told firmly to do his best with the £40,000. The deacons were absolutely ruthless in this. The architect calculated that site acquisition, professional fees, etc, would cost £5,850. That left £34,150 for the building. When the lowest tender came in at £34,500, 'the feeling of the Court was that we must fight at every point the tendency to allow the price to escalate'. The builder was told that he could have the work if he knocked £350 off his tender, which would keep the overall total at £40,000. His final bill was £32,840, and the target was achieved.

### Constitution

The foundation stone was laid on Saturday 22 January 1972. The next challenge was to find a manse for Alex Hardie and his family. The Corporation would not allocate a council house with an additional room for a study. After much heart-searching at a special meeting of the deacons, as to whether the Chapel should take on additional commitments, a detached house, near to the church, was purchased for £7,500, with a 90 per cent mortgage over 25 years. The new church was constituted on Sunday 11 February 1973, free of debt, and the mortgage on the manse was paid off in full nine months later.

The Sunday School in Longstone continued for another year, now under the supervision of the Wester Hailes Church, but numbers dwindled to a dozen, because all efforts were being put into the new area. This was clearly the best use of resources and the new church went from strength to strength. By its second anniversary, membership had doubled, to 92, with between 45 and 50 attending the midweek Bible study and prayer meeting; not many churches have 50 percent of the membership at their midweek meeting. There were 180 children in the Sunday School and Bible Class. Over one hundred attended on Sunday evening; on the second and third Monday of every month, the congregation visited homes in the vicinity of the church.

Baptismal practice – sprinkling and effusion
Baptismal practice, 1962-1999
Derek Prime – conversion of the young
Open-air meetings
Preaching styles
Preaching – audio-tapes (Derek Prime)
Sunday services

*An* Edinburgh Evening News *reporter, writing every Friday under the name Kirker, was a good friend of evangelical causes; he took a keen interest in the new building for the Wester Hailes Baptist Church.*

Within three years of its constitution, the leadership at Wester Hailes had met the conditions that the Chapel had laid down for independence – a satisfactory constitution, stable leadership and financial independence. Exchange of pulpits and occasional joint meetings between the office-bearers continued to be held, for mutual help and encouragement, but the new cause fully vindicated the vision of many years ago.

Additional information on the following topics, mentioned in this chapter, is available on the CD.

Alex Hardie
Associate membership

# Chapter 47
## Changing attitudes (1969–1975)

### New ideas under Derek Prime

#### A time warp
Life in Charlotte Chapel in 1969 was much the same as life in the Chapel had been for decades, excepting the war years from 1939 to 1945. The services followed the same order and used the same hymnals; readings were from the Authorised Version of the Bible; the Sunday School and the weeknight auxiliaries followed their familiar activities from year to year; visiting preachers remarked on the obvious stability, but hinted that a visit to the Chapel was like taking a step back into an earlier era.

As with evangelism (Chapter 46), Derek Prime started where the Chapel was, and tactfully suggested ways in which worship might be made more relevant for the 1970s. One hymnbook replaced the morning and evening hymnals (Chapter 46); the New International Version became the pulpit Bible; prayers to the deity were addressed 'you' instead of 'thou'; family services were encouraged. These innovations are described below.

*The start of a new ministry prompted the deacons to redecorate the sanctuary. Scaffolding made it inaccessible for four weeks in October 1970, during which services were held in the Assembly Hall on the Mound.*

#### Christmas morning family service
In December 1973, Derek Prime suggested holding a 45-minute family service in the Chapel, at 11 a.m. on Christmas Day. Despite the short notice, it was well attended and greatly appreciated, not least because of the relaxed way in which he encouraged the children to participate. It became an annual event, growing in size – sometimes the gallery was required – and friendliness, with children bringing their presents to the platform. Another feature was to ask how many overseas countries were represented – usually about 20. From 1973 to 1979, the offering went to the Algrade School and the work at Humbie (Chapter 44).

*A 45-minute family service on Christmas morning was a welcome addition to the Chapel's festive programme.*

#### Sunday morning family service
Concerned that families should worship together, Derek Prime introduced a family service in December 1975, hoping to attract:

*as many unconverted families as possible with the children in attendance throughout. This would be kept to a duration of one hour and would be evangelistic in approach. Our own members would be expected to vacate the church for the lower hall to make way for the family groups should the need arise.*

---

1 Elders' Minute, 1 October 1975.

It was an instant success, with more than 20 families asking for the booklet *Christian Upbringing*, on offer at the door, and there were calls for another one soon. This was arranged for 22 February 1976, when the Scouts, Guides, Cubs and Brownies paraded and encouraged their parents to come. Family services were then fixed well in advance (September and December 1976, and February 1977) so that Chapel families could plan invitations to neighbours and others. Encouraging though these services were, it was disappointing that not many new families came, especially unconverted ones.

*Family services were held several times a year, with a special focus on the youth activities of the church.*

### New International Version

By 1974, few young people read the Bible in the Authorised Version, although it was still the one used chiefly in the pulpit in the Chapel; Derek Prime explained (below) why this was so. A variety of translations and paraphrases were on the market, some truer to the original text than others; many worshippers brought their personal choice of Bible to the Sunday services, so there was increasing diversity in the pews. The elders debated at length whether other translations should be used in the pulpit; they avoided a decision by saying it was 'the duty of the Pastor to use on any particular occasion that version which, under God's guidance, he finds appropriate.'

Derek Prime convened a committee, which looked at all the issues raised by modern translations, and then set about explaining its recommendations to the congregation. His position, at the end of 1975, was that the New International Version was the best modern translation, but only the New Testament (published 1973) was available. Accordingly, he continued to read from the Authorised Version, whenever it was clear and plain. Where the language of the Old Testament was better expressed in another translation, he used the Revised Standard Version; where the language of the New Testament was better expressed in the New International Version, he used it. He made plain that whenever the whole Bible became available in the New

International Version, he would make extensive (almost exclusive) use of it in the pulpit. This happened in May 1979, and he did.

### Promise boxes

One consequence of the multiplicity of new translations and paraphrases was the disappearance of the promise box from evangelical households. Until the middle of the twentieth century, it was common for guests to be invited to pull out a tightly-rolled piece of paper, from a large number packed into a box, each containing a text; this was given to the guest as a promise for the day. Alternatively, members of a family might, at breakfast-time, pick out their text for the day. Although promise boxes may seem strange now, they were one of many Bible-centered daily devotions for committed Christians; however, the texts were from the Authorised Version, and a new generation, looking for contemporary language, lost interest.

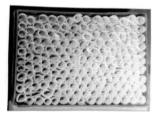

*A promise box in the Chapel archives. The cover reads: "Exceeding great and precious promises" 'Thy words were found and I did eat them.' "Jer.15.16. TAKE ONE AND REPLACE"*

### Language in prayer

When Tom Lawson, the Chapel's assistant pastor, accepted a 'call' to the New Prestwick Baptist Church in April 1975, there was no doubt that the experiment of having an apprentice had been profitable, both for the Chapel and for the individual. Derek Prime contacted London Bible College (now London School of Theology), from which Tom Lawson had come; they recommended a 23-year-old Scot, Alistair Begg, who was just competing his studies. Derek Prime met him in London, and invited him to Edinburgh for a weekend at the end of April. There was mutual drawing, and he started in September 1975 as pastor's assistant – the exact phrase was still important.

When Alistair Begg took part in the Sunday services in April 1975, he addressed God in prayer, as he normally did, by the words 'you' and 'yours', instead of 'thou' and 'thee' and 'thine', to which the Chapel was accustomed. Although this was increasingly practised elsewhere, it was the first time in the Chapel pulpit and the elders were taken aback by the familiarity of it. However, having thought about it, they agreed that guest preachers should pray as they felt led, provided due reverence was maintained.

Shortly afterwards, Derek Prime, having alerted the congregation of his intention to do so, changed once and for all to 'you', and never went back. It was, however, agreed that when the congregation joined audibly in the Lord's Prayer, as they regularly did in those days, it should be: 'Our Father, who art in heaven, hallowed be thy name, …'. Some preferred to use the traditional wording in all their prayers, public and private, and a few continue with it to this day.

### An electronic organ

By 1973, the Chapel's pipe organ was increasingly unreliable. The options were: (1) to repair it (minimum £8,200), (2) to find a second-hand pipe organ (very expensive), (3) to purchase a Hammond (£2,750, but not the best tones for a church) or (4) to purchase an Allen Computer Organ (£4,950, with better tones). After the Hammond and the Allen had been demonstrated, there were an almost equal number of deacons in favour of each. Derek Prime applied the principle of laying the issue before the congregation and discerning God's will by their response. He wrote to all members: 'Which instrument we purchase will depend on the amount received by way of donations by the last Sunday in July 1973.' The congregation's response was much more decisive than that of the deacons, and just enough came in for the Hammond.

*The grey sidewalls of the Chapel were transformed to their present sparkling white in 1974, as crocuses heralded spring in Charlotte Square.*

### Youth activities

In the autumn of 1974, the Sunday School leaders reviewed their wide-ranging responsibilities, which included the Sunday morning crèches, Sunday afternoon School and Bible Classes, the Friday uniformed organisations and Saturday Folkus. They decided that 'Youth Council', and 'executive', were better titles than 'Sunday School' and 'committee', and these names continue to this day.

The 6th Waverley Charlotte Baptist Chapel Scout Troop celebrated its jubilee in October 1971, when 90 former members attended a dinner in the lower hall and the present Scouts paraded for the Sunday morning service. A number of former Scouts played key roles in Chapel life as they grew older, so the link remained a real one.

### Junior YPM / Folkus

While much has been said, and rightly so, about the initiative of the new pastor, others too saw needs and opportunities. As mentioned in Chapter 44, the deaconess and the church officer were concerned that those who were too young for YPM were missing out, so they started a Junior YPM in the spring of 1968, for boys and girls between the ages of 12 and 15. When Derek Prime came to Edinburgh in 1969, attendance averaged 40; they met in the top hall, where they alternated games on one Saturday with Bible study on the next. Soon, they added a weekend away to their programme, over the Edinburgh spring holiday in May.

Reviewing their function in 1974, they dropped the word Junior and restarted after the summer break as Folkus. Numbers and enthusiasm remained steady, and by 1977 the boys outnumbered the girls by 24 to 20 – an answer to prayer, because the leaders had been concerned the boys were losing interest. Folkus remained an independent auxiliary until 1985, when it linked with the Sunday Bible Class and they became two parts of one organisation, called Focus. Two years later, they separated again, with the Sunday meeting reverting to Bible Class and the other becoming Saturday Focus, with the object of winning and nurturing young people for the Lord.

## Regular reviews

### Tradition in the making

It is surprising how quickly a new idea, brought in to break the mould, can become a tradition. To bring variety into the

Sunday evening service, Derek Prime suggested that one of the deacons should give the offertory prayer. When the four deacons brought the offering bags to the front, one of them went to a microphone on the platform to dedicate the gifts. Within a few years, this was regarded as a necessary part of the evening service. Recognising how easily such things happen, Derek Prime instituted a regular review of all Chapel activities, as described below.

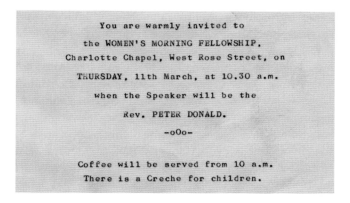

You are warmly invited to the WOMEN'S MORNING FELLOWSHIP, Charlotte Chapel, West Rose Street, on THURSDAY, 11th March, at 10.30 a.m. when the Speaker will be the Rev. PETER DONALD.

—oOo—

Coffee will be served from 10 a.m. There is a Creche for children.

## One a month

He added a standing item to the agenda for the elders' monthly meeting – to look at the function and effectiveness of every Chapel activity, working chronologically through the week. If the leaders of an auxiliary were not elders, they were invited to attend the relevant part of the meeting; this gave the elders an insight into what was happening, and the auxiliaries appreciated the interest shown.

Some meetings were found to have outlived their usefulness, and were discontinued. These included the New Year's Day conference (started 1881), the District Women's Meeting (started 1908), the Girls Own (started 1921), the Rock Mission (started 1923) and the Young Worshippers League (started 1928). Even if it was decided, after review, that no change was needed, the exercise was worthwhile, because people understood better what they were doing and why. This chapter concludes with a comment on nine of these reviews.

*Mrs Prime led the Women's Morning Fellowship, which continued (and still continues) to be very popular. This invitation is from 1971. When she handed over leadership in October 1987, 'aunties' still provided a crèche for toddlers and babies, while young mothers enjoyed the meeting.*

## Women's Thursday Morning Fellowship

At the elders' court in November 1974, Mrs Prime and Mrs Hadden reported regular attendance of between 150 and 175, of whom 75 per cent were Chapel members. Ten young mothers between them brought 13 babies and toddlers to the crèche; it was 1990 before most mothers returned to work shortly after children were born, making the crèche redundant and sharply raising the average age of the meeting.

The meeting was held from 10.30-11.30 a.m., from October to May. Coffee, tea and biscuits were served as people arrived, from 10 a.m. onward, and the half hour of fellowship was appreciated. There was a guest speaker, and the meeting was devotional rather than evangelistic; its purpose was to encourage members and to equip them to share their faith with others.

## Young Peoples Meeting

When the leaders of the YPM met with the elders in the spring of 1973, there was much to encourage. An average of 60 came on Wednesday evening during the winter months, for teaching, discussion, missionary interest and much more. They led a Sunday morning ward service in the Edinburgh Royal Infirmary throughout the year, and about one hundred stayed after the service on Sunday evening, for an informal programme. As described in the last chapter, they ran a well-attended Crosstalk Café in the top hall once a month, with music, an evangelistic talk and opportunity for discussion. In the summer, they switched to outdoor activities, mainly social, but they were responsible for open-air meetings at the Mound on the first Wednesday of the month. At Christmas 1971 and again in 1972, they led two well-attended services there, with a watchman's brazier fire and servings of hot soup to attract the crowds; they gave out copies of John's Gospel and stickers: 'Put Christ back into Christmas'.

At the invitation of the Scripture Union, about 20 from YPM led a summer beach mission at Lamlash, on the island of Arran, in July. For many years, about 60 had gone away together, with an invited speaker, over the Edinburgh autumn holiday weekend. They had only two concerns to share with the elders. They felt that the Junior YPM (mentioned above) was holding onto people for too long at the younger end, and that Group 35 was taking too many away at the older end; they needed young blood coming in, and they needed mature leadership. Their other concern was that while they found it easy to invite people back to the Chapel after the open-air meetings, they felt too inexperienced to talk seriously with them; they asked for some older people to mingle with the hundred or so guests, whom they had brought back for coffee in the top hall.

## District Women's Meeting

The character of this gospel meeting changed in the early 1970s, as the character of Rose Street changed. When normal activities were resumed after the Second World War, the deaconess (who had charge of the meeting) reported excellent and encouraging meetings, with between 60 and 90 in the lower hall of the Chapel at 7:30 p.m. on Wednesday evening, mostly from Rose Street itself. Like most auxiliaries, it broke for the summer months, but social activities and bus outings were arranged. In 1965, it was renamed the Women's Bright Hour; it still attracted about 70 weekly.

However, when the little shops in Rose Street set out to become chic in the 1970s, and the street became a fashionable place to live, many of the poorer residents moved out. Some travelled back into town for the meeting, but it no longer attracted new members. When the elders reviewed the meeting with its leadership, all were agreed that it no longer served a purpose, and it was discontinued.

## Communion

The Lord's Supper was observed at the close of the service on the first Sunday of the month, alternating morning and evening. When the elders reviewed it, two improvements were made. Some found the combined service too long, without a break, so Derek Prime suggested utilizing the fourth Sunday of five-Sunday months, for an additional and more leisurely evening communion, after a break for coffee. The first, on 23 March 1975, was well attended and this became a regular item in the Chapel calendar for many years.

The second improvement was to remove a distraction from the solemnity of the Lord's Table. Offering bags were passed round as part of the communion service, for contributions to the Fellowship Fund, which was distributed in confidence to members in financial need. This was in addition to the general offering, earlier in the service. Mr Prime suggested having a retiring offering, with boxes on the stairs. This had been done in 1917, on the occasions when communion was before the sermon (Chapter 21), but from 1971 it applied to every communion service, a practice that continues to this day. A third suggestion, that the organ should be played quietly during the distribution of the elements at some of the communion services, did not find support; it was many years before this was accepted.

*Until June 1980, the communion table (set with bread and wine in the upper photograph) stood at the front of the platform at all times (except baptisms), with a row of nine chairs behind it. Derek Prime had the chairs removed, and recessed the table under the pulpit (lower photograph), except for communion services. This improved the appearance of the pulpit area, and has been done ever since.*

## New Year's Day conference

Few Chapel activities were reviewed as often or as anxiously as the afternoon and evening conference on 1 January. Should it be changed to 2 January, so as not to clash with family gatherings and the *Messiah* in the Usher Hall (now moved to 2 January)? It was not well supported by members – about three hundred attended, but not many Chapel people; should the Chapel provide a venue for Christians from country areas, particularly older folk, who wanted to do something worthwhile on the traditionally pagan holiday? Unlike the elders, who talked issues through until they reached unanimity, the deacons regularly had to vote on matters within their remit; they decided by a narrow majority to continue the conference on 1 January 1970 and 1971. Then, for three consecutive years, nothing took place; in year one, New Year was a Sunday; in year two, Alan Redpath was speaking at the Carrubbers Close Mission; in year three, nothing was arranged because there had not been a conference for two years. The members were asked, at the 1974 annual general meeting, whether they wanted it to resume. A show of hands proved inconclusive, so nothing was arranged for 1975. The New Year's Day conference, which had been a feature of Chapel life for 90 years, was no more.

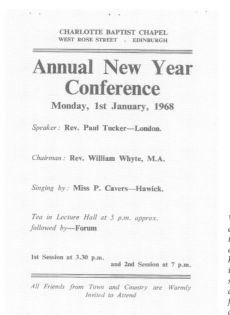

When Derek Prime came to Edinburgh, the New Year's Day conference on 1 January had been a regular item in the Chapel's calendar since 1881. However, demand for it was falling, and the 1971 conference was the last.

## Giving

Until decimalisation in 1971, the half-crown (12.5 new pence) was the commonest coin put into the offering. The nearest equivalent new coin was 10 pence, so there was a 20 percent fall in that aspect of the weekly offering. The treasurer countered by pressing for more covenants. In 1970, 50 covenanters gave £6,034 (including the tax recovered), and the rest of the Sunday offerings totalled £3,623. By 1975, 70 covenants contributed over £10,000 a year out of total church

income of £17,298. In 1976, 93 people covenanted, and by 1979 the number had gone up to 145 – the message was getting through. While everyone else rejoiced as successive chancellors brought down the basic rate of income tax, the church treasurer lamented that he received less by way of refund.

## Doctrinal basis

When he came to the Chapel in 1916, Graham Scroggie added a doctrinal statement to the membership application, which all applicants were required to sign:

*I believe that Jesus Christ is the Son of God, and the Son of Mary, Divine and human; and that, by His sacrifice on Calvary, He is the Redeemer of the world. And I believe the Bible to be the Revelation to men of God's redeeming purpose, Divinely inspired, historically trustworthy, the true and sufficient standard of faith and conduct.*

2 Elders' Minute, 23 October 1916.

That is not the same as the Chapel's 1837 Statement of Belief, which Christopher Anderson adapted from the doctrinal basis of the Bristol Academy, where he was trained (Chapter 2); it focused on the theological issues of his day, but there is no indication that all Chapel members had to subscribe to it. In 1939, Sidlow Baxter replaced Scroggie's statement with one of his own:

*In being received into membership with this Church, do you wholeheartedly subscribe to the doctrines upon which it is built – the full inspiration and Divine authority of the Scriptures; the one Triune God, and the absolute coequality of the Father, the Son, and The Holy Spirit; the real incarnation, atonement, resurrection, ascension, and intercession of the Lord Jesus Christ, the Son of God, and His personal return as King and Judge; the salvation of sinners by grace alone on God's part and faith in Christ alone, on our part?*

3 Membership application forms, 1919-70.

When the membership application was revised in 1970, to take account of associate membership, Derek Prime suggested three advantages in replacing the 1939 statement with the doctrinal basis of the Inter-Varsity Fellowship (renamed UCCF in 1975): (1) the IVF published a booklet,

*Evangelical Belief*, explaining it paragraph by paragraph (now *Ultimate Realities*); (2) the basis was widely recognized throughout the evangelical world; (3) the IVF had amended its basis in 1959, to meet new challenges to the faith, and would continue to update it as necessary. (The UCCF added a new paragraph in 1981, to clarify the deity of Christ.)

The elders accepted the wisdom of this proposal, but insisted on two minor additions; the Chapel's doctrinal basis was now (1970):

*The doctrinal basis of the Fellowship shall be the fundamental truths of Christianity, as revealed in Holy Scripture, including:*

*(a) The unity of the Father, the Son and the Holy Spirit in the Godhead.*
*(b) The sovereignty of God in creation, revelation, redemption and final judgment.*
*(c) The divine inspiration and infallibility of Holy Scripture, as originally given, and its supreme authority in all matters of faith and conduct.*
*(d) The universal sinfulness and guilt of human nature since the fall, rendering man subject to God's wrath and condemnation.*
*(e) Redemption from the guilt, penalty and power of sin only through the sacrificial death (as our Representative and Substitute) of Jesus Christ, the Incarnate Son of God.*
*(f) The bodily resurrection of Jesus Christ from the dead.*
*(g) The necessity of the work of the Holy Spirit to make the death of Christ effective to the individual sinner, granting him repentance towards God and faith in Jesus Christ.*
*(h) The indwelling and work of the Holy Spirit in the believer.*
*(i) The one holy universal Church, which is the Body of Christ, and to which all true believers belong.*
*(j) The expectation of the visible personal return of the Lord Jesus Christ.*

---

4 Membership application forms, 1970-87.

Derek Prime prepared a supplementary statement, dealing with baptism and church government, which were not (obviously) in the pan-denominational IVF basis. The Chapel kept this doctrinal basis until Mr Prime left in 1987; it then adopted the UCCF's revised basis of 1981. When the UCCF rephrased its basis in 1998, to make the clauses gender-inclusive and more understandable to people unfamiliar with theological words, the Chapel followed. This is the statement of belief now printed in the annual report.

## Worldliness

When the stock of membership applications ran out in 1975, the elders agreed that the paragraph about avoiding 'practices and pleasures … of a worldly nature' (Chapter 32) was unduly negative, and replaced it by a more positive question:

*As a Christian do you see the necessity of paying close attention to how you live (Ephesians 5:15; Romans 12:17), so as to lead a self-controlled and godly life (Titus 2:12) and to be an example of a Christian believer in your speech, conduct, love, faith, purity (1 Timothy 4:12) and separation from all that is dishonouring to God (2 Corinthians 6:14-17)?*

---

5 Elders' Minute, 25 June, 1 October 1975.

When Peter Grainger came in 1992, he amended it to:

*Do you pledge yourself, by the grace of God, to live at all times a life that is in keeping with your testimony as a true believer in the Lord Jesus Christ and as a member of this church? (Ephesians 5:15, Romans 12:17, Titus 2:12, 1 Timothy 6:12, 2 Corinthians 6:14-17).*

---

6 Membership application forms, 1993-2000.

and then, in January 2001, to:

*Are you prepared to commit yourself, in reliance on the grace of God, to live in a manner appropriate to a disciple of Jesus Christ? (Ephesians 4:1).*

---

7 Membership application forms from 2001.

That remains the question – there are 22 other questions, about conversion, baptism, Christian service, giving, discipline and doctrine – on the current membership application.

## Young Worshippers League

As the elders reviewed the components of Chapel life, they came to the marking of cards, morning and evening on Sunday, by the leaders of the Young Worshippers League. This had started in 1928, because Sunday School teachers had two concerns: (1) that few of the children attending the afternoon Sunday School came to either of the public Sunday services, and (2) that teachers lost touch with many of the children during the long summer vacation. As has been mentioned several times, good attendance throughout the year earned a book at the annual prize giving in June. During the 1950s and 1960s, between 90 and 100 children were on the roll, with about 60 prizes awarded annually. From 1956, medals were presented as well as books, for good attendance over three years. There was an immediate response to this incentive, and soon perfect attendances were recorded for eight or even nine years.

However, some in the Chapel had two concerns. One was the deliberate absence of any provision for illness; children were brought to the Chapel, when they ought to have been in bed or in quarantine, so as not to lose their prize for perfect attendance. Ministers of other churches were allowed to initial cards when young worshippers attended elsewhere on holiday, but even hospitalisation was not an excuse for non-attendance in Edinburgh. The elders directed in October 1970 that penalising a child who could not attend through genuine illness must cease immediately.

The second concern, anticipating social policy of the later twentieth century, was whether prizes should be awarded at all. This debate went on until November 1971, when all Sunday School prizes were stopped. In their place, scholars were presented with a Bible or a *Daily Light*, when moving from one section of the Sunday School to another. By 1971, nearly all the young worshippers were children of Chapel parents; the Young Worshippers League had served its purpose of getting non-church goers into the habit of church attendance, so the elders discontinued it in May 1973.

**CHARLOTTE BAPTIST CHAPEL**

THE YOUNG WORSHIPPERS' LEAGUE COMMITTEE

request the pleasure of

...............................................................

Company at their Social to be held in the Lecture Hall of the Church on Saturday, 28th February, at 4 p.m.

To facilitate catering please reply before 21st FEBRUARY 1970 to –
Miss G. A. Danson Smith
7 Roseneath Terrace,
Edinburgh EH9 1JS (Phone 229 5900)

*Prizes for (simply) attending church activities were deemed politically incorrect in 1971, so this invitation to the Young Worshippers League prize giving was its last. The ruling did not apply to other league activities, and the annual socials continued until the league was disbanded in 1973.*

Additional information on the following topics, mentioned in this chapter, is available on the CD.

Annual report
Christmas morning
Doctrinal basis
Fellowship fund
Membership applications
Worldliness
Young Worshippers League

**CHARLOTTE BAPTIST CHAPEL**

YOUNG WORSHIPPERS' LEAGUE

As the Annual Prize-giving takes place on Sunday morning, 24th May, you are requested to be present in the Lecture Hall below the Church at 10.30 a.m.

# Chapter 48
## Cameos (1976–1980)

## Events outside the Chapel

### The next five years

The previous three chapters looked thematically at some significant events during Derek Prime's first six years in Edinburgh. This chapter gathers a miscellany of other events, over the next five years of his pastorate. Events away from the Chapel are looked at first, and then those within it, both in chronological order.

### 1976 – Bratislava

The Chapel learned in 1976 that an evangelical church in Bratislava, Czechoslovakia, then behind the Iron Curtain, was putting up new premises despite the restrictions and persecutions of the Communist government; in a special offering, the congregation contributed £550 for an organ. The church invited Derek Prime to visit Bratislava, when the building was complete; he went in May 1978, and was greatly impressed. Fraternal links continued over many years, with Chapel members visiting the church when they were passing through Bratislava on business or on holiday.

### 1976 – Aberdeen

On the weekend of 23-24 October 1976, Derek Prime was in Aberdeen, for the anniversary services of the Gilcomston Baptist Church; the Chapel's former pastor, Gerald Griffiths, took the morning service in the Chapel. The writer was also in Aberdeen where, as the incoming president of the Baptist Union of Scotland, he led the BBC morning radio service from the Assembly.

*At the Baptist Union of Scotland Assembly in October 1976; from left to right, Ian Bremner (Union treasurer), Jim Heron (retiring president), Joyce Balfour, the writer (incoming president), Gerald Griffiths (guest speaker), Derek Prime (opening devotions) and Andrew MacRae (Union secretary).*

### 1977 – The Queen's jubilee

In May 1977, Queen Elizabeth the Second celebrated the silver jubilee of coming to the throne. Derek Prime suggested that the Chapel should hold a Jubilee Thanksgiving Service in the Usher Hall, on the evening of Sunday 29 May, partly to draw out the biblical implications of jubilee in an evangelistic event, and partly 'to give thanks to God for His goodness to us as a nation, and especially during the twenty-five years of Her Majesty's reign.' Christians prominent in public life were invited to declare their hopes for the future of the nation. The grand tier and the area were rapidly filled, and the upper tier had to be opened. Many visitors came in, and the gospel was clearly presented. A number stayed behind to speak with the pastor about salvation.

Encouraged by this, the Chapel took the Usher Hall for Easter Sunday evening 1980, and prepared intensively for it. A series of men's meetings was held in the lower hall, to introduce work colleagues to the gospel; 17 informal home groups took place in a fortnight, trying to interest neighbours; all culminated in invitations to come to the Usher Hall. The Easter Service of Praise almost filled the auditorium, and there was a good response to the invitation at the end; a number came to the discipleship class for further instruction.

### 1977 – A daughter church in Dunbar?

Watching the rapid progress of the Chapel's daughter church in Wester Hailes, and concerned at the absence of any clear-cut evangelical testimony throughout East Lothian, Derek Prime suggested in October 1977 that the Chapel might do something in North Berwick, where he had a holiday home. Others, who attended the churches in the town during their summer holidays, were less enthusiastic about North Berwick, but responded favourably when a building in Dunbar was offered to the Chapel. It was a redundant Church of Scotland, with a hall and garden ground, situated in a prominent and strategic position at the south end of the High Street; the kirk session was keen to see the building used by Christians, and not sold for commercial purposes.

However, the group appointed to investigate the possibilities discovered four negative factors. A small Baptist fellowship, with an American background, had recently started in Dunbar, and the Chapel did not wish to set up in opposition. Secondly, no Chapel members lived in the area; to establish a witness would mean outsiders driving for an hour each way

– unlike Wester Hailes, where there was a resident membership. Thirdly, the building on offer was in poor condition, and not suitable for teams to conduct seaside missions, because there was no overnight accommodation. Fourthly, the population increase, through the building of the Torness power station, was not expected to continue once construction was complete. Although grateful for the offer, the deacons did not let their hearts rule their heads; they thought about it for six months, and then decided, in March 1978, not to proceed.

## 1978 – Successful temperance objections

Over many years, the Chapel publicly opposed moves by the licensed trade to open new premises or to extend opening hours. The Chapel's most high-profile success came during preparations for the Commonwealth Games in Edinburgh in 1970. There was widespread support for the games, but when the City Council suggested having bars in the spectator areas of the stadium, the writer, on behalf of the Chapel and the Free Church of Scotland, successfully lodged objections with the Secretary of State. These objections included:

*it is the experience of the Petitioners [the Chapel] that in dealing not only with the spiritual problems but also with the social ills of this age group, one of the main contributing factors is the degradation of moral character through the abuse of strong drink. Many crimes are committed under its influence, and much anti-social behaviour stems from its influence. Your Petitioners find a very close connection between, for example, drink and sexual immorality. Many a man or woman under its influence has slipped into acts of immorality, because their customary alertness and self-control had been weakened by alcoholic liquor.*

---

1 Elders' Minute, 5 February 1969; Deacons' Minute, 5 February 1969.

In 1972, the Chapel successfully opposed the first modern attempt to open Edinburgh public houses on Sunday. Five years later, Scott's Bar at 202 Rose Street and Elders at 159 applied for Sunday opening; the deacons opposed this, and both applications were refused. Under the legislation then current, neither could apply again for Sunday opening for another two years.

In December 1978, another public house in Rose Street, Rose Revived, applied for permission to change adjoining shop premises to a lounge bar. The Chapel lodged objections, on the basis that Rose Street already had too many public houses; the District Council refused the application, specifically mentioning the comments about the number of existing bars. The Chapel's objection to more public houses in Rose Street, and to longer opening hours for existing ones, was partly on principle and partly because of the security measures necessary when people in the area were under the influence of drink.

*The Chapel premises, which the deacons would have liked to be open and accessible, had to be secured by iron gates to discourage unsociable behaviour on the doorsteps.*

In June 1980, Scott's Bar (202 Rose Street), Elders (159) and Rose Revived (133) all applied again for Sunday opening, to which the Chapel successfully objected. Scott's tried again in February 1985, but withdrew its application when the Chapel lodged objections. The Chapel's last success was in January 1990, when Scott's Bar was again refused a Sunday licence. Shortly after that, the law was changed, and neighbours could no longer object. It was 1999 before Scott's opened on Sunday morning; fortunately, none of the anticipated disruption followed.

## Individuals in the licensed trade

The church's concern was not just about public houses. In November 1976, a couple applied for membership of the Chapel; the husband's job was to serve customers at the licensed counter of a Princes Street shop. When interviewed, he did not share the elders' concern about being associated with the wine and spirit trade. Since it was a multiple store, the elders could not understand his reluctance to transfer to another department; they deferred his application, to give him the opportunity of changing his place of employment. The couple's response was simply to continue attending the Chapel, without pursuing membership. A year later, the husband voluntarily became a warehouse manager, and both applications for full membership were approved.

387

This may seem unreasonable to some today, but Edinburgh's Medical Officer of Health stated publicly in 1969 that Edinburgh's most serious social problem was alcoholism. Chapel members, who worked in the Rock Mission in the Grassmarket (below), knew that drink was usually the downfall of those who were euphemistically described as 'single, homeless men', and whom they sought to help.

## 1979 – The Rock Mission's last move

Every Sunday afternoon, Chapel members prepared sandwiches and gallons of tea for up to one hundred hungry men, some of whom had not eaten for 24 hours. This was followed by a gospel service for an hour, which endeavoured to present the message in ways the men could understand. Many of the men never missed a Sunday. The Rock Mission had met in the Livingstonia Hall from 1923 until the hall was sold in 1952, and then, as described in Chapter 38, in the Grassmarket Mission. Walter Harkness, who was honorary superintendent of the Rock for 13 years from 1966, preferred to use the Church of Scotland's People's Palace. When he stepped down in 1979, Donald Cormack took over and moved the Rock back to the Grassmarket Mission, where it continued until 1987 (Chapter 51). In the Chapel's 64 years of responsibility for the mission (1923-87), there were only five changes in leadership. One young man volunteered in 1931 to help for six months; he was still helping 50 years later, and enthused his wife to serve as well.

*(1) The Grassmarket Mission building, (2) Chapel members assisting with the tea, (3) Donald Cormack leading and (4) Margaret Benington playing the organ. (1983 pictures)*

## Events inside the Chapel

### 1976 – Exceptionally generous gifts

In January 1976, an elderly Chapel member, who was going into a retirement home, donated her fully furnished flat at 16 Falcon Court to the Chapel, to provide accommodation for a deaconess or other full-time member of the Chapel staff or for missionaries on furlough. Its first occupant was a missionary who had no other home, and it proved remarkably useful over the next 12 years.

More problematic was the gift by another elderly member, who left her property at 13 Blantyre Terrace to the Chapel in January 1978. Although the house had been adapted for letting as single rooms, which the Chapel could have used for students and others, it was in a poor state of repair and needed renovation. The Chapel agonized over whether they could or should evict three elderly single ladies and a couple with a family, who were living there, in order to sell the property. The position was amicably resolved when the adjoining nursing home took over the property for £26,000, which the Chapel used for a variety of worthy projects.

There was a third gift, a decade later, when another member left her flat at 4 Balfour Place, Leith, to the Chapel. With commendable foresight, she provided in her Will that the deacons could sell the property, if they did not wish to retain it, and use the proceeds as they thought fit; this turned out to be the best way forward.

### Home Bible study groups

Following the success of pastoral groups, it was suggested from the floor of the annual general meeting in 1976 that something could profitably be arranged for the Thursdays when the Bible School was in vacation; people wanted to combine the friendliness of the home groups with the teaching element of the Bible School. With some reluctance, because of the possibility of fragmentation and the encouragement of cliques, the elders arranged for six groups, of up to 20 per group, to meet in homes between mid-December 1976 and mid-January 1977. There was an open invitation, but nearly everyone who went was already a regular member of the Bible School. The response was positive, so five consecutive weekly meetings were arranged during the Bible School vacations in April, June and

September 1977 and January 1978. Present readers may wonder why so much has been said about them here, but in 1976, home group discussion on biblical topics was novel in the Chapel, and had previously been discouraged as potentially divisive.

Another feature of Chapel life, which is so familiar now that it may not seem worth mentioning here, is a prayer calendar, or prayer diary. This was, however, another novelty in 1976. Alistair Begg suggested it, soon after he came as the pastor's assistant; the experiment was so popular that it became a regular insert in the monthly *Record* until February 1998, when, in order to give more up-to-date information, it was moved in the weekly bulletin – and has continued ever since.

PRAYER CALENDAR FOR SEPTEMBER.

Sun. 5th — Pray for the two young couples – Mr. and Mrs. West and Mr. and Mrs. Sprott – married last Friday and Saturday at the Chapel – as they begin their new life together.

6th — Remember the ladies at Beulah. The Pastor leads the communion service there today.

7th — With four days remaining of the Festival Outreach pray that we may be 'faithful to the last'.

8th — Angus and Eve Noble have now been back in the Philippines for two weeks: pray for wisdom for them as they settle into routine.

9th — Ask the Lord to guide us today as to our own involvement in the life of the church, and thank Him for all those who are making a contribution to the Festival Outreach.

10th — Pray that wisdom may be given to those responsible for drawing up the plans for welcoming new students/ nurses to the fellowship.

11th — Thank the Lord today for all His goodness to us individually and as a company of God's people.

Sun. 12th — Pray for liberty to be given to Pastor and people alike as we seek to worship the Lord in the beauty of holiness.

*The first Chapel prayer diary, familiar nowadays, but a novelty when the pastor's assistant suggested it in June 1976.*

## 1977 – Lunchtime meetings

In October 1977, Derek Prime suggested holding lunch-hour services in the Chapel on Thursday, to fill a need in the city-centre. He proposed serving light refreshments and coffee, so that those coming during their normal lunchtime could have Christian fellowship as well as teaching. Nothing further came of this until the new lounge was opened in 1983; he then had a series of six (Chapter 49), but there was not sufficient support to repeat them.

## 1978 – Broadcast services

Prior to 1978, only two services had been broadcast from the Chapel. The BBC made up for this by recording two separate programmes, one in the morning and the other in the evening, on 29 October 1978. 'Word for Living' was recorded during the morning service and transmitted on Sunday 5 November. 'Sunday Half-Hour' (community hymn singing) was recorded after the close of the evening service, and transmitted on Sunday 19 November, not only in Great Britain but also on the World Service. Letters of appreciation poured in from around the globe, which were both touching and humbling. The morning service on Sunday 1 February 1981 was recorded for transmission, in an edited form, on the following Sunday.

Derek Prime took 'Late Call' on Scottish television in June 1981, as the Heralds had done in 1964 and the writer in 1977. Radio Forth (the local station) asked permission to broadcast a Christmas Watchnight service live from the Chapel on 24 December 1982. It was well supported, but only because of the broadcast; no other Christmas Watchnight services were held at that time, because there was no demand for them. After that, there were no further media invitations to the Chapel or its leaders until Peter Grainger was asked to give four 14-minute talks, with recorded hymn singing, on BBC Scotland's 'New Every Morning' in 1999. BBC Television's policy was to film 'Songs of Praise' only if the congregation was drawn from all local churches, and the Chapel was never asked to be host.

## 1978 – Generosity rewarded

'We have the technology' was a buzzword of the 1970s, but the quality of the transmission from the Chapel to Beulah Home (Sunday services, Monday prayer meeting and Thursday Bible School) deteriorated markedly in the later 1970s. The engineers were perplexed. When a member of the Chapel, who was housebound in Edinburgh, asked whether a landline could be provided to her home at her expense, the deacons were initially reluctant. One of their concerns was that if others made similar requests, with which the system could not cope, this member should not have a benefit not available to all – consistent with the emphasis throughout this ministry of no favouritism. When the applicant agreed to give up the link, if any such problem arose, the deacons provided the facility. Their generosity was rewarded in an unexpected way; when the Post Office engineers installed the second line, they found and rectified the fault in the one to Beulah.

### 1978 – Time of Sunday School

The Youth Council found, toward the end of the 1970s, that 3 p.m. was increasingly unpopular for the Chapel's Sunday School. In 1978, they suggested 9.30 a.m., but the elders were against that for two reasons. If scholars and staff stayed for the morning service (as was expected), three hours of meetings, with just a brief break before the public service, was too much. Secondly, 'it was good for the children to have something spiritually profitable to capture their attention on Sunday afternoons'. To meet the concern of parents who lived out of town, and who had to get the family home for a meal and back again for 3 p.m., lunch facilities were provided on the premises (below). It was another seven years before the church reverted to 12.30 p.m. for the Sunday School, as explained in Chapter 50.

### 1978 – Sabbatical leave

Some of the items recorded here, as innovations in the Chapel in the 1970s, are now so familiar that present readers may wonder why they are even mentioned. They were, however, novel, perhaps even avant-garde, for their time. Derek Prime was completely taken aback when the elders suggested a period of sabbatical leave. Nowadays it is assumed that a minister will be granted a period of study leave every seven years or so, but it was almost unknown in Baptist churches then. The elders proposed that he should have six months away from pastoral duties, between November 1978 and May 1979. Immediately after the two radio programmes just mentioned, he began his first sabbatical from the Chapel. For the first part, he worked in Westminster College, Cambridge and for the remainder of the time he studied the Scriptures at home, free from distraction. He prepared for his future ministry in the Chapel and resumed writing Christian books, which had had to be put to one side during his first nine years in Edinburgh.

### 1978 – Associate pastor

Concerned at the many responsibilities that the Chapel loaded onto its pastor, the office-bearers recommended, in the spring of 1978, that an older man should be appointed, as well as the younger assistant, particularly to help with pastoral matters. His time would be spent in caring rather than in preaching or evangelism and, unlike the younger man, the associate would not necessarily move on after two or three years. The idea was approved in principle, and it was left to Mr Prime to find someone with whom he could work on this basis.

It was three years before there was a meeting of minds. A Chapel member with 30 years' service in Edinburgh City Police, George Smith, felt 'called' in the spring of 1981 to some form of Christian service. He had prepared himself by gaining the Certificate of Religious Knowledge from the University of London and the degree of Bachelor of Arts from the Open University. To give him experience of pastoral work, Derek Prime invited him to join the Chapel team on an honorary basis through the summer of that year. He proved so helpful, both in visitation and in pastoral administration, that he was offered a full-time salaried position from January 1982; he worked as an integral part of the team until November of that year, when he and his wife became wardens at the Kilravock Christian Centre near Inverness. His 18 months on the team had demonstrated the need for a replacement, to help with pastoral care in the Chapel. How his successor, Jim Neilson, joined the team, will be taken up in Chapter 49.

### 1979 – Young Wives Group

This group was started in 1979, to complement the work of the Women's Morning Fellowship. It was primarily for mothers whose children were not yet in senior school, but anyone who considered herself young (defined as 20-40), whether married or single, was welcome. The wife of the assistant pastor was the leader; its aims were to provide fellowship, to encourage mutual care and to give opportunities for witness to friends. It met on the third Tuesday evening of the month, for talks, demonstrations, crafts, missionary evenings, etc. in the winter, and walks and barbecues in the summer, with 50-60 involved.

The name was changed in 1990 to Young Women's Group, and, when there was no longer an assistant minister, the constitution was amended so that the leader could be any full member of the church with appropriate experience. At the end of the vacancy, in 1992, 15-20 were still meeting regularly, one Tuesday evening a month, and the programme continued to cover a wide range of family and social interests.

## 1979 – Partners in Prayer

When two long-standing members of the Chapel retired to the north of Scotland in May 1979, they sought both to join the local Baptist church and also to retain their membership (or at least some formal relationship) with the Chapel. This led to setting up the Partners in Prayer scheme, to send information to 'past members of the Chapel who are now living elsewhere and in membership with another local church'. It minimized the perennial problem of members moving away from Edinburgh and not joining a local evangelical church because they wanted to retain some links with the Chapel – by staying in membership. Under the Partners in Prayer scheme, they received: (1) all documentation posted to Chapel members, (2) the *Record* and (3) an annual (duplicated) letter from the pastor. They were asked every year whether they wished to remain on the list. The response was so favourable that two Chapel members had to be appointed to administer the scheme. It lasted in this form until the end of December 1993; it was then agreed to send the *Record* only.

## 1979 – Coffee after the morning service

Group 35 continued to put forward enterprising ideas (chapter 45). In March 1979, they suggested serving coffee in the lower hall after the Sunday morning service in June, and again during the Edinburgh International Festival in August. They not only chatted to strangers on the premises, but some also prepared a spare place or two at their own lunch tables, and offered hospitality to visitors. This was so successful that it was taken over as a function of the whole church for July and August 1980. To make sure that someone spoke to visitors, after they had been invited from the pulpit to meet the congregation in the hall, the pastoral groups in rotation provided 20 members every week, to look out for strangers and to make them feel welcome. In 1981, Group 35 served light refreshments on the premises for nine weeks between July and September.

## 1979 – Group 45

Group 35 was so successful in integrating people between 25 and 45 into the life of the church, that when the original leaders reached the age of 45, they wanted to provide an equivalent facility for their peers (over 45). There was some opposition to creating yet another group ('sectionalising the congregation', 'potentially divisive', 'cliquey', etc.), and the writer (then aged 46) is amused, now, to see how

passionately he put forward three reasons for it in the March 1979 *Record*: (1) the original members should move on and make way for new blood, (2) some folk at the top end of the original age-range had never come, and so another attempt should be made to involve them, and (3) numbers were now too large to meet comfortably in a private home on Sunday evening – 'older members are increasingly reluctant to squat on what floor space is available' – so, create a second group.

With the reluctant approval of the elders, 30 members launched Group 45 in May 1979. Like Group 35, it had no formal membership, but welcomed everyone of 45 and upward; like Group 35, it met in a home after church, on the second Sunday of the month and had regular summer outings. It took over responsibility for a conducting a service in ward 34 of Edinburgh Royal Infirmary from 4.15-4.45 p.m. on the first Sunday of the month, and did so until 1994.

*Groups 35 and 45 held open house after the evening service on the second Sunday of the month. The objectives were to foster fellowship within the group and to integrate persons within the age group into the life and work of the church. In these 1983 photographs, Group 35 is on the left and Group 45 on the right.*

## 1979 – The new Group 35

The leadership of the reconstituted Group 35 brought fresh imagination and enthusiasm to their remit; their open house on the second Sunday of the month attracted 50-60. On the last Saturday of the month, they had a games activity, trying to bring outsiders into Christian fellowship. The group regularly visited Beulah Home, and remained responsible for an Infirmary ward service. They redecorated the Chapel's flat in Falcon Court, arranged an annual senior members' carol service, and (alternately with Group 45) looked after the catering on summer Sunday mornings and after the Thursday Bible School. Weekends away for the Edinburgh September holiday were very popular.

Going on from their 'coffee after Sunday morning' duty, Group 35 offered to provide lunch in the Chapel after every morning service when Sunday School was in session, so parents and children could stay in town. They were concerned for single people, and especially for lonely overseas students, so they initiated Bible studies and prayer groups, about issues particularly affecting them. They encouraged YPM leavers to move into Group 35; they trained Sunday School teachers, and promoted involvement in social activity. Their overall objective was to bring everyone within their age range into the mainstream of church life. In 1992, they felt that the name Group 2545 (Two Five Four Five) better described their constituency, that is people between the ages of 25 and 45, and it became their formal title.

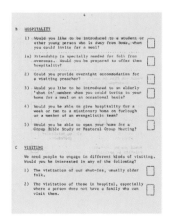

*To encourage members to become involved in the life of the Chapel, a questionnaire was distributed in booklet form, inviting everyone to indicate where they could be of service – pastoral care, hospitality, visiting, speaking and teaching, evangelism, music, administration, etc. In total, one hundred choices were available. At least one person volunteered for every category.*

## 1979 – Opportunities for Service

In October 1979, Derek Prime exhorted every member to take up some new avenue of service within the Chapel; he produced a booklet (popularly called 'The Green Form', from the colour of its cover), for members to identify their

particular gifts. It invited people to support one or more of a hundred areas in church life. By far the most popular, with nearly one hundred offers, was to provide hospitality for a pastoral group or a Bible study group. Baking for church functions was next highest on the list. The booklet was reprinted in September 1982, and nearly three hundred of the second edition were completed and returned. Word processors (the precursor of personal computers) had just become available, so the offers were analysed and lists made available to the elders and to the pastoral team. The booklet filled an important role in the life of the Chapel for nearly 15 years, until the introduction of fellowship groups in 1993.

## 1979 – The year of weddings

Looking back over 1979, Derek Prime counted 16 young couples, whom he had married in the Chapel, and three more couples who had been married in the bride's home church. He called it the year of weddings, and noted that another 11 couples had announced their engagement during the year. He used this as an opportunity to write a lengthy article in the *Record* on 'What constitutes a Christian home?'

*Until Rose Street was pedestrianized in 1990, bride and groom had to be photographed on the narrow (cracked) pavement outside the Chapel, with cars and lorries rumbling by. Lesley Balfour married Graeme Tait in July 1982.*

## 1980 – Pastoral group review

Some of the elders' groups, held three times a year in homes (the same night for everyone, to maximize publicity) were well supported, but others were not. Derek Prime wrote in December 1979:

*These pastoral group prayer meetings have great value in enabling members in their geographical area of the city to get to know each other, and also to pray for one another in a more personal way than is appropriate or possible in the church prayer meeting. But the objective is defeated if we do not make full use of these opportunities.*

2 *Record*, December 1979, p. 3.

There was a sufficiently encouraging response for the elders to increase the groups to four a year, on the last Monday of February, May, August and November 1980. Monday, normally reserved for the congregational prayer meeting, was chosen to avoid yet another meeting. Derek Prime reminded the elders: 'refreshments should be confined to tea and biscuits, to avoid unfair comparison with other groups.' The pastoral groups then settled down, and no further radical changes were needed.

## 1980 – Closed-circuit television

As mentioned in Chapter 42, the Chapel experimented with CCTV in 1962; equipment was improving all the time, and also becoming cheaper, so the deacons decided to wait. They waited for 18 years, and it was early 1980 before they installed two screens in the lower hall and one in the crèche. They were monochrome only; increasing the lighting in the sanctuary, necessary for colour, would have doubled the cost and, it was believed at the time, given the pulpit a theatrical appearance, incompatible with an atmosphere of worship. However, the £3,500 package included equipment to record the services on videotape, and for the pastor to make coloured videotapes in a separate room upstairs, with stronger lighting, for the benefit of shut-in members.

As with the new building at Wester Hailes and the replacement for the organ, Derek Prime invited the congregation to vote with their chequebooks; installation was dependent on sufficient being given to cover the cost. Promises on tear-off slips, collected on Sundays 3 and 10 August 1980, were enough for the project to proceed. One camera was mounted above the north-east door in the gallery, remotely controlled from a room in the southwest corner of the gallery; it swivelled during the singing of hymns to capture the congregation, and focused on the floral display during prayers. Transmission began early in 1981.

```
         SUNDAY, 12th OCTOBER 1980
           MORNING WORSHIP at 11.00 a.m.

Introit
The Word: 2 Corinthians 5:14,15
Paraphrase 48:5-9 The Saviour dy'd
Prayer
Scripture Reading: Romans 6:1-18 read by
                Mr. Osamu Nakahashi
Children's Address
Children's Hymn No. 378 Who is on the Lord's side
(Young children 2½-5 years old leave for the
   Nursery Department, Top Hall)
Intimations and Offering
Dedication of Offering
Message in Song
Prayer
Hymn No. 51 Sovereign grace o'er sin abounding
   Message: The Pastor
   Subject: STUDIES IN 1 PETER
            Living for God (4:1,2)
Hymn No. 487 Jesus, Master, whose I am
Benediction

           EVENING SERVICE at 6.30 p.m.
       (preceded by community hymn-singing)

Hymn No. 86 Jesus, stand among us
Prayer
Hymn No. 110 All hail the power of Jesus name
Scripture Reading: Job 1:13-2:10
Hymn No. 453 Dear Lord, for all in pain
Intimations and Offering
Dedication of Offering
Message in Song
Prayer
Hymn No. 330 How firm a foundation
   Message: QUESTIONS JOB ASKED: Shall we
            accept good from God, and not
            trouble?
Hymn No. 32 My God, I thank Thee
Benediction


              CALENDAR FOR WEEK

SUN:  3.00 p.m. Sunday School & Bible Class
      3.00 p.m. The Rock Mission
      4.15 to   Missionary Band with
      4.45 p.m. Mrs. Charlotte Davis
      4.30 for  Tea in the Top Hall for all
      4.45 p.m. overseas friends
      4.30 p.m. Ladies Fellowship
      5.30 p.m. Prayer Meeting
YPM and GROUP 35 Joint fellowship evening at Bible
House, Hampton Terr. Come along at 8.45 p.m. for an
informal exchange of news and views.
GROUP 45 open house at Mr. & Mrs. R. Armstrong
2 March Grove. Speaker Ian Leitch subject: 'The
Heralds Trust' Anyone requiring transport to and/or
from should contact stewards on duty in vestibule.
MON:  7.30 p.m. City Centre Visitation. Meet in the
                large committee room
      8.00 p.m. Congregational Prayer Meeting
TUE:  7.00 p.m. Women's Missionary Auxiliary
                Speaker: Miss Isabel Wood
      2.30 p.m. Women's Prayer Meeting
WED:  7.00 p.m. Discipleship Class
                No official YPM this week. See
                announcement re Scottish Evangelistic
                council mtg. with Rev. George Duncan.
THU: 10.00 a.m. Women's Morning Fellowship
                Rev. Alistair Ross
                Coffee-Creche
      8.00 p.m. Bible School
                Speaker - The Pastor
                Subject - Studies in the Life of
                Elijah. Coffee served afterwards.
FRI:  6.00 p.m. Cubs
      7.30 p.m. Guides and Scouts
      7.30 p.m. Rangers - Chinese Cooking. Meet large
                Committee Room
      7.30 p.m. Venture Scouts - Games evening Lower
                Hall
      8.00 p.m. Choir Practice
```

*This bulletin for the second week in October 1980 set out the details of the two Sunday services and the activities during the week to follow.*

393

## 1980 – The missionary family

In 1980, 23 Chapel members were overseas as missionaries, two in Brazil, one in Indonesia, three in the Philippines, two in Hong Kong, two in Thailand, two in India, two in Nepal, one in each of South Africa, Kenya, Nigeria, Ivory Coast and Central African Republic, one in each of Afghanistan, Yemen and Israel and one in Austria. Nine were engaged in evangelism or church planting, eight in medical work and six in teaching or literature distribution. Although the Chapel also encouraged members to take paid secular employment in developing countries, where they could have Christian influence, in 1980 all 23 were with missionary societies.

The Chapel tried annually to increase its support for its missionary members. In 1980, £250 per person was sent every quarter to their society, but the aim was to raise this to £300. That this was achieved by 1982 is remarkable because of two factors. Five new missionaries were commissioned in 1980, so just to maintain a quarterly disbursement of £250 required a 17 per cent increase in giving. To raise it to £300 needed a 40 per cent increase, but the congregation responded magnificently. Secondly, when faith missions, which had previously not made known the support needs of their missionaries, began to ask new candidates to gather promises from sponsors, some Chapel members sent that part of their missionary offering directly to the individual, and not through the Chapel's missionary fund, because it was distributed equally among all the missionaries.

*The Chapel's contribution to the support of its missionary members in 1979-83. When the treasurer achieved his aim of sending £300 a quarter to every missionary in 1982, he said: 'Well done – now let's make it £350', and this was achieved in 1983.*

Ian Finlayson, the convener of the Chapel's missionary committee, was invited to contribute a chapter to a book, published by the Evangelical Missionary Alliance in 1985, entitled *Ten Sending Churches*. It described how ten different churches, in all parts of Great Britain, had caught and responded to the vision for mission. Rather than précis the chapter here, it is reproduced in full on the CD, under *Ten Sending Churches*.

## 1980 – Administration

Administration is like the digestive system – when it works, you take it for granted; when it goes wrong, you think about little else. The cameos in this chapter would not be complete without mention of the dedication of dozens of lay members of the congregation. On Sunday morning, every Sunday for 52 weeks in the year, bulletins and copies of the *Record* were handed out, both prepared entirely by volunteers, visitors were welcomed and shown to their seats, prayer meetings were led, the choir performed, the crèche was staffed, and coffee was served in the lower hall. Two hours later, a new group of volunteers prepared the building for the Sunday School. The morning activities (except crèche and coffee) were repeated every Sunday evening, The congregation took this for granted, because it went so smoothly, but those involved were regularly reminded, by reference to Acts 6:3-6 (appointment of the first deacons), that good administration is a spiritual gift.

## 1980 – Year-end

Another new idea for 1980 was an open-air carol service in Rose Street, on 19 December. It was well received and four hundred invitations were given out for the Chapel's Christmas services. During 1980, there were 5 baptismal services, with 32 baptized; 15 Chapel members were married, 15 babies were born and there were 12 dedications; the membership increased by 20, to 820. It had been a busy year.

Additional information on the following topics, mentioned in this chapter, is available on the CD.

Alex Hardie
Derek Prime's publications
Divorce
Marriage
Opportunities for Service
Temperance – Commonwealth Games, 1970
*Ten Sending Churches*
Young Wives Group

# Chapter 49
# The early 1980s (1981–1984)

## Auxiliary activities

### 1981 – Link with elders

It seems fairly obvious, looking back, to link every church auxiliary with an elder, who would take a prayerful interest in its work and liase on its behalf with the other office-bearers. It was, however, only when Derek Prime suggested this in January 1981, as an extension of the elders' pastoral care, that such links were made. The list is worth reproducing, as anyone familiar with the Chapel now will recognize some names, more than a quarter of a century later:

| Auxiliary | Leader | Elder |
|---|---|---|
| Bible Class | Graham Baker | George Nash |
| Brownies | Judi Wilson | Hans Clausen |
| Choir | Jim Monihan | Jim Monihan |
| Cubs | Brian Wilson | Angus Ferguson |
| Folkus | Barry Sprott | Robert Armstrong |
| Group 35 | David Clement | Angus Ferguson |
| Group 45 | Malcolm Fisher | Ian Balfour |
| Guides | Margaret Michie | John Gordon |
| Ladies' Sunday Fellowship | Kate Young | Douglas Macnair |
| Overseas Student Fellowship | Sheila Masterton | Norman Hunt |
| Rangers | Jenny Liddell | Alan Wilson |
| Rock Mission | Donald Cormack | Jim McCall |
| Scouts | Norman Wilson | Colin Simpson |
| Student Work | Kenneth Armstrong | Norman Hunt |
| Sunday School – Juniors | Bill Dowall | Charles Dick |
| Sunday School – Primary | Angela Inchley | Charles Dick |
| Venture Scouts | Robert Naysmith | Robin White |
| Women's Missionary Auxiliary | Bessie Barnie | John Holburn |
| Women's Morning Fellowship | Betty Prime | Robert Hadden |
| Women's Prayer Meeting | Diana Guthrie | David Wallace |
| YPM | Jimmy Hughes | Alex Cameron |
| Young Wives Group | Margaret Armstrong | Russ Murray |

The Guides, whose last reunion was in 1966 (Chapter 44), celebrated the jubilee of their foundation in 1931 by 130 gathering in the lower hall on Saturday 21 February 1981, some having come from Alness and others from London.

### 1981 – Bible Class

The first of the auxiliaries listed above, the Bible Class, met at the front of the sanctuary on Sunday afternoon from 3-4 p.m., with over 50, aged 12-17, on the roll. They stayed together for the first half-hour, for singing and general topics, and then broke into eight groups for Bible study with their teachers. The class project was to collect halfpenny coins for Bible societies or youth outreach; since there were 240 pennies in a pound sterling (old money), and since donations topped £100 every session, the leaders had to count and bank about fifty thousand halfpennies a year.

*Opening devotions at the Bible Class, which met at the front of the church on Sunday afternoon. It was not an ideal location for a group of 50, but everywhere else in the building was occupied with Sunday School activities.*

### 1981 – Overseas Student Fellowship

When Sheila Masterton retired from missionary service in Calcutta in 1978, she started an informal meeting on Saturday evening, every six weeks, for young people from overseas. It was an opportunity to get to know one another over a meal, to have games, sometimes a film, a barbecue in the summer and carol singing at Christmas. The evening ended with an epilogue; even those who were not Christians appreciated the friendship and some of them came to the Chapel regularly on Sunday.

In 1981, the group was formally recognized as the Overseas Student Fellowship, meeting on the last Saturday of every month, indoors during the winter and outdoors in summer. Derek Prime, with his usual pastoral concern that no Chapel activity should be exclusive, suggested it should be open to anyone wishing to meet overseas folk. It provided a valuable forum for integration into the Chapel, as well as for evangelism and fellowship. In 1988, it was tactfully renamed the International Fellowship; 23 countries were represented, and by 1993 this had grown to 41.

During the vacancy of 1987-92 – or perhaps because of it – numbers continued to grow, with a Bible study every Friday evening in Sheila's home and imaginative programmes once a month on Saturday throughout the year. Every Tuesday morning, the wives of overseas students met for Bible study. A weekend away to a youth hostel was arranged in April 1993, attended by 60; it was a great success and became an annual event. Numbers at the monthly gatherings outgrew even the largest private home available, so the Saturday evening meeting was moved to the Chapel lounge (described below), and attracted up to 150 students from around the world, rising to two hundred by 1993.

### 1981 – Tape library
In the spring of 1981, Charlotte Recordings' tape library, containing over six hundred master tapes of Sunday services and Bible School lectures, was given a new home in the former organ loft at the southwest corner of the gallery. The library was open after both Sunday services and copies, either on reel or on cassette, were lent free of charge; in addition, copies were posted all over the world. When some shut-in elderly members found that a full service, including a 30-minute sermon, was too much for their concentration, tapes were run off with one or two hymns, a Scripture reading and a short message, recorded specially for them by Derek Prime, and a prayer.

*The library of master tapes, located off the southwest gallery of the church, from which Henry Kaminski, in the photographs, distributed copies worldwide. The master tapes are in the Chapel archives.*

### 1981 – Women's Missionary Auxiliary
The Women's Missionary Auxiliary met weekly from 7-9 p.m. on Tuesday evening, knitting and sewing for missionaries and listening, while they worked, to a missionary speaker or to letters from missionaries being read; every evening closed with family worship. Once a year, the goods were on display for the rest of the church, prior to despatch to the mission field.

*The Women's Missionary Auxiliary in 1982. The scene is typical of the work that different generations carried on, continuously from 1916 to 1991.*

## A lounge at street level

### Problems with the lower hall
When the uniformed organisations met on Friday evening, they were hampered by lack of space; the deacons seriously considered purchasing additional property – but where? One possibility was a former Church of Scotland hostel at 38 Greenhill Gardens, which would have provided much-needed accommodation for overseas students as well as a meeting-place for Chapel auxiliaries. Another was the former Chalmers-Lauriston church and hall at 77 Lauriston Place, Tollcross – still vacant and now (2007) sadly derelict. There was, however, concern at running Chapel activities so far away from the Chapel; the auxiliaries likely to be evicted (as they put it) were particularly concerned. The deacons redoubled their efforts to purchase or rent something in the vicinity of Rose Street; the answer turned out to be even nearer than they had hoped (below).

*The Brownies and the Cub Scouts were among the organisations hampered by lack of space on Friday evening, until the lounge was built.*

There was also increasing pressure to separate the multi-purpose functions of the lower hall. When church members invited visitors for coffee after the Sunday service, they wanted to take them into an attractively furnished venue, but the youth organisations needed facilities for lively indoor games during the week; these two uses were incompatible with one hall. Furthermore, the acoustics in the lower hall were not satisfactory for the closed-circuit television overflow on Sunday morning (Chapter 48).

## Concept of a lounge

Accordingly, Derek Prime contacted a London architect, who specialized in church design. He suggested inserting a new floor (the present lounge) at street level. As well as giving more space, it would overcome two psychological disadvantages (as he expressed it) of the present building. One was the need to go up stairs to the sanctuary or down stairs to the lower hall, before coming to any seating accommodation – not very welcoming for visitors and quite unsuitable for invalids. Secondly, while people were encouraged from the pulpit to stay for refreshments after the service, they had to walk past the front door on their way to the lower hall; they were as likely to walk out, when they came to the door, as they were to go on downstairs.

The architect's proposal was brought to a members' meeting in August 1981. He was confident that the planning requirement of .45 square metre per person could be met, and still provide 280 chairs in the new lounge. The concept was so novel that numerous questions were asked, about headroom, acoustics, ventilation, cost and (particularly contentious) the need to drop the centre section of the floor in the lower hall by 21 inches, with three steps. There was some fairly vocal opposition to the whole scheme; the members asked for time to think about it, and three hundred reconvened a fortnight later.

On the day when the decision was to be made (Monday 14 September 1981), the Chapel was open for prayer from 7 a.m. through until 5 p.m., with a pause every half-hour for people to come and go. A good number attended throughout the day, with an office-bearer leading the sessions and everyone seeking guidance for the decision to be made that evening. The deacons, recognising the enormity of the project, recommended that it should proceed only with the approval 'of at least 75 per cent of those present and voting'; the Pastor wished to make it clear, therefore, that even if 74 per cent were in favour, the motion would fall.' After many questions were asked and answered, 298 votes were cast, 227 for the motion and 71 against – 76 per cent in favour.

## Financing the project

Sunday 15 November 1981 was designated as gift day; £149,500 was required for the building work and a further sum for the furnishings. Another day of prayer was held on Saturday 14 November, from 8 a.m. to 4 p.m. Six hundred people contributed to a special offering after the morning service on the Sunday, £60,000 in cash and a further £83,000 in promises (pledge card below). When other donations of £10,000 came in during the week, the project was viable.

It is not often that the intimations during a church service are interrupted by the congregation singing the doxology, but when the writer announced at the evening service exactly a year later, on Sunday 14 November 1982, that redeemed promises had that day brought the total in hand to £153,625, the pastor invited the congregation to stand and to respond in this way.

*Many worshippers regularly chatted outside the front door after Sunday services, but the absence of hall accommodation, during the building work, meant that more than usual had to use Rose Street to catch up with their friends' news.*

Work had commenced on 9 August 1982, with a target completion date for the end of February 1983, but it was Saturday 7 May before the lounge was ready for occupation.

## 1982 – Weeknights without the lower hall

While the lounge was being constructed, the lower hall was not accessible, so rooms were rented for the auxiliaries from the YWCA and St Cuthbert's church. The elders arranged two sessions in the Chapel, for six consecutive Thursday evenings in the autumn of 1982. One group, meeting in the top hall to study evangelism, attracted 60 people; the other, conducted by the pastor in the sanctuary, studied the life of Samson and was attended by between 70 and 100. In addition, ten Bible study groups met in homes around the city. In all, 130 chose these home meetings, and four of the ten groups wanted to continue; all expressed the wish to repeat the experiment in the spring of 1983.

*David Hunt conducting a Monday evening prayer meeting in the sanctuary in the Chapel in the spring of 1983, while reconstruction of the lower hall was under way.*

Derek Prime was, as ever, anxious for the whole congregation to meet together from time to time, in case the small groups became cliques. He established a pattern in the spring of 1983, which endured, with variations, for the rest of his pastorate. Every term (January, April and October) started with three Thursday congregational gatherings, followed by six Thursdays when there was a choice of home groups or a central study. The combined sessions included some popular Bible workshops. A hundred or more gathered in the Chapel and suggested topics they would like to explore. Derek Prime led a discussion on them, there and then, based on the Scriptures; it was possible to deal with subjects that would have been inappropriate at Sunday services.

CHARLOTTE BAPTIST CHAPEL
RECONSTRUCTION OF THE LOWER HALL

I propose to give by 31st December, 1982 a total sum of £ _____ to the project.

EITHER I enclose £ _____ now and will give the remainder by 31st December, 1982.

OR I wish the Treasurer to send me the explanatory letter and necessary papers regarding the "loan and waiver" covenant scheme.
(Mr, Mrs, Miss)

NAME .......................................

ADDRESS ...................................
.............................................

SIGNED ....................................

DATE ......................................

THIS INFORMATION IS CONFIDENTIAL TO THE CHURCH TREASURER AND HIS ASSISTANT ONLY.

*1*

*2*

*3*

*4*

*5*

The members of

CHARLOTTE BAPTIST CHAPEL

warmly invite you to the

DEDICATION and OPENING

of the

NEW LOUNGE AND LOWER HALL

on

Saturday, 7th May 1983

at

2.30 p.m.

The new premises will be open for viewing after the Service of Thanksgiving and Dedication, and tea will be served.

*6*

*(1) The pledge to meet the cost of the alteration. (2) Lowering the floor by three steps, to provide headroom in the new lower hall. (3) Inserting the mezzanine – the floor of the lounge and the ceiling of the lower hall. (4) The new lounge, before the chairs were delivered. (5) The new lower hall. There is now one step less, as the floor had to be raised in 1992 for the installation of a pump to take away water ingress. (6) The opening service. (7) The Week of Special Events that followed.*

We would like to invite you to join us in a

**Week of Special Events**

to mark the opening of our **NEW LOUNGE AND LOWER HALL**

**Charlotte Baptist Chapel, Edinburgh**

*7*

## 1983 – Outreach through the lounge

In the summer of 1983, the new lounge was turned into an outreach café between 10 a.m. and noon on Saturday morning. Christian music was played in the background and visitors were impressed with the warm welcome, the décor, the food (especially the modest prices), the free literature and the books on sale. The café was held throughout the summer, until the last Saturday of the Edinburgh International Festival.

Creation of the lounge also prompted the Chapel to arrange a series of six lunch-hour meetings in the autumn of 1983. It was open for snack lunches from 12 noon to 2 p.m., and a fifteen-minute talk was given twice, at 12.35 and again at 1.05. The talks were aimed at people who worked in the city centre, with a devotional content for Christians and a challenge for those who were not. About 20 came each week, and as half of them were not Chapel members, the venture was felt worthwhile. There was not, however, sufficient support to repeat the series.

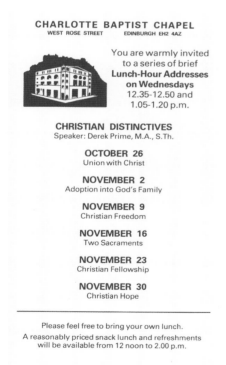

*The attractive new lounge prompted the Chapel to arrange lunch-hour meetings in the autumn of 1983.*

Coffee and tea, which had been served to visitors in the lower hall after the Sunday morning service during the summer

months before the reconstruction took place, was now available in the lounge every Sunday. The bulletin reminded the pastoral groups which of them was on smiling duty (welcoming) that Sunday, with the specific aim of looking out for strangers.

At Christmas 1984, the young people held an open day in the lounge on Saturday 21 December, from 10 a.m. to 5 p.m. They sang carols in Rose Street, with police permission, and invited shoppers to coffee and mince pies in the lounge, where they gave a short Christmas message every half hour. The visitors' book recorded 105 non-Chapel people, who were encouraged to come back on Sunday. The YPM repeated the outreach on the following two Christmases, and 90 signed in as visitors in both 1985 and 1986. They also held outreach cafés on Saturday evening once a month, hoping to bring in young people who were wandering aimlessly along Rose Street.

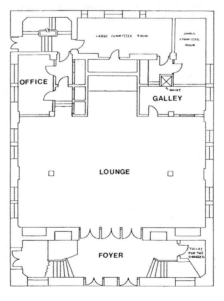

*The ground floor in this 1983 plan was altered in two ways in 2005 – the galley was expanded into a full kitchen and the office was divided into two.*

## 1983 – Babies, toddlers and nurseries

During the early 1980s, there was one apparently insoluble problem every Sunday morning; work on the new lounge turned it temporarily into two insoluble problems, but completion of the lounge solved both. The first was the double occupancy of the large committee room, as the plan above describes it. The choir met for a final rehearsal, leaving at 10.50 a.m. to take their places in the church. The aunties who ran the crèche wanted in by 10.30 a.m., so that children would settle with toys and books as they arrived; children kept waiting on the stair became fractious and parent-demanding. The choir were asked to practice in the top hall, but protested that some were unable to climb that far; the deacons were still trying to find a solution to this problem when the construction of the lounge threw up an even bigger one.

The CCTV overflow from the sanctuary to the lower hall was moved to the top hall for the nine months of building work, displacing the nursery for two-and-a-half to five-year-olds. Parents and children, who had settled into the routine of keeping this age group in church for 20 minutes and then going upstairs in the top hall for an hour, were appalled. Children of this age could be kept reasonably quiet for 20 minutes in church, in the knowledge that they could unwind in the less formal atmosphere of the nursery. To require them to stay in church for an hour and 20 minutes would, the parents said, make impossible demands on them, and would be distracting for the congregation round about. They said they would keep their children at home until the alterations were done.

Completion of the lounge in May 1983 solved both problems. The CCTV was shown there, the choir had unlimited use of the committee room, a new category of 'under 3s' got exclusive use of the lower hall from 10.30 a.m. and the nursery (renamed the Beginners' Sunday School, for ages three to five), had the top hall to themselves. They left the main service after the children's talk; because of their isolation at the top of the building, Youth Council arranged one adult for every four children, in case of fire. That threw up another concern – the number of grown-ups who had to miss the sermon, but tapes of it were readily available for them.

*When the alterations were complete, a Beginners' Sunday School was created for ages three to five; they left the sanctuary after the children's talk, about 20 minutes into the service; children over that age were expected to stay with their parents through the service.*

## Experiments and more experiments

### 1982 – Ingliston Sunday Market

In 1982, the biggest Sunday market in Scotland was held at Ingliston, beside Edinburgh airport, from 10 a.m. to 4 p.m.; it attracted thousands of people every week, from all over the country. The Chapel obtained permission to hold an open-air service in the grounds for an hour on Sunday afternoon, from 1-2 p.m. throughout the year, with singing, speaking and giving out gospel literature, continuing longer if interest was shown. Although permission was for all year round, services were held only in the summer months of 1982 and 1983. A proposal to set up a bookstall at the market was not approved – selling on the Lord's Day could be a reflection on the name of the church; without it, the enterprise was deemed not to be worthwhile, and it was not repeated in 1984.

*In 1982, the Evangelical Times obtained permission to take photographs during the morning service, for an article. The pulpit and pews were still covered in the original dark paint; it was 1989 before they were scraped back to the natural wood.*

### 1982 – Experiments at the Mound

The Chapel's Wednesday evening open-air meeting at the Mound was increasingly poorly supported in the early 1980s, despite every encouragement – and occasional chastisement – from the evangelistic committee. In 1982, the meeting was switched to Thursday for three reasons. One was that late night shopping was catching on, and Princes Street was much busier on Thursday than on other weeknights; secondly, Chapel members had a long tradition of supporting the Bible School on Thursday evening, and were more likely to keep coming on Thursday when the school stopped for the summer; thirdly, it did not conflict with the YPM on Wednesday evening. There were not many cities where it was still possible to have an effective open-air evangelistic outreach right in the middle of the city, but until the Mound was turned over for car parking, it was an ideal place to draw crowds. To catch shoppers, the time was advanced to 7.30 p.m., in place of the traditional eight o'clock. The meetings in 1982 were satisfactory, but with poor support from office-bearers and the membership.

## 1983 – Experiments with the choir
Following the resignation of the choirmaster in October 1982, the elders hoped that the choir would continue on traditional lines, singing an introit as the minister entered the pulpit, an anthem after the offering and a suitable requiem (morning) and vesper (evening) to conclude the service. However, that required a leader, so the choir disbanded, with a view to re-forming in due course. In the meantime, the elders arranged for four *ad hoc* groups to lead the praise, and, as they gained confidence, to sing an introit in the morning and a choir-piece at night:

(a) YPM on the first Sunday in the month,
(b) Group 35 on the second Sunday,
(c) Group 45 on the third Sunday,
(d) a praise group, led by former choir members,
    on the fourth (and fifth) Sunday.

The choir re-formed in October 1984, under the leadership of the Chapel deaconess, Jessie Bell. It was not ideal for her to be in the choir stalls, as normally the deaconess mingled with the congregation before and after the services, but she carried on until Donald Cameron was appointed in 1988, with the title of music convener. He recruited new members, and they sang every second Sunday. With tuition available in schools, more and more young people were becoming proficient on a variety of musical instruments. There was a scratch orchestra of fifteen, six strings, five woodwinds and four brass, at the farewell service for Derek Prime in October 1987 (Chapter 50), but Donald held over changing the style of worship until the new pastor was in post. When that happened, in 1992, the orchestra led the congregational singing on four Sundays in the year, the choir sang on twelve, with soloists, groups or the YPM choir on the other Sundays.

## 1984 – Combined mid-week meetings
In the autumn of 1984, the (Monday) prayer meeting was held after the Bible School on Thursday, so that conscientious people would not be away from home for two evenings in the week. Although well supported, the experiment was not continued after a month, because there was no significant increase in numbers over a normal Thursday Bible School, and the combined meeting did not attract the young married couples who had asked for it. Some felt that the study had to be rushed, in order to finish in time for the prayer, but the break for refreshments between the two sessions was a valuable opportunity for fellowship.

The remainder of the autumn term in 1984 was given over to seven Bible study groups, six in homes, on Philippians, and one in the Chapel lounge, on the life of Samuel. When the elders felt that the whole church should focus on one particular subject (for example, lessons from the book of Acts), all the groups followed the same syllabus for all ten weeks of the term.

Pastoral groups – all members were expected to attend – continued to meet three times a year, for fellowship, information, prayer and a Scripture reading by the leader, but not for Bible study. Calls by some groups to meet more often were resisted by the elders on two grounds; one, that the *raison d'etre* of the groups was for the whole church to meet around the city on the same night, and secondly, that more meetings would detract from the Monday prayer meeting and the Thursday Bible School.

## Pastoral matters

### 1982 – Concern for the unemployed
In 1982, a number of Chapel members were unemployed. One of the deacons set up a register, so that any Chapel member looking for staff could consult it. The same deacon offered to work with the government's Manpower Services Commission, which met the full wages of unemployed people prepared to work on an approved scheme. As only 6 of the 16 unemployed members of the congregation responded, the Community Project could not proceed, but the register remained available.

*The pastoral team in the autumn of 1982 – from left to right, Jack Ansdell (church officer), David Hunt (pastor's assistant), Derek Prime (pastor), Ella Bruce (pastor's secretary), George Smith (pastoral care) and Diana Guthrie (deaconess).*

*The lounge of the Chapel's Beulah Home in 1982; it was opened in 1956 (Chapter 39), but Douglas Macnair was the first male resident; it was managed at this time by Chapel members Gordon McAndrew, Alex Cameron (convener), George Nash, Barry Sprott, Kath Cameron, Mabel McLean (matron), Joyce Balfour and George Harley.*

In the autumn of 1983, David Hunt, having made an outstanding contribution to the life of the Chapel during his two years as trainee minister, accepted a call to the pastorate of the Renfrew Baptist Church. Jim Murdock replaced him as the pastor's assistant, in November 1983. Although the elders would have liked Jim to stay for longer, because of his all-round usefulness in the pastoral team, he felt it right to accept a 'call' to the Baptist church in Lincoln, and left in December 1985. The appointment of the eighth and final assistant during Derek Prime's pastorate is described in the next chapter.

### 1983 – Another pastoral assistant

George Smith, mentioned in the last chapter, dealt so ably with pastoral care in the church that when he resigned in October 1982, to take up an appointment at Kilravock Castle conference centre near Inverness, there was no doubt that someone similar was required, to supplement the work of the pastor. Intimation was made in the church and to Bible colleges and to missionary societies. The person who commended himself wholeheartedly to the elders was one of the Chapel's own members, James (Jim) Neilson. He was 40 years of age, and after eight years' experience in the audit department of Lanarkshire County Council, he had served in Bolivia, doing missionary work, for ten years. Since January 1978, he had been an accountant with the National Bible Society of Scotland, and had helped with administrative duties there as well. The congregation unanimously called him on 14 March 1983, to join the pastoral team on 1 May.

*Jim Murdock during his time as pastor's assistant in the Chapel, with his wife Elizabeth and one-year-old Peter.*

### 1984 census

The National Bible Society of Scotland asked churches throughout Scotland to conduct a census on all four Sundays in March 1984. Unlike subsequent surveys, where the congregation was given a questionnaire to fill in, this was to be done by observation. At the time, membership stood at 880. The writer estimated attendance (averaging the four Sundays) at 780 in the morning and 500 in the evening.

Because the only unobtrusive time to count the congregation was during the offering, the morning figure excludes children up to the age of five and the adults who supervised them, as they had left after the children's talk. The Bible Society asked for breakdown by age for the morning service; the writer is poor at guessing ages, but he estimated:

|  | Male | Female | Total | % |
|---|---|---|---|---|
| Under 15 | 12 | 19 | 31 | 4 |
| 15–19 | 24 | 43 | 67 | 9 |
| 20–29 | 115 | 127 | 242 | 31 |
| 30–44 | 59 | 67 | 126 | 16 |
| 45–64 | 68 | 80 | 148 | 19 |
| over 65 | 43 | 123 | 166 | 21 |
|  | 321 | 459 | 780 | 100% |

This obliged the Chapel to reconsider the popular belief that there were about a thousand at the regular services. The pastor and elders were particularly challenged by the Sunday evening attendance. Three series of sermons, one on Genesis, another on Revelation, and one on hard questions in the Bible, caught the imagination of many; some students delayed going home, at the end of the university term, to hear the end of the series. Earnest prayer was no doubt foundational, but a new hymnbook and better lighting also lifted spirits; one hesitates to say when and why the tide turned, but by the spring of 1985 the evening service was better attended, and there was an enthusiasm and a desire to be involved.

The new hymnbook was *Mission Praise*, which was used in place of *Hymns of Faith* as the pastor or guest preacher felt appropriate. At the request of the deacons, who gave out the books at the door and collected them again after the service, the preacher could choose either book but not hymns from both at the same service. The flaps of the plastic (Chapel) covers held visitors' cards, for completion and handing in.

Two more volumes of *Mission Praise* quickly followed, so in December 1991, the Chapel purchased copies of the composite edition, covered them with plastic bindings and inserted visitors' cards; they became the main congregational hymnbook. *Hymns of Faith* was still available, and was used occasionally – for example at the church anniversary in October 1999, and it is still used from time to time at mid-week meetings.

*At the end of 1984, the Chapel purchased fifteen hundred copies of the hymnbook* Mission Praise, to be used in place of Hymns of Faith *on such occasions as the pastor felt appropriate.*

### 1984 – Holiday club

Holiday clubs are now fairly common, but it was novel, at least for the Chapel, when the Youth Council ran one in the lounge for a week during the school holidays in the summer of 1984. It was open from ten o'clock in the morning to three in the afternoon, and attracted children from the Chapel and their friends, and also children from the area around Rose Street. There was singing, quizzes, stories, study groups, games and refreshments, with one evening activity for all the family. It was not repeated until August 1990, when two holiday clubs were held, one from Monday 6 to Friday 10 August, for secondary school children, and the other from Saturday 4 to Saturday 11 August, for primary school age, both in the afternoon only.

Additional information on the following topics, mentioned in this chapter, is available on the CD.

Charlotte Recordings Ltd
*Evangelical Times* Report 1982
Lower hall
Open-air meetings
Preaching – audio-tapes (Derek Prime)
Sheila Masterton
Trustees

# Chapter 50
# Responding to new situations (1985–1987)

## Membership and outreach

### Three positive years

During the last three years of Derek Prime's pastorate, the Chapel not only expanded its use of the new lounge, but also held a major Commonwealth Games outreach in July and August of 1986 and established a daughter church in Barnton in 1987. Help with these and other new ideas came from the 84 new members in 1985, ranging from teenagers to senior citizens. Who were they?

### Who wanted to join?

Testimonies given at membership interviews during 1985 fell into four groups. A dozen had been converted during large city crusades; this was an encouragement to Chapel members who had worked tirelessly over the years at the crusades led by Billy Graham, Stephen Olford, Arthur Blessit and Dick Saunders. Some of the dozen had no Christian background, but had come to faith after their friends invited them to one of the rallies.

Another dozen were converted through school camps or school missions; these were less dramatic than crusades, but equally effective. Again, this was an encouragement to those who had, over the years, prepared messages for school Scripture Unions, given up holidays to be leaders at camp, and so on. Another 24 new members had first professed faith in Christ at home, typically between the age of 8 and 12 and now, a decade later, they were ready for church membership. Their parents' quiet testimony, together with family Scripture reading and prayer, had borne fruit.

Sixteen others had received the Lord in the Chapel, during a Sunday service or in Sunday School, Bible Class, Folkus or in one of the uniformed organisations. The leaders of these groups were delighted to know that their faithful work had been rewarded. The remaining 20 had been converted in other churches and had then come to Edinburgh. Of the 84 new members (48 women and 36 men), 14 had no previous church connection before their conversion; 3 had come to Edinburgh to study and had been invited to the Chapel by fellow students. Seven of the new members were in their teens, 46 in their twenties, 18 in their thirties, 8 in their forties, 1 in their fifties and 4 were over 60. No generation was unrepresented; the average age was 28.

On the other hand, 68 names had to be deleted from the roll during the year, 21 by death, 28 by transfer away and 19 by roll revision. There was therefore a net gain of 16, bringing the total membership at 31 December 1985 to 888.

### Charlotte Baptist Chapel

ROSE STREET, WEST,
EDINBURGH.

Dear Brethren,

In accordance with your request, we hereby transfer to your membership and fellowship,

............................................................ who for a period of ............ years, held membership in good standing in this Church.

As we commend our friend(s) to your welcome and kindness we take opportunity of expressing our good wishes to you in all your work for our dear Lord. May rich blessing be upon you.

On behalf of Charlotte Chapel,

Cordially yours,

*Secretary.*

*Printed letters of transfer were commonly used in Baptist churches until word processors made standardized yet personal letters possible.*

### Beach missions

During the Julys of 1985-87, about 20 from the Chapel YPM led a fortnight's beach mission, on behalf of Scripture Union, as they had done every summer since 1976. At first, they went to Lamlash, on the island of Arran, and then moved to St Andrews. In 1988, Scripture Union decided it was not appropriate for one congregation to run a mission in the name of an interdenominational society, so some of the YPM went to different Scripture Union camps around Scotland, while others arranged a beach mission under the Chapel auspices, with Ayr as a favourite spot year after year until 1995.

*The Chapel young folk conducting a beach mission at St Andrews in July 1982.*

## Drama

In 1985, the elders had to consider the place of drama in the presentation of the gospel. Some of the younger people in the Chapel, influenced by the Fisherfolk from Houston, Texas, who had settled on Cumbrae, off the Ayrshire coast, were keen to put on sketches. Experience elsewhere made the elders cautious. Their reasons may not convince present readers, but they were concerned at: (1) the diversion of scarce resources into the time that was needed for rehearsing and presenting drama, (2) the lessening impact of the gospel, presented in this way, as opposed to direct evangelism, (3) the difficulty of being good enough to attract respect (the cringe factor) and (4) the danger of the message being lost in entertainment.

The Chapel young people accepted the need for caution, but still saw a niche for their acting talent. By 1991, they had seven evangelistic pieces, which they performed in the open air at the Cameron Toll shopping centre and in any church that invited them. At the March 1992 missionary conference, they contributed very acceptably to the Saturday evening rally. In November 1993, they were recognized as an official Chapel auxiliary, and took the name Jigsaw.

## The charismatic movement

### Speaking in tongues

The modern charismatic renewal movement came to Scotland in the early 1960s; at first, it was characterized by speaking in tongues. Sympathetic ministers exercised their gift only in private or at prayer groups during mid-week meetings; at that time, they conducted traditional services on Sunday. Those who came as guest preachers to the Chapel had the good manners, knowing the Chapel's reservations about the movement, not to speak about it from the pulpit. Although these men believed they were promoting charismatic renewal for the welfare of the whole church, it was a sad reality that renewal could be (and sometimes was) divisive; if some members (charismatics) were for it and others (kerygmatics, to use the buzzword of the time) were against it, tensions developed. The main reason given by men leaving the Baptist ministry in Scotland in the 1960s and 70s was the disruption that had followed charismatic renewal in their congregation.

In June 1971, the Chapel elders quietly discouraged what they regarded as a potentially disruptive situation within the fellowship. Edinburgh was large enough for them to suggest that those drawn to the new Pentecostalism should transfer their membership to a local church that encouraged this gift, rather than promoting it in the Chapel. Invitations to inter-denominational rallies in the city with a charismatic emphasis were courteously declined.

From 1979, Spring Harvest, an annual week-long training conference, brought together charismatics and non-charismatics in a way reminiscent of the Keswick Convention in an earlier era. The younger generation in the Chapel supported Spring Harvest enthusiastically; in June 1979 it was evident that a number in the Young Peoples Meeting, and in the younger Focus group, were under charismatic influence. The elders wisely decided not to make an issue of it, which could have been divisive; instead they pointed the young folk to the person and work of the Lord Jesus Christ, emphasising that the main function of the Holy Spirit was to glorify him.

### Sunday 24 March 1985

While Derek Prime was leading the opening prayer at the morning service on Sunday 24 March 1985, a woman in her forties, sitting at the back of the upstairs gallery, began to speak loudly in tongues, that is in language unintelligible to anyone else. One of the elders asked her to desist and to leave the sanctuary, which she did; while he was doing this, a member of the congregation struck up a well-known hymn, and others joined in. While some felt afterwards that the proper response, in light of 1 Corinthians 14:27, would have been to call for an interpreter, most members approved of the action taken.

The senior assistant pastor, Jim Neilson, together with the writer and his wife, Joyce, called on the woman at her home in West Lothian. They ascertained that her interruption had been deliberate – she had intended to intervene on the previous Sunday, but had not got round to it; having said nothing on that occasion, she was determined to speak out on 24 March. Her actions were controlled, in that she had the ability to resist the impulse, if she wished. Initially, she refused to give an undertaking not to do it again, because she felt that she had a mission to bring charismatic worship into the Chapel. Jim Neilson and the writer presented theological arguments, which left her unmoved; however, when Joyce said that to interrupt the preacher was rude – simply bad manners – she was immediately contrite, and agreed not to do so again. She accepted that there was a difference between the use of tongues in private devotion and in public worship.

Derek Prime then spoke to the YPM at their Wednesday meeting about the charismatic movement, and there were no further problems. At this time, the Gay Rights Movement were disrupting services in churches where their views were unacceptable, so letters to visiting preachers, with details of the services, included a paragraph about how to respond to any banner-waving demonstration. Fortunately the provision (to announce a hymn, and not to lay hands on the protestors) never had to be invoked.

## John Wimber

Through the 1980s, John Wimber's Association of Vineyard Churches had a significant impact on some Anglican and Baptist congregations in the United Kingdom. Wimber himself, whose ministry was 'to equip the saints with the gifts of the Holy Spirit, accompanied by signs and wonders', came to the Usher Hall in Edinburgh in September 1988, that is during the Chapel's vacancy. A number of members attended his four-day conference, and some were impressed by his concept of power evangelism. The Chapel 'signs and wonders' people were mature enough not to cause division between themselves and those who were wary of John Wimber's teaching; everyone learned from the courteous exchange of views that followed the conference.

Before the most extreme form of Wimber's ministry, later called the 'Toronto Blessing', came to churches across the British Isles, the Chapel had a new minister, who understood the dangers of it and who cautioned the Chapel against any involvement with it.

## Charismatic influence

Many Scottish churches, including the Chapel, which were outside the charismatic renewal movement, began to do charismatic things in singing, in worship and in other areas. Worship leaders and worship groups appeared in Baptist churches across Scotland in the middle 1980s. The Chapel office-bearers and their wives held a seminar on: 'Is there an alternative to the hymn sandwich?' – that is, the traditional hymn-prayer-hymn-reading-hymn-sermon-hymn

-benediction. By 1990, it was not uncommon for guest preachers to announce three or four consecutive worship songs on a Sunday, especially at the evening service, together with testimonies. The Chapel printed its own song sheet, with 35 modern hymns, and gave it out on Sunday along with *Mission Praise*; 11 of the hymns were by Graham Kendrick, including 'The Servant King', 'Shine, Jesus, 'Shine', 'Meekness and Majesty', 'Rejoice! Rejoice!', 'Such love' and 'Who can sound the depths of sorrow?' There was much less formality, without a loss of reverence.

## 'There is Hope'

From 1985 to 1992, a loose grouping of 40 Edinburgh churches, under the leadership of an independent organiser, advertised the Christian message on Lothian buses, and distributed evangelistic literature, under the title 'There is Hope'. They organized marches of witness along Princes Street, up the Mound and down the High Street – 'come with the family and brightly dressed'; they held praise nights in the Usher Hall on Easter Saturday from 1986 onward.

The choir practice for these events, attracting about three hundred, was held in the Chapel on Saturday morning. There were two difficulties about further (official) involvement; one was that they met for planning and for their devotional meeting on Monday evening, which clashed with the Chapel's main prayer meeting. As a gesture, the Chapel invited them to combine their meeting with the Chapel prayer meeting, but the result was not satisfactory for either group. The other difficulty was the Chapel's reservation about the charismatic emphasis of some of the leaders. In consequence, Charlotte Chapel did not officially participate in 'There is Hope' after Easter 1987, but many members, especially younger ones, remained active in it. The church still contributed to the cost of putting the Christian message on buses, made the lounge available for meetings, and publicized 'There is Hope' activities in the Sunday bulletin. Their March for Jesus in Edinburgh in September 1989 was one of 48 similar events throughout Great Britain; with half a million taking part in total, it was reckoned to be the largest single Christian event in the United Kingdom in the twentieth century. The Edinburgh group was still arranging Marches for Jesus in the summer of 2000, and holding meetings in the Chapel up to October 1992.

## Responding to a changing society

### 1985 – Easter communion

There had been no weekday Easter communion in the Chapel since Derek Prime came to Edinburgh in 1969. At a members' meeting, someone suggested coming together for the Lord's Supper, with nothing else to detract from it, on Good Friday, 1985. It was well attended but, as mentioned in Chapter 36, the Emmaus choir, which included many Chapel members, gave a sacred concert every Good Friday; accordingly, from 1987 onward, the Easter communion in the Chapel was on Thursday evening, which was, in any event, a more appropriate time to remember its institution. Initially, numbers were small enough for everyone to sit around a table in the lounge, in the traditional Scots (and Brethren) way; soon, however, the Thursday communion grew in popularity, until it had to move from the lounge into the church itself, as continues to this day.

### 1985 – Time of Sunday School

The Chapel has always had a scattered congregation, but with new housing in the suburbs, parents found it increasing difficult to take the family home for lunch and be back at the Chapel for 3 p.m., collect the children at 4 p.m., and return for the evening service at 6.30 p.m. Lunch on the premises (Chapter 48) did not go to the root of the problem; to arrive at the Chapel before 11 a.m. and not to leave until after 4 p.m. was inordinately long.

So, why not hold the Sunday School after the opening devotions and the children's talk, as is done now? Derek Prime believed, and nearly all the leaders agreed with him, that there were three disadvantages. One was that children should grow up to regard attending church with their family as the norm. The second was the spiritual welfare of the teachers; either they would rarely attend the whole morning service – not good for them – or they would work on a rota – not good for teacher-pupil relationships, even if enough members could be found to form a rota. Thirdly, with the lower hall (and then the lounge) required every Sunday for an overflow of adults, there was insufficient accommodation for individual classes; 13 South Charlotte Street was not available, being the caretaker's house.

A questionnaire to parents and teachers in March 1983 showed significant support for moving the Sunday School from 3 p.m. to 12.30 p.m. There were, however, contrary views, so the elders moved cautiously. At a meeting for all interested parties in January 1985, 56 wished to change the time, 25 did not wish a change and 18 were undecided. Accordingly, the Sunday School was held, as an experiment, from 12.30 p.m. to 1.15 p.m. between April and June 1985. Parents, teachers and children enthusiastically supported this, and there was no thought of returning to the afternoon. Most parents enjoyed a time of fellowship together, over coffee in the lounge, while waiting for the children; they were then free, as a family, until the evening service.

Children aged between three and five had, for some years, left the morning service before the sermon and gone to the top hall; this continued and, as mentioned in Chapter 49, it became known as the Beginners Sunday School. There was, therefore, no further provision for them at 12.30 p.m. On the first Sunday in January, March, May, etc., when communion followed the morning service, the Sunday School met as usual at its new time of 12.30-1.15 p.m.; no coffee was provided for the parents, as it was often 1 p.m. before the service concluded.

### 1986 – Beavers

Youth Council noted that the Scout movement had, nationally, created Beaver Colonies for boys of six and seven, that is before the age of Cubs. Always looking for new ways to involve young people, they started Beavers in the Chapel in 1986. The maximum number was 24, and soon there was a waiting list (Chapter 52). The Beaver Colony had the use of Canty Bay, so a new generation of younger parents were asked (by their children) not to arrange a family holiday at the beginning of July, in case it clashed with the Beaver camp.

*One of the incentives for joining the Beaver Colony was the prospect of camping at Canty Bay, North Berwick.*

*Charlotte Baptist Chapel, West Rose Street, Edinburgh.*

*We warmly invite you to a*
**MENS MEETING**
*on Thursday 2nd October, 1986*
*7.45pm for 8pm.*

*speaker: Professor David Short (Aberdeen)*
*subject:*
**'DO YOU REALLY WANT TO SEE YOUR MEDICAL RECORDS ?'**

*further dates for your diary:*
*12 February, 1987. speaker: Professor Verna Wright*
*22 May, 1987. speaker: Mr. John Chapman*

*The lounge was an ideal venue for meetings like this one, where a talk based on the speaker's profession led easily into the relevance of the gospel to individual lives.*

### 1986 – Six objectives

At the beginning of 1986, Derek Prime set six objectives for the year – Caring for People, Bible Study, Adequate Finance, Openness to Change, Evangelism and the Best Use of Gifts. Toward the end of the year, progress was 'marked' in all six areas. There was much to encourage; although, under the first, more needed to be done to welcome students and nurses: they came to Edinburgh as strangers, often shy and lonely, and tea in the lower hall on Sunday afternoon was no substitute for inviting them into homes. On the second, the balance between central Thursday Bible schools and home Bible studies was about right. On the third, the treasurer had set a weekly target of £1,400, exclusive of covenanted giving, and he printed the result in the bulletin week by week; this was another area where he said: 'Thanks, well done, but keep up the good work'.

On Openness to Change, a glance at the weekly bulletin from only a year or two previously showed how quickly the congregation was adaptable to new ideas. Opportunities abounded for evangelism, with guest services, visitation of the district, the festival café, men's meetings and many more, although, as always, personal contact was needed to follow up the opportunities provided. On the last of the six objectives – making the Best Use of Gifts – too few people were doing too much of the work; they were not involving others, to work with them and share the load. As this goal was not being met, the challenge went out: 'Find a deputy'.

The festival café was a good example of old ideas and new ideas blending together. From Monday to Friday on the middle week of the Edinburgh International Festival in August, the lounge was open for snacks and conversation from 10.30 a.m. to 2.30 p.m. The novel feature was that the traditional open-air meeting at the Mound, from 8-8.45 p.m., and the distribution of Christian literature along Rose Street, from 7.45-9 p.m., both focused on getting passers-by to come into the evening café in the lounge, open from 7.45 -10 p.m. Short evangelistic programmes were put on throughout the evening, and, as always happened on such occasions, others gathered for prayer in the lower hall, for an hour from 7.45 p.m., to support the public outreach upstairs.

### 1986 – Charlotte Chapel football team

In 1934, some young men in the Chapel asked the deacons for permission to field a team in the East of Scotland Churches Football Association; they were told: 'it would not be in the highest and best interests of the Church'. Although attitudes had changed in many ways over 50 years, their successors in 1986 did not risk a refusal and simply joined the Association. There were eleven churches in the league, so there was a game every Saturday for all except one of them in rotation. The Chapel team competed successfully, although it was so loosely connected with the Chapel that it did not feature in any printed reports and few, apart from those taking part, know of its existence. Players did not have to be members of the church, nor even to attend its services; many came through personal contact, for example with Scouts at camp.

In 1994, the team was mentioned in the *Record* for the first time; in 2002, it achieved a two-page spread on winning the Association cup. Then, in 2005, the team was taken over by the Chapel office-bearers under the title Charlotte Sports, a new auxiliary formed to develop sport as an outreach ministry (Chapter 56). The team's fixtures were then included in the Sunday bulletin, with the exhortation: 'please pray that the potential for outreach and discipleship may be truly fulfilled'; the score was printed on the following Sunday.

### 1986 – Deaf Christian Fellowship

As mentioned in Chapter 40, deaf people attended the Chapel on Sunday evening, and Robin White 'signed' for them. From 1958, some came on Sunday morning as well, and he interpreted for them in a reserved pew; after the lounge was built in 1983, he did it there. A number of deaf people also met fortnightly in the Chapel on Wednesday evening, for Bible study.

By 1986, Robin White had been doing it for 30 years; he was finding it difficult to attend every week, but no one could be recruited to help. Six deaf folk were so appreciative that he continued for another 17 years, meeting in a side-room for three Sundays in the month and in the sanctuary on the fourth (including communion). In 2003, he asked the Chapel to stop advertising the facility of deaf signing in the bulletin, as he was aged 89 and could not be sure of getting to the Chapel: no one else would take it on.

## 1986 – Fund raising

In December 1986, Youth Council asked the elders for guidance about bring-and-buy sales, to raise money for a Blue Peter appeal for vehicles for relief purposes. Although sympathetic to the project, and recognising that most teenagers do not have income from which to support worthy causes, the elders were cautious. They wanted the young people to think through the principles, now, that would influence their future attitude to giving; the Chapel had found, over the years, that direct giving by the Lord's people was more effective than bring-and-buy sales.

The elders drew a distinction between raising funds for the Chapel's own work and raising funds for others. For the former, it was the duty of the church to supply all necessary resources for the Chapel auxiliaries. If young people wanted their auxiliary to have something extra, which could not be classified as necessary, they could raise money for it by washing cars or by sponsored gardening and the like. Selling goods for profit within the church fellowship was a second best, and selling outwith the church, to raise money for the church, was unacceptable, because (the elders believed) it was difficult to fix a just price and there was too much scope for misunderstanding.

For appeals by outside organisations, and specifically for the Blue Peter appeal, the elders said they would have preferred direct giving, including approaches to sympathetic adults within the Chapel, but they would consider bring-and-buy sales on the merits of individual requests. These principles

were shared with the church at the next members' meeting, and agreed as church policy.

## Thirteenth Commonwealth Games

In January 1985, the Chapel began planning an evangelistic outreach to visitors coming for the Commonwealth Games, to be held in Edinburgh from Thursday 24 July to Saturday 2 August 1986. With heightened security after terrorist activity at the 1970 games, there was little access to the competitors.

Sunday evening 26 January 1986 was set aside for a special offering for the costs. Recognising that the key to success was not organisation but spiritual preparation, the Chapel was open for prayer on Saturday afternoon from 2-5 p.m., with a brief pause every half-hour for people to come and go. The budget, to include two large marquees in Charlotte Square Gardens and ten thousand leaflets, was £12,500. Members were challenged to meet the entire budget on this one evening; the offering was £12,600. The Chapel's prayer meeting on the third Monday of every month was given over to the outreach, and prayer triplets were formed, to bring specific requests to the Lord.

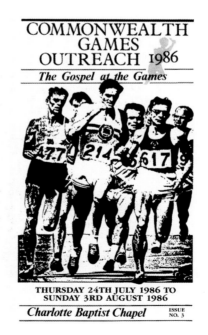

*Monthly information leaflets encouraged support for 'The Gospel at the Games'.*

The marquees in Charlotte Square Gardens were open all day throughout the games. One had five hundred seats and a platform for a choir of 50, together with an area for counselling; the other was the Tea Garden, where refreshments were served daily (except Sunday) from 10 a.m. to 5 p.m. The National Bible Society of Scotland displayed Bibles in languages from countries around the Commonwealth, and Scripture Union had a bookstall, with Bibles and Christian literature for sale.

Evangelistic lunchtime and evening rallies were held every day in the larger marquee, which was well filled. Prom Praise, the 70-strong orchestra from All Souls, Langham Place, London, gave two concerts in the marquee; they also took part in the Sunday evening service in the Chapel, with their rector, Michael Baughan, as the preacher. It was a warm summer evening, and there have probably never been more people in Charlotte Chapel at one time – every seat in the sanctuary was taken, with overflows linked by CCTV to the lounge and lower hall; the vestry was packed (with the door open), and there were loudspeakers in the vestibule and the top hall. With the windows open, the music and the message could be heard in the street outside as well.

About 30 people made commitments during the 10 days. One man, who had come from England with tickets for many of the games, was invited to the marquee and attended several times between events at Meadowbank; after one of the rallies, he committed his life to Jesus Christ for the first time. Chapel members involved in the outreach developed a deep sense of fellowship – through mounting security over the marquees for 24 hours a day, preparing hundreds of meals, participating in the choir, distributing literature and praying together.

## Barnton Baptist Fellowship

### The vision
In October 1985, some Chapel members living in Barnton, on the western outskirts of Edinburgh, told the elders they would like to start an outreach in their neighbourhood, leading, if possible, to the formation of a church. They pointed out the practical difficulty of inviting non-Christian friends to drive into the centre of town, and the advantages of a local meeting. This was different from the Chapel's outreach to Wester Hailes (Chapter 46), where there was no evangelical witness in the area and Chapel members travelled

into it in order to establish one; in the Barnton situation, there was a felt need by Chapel members already in the area. On the second and fourth Monday at the month, they held their own prayer meeting, at the same time at the Chapel's one; about 20 attended, clearly indicating their commitment to a distinctive work.

The Chapel carried out a door-to-door survey of Barnton and Cramond in May 1986, asking householders if they would support a new church in their locality, and/or send their children to a Sunday School? The canvassers experienced no hostility, but a great deal of apathy; only 10 per cent of those questioned regularly attended a place of worship, but 12 per cent of them said they would be interested in a new community church.

### Constitution
It was decided to test the water by holding a Sunday morning family service for four months in the Cramond Primary School, from Christmas 1986 to Easter 1987. A crèche provided for infants and a Junior Sunday School for ages two to five; otherwise, families sat together. Between 120 and 150 came at 10.30 a.m. for an hour's service, with a good spread of ages; 35 per cent had no Chapel connection. Bible studies were held on Thursday, initially with four groups of ten each.

*The Barnton Baptist Fellowship held praise and worship services for all ages in the local school on Sunday morning, starting on 21 December 1986.*

As the four months drew to a close, there was no hesitation about continuing. The Chapel elders suggested the same three criteria for Barnton as they had laid down for Wester Hailes, that it should become an independent church when it had: (1) responsible leadership, (2) financial independence and (3) a constitution. These were in place by the autumn of 1987; Derek Prime led a thanksgiving service in the school on Saturday 5 December 1987, incorporating the constitution of the Barnton Baptist Church.

While the Chapel was pleased to see the establishment of the new witness in Barnton, 42 of the 50 founding members of the Barnton Baptist Church were from Charlotte Chapel and, by definition, they were people of leadership and initiative. It was not just adults whose contribution to Chapel life had to be replaced – half of the 36 young folk who attended Focus on Saturday evening joined the equivalent group in Barnton.

## Relinquishing the pastorate

### 12 months' notice

During 1985, both assistant pastors were 'called' to Baptist churches of their own, Jim Neilson to New Prestwick and Jim Murdock to Lincoln. Peter Firth replaced Jim Murdock in September 1986, but the elders were still actively searching for a senior assistant for pastoral visitation. The older man would normally be invited for a number of years, so Derek Prime felt it right to advise the elders, in October 1986, that he had in mind to relinquish the pastorate in twelve months time. He used the word 'relinquish' rather than 'resign'; there were no problems, hidden or otherwise, but incipient health difficulties made him realize that he could not indefinitely maintain the pastoral office at his own high standard. In twelve months, Peter Firth would have been with the team for a year, and could assume significant pastoral responsibilities. Furthermore, Mr Prime hoped that the church would utilise the year to look for a new pastor, and work toward a smooth transition.

The deacons received the news with great regret, but heeded his advice and asked the church to form a search committee. In previous vacancies, the whole diaconate had been appointed; this time, the members took the view that the elders had recently been elected by the congregation to look after the spiritual welfare of the church, and that this included finding and recommending a new minister.

*Derek Prime, as he relinquished the pastorate in October 1987.*

Charlotte Baptist Chapel 179th Anniversary Weekend 1987

Saturday 3rd Oct. 3 - 4.30pm
"Farewell" to Rev. Derek Prime and Mrs. Prime. All ages welcome. A time of thanksgiving to God for the last 18 years of ministry. Followed by refreshments and informal fellowship.

Sunday 4th Oct.
11am - Morning Service (Crèche facilities available)
6.30pm - Evening Service (Leading into Communion Service) Both services conducted by Rev. Derek Prime, M.A., S.Th. All events of the weekend to be held in Charlotte Chapel, West Rose Street, Edinburgh.

*The farewell services, on Saturday and Sunday 3-4 October 1987, expressed the Chapel's gratitude to God for 18 years of outstanding pastoral ministry.*

### 'A multitude of things that he made better'

The Chapel was packed almost to capacity for the first farewell service, on Saturday afternoon, 3 October 1987. Among the many tributes paid, Rev. James Philip, minister of Holyrood Abbey Church of Scotland, spoke on behalf of 'the considerable group of evangelical men and congregations in the city':

*The word that most readily comes to my mind, in trying to describe what we have felt about this ministry and about the man, is complete and utter integrity. Even to sit and listen to him, as I did not so very long ago at Keswick, one sensed the integrity even as he stood up and before he said a word. He is and has been that kind of man. Describing one of his great friends, John Buchan spoke about 'a multitude of things that he made better by simply existing among them'. I think that that sums up what many of us have felt about Mr Prime*

**Chapter 50**
Responding to new situations (1985-1987)

*and his presence here in Edinburgh over these 18 years. The apostle John recorded, at the end of Chapter 10 of his Gospel: 'all things that John the Baptist spoke of this man [Jesus] were true'. All things that Mr Prime has spoken about Jesus Christ have been true, and to speak true things truly about the Son of God is the greatest joy and the greatest accolade that any man could have, and this is the man to whom you bid farewell this weekend.*

1 Quoted from Rev. James Philip's tribute at Derek Prime's farewell service, 3 October 1987

Derek Prime conducted both services on Sunday 4 October, including communion at the close of the evening service. He then slipped away, not shaking hands at the door, at what was an emotional time for him and for the congregation, who had come to love him in the Lord. He had baptized 734 and received 1057 into membership; every one of them had received a card, with a verse of Scripture that Derek Prime had chosen with the individual in mind.

He has had a busy retirement; he continues to live in Edinburgh, and attends an evangelical church near his home. He has written several new books, spoken frequently at churches and conferences, and acted as pastor to many in the ministry. Families have often asked him to conduct the thanksgiving service for members who had grown up under him, and, both during the vacancy and then in co-operation with the Chapel's new pastor, he has done this supremely well.

Additional information on the following topics, mentioned in this chapter, is available on the CD.

Baptism in the Holy Spirit
Charlotte Chapel football club
Church officers from 1912
Elders' duties
Fund raising
Sunday School
Worship leaders

# Chapter 51
# First part of the vacancy (1987–1989)

## Early vacancy experiences

### Strategy report

In October 1987, the Chapel went into (what turned out to be) the longest vacancy in its history, nearly five years. Shortly before that, the office-bearers had hammered out a ten-year plan. Should the church remain in Rose Street? Yes, but improve the top hall. Should the Chapel be a preaching centre? No, because that implied a place to which people did not belong. Should more be done for students and visitors? Not much more – they should be welcomed, encouraged and taught, but their loyalty was elsewhere. Should the style of services be altered? Not at present. Should the premises be open during the day, as a book-room or for meditation? Not for a book-room, but possibly for something else; meantime, remove the formidable iron grills from the front doors during the day. Should the uniformed organisations look for separate property? No, they must feel part of the Chapel. Should they meet on different evenings to lessen the pressure on accommodation? No, because parents brought them and waited for them, and it would be unreasonable to expect this on different evenings for different age groups.

Should a church family holiday be arranged? Yes. Should the Sunday School picnic cater for the whole church? Yes, with immediate effect. Should the church recognize home missionaries as well as overseas missionaries? Yes. Should house groups be set up, for Bible study, prayer and fellowship, based on common interest rather than on age or geographical area? Yes, if leaders could be trained. What about those who did not like small groups? There should be more church fellowship evenings. What were the staffing requirements? A pastor, two pastoral assistants, a deaconess, a pastor's secretary, a caretaker, an assistant caretaker and two part-time cleaners. Was that sufficient? Emphatically yes; many lay people were dedicated to the Lord's work in the Chapel, and it was important to encourage their loyalty.

> **Church Picnic**
> **When? Saturday 24 June**
> **Where? Callendar Park Falkirk**
> **Cost? Bus £1.00 Food £1.00 (for children only)**
> **Time? Bus leaves West Register House 10.30 am and leaves Falkirk 4.30 pm**
> **Attractions 9 & 18 hole Pitch & Putt, Crazy Golf, Putting, Playground,**
> **Bouncy Castle, Boating Pond, Mini-cars, Races.**
> **Tickets from Albert Peterson or Section Leader 4 & 11 June.**

*The strategy report recommended remodelling the Sunday School picnic, by making it for all ages and by encouraging everyone to participate; this was implemented in 1989.*

## Lay leadership

Derek Prime's preaching through 1 Corinthians on Sunday morning for a year, from the spring of 1983 to Easter 1984, had caught the imagination of regular worshippers in a new and personal way; they were challenged by the exhortations: 'Working together' (Chapters 1-3), 'Responsibility for each other' (Chapters 8-9) and 'The use of spiritual gifts' (Chapters 12-14). When the pastoral team was reduced from four to two (as described above) and then to one (below), an unprecedented number of lay people took on leadership roles – one prepared candidates for baptism, another arranged membership interviews and welcomed new members, another led the eight-week discipleship class, another looked after communion and others ran the Thursday Bible School, and much more. Previously, they had been involved; now they took responsibility.

*In February 1989, assistant pastor Peter Firth accepted a 'call' to the Peebles Baptist Church, leaving only the deaconess in what had been, until recently, a pastoral team of four.*

This enhanced involvement was repeated throughout the church, as members got on with the job in the absence of full-time pastoral leadership. People were excited by the opportunities, and the annual meeting in April 1989 noted:

*As a result of this Vacancy, and the discussions that have taken place, and examination of Scripture as to the role of the various Office-bearers, is clear that the Chapel will 'never be the same again'. With the many talents available throughout the congregation, it is now much clearer what style of leadership will best fit into the framework of the Chapel for the 1990s.*

1 Members' meeting, April 1989.

Another recommendation in the strategy report was to have a church family holiday, from Friday to Sunday afternoon. The first was held at the Nethy Bridge hotel near Aviemore (130 beds) from 5 to 7 May 1989; it has been repeated every year since, in Nethy Bridge (until 1993 and again in 2000-02, in October), or in Aberfoyle (2003-4) or in Blair Atholl or in Aviemore itself (2005-7).

*The first church family holiday weekend was held at the Nethy Bridge hotel near Aviemore in May 1989.*

### Going and coming

The fluidity of late twentieth-century society is illustrated by the membership figures for the 1980s. During that decade, 602 joined the Chapel, an average of 60 a year, but 697 names had to be deleted through death, transfer away or roll revision. During the first seven years of the 1980s, when Derek Prime was pastor, the membership rose steadily, but it dropped back during the vacancy (including 42 who went to Barnton as the vacancy began, Chapter 50). Those seeking consecutive Bible ministry drifted to other churches, as the elders deliberately asked guest preachers to choose their own

subjects rather than follow a syllabus drawn up here. On the other hand, the discipleship class, for those enquiring about the Christian faith or seeking baptism, ran almost continuously, and 12 were baptised on Easter Sunday 1989. There was only one month in the first two years of vacancy when no new members were received – 76 in all. The roll at 31 December for the years 1980 to 1989 was: 843, 850, 868, 880, 888, 908, 881, 811, 786, 754.

## Early vacancy experiments

### The Mustard Seed

In the spring of 1987, the leaders of the Rock Mission in the Grassmarket recommended that the time had come to transfer the Chapel's resources to some other work. At the same time, there was growing concern (as mentioned in the strategy report) that the Chapel had iron gates across its doors during the day from Monday to Saturday, while people were streaming along Rose Street, and that these came down only after the crowds had gone home. Why not invite them in while they were there? Why not serve light meals in the lounge for six days a week, to build bridges with the city-centre population? The congregation was invited to suggest a name and the Mustard Seed was the popular choice; great things can come from small beginnings, as the Lord explained in Matthew 13:31-2: this text was the headboard in the lounge, as seen in the first photograph in Chapter 55.

It opened in June 1988, with enthusiastic voluntary cooks and waitresses, whose aim was not just to serve tables but also to engage visitors in conversation, and to introduce them to the church. It was always described in Chapel publications as the 'Mustard Seed Café Outreach'; Christian literature was on display. The first hundred response cards (disregarding Chapel members) showed that 60 per cent of the café users lived in Edinburgh, 29 per cent worked in the city centre, 25 per cent were visitors to the city and 23 per cent wanted to see around the building; 25 per cent wrote that they would like someone to speak publicly about the Christian faith, while the meals were being served, and 95 per cent gave their name and address and asked for further information.

Visitors became regulars and many constructive discussions took place over lunch. From time to time, an invited speaker gave a short talk during the meal-service in the lounge; on special occasions, such as Easter or Christmas or during the Festival, people were invited to have a meal and then to attend a service in the sanctuary.

After five years, the Mustard Seed had settled into a pattern, which met certain criteria but not its original vision. On the positive side, there was a pleasant atmosphere, good literature on the tables, and a five-minute talk once or twice a week; gospel music was played on the piano, with requests for favourite hymns. It was popular with the elderly and lonely, but since most of the customers were regulars, and most were either Christians or church attenders, there was a fairly limited field for evangelism. On the negative side, the café was not reaching office people, partly because the service was not fast enough, partly because there were not enough small tables where business people could talk privately, but chiefly because most of the surrounding offices did not know the café existed. There was, however, no doubt that the Mustard Seed had a role and should continue.

*The invitation at the door of the Chapel, for passers-by in Rose Street to come in to the Mustard Seed Café.*

Seventeen years later, the voluntary workers, many of whom had been mature when they started, had grown old gracefully together. The younger generation returned to secular work

shortly after children were born, so although the workers enjoyed great fellowship through their volunteer service, it became increasingly difficult to staff the Mustard Seed adequately. From 2003, it did not open on Friday, although the weekly 'thought for the day' was still given on other days. Stringent hygiene regulations were not the reason for closure, as the Chapel spent large sums to comply with them; by the end of 2005, it was no longer possible to provide personnel for preparing and serving the food and administering the café. With reluctance, as it had been a wonderful fellowship for the workers as well as an effective service for the community, it closed its doors in December 2005.

## Monday and Thursday

In the spring of 1988, six locations were arranged for a seven-week Thursday study on 'The Seven Churches of Asia', one in the lounge and five in homes around the city. At the same time, a Homemakers Bible Study Group catered for those recently married or about to be married. For the autumn of that year, as another experiment, the prayer meeting and the Bible School were held consecutively on Monday, each with a minimum of preliminaries. A guest lecturer took the Bible School from 7.30-8.10 p.m., followed by five minutes for refreshments and for coming and going, then prayer from 8.15-9 p.m.

For the spring of 1989, the experiment was reversed, with the combined meeting on Thursday. Some older members, who had attended the Monday prayer meeting faithfully since Graham Scroggie's day, were vocal in protest, saying that the Chapel had prospered because the members met on Monday to pray home, as soon as possible, the messages of the previous day. Other traditions changed as well – when there was no Bible School, the prayer meeting opened as one, but then divided into three, with one group in the lounge, another in the committee room and the third in the lower hall, so that more could participate.

When the summer open-air outreach restarted in June 1989, at 7.30 p.m. on Thursday at the Mound, the prayer meeting went back to Monday, with prayer for the vacancy at 7.30 p.m. and the regular meeting at 8.00 p.m.; both were well supported. The open-air, preceded by prayer in the Chapel, continued until the end of August, which gave 11 or 12 consecutive Thursdays throughout the vacancy. Although public speaking ended at 9 p.m., individual conversations went on much longer and these were the most worthwhile part of the evening. This pattern continued until the summer of 1993; the evangelism committee then reported that although the open-airs 'were well conducted by those involved, few came to swell the crowd and little interest was shown by those who passed by.' They decided to concentrate instead on the Festival Outreach in 1994 (Chapter 54), and there were no more open-air meetings at the Mound.

### Small groups

One of the reasons for experimentally combining Monday and Thursday evening was to free up a night in the week for a network of regular home group meetings – 'every growing church has small groups', they said. However, no one was available to train leaders or to organize groups at this stage, so the pattern of a Monday prayer meeting and a Thursday Bible School was resumed in the autumn of 1989. There was, however, one tentative step toward a small group structure, in that the Bible School alternated between a central meeting, with a guest lecturer, and small groups in homes. Five practical topics (use of time, attitudes to money, environmental issues, work and unemployment, injustice and oppression) were expounded in the Chapel one Thursday and then teased out in four groups in homes, plus one in the Chapel, on the following Thursday.

This pattern, which continued through the spring and autumn of 1990 and the spring of 1991, became the training ground for new hosts and leaders, who formed the nucleus for the fellowship groups, described below. However, a surprise discovery in the summer of 1991 compelled the elders to act more quickly than they had intended.

### A network of small groups

In 1991, the elders became aware that 11 home groups for Bible study and prayer, organized and held outwith the formal structure of Chapel life, were meeting in homes during the day or in the evening (but not on Monday or Thursday). These catered for niche needs: for new Christians (introduction to Scripture Union material), for mothers with young children, for older women, for international students, for the wives of international students, for post-graduate students, and so on. In addition, two groups of mature Christian men met on Saturday morning for Bible study in depth, and mature Christian women met on Friday morning for prayer; there were also two groups focusing on overseas mission. Charlotte Chapel was diversifying and learning by doing instead of by listening only; the leadership had delayed setting up a network of small groups, so the membership had created them instead.

### Restructuring

Barry Sprott, who had been pressing for years for a Chapel-wide home group structure, urged the elders to regain the initiative and to use Thursday evening to establish a small group infrastructure within the life of the Chapel. Desirable as that might be – and nearly everyone supported the principle – no one in leadership had the time or the resources to train enough leaders or to organize enough small groups for everyone to attend on a regular basis.

As soon as Peter Grainger came to Edinburgh in August 1992, he identified this as a gap in Chapel life. It was not that he imposed a small group structure on the Chapel; the Chapel was waiting for someone to organize it. His first members' meeting endorsed his proposal to establish a network of fellowship groups – a new name for a new concept – for Bible study and prayer, to start in April 1993. They were to meet twice a month on Thursday evening, but not all on the same Thursday, so that married couples with small children could share baby-sitting facilities or attend different groups. These groups were no longer led by elders, but by trained leaders, with an elder looking after two or three groups. The small group structure replaced the Thursday Bible School.

## Sunday

### Sunday morning

The elders wanted as much continuity of teaching as possible for the young folk, so Youth Council provided the speakers for the children's talk during the Sunday morning service, unless the guest preacher specifically said in advance that he wished to do it. Only children up to the age of five left after the talk, so it was important for those just over that age to 'own' at least part of the service; a familiar face for the chorus and talk, just after the service started, helped. The invitation to hand in some 'object found in the Bible', together with a Biblical reference for it, was very popular and stretched the imagination of both the youngsters and the leaders.

## Sunday evening

By the spring of 1988, half a dozen or fewer attended the public prayer meeting at 5.30 p.m. on Sunday, specifically to pray for the evening service. The elders, who led it on a rota basis, proposed to discontinue it, but the faithful few found a champion in a Chapel member, Arthur Masson, who led a new-style prayer meeting, starting at 5.45 p.m., until he left Edinburgh at the end of 2000.

Community hymn singing, from 6.10 p.m. until the service started at 6.30 p.m., had been started in the days when all the good seats were taken by 6.10 p.m.; singing filled in the waiting time. During the vacancy, there was, unfortunately, no difficulty in getting a seat and most people arrived about 6.25 p.m.; some came at 6.28 p.m. in order to avoid the cringe factor in the community singing. The director of music proposed in 1989 that it should cease, although the organist would play familiar hymns and choruses from 6.10 p.m. When this was put to a members' meeting, 75 per cent voted to continue with community singing, although they did not promise to be there to participate. It continued right through the vacancy, with a rota of leaders. One of Peter Grainger's first acts, when he came in August 1992, was to regularize this, as described in Chapter 53.

Guest preachers during the vacancy were invited to tell the congregation something about their own situation, for five or ten minutes as part of the evening service, concluding with a couple of topics for prayer; widening of horizons in this way was one of the features of the vacancy. The after-church fellowship for everyone, on the fourth Sunday of the month, was an important time for sharing information, and generally it filled the lounge.

## Baptismal services

Despite the absence of a pastor, an encouraging number came to faith and were baptised during the vacancy. There were three baptismal services in 1988, with 10 candidates in January (6 women and 4 men), 11 candidates in April (6 and 5), and 6 candidates in November (4 and 2). In 1988, the Chapel finally abandoned its heavy baptismal robes for men and waders for those conducting the baptisms, in favour of a white shirt and trousers. There were two services in 1989, with 17 baptised, 12 women and 5 men. As mentioned in

chapter 46, the pastoral studies class from the university's New College came to the autumn service, and asked penetrating questions over coffee afterwards about believers' baptism and the Chapel's style of leadership.

In 1988, Christmas Day fell on a Sunday. Over the previous year, 120 overseas students from 36 countries had filled in visitors' cards. They were invited to spend Christmas Day with a Chapel family, and over 40 accepted. This became a regular feature, whatever day of the week was Christmas Day.

**CHRISTMAS DAY AT CHARLOTTE CHAPEL**

Some Chapel families wish to share their Christmas Day with those away from home. Would you like to spend the day with a family? Please indicate yes, or no, so that suitable arrangements can be made early and that you can be introduced to the family beforehand.

PROGRAMME

Morning Worship at 11.00am led by the Rev. Derek Prime.

Go to your hosts' home for lunch and tea.

Evening Worship led by the Rev. Derek Prime.

Light supper and Carols at the home of Mr. & Mrs. Ian Balfour.

*Christmas Day 1988 was a Sunday, and all overseas students were invited to spend the day with a Chapel family.*

## Sunday crèche

Facilities for children on Sunday morning will be detailed in the next chapter, but an innovation in December 1989 deserves mention here. For some years, there had been a crèche for babies and toddlers, from 10.45 a.m. until the end of the service; youngsters aged 3-5 came into church with their parents and left after the children's talk, for Beginners Sunday School. The new feature was a quiet room on the top floor for children of primary school age who did not go to the Sunday School, but who stayed with their parents until just before the sermon; children at secondary school stayed in for the whole of the morning service, and many of them attended the Sunday School afterwards as well.

## Who is an evangelical – now?

The Chapel was fortunate in the number of distinguished preachers, from many parts of Great Britain, who were prepared to come to Edinburgh for the Sunday services during the vacancy. Many of them accepted the invitation to bring their wife and to make a long weekend out of it; this gave their hosts the opportunity of learning about developments in the wider evangelical scene.

Discussion with visiting preachers made the Chapel leadership aware of the changing boundaries of evangelicalism in the late 1980s. Most of the office-bearers had grown up when evangelical Christians were a minority in the wider church, with something of a ghetto mentality. They were 'unworldly, diligent in attendance at weekly prayer meetings, meticulous about quiet times, suspicious of the arts, missionary-minded, hostile to new liturgical ideas'. Their energies were concentrated on safeguarding the essentials of the faith, and maintaining a firm discipline among themselves. The distinctives of evangelicalism were clearly defined.

However, during the 1980s, both the numerical strength of evangelicals and their proportion of the total number of Christians increased; evangelicals began to interact with other traditions and, in turn, they were recognised by others in the wider religious scene. This gave evangelicals a new confidence to be bold. The first available figures are from 1984, when 28 per cent of churchgoers in England and 23 per cent in Scotland said that they were evangelical. Festivals like Spring Harvest, attended by seventy thousand a year, including one in Ayr for Scots and Northern Irish people, gave an enormous boost to evangelical morale.

The Chapel leadership learned from their weekend guests that the evangelical community was becoming increasingly diverse. This was not unhealthy – diversity around an agreed doctrinal position is no bad thing. There was, however, a growing doctrinal diversity; a new liberal evangelicalism was emerging, although it preferred to call itself 'open evangelical'. It was not traditional evangelicalism, yet it wanted to use the title. What did one say to people from a variety of backgrounds, or from no background at all, who wanted to work with Charlotte Chapel, because they liked its evangelical dynamism, but who did not subscribe to substitutionary atonement, or who questioned the authority of the Bible?

The elders had to ask themselves, in the late 1980s, what was non-negotiable among evangelical distinctives? How should they respond, not just to the Christian gay and lesbian movement, but also to the formation of an evangelical wing within it in 1987? Where was the line between 'welcoming' gay and lesbian people, as fellow-sinners saved by grace, and 'affirming' their lifestyle? How closely should evangelicals work with Roman Catholics on moral and ethical issues, on which they shared a common approach – marriage, embryo-research, etc. – while other branches of the Protestant church took a liberal view? It was a fascinating learning-experience for the hosts of guest preachers to talk with evangelical leaders, from a wide variety of places, who came to the Chapel as pulpit supply.

### October 1989 – 104 Sundays with 72 preachers

A meeting of members was held in October 1989, on the second anniversary of Derek Prime's leaving. The vacancy committee reported that everyone, whose name had been suggested to them, had either been in the pulpit, or had declined to come, or was due to preach in the near future; the elders had also gone to hear some pastors in their own churches. In the two years of vacancy, 72 men had taken services in the Chapel. Some were from other denominations or were retired, and so they were not candidates for the vacancy, but every preacher came initially as pulpit supply – the committee had no mandate to invite them on any other basis.

That second anniversary meeting, attended by 292 members, made a serious approach to a man who had already made it clear that he had no wish to move from his present church – but Sidlow Baxter had said that when the Chapel invited him in the early 1930s. It was no surprise, but nevertheless a disappointment, when he declined the formal invitation.

## Outreach

### Livelink

When the Chapel heard about the satellite link from the Billy Graham mission in Earls Court in London in July 1989, and the final rally in Wembley Stadium, the evangelism committee approached other Edinburgh churches. St George's West in Shandwick Place agreed to be host and Chapel members were active in stewarding, counselling, inviting friends and subsequently leading nurture groups. The building was completely or nearly filled every evening, and 150 were counselled. The fellowship among the various churches was good for everyone involved.

*Livelink provided satellite transmission from Billy Graham's crusade in London, to centres around the country. The Chapel took the initiative in arranging an Edinburgh venue.*

### 'Crosstalk'

Quarterly from Easter 1988, the evangelism committee printed 6,500 copies of an attractive news-sheet 'Crosstalk' giving details of Chapel activities and carrying an evangelistic message. It was given away at the Mustard Seed café, delivered to homes in the Stockbridge area, made available for Chapel members to distribute and the YPM went along Princes Street on Saturday morning, handing it to passers-by.

*The news-sheet 'Crosstalk' publicized Chapel activities as well as carrying an evangelistic message.*

### The *Record*

From 1971 to 1988, the monthly *Record* was produced in-house, to save the subsidy needed from general church funds for a professional publication (Chapter 46). In 1989, the deacons embarked on a half-way-house; the text was set by an outside printer, at a cost of £500 for 1,000 copies, but everything else, including collating and stapling, was done by

volunteers. From 1989 to 1992, the cost (50 pence per copy) was shown on the cover, to encourage donations; it then seemed inappropriate to hand the *Record* to visitors, with a price showing, so this was omitted. Members donated generously, and there was no need to sell advertising space. Of the 1,000 monthly copies, 135 were posted to the missionary family and others away from Edinburgh.

Additional information on the following topics, mentioned in this chapter, is available on the CD.

Deaconess
Rock Mission
Vacancy 1987-1992

# Chapter 52
# Second part of the vacancy (1990–1991)

## Chapel life in 1990

### Peeking through scaffolding

The sanctuary was redecorated in January 1990, as is necessary every 20 years or so. On previous occasions, the congregation had to vacate the building for several weeks, while heavy scaffolding was erected. This time, it was sufficiently lightweight for services to continue, even if worshippers had to peek around bars and planks to see the pulpit. The convener of the house committee asked the contractors to provide a mock-up of a colour scheme; he presented this to the congregation as 'what the professionals advise'. It was accepted without dissent; since it is still the décor at the time of writing (2007), readers can judge whether they agree.

*Gas-lighting globes were removed as part of the 1990 redecoration; until then, this one was prominent on the back stair, although it had been disconnected from the mains for many years.*

The house committee took the opportunity of: (1) upgrading the CCTV cables to carry coloured pictures, (2) removing the tiered choir stalls and creating a flat area, which involved re-positioning the organ console and (3) removing the last remaining gas-light globes. These had not worked for fifty years, but they were a tourist attraction. Seeing them go, one older member recalled a winter Sunday evening when he was a youngster and when the globes still functioned. During the service, the electricity supply failed, so gaslight was needed to evacuate the building. He, like most in the Chapel, had been brought up to believe that smoking was a great evil; how, then, he asked his parents, could some church members produce cigarette lighters to ignite the gas?

*Photograph by a professional photographer, Fiona Good, after the dark varnish had been stripped off the pulpit and the pews in January 1990 and the natural wood had been waxed; the south window had not yet been blanked out to assist PowerPoint projection.*

```
            MORNING WORSHIP AT 11.00 AM

The Word
Hymn 525            O Thou who camest from above
Prayer
Scripture Reading   Gal. 5: 16-26
Children's Chorus
Children's Talk
Children's Hymn 766  Who can sound the depths of sorrow
(Pre-school children leave for the Beginners' Sunday School
  in the Top Hall.  Visitors welcome.)
Intimations and Offering
Dedication of Offering
Prayer
Hymn 37             As the deer pants for the water
Message:            Mr Charles W Price
Subject:            CIVIL WAR IN THE SOUL
Hymn 495            O for a heart to praise my God
Benediction
```

*Throughout the vacancy, the weekly bulletin included the order of service, which was helpful both to the congregation and to the visiting preacher.*

### Sermon outlines

The weekly bulletin included the order for the Sunday services, as in the sample above. In 1990, a visiting preacher introduced a further idea, which became instantly popular, printing an outline for the sermon. Rev. Allan Bosson, pastor of a Baptist church in Savannah, Georgia, kindly gave the whole month of July 1990 to the Chapel, preaching, leading and visiting, without any suggestion of his moving to Edinburgh. He provided a sermon outline for the morning and evening services throughout the month. The elders encouraged others to do this, and it became standard when Peter Grainger came to the Chapel in August 1992. They were included as inserts in the bulletin until PowerPoint took over a decade later; Peter Grainger's outlines were so much appreciated that Christian Focus published 150 of them in book form in 2003.

## Candles in the Chapel?

The young people were among the most enthusiastic supporters of the Watchnight service, to bring in the New Year. They went on to a party and a meal in a convenient hall (unless 1 January was a Sunday), and then, as a group, began 'first footing'. In 1990, they wanted to light candles on all the window ledges in the Chapel. The deacons had no theological objection, but were concerned about the fire risk, and said 'No'. By the following year, safety conditions were satisfied, and the YPM lit the sanctuary with candles at both the Christmas service and the Hogmanay gathering. Ninety set off for the 1 January party, and 39 of them were still first footing when they arrived (by arrangement) at a member's home for breakfast at 8 a.m.

The YPM, which was for everyone attending the church between the ages 15 to 30, held up well throughout the vacancy. Sunday evening, after church, attracted over 70, although there were not so many on Wednesday evening; this was divided between a winter programme for teaching and learning from the Bible and a summer programme of outdoors activities. Asked why so few came to the church prayer meeting on Monday, the vice-president gave two reasons: that YPMers gave priority to their own prayer time for half an hour before the meeting on Wednesday evening, and that they preferred to pray in smaller groups than the Monday night format. He went on:

*The spiritual temperature is high in YPM at the moment. We have weekly Wednesday prayer meetings as well as additional prayer breakfasts, lunches and suppers. We have boys' and girls'*

*camps. Spiritual and social activities overlap. We do regular tract distribution, visit Beulah weekly, sponsor four Third World children (we have just collected over £1,000 for World Vision by going without food for 24 hours) and maintain an Elderly Link with older Chapel members, to name but a few activities.*

1 *Record*, May 1992, p. 5.

The highlight of the year remained the September holiday weekend, when they went, with a guest speaker, to a youth hostel or conference centre.

## Student lunches

Many regular events are now taken for granted, and it is easy to assume they have always happened. While the Chapel had held monthly tea meetings for students and others away from home, for many years, the first open invitation for students to stay for Sunday lunch in the lounge was on 14 October 1990. It became a regular monthly event during term time, and an important part of the Chapel's welcome to students. As the pastoral team grew in number, in the later 1990s, a time of Bible study was provided after the meal. No prior notice was required, but numbers never fazed the hospitality team, not even when 240 stayed for lunch on Student Sunday in October 1993. Between October and May, students were invited to the Chapel at four o'clock on Sunday afternoon, for discussion followed by tea before the evening service. Students were also invited to join a Chapel family at home for lunch on the last Sunday of the month, but that required advance notice and planning.

## Sunday morning – Sunday evening

The Sunday morning service was so well supported in 1990 that there were usually some in the lounge, watching the closed-circuit television, not by choice. They had the opportunity of coming upstairs when the younger children went out, but the relay was always on, anyway, for those who could not manage the stairs, or who had a cough or restless children. Typical attendance on a Sunday morning was about eight hundred, but with CCTV available, the stewards no longer had to pack seven into each side pew in the sanctuary and thirteen in the middle.

The greatest disappointment was the decreasing attendance on Sunday evening; it was a national trend, but the elders would not give in and close the gallery. One Sunday evening in March, there were 160 in the gallery and 120 downstairs; they would have looked better downstairs, together, and they might have felt better as well, but the elders insisted that the whole church should be open. Only on three occasions throughout the whole vacancy, when bad weather and holidays combined to make numbers very low, did the writer override these standing orders and rope off the gallery.

### Baptismal services

Two or three baptismal services were required every year during the vacancy; 27 were baptized in 1998, 17 in 1989, 21 in 1990, 28 in 1991 and 13 prior to the new pastorate in August 1992. There was much to encourage – the number attending the discipleship class, the many involved in pastoral care, the variety of midweek meetings, the youth activities, the evangelistic outreaches, the International Fellowship, the literature produced and much more.

## Commitment, 1990s-style

### Home mission

Prior to 1990, the Chapel gave a high profile, often coupled with financial support, to members serving overseas as missionaries, but full-time workers with home-based organisations like the Edinburgh City Mission, Scripture Union and the Faith Mission were rarely mentioned. The strategy report, noted at the beginning of the last chapter, recommended that this anomaly should be remedied. One way forward was to make the missionary committee into the mission committee, with overseas and home branches, but that did not find favour; the committee had enough on its plate in looking after 20 members overseas.

Accordingly, a home mission committee was formed in May 1990, to support, by prayer, publicity and finance, members in Christian service in Great Britain. It arranged an annual home mission event, similar to the overseas mission weekend, that is, a Saturday evening programme, a guest preacher for the Sunday and an after-church fellowship. The first was held on 25 November 1990, when the guest preacher was one of the Chapel's old boys, now director of a UK mission. The offerings at both services established a home mission fund. From then on, home missionaries were

included in the prayer of intercession on Sunday, and every three months the Monday prayer meeting concentrated on them. Five years later, the overseas and home mission committees merged (Chapter 54).

### Short-term missionary service

In the early 1990s, the Chapel, along with other missionary-minded bodies, began to receive offers from newly qualified, professional young people, anxious to help for a year or so in established missionary situations, without committing themselves for life. The concept was not new – Norman Wallace, having spent his medical elective at the EMMS hospital in Nazareth, went back with his wife for the year July 1978-July 1979 as a doctor – but this was not described as missionary work; there was no valediction, and it was not organized through the missionary committee. When two of the Chapel's young people made similar offers in 1990, a new phrase was coined – 'short-term missionary service'. Lynne Ager, who had recently qualified in opthalmics, went in January 1991 for six months to Kano, Nigeria, with the Sudan Interior Mission, and Shirley Glendinning went as a midwife to Kenya with the Africa Inland Mission. At the same time, Steve Begarnie offered to work with Scripture Union in Dundee for a year, and the Young Peoples Meeting regarded all three of them as 'our missionaries'.

Short-term missionary projects are common now (below), but this should not detract from the significance of what was happening in the early 1990s. Until then, missionaries went abroad for life, or for a substantial part of it. Here were Chapel young people, none of them 'called' as career missionaries, offering the first six or twelve months of their professional lives to missionary societies. In August 1991, Drs Robin and Frances Balfour went on this basis to Chogoria Hospital, Kenya; in 1992, Bryce Crawford, Junior, spent a year in Uganda, nursing with the Africa Inland Mission, while Catriona Fulton worked with Interserve, and Becky Todd did her medical elective in Thailand and later went for a year with Operation Mobilisation. Sandy Balfour taught English for a year in a school near Tokyo and then went to China for two years, with his wife, through a Norwegian missionary society. In 1993, Diane Harry worked for three months with TEAR Fund in South Africa, Colin Saunders spent the summer on a placement in Nepal and Scott Ross joined the YWAM ship.

Ten years later (2001), ten Chapel members spent the summer working overseas with missionary societies; by 2006, this had risen to 20, some on medical electives, others for their university summer holiday (Chapter 56). Short-term service had become increasingly significant, both for missionary work overseas and for the spiritual development of the volunteers.

## Career missionaries

In the 1990s, many missions reported dwindling numbers of applicants for long-term (career) missionary service; most offers were for short-term assignments. There were, however, a number of Chapel young people who answered the traditional 'call' to long-term missionary service. In March 1990, Joanne Muir joined Operation Mobilisation's ship, *Logos*. In October 1990, Colin and Karen Finlayson went to work for one month in the Colentina Hospital and Orphanage in Bucharest and stayed for three years. In 1992, Karen was named British Nurse of the Year for her devotion. In February 1992, three other Chapel members (Dai and Morag Eddyshaw and Peter Hsu) were valedicted for full-time missionary work, in Ghana and the Seychelles respectively. Financial support was growing all the time; in 1986, the Chapel sent £1,800 a year to every Chapel missionary, but in 1991 the congregation gave enough for £2,400 to be remitted.

## 1990 quinquennial election

Another feature of the early 1990s, both in the Chapel and in society at large, was the problem that many, especially younger people, had in finding time for voluntary work. Their days were steadily eaten into, by employers' demands in the workplace, by working wives' need for family life, and by everyone's expectation for more leisure. It was not just a Chapel problem – even the most popular charities found it hard to get volunteers – but the five-yearly election of elders and deacons in the Chapel, in the spring of 1990, illustrated the growing dilemma.

Until then, the election of elders and deacons had been keenly contested, indeed competitive, and there were many more candidates than vacancies. In 1990, only 22 were prepared to stand for the 22 vacancies for elder and only 19

for the 18 vacancies as deacon. The situation did not get any better, and in 2005, only 9 were prepared to stand as elders in a new structure where a dozen or more were needed.

## The vacancy situation

### A week of prayer

Challenged by the outcome of the elections, and the continuing vacancy in the pastorate, the congregation responded warmly to the elders' suggestion that every evening from Monday 18 to Friday 22 June 1990, members and regular worshippers should come together for an hour and a half of prayer. There were different topics every night, covering all aspects of Chapel life and beyond. Numbers were so large that after opening devotions together, the meeting split into groups in different parts of the building. Over the years, up to the present, some like to divide and some do not, but the verdict at the end of June 1990 was that prayer in groups had been a great success and should be repeated.

### 'Is there someone out there?'

Derek Prime had chosen, as the Verse for the Year 1987: 'God acts on behalf of those who wait for Him (Isaiah 64:4)'. In introducing it, he urged the Chapel: 'to know the way forward in seeking the one whom God has already chosen to be the next pastor.' The elders approached the vacancy in the firm belief that there was one man 'out there', whom God had prepared for Charlotte Chapel, and that the function of the vacancy committee was to identify him. As the years went by, some members asked the elders whether they really believed this was so; the writer always answered in the affirmative, right up to the end of the vacancy.

Other members asked whether it was necessary to appoint the pastor before filling the other two vacant positions? Those with experience of team ministries elsewhere advised that it was, because there should be no doubt as to who was in charge, namely the pastor, and that he should be involved in choosing the team. Accordingly, the vacancy committee, supported by the church, put aside any thought of 'calling' an associate or assistant minister before the pastor was in post.

### 4 October 1990

The church anniversary was celebrated, as usual, on the first Sunday of October 1990. It was also the third anniversary of the vacancy, and it saw the hundredth guest preacher in the pulpit. The church was in good heart, well attended (at least on Sunday morning) and active on many fronts. The faithful preaching of the Word from the pulpit was the reason given by most people, who had no other Chapel connection, applying for membership. The lack of systematic teaching had been compensated to some extent by the individual insights of a hundred men, from many parts of Great Britain, Australia, Canada, America and South Africa. In their individual ways, they had taught, challenged, encouraged and rebuked from many different passages of Scripture. Through them, the Chapel had deepened fellowship with several colleges, alliances, unions and missions.

What no one knew, on the anniversary Sunday on 4 October 1990, was that the end of the vacancy was in sight. The guest preacher on 16 September 1990 had attracted much favourable comment, and the elders had invited him back for Sunday 27 January 1991. Within two years, the vacancy would be over and the Rev. Peter Grainger would be the new pastor (Chapter 53).

### PowerPoint

Can one imagine a service in the Chapel, now, without intimations, hymns, sermon outlines and photographs appearing on the screen and its satellites in the sanctuary? From time to time during the vacancy, visiting preachers asked whether there were such facilities. Until April 1991, the answer was 'not possible', because sightlines to the organ gallery and to the platform (the two possible locations for a screen) were poor from many parts of the building. However, when David Smith, then principal of Northumbria Bible College, preached on the prodigal son for three consecutive Sundays in April 1991, he brought his own equipment and experimented with it. To the pleasant surprise of the office-bearers, a screen in the choir stalls was not obtrusive, and it was reasonably visible. This did not, however, inspire the Chapel to do anything permanent until the autumn of 2001, when PowerPoint was installed, as described in Chapter 56.

## Youth Council, 1991

### Responsibility

In 1991, Youth Council was responsible for 14 weekly activities. It is worth mentioning them briefly, because 5 of them were replaced by junior church under the new ministry that began in 1992 (Chapter 53).

### Sunday morning

1. A crèche for babies and toddlers was available as parents arrived; babies (usually 9) were cared for in one room, while toddlers up to the age of 3 (usually 18) went to the lower hall. This required 7 leaders and some helpers; a rota ensured that no one missed the sermon more than once every six weeks, so about 60 in all were needed for crèche duties.

2. After the children's talk, pre-school children left for Beginners Sunday School in the top hall; after some choruses, they divided, with 3- and 4-year-olds (usually 11) going to their own class, and pre-school 5-year-olds (usually 6) remaining in the hall. Nine leaders and helpers were required, on the same rota basis as mentioned above. Every child took a leaflet home, to show their parents what they had learned. Just before the sermon, parents with restless children of primary school age could take them to a quiet room on the top floor (Chapter 51). Children of school age were expected to stay in for the whole service.

### Sunday at 12.30 p.m.

3. Children aged 5 to 8 had a glass of juice and a biscuit in the lower hall after the morning service, and then met as the Primary Sunday School from 12.30-1.15 p.m. There were usually 28 youngsters and 6 teachers; again, the children took a leaflet home, and they had a memory verse. Pennies were collected weekly, to help the Chapel missionary, Mary Wight, keep her adopted son, Andrew, at school.

4. Junior Sunday School followed the same pattern, for 30 children aged from 8 to 12. They were together for the first 15 minutes, and then formed 5 classes. Pennies for

Peru were collected, to help a Sunday School in a shantytown on the outskirts of Lima; in 1991, over £100 was given. The leader, Mary Harrison, appointed in October 1990, was the first-ever woman leader in the Chapel's Sunday School, and she had 5 helpers.

5. Bible Class was for ages 12 to 15, about 30 young people, half boys and half girls and 4 teachers. When the church office at 13 South Charlotte Street became available in late 1992, they were delighted to use it instead of the main sanctuary, where people kept wandering through. As with the other groups, Scripture Union material was the foundation of the teaching.

## Friday evening

6. Rainbow Guides were started in 1991, for girls aged 5 and 6; they met in the deacons' counting room on the top floor from 6.15-7.15 p.m. Thirteen attended, of whom 8 had no other church connection, with 5 warranted leaders.

7. Beavers, for boys aged 6 and 7, also met from 6.15-7.30 p.m. The maximum number was 24, and there was usually a waiting list. Less than half of the Beavers had any other link with the Chapel, so the Bible-story time at the end of every meeting was important. There were 5 leaders.

8. Cub Scouts met in the lower hall from 6.00-7.30 p.m., for boys aged 8 to 11. Numbers varied from 20 to 28, with 6 leaders. Two-thirds came from non-Chapel families. They had 3 camps a year at Canty Bay, at Easter, summer and Christmas.

9. Brownies were girls aged 7 to 10, who also met from 6.00-7.30 p.m.; 18 girls were enrolled, with 15 regularly attending, and there were 3 leaders. Activities included swimming, trampolining, cooking, games, badge evenings and many more. Half were from non-Chapel families.

10. Guides met from 7.30-9.15 p.m., for girls aged 10 to 14. Twenty-three were on the register, of whom 20 attended regularly, several with no church connection, and there were 3 leaders.

11. Scouts, also meeting from 7.30-9.15 p.m., were boys aged 11 to 15. Numbers were steady at 37, of whom 20 were from non-Chapel families and 13 had no church connection; Scouts brought their friends from school. There were 6 leaders, and every Friday evening ended with a Scripture Union Bible reading and prayer. Camps at Canty Bay were held in July, October and at Christmas.

12. Venture Scouts started at 7.30 p.m., for boys aged 15 to 20. There were 17, soon rising to 24, of whom 7 had no other church connection, and 3 leaders.

13. Ranger Guides also started at 7.30 p.m., but only on alternate Fridays; they were for girls aged 15 to 20. Between 6 and 11 attended regularly, with 2 leaders; about one-thirds of the girls were from non-Chapel families.

In all, about 100 boys and 60 girls attended the uniformed organisations on Friday evening, which, along with camp, was seen as a real opportunity for evangelism. Parents were invited to family and birthday services.

## Saturday

14 Focus met on the first and third Saturday of the month at 7 p.m., to provide the Chapel's 12- to 15-year-olds with a social setting in which to develop Christian friendships. Forty regularly attended, 21 boys and 19 girls, with 7 leaders; camp in May was the highlight of the year.

In addition, 2 discovery groups were set up, one on Friday evening, the other on Sunday, for 8 young people who went forward during Mission Scotland at Murrayfield in May 1991 (below).

As Christmas drew near, the Chapel's top hall, lounge and lower hall were booked more or less continuously on Saturday, as the various groups put on their seasonal parties.

## Visitors' emblems

Early in 1992, a member returned from holiday in America with some small self-adhesive roses, which he had seen used to identify visitors to churches. The Chapel imported boxes of them from May 1992 to May 1994; visitors were asked at the door whether they would accept one and affix it to their lapel or dress. As members looked around, before and after the services, it was easy to welcome the wearers without risking the put-down: 'I've been coming here longer than you have'.

*Visitors were asked at the door whether they would affix this emblem to their lapel or dress, so that regular worshippers could say hello.*

## Outside events

### Keep Sunday Special

A government Bill in 1990, to remove all restrictions on Sunday trading in England and Wales, was the only legislation put forward by Margaret Thatcher's government to be defeated on the floor of the House. Although it did not directly affect Scotland, the Chapel threw its weight behind the opposition to it, with prayer and the canvassing of members of parliament. As the Chapel's representative on the Keep Sunday Special committee put it: 'Christians cannot be neutral in this matter. A day of rest is part of God's plan for all men. God cares about family and community life. A day in the week when almost everyone is free from work is essential for family life and for friendships to flourish by having time to spend together.'

### Rose Street

In July 1990, the Council pedestrianized Rose Street and banned traffic from it. For some years, it had been a busy through-road for cars, with 'no parking' signs, so it was not popular with either motorists or pedestrians. The Council agreed to suspend noisy renovation work during the Chapel's Sunday morning and evening services; if heavy equipment was operating as the service time approached, production of the Council's letter ensured a 90-minute tea break – not that the workmen objected to that.

*Before Rose Street was pedestrianized in July 1990, it was a busy through-road for cars, with 'no parking' signs, so it was not popular with either motorists or pedestrians.*

### Keswick in Edinburgh

The week of meetings in June, which Graham Scroggie had started in 1917, and which the Edinburgh Evangelistic Union had taken over in 1925, were popularly known as the Keswick Week, although the official title was the Edinburgh Convention (Chapter 29). There was no need to have them from 1956 to 1968, because the Monday-Thursday evening meetings from the large tent in Keswick were relayed to the Chapel by telephone link, but they resumed in the Chapel after the landline was discontinued (Chapter 39). They were reasonably well supported by Chapel people and others, with a guest preacher from Monday to Friday. In 1995, the venue was moved to the Bristo Baptist Church, but the Chapel still publicizes (and a few members attend) the Annual Bible Convention, as it is now known.

### Billy Graham – Mission Scotland, 1991

*Billy Graham spoke twice at the Murrayfield Rugby Stadium, as part of Mission Scotland, 1991; 46 of those who went forward, and who had no church connection, were referred to the Chapel for follow-up.*

The Chapel was involved in every aspect of Billy Graham's visit to the Murrayfield Stadium on Saturday 25 and Sunday 26 May 1991, at 4 p.m. – praying, stewarding, counselling, singing in the choir and much more. A Chapel member, who was a police traffic officer, was Graham's chauffeur throughout his visit to Edinburgh. Younger Christians, who had heard about the response to the appeals in the 1955 Crusade, were astonished, impressed and humbled to see hundreds come forward for counselling at the conclusion of the message. Forty-six people, with no active church connection, between the ages of 7 and 60, were referred to the Chapel for follow-up.

*The Chapel enthusiastically supported the work of Billy Graham and he, for his part, was grateful to the Chapel. From left to right: Kath and Alex Cameron, Billy Graham, the writer and his wife, at a reception for the Grahams.*

## Romania

In the spring of 1990, one of the Chapel's former assistants, Tom Lawson, felt a burden for Christians in Romania, which had recently opened its borders to the west. The Chapel responded with enthusiasm in half a dozen ways. The first was to supply Tom with as many Bibles as he could take to Romania in April 1990. The second was to fill two lorries, one carrying 7 tons and the other (refrigerated) carrying 16 tons, with £4,000 of medical supplies, £4,000 of food, £2,000 of Bibles, £2,000 of clothing and bedding, £1,000 of toiletries and £1,000 of spare parts, together with a huge amount of toys, shoes, books and other items. Chapel members Jeremy Landless and Brian Wilson (along with several non-Chapel men) drove these lorries from Edinburgh to Bucharest, where Chapel members Colin and Karen Finlayson were nursing in an orphanage. Another consignment of medical supplies for the orphanage followed in August 1991; Jeremy and Brian set off again in December, and this time they also delivered a lorry-load to Doru Popu in Arad (below).

Thirdly, the Chapel supplied Bibles and literature to churches in Arad and Timiurlra over a number of years. Fourthly, a retiring offering of £7,000 in June 1992 enabled the Chapel to sponsor four pastors in Arad for four years; after that, two of them received local support, but the Chapel continued to finance the other two. Fifthly, the Chapel gave hospitality for Romanians coming to Edinburgh; Rev. Doru Popu, pastor of the Arad Baptist Church, conducted a university mission here in 1992, and choirs from Romanian churches sang in the Chapel in 1996, 1997, 1998 and 2000.

Sixthly, many Chapel members have gone to Romania over the years since 1990, to help in a variety of Christian projects. Kirsty Dennis was the first, for four weeks in January 1992, followed by Stephen Lawson and wife for three weeks, and Ian and Sheila Finlayson for ten days in April. Colin and Karen Finlayson stayed in Bucharest until 1993; John Easton filmed a documentary about Romanian orphanages in 1997; John and Emily Smuts visited in 1998; the Chapel's assistant pastor, John Percival, lectured in Romania for two weeks in 2002. Chapel member Hamish MacRae (Andrew's brother) still goes regularly throughout the year to teach, for a fortnight at a time, in the pastors' colleges there.

## Festival kiosk, 1991

Twenty-six Chapel people took turns to give out evangelistic literature from an outreach kiosk in Rose Street, throughout the three weeks of the Edinburgh International Festival in August 1991 – they were well received and there was a good response.

## Care caravan

From 1991 onward, two of the Chapel's peer groups, YPM and Group 35, provided personnel, on a rota basis, to staff a care caravan, a joint venture between the Bethany Christian Trust, Edinburgh City Mission and several local churches. Edinburgh had a growing homelessness problem, with about four thousand people sleeping rough. On the basis that 'one person sleeping rough in Edinburgh in our day is one too many', teams parked the caravan on Waverley Bridge, initially between midnight and 2 a.m. on Friday and Saturday and 5-7 a.m. on Wednesday. About 20 homeless people came into the caravan on a typical night, to be given hot soup and freshly baked rolls, and to have a talk with the six helpers, who offered advice and who supplied fresh blankets for those in need.

427

The need was so great that by 1993, the Care Van (its new name) was in place from 9.30-11.30 p.m., 365 nights in the year, and about 40 people were served every evening. This was a heavy commitment – Group 35 were responsible for six Wednesdays in May and June. The van then became mobile, and made regular stops in central Edinburgh, which gave up to 60 homeless men and women every evening the opportunity of help. One Chapel member described a typical evening in 2001:

*The Care Van used to be a mobile bank; now it's a mobile soup kitchen, serving the homeless people of Edinburgh every night of the year. It's stocked with tracts, Bibles and information on where the homeless can get accommodation, clothes and food. It is run by two Christian organisations, Bethany Christian Trust and Edinburgh City Mission, but is manned by teams (of at least six volunteers) from thirty different churches....*

*We aim to be at Waverley Bridge for 9 p.m., where we open the back doors and offer homeless people tea, coffee or cup-a-soup and a roll. We hand out clothes. There is usually a demand for gloves, scarves and hats. On an average night there will be 20-30 people. We get the chance to talk to them, lend a listening ear, and from time to time, share the Gospel with them.*

*We head along Princes Street to King Stables Road. We go out on foot here, as well as into St. Cuthbert's graveyard to see if anyone is bedding down. We go to Lothian Road and then the Grassmarket. The next stop for the van is Bristo Square but on our way through the Cowgate we may see someone at West Nicholson Street and will stop to serve. When we get to Bristo we go out on foot to check if there are any homeless people in the area. North Bridge is our next stop before our final stop at Canongate Kirk. Back at Jane Street we clean the van and finish the night with a time of prayer before heading home at midnight.*

---

2 *Record*, April 2001, p. 12.

The Young Peoples Meeting provided a team on the second Saturday of every month, through to the spring of 2003. By then, the clientele were no longer under the influence of drink (with which the YPM could cope) but displayed the violent and irrational behaviour of drug abusers. The Chapel felt it inappropriate to ask young people to deal with this, and experienced helpers took their place. At the time of going to print (2007), the Chapel is providing a team of five every second Saturday evening.

## 'Call' to Rev. Peter Grainger

### 16 September 1990

The third Sunday in September is part of the Edinburgh autumn holiday, and the Chapel is fairly thinly attended. The Young Peoples Meeting take as many as possible away for the weekend, and families have a break before the winter sets in. During the vacancy, the writer, as church secretary, usually invited a local person to be the guest preacher. However, when the representative of a missionary society (who had preached before) offered to take the services on Sunday 16 September 1990, because he was to be in Scotland anyway, his offer was gratefully accepted and hospitality arrangements were made.

Shortly before the weekend, his minister telephoned from Swindon to the writer, to say that the man was no longer available, but that he (the minister) could come in his place. The writer, embarrassed at the comparatively modest number who would attend the Chapel on that Sunday, suggested he might come on some other occasion. However, he replied that even a few hundred was more than many churches had for special occasions; the air ticket was non-refundable and, anyway, he would like a weekend in Edinburgh.

When a guest preacher's ministry made an impression on the congregation, the elder giving hospitality often invited other elders and their wives to drop in for coffee, after the evening service. Those who gathered that evening were insistent that Peter Grainger be invited back, as soon as possible, so that others might meet him. The first available date was Sunday 10 February 1991. On the Friday before the Sunday, he phoned to say that Swindon was cut off by snowstorms and that there was no possibility of getting through by train, air or in any other way. The next mutually convenient date was 25 August 1991.

## 25 August 1991

After Peter Grainger's second visit, on 25 August 1991, this time accompanied by his wife, the elders came quickly and without hesitation, to the unanimous recommendation that he should be invited for a week in October, and that members should be told this was 'with a view'. Peter Grainger was surprised. At his induction, he said that his wife had asked him, as the train drew out of Waverley station on their return to Swindon in August 1991, whether he thought there was anything more behind the visit. Peter's reply was: 'Put it out of your mind. I doubt whether these 22 elders will ever be unanimous about the vacancy on this side of eternity.' They were – for the first time as a vacancy committee.

When the Graingers came back to Edinburgh for the last week in October, they spoke at the prayer meeting, got to know the elders and deacons and the staff and the residents of Beulah, attended the YPM and the Women's Morning Fellowship and the Bible School. On Tuesday 5 November, the congregation endorsed the unanimous and enthusiastic recommendation of the vacancy committee, to issue a 'call'. After much prayer and heart-searching and consultation with friends and the elders at Freshbrook, he graciously accepted. When this was announced (simultaneously in Edinburgh and in Swindon) on Sunday morning 24 November 1991, the congregation in the Chapel spontaneously sang the doxology. Delighted though they were for themselves, they were concerned that the young congregation at Freshbrook would soon go into a vacancy situation. To allow the children to complete the school year, it was arranged that the Graingers would move to Edinburgh as a family in July 1992, with the induction on Saturday 22 August.

*Elders and deacons at the end of the vacancy, August 1992. Tim Prime, Derek Liddell, Ian Finlayson, Jim Landels, Donald Cameron, Sid Harrison, Philip Murray, Harry Robertson, Bill Walker, John Grant, John Shepherd, Angus Ferguson, Derek Finlayson, Johnny Prime, Barry Sprott, Bryce Crawford, David Whitlie, Albert Peterson, Robert Shaw, Robert Naysmith, Alastair Hay, Norman Wallace, Norman Wilson, Adrian Todd, Stewart McLeod, Ian Balfour, Jonathan Bartlett, George Haig, Russ Murray, David Fairlie, David Dennis, Jim McCall, (inset left) Eric Smith  (inset right) George Nash.*

## Reflections on the timetable

Looking back, it is evident why 1991 was the appointed year, both for the Chapel and for Peter Grainger. The elders never departed from two fundamental principles: (1) not to consider two names at the same time, and (2) complete unanimity would signify they had met the man of God's choosing. If snowstorms had not isolated Swindon on Saturday 9 February 1991, delaying Peter Grainger's second visit until August, it is doubtful whether the committee, or the church, would have known what to do. A week of ministry had been arranged for the end of April 1991, and many hoped that the guest preacher might be persuaded to fill the vacancy. At the end of that week, there was no unanimity, and the visitor said he wanted to stay in his present church. Only after that week – a necessary week to focus their thinking – did the vacancy committee accept that the someone 'out there', whom God had prepared for the Chapel, might not be widely known (yet) in Baptist churches. The way was prepared for 25 August 1991.

Peter Grainger, for his part, could not have considered a 'call' any earlier than 1991. He had gone as pastor to the Freshbrook Evangelical Church in Swindon in 1988; by 1989, the church had outgrown the community centre, and a new church building was opened in June 1990. Until that was established, it would have been unthinkable to leave.

## Membership

Before the new pastor arrived, the elders reviewed the roll and deleted 51 names of those with whom they had lost touch or who could not be persuaded to attend. The vacancy ended with a lean but healthy membership of 663:616 full members and 47 associate.

Additional information on the following topics, mentioned in this chapter, is available on the CD.

Girl Guides
Vacancy, 1987-1992

# Chapter 53
## Challenges bring change (1992–1995)

### The new pastor

**The Grainger family**

Peter Grainger was aged 45 when he became the eighteenth pastor of Charlotte Chapel. He was brought up in a Christian home and in a Baptist church (FIEC) in Chesterfield in Derbyshire; he was converted in his early teens at a Youth For Christ rally. On leaving school, he read Biblical History and Literature at the University of Sheffield, and in 1968 he joined Wycliffe Bible Translators. After linguistic training and a year at the Bible Training Institute in Glasgow, he became Wycliffe's first student secretary. He did deputation work among college and university students in Great Britain for two years.

In 1972, Wycliffe asked him to go to Nepal, and then to India, where his work included language surveys and initiating a programme for training Indian nationals. After one year of full-time study at Reading University (1974-5) and two more years of part-time study while back in India, he obtained a Masters degree in linguistic science.

Mrs Nita Grainger was a linguist in her own right, having graduated with honours in Spanish and Latin American Studies from the University of Newcastle. She became a Christian in her late teens, through reading the Bible; her involvement with the university Christian Union greatly strengthened her faith. As part of her course, she spent several months in Mexico and Brazil with Wycliffe. Although she too was from Chesterfield, she and Peter did not meet until they were at the Wycliffe Centre near High Wycombe in 1976. They married a year later, in June 1977, after she had completed a one-year course at All Nations Bible College; they served together overseas for the next eight years.

While in Nigeria, Nita became very ill with a series of viruses. When they returned to England in 1985, she was hospitalised in the London Hospital for Tropical Diseases. They were advised not to go overseas in the near future. During recent furloughs, they had linked up with the Long Crendon Baptist Church in Aylesbury, Buckinghamshire. Peter was invited to join its pastoral team, as well as teaching at Wycliffe. For three years he worked with the pastor and gained valuable experience; the church ordained him to full-time ministry.

In 1988 they were 'called' to the Freshbrook Evangelical Church in Swindon. Started six years previously in a community centre, it had only 40 members when the Graingers arrived, but together they put up a building to seat 600, on a cosmopolitan new estate, at a cost of £600,000. The membership grew to 120 during their time; they were not anticipating a move from Freshbrook, but they knew there is never such a word as 'never' in Christian service.

When they arrived in Edinburgh in July 1992, having accepted the 'call' to Charlotte Chapel, they moved into the manse at 11 Midmar Gardens, which the Redpaths had chosen in 1963 (Chapter 42) and which the Chapel had used or rented out through the long vacancy. They occupied it until November 2006, when they downsized into property of their own (Chapter 58).

*The Grainger family as they came to Edinburgh in the summer of 1992. Benjamin was born in 1980, and Rebecca in 1981.*

### Induction

The induction service, on Saturday 22 August 1992, was a joyful occasion in a full church. About 50 had come from Freshbrook, and Peter Grainger spoke frankly, but with humour, about the events leading up to his 'call' (Chapter 52). Rev. George Mitchell from Kirkintilloch, who had been Peter's mentor in the Bible Training Institute in 1968, led the dedication. Prayers of commitment were followed by choral, orchestral and solo pieces. Rev. Beverley Savage from Swindon brought the message.

After tea (served in the lounge, lower hall and top hall, to accommodate the numbers), a welcome social added a lighter touch, with musical items and a recitation. It was a typical induction into a Scottish Baptist church of the 1990s, including greetings from many places, a beautiful flower arrangement for Nita Grainger, an epilogue and a benediction pronounced by the new pastor. A souvenir edition of the *Record* included the programme, the hymns, additional greetings and the names of the 148 men who had occupied the pulpit during the 253 Sundays of the vacancy. The day concluded with a well-attended ceilidh and a buffet meal in a marquee in Murrayfield Road.

## 'Is there a better way?'

Peter Grainger added a new word to the elders' and deacons' agendas – 'Why'? 'Why do you do this, and why do you do it this way?' It was fascinating to examine issues from two different backgrounds. When the elders or deacons demurred at some proposal, he would ask, 'Why not?' Some were fundamental changes, such as home groups replacing the Thursday Bible School, gospel preaching on Sunday morning and teaching for Christians at night, holding communion as an integral part of the Sunday service (not as an optional extra at the end) and the creation of junior church during the Sunday morning service (all examined below). Others involved a different way of carrying out existing practices, such as candidates for baptism giving oral testimony from the pulpit and applicants for membership undergoing a rigorous training programme (also examined below).

Other new ideas were minor by comparison, but very effective. For Student Welcoming Sunday in October 1992, the whole congregation was issued with adhesive labels on which to write their names. At a point in the service, everyone was asked to greet those around them; many regular attenders were delighted to be able to put a name to familiar faces, as well as welcoming strangers personally. Following that, colour coded badges were provided every week for elders, deacons, stewards and counsellors, and this has continued ever since.

'Churches are good at starting things', said the new pastor, 'but poor at stopping them when they have outlived their purpose'. The remainder of this chapter looks at some of the challenges and changes that he brought to Chapel life between 1992 and 1995. Initiatives by the laity, over the same period, are mentioned in the next chapter.

## Statement of purpose

The office-bearers and their wives held a retreat on a Saturday at the beginning of October every year. Peter Grainger set the agenda for October 1993 by asking: 'For what purpose did the Lord bring our church into being?' or, more simply, 'Why are we here?' The participants hammered out a rudimentary statement of purpose, by which to evaluate the Chapel's many activities. This was refined over the next few months, and approved at a members' meeting as follows:

*Charlotte Baptist Chapel exists to glorify God as we endeavour to:*
*honour God's name, by worshipping Him together in spirit and in truth, so that we please Him in all we say and do,*
*teach God's Word, by seeking to understand and apply all of the Scriptures to our lives, so that we become more like our Lord Jesus Christ,*
*serve God's people, by caring for one another and building one another up in the faith, so that we reach maturity in Christ,*
*extend God's kingdom, by proclaiming the good news of Jesus Christ and demonstrating His love in action, so that others might confess Christ as Lord.*

1 Charlotte Chapel Annual Report, 1993.

This complemented the doctrinal statement, which every member accepted on joining the church (Chapter 47); the statement of purpose focused on the Chapel's activities rather than on its core beliefs.

## New ideas for Sunday

### Sunday morning

The congregation was delighted to get back to consecutive Bible teaching, with a series on Revelation on Sunday morning through to November 1992, followed by the life of Jacob; in the evening, studies in the book of Ruth were interspersed with special events like baptisms. However, change was not long in coming. The tradition had been for a teaching ministry on Sunday morning and a gospel message at night. Peter Grainger, recognizing that there were more unconverted people in most churches on Sunday morning than on Sunday evening, embarked on a morning evangelistic series from January to May 1993, entitled

'Encounters with Jesus'. This focused on people whom Jesus had met when he was on earth; to bring the historical encounters up to date, a member of the congregation was interviewed every Sunday about his or own personal encounter with Jesus. The children's talk and the hymns and music were tied in with the theme, which caught the imagination of the congregation. Stewards recruited during the vacancy, when there were more seats than people, soon learned how to pack the building and to direct latecomers politely to the televised overflow in the lounge.

In Swindon, Peter Grainger had not normally both led a service and preached at it. From his arrival in Edinburgh, he usually invited one elder to give the children's talk and another to lead the pastoral prayer. On Sunday evening, he sometimes sat in the congregation until it was time to preach. He was not impressed with other churches, which he had visited, where one man was expected to do everything; he wanted to work in a team.

### Children's worksheets

Children of school age were expected to sit through the whole Sunday morning service. With the start of the morning evangelistic services in January 1993, children aged 5-11 were offered worksheets, linked with the theme of the sermon, to be completed during the service and handed in. There were prizes at the end of the series. This lasted for 18 months, until the creation of junior church during the morning service, as described below.

### Bibles in the pews

So that visitors could follow the Scripture reading during the service, Peter Grainger purchased three hundred Bibles and placed them in the pews. From then on, announcement of the passage to be read included: 'on page __ in the pew Bibles'. Chapel members, brought up to know their Bibles, listened with incredulity (but with growing understanding) when Peter Grainger told them about a man, who had begun to attend church and to read the New Testament. Peter asked him, one day, how far he had got; he replied, 'to page 108'.

### Sunday evening

On his first Sunday, Peter Grainger tackled the vexed question of community hymn singing before the evening service started at 6.30 p.m. As mentioned in Chapter 51, the congregation insisted on this during the vacancy, although some deliberately arrived at 6.28 p.m. in order to miss it. The new pastor had a masterly answer to the various points of view. The evening service was re-timed, to start at 6.20 p.m.; he went into the pulpit, and announced and led three or four worship songs in succession. Not earlier than 6.30 p.m., he read some Scripture verses, as a call to worship, and announced a hymn; most people were now in their seats by 6.20 p.m., everyone by 6.30 p.m.

The 6.20 p.m. experiment was suspended during the pastor's holiday month in July 1993, and not restarted – it had served its purpose. For a while, the evening service again began with a hymn, prayer, welcome and another hymn, but it was not long before Peter Grainger established a pattern that pleased most of the people most of the time. He started with several songs or hymns together, and the young people loved it. Student numbers had always been good, but they doubled in the academic year 1993-4. There was nearly always a mission spot, where members involved in home or overseas evangelism were interviewed about their work, followed by prayer for it. Like all good new ideas, it was reviewed after a couple of years, and from 1995, it was used only when someone special was passing through.

Before the introduction of PowerPoint in 2001 (Chapter 55), the bulletin included the full order of service; a typical Sunday evening during Peter Grainger's third year was:

| | |
|---|---|
| *Welcome* | |
| *287* | *I love you, Lord* |
| *570* | *Reign in me, Sovereign Lord* |
| *388* | *Jesus, we enthrone you* |
| *335* | *In my life, Lord* |
| *Prayer* | |
| *77* | *Christ triumphant* |
| *Intimations and offering* | |
| *Dedication of offering* | |
| *Mission spot* | *Ian Finlayson with Kate Jackson* |
| *Prayer* | |
| *Band and singers* | *Amazing love* |
| *Reading* | *I Kings 18:16-29 (page 359)* |
| *359* | *Jesus calls us* |
| *Message* | *Elijah – No answer* |
| *476* | *My Lord, what love is this?* |
| *Benediction* | |

2 Order of service for Sunday evening, 20 November 1994.

With the new ministry, there was less need for monthly after-church fellowships, which had been popular (and useful) during the vacancy; the members' meeting in January 1994 voted to have them only if and when some special occasion came along.

## Series

For the calendar year 1994, the pastor preached in the morning through the Letter to the Hebrews, drawing out encouragements, challenges and lessons for daily living. In the evening, he expounded the parables in Matthew's Gospel from January to June, and then the life of Elijah from August to December – a series that continued into 1995. As these themes were developed, the benefits were evident in two ways – first, in large numbers attending, with the sanctuary often filled nearly to capacity in the evening as well as overflowing in the morning and, secondly, in the lively interest in what came next in the series. Pulpit exposition was supplemented by guided discussion of the same passage in fellowship groups during the week (below).

## Testimony at baptisms

In Peter Grainger's first 21 months in the Chapel, there were 14 baptismal services, at which nearly all of the 51 candidates gave testimony from the pulpit in the earlier part of the service. He explained what was behind this innovation: 'public confession of the faith of a new Christian is a great encouragement to all the others.' For the same reason, he printed a précis of every candidate's journey to faith in the *Record* from January 1994 onward, along with the testimony of new members. Of the 51 baptized, 28 were male and 23 were female; 33 were under 23; 12 were aged 23–30; 3 were aged 31–40; 3 were over 40; 33 were students; 43 were British; 7 were children of Chapel members; 49 were unmarried.

Radio microphones are now taken for granted, but the Chapel's first purchase was in 1995 (cost, £359), for the pastor's use at baptismal services. The writer was relieved, because until then one of his more anxious duties as church secretary was to make sure that the microphone stand, connected to the electric power supply, was near enough to the baptismal pool to pick up the pastor's voice without being so near as to topple into it.

## Junior church (Sunday morning)

The timing of Sunday School (12.30-1.15 p.m.) was far from ideal; the bulk of the morning service was not tailored for children, and those who had sat through it were tired and ready for lunch. Peter Grainger asked the elders: if adults were being taught in a manner appropriate for them (the sermon), why should children not be taught at the same time in a way appropriate for them (junior church)? This was revolutionary thinking for Charlotte Chapel; he raised it in August 1993, and kept it on the agenda until the new scheme was approved by the membership in June 1994.

Some parents were initially opposed to junior church during the morning service, but the majority supported it, provided it catered only for primary school age. The original plan had been for children up to secondary 2 to leave after the children's talk, but the parents' strong preference, at the consultation stage, was for all secondary school children to stay with them. At a members' meeting in June 1994, the choice was whether all primary children should go out, or only children up to primary 4 (age approximately eight); the majority vote was for the latter. It was agreed to experiment with the following programme for a year, commencing on 28 August 1994, and then to evaluate it.

## The experiment

The baby crèche (15 babies in the committee room) and the toddler crèche (26 in the lower hall) continued as before, from 10.45 a.m. to the end of the service. Between them, they catered for children until their third birthday. Fire regulations required a ratio of one adult for every two children, so 21 adults were on duty on Sunday, on a rota of once every six weeks.

After the children's talk, two groups left for junior church. Discoverers (formerly the Beginners Sunday School, plus one extra year) were children aged from third birthday to primary 1. They went to the top hall where, after an initial time together, they divided into classes for three-, four- and five-year-olds. Numbers doubled in the first year from 20 to 40. Twelve teachers per Sunday were on a four-week rota.

The other group to leave was CID (Christian Investigation Department), for children of primary 2-4; they met in the church office in 13 South Charlotte Street. After an initial time together, the children divided into three classes. There were 40 on the roll and attendance averaged 35.

Teachers were provided with a tape of the service they had missed, and they were encouraged to attend on Sunday evening. Six times a year (Christmas, Thinking Day, Easter, Youth Council Birthday, Harvest and Remembrance Day) all children over three stayed in for a family service, usually participating in it. On these Sundays, only the crèches were held.

Two groups still met at 12.30 p.m., after the morning service. FBI (Fearless Bible Investigators), formerly the Junior Sunday School, was for primary 5-7 (ages 8-11); after a glass of juice in the lower hall, they went to classes in the top hall. There were 34 on the roll and about 25 attended regularly. Bible Class (secondary 1-3, no change of name) went to the church office, where, after a short time together, they split into groups of five or six for serious Bible Study, with three teachers. Their parents chatted in the lounge over a cup of coffee until the family was reunited at 1.15 p.m.

### Everyone out

It was not long before junior church was extended to include FBI and Bible Class; they were too tired and hungry, after sitting through the morning service, to concentrate. From October 1996, FBI left during school term along with the younger children; they did not go out during the school holidays, so they could become accustomed to attending the whole service. The elders had a real concern that if youngsters were not gradually introduced to adult services, they might stop coming altogether when they reached the end of junior church at the age of 12. For the same reason, Bible Class went out for half of the Sundays in the year; for the other 26, they stayed in. In all, about 150 children attended the Chapel on Sunday morning, and this number grew under the new arrangement.

### Communion

In February 1993, Peter Grainger asked the elders to consider incorporating the monthly communion into the main service, as a seamless part of one whole. For many years, people in the gallery had been invited, on the first Sunday of the month, to come downstairs to the area during the hymn after the sermon, in order to participate in the Lord's Supper. Visitors were told that all who loved the Lord, irrespective of

membership, were invited to stay. Despite that exhortation, about half the congregation left during the hymn, including many members – a habit formed, and not corrected, over years. It was rare for the area of the church to be full.

In the summer of 1995, Peter Grainger took the first step towards his suggestion. He did not yet have communion before the sermon – that came later, in the autumn of 1998 – but in 1995, he moved directly from the sermon to the Lord's Supper, with elders serving communion in the gallery as well as in the area. The *Record* subtly drew attention to the change; at the beginning of the year, it announced: 'communion is after the service', then the word changed to: 'during the service'. This made for seamless worship, which was appreciated; people in the gallery did not have to move, and only a few slipped out during the hymn after the sermon. When that hymn was sung sitting down (as the hymn before communion traditionally was), it took a bold person to stand up and go. Those who did not wish to participate were told to pass on the bread and the wine.

This had implications, both practical and theological. Practical: were there enough glasses to serve everyone? Hamilton & Inches, the silversmiths in George Street, were asked whether they could manufacture some more (matching) silver trays; they replied that they had been holding two trays in their vaults since the Chapel placed an order many years previously, which had not been collected. With these extra trays, the elders were able to prepare 672 glasses (28 trays with 24 glasses); normally that sufficed, although occasionally the duty elder had to replenish empty trays in the vestry as elders came to the front with people still to be served. Ten years later, with the same system operating, only 26 trays were needed, giving 576 glasses in the sanctuary and 48 in the lounge; some came back unused, so (say) five hundred were taking communion at morning services. There were less at evening communions – the total congregation on Sunday 6 June 1999 was 327.

Theological: should one 'fence the table'? There were people in the pews who would not have described themselves as believers and, in the morning, there were a hundred or more children from the age of nine. The pastor always explained the implications of participating in the Lord's Supper but later, when people had become accustomed to the new format, communion became what the Scots divines used to call 'a converting ordinance'.

*Let me say two things in conclusion, before and in preparation for coming to the Lord's Table. First of all, if you are not a Christian, then whatever you may have done, whatever lifestyle you may be leading … I have good news for you. The good news of Jesus Christ is that God has made a way by which you can be washed, by which you can be set apart, by which you can be put right with God….*

*God can do something that you will never do by your own efforts. He can transform you, he can change you, he can set you apart, he can use you in his service and he will declare you right on that day of judgement when you stand before God, because Christ stands in your place – the just for the unjust, to bring you to God.*

*So if you are not a Christian as you come to this table, the challenge of God's word is this – 'be reconciled to God', 2 Corinthians 5. The apostle Paul says: 'as ambassadors for Christ, we implore you, be reconciled to God.'… And if you are not, this evening you have an opportunity. You can come to this table for the first time, in repentance and faith, with nothing in your hands, in confession of your sin, and ask Christ. He will receive you, he will reconcile you to God, he will put his Spirit within you, and he will give you the hope of eternal life. That's the first thing I want to say at the Lord's Table. Here's the second one. If you are a Christian, then you cannot afford to be in any kind of dispute with any other Christian, especially one within the same fellowship, the same church.*

---

3 Evening service, 6 April 2003.

For communion during the evening of the anniversary weekend in October 1998, Peter Grainger went further. After opening devotions, he conducted the Lord's Supper almost at the beginning of the service, followed by the sermon (as Graham Scroggie had done in 1917 (Chapter 21)); he repeated this at the next evening communion, in December, and occasionally after that, but it did not become a regular pattern.

At Easter 1997, the communion service on Maundy Thursday evening, which consisted of nothing but Scripture reading and comment before the bread and the wine, was so well attended that it had be held in the sanctuary, not in the lounge; that has been the pattern ever since.

## New ideas for weekdays

### Fellowship groups

The traditional Thursday evening Bible School met for the last time during the autumn of 1992. The theme was 'sharing your faith', particularly in personal counselling; one of the weaknesses that Peter Grainger had identified in the Chapel was how few people were available, or at least willing, to speak with enquirers after the Sunday services.

That was just the beginning. It took all of Peter Grainger's enthusiasm to persuade the Chapel to replace the Thursday Bible School permanently with small groups, meeting in homes, for Bible study and pastoral care. This was achieved in three stages. From January to April 1993, 60 potential leaders were invited to meet on Thursday evening, to learn the dynamics of group study; because of this, there was no Bible School. This produced 25 leaders and a dozen deputies. From April to June, Peter Grainger led a short Bible Study in the Chapel on Thursday evening, to which everyone was invited; the meeting then broke into study and prayer groups, for the leaders to practice what they had learned over the previous months. This was in addition to four Navigator 2:7 groups, which were already running and which had their own agenda over an eighteen-month discipleship course.

The name fellowship groups was chosen for the third and final stage. Members and regular worshippers were exhorted to signify willingness to be involved, and 380 did so, in addition to the 40 already in Navigator groups. They were divided into 22 groups, scattered around the city, and meetings began in September 1993. Two were held during the day; the other groups met twice monthly, either on a Tuesday or a Thursday evening. With 22 elders in the church, one was linked to every group, although not necessarily to lead it. Average attendance was 13-14 per group. Many found the groups were a gateway to wider fellowship in the church – there were now people to whom they could relate among the sea of faces on a Sunday; others discovered their voice for the first time, as they contributed to the discussion.

*Nearly 400 signed up for a fellowship group as soon as the leaflets were available in the summer of 1993.*

fellowship groups, of whom 320 were church members; in 1998, the total dropped to 294. It took '40 Days of Purpose' in 2006 to get five hundred people involved (Chapter 58).

### Pastoral groups

The existing pastoral groups, which had met three times a year since 1970, all on the same evening, were to be phased out when fellowship groups got under way. However, members appreciated the opportunity of discussing church business in a home context (members only), so pastoral groups were retained as mini business meetings. The significance of this is taken up in Chapter 55.

### Peer groups

The growth of fellowship groups (all ages) undermined, but did not eliminate, the role of peer groups. Group 45, for those over 40, provided a welcoming environment for newcomers and fellowship for members on one Saturday and one Sunday evening a month; it continues to this day, under the name Apex from November 2003.

Group 2545 remained popular for another few years, with a weekly programme during summer and monthly Saturday and Sunday meetings during the winter. Most who attended were single; young marrieds, especially those with children, were drawn to the new 'Family Matters' ministry. Even for singles, Group 2545 was too successful for its own good; as newcomers integrated into the Chapel through the group (which was its purpose), they linked up with fellowship groups instead. Group 2545 disbanded in 2000, and despite initiatives called 'Moving Beyond 2545' and 'Son of 2545', it was 2002 before it was re-launched as 'Matrix' (Chapter 57).

### Mothers and Others

Nita Grainger started a new group in August 1993, for younger women. A Young Women's Group had been started some years before, to provide fellowship and to discuss topics relevant to their age. However, evenings were proving difficult for them, so Nita Grainger: (1) changed the time to Tuesday morning, 9.30-11.00 a.m., (2) increased the frequency from monthly to weekly, and (3) changed the name to Mothers and Others. It was for mothers with pre-school or school age children, and other women in that age range. About 30 gathered in the lounge, initially for coffee and a chat; older women looked after the babies and toddlers in a crèche. On the first and third Tuesdays of the month,

Over time, the fellowship groups became the primary agency for pastoral care. By 1995, 459 had signed up for a group, of whom 350 were Chapel members; deducting those who could not attend for geographical or health reasons, 459 represented 70 per cent of the membership. Most now applying to join the church had come via a fellowship group. The ideal was for a group to divide when numbers reached 15, but some groups had gelled so well that they were reluctant to do this. At the end of 1995, nearly all the groups had 20 or more members and 5 groups had over 25. The major change during 1995 was to study the passage on which the pastor preached on Sunday morning, instead of using independent material; there was much debate as to whether it was more profitable to study the passage before the pastor preached on it or afterwards.

Over the next five years, about half of the groups flourished, but the other half struggled. In 1997, four hundred attended

Mothers and Others divided into small groups for Bible study, using *Parents and Children* as a guide; on the second Tuesday, they had a speaker on some relevant topic.

On the fourth week of the month, they joined the Women's Thursday Morning Fellowship; the two meetings were complementary, not competitive. Over the years, society had changed and it was increasingly difficult for younger women to attend; if they were not collecting children from nursery school, they were back at work after their children had started school. The Thursday meeting still attracted over a hundred; although the average age was 73, numbers did not decrease as new people kept coming. Many were from other churches, and they appreciated both the warm pre-meeting fellowship and the excellent quality of the speakers. The meeting continues to this day, with the members growing older gracefully together; newcomers are still made welcome – and they become regulars.

As Mothers and Others grew throughout the 1990s, there were three developments. A group of Koreans met separately, weekly in homes, to study the Bible from the perspective of a different culture (they still do). Secondly, working mothers began to meet on Friday evening, to investigate the Christian faith as worked out in their situations. Thirdly, the name Mothers and Others was changed to Oasis in 2001. The Tuesday morning meeting continues weekly, with the regular support of 20-30 mothers, and others helping in the crèche.

### Tuesday prayer meeting

The lounge was regularly filled, sometimes almost to capacity, for the Monday evening congregational prayer meeting. The last of Peter Grainger's new ideas for weekday activities came in February 1995. He proposed that the prayer meeting should move from Monday to Tuesday. He wanted to clear one day in the week of all church activities, and Monday was the only possible day; fellowship groups met on Tuesday and Thursday, the YPM on Wednesday and the uniformed organisations on Friday. He suggested that Monday should be used to digest what had been learned on Sunday, to relax after the busyness of the previous day, to have time with families and to build bridges with non-Christians.

He introduced a four-week Tuesday cycle, unrelated to the calendar month: week one was a missionary prayer meeting,

at 7.30 p.m.; on weeks two and four, Tuesday fellowship groups met in homes and the prayer meeting in the church was for all others, at 8 p.m.; on week three, the prayer meeting in the church was for all, at 8 p.m., on general topics. Reaction was generally positive. As with most of Peter Grainger's innovations, people initially said 'Why?' and he said 'Why not?' A trial period was fixed for January 1996; it was reviewed and confirmed in July 1996, and this pattern lasted for a decade, until September 2006, when it moved to Wednesday (Chapter 58).

## New ideas in pastoral matters

### Pastoral assistant

Peter Grainger was anxious to bring the pastoral team up to its full establishment. The vacancy committee had looked primarily for a preacher, and had deliberately refrained from making any settlement on the pastoral side until the senior pastor was in post. Rev. Angus Noble, who had recently returned after 25 years as a missionary in the Philippines, helped out from October to December 1992 and formally joined the team on 1 January 1993. His title was 'Pastoral Assistant'; his experience and spiritual gifts equipped him admirably for pastoral care and visitation. He was also chaplain to the Mustard Seed Café.

### Deaconess

In August 1995, the Chapel welcomed a new deaconess, Miss Eilish Agnew. In the 18 months since Jessie Bell had moved to other areas of Christian service, a Chapel member, Mrs Jess Talbot, had assisted the team while her husband worked with the Edinburgh City Mission. Over the 18 months, the elders tried to find a better title for the post, but eventually decided that most Chapel folk knew what a deaconess was – a lady worker, whose gifts were pastoral and encouraging, and who ministered to the sick and elderly, cared for single mothers, supported new and young mothers and was generally available to counsel women as needs arose.

Eilish came with the warm commendation of her home church in Ballymena, Northern Ireland. It was there that she put her faith in Christ in her teens, and soon developed an interest in overseas mission. After working for some years as a school secretary, she trained at the Belfast Bible College and then served for 16 years with the Overseas Missionary Fellowship in the Philippines. When her role in urban church-planting there was phased out, she worked full-time with her home church; when they offered her sabbatical leave, she enrolled for a course in counselling skills at St John's College in Nottingham. While she was there, Angus Noble, who had been her field director in Manila, recommended her for the vacancy on the Chapel's pastoral team; she came to Edinburgh as soon as her course was complete. During her eleven years in the Chapel, her job-title was changed from 'deaconess' to 'pastoral assistant'; she retired in July 2006 and returned to her family in Northern Ireland.

Eilish's conscientious attention to those confined in their homes soon threw up the need for more help, so a pastoral visitation team was formed, with eight women who visited two or three shut-in members once or twice a month.

*The pastoral team in October 1995 – Nic Roach, Peter Grainger, Eilish Agnew, Angus Noble.*

## Two associate pastors

With the pastoral side well covered, Peter Grainger urged the elders to look next for an experienced associate pastor, instead of (as traditionally) a young man straight out of college, who was seeking experience before going to a church of his own. The associate would be expected to stay for five years, and would immediately take a major role in the pulpit and in leadership. Rev. Nic Roach, a pastor in Canterbury, was recommended to the Chapel and he agreed to start in October 1995; he quickly settled in, together with his wife, Helen, and their children Katy and Simon. Angus Noble's role was renamed 'associate pastor', so the team now consisted of a senior pastor, two associate pastors and a deaconess. Sadly, both of the associate pastors had only a

short time with the team. Angus moved on to other Christian service in April 1996, and, tragically, Nic suffered a brain tumour six months later; he died in hospital on 3 January 1997, aged 38. The esteem in which he was held was shown by the Chapel being filled almost to capacity, including the gallery, for a thanksgiving service for his life.

## Divorce and remarriage

Until the 1960s, divorce was almost unknown in evangelical families in Scotland; whether a Christian should marry someone who had been divorced was rarely an issue. It was 1984 before these became pastoral concerns in the Chapel. The elders distinguished between those who had been divorced before conversion, in which case, on the basis of I Corinthians 6:11, their conversion had 'washed, justified and sanctified' them, and those who, as Christians, had been involved in marriage breakdown.

Peter Grainger and the elders drew up guidelines, early in his pastorate in Edinburgh. Their goal at all times was the spiritual welfare of the members concerned, either by dissuading them from Scripture from taking a wrong step, or restoring those who had taken one. The guidelines, revised in 1999 and again in 2003, are set out under 'Divorce' on the CD.

## Membership

At Peter Grainger's first elders' meeting, he recommended, and the elders approved, a more rigorous procedure for membership. Until then, people took an application form from the rack on the stair and sent it to the elders; unless any concerns were expressed, they arranged a 15-minute interview. If that was satisfactory, the application was accepted, subject to the person attending a 30-minute talk on a Sunday morning before being received at the next communion service.

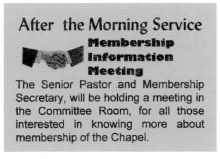

**After the Morning Service**
**Membership Information Meeting**
The Senior Pastor and Membership Secretary, will be holding a meeting in the Committee Room, for all those interested in knowing more about membership of the Chapel.

*Peter Grainger introduced an information meeting, with no commitment on either side, as an essential first step toward membership.*

Under the new system – still operating – the essential first step was to attend a membership information meeting, held monthly after a Sunday service. Peter Grainger and others gave a brief history of the Chapel, its practice and procedures, and outlined the implications of membership; there was no commitment on either side at that stage. Application forms were available only at the conclusion of this meeting. Completed applications were brought to the elders for comment. In the meantime, applicants had to read a booklet, *Evangelical Belief*, explaining the Chapel's doctrinal basis. Far from being off-putting, this stringent new procedure attracted up to 20 at the monthly information meetings. Over a five-year period, 211 applications were received, of which 196 were accepted, 5 were withdrawn and 10 were refused.

Interviews were now scheduled for half an hour as the norm, and were conducted by three elders or, in the case of female applicants, by two elders with the deaconess or an elder's wife. Successful applicants were welcomed into membership at the next communion service. Another improvement in the procedure was to give every accepted member a photocopy copy of the application form, which they had completed, as a reminder of the commitment made. The final new idea was to print biographical details of all new members in the *Record*.

## In association

The lengthy new procedure threw up a problem. While students' applications were being processed, they had no meaningful relationship with the Chapel; by the time they were accepted, many did not have long to enjoy (associate) membership before they finished their studies and left Edinburgh. A phrase was therefore coined – 'in association' – and student applicants were allocated immediately to a fellowship group, without any formal procedure; this was formalized as 'student link' in 1998 (Chapter 55).

Applications for associate membership were dealt in the same way as full membership applications. Associate membership was useful (and popular) for two reasons. Some, who lived permanently in Edinburgh, wished to be involved in, and to receive pastoral care from, the Chapel although they did not accept believers' baptism by immersion for themselves. Provided they did not undermine the Chapel's position by word or action, they were welcomed. Others, baptized believers, did not expect to settle in Edinburgh and wanted to retain their membership in their home church (Chapter 46). One could not be a member of two churches at the same time, but full membership at home and associate membership in the Chapel was acceptable to all concerned; when they left Edinburgh, they automatically dropped off the Chapel's roll because they were already in another pastoral relationship. Those in full membership who moved away from Edinburgh were kept on the Chapel's roll until they found a spiritual home elsewhere, so that they could be transferred to a new church.

## What an example ...

At 1 January 1993, the Chapel membership was 663 (616 full members and 47 associate). At every communion service in that year, some new members were received, 56 in all; 13 of them joined following baptism, 17 transferred from elsewhere, and 1 rejoined after an absence of some years. The other 25 (11 full members and all 14 associate members) joined on 'confession of faith', meaning they had no current membership elsewhere or that their former church had no formal transfer arrangement with Baptist churches.

During the year 1993, 12 members died (10 full and 2 associate). They had been in membership for a total of 676 years, that is an average of 54 years – what an example to follow.

Additional information on the following topics, mentioned in this chapter, is available on the CD.

Associate membership
Baptismal practice, 1969-1999
Communion under Peter Grainger
Deaconess
Divorce
Eilish Agnew
Nic Roach
Pastoral groups
Peter Grainger before Charlotte Chapel
Peter Grainger's induction

# Chapter 54
# Changes bring challenge (1992–1995)

## Familiar ideas developed

### Lay initiatives

The last chapter looked at some of the challenges and changes introduced by the new pastor during the first three years of his ministry. Other aspects of Chapel life were developing as well, under the initiative of a committed and active laity.

### 13 South Charlotte Street

When the church officer vacated the Chapel's flat at 13 South Charlotte Street in July 1990, the original plan was to renovate it and rent it commercially to produce income. However, a recession in the property-letting market was providential for the Chapel; it made the deacons think again, and they realized: (1) the flat would provide greatly improved office accommodation for the pastoral team, and (2) youth organisations could use it after office hours. In the spring of 1992, the flat was turned into five offices, with kitchen facilities, toilets and a storage area. The office in the Chapel, which was off the corridor from the lounge to the back stair, became the home of the tape ministry until it was divided in 2005, to give the duty caretaker a base as well.

*Until March 1993, the Chapel bookstall had to be laid out on tables and then stored away again in boxes. Here, June Ferguson is selling from the first purpose-built display cabinet, which is still in regular use.*

## International Fellowship

In the 1970s, most overseas students attending the Chapel were undergraduates. Twenty years later, many were post-graduates, some of them married with families. The Chapel was in touch with about two hundred, from 39 overseas countries. The International Fellowship had to be diplomatic, because of the diversity of their backgrounds. Some students came to Scotland with no personal knowledge of Christ, but a belief that this was a Christian country – they had many questions to ask. Others came as young Christians, and were eager for as much Bible study and fellowship as possible. Others were mature Christians, who had served in their home churches, and who challenged the fellowship here by their eagerness to reach out for Christ.

Bible study groups met in different homes around the city, modelled on the one in Sheila Masterton's flat on Friday evening. There was a monthly Saturday gathering (wintertime) or outing (summertime), attended by over one hundred; many of them were not Christians, but they warmed to the Christian love shown to them. Five Chapel members assisted wives to improve their English. The fellowship had its first weekend away at a youth hostel in the spring of 1993; 50 attended, and it has been repeated every spring since, growing in number. Many students return to their own countries expressing appreciation for the hospitality given here, especially for meeting Chapel families in their homes.

## Christmas activities

On the Saturday morning before Christmas, from 1992 to 1995, Chapel members went along Rose Street, offering evangelistic literature and inviting passers-by and shoppers to coffee and mince pies in the lounge. In 1992, they also sang carols in Rose Street from 10 a.m. until 1 p.m., interspersed with tract distribution and invitations to the café. On the Saturday evening before Christmas in 1993, the Chapel was almost filled for a programme of Christmas music by Kids' Praise, the Chapel Praise Singers and the Band and Singers, accompanied by the orchestra, organ, piano and electric piano. There was also congregational singing, a challenging gospel message, and more coffee and mince pies in the lounge. On the Sunday before Christmas, all these groups presented more music and carols at a family service in the morning and an evangelistic service in the evening, concluding with yet more coffee and mince pies.

On Christmas Eve 1992, the YPM held open house in the lounge at 10.45 p.m., for fellowship over (more) coffee and mince pies, followed by a Watchnight service in the church at 11.15 p.m., led by themselves and attended by about three hundred. In 1993, they put on a slide presentation of Christmas scenes around Edinburgh, with background music, followed by musical items, readings and a dramatised challenge to the commercial and sentimental pressures of Christmas. On Christmas Day, 80 of the International Fellowship were entertained in homes for lunch, after a short family service in the Chapel; about 40 of them, representing a dozen countries, gathered in the evening for a party in the lounge.

For many years, the elders had felt it inappropriate to have a Christmas tree in the sanctuary. In the early 1990s, a small one was permitted; it increased annually in size and illumination until the 1999 tree (in the photograph below) filled one of the stairs into the pulpit.

*During the 1990s (and continuing), a short family service about 11.15 on Christmas morning filled the area of the Chapel. The children responded to the pastor's invitation to bring their toys to the platform, from dolls to computer games.*

Christmas Day fell on a Sunday in 1994, but there was sufficient demand, from those who had no other arrangements, to have an evening service on both 25 December and 1 January. It was also a convenient way for the Chapel families who had entertained overseas students on Christmas Day to bring them back into town to meet up with others for the evening. The evening service also provided a focal point for Christians from other parts of Edinburgh, whose home churches did not have one. However, in 2005, when Christmas Day and New Year's Day were again Sunday, there were morning services only. Peter Grainger had his usual roll call during the Christmas Day service in 2005, and 23 countries were represented in a congregation that packed the area of the church.

**The last Hogmanay Watchnight**

The exuberant Hogmanay gathering in 1991, described in Chapter 52, was almost the last of such services. On Saturday 31 December 1994, only 83 people attended, many of whom were not Chapel members, but it was not low numbers that spelled the end. Hogmanay 1995 was a Sunday so, contrary to earlier practice, no service was held. In 1996, the YPM led a Christmas Watchnight service in the Chapel, but the anticipated noise and disruption from the biggest New Year party in the world obliged the Chapel to move to the Bristo Baptist Church. That did not attract many, and it was not repeated.

For 31 December 1997, the police restricted access to Rose Street to those who had previously obtained armbands, as part of their measures to control large numbers of inebriated people. The YPM held a Christmas Watchnight in the Chapel, but went out of town for New Year. The distinctive way in which the Chapel had brought in the New Year since 1903 was over. The Chief Constable asked for the use of the lower hall as a rest centre for police on duty; this was readily granted, not only in the interests of good community relations but as an opportunity to give them copies of a TELit leaflet (below), written specially for police men and women. It was a new way to end the year – Chapel members distributed evangelistic literature to a captive audience as they came in for their break, and the Chief Constable sent a cheque and an appreciative letter of thanks for the use of the building.

**Church music**

Congregational singing in the Chapel, led by the choir, was a source of inspiration to both pulpit and pew throughout most of the twentieth century. However, visiting preachers during the vacancy commented on two aspects: first, that it was now unusual in evangelical churches to have a choir sing a formal anthem during services, and secondly, could a church of seven hundred members not muster more than a dozen for its choir?

Toward the end of the five-year vacancy, choir numbers and morale dropped, and did not pick up in the new pastorate. Accordingly, a year later, the choir decided to sing a formal piece only at Christmas and Easter. Various small singing groups came into being, including the Chapel Praise Singers (formed on 21 February 1993 and still singing regularly), Kids' Praise, the Band and Singers and, occasionally, an orchestra (15 members in 1993); when none of these was available, former members of the choir met at 10.30 a.m. on Sunday morning, to practice the hymns for the day, because it helped the congregational singing to have a lead from the choir stalls.

## Church anniversary, October 1994

Some members expressed concern, early in 1994, that the first weekend in October had become a formality, with an outside speaker but only an occasional backward or forward look. The elders accepted this as valid comment, and arranged a week of special events for the one hundred and eighty-sixth anniversary, for thanksgiving and rededication. Particularly encouraging were the 7.30 a.m. prayer meetings, for an hour from Monday to Friday (an innovation for the anniversary week, with about 50 attending), the extended prayer and testimony meeting on the Monday evening, the open doors at both Mothers and Others on Tuesday morning and the YPM on Wednesday evening, a special Women's Morning Fellowship on the Thursday and a lively ceilidh on the Saturday evening in a school hall. The pastor's pulpit ministry on Sunday 9 October, and communion after the evening service, provided a memorable end to a memorable week. The pattern was repeated in 1995, with two additions on the final Sunday; family lunch on the premises attracted well over two hundred, and the anniversary closed with an evangelistic family service.

The morning prayer meeting was so much appreciated that the church was open every Friday from then on, from 7.30-8.15 a.m., when more than 30 regularly gathered for prayer, followed by a light breakfast.

OH GOOD! IT'S PETER GRAINGER ON T.V., INSTEAD OF HARRY SECOMBE

*From 1994 to 1996, the residents of Beulah Home viewed services in the Chapel by live television, instead of just hearing the voices over the landline. Transmission varied in quality from week to week, and was discontinued at the end of 1996; the expense of installing a cable TV link was prohibitive.*

## How the Chapel functioned

### Annual report

Because of pressure on time at the annual business meeting, most of the 30 Chapel auxiliaries (below) had no opportunity of reporting to the members. Norman Hunt recommended, in the early 1990s, printing an annual report. At that time, he was spending several months of the year in Hong Kong, assisting one of the Bible Colleges to upgrade to university status. While there, he worshipped at the Anglican St George's Church, and he brought back copies of their reports. He urged the writer to do something similar in the Chapel, but it was quite an undertaking, especially to launch the project; neither the writer nor anyone else felt able to do it. Eventually Norman Hunt was persuaded to be the answer to his own suggestion. At the end of 1993, he invited all Chapel leaders to submit a given number of words, which he then edited, collated and printed; the problem was keeping contributors from saying too much. The first printed annual report was for the year 1993; it grew in size and popularity until, in 2007, the 2006 report was renamed 'annual review' and appended to the Chapel *Record*.

*Professor Norman Hunt, who, among many other innovations, produced the Chapel's first printed annual report.*

## One body – many parts

Prior to the introduction of the printed annual report (above), the editor of the *Record* commissioned a series of articles, one every month from October 1992, to explain the role of auxiliaries and individuals in Chapel life. The fact that it took three years to cover even the main functions of the Chapel was a reminder that the body had many parts.

| 1992 | October | PA / CCTV System |
| | November | Bookstall |
| | December | Stewarding |
| | | |
| 1993 | January | Tape ministry |
| | February | Property committee |
| | March | Discipleship class |
| | April | Finance committee |
| | May | Beulah Home |
| | June | Mustard Seed Café |
| | July | Deaconess |
| | August | Elders' court |
| | September | Group 45 |
| | October | YPM |
| | November | Music ministry |
| | December | Church flowers |
| | | |
| 1994 | January | Pastor's secretary |
| | February | Group 2545 |
| | March | Missionary committee |
| | April | Membership secretary |
| | May | Communion services |
| | June | Caretakers |

| | July | International Fellowship |
| | August | Church secretary |
| | September | Deacons' court |
| | October | Youth council |
| | November | Home mission committee |
| | December | Evangelism committee |
| | | |
| 1995 | January | Pastoral assistant |
| | February | Quinquennial election |
| | March | Church treasurer |
| | April | Chapel prayer meetings |
| | May | Women's A.m. Fellowship |
| | June | Mothers and Others |
| | July | *Record* |
| | August | Fellowship groups |
| | September | *Junior Record* |
| | October | Pastor |

## Mission service committee

By early 1994, both the overseas mission committee and the home mission committee agreed that the distinctions between: (1) long-term overseas service, (2) short-term overseas service and (3) home mission were increasingly blurred, and that in due course there should be one committee, supporting both overseas and home missionaries. The practical difficulty was funding; gifts for overseas mission were designated for that work and home mission, a fairly new concept, did not have a high profile.

Four new overseas missionaries were added to the Chapel's support list in 1994, bringing the total to 15 on active service and 12 others who were either on home leave or retired. In that year, the Chapel sent £2,400 a year toward the support of every overseas missionary, plus payments for children and retired missionaries, a total of £46,279. There was no possibility of matching this, in the short term, for home mission.

Accordingly, a mission service committee was formed, to encourage Chapel members to see the two branches of mission as equally deserving. It did this through church events and articles in the *Record*, but in the meantime, until the home mission committee could generate sufficient funds to equalize payments, £12,000 was transferred annually from general church funds toward the support of home missionaries. At the quinquennial election of May 1995, when all committees stood down and were reappointed, the two committees agreed to merge on 1 January 1997 into one mission board, incorporating the mission service committee. The progress of the board is taken up in the next chapter.

### Jigsaw

As mentioned in Chapter 50, the Chapel's drama group, which had met informally since 1985, was established as 'Jigsaw' in 1993. The name reflected their perception of themselves as a small piece in the bigger pattern of evangelism of the Chapel, usually as a prelude to preaching, which they recognized should be paramount. Their aim was two-fold: to reach non-Christians with the gospel, by visual presentations, and to encourage Christians to use similar methods in evangelism. They took part in seeker services, the Festival outreach, the Christmas music evening, Bible Class and Group 2545. They had ten committed members and a number of thought-provoking sketches.

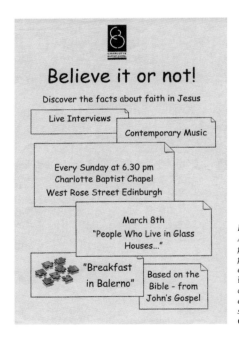

*From January to April 1998, Jigsaw presented a thought-provoking sketch, entitled* Breakfast in Balerno, *as part of the Sunday evening evangelistic series from John's Gospel.*

Jigsaw disbanded in 1999, but during the Edinburgh International Festival in 2002, the Chapel sponsored the (Christian) Saltmine Theatre Company. The Chapel building became an official venue for the Festival Fringe in 2003 and subsequent years (Chapter 57).

### Festival cafés, 1994-1995

Until the autumn of 1993, open-airs were held throughout the summer at the Mound, latterly on Thursday evening only. In 1994, the evangelism committee decided to concentrate on festival outreach instead, and opened the Chapel on two Wednesdays and two Thursdays from 8 p.m. and one Saturday from 10 a.m. Encouraged by the response, they focussed on the middle week of the festival in 1995, from Tuesday 22 to Thursday 24 August. Every evening started with 30-40 gathering in the lower hall, to pray for the events of that night. Most of them then moved off to their own areas, open-air or literature distribution or staffing Café Life, but some continued to pray in 20-minute periods throughout the evening; this was seen as the foundation of the outreach.

A new format was tried for the open-airs, and proved useful; proclamation was interspersed with opportunity for discussion, and this was repeated several times every evening. From 7.30 p.m., a team distributed leaflets and invitations to the café; it was encouraging to see strangers come into the building holding their invitation (with map). The café was busy on all three evenings, from opening time at eight o'clock until well after the official closing time of ten o'clock Free coffee, tea, juice and home bakes, contemporary music, drama sketches with a relevant challenge and literature on the tables, led to many meaningful conversations. The same pattern was followed during the festivals of 1997, 1998 and 1999, with 50-60 visitors every night.

### Five years of the Mustard Seed Café

In 1993, on the fifth anniversary of the opening of the Mustard Seed Café, its leader reported:

*Little did we think this venture would be a real café outreach. The opening time is 12 noon, closing 2 p.m., but work starts around 9.30 a.m. A lot has to be done before 12 noon, and equally a lot of clearing is needed after 2 pm. At around 11.30 a.m. each day, the workers gather for a cup of coffee and we have a short devotional time, committing our day to the Lord and asking blessing on our work, praying that the service we give and the happy atmosphere will be a testimony to all who come in for lunch. As time permits we ask the customers if they have been to the cafe before. Many have. Others say they have been recommended by a friend, as the atmosphere and the food are excellent. 'Best potatoes in town' is often the answer. We are so encouraged that good contacts are being made, and some of our customers attend Chapel services. We also have a five minute 'spot' talk once or twice a week, when the gospel is told in a clear yet simple way. Another feature is a pianist who comes as available and plays gospel music, often getting requests for favourite hymns.*

---

1 *Record*, June 1993, p. 11.

*The Mustard Seed Café continued to be well patronized, with an evangelistic message once a week. Jim Monihan provided live music on Wednesday and gave away two hundred copies of the New Testament to enquirers in one year.*

### The *Junior Record*

For 88 years, since the first edition of the *Record* in January 1907, there had been a page for children and young people, originally called 'The Children's Corner'. In 1994, Youth Council queried how many actually read it, and decided to launch its own magazine from January 1995. Using desktop publishing software, the young people wrote the *Junior Record* themselves, with a mixture of news, puzzles and items of interest for the ages 4 to 14. At first, 350 copies were available on the first Sunday of the month, along with the main *Record*, but the greater demand came from the uniformed organisations on Friday evening. Contributors, whose pieces were accepted, sent copies to grandparents, aunts and uncles. Many of the children were from non-church families, so a new dimension was added, with an evangelistic message.

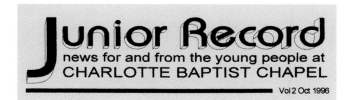

*The young people themselves wrote the* Junior Record.

## Census and elections

### Census Sunday, 30 October 1994

At an evening service early in 1994, Peter Grainger asked the congregation how many had attended the Chapel that morning; far fewer hands were raised than he had expected. As arrangements were already under way for the ten-year census of all Scottish churches, to be held in October, the Chapel prepared its own (more detailed) questionnaire, to be used on Census Sunday, 30 October 1994.

It was completed by 912 adults; youngsters under the age of 15 (164 were present) did not participate. There were 729 adults at the morning service and 507 at the evening service. Of the 550 able-bodied members living in Edinburgh, 434 (79 per cent) attended at least once; the elders thought this was disappointingly low, but the statisticians were impressed that the number was so good.

The leadership were taken aback by two analyses of the forms. First, less than half of the 912 were Chapel members; 43 per cent were full members and 5 per cent were associate members, but 29 per cent of the congregation had their membership elsewhere although they came regularly to the Chapel. The remaining 23 per cent classified themselves as visitors, but 32 per cent of the 'visitors' had been coming for up to three years and some for even longer; only 8 per cent were really passing through.

The second surprise was that only one-third of the 912 attended both morning and evening services; 44 per cent came in the morning only, 20 per cent came in the evening only and 36 per cent came twice. Taking the day as a whole, 41 per cent of those attending were men and 59 per cent were women, about the norm for other Baptist churches in Scotland and not greatly different from all churches throughout Great Britain. One-quarter were aged 15-24, one-third 25-44, one-fifth 45-64, and the remaining one-sixth were over 65. The average age was 42, considerably younger than the average of all Scottish churchgoers at the time. On the other hand, 19 per cent of the congregation had attended the Chapel for over 30 years, 12 per cent for 21-30 years, 25 per cent for 6-20 years, and 44 per cent for up to five years.

## Chapter 54
Changes bring challenge (1992-1995)

Of the 164 youngsters under age 15, who were not included in the questionnaire, 8 were in the baby crèche and 14 in the toddlers' crèche (ages 1-3). After the children's talk, 23 Discoverers and 27 CID went to Junior Church; FBI did not go out that morning, leaving 92 youngsters in church. Of these, 36 were in the age range 9-10 and 56 aged between 11 and 15.

Over the next decade, the number of 'oncers' increased, both in the Chapel and nationwide; by 2005, only one in five attended both services in the Chapel. In the autumn of that year, the elders were able to ask Peter Grainger to repeat, on Sunday evening, the sermons on the Ten Commandments that he had given on Sunday morning in the spring of 2004 – because there was almost a different congregation.

### Where people lived
People still came to Rose Street from all over the city. Chapters 23 and 31 listed the homes of the elders and deacons in 1916, 1933 and 1935. On Census Sunday, the congregation had travelled from almost every postal district up to EH30, but only one-third of one percent lived in EH2, where the Chapel is located.

| | 1994 | 2004 | | 1994 | 2004 |
|---|---|---|---|---|---|
| EH4 | 15% | 14% | EH21 | 1% | 1% |
| EH10 | 10% | 11% | EH26 | 0.4% | 0.5% |
| EH12 | 10% | 12% | EH2 | 0.3% | – |
| EH13 | 6% | 4% | EH28 | 0.3% | – |
| EH14 | 6% | 9% | EH49 | 0.3% | – |
| EH9 | 5% | 5% | EH22 | 0.2% | – |
| EH3 | 5% | 7% | EH25 | 0.2% | – |
| EH6 | 4% | 5% | EH29 | 0.2% | – |
| EH8 | 4% | 2% | EH41 | 0.2% | – |
| EH16 | 4% | 4% | EH52 | 0.2% | 1% |
| EH11 | 4% | 6% | EH18 | 0.1% | 0.5% |
| EH17 | 3% | 1% | EH20 | 0.1% | 0.5% |
| EH7 | 3% | 2% | EH23 | 0.1% | – |
| EH1 | 2% | 1% | EH32 | 0.1% | – |
| EH15 | 2% | 1% | EH35 | 0.1% | – |
| EH5 | 1% | 2% | EH44 | 0.1% | – |
| EH30 | 1% | 1% | Non-EH | 10% | 8.5% |
| EH54 | 1% | 1% | | | |

_____
1 **Analysis by the Christian Research Association.**

As may be seen, the catchment area did not change substantially between the census of 1994 and the next one in 2004 (Chapter 57)

### Response to the census
Analysis of the figures set the leadership various challenges. If 44 per cent of the congregation were not members, but only 8 per cent were visitors, why would the other 36 per cent not join? If nearly everyone present claimed to be a believer, how effective was the outreach? If 28 per cent were students – a huge percentage for any church – were their particular needs (away from home, many from overseas) being met? If the respondents had nearly six hundred children in total, why were only 164 of them in church that Sunday? If over a quarter of the married people came on their own, were their spouses not interested?

Until the census, it had been popularly said that most students slept in on Sunday morning and came to church at night; in fact, 83 per cent of undergraduates came in the morning only, 54 per cent in the evening only, and 37 per cent twice. Only 40 per cent of them went to a student Christian Union – a trend, which is now (2007) more pronounced than ever; students were being encouraged to seek teaching in local churches rather than in meetings organized by their peers.

### Women deacons
In preparation for the quinquennial election of deacons, due in the spring of 1995, the elders looked again at the teaching and practice of the New Testament about women deacons; they recommended to the members in December 1994, that the election should be open to everyone over 18. The members, after a careful and good-natured debate, voted in favour by a simple majority but not by the required two-thirds, so the former practice (men only) continued; before the next election, five years later, the elders renewed the recommendation. This time, on the assurance that there were no plans to extend the franchise to the office of elder, 75 per cent of the members voted in favour, and by the summer of the year 2000, the Chapel had its first women deacons.

### Committees become ministries
The 1995 election of office-bearers proceeded smoothly, with the welcome addition of a photograph and a short word-picture of the candidates on display in the lounge. However,

once elected, the 22 elders and 18 deacons did not immediately launch, as their predecessors had done, into appointing half a dozen committees. They recognised the need for a new structure; everyone elected, together with wives who wished to be involved, embarked on a careful appraisal over the summer months of their spiritual gifts – not as they imagined them, but as others saw them. They then formed themselves, at the end of 1995, into 13 ministries, deemed a more appropriate word than committees. Co-ordinators, rather than chairmen, led the ministries, because their task was to draw together and inspire those who gave their time and energy so willingly to the Lord's work.

*Every five years, all Chapel office-bearers retire and are eligible for re-election. This chest has served as the ballot box for as long as anyone can remember.*

*Many Chapel members supported the Heralds (Chapter 43), although the group were never part of the Chapel as such. They celebrated their twenty-fifth anniversary in November 1995 with services in the Usher Hall and in the Chapel.*

### TELit, Thematic Evangelistic Literature

Like the Heralds, TELit had close links with the Chapel, although never formally part of it. As with the Heralds, the leader (Barry Sprott) was a Chapel member and the annual supporters' meeting was held on the Chapel premises. Barry, a social worker and an elder in the Chapel, who was active in evangelism and teaching, felt 'called' in 1986 to full-time Christian service, particularly to design, produce and publish evangelistic folders woven around a theme – a place, an event or some other feature of everyday life.

*The folder that best represents the work of TELit over the years, and which has been kept in print from the very beginning, is* A Cross the Bridge.

Working from home, he quickly established a market for well-produced literature, blending thematic text, full colour illustrations and a clear gospel presentation, using the actual words of Scripture. In 1990, TELit became a charitable trust. When, in the first three months of 1995, he and his helpers dispatched a quarter of a million folders from his home, and he still had three hundred boxes of stock in 50 different titles, the need for office premises was acute. A shop at 144 Ferry Road came on the market late in 1995; it had bare floorboards and no shelving, but the team refurbished it and provided not only office and storage facilities, but also an attractive shop window for the literature. TELit now provides thematic evangelistic publications for a wide range of churches and Christian organisations, not only throughout the United Kingdom but also worldwide. In the millennial year, over one million folders were ordered, and by 2007, more than ten million had been produced in all.

### Peter Barber

Peter Barber, one of the Chapel's old boys and now the general secretary of the Baptist Union of Scotland, knew from May 1994 that a cancerous growth was terminal. He died at home with his family around him on 1 September 1994, a few days after his sixty-fourth birthday. Since he joined Charlotte Chapel as a teenager, it had been the Chapel's privilege to be associated with his memorable life. He was active in the Young Peoples Meeting and was their vice-president in 1951-52. Under the influence of Sidlow Baxter, Peter was 'called' into Baptist ministry. He last occupied the Chapel pulpit for both services on Sunday 24 February 1994.

Charlotte Chapel Baptist Church
Rose Street, Edinburgh
Friday 9th September, 1994
at 7.30pm

*A large and representative congregation gathered in the Chapel on Friday 9 September 1994 for a thanksgiving service for the life of Peter Barber.*

A large and representative congregation filled the Chapel on Friday 9 September 1994 for a thanksgiving service. Peter and his wife, Isobel, had chosen the hymns and they all spoke of Christ: 'Crown him with many crowns', 'Jesus shall take the highest honour', 'How sweet the name of Jesus sounds' and 'With harps and with viols'. Many present readers will not know those who took part, but to mention their names will bring back memories for some. Douglas Hutcheon, the Union's superintendent, led the service. Eric Watson, the previous superintendent, read the Scriptures and prayed. Karl Heinz Walter, secretary of the European Baptist Federation, David Coffey, general secretary of the Baptist

Union of Great Britain, and Donald McCallum all gave tributes. Alex Wright, the minister of the Glenrothes church, prayed. Andrew MacRae, Peter's predecessor at the Union, gave the address, based on the faith of Paul as expressed in Philippians 3, which he related to Peter's life. Kathie White sang 'People need the Lord', a favourite of Peter's. Ian Mundie took the closing prayer.

Three weeks earlier, there had been a thanksgiving service in the Chapel for the life of David Wallace, the honorary treasurer for 22 years, 1961-83. Born in 1913, he had sat under six ministries, Graham Scroggie, Sidlow Baxter, Gerald Griffiths, Alan Redpath, Derek Prime and Peter Grainger. The *Record* rarely printed obituaries, which is why so few office-bearers are named on the CD, but there was a fine tribute to David Wallace from his successor as treasurer and it is copied there.

Additional information on the following topics, mentioned in this chapter, is available on the CD.

Annual report
Church office
Church officers from 1912
David Wallace
Elders and deacons – history
International Fellowship
Jim Monihan
Management Review, 1993
Norman Hunt
Peter Barber
Women deacons

# Chapter 55
# Maintenance or mission? (1996–1999)

## Where do we grow from here?

### A full church

The first three years of Peter Grainger's pastorate saw steady growth in nearly all aspects of Chapel life. The question for the last four years of the twentieth century was whether the Chapel was simply maintaining its position, or whether there was still an appetite for mission. This chapter looks first at the ongoing work, and then at some of the innovative ideas for outreach.

Many Sunday mornings were filled to overflowing, with no room in the sanctuary by 10.55 a.m.; late comers had to sit in the lounge until the children went out to junior church. It is said that when a church building is filled to 80 per cent of its capacity, its growth plateaus out, for two reasons: (1) the members tend, even subconsciously, to become complacent and so lack urgency in evangelism, and (2) if newcomers cannot easily find a seat, they tend not to return.

*In 1996, the televised picture-link to the lounge was displayed on two 22-inch screens, like domestic TVs; this was scarcely attractive, especially to those who were there not by choice. It was 2001 before one large (seven-foot square) screen was installed.*

In 1996, the Chapel office-bearers seriously considered looking for larger property – either building from new or buying and adapting an existing building. If (as they decided in October 1997) the Chapel should remain on its present site, should there be two services on Sunday morning? The space-problem was chiefly on Sunday morning and Friday evening (for the uniformed organisations), but numbers at the Sunday evening service were also growing, with many younger folk in attendance.

### Pulpit ministry

*The Scotsman* asked its readers: 'Have we really become a nation that puts feelings first and prefers image to reality?' Regrettably, the answer was 'Yes'. In that climate, the exposition of Scripture from the pulpit, followed by discussion of it in fellowship groups, was crucial to the spiritual development of the congregation. On Sunday morning for the whole of 1997, the theme was 'Building on the Rock' – the teaching of Jesus in the Sermon on the Mount. To counteract the danger of settling down snugly inside houses built on rock, while the rains came down and floods came up, the 1998 Sunday morning sermons focused on the people of God as pilgrims, based on the book of Joshua and its New Testament counterpart, the Acts of the Apostles.

The Sunday evening service was directly evangelistic, and usually developed a theme over several weeks, in order to encourage attendance. Subjects included: 'Real Answers to Real Questions', from the life and teaching of Jesus, 'Overcoming ... guilt, doubt, anger, pride, fear, the tongue, lust and fear', and 'A sting in the tale', based on the parables in Luke.

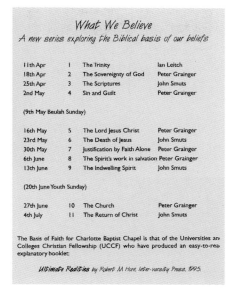

*What We Believe*
A new series exploring the Biblical basis of our beliefs

| | | | |
|---|---|---|---|
| 11th Apr | 1 | The Trinity | Ian Leitch |
| 18th Apr | 2 | The Sovereignty of God | Peter Grainger |
| 25th Apr | 3 | The Scriptures | John Smuts |
| 2nd May | 4 | Sin and Guilt | Peter Grainger |

(9th May Beulah Sunday)

| | | | |
|---|---|---|---|
| 16th May | 5 | The Lord Jesus Christ | Peter Grainger |
| 23rd May | 6 | The Death of Jesus | John Smuts |
| 30th May | 7 | Justification by Faith Alone | Peter Grainger |
| 6th June | 8 | The Spirit's work in salvation | Peter Grainger |
| 13th June | 9 | The Indwelling Spirit | John Smuts |

(20th June Youth Sunday)

| | | | |
|---|---|---|---|
| 27th June | 10 | The Church | Peter Grainger |
| 4th July | 11 | The Return of Christ | John Smuts |

The Basis of Faith for Charlotte Baptist Chapel is that of the Universities and Colleges Christian Fellowship (UCCF) who have produced an easy-to-read explanatory booklet:

*Ultimate Realities by Robert M. Horn, Inter-varsity Press. 1995.*

*In the hope, which was fulfilled, that some would come to faith through the Sunday evening series 'A sting in the tale', the next series explored the Chapel's doctrinal basis.*

### Standing to sing

It is said that ventures prosper by paying attention to detail, without getting bogged down in it. In July 1996, the elders discussed what may appear to be the most trivial item ever to appear on their agenda – when to stand for the hymns. Some people stood up right away, others waited until the organ introduction was complete, and others didn't know what to do. The confusion was compounded when a modern song had a brief introduction, followed by a quick start; it was embarrassing, particularly for visitors, when the announcement of a hymn was followed by what looked like a Mexican wave. It was decided that everyone should stand, for all hymns, as soon at the music began. This was earlier than in many churches, but it made for consistency and demonstrated some enthusiasm to participate.

## Baptisms

As mentioned in Chapter 53, one of the innovations of Peter Grainger's pastorate was publishing in the *Record* the testimony of baptismal candidates – 177 in the first nine years of his ministry. They comprised: (1) children of Chapel members, who had grown up in the church, (2) students, who had come to faith in Edinburgh, and (3) others converted through the Chapel:

| Year | Total | CC | Students | Others |
|---|---|---|---|---|
| 1992 | 14 | 3 | 4 | 7 |
| 1993 | 19 | 6 | 2 | 11 |
| 1994 | 27 | 9 | 11 | 7 |
| 1995 | 25 | 2 | 9 | 14 |
| 1996 | 29 | 5 | 10 | 14 |
| 1997 | 13 | 3 | 3 | 7 |
| 1998 | 16 | 5 | 5 | 6 |
| 1999 | 23 | 5 | 6 | 12 |
| 2000 | 11 | 6 | 3 | 2 |
| Total | 177 | 44 | 53 | 80 |
| Percent | 100% | 25% | 30% | 45% |

*John Smuts (left) baptizing in the spring of 1999. Children were encouraged to sit in the front row or on the pulpit steps. Until Peter Grainger came, candidates had their backs to the congregation, so water often splashed onto the front row as they were baptized.*

## Infant dedication

In the spring of 1999, when 16 Chapel couples were expecting additions to their family, the elders reviewed the practice of asking everyone to stand for the dedicatory prayer. It was recognized that visitors could not meaningfully commit themselves to support these particular parents in the upbringing of their child. From then on, only members were invited to stand and to identify with the family – although, in practice, most visitors stood up as well, rather than be left sitting when all around were standing.

## A snapshot of the congregation

The Baptist Union of Scotland asked all congregations to carry out a survey on the first Sunday of June 1999. The result was a salutary reminder that the building was not always overcrowded. The figures for the two Sunday services were:

| | Morning | | | Evening | | |
|---|---|---|---|---|---|---|
| | male | female | total | male | female | total |
| Under 12 | 75 | 85 | 160 | 1 | 5 | 6 |
| 12–19 | 18 | 23 | 41 | 5 | 20 | 25 |
| 20–39 | 102 | 129 | 231 | 75 | 65 | 140 |
| 40–59 | 75 | 78 | 153 | 40 | 45 | 85 |
| 60–79 | 38 | 81 | 133 | 22 | 46 | 68 |
| 80+ | 3 | 11 | 14 | 0 | 3 | 3 |
| Totals | 311 | 407 | 718 | 143 | 184 | 327 |

Membership in June 1999 was 740 but, as always, a number lived too far away to attend on a regular basis, and 110 were permanently shut-in. About half of the congregation on that Sunday were not members, but, as commented earlier, both church and secular voluntary organisations were finding it increasingly difficult to persuade people to commit themselves – more and more wanted to attend but not to join. Although attendance remained steady, indeed encouraging, throughout 1999, particularly in the number of younger people coming to the services, membership dropped by 20 at the end of the year to 651 full and 69 associate members – the first negative figure since Peter Grainger came to the Chapel in 1992.

The reluctance of younger people to join the Chapel meant that members' meetings became increasingly unrepresentative of the age and social mix attending the Sunday services – older people had to make decisions affecting younger ones, without input from them. The elders racked their brains for ways to encourage membership, while also getting across the message that membership involved commitment.

## Publicity and technology

### Signposts

In January 1996, the deacons learned that the city was raising money by offering personalized signposts for £250 a time. The Chapel applied for two, one at each end of Rose Street, to direct visitors and to increase awareness about the church in the city-centre.

*Signposts at the junction of Rose Street with Castle Street (left) and South Charlotte Street (below) directed visitors to the church from 1996 until Castle Street was pedestrianized in 2005 and a lorry knocked down the one in South Charlotte Street.*

### PowerPoint

Members attending the Keswick Convention in July 1996 were impressed when PowerPoint projected hymns and intimations onto wide-screen monitors. Would it work in the Chapel? The church treasurer made a modest start at the next members' meeting, using PowerPoint to illustrate the financial report, but it was 2001 before it replaced hymnbooks and sermon outlines every Sunday (Chapter 56).

During 1997, the YPM set up a website, the first in the Chapel, to publicise outreach events and to raise their profile in Edinburgh. The church followed, but not until the spring of 2001, as set out in the next chapter.

*The Chapel's logo from January 1998 to October 2005, used on letterheads, cards, the Record and many more.*

### Logo

By January 1998, the Chapel's logo, the exterior of the building set against an Edinburgh skyline (Chapter 48), was more than 20 years old and conveyed a message only to those who recognized the building. A Chapel member, who was a professional graphic designer, came up with a new logo, incorporating the letters CBC and the name Charlotte Baptist Chapel. This was used on all publicity material until October 2005, when another format was adopted (Chapter 57).

Nothing in the Chapel's new logo attracted the censure of the politically correct. The Baptist Union of Scotland was not so fortunate. It had adopted the motto 'Jesus Christ – the only Hope' for its centenary in 1969, and retained it ever since. When franking machines became popular in the 1980s, it used the motto, with an appropriate logo, on outgoing mail. When the Union upgraded its machine in 1997, Pitney Bowes refused to transfer these words to the new machine. Royal Mail confirmed that the word 'only' was unacceptable; 'Jesus Christ our Hope', was alright, but the Union's alternative suggestion, 'Jesus Christ, Hope of the World', could (said Royal Mail) cause possible offence.

## Eighty years young

On Remembrance Day 1998, the Young Peoples Meeting celebrated its beginning, in its present form, in November 1918. Its motto over all the eighty years had been 'The Utmost for the Highest', but the guest preacher for the anniversary thought this was not sufficiently personal, and spoke on 'My Utmost for His Highest'. The young people led a well-attended Sunday evening service.

*David Murray cutting the cake at his ninetieth birthday celebration, held in the Chapel lounge in May 1999, with his daughter Irene watching.*

## 5 a.m. on Sunday

On Sunday 1 November 1998, three Home Counties Baptist ministers embarked on a preach/drive, to raise funds for the Baptist Missionary Society in Nepal. They left John o' Groats at one minute past midnight, aiming to preach in Scotland, Wales and England and to reach Land's End before midnight (which they did with 50 minutes to spare).

Their first stop was at 5 a.m. in Charlotte Chapel, where they preached from the pulpit to a dozen supporters; after bacon

rolls and coffee, they drove on to preach in Penarth Tabernacle, Cardiff, at 3 p.m., and Upton Vale Baptist Church in Torquay at 7 p.m., before going on to Land's End. With the car sponsored and the petrol sponsored, they raised £2,000 for the work of BMS, and got themselves into the *Guinness Book of Records.*

*Three Baptist ministers preached briefly to a congregation of a dozen Chapel members at 5 a.m. on Sunday 1 November 1998, on a sponsored one-day drive from John o' Groats to Land's End; they then had breakfast before setting off for Wales.*

The BMS had other innovative ideas at this time – a meeting in the Chapel in April 1997 included a live telephone conversation with a BMS family in Zimbabwe, backed by PowerPoint photographs. Questions and answers were clearly audible over the Chapel's loudspeaker system, culminating in requests for prayer; the president then prayed with them and for them over the phone, concluding with a united amen from Zimbabwe and the Chapel together.

It was Harvest Thanksgiving in September 2006 before the Chapel copied the idea. During the morning service, Chapel missionaries Daniel and Barbara Zeiden, who had just been moved from Bolivia to Washington DC by their mission, Food for the Hungry, answered questions about their work while photographs on the screens illustrated what they had to say, and they stayed on line for the prayers for them.

## Pastoral care

### Student link

The phrase 'in association', coined in 1994 for students who were not members of the Chapel (Chapter 53), was unsatisfactory. Early in 1998, the elders introduced a fast-track special relationship called Student link.

It ran for one academic year at a time, with students encouraged to sign up afresh for each year of their studies. The three requirements were: (1) an interview with an elder, to make sure of a clear Christian commitment, (2) a promise to worship regularly at the Chapel while in Edinburgh, and (3) acceptance of the doctrinal basis. They were then received at communion and could serve as stewards, musicians, teaching children, etc., and received pastoral oversight and encouragement. During the first year, 11 took advantage of it; they could, of course, seek full membership at any time.

*John Smuts came from London Bible College (now London School of Theology) in the summer of 1997, to be assistant pastor for two years, before going on to a pastorate of his own in Cheltenham.*

### The pastoral team

Following the death of Nic Roach in January 1997, the elders reviewed the make-up of the pastoral team. They reverted to the former practice of inviting a student, about to graduate

from theological college, to come for two or three years and then move on to a church of his own. John Smuts, with his wife Emily, took up the duties of assistant to the pastor on 1 August 1997.

On the same day, a new post of pastoral assistant was created, to work alongside the deaconess, Eilish Agnew; Judy White filled it admirably from August 1997 to March 1999. At this time, 110 Chapel members were unable to attend services, through infirmity. If all of them received one visit of one hour per week, it would require (including travelling) three full-time members of the pastoral team. Accordingly, visiting teams of lay people were invaluable, as they made regular calls on the shut-in members.

When Judy White left in March 1999, to work with the homeless at Bethany, it was decided not to seek a successor but to appoint an associate pastor for pastoral care. The change in name, from director of pastoral care (Dr Ronnie McVicker's title from September 1996 to November 1997) implied more general care and less specialist counselling. Bill Denholm started in April 1999; his professional background was in business personnel, counselling and training. He had been made redundant in October 1992, and had undertaken a three-year degree course at Glasgow Bible College (now International Christian College). With a BA degree in theology, he became part-time assistant at St David's Church of Scotland, Glasgow and worked there, assisting primarily with pastoral work for almost three years, before coming to the Chapel.

*Bill Denholm was associate pastor for pastoral care from April 1999 to December 2005.*

In 2003, the elders decided it would be helpful if Bill Denholm's gifts were recognized by ordination to the ministry, and this took place during the morning service on 14 December.

### Winter care shelter

In addition to the Care Van (Chapter 52), Bethany Christian Trust arranged a night shelter for the homeless, every evening between 23 December 1996 and 6 January 1997, from 8 p.m. to 8 a.m. Seven churches opened their halls, which were transformed by camp beds and blankets into sleeping accommodation. Every night was staffed by a group of volunteers from different churches, who cooked an evening meal and breakfast. The Chapel provided two teams from Christmas Eve to Christmas morning in the Buccleuch and Greyfriars church hall; one team covered from 8 p.m. to 12 midnight, and the other through to 8 a.m. The first team set up the hall, served an evening meal and bedded folk down; the second served breakfast, cleared up the hall and returned the camp beds to Bethany House. Fourteen in total took advantage of the shelter that night, twelve men and two girls.

That was the beginning of an involvement that still goes on. In 1997, Bethany asked the Chapel to take its turn, along with other churches, of opening its building overnight during the winter months (December-February), as well as providing a team of six people to feed those who came in and to spend time chatting to them. The lower hall was available on Monday night – the only free evening at that time – and up to 25 people came in every night. As other churches opened their doors, the Chapel was required for only four or five nights every winter. In 2001, up to 40 (aged 17-70) came nightly, some to eat and then go back to the streets, others to stay overnight. It then became more convenient to offer Thursday night; in 2002-3 and again in 2003-4, the Chapel was host on five Thursdays between December and February.

In 2005-6, the winter care shelter ran for 22 weeks, from the beginning of November to the beginning of April. Forty Edinburgh churches participated, and the Chapel was responsible for six nights. About two-dozen homeless people came every night, and the Chapel provided a team of seven (at least two men) to look after them. When the Chapel prayer meeting moved from Tuesday to Wednesday in September 2006 (Chapter 58), the Chapel team provided both the venue and the team for six Tuesday nights in November and December 2006 and January and February 2007.

### Fellowship groups and pastoral groups

Meaningful participation at members' half-yearly meetings had always been a problem, because two hundred or more people facing the platform cannot easily communicate with each other. Fellowship groups were therefore asked, in the autumn of 1996, to become sounding boards for church business, discussing the agenda for forthcoming members' meetings. The church diary was structured so that the elders could meet after the groups and before the church meeting; responses were co-ordinated and recommendations to the members' meeting finalized. Since about a hundred non-members attended the fellowship groups, they were (until November 2006, when non-members who usually attended the group were invited) redesignated, twice a year, as pastoral groups and open to members only. Quite a few members, who did not go to fellowship groups, made a special effort to be there.

The first topic discussed in this format was whether to move the church weeknight prayer meeting from Monday to Tuesday (Chapter 53). A full but informal discussion took place in the 23 homes where the groups met, under the chairmanship of an elder. The fact that every group favoured Tuesday influenced the next church meeting to finalize that day. Typical attendance at members' meeting at this time was 175, whereas about 330 attended pastoral groups.

There was, however, an unforeseen negative consequence of the new arrangement. Some members, who had discussed everything that was to be raised, did not bother to come to the members' meeting, even although that was where decisions were taken. Attendance fell from the figure just mentioned to 120, 110, and then, in June 2004, to 90. For the November 2005 meeting, there was only half an hour of business (members only), and then the doors were opened for everyone to hear reports on the work in Niddrie (below) and other items of general interest. This boosted attendance back to the two hundred mark.

| ACTIVITY | TIME/DETAILS |
|---|---|
| **SUNDAY** | |
| Morning Service | 11:00am |
| Junior Church | 11:20am |
| Evening Service | 6:30pm |
| YPM (15-30 years) | |
| 2545 (25-45 years) | See Bulletin for details of these |
| Group 45 (40+ years) | three groups meeting after church |
| **TUESDAY** | |
| Mothers and Others | 9:30am |
| Prayer Meeting | 8:00pm |
| Fellowship Groups in Homes | Alternate weeks, see Bulletin |
| **WEDNESDAY** | |
| Ladies Prayer Meeting | 2:30pm |
| YPM | 8:00pm See Bulletin |
| **THURSDAY** | |
| Womans' Morning Fellowship | 10:00am |
| Fellowship Groups in Homes | Alternate weeks, see Bulletin |
| **FRIDAY** | |
| Prayer Meeting | 7:30-8:15am |
| Evening Mothers & Others | 6:15pm |
| Uniformed Organisations | Various (see Bulletin) |
| **SATURDAY** | |
| Men & Brothers Breakfast | 7:30am Monthly (1st Saturday) |
| Focus (12-15 years) | Various (see Bulletin) |
| International Fellowship | 7:00pm Monthly (2nd Saturday) |
| **DAILY MONDAY TO FRIDAY** | |
| Mustard Seed Cafe | 12 - 2:00pm |

*The fellowship groups unanimously voted to change the night of the prayer meeting from Monday to Tuesday; this was, therefore, a typical week in the Chapel from 1997 to 1999.*

## The midweek prayer meeting

The Tuesday fellowship groups were keen to keep their evening, so when the central prayer meeting moved to Tuesday, the pattern developed of a smaller central meeting (60 or more still came) on one Tuesday and a larger one, for everyone, on the next. Over the ensuing eight years of this compromise, the elders kept suggesting either moving all mid-week activities to Tuesday, alternating home groups with a prayer meeting in the lounge, or concentrating everything on Wednesday; the eight fellowship groups that met on Tuesday and the eight that met on Thursday all wanted to stay the way they were, so in September 2006, a partial solution was found – the central prayer meeting was held fortnightly, on Wednesday, with fellowship groups on Tuesday or Thursday on the alternate weeks.

## New ideas

### Men and Brothers

An invitation to men of all ages to come to the lounge at 7.30 a.m. on the first Saturday of the month, for breakfast, followed by an arranged speaker and a time of prayer,

attracted between 30 and 40 of various ages from its inception in June 1997. The purpose of Men and Brothers was to provide fellowship, teaching, encouragement and an opportunity for evangelism. The meeting closed at 9 a.m. From September 1998 onward, the group also had an annual weekend away. In 2001, a breakfast outreach, with Eddie Stobart as speaker, attracted 65 men, 12 of whom were invited guests. The group continues to flourish.

### History and Theology

At the beginning of 1998, one of the Chapel elders, Angus Ferguson, sought permission to have an open meeting on Thursday evening, six times a year, when no other activities were planned. Invited speakers took up some aspect of either the history or theology of the Christian faith. The first meeting, in February 1998, attracted 30, including some from other churches, and that has been the pattern ever since. When the subject has been of special interest, 50 or more have attended. Some have a standing order for a tape of the meeting.

*The Chapel was visible from George Street, and vice versa, for some months at the end of 1998, during reconstruction at the Roxburghe Hotel.*

### Views to the north

Part of the Roxburghe Hotel was demolished in 1998, to be replaced by modern suites. At the Chapel's request, the building warrant for the reconstruction forbad any noisy work during Sunday morning and evening; the contractors were not only scrupulous in observing this, but also were helpful during weddings and funerals. They even offered to wash the Chapel windows from time to time.

*The builders allowed the writer access to the scaffolding, to take photographs of the Chapel with Edinburgh Castle in the background.*

### 'Each One Bring One'

The Chapel had traditionally used open-air preaching and tract distribution as part of its evangelistic outreach. That was about to change. 'Imagine the following situation', said Peter Grainger in June 1996:

*A man is walking down Princes Street when he is accosted by one of those people with a clip-board. 'Excuse me, Sir. May I ask you a question – are you married?'. 'Actually, no,' replies the man. Then the interviewer responds with a big smile: 'I have just the girl for you,' he says, and introduces him to a young lady standing nearby. Now, what would you think about him if he agreed to marry her on the spot?… Yet there are some Christians who believe that it is normal to accost a total stranger in the street and expect him or her to make a far more life-changing decision than getting married – to receive Jesus Christ as Saviour and Lord immediately. We are now, I believe, in a missionary situation which involves considerable pre-evangelism…. Recent surveys (and testimonies in our own church) suggest that it usually takes a minimum of a year's exposure to the message and messenger before a person makes a response of faith.*

1 *Record*, June 1996, p. 2.

To meet this valid criticism, the Chapel arranged a week in June 1996 with 17 informal evangelistic meetings, all based around a meal, under the title 'Each One Bring One'; hosts purchased a double ticket, so the guest came free. More than a hundred non-Christians attended the June 1996 'Each One Bring One' meetings. Ian Leitch spoke at breakfasts, coffee mornings, business lunches, seniors' lunches, supper evenings, pizza parties and a couples' dinner, catering for all ages. Most events were well supported and some were sold out.

Nearly 80 of the 100 asked for further information. A smaller number joined a 'Just Looking' group, to work through questions such as 'Who is God?' and 'How to be right with God'. About 20 indicated that they had asked Christ into their lives. Some of these were reaffirmations of a decision made previously, but others committed their lives to Christ for the first time; signs of changed lives were obvious. Involvement in the week made Chapel members realize what could be done in this way.

*'Each One Bring One' brochure; the outreach was repeated in May 1997, May 1998 and September 2002.*

### 'Open to Question'

'Each One Bring One' led, in the spring of 1998, into 'Open to Question' (below), and then into another course entitled 'First Steps'. This covered the basics of the Christian faith, especially for new Christians and for those considering baptism. It met in the church office at the time that best suited the participants – Monday or Thursday evening or Sunday afternoon. In 2000, 'Second Steps' was added, as described in the next chapter.

'Open to Question' was based on material from Campus Crusade, and ran for eight consecutive Monday evenings. It promised: 'There will be a relaxed atmosphere with no requests to speak publicly, to sing, pray or do anything "religious"'. Every session began with a thought-provoking talk for about 35 minutes, followed by refreshments and analysis of the subject for the evening in small groups. Although the series breached the 'no meeting on Monday' rule (Chapter 53) for the first time, there was no other day in the week; the responses at the end of the course fully vindicated the effort put into it. It was repeated several times a year over the next four years, with an average of 32 attending; in 2002, it was replaced by 'Christianity Explored' (Chapter 57).

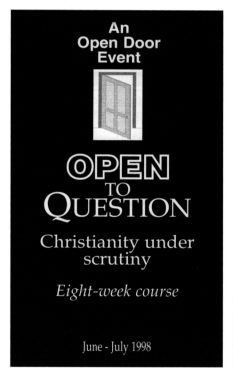

*'Open to Question' was held in the Chapel for eight consecutive Monday evenings, several times a year, from 1998 to 2001.*

## Christmas outreach

Christmas outreach, described in the last chapter for the years 1992–5, was expanded considerably from 1997 onwards. To capture the interest of shoppers flocking into the centre of Edinburgh, and of city workers looking for something different during their lunch break, the Chapel advertised a lunchtime carol service in Christmas week in 1997; one hundred attended, of whom three-quarters had no Chapel connection. A cafe in the lounge on the Saturday brought in 50 visitors for a gospel talk.

A programme entitled 'Christmas Encounters', presented on the Friday and Saturday evenings of Christmas week, involved the Chapel Praise Singers, the Band and Singers, Kids' Praise, the Youth Choir, the Male Voice singers and Jigsaw. There was a Watchnight service on 24 December and a family service on Christmas Day. 'Christmas Encounters' was repeated, with great success, on the Friday and Saturday of Christmas week from 1998 to 2000. From 2000, the lunchtime carol concert was made even more attractive by offering free lunch in the lounge before and after the service.

## Origin Scotland

Origin Scotland came into being in 1996, combining the musical talents of the younger generation of Carrubbers Christian Centre, Bellevue Chapel and the Chapel. Initially it aimed to reach students and young people with the gospel, and to promote unity in the church through worship and outreach, but it soon held praise nights for everyone in the Usher Hall. As these were not Chapel events, this is not the place to go into detail, but many Chapel members were involved, and still are.

## Niddrie mission

In April 1996, one of the Chapel elders, who was also a trustee of the Niddrie mission at 12 Hay Drive, advised the elders that the work, opened in 1896, was likely to close unless help was given. The area was undergoing massive redevelopment, with new and better quality housing; he saw the potential if the Chapel could supply a secretary, treasurer, music leader, youth worker and, as soon as possible, a full-time pastor, who would be part of the Chapel team, so as not to feel isolated.

The elders arranged an after-church fellowship in September 1996, when a video was shown, and the implications of the Chapel taking up a work in Niddrie were considered. Fourteen Chapel members (including two couples) volunteered to become involved. The November 1996 members' meeting gave authority, by an 83 per cent majority,

457

to treat Niddrie as a daughter church and to advertise for a pastor, funded by the Chapel. The priority was for a pastor, not for a new building.

The Chapel provided a rota of leaders and speakers for the Sunday morning service, and by January 1997 about 40 were attending, 15 of whom were from the Chapel. Four of the Chapel elders provided oversight, and about 20 Chapel members helped with the Sunday School (during the service) and with three children's clubs during the week, attended on a regular basis by 60-70 children aged 5-16. In addition, the Chapel's Young Peoples Meeting, which had not managed to put together a team for a summer beach mission in 1996 – they had been at Ayr until then – spearheaded an outreach in the Niddrie district in the summer of 1997.

A number of applications were received for a full-time pastor, and from these, one man was appointed. Although he took up the work, he could not find suitable accommodation and the appointment was terminated by mutual consent in October 1997. This is not the place to detail the difficulties and disappointments of the next three years. Further attempts to find a suitable pastor were abortive; the City Council were ambivalent about the mission property; only a small number of people from the Chapel got involved. Nevertheless, and in knowledge of the problems, the December 1998 members' meeting voted by a majority of 91 per cent to continue to seek a pastor and to draw up plans and costing for the upgrade or replacement of the building. What happened next is described in Chapter 57.

### Mission board

As mentioned in the previous chapter, the overseas and the home mission committees merged into one mission board on 1 January 1997. The new board had to be cautious, because it inherited two quite different policies on the handling of money. The overseas committee had clear rules about equal distribution of funds, £2,640 per missionary overseas in 1996, four-fifths to the mission for support and one-fifth to the individual as a personal gift. The home committee had a discretionary approach, taking into account individual circumstances; it made gifts personally to Chapel members engaged in home mission (not to their societies), averaging £400 a year, and also send money to organisations in which the Chapel had a particular interest, such as Scripture Union, even if no Chapel members were serving

with them. The overseas committee provided additional support for children (£528 per child per annum in 1996), which was not the policy of the home committee.

The overseas mission committee had supported Chapel members as follows:

|  | 1993 | 1994 | 1995 | 1996 |
|---|---|---|---|---|
| Missionaries | 13 | 18 | 18 | 20 |
| Retired missionaries | 7 | 8 | 8 | 8 |
| Missionary's children | 5 | 9 | 9 | 11 |

It took the new board six years to achieve parity of support (Chapter 57), but they found themselves with parity in another area almost immediately. It was not pre-planned, but at the end of the calendar year 1997, the Chapel's monthly magazine, the *Record*, had carried 144 pages of mission news and 144 pages of other news. The mission news divided into four categories: 71 pages from members working overseas, 32 pages from members in Britain, 34 pages about overseas missions where the Chapel had no present members, and 7 pages about evangelistic work at home.

*With the merger of overseas and home mission, one combined prayer card was issued for the mission family; this one is from March 1998 and there were another 32 names on the reverse of the card.*

Prior to the merger, both overseas mission and home mission had a weekend in the church calendar, one in February and the other in November. Both dates were retained, and there were now two Mission Focus Weekends, although the organisations had merged. The pattern has been broadly similar over the decade since the merger – something on Saturday evening, a guest speaker for both services on Sunday, and afternoon tea with mission personnel on Sunday. The weekend in November 2005 was special, as Operation Mobilisation suggested a joint venture to focus on a particular people-group in India. The monthly Men and Brothers breakfast was incorporated into the weekend, workshops were held throughout the Saturday afternoon, and then there was a meal at 6 p.m., followed by a contribution from the mission folk present – and the Sunday services as well.

## The millennium

There was a Christmas Day family service on Saturday 25 December 1999, followed by a morning service at the usual time on the Sunday, but no evening service on Boxing Day. The special services to celebrate the millennium are described in the next chapter.

*The YPM brought in the millennium in a marquee; the weather was so mild that there was no need for cardigans as they queued for the buffet in an adjoining tent.*

The YPM scoured Edinburgh for somewhere to hold a party on 31 December 1999, to bring in the new year and the new millennium, but everything suitable was booked up. They pitched a marquee in the writer's garden in Murrayfield Road; the weather was so mild that after midnight they queued for the buffet without a cardigan in sight.

Additional information on the following topics, mentioned in this chapter, is available on the CD.

Associate membership
Baptist Missionary Society Road Show
Census of 1999
Deaconess
Dedication of infants
Divorce
Maintenance or mission?
Mission board
Niddrie Mission
Pastoral groups
Seven-year review (1992-1999)

# Chapter 56
## Into the twenty-first century (2000–2001)

### The Chapel in the millennial year

#### 'The Man behind the Millennium'

On Sunday 2 January 2000, there was a short morning service in the Chapel, and then the congregation joined with four other city-centre churches for two rallies in the Festival Theatre. The theme at both was: 'Jesus – the Man behind the Millennium', celebrating the two-thousandth year of his birth (AD 2000 = anno Domini, in the year of our Lord). The Millennium Celebration at 4 p.m. was primarily for Christians from all over the city, followed by an evangelistic outreach at 8 p.m. The area of the theatre and the dress circle were filled on both occasions, with 1335 tickets sold for the former and 1376 for the latter, occupancy rates of 71 per cent and 73 per cent respectively. Special millennium editions of Mark's Gospel were distributed to adults, teenagers and children.

Sunday 9 January was entitled Amnesty Sunday in the Chapel; a real effort was made to encourage those who had ceased to attend church on a regular basis to make a fresh start, with no enquiry as to when or where they had lost the good habit of regular attendance. With that emphasis in the morning, it was appropriate to have the January communion in the evening of Sunday 9 January.

Mark's Gospel was the focus of the pulpit ministry right through the year 2000, taking up Jesus' question to his disciples: 'Who do you say that I am?' The Sunday morning service looked at 36 answers to that question, progressing through the New Testament from Gospels to epistles, and ending with the book of Revelation. Junior church followed the same theme, as did the fortnightly fellowship groups. The evening service studied the book of Genesis, first a series of 10 on the opening chapters, followed by a series of 14, 'From Jacob to Israel'. A new series of 'Open to Question' was held in the lounge on Monday, to help seekers find answers in a non-threatening environment.

#### Discipleship and training courses

In 2000, the discipleship group 'Building Up and Living Out' divided into: (1) 'First Steps', which ran for 7-8 weeks on Sunday afternoon, covering the basics of the Christian faith for new Christians and for those considering baptism (renamed 'Building Blocks' in March 2006) and (2) 'Second Steps', for growing Christians, to help them understand the fundamentals of the Christian life. This was a 13-week course, also on Sunday afternoon; both courses were regularly repeated.

Some went on to the Navigators 2:7 series, over four ten-week terms, with an option of one or two further ten-week terms. Alternatively, the network of 16 fellowship groups, meeting fortnightly in homes across the city, nurtured members and non-members alike as they shared in prayer and fellowship around God's Word. John Percival, who joined the pastoral team in October 2000 as assistant pastor for three years when John Smuts went to Cheltenham in June 2000, arranged Discipleship Group Bible Studies, for students to meet regularly with older Christians, to study the Bible and to pray together. John was aged 26 when he came back to Edinburgh; he had studied medieval history at the Universities of St Andrews and Cambridge, where he also worked with Eden Baptist Church.

*John Percival, assistant pastor from 2000 to 2003, had been brought up in the Chapel but had been away from Edinburgh, studying, for some years.*

#### Youth Council

Youth Council entered the new millennium in good heart. It still had 14 departments (Chapter 52), 5 of them now in junior church (Chapter 53), with about 160 meeting on Sunday; another 8 departments made up the uniformed organisations, with about 170 meeting on Friday; the fourteenth was Saturday Focus (school classes secondary 1-3, with secondary 4 added in 2003), with about 25 meeting in homes fortnightly during school term. A number attended more than one activity, so about 220 youngsters in all were involved in the Chapel. This required over a hundred leaders, more than half of them working on a rota basis in the crèche. The Council's twin aims were: (1) to encourage young people to know Christ personally and to start following him, and (2) to let them know that attending church should be 'cool' – normal and enjoyable,

In the summer of 2001, the Young Peoples Meeting (not part of Youth Council) raised its minimum age from 15 to 16. This left a gap for those aged 15, the age that many youth organisations found the most challenging. (The Scout Association made a number of alterations to its structure about this time, in an attempt to keep this age group.) Youth Council created YCC (Young Charlotte Chapel), open to secondary day school classes 3 and 4. Meeting on alternate Saturday nights, its aim was social activity and Bible teaching. It had peaks and troughs; from the summer of 2003 to the spring of 2004, it almost closed through lack of numbers and shortage of leaders, then it changed to meeting only two or three times a term, and seven or eight attended regularly.

### The section 28 debate
The Chapel supported the widespread opposition by Christians throughout Scotland to the Scottish Government's determination that local authorities should promote homosexuality as a family relationship (by repealing a 1986 Act that precluded such teaching). By letters to the Scottish Parliament, they protested that children should not be forced to attend lessons where homosexuality was put on the same footing as heterosexuality; what was taught in school should not undermine what was taught at home. The Executive bulldozed their repeal through Parliament, but the amendment to the law was largely symbolic and the practical consequences were minimal.

### Men's Fellowship
The associate pastor for pastoral care, Bill Denholm, saw the need to re-establish a meeting for retired men. He suggested alternate Friday afternoons, starting in March 2000. There was usually an invited speaker, on a subject that was devotional or of missionary interest or of social concern; the format was informal and discussion was encouraged. There were also walks and visits to places of interest in Edinburgh and in the Borders and Fife. Forty names were on the roll, and the meeting, which continues to this day, had (and still has) a regular attendance of about 25.

### Ambassadors in Sport
In 2000, the Chapel invited Ambassadors in Sport to run a four-day evangelistic Sport Soccer School on the Meggetland playing fields from 10 a.m. to 3:30 p.m. during the Easter school holidays, from Tuesday 11-Friday 14 April. It was open to boys and girls aged 7-15, and was fully subscribed. Ambassadors in Sport was a Bolton-based ministry that focused on outreach and evangelism through football. Their soccer schools gave young people an opportunity to learn basic and advanced football skills in a positive and encouraging environment, with emphasis on sportsmanship and character, based on biblical principles.

Like the Men's Friday Fellowship, just mentioned, which was started as an experiment in the previous month, the Soccer School continued, and has expanded to this day. From 2002, it offered advanced coaching to 14-16 year olds, and was always over-subscribed, with more than 50 attending. In 2005 and 2006, the Gyle Park playing fields and the adjoining St Thomas' church halls provided an excellent venue.

### Charlotte Sports
Encouraged by the interest shown in the Ambassadors in Sport soccer schools, the Chapel officially recognized its own football team (Chapter 50), and brought it under the umbrella of Charlotte Sports, a new auxiliary formed to develop sport as an outreach ministry. By 2006, this auxiliary was running golf outings and hockey matches and entered Team Charlotte in a nationwide effort to raise £100,000 for Tearfund in September 2006.

*Miss Agnes Blyth, who was baptized in the Chapel in 1918, celebrated her one-hundredth birthday in Beulah Home in April 2000. She showed her well-wishers the message of congratulation she had received that morning from Her Majesty the Queen.*

460

## Chapter 56
Into the twenty-first century (2000-2001)

### Two more centenarians

On 10 February 2000, Miss Margaret Tullis, whose baptism in the original Chapel building was mentioned in Chapter 18, and who was now the oldest member (she joined in 1911), celebrated her one-hundredth birthday in an Edinburgh nursing home. Two months later, Miss Agnes Blyth, one of the residents of Beulah, reached the same milestone on the 6 April.

Some events in Agnes Blyth's life are worth recording, because they were shared by many of her generation in the Chapel, and they illustrate how much society changed during her lifetime. She told those who gathered in Beulah for the birthday celebration a little about her life. She was brought up to walk the two miles to church every Sunday (a Presbyterian church in Kelty in Fife) and apart from writing letters, no activity was permitted throughout Sunday except reading and learning poetry; the older children walked back to the church for Bible Class after supper. Every member of the family took turns to say grace before meals; Agnes recalled that when it was her turn, her favourite was: 'For what we about to eat, we thank the Lord and the British Fleet.' Three of her five sisters emigrated, to Australia, Canada and the United States; she kept in touch with them weekly through the Sunday afternoon writing sessions.

On leaving school, she became a nursery maid in a Borders mansion. She was given one match a day, with which to light the nursery fire at 6 a.m. She then came to Edinburgh and was baptized in the Chapel in 1918. Five years later, she obtained a post as governess to the children of an Edinburgh lawyer at 38 Heriot Row. She successfully brought up the three boys, all of whom joined the Royal Air Force during the Second World War. She then ran a crèche in Edinburgh and looked after her elderly parents, until she was asked back as nanny to the children of the boys whom she had brought up. When they too left home, she went back to 38 Heriot Row, as companion to the lawyer's widow. Many Chapel members in the inter-war years were in service in the New Town, but few served four generations; she was invited to the christening of the grandchildren of her original charges.

### Conference ministry

It has always been the privilege of the Chapel to give leave of absence to its ministers, to address conferences elsewhere, recognising not only the benefit to the other congregation but also the enrichment of the minister's own life and the consequent blessing coming to the Chapel on his return. What was new in Peter Grainger's time was the speed with which such visits could take place. He and his wife flew to the Ivory Coast on 30 March 2000, to take part in Wycliffe devotional conferences for the first fortnight of April, then on to Mali for further ministry, and yet he was back in his own pulpit for Sunday 23 April. Similarly, they left Edinburgh on 13 March 2003, for conferences in Nigeria and to revisit the places where they had worked in 1983-5, but Peter conducted the services in the Chapel on 30 March. They went in November 2004 to an isolated part of the Philippines, for the dedication of the translation of the complete New Testament into the Mayoyao langauge by Barbara Hodder, one of the Chapel missionaries; in April 2006, they went to Papua New Guinea, for the celebration of 50 years of Wycliffe's work there and to visit a project involving Teresa Wilson (another Chapel missionary), and in both cases they were back almost before most members realized that they were away.

### Gift Aid

As mentioned in Chapters 35 and 47, the years between 1952 and 2004 saw tax recovery, through deeds of covenant and, later, Gift Aid, become an increasingly important part of the Chapel's budget; the number of members participating rose from 3 to 430. Gift Aid, in its present form, dates from 6 April 2000. Until then, gifts had to be of £250 or more to qualify; the alternative, a deed of covenant, required a commitment of four years or longer. In 2000, the chancellor brought all charitable giving under one umbrella, removing the four-year term for covenants and making Gift Aid available on any amount from £1 upward – for every pound given, the treasurer received another 28 pence from the Inland Revenue.

Chapel members responded enthusiastically; they had got the message at last. In 2004, the Chapel received £354,760 in cash (to which a tax refund of £93,200 was added) for its general and missionary funds, a total of £447,960, and a further £317,440 in cash (plus tax refund of £86,160, total £403,600) toward the new building at Niddrie, a total of £851,560 from the 430 members and regular attenders who used Gift Aid. The weekly offerings, not through Gift Aid, added £15,907 and £9,669, respectively; gift-aided donations now accounted for 85 per cent of the Chapel's income.

## Quinquennial elections, spring 2000

The Chapel operated with virtually the same leadership structure from 1877 to 2000. Elders were elected every five years, to share with the pastor in the spiritual oversight of the congregation, and to act along with the deacons (also elected every five years) in the practical running of the church. In 1995, the relationship was amended slightly, to allow the deacons to meet and to take decisions on their own. However, as the twentieth century drew to a close, there was a move to separate pastoral oversight from management – to have pastoral elders and ministry elders – and the elders would nominate the deacons. After much discussion, the congregation approved this, for the quinquennial election in 2000.

It looked good on paper, but it did not work in practice; since the structure was radically altered for the 2005 elections (Chapter 57), no more need be said here. However, the value of women deacons, appointed for the first time in 2000 (Chapter 54), was recognized, and they had come to stay.

*In 2000, the congregation elected elders only, not deacons; the elders then brought nominations to the congregation for all other offices.*

## Café Rendezvous

Café Life, which had reached many during the Edinburgh International Festival from 1994 to 1999 (Chapter 54), was renamed Café Rendezvous and held again on three

Thursdays in August 2000. Following half an hour of prayer together, some went out to distribute invitations to the lounge, which opened at 7.30 p.m., while others greeted visitors and spoke with them, or prepared and served refreshments, or provided background music. Every hour, there was an evangelistic talk for about ten minutes; about 60-70 strangers came in and were challenged by the gospel message. For 2001, it was felt better to concentrate on six successive evenings in August, and to be open from 8 p.m. until midnight. About 350 visitors came in during the week, from 18 countries; 109 of them were sufficiently interested in the message to give the Chapel their names and addresses, so that they could be prayed for and literature sent. Three made definite commitments to Christ; the Chapel members ended the week exhausted but delighted at the response.

## Mystery worshipper

Since 1998, teams of mystery worshippers have travelled incognito in the British aisles [sic] and beyond, reporting on the comfort of the pews, the warmth of the welcome and the length of the sermon. One attended both services in the Chapel on Harvest Thanksgiving Sunday in September 2000, and posted his or her report on their website in the usual way. It is reproduced in full on the CD, but on the three specific areas mentioned, the comments were:

*Was your pew comfortable? Fairly comfortable, consisting as it did of a wooden seat with a layer of cushioning.*

*Did anyone welcome you personally? A young man on the door greeted me with a handshake and a hymn book and explained the unusual layout of the building. An elderly lady chatted to me on the stairs and, discovering that I came from London, spent a few minutes recalling her wartime experiences there.*

*Exactly how long was the sermon? 43 minutes.*

---

1 http://ship-of-fools.com/Mystery

Another of the standard items in their reports is: 'Was the worship stiff-upper-lip, happy clappy, or what?' The answer for the Chapel was: 'Traditional non-conformist with a couple of choir items. The hymns were mainly traditional, with one or two more contemporary songs. The evening service at the same church, however, was led by a band with sax and drums, and the style of worship was more contemporary.'

## Flexible anniversaries

The church anniversary was usually celebrated over the first weekend in October. However, in 2000 it was known that Dr Howard Hendrix, of the Dallas Theological Seminary, would be in Edinburgh in mid-June, so an anniversary weekend was built around his visit. He spoke seven times in three days – at an evening meeting on Friday, a men's breakfast, a ladies' coffee morning and a gathering for the whole church on Saturday, at both of the Sunday services and at an after-church concert.

In 2001, the date went back to October but the format was even more experimental. Wednesday was a day of prayer, preparatory to a members' meeting that evening (about purchasing additional accommodation, below). The 'Family Matters' ministry held workshops on Christian living on Thursday evening and on parenting on Friday evening. The anniversary concluded with special services on Sunday, including the Thankoffering and communion.

Perhaps because of the extra activities, no one except the leader turned up for the public 10 a.m. prayer meeting on Sunday 7 October 2001, the first time this had happened since Joseph Kemp started it in 1902. The elders refused to be discouraged, and continued the meeting, although attendance was usually about five. However, in April 2006 they decided that everyone who wanted to attend knew about it, and that mention of it in the weekly bulletin was not attracting any newcomers, so it was no longer printed in the bulletin. That did not discourage Jeremy Landless, whose dedicated leadership kept the meeting alive, and in 2007, when numbers were again into two figures, the 10 a.m. meeting rejoined the weekly calendar in the bulletin.

The 2002 anniversary was different again. It started on the first Sunday in October and ran through to the following Thursday. The theme was 'Prayer, the untapped resource', with prayer meetings from 7.30 to 9 p.m. on Tuesday and Wednesday, then tea at 6 p.m. on Thursday, followed by prayer in small groups from 6.45 p.m., and activities for the children, through to 9 p.m. The size of the groups was noticeably measured by age; younger people preferred the informality of very small groups, three or four, while older people formed themselves into clusters of ten or more.

When a speaker with special appeal to students became available for the first Sunday in October 2003, it was designated Student Sunday; the anniversary was to be marked at the end of November, but when baptisms were arranged for that Sunday morning, the one hundred and ninety-fifth anniversary passed almost unnoticed. The 2004 anniversary was also low-key, at the end of October.

The 2005 anniversary was in two parts. Since Dr Don Carson was to be in Edinburgh on Sunday 28 August, that was designated anniversary Sunday, with a birthday cake in the pulpit and a brief history of the Chapel for the children's talk. The Thankoffering, normally part of the anniversary, was received on Wednesday 23 November during a praise and thanksgiving service at the conclusion of a shortened half-yearly members' meeting. As always on Thanksgiving days, the fund remained open for those who had forgotten their envelope on the appointed day.

The 2006 anniversary, on the last Sunday of October, was different again, and is described in Chapter 58.

## 'Not The Usual Prayer Meeting'

The experimental prayer meeting on the Thursday of the 2002 anniversary (above) was so well supported that the elders kept the format (and the name, 'Not The Usual Prayer Meeting') for the third Tuesday of every month. The ministries (committees) took it in turn to lead. A buffet tea was served at 6 p.m., for those coming straight from work; there was then a session of information, and prayer from 6.45-7.25 p.m. in small groups (with a separate section for children), and another from 7.30-8.20 p.m., this time together. People came and went at the breaks; the final time for prayer was from 8.20-9 p.m.. The usual Tuesday prayer meeting on fellowship group weeks averaged about 35 during the early 2000s, with double that number when the fellowship groups were not meeting; NTUPM brought out over a hundred, to learn about particular activities in the church.

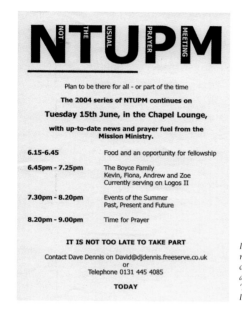

*In 2004, every ministry had at least one Tuesday evening a year to lead the 'Not The Usual Prayer Meeting.'*

## Review of 2000

The year 2000 saw solid progress, with a number of fresh initiatives. Although the trend to 'once-ism' on Sunday continued, membership remained stable, with challenging Bible-based ministry. The revival of the work at Niddrie was an encouragement, as was the number of young people offering themselves for full-time Christian service. Student work flourished, changing its approach in response to the changing needs of students. Pastoral care became increasingly complex in the face of pressures on every aspect of daily living, especially as marriage and family life were being aggressively undermined by secularism in society. There were five baptismal services during the year with a total of 16 confessing their faith in this way. Most, but not all of them, came into membership at the same time.

## 2001

### Growing in Christ

The Verse for the Year 2001 was: 'Grow in the grace and knowledge of our Lord and Saviour Jesus Christ' (2 Peter 3:18). This was expounded in three series of sermons on Sunday morning. Up to Easter, they were based on 2 Peter, 'Growing in Christ'; during the spring and early summer, Rev. Derek Prime, a former pastor, explored 'The Fruit of the

Spirit' (Galatians 5:22-23) during Peter Grainger's sabbatical leave; in the autumn, Peter Grainger continued the theme in a series on relationships, 'Growing Together'.

Sunday evening for the first part of the year was based on 'Ten Tough Questions, answered from the Psalms', followed by an evangelistic series, 'Ultimate Questions', dealing with the essentials of the Christian faith. The final months of the year brought studies in Amos, entitled 'The Lion Roars'. The book of Amos might not seem evangelistic, but several young people came to faith during these weeks. For most of the year, the morning service was almost packed out; attendance at the evening service continued to grow, with a quite different feel from the morning, and with a largely different congregation.

### Onlinewithgod@charlotte

This was not an e-mail address, but an opportunity, every third Sunday evening, for students and other young people who wanted to think more deeply about their faith, to grill the preacher. John Percival, the assistant pastor, started it in November 2000. After the evening service, coffee and cakes were served in the lower hall, and then there was an opportunity to look in depth at the issues raised by the sermon that evening.

There was plenty in the Sunday evening services from January to April 2001 to discuss. 'The Ten Tough Questions, answered from the Psalms', included:

Does God watch 'News at Ten'?
How can I be forgiven when I've done something terrible?
Where is God when I need him most?
Why do drug barons always have big houses and nice cars?
What do I do when none of my friends believe in God?

The YPM were sufficiently impressed to join in, rather than have their own Sunday evening activity. The YPM normally had 50-75 at their informal (and lively) Sunday evening meetings in 2001; on Wednesday, numbers varied from 30 to 40.

There was, as mentioned earlier, an increasing need to provide ministry for students. University Christian Unions had changed their emphases by 2000, seeing their role more in terms of evangelism than discipleship. This meant greater responsibility for local churches; the Chapel set up discipleship groups for students, with a recent graduate as leader, and students were encouraged to attend both services on Sunday.

In the autumn of 2003, Onlinewithgod@charlotte moved to the early afternoon, for six consecutive weeks, after lunch for students in the lower hall, and it was renamed Down 2 Earth. Instead of questioning the preacher from the evening service, they had talks from the Chapel team and group discussion.

## cbcOnline

Another facility, also started in 2000, and also nothing to do with personal computers, was 'cbcOnline'. A member collated news from the mission family, home and overseas, and made ten A4 pages available on the first Sunday of every second month. It was essentially a prayer diary, with an entry for every day of the month. Copies were distributed without charge at the Sunday services. Those who were mystified, on coming to the mission prayer meeting on the first Tuesday of the month, to be handed a piece of paper with a number between 1 and 30, learned that it was their privilege to pray, during the meeting, for the person listed for that day of the month.

## Church family picnic

'This year's annual church family picnic took place on 24 June 2001 at Penicuik Public Park…. As always there were a number of activities for everyone to enjoy, such as a bouncy castle, jousting, football, rounders, face painting and football. Lunch was hamburgers, crisps and juice, etc., rounded off with ice cream…. After lunch the family races were held. This is when you realise how unfit you are!'

## Summer action around the world

As mentioned in Chapter 52, the early 1990s saw a new concept, of professional people offering to help in established missionary situations, for a year or so, without longer-term commitment. A decade later, some still went for a year but many more gave up their summer vacation to work overseas. In 2001, and again in 2002 and 2003, ten Chapel members scattered across the globe for the summer months, to Ecuador, Malawi, Nairobi and Niger in 2001, to Ecuador, Ghana, Kiev, Mexico, Nicaragua, the Philippines and Uganda in 2002, and to Ethiopia, Kenya, Kosovo, Italy, Mexico, St Petersburg, Tanzania and Togo in 2003.

In 2006, six Chapel young people were on a year's short-term service, two abroad and four in Britain, while another 20 went for the summer to Brazil, the Czech Republic, Germany, Hungary, India, Lithuania, Malawi, South Africa, Spain, Switzerland, Ukraine or Tanzania; 32 more were leaders at Scripture Union and other summer camps in Scotland. Apart from the help that they gave in these places, they grew immeasurably in their own personal faith by contact with other Christians. At the same time, 'cbcOnline' (above), gave bimonthly prayer details from 58 members (including spouses) who were in full-time, long-term Christian service, 36 at home and 22 abroad.

## Sabbatical leave, April-June 2001

By the late twentieth century, churches were giving their ministers a period of sabbatical leave every seven years. Peter Grainger was due one in 1999 or 2000. He wanted to see the new elders and deacons settled into office after the quinquennial elections in the spring of 2000, so he postponed his well-deserved break until after Easter 2001. He and his wife spent three months at the Whitefield Institute in Oxford, considering challenges facing the church in Britain at the beginning of the twenty-first century. As mentioned, Rev. Derek Prime took nine Sunday morning services on 'The Fruit of the Spirit', while the pastor's assistant, John Percival, and the evangelist, Ian Leitch, brought messages on apologetic themes in the evening. The Graingers' reports on the insights they gained from this study-leave are on the Chapel website.

## Multi-media

Upgrading the electronics in the Chapel, particularly the quality of the picture to the lounge, had been discussed for years. Outside consultants recommended a completely new system. This would allow coloured projection onto an electrically operated eight-foot-square screen above the choir and a seven-foot-square pull-down screen in the lounge. The words of hymns, sermon outlines and pictures could be projected onto the screens and, in the lounge, superimposed on the picture of the pulpit and preacher. Whatever was seen on the screen could also be video-recorded.

Those in favour gave a demonstration on Christmas Eve, 2000. Feedback was generally positive, but the elders still hesitated. Would TV-type lighting (necessary for colour) make the building more welcoming, or would it turn the pulpit into a theatre? Fortuitously, the elders were given an easy way to find out. Derek Prime asked if the Chapel could make data projection equipment available for the nine morning services during Peter Grainger's sabbatical leave, as he thought it added value to the preaching. The church hired what was necessary for the nine weeks, and the elders evaluated the system.

When Peter Grainger came back at the end of August, refreshed by his sabbatical leave and enthusiastic about multi-media, the elders installed it permanently. The pews at the back of the church, in the area known as the bed recess, were removed and sold to souvenir-hunters in the congregation, so that the audio, video and data controls could be installed together in one accessible place.

The package included replacement of the audio system, the pulpit microphones and the loudspeakers, which were ten years old. They were controlled from another console, on the west of the bed recess (not in the picture below). It had originally been proposed to bolt four 29-inch flat-screen monitors onto the downstairs pillars in the sanctuary, as people sitting under the gallery could not see the large screen; this was not implemented, partly because large monitors were unsightly and partly because they cost £5,000 each in 2001. Projection of a five-foot image onto the two end walls (just visible in the bottom photograph below) has proved almost satisfactory, except for those close to the wall.

466

*The console on the east of the 'bed recess' (top); the lounge, with the words of a hymn superimposed on a view from the roving camera upstairs (centre); the screen above the choir stalls and, just visible, the repeater on the wall under the gallery; the preacher is looking at the monitor in the pulpit (bottom).*

*The evening sun pours through the west windows of the church at certain times of the year, blinding the speaker and the choir. With the installation of PowerPoint (below), roller blinds had to be fitted for the screens to be readable.*

## 15 South Charlotte Street

While the multi-media experiment was being evaluated in June 2001, a 'For sale' board appeared at 15 South Charlotte Street, almost adjoining the Chapel. The upset price was £575,000 although the owners said they expected £620,000, approximately the Chapel's own valuation. It could provide rooms for youth activities and a better office; the ground floor, opening directly onto South Charlotte Street, could make user-friendly access to (say) a bookroom and coffee lounge. The price included five parking spaces, over which it might be possible to build a bridge to the Chapel, and to install a lift. At that time, the parking area was open to Rose Street; the new owner built the steel shuttering that now runs from their building to the Chapel.

*15 South Charlotte Street, which backed onto the Chapel and had five car-parking places in the space between two buildings, came on the market in June 2001.*

The opportunity could not have come at a worse time. The Chapel had just finalized the multi-media system at a cost of £51,000, and had made a commitment to the outreach in Niddrie, where there was now a full-time pastor and around 40 members. The Niddrie leadership recommended: (1) their building needed to be replaced, not just renovated, (2) renting accommodation in the community centre, instead of putting up a purpose-built church, was not desirable in the long term, and (3) an adjoining plot of land was for sale, and a very attractive church complex could be built on the combined site. No firm costs were available, but £500,000 was a guesstimate.

The position was put to the members at a special meeting on Wednesday 3 October 2001. There was no competition for 15 South Charlotte Street, but the owners were not prepared to reduce the price. Ninety-six per cent of the 231 members at the meeting decided that the Niddrie building must go ahead; they also decided, by a majority of 75 per cent, to put in an offer for 15 South Charlotte Street if, but only if, pledges (not cash) of £500,000 were received by Sunday 21 October. It was assumed that the present church office on the second flat at number 13 would sell for about £100,000.

Part of the difficulty, apart from finding the money, was that many could not visualize how the three-storey building could be efficiently used and managed. Two hundred and two pledges were received, totalling £351,788, so that was that. The elders felt directed to invest in people rather than in property, and a year later appointed the first student and youth worker (Chapter 57). Two sobering statistics came out of the appeal: (1) only a third of the members responded to it, and (2) two hundred of the personally addressed letters about it had not been collected from the lounge. If one wanted to reach the whole membership, letters had to be posted, or at least the ones still left uncollected after a couple of Sundays.

The building was renovated, and the penthouse, with two car parking spaces, came on the market in 2006 at an upset price of £400,000. The deacons looked at it, but the fire hazard of taking dozens of young people to a top flat with only a common stair for an exit, and its total unsuitability for disability access, made it a non-starter for the Chapel.

*To finance the purchase of the whole building at 15 South Charlotte Street – the farthest-away 'For sale' board in the picture – the Chapel would need to sell its flat at number 13; clearly this was not an easy time for selling commercial property in the street.*

**Hogmanay Hootenanny (their phrase)**

The Chapel booked the Scripture Union conference centre at
Lendrick Muir, near Kinross, from the evening of Monday 31
December 2001 to the afternoon of 1 January, and about 150
attended. There was a church family party from 8.30 to 11.15
p.m. on Hogmanay, followed by a Watchnight service to
usher in 2002, and then the ceilidh started. Officially it
ended at 2 a.m., but many were still dancing at 3 a.m.;
dormitory accommodation and breakfast and activities
through to noon on Tuesday cost a modest £22 for adults
and £8 for children. This was repeated from 2002 to 2005,
but since 1 January was a Sunday in 2006, it was felt
inappropriate to bring in New Year in this way.

Additional information on the following topics,
mentioned in this chapter, is available on the CD.

Gift Aid, 2004
Mystery worshipper
Niddrie Mission
Summer action, 2006

# Chapter 57
# Conspicuous for Christ (2002–2005)

## 2002

### Prayer meetings

The Friday pre-breakfast prayer meeting in the Chapel, started after the October 1994 anniversary (Chapter 54), had fallen into abeyance. To capture the opportunities of 2002, 45 minutes of praise and prayer were restarted, from Monday to Friday, 14-18 January, at 7.30 a.m., concluding with coffee and rolls. This was so much appreciated that the meeting was continued, once a week, on Friday. It is still (2007) held during the autumn, winter and spring, although support for it varies – typically about ten.

This had an impact on attendance at the Tuesday evening meeting. Although older people still regarded it as the church's main prayer meeting, others, who were coming into town anyway for work, preferred the Friday morning, and attendance on Tuesday declined. When there were no fellowship groups, about 70 attended, down from 80-90 before the move from Monday to Tuesday; about 15-18 people took part audibly on a typical evening, although 45 participated at one missionary prayer meeting when the topic aroused particular concern. Often the Tuesday meeting divided into smaller groups, after an opening time together, so that more could take part; the younger people liked it, the older ones did not. On the alternate Tuesday, when about half of the fellowship groups were meeting, around 35 came to the central meeting. The home groups continued to be one of the main strengths of congregational life, and prayer was an important component at them, along with Bible study and friendship.

### 'Good News for Bad People'

The Verse for the Year (below) was expounded in 32 sermons throughout 2002, going through the Letter to the Romans under the title 'Good News for Bad People'. The first 20 sermons were preached at the evening service up to June, with a further 12 in the morning from August to December. (The other 20 Sundays were taken up with regular events in the Chapel calendar.) The morning messages from January to March were studies in Proverbs called 'Wisdom for Living', followed in the second quarter by a series in Jonah entitled 'The Reluctant Missionary'. During the autumn months, the evening service brought 'Good News for Europe', based on Acts 15-22. In the first ten years of Peter Grainger's ministry,

he covered almost every book of the Bible, giving the congregation not just head knowledge (although that was greatly appreciated) but also challenges to Christian life and spiritual growth.

There was good reason for switching the series between Sunday morning and evening. When Peter Grainger came to Edinburgh, over a third of the congregation attended the Chapel twice on Sunday. He could therefore plan a balanced diet of Old Testament at one service and New Testament at the other. Ten years later, less than a quarter came twice (census, below); furthermore, some people now took one or two weekends a month away from Edinburgh, which made a series difficult for them – and for the preacher.

*The Verse for the Year was the basis for 32 sermons from the Letter to the Romans.*

Throughout 2002, the Chapel appeared to be all but full on the average Sunday morning, which makes one wonder whether a number did not complete the forms handed round for a census in November (below). The morning service attracted all ages, but the majority at the evening service were young, especially students, with a flavouring of older people. The November census illustrated the difference between the two services – 44 per cent in the morning service were over 45, while 45 per cent in the evening were under 25. The style of the two services was now quite different. While the ministry of the Word remained central to both, the morning service was traditional in style and appeal, whereas the evening service had a contemporary feel, both in structure and music.

A visitor at this time, the president of the Baptist Union of Great Britain, reported:

*I was able, completely incognito and in the guise of an English tourist, to pay a visit [August 2002] to Charlotte Chapel, one of the largest UK Baptist churches and one with a great history. It was packed to the gunnels of course with a wide cross-section of people and is in a splendid position in the town. Unlike some churches with a notable past this one seems to have a great future as well!*

1 Nigel Wright, *Baptist Times*, 29 August 2002, p. 7.

### 'Christianity Explored'
'Open to Question', held on Monday evening from the mid-1990s to 2001 (Chapter 55), was replaced in 2002 by 'Christianity Explored', a ten-week evangelistic course that also covered the basics of the Christian faith, but in a less academic way. Written in 1995 at All Souls Church in London, it explored three areas: Who was Jesus? Why did he come? What does he require? The Chapel has run this course twice a year, from January to March and October to December, ever since.

Over 60 'explorers' attended the first course, in addition to the 20 needed to lead, speak, cater, administer and work the electronics. Several, who had no Chapel connection, came through press advertising. In every course, some have realised their need of the Saviour, a necessary starting point for a generation that largely has no concept of the need to repent, and accepted Christ. While never turning anyone away, the team have sometimes been quietly anxious, in the dozen courses run so far, whether they could cope with any more in the friendly atmosphere of the Chapel lounge.

### Matrix, Synergy, Apex and others
Following the demise of Group 2545 (Chapter 53), there was nothing specifically for the mid-twenties to mid-forties. Accordingly, the 'Family Matters' ministry launched Matrix in March 2002, for singles, and Synergy in August 2002, for young marrieds. Seventeen couples attended Synergy on Saturday evening, initially once a month but later every second month, because of babysitting problems.

Matrix was more ambitious, perhaps too ambitious; it met on the first Saturday and the second Sunday of every month, and also arranged lunches in homes on the last Sunday.

Sadly, it ran out of steam by the summer of 2003, because those involved were busy elsewhere in the church, and disbanded. Nothing like it was available for Chapel people in their 20s and 30s for the next four years. Then, in June 2007, a group calling themselves 'CC2030+' issued an open invitation to a Sunday lunch, in the hope of establishing 'a network of opportunities for making contact with other people their age, building a sense of community and using their gifts to serve others'. Forty attended the first meeting.

Group 45 (for everyone over that age) wanted to broaden its base, so it wound up early in 2003 and reformed as a new peer group with the title Apex. It provided fellowship, integration and evangelism, meeting on Saturday, sometimes in the Chapel lounge and sometimes for outside activities.

The 'Family Matters' ministry was also concerned for single parents; seminars were held and support offered under the umbrella of the lone parent network. In 2004, this became a group in its own right, for mutual support, fellowship and encouragement for those who, for whatever reason, found themselves grappling single-handedly with the responsibilities of parenthood. Meetings were held monthly, and included social activities on Saturday afternoon.

### 'Each One Bring One'
A new series of 'Each One Bring One' (Chapter 55) was arranged for a week, Tuesday to Saturday, in September 2002, replacing the festival café. Much prayer, planning and preparation went into the week, so it was disappointing that only 36 people brought a total of 85 guests to the various events. Nevertheless, the feedback was encouraging, with 40 requesting a copy of *Ultimate Questions* and a number committing themselves to Christ. For the summer of 2003, the evangelism ministry took a totally different line, as set out below.

*As Peter Grainger came out of the vestry for the morning service on Sunday 25 August 2002 (the tenth anniversary of his induction), this picture was projected onto the screen. It took him by surprise, as did a presentation of flowers to Nita.*

# Chapter 57
## Conspicuous for Christ (2002-2005)

### Census Sunday, 17 November 2002

On Sunday 17 November 2002, a further census produced two similarities and two disturbing differences, compared with the one on Sunday 30 October 1994 (Chapter 54). In both, only half of those attending were members – 335 out of 665 completed questionnaires in 2002; membership was 663. Over one-quarter of non-members (190 people) regarded the Chapel as their church; 43 per cent of them had been coming for six years or more. Asked about this, some answered the questionnaire quite openly: 'We are getting all the benefits without being members, so membership is irrelevant.' That resonated with comments heard across the Baptist denomination at this time.

The proportion of men was still on the increase, up from 41 per cent of the 1994 congregation to 44 per cent in 2004. This matched the pattern of church life in Scotland generally, where male attendance increased from 37 per cent in 1984 to 39 per cent in 1994 and to 40 per cent in 2002.

There were two worrying differences between the surveys. As mentioned above, the number of 'twicers' had fallen from 36 per cent to 24 per cent, disturbing but nothing like the decline across the country as a whole. Secondly, there was a big drop in the number of newcomers making the Chapel their home. In 1994, almost half of those attending had been coming for less than six years; in 2002, this had dropped to about a third, and the number attending for between six and ten years had doubled – less new blood was coming in. The intense loyalty of many members was illustrated by adding up the years in membership of the 11 who died during the year – 524, which gave an average of 48 years.

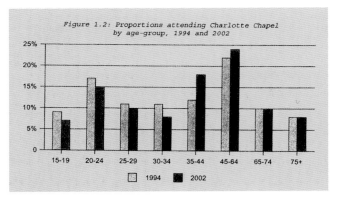

*Figure 1.2: Proportions attending Charlotte Chapel by age-group, 1994 and 2002*

*Over the eight years 1994-2002, the average age of the congregation increased from 42 to 44.*

The age-range and the number of those attending the Sunday morning service at the visual survey in 1984 and the surveys by questionnaire in 1994 and 2002 was:

|       | 1984 | | 1994 | | 2002 | |
|-------|------|------|------|------|------|------|
|       | no.  | %    | no.  | %    | no.  | %    |
| 15-19 | 67   | 9    | 58   | 9    | 32   | 7    |
| 20-29 | 242  | 32   | 189  | 28   | 112  | 25   |
| 30-44 | 126  | 17   | 168  | 23   | 154  | 26   |
| 45-64 | 148  | 20   | 168  | 23   | 123  | 24   |
| 65+   | 166  | 22   | 146  | 17   | 112  | 18   |
| Total | 749  | 100  | 729  | 100  | 533  | 100  |

At the beginning of 2002 there were 718 members – 647 full plus 71 associate or student link. During the year, 28 new members were received (15 plus 13), 7 members died (6 plus 1) and 76 were removed from the roll because they had left Edinburgh or for other reasons. The membership at the end of 2002 was therefore 663 (590 plus 73), exactly the number when Peter Grainger came to Edinburgh.

### Student and youth worker

When the congregation said 'No' to the purchase of 15 South Charlotte Street (Chapter 56), the elders decided to invest in people rather than in property. The two most obvious needs were for an additional member of the pastoral team to work with: (1) British young people in the 16-25 age bracket, and/or (2) international students. These were two distinct groups within the life of the church, with different needs and opportunities. Sheila Masterton had given herself (and her home) unstintingly to looking after 'international' students for 25 years, after retiring from missionary work in India, but she had to go into a nursing home in June 2004. The social habits of international students were different from those of British students and young people – 'international' students were usually older and sometimes had families with them.

A members' meeting in June 2002 agreed to give priority to the appointment of someone to work with British students and also to help the Young Peoples Meeting with training and discipleship. His title was to be student and youth worker. Historically, the Chapel's YPM had catered predominantly, but not exclusively, for Chapel families and others who lived at home in Edinburgh. They had an intensive programme of activities, often meeting up to three times a week. The YPM did not (generally) attract young people who had come to Edinburgh to study; the latter had less time during the week, and they were away from Edinburgh for several months of the year. Accordingly, the Chapel had, again historically, arranged different programmes for students, offering a mix of training and social activities, usually on Sunday and only during term time.

*The two key groups have radically different cultures and lifestyles compared with each other. The student group could be termed 'outsiders' and the YPM group 'insiders'. This is a generalisation obviously but nevertheless the differences between the two groups are real. The student group comes from a largely non-Christian background and sees itself interacting with the world on the world's terms, hence the few activities each week. YPM acts as a sort of protection for our young people supplying social interaction, deeper Bible study and Christian service opportunities. The student group can appear to be barely separate from the world in lifestyle while the YPM group can appear to be isolated from the real world having an alternative lifestyle supplied for them.*

2 Ministry Elders' Minute, 8 January 2003.

The remit of the student and youth worker was to support both groups, and to foster a joined-up relationship, recognising their different strengths. Each was to retain its identity and to be led by its own committee, but without tension or competition. The student and youth worker was not to replace the assistant pastor, but was an additional staff appointment. To finance this, an ambitious target of £25,000 was set for the October 2002 Thankoffering; the congregation responded with £34,600, the largest Thankoffering ever, so far. Average wages in Scotland were £24,500 a year at the time. There was sufficient to send the usual Christmas gift to missionaries (£4,500), to replenish the fund for students training for ministry, and to go forward with the new post.

Colin Adams, originally from Kirkintilloch, was appointed in January 2003 and moved to Edinburgh, with his wife Nicki, on completion of his studies at the International Christian College in Glasgow in June. He quickly settled into this complex role. Under his leadership, the student and youth work became closely integrated; this was a remarkable achievement, considering the historical differences between them. Two years later, his valuable contribution was

recognized by changing his title to assistant pastor for student and youth, and offering him a further three-year contract.

*Colin Adams, student and youth worker (2003-5) and then assistant pastor for student and youth (2005-7) and then, ordained on 20 May 2007, associate pastor (to date).*

## Women's Morning Fellowship

Although those attending the Women's Thursday Morning Fellowship were growing gracefully but steadily older, the leaders were prepared to experiment. From October 2002, the first Thursday of the month was given over to a series on 'Coping with... suffering, fear, bitterness, loneliness, depression, bereavement and anger.' Many of the 80 who attended said how helpful these topics had been. The weekly meeting was supplemented in December 2002 (for the first time since it began) by a Christmas lunch and carol singing at an Edinburgh restaurant, attended by 60. The jubilee in January 2007 included a typed message from Kitty Griffiths, who had started the fellowship in January 1957 (Chapter 40); over one hundred attended, including four who had been at the inaugural meeting.

## Communion

The elders constantly re-examined Chapel tradition in light of biblical criteria. In the autumn of 2002, they accepted that there were no biblical or theological reasons – only cultural ones – for elders (men) serving communion. There was a generation difference here; the writer was among those who had never thought of questioning existing practice, but one of the younger elders said:

*The way in which we celebrate communion is a good example of how perceptions within the Chapel can vary. The tradition*

473

*of having an array of elders sitting an the platform and serving the congregation is undoubtedly seen as quite acceptable by a significant section of the congregation, particularly those most steeped in Chapel culture. However, to others, the procedure seems at best faintly ridiculous and at worst offensive. Peter makes every effort to explain that this procedure has nothing to do with status but the subliminal message we present is one of control, status and, since no women are involved, of male domination. This is far from the leadership style required and exemplified by Jesus.*

3 'Membership – a Discussion Paper', August 2003.

For the Maundy Thursday communion in 2003, non-elders, both men and women, were invited to serve the congregation. To emphasise that there was no status factor, only the two giving thanks sat on the platform with the pastor; all the other servers sat on the front pews with the congregation. Many positive comments were made, and no objections were noted, so the pastor extended the experiment to Sunday evening communion, asking fellowship groups to take it in turn to choose people (men and women) to serve. In deference to the feelings of older members, it was agreed that initially only elders would lead the prayers at the communion table.

In a separate development, the leaders of some of the fellowship groups asked whether there was any objection to their occasionally conducting the Lord's Supper in the home when the group met. The elders advised that provided a responsible person led the worship, and explained the significance of it to any who were on the fringe of the group, they could see no reason to object, either for fellowship groups or for any other groups within the Chapel family.

## 2003

### Devote yourselves to prayer
Peter Grainger proposed that the focus for the year 2003 should be on prayer:

*If you ask people what we are known for, then most people would say 'Charlotte Chapel is a preaching church'. My wish for 2003 is that many more people might also say, 'Charlotte Chapel is a praying church'. The verse I have chosen for the*

*year is Colossians 4:2: 'Devote yourselves to prayer, being watchful and thankful.'*

4 *Record*, January 2003, p. 5.

From Monday 13 to Friday 17 January, the lower hall was open for prayer between 7.30 a.m. and 8.15 a.m., as it had been at the beginning of 2002, again followed by coffee and rolls. This was repeated in January 2004 and 2005.

The Sunday morning sermons up to Easter were on 'People in Prayer', with examples from Old Testament characters. This was followed by six messages on the Lord's Prayer and six studies on 'The Man who Prayed' (Elijah). Simultaneously, the fortnightly fellowship groups studied the subject of prayer and prayed together. The year concluded with a series entitled 'The Church that Prayed', studies in the book of Acts. In the evening throughout the year, there were 27 messages on 1 Corinthians, entitled 'Keeping First Things First'.

*For the Saltmine Theatre Company's evangelistic plays, the front pews in the Chapel were taken out and replaced by staging.*

### Corporate prayer
Among those who supported the pastor's clarion call for more prayer, there was a good-natured difference of opinion, mostly along generation lines, as to when and how corporate prayer should take place. Some felt that the central (Tuesday) meeting should have the highest profile, while others said that fellowship groups were preferable, because they felt uncomfortable in praying with people they did not know. Of those who came on Tuesday evening, some liked breaking into small groups, and others did not. Even the topics for prayer evoked different views; some said that there was too much emphasis on pastoral matters and not enough on major areas affecting the church and nation; others felt that the purpose of prayer meetings was to share pastoral concerns, and to pray for them.

To cater for all views, the elders encouraged both the weekly central meeting and also the fortnightly fellowship groups, as well as the Friday early-morning meeting and the Wednesday afternoon women's prayer meeting, usually attended by about a dozen. Members were exhorted to be at one of them, at least, every week. The 'breaking into small groups' debate was dealt with in a very practical way – on the Tuesday when fellowship groups met, numbers at the central prayer meeting were smaller, so it did not divide; on the alternate Tuesday, when numbers were larger, it often did. This arrangement continued until the radical reorganisation in September 2006 (Chapter 58).

## CBC at the fringe

During the Edinburgh International Festival in 2002, the Chapel sponsored the (Christian) Saltmine Theatre Company. In 2003, the evangelism ministry took the bold step of applying to the Festival Fringe Society, for the Chapel (for the first time) to be an official festival event (Venue 251), advertised on the Fringe programme and selling tickets. Saltmine produced a play called *The Vigil*, in which a gardener was accused (as in a court trial) of stealing the body of a convicted criminal. The jury was the audience; about five hundred (the biggest number to attend a Chapel festival event for years) came to the seven performances between Monday 18 and Saturday 23 August, with a matinee on the Saturday afternoon. Café Rendezvous was open after the performances, and to the delight of the organisers, 90 Chapel members volunteered to help.

In the following year, 2004, the venture was repeated with a different play, C.S. Lewis' *The Screwtape Letters*; after the seven performances, the Chapel was given the coveted 'sold out' accolade, awarded by the Fringe Society for productions where all seats were sold for all performances. The Chapel also premiered a new play, *Emma's Mystery*. A young student was preparing for a religious education exam; as she puzzled about the biblical characters in the syllabus, they came to life on the stage and explained themselves. Over one hundred came to the three lunchtime performances.

In 2005, the Chapel invited Saltmine to perform *The Screwtape Letters* again and also *The Hiding Place* (the story of Corrie Ten Boom). In August 2006, a second week was added, with *Joy Observed*, a play about an American writer and poet, Joy Davidman, an atheist and Marxist who was

converted though reading C.S. Lewis' works and who subsequently married him. *The Screwtape Letters* and a hilarious musical, with a Christian challenge, were then performed, and the total audience over the fortnight was about fifteen hundred – only part of the area of the church could be used, because of the stage and the equipment.

One thing did not change over all the years; during the festival outreach, groups met in the lower hall for prayer throughout the activities (even the matinees); the aim was, as ever, the conversion of friends, colleagues, neighbours and strangers. Some among the Chapel leadership would have preferred a more directly evangelistic outreach, but most agreed that, given the Chapel's position, drama, supplemented by personal conversation in the café afterwards and the distribution of literature, was the most effective use of resources.

*Since 2003, the Saltmine Theatre Company have presented evangelistic drama in the Chapel, as part of the Edinburgh International Festival Fringe – this in 2006.*

474

The festival productions all publicized the next 'Christianity Explored' course, which started shortly afterwards. Fourteen non-Christians attended the 2003 course, four of whom made a personal commitment to Christ and went on to attend 'First Steps' and joined a fellowship group. Over 50 attended the course in the autumn of 2005, of whom two, who had no previous Chapel connection, became Christians. 'Christianity Explored' was followed by 'Discipleship Explored' for nine Monday evenings in the spring of 2006, and 36 attended.

In addition, the Chapel was the venue, on a Saturday or a Sunday evening in August 2004, 2005 and 2006, for the inter-church group Origin's praise night, which completely filled the building.

## Website

As mentioned in Chapter 55, the Chapel opened its first website in the spring of 2001, four years after the YPM; in its first year, it received almost 2,500 hits. It was expanded in January 2003, to include the Sunday sermons, both the words and the PowerPoint illustrations for them. Soon the site was averaging one hundred hits every day, from all over the world; more than half of the visitors stayed online for over half an hour. The first Chapel 'blog' was in 2006 (Chapter 58).

For over a hundred years, the Chapel had advertised its Sunday services and the name of the preacher in the church notices section of *The Scotsman*. With this information available on the website, it was decided in 2005 that weekly press advertisements – which cost more than £1,000 a year – were no longer value for money, and they were stopped at the end of 2005.

## 31 countries

At the annual Student Welcoming Sunday, which was on 12 October in 2003, Peter Grainger asked people at the morning service to call out their home country; 31 countries were represented:

Africa: Ghana, South Africa, Zimbabwe
Middle East: Bahrain
Indian sub-continent: Bangalore
Asia: China, Hong Kong, Korea, Macau,
    Malaysia, Philippines, Singapore

Australasia: Australia, New Zealand
North America: Canada, Mexico,
    United States of America
Caribbean: Jamaica
South America: Peru
Europe except UK: Eire, France, Greece, Holland,
    Norway, Russia, Ukraine
UK: Northern Ireland (40 people), Wales,
    England, Scotland, Channel Islands.

## Niddrie Community Church

The long search for the right man to lead the Chapel's Niddrie mission (Chapter 55) ended in July 2000 with the appointment of Rev. John Lowrie. He qualified as an electronic development engineer before studying at Northumbria Bible College. He then spent three years working as a full-time elder (mainly in evangelism) with a Grace Baptist church in southeast London, followed by six years as pastor of a Baptist church in Ballymena, Northern Ireland. His wife, Lucille, was a graduate in languages from Edinburgh University.

*John Lowrie, leader of the Chapel's Niddrie mission and, later, of the Niddrie Community Church (2000–07).*

On Sunday 9 September 2001, in the presence of many supporters from the Chapel, the mission was formally constituted as a church, with 38 members. Some had attended the mission for years, long before the Chapel came on the scene; others (22 of the 38) retained their membership in the Chapel, meantime, but committed themselves to the outreach. It took another four years to get a building project under way, but in September 2001 those who had worked and prayed together were no longer running a mission hall – they comprised a church.

This is not the place to detail how the Niddrie church became the Niddrie Evangelical Church in August 2003 and then the Niddrie Community Church in November 2004, but the Chapel's contribution to the new building must be noted. It was decided to demolish the old mission building and to rebuild on the existing site and on the adjoining land (Chapter 56). By the summer of 2003, the necessary permissions had been obtained. To put up a building with a sanctuary/multi-purpose hall seating 150 people, together with a café, office and meeting rooms, was costed at £600,000, to include construction, furnishing, fees and VAT. The plans included scope for the building to be extended at a later stage and a sports hall added.

An appeal was launched at the Chapel's anniversary weekend in October 2003, on the basis that no work would be instructed until at least 90 per cent of the estimated cost had been received in cash or in promises; no public funds or grants were available. The Thankoffering went entirely to the Niddrie project; Sidlow Baxter's widow sent £18,000 in his memory, £1,000 for every year of his ministry in the Chapel from 1935 to 1953; the Wester Hailes Baptist Church, which the Chapel had built in 1972 at a cost of £32,840 (Chapter 46), sent £10,000. The necessary 90 per cent was given or promised by the end of February 2004, and the full £600,000 was achieved by October.

The aim was to complete the building by the end of 2004. Sadly, the tenders received were hugely in excess of the budget figure, because builders were at a premium in Edinburgh at the time and could name their price. Negotiations to trim the cost, without reducing the size of the building, took place through the autumn of 2004 and the spring of 2005; a contract was placed in March for £632,984 (£541,406 for construction, £91,576 for fees, etc.; this did not include £50,000 for equipment and furnishings). Work to clear the site began at Easter 2005 and, as costs escalated, the Chapel's 2005 Thankoffering (£36,800) was given entirely to Niddrie; this brought the fund up to £681,000. The opening of the building is described in the next chapter.

### An honest appraisal
The generosity for the Niddrie building was encouraging, but in his annual report for the year 2003, the church secretary expressed some concern about the spiritual temperature in the Chapel. Having listed the encouragements, of which there were many, he went on:

*There continues to be relatively few coming forward for baptism [14 in 2003, against an average of 21 a year since Peter Grainger came in 1992] and applying for membership [31 against an average of 46]. Thus we are not seeing a net increase in the number from which our active workers are drawn, and as was pointed out last year, the average age of our members is increasing. Generally speaking attendance at the various prayer meetings is low, it would seem that the number of 'twicers' on Sunday continues to fall and, although many of our Fellowship Groups are thriving, others are less healthy.*

5 Annual report, 2003, p. 8.

Peter Grainger had expressed similar concerns at the members' meeting in November 2003. He suggested that the answer was to seek a fresh encounter with the Lord Jesus in 2004. Under the title 'Following Jesus', he used Sunday morning to go through Mark's Gospel, getting back to basics. Again, the fellowship groups studied the same passage as the Sunday sermon. The Verse for the Year 2004 was Mark 8:34: 'Jesus said: "If anyone would come after me, he must deny himself and take up his cross and follow me."'

## 2004

### Burns' Supper
On Saturday 24 January 2004, the Young Peoples Meeting used the popularity of Burns' Night suppers for an evangelistic event for the age range 15-30. There had been such celebrations before, for members only, but this was an outreach event. They took a neutral hall and invited the student and youth worker to give an appropriate message; he chose 'My love is like a red, red rose'. It was so successful that it was repeated in 2005.

### Associate or assistant pastor?
As mentioned in Chapter 55, the Chapel reverted to a three-year appointment of an assistant pastor, after the death of the first long-term associate pastor, Nic Roach, in 1996. John Smuts was followed by John Percival; when the latter's three years were coming to a close, in the spring of 2003, the elders thought again about the benefit of a long-term associate, who would share the pulpit ministry and spearhead evangelism. The post was advertised, many enquiries were

received and a number of leads were followed up, but no one with the necessary qualifications and experience was found. The elders decided to have another assistant pastor, and appointed Richard Gibb, a member of the Chapel.

Richard became a Christian as a child. Prior to studying theology at Wheaton College, Illinois, he worked for six years as a business consultant for Ernst & Young based in Edinburgh. He completed his doctorate in Systematic Theology at the University of St Andrews in December 2004 and joined the pastoral team on 1 January 2005. His wife, Alison, who is from Northern Ireland, works as a dietician at Queen Margaret Hospital in Dunfermline.

*Richard Gibb, assistant pastor (2005–06)*

### No tie?

As described in Chapter 44, a specific, unplanned, event in 1968 led to women coming to the Chapel on Sunday without hats. Another unplanned (and more traumatic) event in 2004 led to preachers coming without a tie. While fishing on Deeside in early July, Peter Grainger slipped and fell heavily, smashing an elbow. Despite jocular references to his ministry 'before the fall' and 'after the fall' (Genesis 3), the injury was serious and he was unable to preach or carry out pastoral duties for three months.

On his return to the pulpit, with his arm in a sling, it was not possible to wear a tie. Older members raised their eyebrows, but by the end of 2004, he regularly wore an open-neck white shirt in the evening, not from necessity (as in the early autumn) but from choice. When Richard Gibb started in January 2005, his pulpit dress was often a jacket and a white shirt without a tie. Present readers may wonder whether this

is worth mentioning, but it was innovative in the Chapel at the time. It was picking up a trend that had been gathering force among the younger generation for a while – no tie on Sunday.

Peter Grainger's enforced absence gave the elders time to look seriously at his workload. On his return, it was agreed that normally he would preach only once per Sunday, and devote more time to other aspects of leadership.

*A summer Sunday morning after church in 2004. If the weather was fine and the congregation was chatty, cars just had to wait.*

### The mission family

Gifts to the Chapel may be allocated by the donors among various funds; for several years, including 2004, 34 per cent of all giving was designated for the mission family. This enabled the Chapel to send £3,200 to everyone on the mission support list in 2004 – overseas and home workers had achieved parity in the previous year. There were 33 adults, and among them they had 22 children, for whom £656 each was sent as well; 13 had retired from overseas service and received £1,480 each. A further £8,500 was distributed as Christmas presents to the mission family. Not everyone mentioned in the bimonthly prayer calendar cbc.Online, as engaged on full-time Christian service, was supported financially – some were self-sufficient and wished only prayer support. Members in training received grants on a needs basis.

The paper distinction between 'home' and 'overseas' was maintained only because there was, historically, a retirement fund for overseas missionaries and no equivalent, yet, for home workers. Apart from that, they were treated equally. A seven per cent increase in Chapel giving to mission in 2005 enabled the treasurer to send quarterly disbursements of £850, that is £3,400 for the year, plus something for children and the retired. He challenged the congregation to increase mission giving by another six per cent in 2006; in faith he increased the quarterly disbursement to £900, and his faith was rewarded by a surplus of nearly £1,000 a month on his budget.

## 2005

### Descriptor for the Chapel
Throughout 2004, the elders discussed a new vision statement and a new logo for the Chapel. The idea of dropping the word Baptist from the name, and using the slogan 'Conspicuous for Christ', to mirror Charlotte Chapel, gradually emerged. The aim was to be different and to make a difference, 'to impact our world as a distinctive community of believers transformed by the power and message of Christ'. The Verse for the Year 2005 was therefore: 'Shine like stars in the universe as you hold out the word of life (Phil. 2 v. 15/16)'. The new logo, with its accompanying slogan (below) was launched in the autumn of 2005.

*The new logo, which picked up the four Cs: Charlotte Chapel – Conspicuous for Christ. It was sometimes printed in white, against a black background – the light shining through.*

### Major lessons from the minor prophets
By the beginning of 2005, two factors were shaping the Chapel's evening service: (1) only one in five of those attending on Sunday morning now came back on Sunday evening, and (2) more and more people came from churches that no longer had their own evening service. For example, St Thomas's Episcopal Church discontinued their evening service in mid-January 2005, so their young folk flocked to

the Chapel and then went back to Costorphine for their own youth fellowship. The Chapel had become, more than ever, a service provider for other churches, and numbers increased accordingly.

Some distinctive features on Sunday evening from January to March 2005 (mentioned below) attracted considerable interest. Except for the third Sunday in the month, which was an overtly evangelistic guest service under the title 'If everything Jesus said were true…', the other evenings explored the 12 minor Old Testament prophets. The message was essentially teaching, although there was always an application, including a word to non-believers, towards the end. The gallery was well filled (perhaps about 300) and the area respectably so (about 150).

A layperson usually chaired the opening part of the service, which included half a dozen modern songs, often led by a band and singers. When the subject was Jonah, three members read the entire book, taking parts in a dramatised reading, supported by PowerPoint illustrations. After the sermon (35 minutes), two members of the congregation led publicly in prayer for the topics that had been expounded. Some of the older generation attended faithfully; the young people turned out in force, but middle age was not well represented.

### Love in action
In addition to the magnificent contribution to the cost of the Niddrie building (above), the congregation responded generously to the series of natural disasters during the year 2005. Following the tsunami devastation on Boxing Day 2004, £18,200 was given in a few weeks. A Chapel member told the congregation in June about the need for a 4-wheel vehicle for her work among orphan children in Malawi; she wondered (privately) whether the Chapel might contribute £500 toward it, but £6,000 was put into the boxes on the stairs. The congregation was challenged from the pulpit in August 2005 about the failure of the harvest in Niger, and gave £4,650 for the work of Tearfund; the retiring offering on Harvest Thanksgiving Sunday in September (£4,000) went there as well. (All these appeals were topped up from general funds to a round figure.)

When an earthquake devastated North India, Pakistan and Kashmir on 8 October, £6,000 was contributed right away.

## Chapter 57
Conspicuous for Christ (2002-2005)

Christmas Day was a Sunday in 2005, but there were still enough at the morning service to give £2,616 to the Bethany Christian Trust. That brought the Chapel's total 'love in action' for the year 2005 to £41,466; with tax recovered through Gift Aid, a total of £50,233 was sent to these good causes.

*The Chapel's logo – 'Conspicuous for Christ' – was printed in white against a black background. On a sunny day, the Chapel building is conspicuous from Edinburgh Castle as a white-painted building among the darker stone of its neighbours.*

### Election of office-bearers, 2005
The new structure for office bearers, introduced in May 2000 (Chapter 56) created three problems. (1) It needed 34 elders, and pressures of business, family and other commitments made it impractical to find anything like that number. (2) Separating pastoral elders and ministry elders was confusing and everyone wanted to revert to a unitary court. (3) Too many were involved in decision-making for effective management.

The 2005 solution was greatly to increase the role of fellowship group leaders. Elders (only) were directly elected; it was hoped to have a dozen, but only nine agreed to take office. They were responsible for membership, planning and pulpit ministry, but had no direct pastoral link with the congregation. They recommended names for fellowship group leaders and deacons (male or female) to the membership. Fellowship group leaders maintained contact with the members in their group, irrespective of attendance at the fortnightly meetings, and informed the elder (attached to the group) and the pastoral team about any special needs. (There were also pastoral group leaders, who supervised fellowship groups, but their role is not pursued here.)

Seven ministries (committees), led by elders and supported by deacons, gathered a team around them to look after seven areas of church life: Christian living, evangelism, mission, student and youth, support services, worship and witness, Youth Council. An administrator replaced the church secretary. The elders and deacons both dropped the name 'court' for their meetings. It was all change.

*For family services, Peter Grainger invited a Chapel family to lead the intercessory prayer. For harvest thanksgiving in 2005, Roger and Anna Pagan and their children, Robert, Philip and Sam, all contributed.*

### Church and congregation
At the farewell for Lawrence Carter in 1875 (Chapter 9), and regularly after that, the phrase 'church and congregation' was used to distinguish members from those who attended regularly but who did not join. The exact proportion was not known until the censuses of 1994 and 2002, which demonstrated that on a typical Sunday, about half of those present were members, although many of the others regarded the Chapel as their church.

There were illustrations of this, in 2005 and again in 2006. When the new leadership structure (above) had been finalized, the elders, deacons and leaders of pastoral groups were 'recognized' during the morning service on Sunday 2 October 2005. They, with their spouses, occupied the front seats downstairs. After they had affirmed their acceptance of office, the pastor asked the members (only) to stand for a prayer of dedication. The west gallery was in the writer's view; of the 56 people occupying it, 9 were standing. Young people tend to go to the gallery, so this ratio was not reflective of the whole congregation, but nevertheless it was significant.

The other illustration was during Rodney Stout's induction, on the last Sunday in July 2006. For the act of induction, Peter Grainger asked not just members, but all who regarded the Chapel as their church to stand; less than 50 per cent of the congregation got to their feet – there was scarcely a pew without someone seated, and whole rows sat together. Again, this may not have been typical, as many members were on holiday and there were summer visitors, as well as friends who had come for the occasion. Nevertheless, the response to the pastor's wide invitation underlined just how many attended the Chapel without any sense of belonging to it.

## One Sunday morning

While Sunday evening services were less formal, as mentioned earlier in this chapter, and morning services were generally traditional in style, the 11 a.m. service on 27 November 2005, led by Colin Adams, Pip Harry and Harry Robertson, was rather different:

Welcome and intimations by CA
Drama – a plug, by two children, for the
    Christmas services
Prayer, by a member of junior church
Hymn 237: Holy, holy, holy
Drama, on theme of stealing, introduced by PH
Song with PowerPoint (listening, not singing):
    You raise me up
Song: My God is a great big God
Children and young people up to secondary 3
    leave for junior church
Offering with Hymn 319: I'd rather have Jesus than
    silver or gold
Dedication of Offering
Interview with Anthony Andrew about
    persecuted Christians (HR)
Prayer led by Anthony Andrew
Chapel Praise Singers
Intercessory prayer (HR)
Hymn 806: Beauty for brokenness
Message: Exodus 20:15, the eighth commandment,
    'Begged, borrowed or stolen?' (Richard Gibb)
Hymn 624: Take my life and let it be
Benediction: the Grace, said to one another

*During hymn singing, the operators of PowerPoint projected images from a camera panning around the congregation in the sanctuary, to make those in the lounge feel part of the congregation, and also superimposed the words of the hymns on the screen in the lounge.*

## 'Light a Light' – Monday 5 December 2005

For many years, St Columba's Hospice put up a Christmas tree in Charlotte Square Gardens and invited people to buy a white bulb for it, in memory of a loved one – hence the name 'Light a Light'. They were switched on at a public ceremony at the beginning of December, followed by a minute's silence. In 2003, the Chapel was asked to host a carol service, after the event in the gardens. This was little known for a couple of years, but it was widely publicised in 2005. After Sir Tom Farmer had announced that 657 bulbs had been donated, and switched them on, he invited everyone to walk across to Rose Street; well over two hundred did so, less than a dozen with any Chapel connection.

An Edinburgh operatic group with 30 voices led the congregation in singing three carols; Bill Denholm, the Chapel's associate pastor, opened in prayer; Father James, the Hospice's Roman Catholic chaplain, read the Scriptures; a Chapel member sang a delightful solo and Peter Grainger brought a closing message. The whole programme was superbly presented, technically and spiritually, and many visitors expressed their gratitude; they must have meant it, because nearly everyone asked for the leaflet about the Chapel's Christmas programme.

In December 2006, over twelve hundred were in the Gardens when Jackie Stewart switched on the lights, of whom more than four hundred came across to the Chapel, where the carol singing and the message were warmly appreciated.

## 'Christmas is all about me'

When multi-media equipment was proposed in 2001, some wondered whether the necessary lighting would turn the pulpit into a theatre. Events on weeknights, especially during the Edinburgh International Festival, were spectacular, but even the most traditional members were impressed with what was sympathetically achieved at Christmas 2005. On three consecutive Sunday evenings in December, music, carols, drama and narration were skilfully blended to give three different perspectives on the meaning of Christmas, under the title 'Christmas is all about me' (Jesus).

The sanctuary was darkened, with spotlights on a Christmas tree and a crib on the platform. The services opened with video clips of typical festive events, and then the narrator set the scene in simple but effective rhyme. Typical drama was a piece entitled 'Away with the Manger'; shepherds, angels, wise men, oxen and donkeys crowded around the baby in the crib, until a photographer (in the skit) from the *Bethlehem News* moved them away from the manger in order to get a better group picture – without the baby Jesus. Point taken: Christmas is all about me.

Carols, prayers and readings followed, with spotlights on the band and singers in the choir stalls, then a challenging message. One evening, the crib was dismantled as part of the drama, and cunningly put together again in the shape of a cross. The building was filled almost to capacity, with all ages present, several octogenarians and hundreds of young people. Many stayed for refreshments in the lounge. It was a fitting end to a memorable year.

## Christmas 2006

Encouraged by the response to the three Sunday evenings before Christmas 2005, just described, the musicians and the drama group built a series around the word 'history' for the corresponding three evenings in December 2006: 'History – prophesy fulfilled', 'His story – Jesus Christ' and 'Is His story now history?' Again, dramatized readings from Scripture (by young people taking a verse each), sketches, carols, a silent slide show to challenge comfortable assumptions, carols, prayers and a message were skilfully blended, to focus the attention of a packed church on the meaning of Christmas for today.

Additional information on the following topics, mentioned in this chapter, is available on the CD.

Elders and deacons, 2005
Sheila Masterton
Sunday services

# Chapter 58
## Belief, behaviour and belonging (2006–now)

## 2006

### '40 Days of Purpose'

The title for this last chapter – 'Belief, behaviour and belonging' – was the subject of a recent sermon, in which the preacher showed how all three are needed for a healthy church. It is an appropriate focus for the last years covered in this history of Charlotte Chapel so far.

From Sunday 15 January to Sunday 26 February 2006, five hundred Chapel people undertook a seven-week course of intensive Bible study, entitled '40 Days of Purpose'. The object was to help every member of the congregation focus on the purpose of life and the purpose of the church. The study was in three parts:

Pulpit ministry for seven consecutive Sundays
Fellowship groups meeting once a week for seven weeks
Individual reading of a chapter a day, for 40 days, from *The Purpose Driven Life*.

The foundation was laid in a week of prayer, starting on Saturday 7 January from 9 a.m. to 4 p.m., (lunch from 12 to 1), with people coming and going. PowerPoint projected items for prayer onto the screen in the lounge, automatically changing the topics every ten minutes, so that people prayed for specific areas as the titles rolled across the screen. From Monday 9 to Friday 13 January, there was a prayer meeting in the lounge from 7.30-8.15 a.m., with a different focus every morning.

Over the seven Sundays, and in the groups during the week, participants explored:

What on earth am I here for?
You were planned for God's pleasure – worship
You were formed for God's family – fellowship
You were created to become like Christ – discipleship
You were shaped for serving God – ministry
You were made for a mission – evangelism
Celebration Sunday

The evening service continued the theme from a different Scripture passage. A fellowship meal, attended by 480, and served by the group leaders in the Assembly Rooms, followed the last Sunday morning of the series.

### Fellowship groups

Weeknight fellowship groups were an integral part of '40 Days of Purpose'. Before it started, there were 15 groups, meeting fortnightly in homes around the city. To cater for everyone who signed up for the course, the number of groups was expanded to 40, and about five hundred people met weekly over the seven weeks. They listened to a DVD and then went through the Group Study Guide provided.

Thirty-five of the groups continued, but on the more usual fortnightly basis, when '40 Days' was over. Following the same pattern, that is a DVD and a study book, the spring series was 'Six Steps to Encouragement', and then, after the summer break, studies in the Book of James. By this time, some of the fellowship groups had consolidated, but at the end of 2006, there were 29 home groups, with 433 on their roll, nearly double the number of groups that existed before '40 Days'. In addition, a seven-week course was started in March 2006, called 'Building Blocks', to cover the basics of the Christian faith. It ran on Wednesday evening, and every session involved discussion in small groups, a talk, and then further group discussion, focused on a relevant Bible passage.

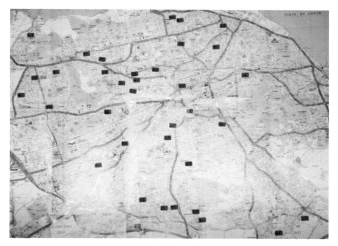

*Twenty-five new fellowship groups were created, bringing the total number to 40, to cater for the five hundred who were involved in '40 Days of Purpose'.*

### A quarterly *Record*

Volume 100, issue 1, of the *Record*, published in January 2006, was an up-market colour magazine, in a square format in place of the book style which had been used since its inception in 1907. Until 2001, it came out on the first Sunday of the month, then it became bimonthly, and the 2006 format, continuing, is quarterly. It is still distributed without charge, paid for from the general funds of the church – £5,626 in total in 2006.

## Niddrie Community Church

The Niddrie congregation took possession of their new building in February 2006. Shortly afterward, they were troubled by serious vandalism, which was given citywide and sympathetic publicity on the front page of the *Edinburgh Evening News* and necessitated the installation of electric shutters.

The new building was a tremendous asset in the work. The impressive main hall was ideal for the Sunday and midweek services, and also for youth and children's ministries and a parent and toddler group. The café attracted people of all ages from the area, particularly for butties (filled hot rolls) in the morning.

*The new building for Niddrie Community Church in February 2006.*

In May 2006, the church appointed a full-time youth and community worker, Michaela Forbes, from Kansas, USA. She had come to Scotland in 2002, after two years on the Operation Mobilization ship *Doulos*, to study at the International Christian College in Glasgow; while there, her practical experience included working with young people in Penicuik.

## Gift Aid

Gift Aid continued to benefit the Chapel in two ways – tax recovery added 28 pence to every pound given, and Gift Aiders' preferred method of giving, by bank standing order, ensured a steady cash flow. For the year 2005, 350 households contributed £279,855 to the general fund through Gift Aid, while cash in the offering bags brought in another £42,000. The average household gave £800 over the year to the general fund, which is £73 a month or £17 a week. In addition, half as much again was given and designated for mission (Chapter 57). Average Scottish wages at this time were £24,960 a year, £2,080 a month, £480 a week, so £1,200 a year per Chapel household (£800 general and £400 mission), together with support for other worthy causes, brought many up to a 'tithe' of their income – especially if one calculated the tenth on net income, not gross.

The year 2006 saw more and more people designating their gifts for particular aspects of the Chapel's work. This was good news for the ministries concerned – mission received (in round figures) £175,000, which was, for the first time, more than half of the corresponding figure for the general fund (£334,000) – but the treasurer cautioned against being too 'choosy'; the general fund had to cover the essential (if less exciting) services, and with the pastoral team at full strength, 62 per cent of expenditure went on staffing – a comparable figure with similar organisations.

## 75 years of Guiding

The seventy-fifth reunion of the 186th City of Edinburgh Company of Girl Guides (Charlotte Baptist Chapel) was held in the lounge on Saturday 4 March 2006. About 120 attended, including old girls, children and current leaders. The Rainbows told what they did each week in the form of an acrostic poem; the Brownies put on a fashion show of uniforms through the years; the Guides gave a timeline performance from 1930 to 2006; the Rangers helped with the refreshments. After each section had taken part, a former leader gave thanks for that group and prayed for God's continued blessing on it.

There were 36 enthusiastic girls in current Guide membership, with a waiting list. Guide programmes now centred on five areas: Healthy lifestyles, Global awareness, Skills and relationships, Celebrating diversity and Discovery. The promise remained central: 'I promise that I will do my best: To love my God, To serve my Queen and my country, To help other people and to keep the Guide Law.'

*The Girl Guides' seventy-fifth reunion, in the lounge in March 2006, and the badge to celebrate it.*

## Pastoral team

Rodney Stout joined the team in January 2006, replacing Bill Denholm as associate pastor for pastoral care. A native of Orkney, and brought up in the Sunday School in the Baptist church there, Rodney had a conversion experience at the age of 11. After three years in the building trade and twelve in the power industry, he answered a 'call' to ministry and went to Northumbria Bible College and then to the Scottish Baptist College. For two of these years, he was student pastor at Airdrie Baptist Church and then, from 1994 to 2005, pastor of Dalkeith Baptist Church.

*Rodney Stout, associate pastor, and Isobel Dudgeon, pastoral care worker, joined the Chapel team in 2006.*

Eilish Agnew, the pastoral assistant, retired to Northern Ireland in July 2006. During her time, the title 'deaconess' had been changed to 'pastoral assistant', but that was felt to be too vague. Mrs Isobel Dudgeon started in September as 'pastoral care worker'. Born into a fifth-generation Christian family in Northern Ireland, she made her own profession of faith at the age of 15, during a mission in her church. After university, she taught missionary children in Brazil for two years, then studied at the Northumbria Bible College, where she met her husband, Martin. They spent ten years in Bolivia with SIM International, retuning to Britain when their two children, James and Joanne, reached secondary school age. Isobel then worked with students at the University of Central Lancashire, living in Preston, while Martin served with a missionary organisation; his work could be done as well from Edinburgh as from Preston.

## Wednesday evening prayer meeting

The Chapel's main/central prayer meeting, which had been held weekly on Monday for most of the twentieth century, and then weekly on Tuesday from 1996, underwent a radical transformation in the first week of September 2006. It moved to alternate Wednesdays, with concentration on the home groups on the other weeks; it started at 7.30 p.m., for a time together, and then divided into smaller groups; the YPM also moved to fortnightly midweek meetings, joining the central prayer meeting when it was on, and having their own meeting on alternate weeks.

At the request of a dozen members, who felt strongly that there should be a mid-week evening prayer meeting every week, the building was made available, provided they organized it themselves for the second Wednesday of the month; members of the pastoral team agreed to lead on the fourth Wednesday.

The first Wednesday of the month concentrated on mission, and the third one on other topics. For 20 September 2006, when the focus was on schools and teachers, nearly one hundred attended. After a challenging call to prayer by a school chaplain, and about ten minutes of collective intercession for the areas outlined by him, Peter Grainger asked the teachers present to stand and to spread themselves around the lounge. He then asked the meeting to group themselves in fours or fives around every teacher – and to ask that teacher for personal prayer topics. This was remarkably effective for another ten minutes. Then, having prayed in one large group, and about 20 small ones, four members of the pastoral team led middle-sized groups in four different rooms, concentrating on the Chapel family. Coffee was served for all at nine o'clock. For the third Wednesday of October, the pattern was repeated, with the focus on the medical profession and, in November, on the legal profession.

### Student welcome
University freshers' weeks now begin early in September. The second Sunday of September 2006 reminded those who had become casual over the summer about the difference that an intake of students makes to a Chapel morning service. The sanctuary was packed well before eleven o'clock, with crowds of new students (unaware of the need to be early) coming up from the lounge as the children left for junior church after 20 minutes.

The Chapel, for its part, made every effort to welcome students. On that Sunday, a home was open for lunch – no prior notice required – and on the following Sunday, lunch was provided on the premises, followed by a (professionally guided) walking tour of the city centre. A full student programme then took shape for the rest of the semester, including Sunday lunches followed by Bible study, '121 discipleship' and a home-from-home initiative – 20 Chapel members offered regular hospitality, prayer support and general encouragement for everyone studying away from home.

### The Greenhouse
A new training programme, The Greenhouse, was launched in September 2006, aiming to nourish and nurture tender shoots among Chapel leadership. By teaching biblical truth and practical skills, it equipped Christians to serve better, and sought out those who would not put themselves forward, but whom others saw as potential leaders. It was an intensive course, meeting from 8-9.15 p.m. for four consecutive Thursdays, nine times a year, with a break between blocks, 36 sessions in all. Within a few weeks of its launch, 22 were attending and there was so much to cover that it was hoped to continue into a second year – and then to repeat the course.

### A novel anniversary
The one hundred and ninety-eighth anniversary, held on the last Sunday of October 2006, was a one-day in-house celebration, focusing on prayer. At the morning service, Peter Grainger preached on prayer under the acronym Acts (adoration, confession, thanksgiving and supplication), and concluded the service by inviting everyone to join in four prayers, on these four aspects, displayed by PowerPoint, including Psalm 51 for confession.

An enjoyable communal lunch in the lounge – 'bring a little extra for visitors' – was followed by every ministry (committee) laying out its wares in a room in the Roxburghe Hotel, given without charge by the sympathetic general manager. At 1.30 p.m., four areas of the lower hall were focal points for group or personal prayer, followed at 2 p.m. by an hour of singing and interviews. Google Earth zoomed in to Aix-en-Provence as the chairman chatted live on the phone with a Chapel missionary there and prayed for his family; the screen then refocused on Macau as Donald Fleming, who was present but who had recently served there, talked about his experiences. Three others were interviewed about prayer, and finally another member responded to specific requests for prayer. About 160 were present, but not many under 30.

Before the evening service, Peter Grainger said that if you went to a football match, and extra time was required after 90 minutes, you didn't grumble and you didn't leave; you enjoyed the additional play as much, if not more, than the game you had expected. It was a timely introduction to a marathon evening, with seven songs, two more video-prayers with Google Earth, two presentations (Niddrie and '40 Days of Purpose'), and the sermon.

### 11 Midmar Gardens
In the autumn of 2006, the Graingers and the Chapel leadership agreed that it was time to sell 11 Midmar Gardens, which had been the manse since 1963 (Chapter 42). It was now too large for them, and it needed substantial refurbishment. They bought their own property in Newtongrange, and moved to it at the end of November. The manse, bought in 1963 for £5,500, was sold by the Chapel for £963,000; the proceeds were partly earmarked for additional accomodation in Rose Street (below), partly used to purchase a manse for the Adams family and partly invested against future needs.

### The first Chapel 'blog'

Various women's activities in the Chapel – evangelistic, teaching, caring and others – were brought together on Tuesday 14 November 2006 under a formally-named and newly-created Women's Ministry. It was for all ages, and was publicized through the first-ever Chapel 'blog' (short for 'weblog', a world-wide-web that, unlike a static website, invites online responses), www.titus2talk.blogspot.com.

## 2007

### Sunday morning

The Sunday morning service continues to be the best supported of all Chapel activities. There has been no census since 2002 (Chapter 57), but a typical morning communion is a good guide to attendance. About 105 youngsters (25 Discoverers, 25 CID, 30 FBI and 25 Sunday Focus), accompanied by 25 leaders, leave for junior church after the children's talk, and take no part in communion. Twenty-four trays with 24 glasses each are prepared for the sanctuary, and a further three trays for the lounge, so 648 individual glasses are available. (The lounge can hold over a hundred, but quite a number come upstairs when the children leave.) Servers sometimes have to ask other servers for help as their trays empty, and between five and six hundred participate; a number of others pass the tray, as they are invited to do if they are not comfortable in taking part. With 130 at junior church, it follows that an average of about 680 now attend the morning service, plus adults who go straight to supervise the crèches before the service starts. That is less than in 1984 and 1994, because the figures then (749 and 729, Chapter 57) did not include anyone under 15, so there is no room for complacency.

### Charlotte Running Group

It might be thought that every imaginable auxiliary now existed under the Chapel's umbrella, but January 2007 saw the launch of the Charlotte Running Group, meeting every Monday evening. A dozen or more gather, with activity suitable for all levels. Progress may be followed, as with all auxiliaries, on the Chapel's website, where it appears, along with football, hockey and golf, under Charlotte Sports ministry.

At the same time, another group was started, 'Helping mums', to provide practical support for mums and dads as they adjust to life with a new baby – visiting at home, providing meals, and helping in practical ways; again, details are on the Chapel's website.

### Niddrie

In March 2007, Mez McConnell accepted a unanimous 'call' to be pastor of the Niddrie Community Church. His autobiography, *Is There Anybody Out There?: A Journey From Despair to Hope* (Christian Focus, 2006), describes his early life of abuse, violence, drugs, thieving and prison, his conversion and his recent work as a missionary among street children in Brazil. He is married with two children of his own, and expects to start in Niddrie in September 2007.

## Constant change is here to stay

### Property

As this book goes to the printer in July 2007, substantial changes are under way. The sale of the manse released sufficient capital for the Chapel to begin looking for additional accommodation in Rose Street – to meet acute overcrowding on Sunday morning and Friday evening and at other times as well. The garage and offices facing the back door of the Chapel came on the market, and applications have been made to the planning and listed building departments. Unless pressed by competition, the Chapel will await the outcome of these applications before finalizing the purchase.

Plans have been drawn up to remodel the front of the Chapel sanctuary. These are so provisional at this stage that nothing useful can be said – except that 'constant change is here to stay'. When it comes, sceptics and opponents of change are sometimes pleasantly surprised. In the spring of 2007, the leadership of the Young Peoples Meeting moved its traditional Sunday evening gathering to Saturday evening. There were misgivings – what would people do after the evening service? Was it a mistake – who would come to a 'meeting' on a Saturday evening? Three months later they reported: 'This is going really well and everyone enjoys having a bit more time without the threat of school or work hanging over things.'

## Constitution

The recently-created Office of the Scottish Charity Regulator requires every charity to have a formal written constitution – until now, the Chapel has worked on precedent and practice. Framing this requires, among other things, defining 'membership' – which means looking at the place of associate members in a twenty-first century constitution. Given their involvement in the work of the Chapel and their financial contribution, should associate members have a say in how funds are disbursed and how the church develops its ministry? If so, they should be able to vote at church business meetings; current thinking is, however, that only full members (baptized believers) should be eligible for election as elders.

## Disclosure Scotland

Everyone working with children and vulnerable adults must go through the Disclosure Scotland process, to ensure that any past criminal convictions are identified. It is proposed that this should be done automatically, as part of the membership application process, as is done in some other Baptist churches; but should the entire membership be 'disclosed' on a rolling basis?

## October 2008

In the same way as the Chapel celebrated its centenary with a series of meetings in October 1908 (Chapter 16), although the church was constituted on 24 January 1808, so the Chapel will (God willing) commemorate its bicentenary with a weekend of activities in October 2008. One of the former assistants, Rev. Alistair Begg, has accepted an invitiation to be the guest preacher; it is hoped that many others, former assistants and deaconesses (Appendix One), will come to Edinburgh for the occasion.

## What else?

The Chapel website www.charlottechapel.org includes the full text of the *Record* and the annual reports from 2001 to date, and the Sunday sermons from 1992 – the PowerPoint illustrations, the sermon outlines and the sermons themselves. Details of the many, many people, whose contribution would have been mentioned in this book if there had been space, can be found (often with photographs of them) in the *Record* and the annual reports online.

*Alistair Begg has accepted an invitation to be the guest preacher at the Chapel's bicentenary celebrations, including a service in the Usher Hall on Sunday 26 October 2008. After study at London Bible College (now London School of Theology), he was assistant pastor in the Chapel from 1975 to 1977 (Chapter 46), then pastor of the Hamilton Baptist Church. In 1983 he moved to become the senior pastor at Parkside Church near Cleveland, Ohio, and has been there ever since.*

## What of the future?

What type of community will Charlotte Chapel be in its third hundred years? If members and regular worshippers are truly Conspicuous for Christ, as the current logo exhorts, the writer sees three challenges and three encouragements.

Challenge one: to affirm the uniqueness of Jesus Christ. Successive ministers have contended for this, for all the years of the Chapel's existence, but it is under attack as never before. To assert with confidence the truth of John 14:6: 'I am the way and the truth and the life. No one comes to the Father except through me', invites accusations of arrogance, or even racism; it is essential to proclaim the uniqueness of Christ with certainty, but with humility.

Challenge two: Fewer and fewer children and young people have any experience of Sunday School or church. At the same time, multi-faith teaching of religious education means that basic knowledge of Christianity is much less than in previous generations. A school chaplain told the Chapel in 2006 that he estimated only one young person in 25 in Edinburgh was receiving adequate tuition in the Christian faith. Not only does this make it harder to interest the other 24 in the gospel, but it means starting with the rudiments of the faith when people do express an interest.

Challenge three: How can moral convictions, based on biblical principles, be expressed with grace and tact in a culture that increasingly promotes hedonism, self-indulgence, cohabitation and same-sex partnerships? As discussed in Chapter 51, there is a sensitive balance between 'welcoming' gay and lesbian people, as fellow-sinners saved by grace, and 'affirming' their lifestyle. Jesus advised his disciples, when sending them into situations that challenged the prevailing culture, 'to be as shrewd as snakes and as innocent as doves' (Matthew 10:16).

Encouragement one: Over the last 50 years, the Chapel has, without breakdown in fellowship, faced and come to terms with some major issues, including the ecumenical debate, the charismatic movement and the role of women. These were resolved in the conviction that the Bible should – must – be central to the discussion, the governing principle of the debate, the guide to family life and the framework for society. A Bible-centred ministry lay at the foundation of Charlotte Chapel, and the conviction that supreme authority is to be found in Scripture (or, more accurately, in the Christ of whom the Scriptures speak) has energized the Chapel through two centuries of upheaval and change. The Bible is the only book in the world where the author is present every time it is read.

Encouragement two: Evangelism and outreach, which have been at the heart of every ministry, are constantly reviewed and renewed, to meet the circumstances of the day. In the past, adaptation may not have been as spontaneous as the occasion demanded, but the Chapel now seeks to make evangelism, whether in the church or outside it, as relevant as possible to society around.

Encouragement three: Throughout the lifetime of the present members, the Chapel has known God's abundant blessing on its work and ministry. At the bicentenary, there is, in the goodness of God, a committed pastoral team, a dedicated laity, a large congregation and a vision. The Chapel must never be complacent, so a look at the past may help in planning for the future – after all, Paul told the church at Corinth about the wanderings of the children of Israel through the desert, and concluded: 'These things happened to them as examples and were written down as warnings for us' (1 Corinthians 10:11).

Additional information on the following topics, mentioned in this chapter, is available on the CD.

Girl Guides
Greenhouse
Prayer meetings
Visitors on 30 July 2006
Website

# Ministers and assistants

| Ministers | | Assistants | |
|---|---|---|---|
| Rev. Christopher Anderson | 1808-51 | Alfred C. Thomas | 1851 |
| Rev. Alfred C. Thomas | 1851-55 | | |
| Rev. James Martin | 1857-58 | | |
| Rev. William Stacey Chapman | 1859-60 | | |
| Rev. John Edward Dovey | 1862-66 | | |
| Rev. William Christopher Bunning | 1866-72 | | |
| Rev. Lawrence George Carter | 1872-76 | | |
| Rev. Owen Dean Campbell | 1877-84 | | |
| Rev. Samuel George Woodrow | 1885-88 | | |
| Rev. Thomas Wreford Way | 1888-96 | | |
| Rev. Foster Henry Bardwell | 1897-01 | | |
| Rev. Joseph William Kemp | 1902-15 | James Johnston | 1906 |
| | | James Scott | 1906-12 |
| | | Archibald B. Jack | 1912-13 |
| | | J.R. Hewison | 1914 |
| | | B. Murdoch McLaren | 1915-16 |
| Rev. William Graham Scroggie | 1916-33 | | |
| Rev. J. Sidlow Baxter | 1935-53 | | |
| Rev. Gerald B. Griffiths | 1954-62 | | |
| Rev. Alan Redpath | 1963-66 | Bryan Thomson | 1964-66 |
| | | Alex Hardie | 1966-73 |
| Rev. Derek James Prime | 1969-87 | Tom Lawson | 1973-75 |
| | | Alistair Begg | 1975-77 |
| | | Kenneth Armstrong | 1978-81 |
| | | David Hunt | 1981-83 |
| | | George Smith | 1981-82 |
| | | James Neilson | 1983 |
| | | Jim Murdock | 1983-85 |
| | | Peter J. Firth | 1986-89 |
| Rev. Peter James Grainger | 1992-date | Angus Noble | 1993-96 |
| | | Nic Roach | 1995-96 |
| | | Ronald McVicker | 1996-97 |
| | | John Smuts | 1997-2000 |
| | | Ken Gordon (Niddrie) | 1997 |
| | | Bill Denholm | 1999-2005 |
| | | John Percival | 2000-03 |
| | | John Lowrie (Niddrie) | 2000-07 |
| | | Colin Adams | 2003-date |
| | | Richard Gibb | 2005-06 |
| | | Rodney Stout | 2006-date |
| | | Mez McConnell (Niddrie) | 2007-date |

## Deaconesses

| | |
|---|---|
| 1907-16 | Miss Elizabeth C. Boyle |
| 1916-21 | Sister Lilian E. Tipper |
| 1921-49 | Miss Elizabeth C. Boyle |
| 1949-67 | Miss Margaret Gillon |
| 1967-71 | Miss Joan Wragg |
| 1971-72 | Miss Dorothy Somerville |
| 1973-75 | Miss Shirley Tory |
| 1976-82 | Miss Diane Guthrie |
| 1983-84 | Miss Barbara Hodder |
| 1984-93 | Miss Jessie Bell |
| 1993-95 | Mrs Jess Talbot (part-time, visitation) |
| 1992-2006 | Miss Eilish Agnew (pastoral assistant) |
| 1997-99 | Miss Judy White (pastoral assistant) |
| 2006-date | Mrs Isabel Dudgeon (pastoral care worker) |

## Evangelists

**Scotch Itinerant Society**

| | |
|---|---|
| 1808-20 | Alexander McLeod |
| 1810-24 | Dugald Sinclair |
| 1810-24 | David Gibson |
| 1821-24 | John Gilmore |
| 1821-22 | David Douglas |

**CC Evangelistic Association**

| | |
|---|---|
| 1920 | Mr & Mrs William Whyte |
| 1920-25 | Mr & Mrs William Park |
| 1924-28 | Walter J. Main |
| 1925-30 | William A. Cottingham |

# Bibliography of cited works (Full bibliography on the CD)

491

Hugh Anderson, *The Life and Letters of Christopher Anderson* (William P. Kennedy, Edinburgh, 1854)

J. Sidlow Baxter, *Britain's Greatest Need* (Warwick, Edinburgh, n.d.)

Andrew L. Drummond and James Bulloch, *The Church in Victorian Scotland, 1843-1874* (The Saint Andrew Press, Edinburgh, 1975)

Mary R. Hooker, 'Mrs W. Graham Scroggie', *The Sword and the Trowel*, 76 (1940)

Winnie Kemp, *Joseph W. Kemp, by his wife* (Marshall, Morgan and Scott, London, 1936)

Timothy Larsen (ed.), *Biographical Dictionary of Evangelicals* (Inter-Varsity Press, Leicester, England, 2003)

Eric Lomax, *The Railwayman* (Cape, London, 1995)

Donald E. Meek (ed.), *A Mind for Mission: Essays in appreciation of the Rev. Christopher Anderson* (Scottish Baptist History Project, Edinburgh, 1992)

Godfrey Holden Pike, *Seven portraits of the Rev C.H. Spurgeon* (London, 1879)

Derek J. Prime, *Pastors and teachers: the calling and work of Christ's ministers* (Highland Books, Crowborough, East Sussex, 1989); revised edition with Alistair Begg, *On Being a Pastor: Understanding Our Calling and Work* (Moody Press, Chicago, 2004)

'Report of the Commission of Enquiry into the Opportunities of Public Religious Worship, and means of Religious Instruction, and the Pastoral Superintendence afforded to the people of Scotland 1837-8', 9 vols (House of Commons, London, 1838)

K.B.E. Roxburgh, 'The Fundamentalist Controversy Concerning the Baptist Theological College of Scotland', *Baptist History and Heritage*, 36 (2000)

W.J. Seaton, *A short history of Baptists in Scotland* (Fauconberg, Dunstable, 1983)

C.H. Spurgeon, *Autobiography, vol. 2: The Full Harvest 1860-1892*, revised edition (Banner of Truth, Edinburgh, 1973)

Brian R. Talbot, *The Search for a Common Identity: The Origins of the Baptist Union of Scotland 1800-1870* (Paternoster Press, Carlisle, 2003)

A.E. Taylor, *The Faith of a Moralist*, vol. i. (Macmillan, London, 1930)

Ralph G. Turnbull, *A Treasury of W. Graham Scroggie* (Baker Book House, Grand Rapids, 1974, Pickering and Inglis, London, 1975)

Rev. Dr Ralph Wardlaw, 'A Sermon preached in Albany Street Chapel, Edinburgh, on Lord's Day evening, February 29th, on occasion of the death of the Rev. Christopher Anderson' (London, 1852)

Stephen F. Winward, *The Dedication Service* (The Baptist Union of Great Britain and Ireland, London, 1960)

Anon, 'Statement of the Circumstances Relative to the Church lately under the pastoral care of the Rev. Christopher Anderson' (Edinburgh, 1852)

## Periodicals and newspapers

*Baptist Handbook*
*The Baptist Quarterly*
*The Baptist Times*
*The British Weekly*
Charlotte Chapel Handbook
Charlotte Chapel *Record*
Charlotte Chapel Annual Report
*The Christian*
*Daily Record*
*Edinburgh Evening News*
*Free Church Magazine*
*Scottish Baptist Magazine*
*The Scots Magazine*
*The Scotsman*
*Sunday School Times*

# Additional information on CD

# Index (Fuller index on the CD)